SPHERICAL ASTRONOMY.

SPHERICAL ASTRONOMY.

BY

F. BRUNNOW, PH. DR.

TRANSLATED BY THE AUTHOR FROM THE SECOND GERMAN EDITION.

NEW YORK:
D. VAN NOSTRAND, 192 BROADWAY.
LONDON: ASHER & CO.
1865.

DEDICATED

TO THE

REV. GEORGE P. WILLIAMS, L. L. D.

PROFESSOR OF MATHEMATICS IN THE UNIVERSITY OF MICHIGAN

BY THE AUTHOR

AS AN EXPRESSION OF AFFECTION AND GRATITUDE FOR UNVARYING FRIENDSHIP AND A NEVER CEASING INTEREST IN ALL HIS SCIENTIFIC PURSUITS.

PREFACE.

During my connection with the University of Michigan as Professor of Astronomy I felt very much the want of a book written in the English language, to which I might refer the students attending my lectures, and it seems that the same want was felt by other Professors, as I heard very frequently the wish expressed, that I should publish an English Edition of my Spherical Astronomy, and thus relieve this want at least for one important branch of Astronomy. However while I was in America I never found leisure to undertake this translation, although the arrangements for it were made with the Publishers already at the time of the publication of the Second German Edition. In the mean time an excellent translation of a part of the book was published in England by the Rev. R. Main; but still it seemed to me desirable to have the entire work translated, especially as the Second Edition had been considerably enlarged. Therefore when I returned to Germany and was invited by the Publishers to prepare an English translation, I gladly availed myself of my leisure here to comply with their wishes, and having acted for a number of years as an instructor of science in America, it was especially gratifying to me at the close of my career there to write a work in the language of the country, which would leave me in an intellectual connection with it and with those young men whom I had the pleasure of instructing in my science.

Still I publish this translation with diffidence, as I am well aware of its imperfection, and as I fear that, not to speak of the want of that finish of style which might have been expected from an English Translator, there will be found now and then some Germanisms, which are always liable to occur in a translation, especially when made by a German. I have discovered some such mistakes myself and have given them in the Table of Errors.

I trust therefore that this translation may be received with indulgence and may be found a useful guide for those who wish to study this particular branch of science.

JENA, August 1864.

F. BRÜNNOW.

TABLES OF CONTENTS.

INTRODUCTION.

A. TRANSFORMATION OF CO-ORDINATES. FORMULAE OF SPHERICAL TRIGONOMETRY.

B. THE THEORY OF INTERPOLATION.

C. THEORY OF SEVERAL DEFINITE INTEGRALS USED IN SPHERICAL ASTRONOMY.

D. THE METHOD OF LEAST SQUARES.

E. THE DEVELOPMENT OF PERIODICAL FUNCTIONS FROM GIVEN NUMERICAL VALUES.

SPHERICAL ASTRONOMY.

FIRST SECTION.

THE CELESTIAL SPHERE AND ITS DIURNAL MOTION.

I. THE SEVERAL SYSTEMS OF GREAT CIRCLES OF THE CELESTIAL SPHERE.

II. THE TRANSFORMATION OF THE DIFFERENT SYSTEMS OF CO-ORDINATES.

SECOND SECTION.

ON THE CHANGES OF THE FUNDAMENTAL PLANES TO WHICH THE PLACES OF THE STARS ARE REFERRED.

THIRD SECTION.

CORRECTIONS OF THE OBSERVATIONS ARISING FROM THE POSITION OF THE OBSERVER ON THE SURFACE OF THE EARTH AND FROM CERTAIN PROPERTIES OF LIGHT.

Page

III. THE ABERRATION.

FOURTH SECTION.

ON THE METHOD BY WHICH THE PLACES OF THE STARS AND THE VALUES OF THE CONSTANT QUANTITIES NECESSARY FOR THEIR REDUCTION ARE DETERMINED BY OBSERVATIONS.

I. ON THE REDUCTION OF THE MEAN PLACES OF STARS TO APPARENT PLACES AND VICE VERSÂ.

II. DETERMINATION OF THE RIGHT ASCENSIONS AND DECLINATIONS OF THE STARS AND OF THE OBLIQUITY OF THE ECLIPTIC.

III. ON THE METHODS OF DETERMINING THE MOST PROBABLE VALUES OF THE CONSTANTS USED FOR THE REDUCTION OF THE PLACES OF THE STARS.

A. Determination of the constant of refraction.

B. Determination of the constants of aberration and nutation and of the annual parallaxes of stars.

FIFTH SECTION.

DETERMINATION OF THE POSITION OF THE FIXED GREAT CIRCLES OF THE CELESTIAL SPHERE WITH RESPECT TO THE HORIZON OF A PLACE.

SIXTH SECTION.

ON THE DETERMINATION OF THE DIMENSIONS OF THE EARTH AND THE HORIZONTAL PARALLAXES OF THE HEAVENLY BODIES.

I. DETERMINATION OF THE FIGURE AND THE DIMENSIONS OF THE EARTH.

II. DETERMINATION OF THE HORIZONTAL PARALLAXES OF THE HEAVENLY BODIES.

SEVENTH SECTION.

THEORY OF THE ASTRONOMICAL INSTRUMENTS.

I. SOME OBJECTS PERTAINING IN GENERAL TO ALL INSTRUMENTS.

A. Use of the spirit-level.

B. The vernier and the reading microscope.

C. Errors arising from the excentricity of the circle and errors of division.

D. On flexure or the action of the force of gravity upon the telescope and the circle.

E. On the examination of the micrometer screws.

ERRATA.

page 23	line 5 from bottom	*for* for a	*read* a
31	line 5 from bottom	*for* one	*read* unity
33	line 13 from top	*for* formulas	*read* formulae
48	line 19 from bottom	*for* as near	*read* as nearly
57 and 58	line 13 from bottom, line 17 from top	*for* at last	*read* finally
59	line 12 from bottom	*for* to	*read* too
60	line 6 from bottom	*for* constant quantity	*read* constant
71	line 17 and 19 from top	*for* North-Pole	*read* North Pole
—	line 20 from top	*for* South-Pole	*read* South Pole
—	line 9 from bottom	*for* Parallel-Circles	*read* Parallel Circles
73	line 10 and 12 from top	*for* vertical-circle	*read* vertical circle
—	line 13 from top and line 2 from bottom	*for* point South	*read* South point
—	line 17 from bottom	*for* point West	*read* West point
74	line 14 from top	*for* polar-distance	*read* polar distance
75	line 6 from bottom	*for* right-ascension	*read* right ascension
76	line 4 from top	*for* vertical axes	*read* axes
—	line 3, 8, 9 from top and 8, 9, 14 from bott.	*for* right-ascension	*read* right ascension
—	line 3 from bottom	*for* multiply	*read* divide
77	line 19 from bottom	*for* vertical	*read* perpendicular
78	line 10 from top	*for* vertical	*read* perpendicular
81	line 9 from bottom	*for* point North	*read* North point
84	line 17 from bottom	*for* at last	*read* finally
93	line 8 from top	*for* $a\,(1 - \cos E)$	*read* $a\,(1 - e\cos E)$
100	line 6 from bottom	*for* sidereal time	*read* of sidereal time
—	line 5 from bottom	*for* mean time	*read* of mean time
101	line 11 from top	*for* on a	*read* to the
103	line 6 from bottom	*for* in	*read* is
107	line 18 from top	*for* star	*read* stars
116	line 18 from top	*for* against	*read* to
127	line 3 from bottom	*for* at last	*read* finally
135	line 12 from bottom	*for* $\cos\beta$	*read* on β
138	line 4 from top	*for* the light	*read* light
139	line 11 from top	*for* the light	*read* light

page 140 line 16 from bottom 144 line 10 from bottom 147 line 2 from bottom 148 line 1 from top 154 line 11 from bottom 155 line 8 from bottom	*for*	at	*read* on
169 line 9 from top 171 line 4 from top 173 line 1, 2, 18 from top 174 line 13 from top	*for*	stand	*read* height
176 line 14, 11 from bott.	*for*	the refraction	*read* refraction
178 line 11 from top	*for*	at	*read* on
181 line 12 from top	*for*	vertical	*read* perpendicular
190 line 11 from top	*for*	at	*read* on
209 line 5 from top	*for*	vertical	*read* perpendicular
210 line 4 and 5 from top	*for*	vertical	*read* perpendicular
214 line 8 from top	*for*	usually	*read* and as usually
226 line 10 from top	*for*	at last	*read* finally
232 line 14 from bottom	*for*	Now	*read* Now let
272 line 13 from bottom	*for*	$-\frac{1}{6}p^3 \sin t \cos t$	*read* $-\frac{1}{6}p^3 \sin t \cos t^2$
286 line 18 from bottom	*for*	$\cos \delta \sin \lambda$	*read* $\cos \delta' \sin \lambda$
331 line 9 from top	*for*	$= \frac{x}{\text{tang } \pi}$	*read* $= -\frac{x}{\text{tang } \pi}$
397 line 18 from top	*for*	a	*read* an
399 line 1 from bottom	*for*	i and i'	*read* $2i$ and $2i'$
425 line 14 from bottom	*for*	of	*read* between
450 line 4 from bottom	*for*	of	*read* between
456 line 16 from top	*for*	form	*read* from

INTRODUCTION.

A. TRANSFORMATION OF CO-ORDINATES. FORMULAE OF SPHERICAL TRIGONOMETRY.

1. In Spherical Astronomy we treat of the positions of the heavenly bodies on the visible sphere of the heavens, referring them by spherical co-ordinates to certain great circles of the sphere and establishing the relations between the co-ordinates with respect to various great circles. Instead of using spherical co-ordinates we can give the positions of the heavenly bodies also by polar co-ordinates, viz. by the angles, which straight lines drawn from the bodies to the centre of the celestial sphere make with certain planes, and by the distance from this centre itself, which, being the radius of the celestial sphere, is always taken equal to unity. These polar co-ordinates can finally be expressed by rectangular co-ordinates. Hence the whole of Spherical Astronomy can be reduced to the transformation of rectangular co-ordinates, for which we shall now find the general formulae.

If we imagine in a plane two axes perpendicular to each other and denote the abscissa and ordinate of a point by x and y, the distance of the point from the origin of the co-ordinates by r, the angle, which this line makes with the positive side of the axis of x, by v, we have:

$$x = r \cos v$$
$$y = r \sin v.$$

If we further imagine two other axes in the same plane, which have the same origin as the former two and denote the co-ordinates of the same point referred to this new system by x' and y' and the angle corresponding to v by v', we have:

$$x' = r \cos v'$$
$$y' = r \sin v'.$$

If we denote then the angle, which the positive side of the axis of x' makes with the positive side of the axis of x, by w, reckoning all angles in the same direction from 0^0 to 360^0, we have in general $v = v' + w$, hence:

$$x = r \cos v' \cos w - r \sin v' \sin w$$
$$y = r \sin v' \cos w + r \cos v' \sin w,$$

or:

$$\begin{aligned} x &= x' \cos w - y' \sin w \\ y &= x' \sin w + y' \cos w \end{aligned} \quad (1)$$

and likewise:

$$\begin{aligned} x' &= x \cos w + y \sin w \\ y' &= -x \sin w + y \cos w \end{aligned} \quad (1\,a)$$

These formulae are true for all positive and negative values of x and y and for all values of w from 0^0 to 360^0.

2. Let x, y, z be the co-ordinates of a point O referred to three axes perpendicular to each other, let a' be the angle, which the radius vector makes with its projection on the plane of xy, B' the angle between this projection and the axis of x (or the angle between a plane passing through the point O and the positive axis of z and a plane passing through the positive axes of x and z, reckoned from the positive side of the axis of x towards the positive side of the axis of y from 0^0 to 360^0), then we have, taking the distance of the point from the origin of the co-ordinates equal to unity:

$$x = \cos B' \cos a', \quad y = \sin B' \cos a', \quad z = \sin a'.$$

But if we denote by a the angle between the radius vector and the positive side of the axis of z, reckoning it from the positive side of the axis of z towards the positive side of the axis of x and y from 0^0 to 360^0, we have:

$$x = \sin a \cos B', \quad y = \sin a \sin B', \quad z = \cos a.$$

If now we imagine another system of co-ordinates, whose axis of y' coincides with the axis of y, and whose axes of x' and z' make with the axis of x and z the angle c and if we denote the angle between the radius vector and the positive side of the axis of z' by b and by A' the angle between the plane passing through O and the positive axis of z' and the plane passing through the positive axes of x and z, reckoning both angles in the same direction as a and B', we have:

$$x' = \sin b \cos A', \quad y' = \sin b \sin A', \quad z' = \cos b,$$

and as we have according to the formulae for the transformation of co-ordinates:

$$\begin{aligned} z &= x' \cdot \sin c + z' \cos c \\ y &= y' \\ x &= x' \cos c - z' \sin c, \end{aligned}$$

we find:

$$\begin{aligned} \cos a &= \sin b \sin c \cos A' + \cos b \cos c \\ \sin a \sin B' &= \sin b \sin A' \\ \sin a \cos B' &= \sin b \cos c \cos A' - \cos b \sin c. \end{aligned}$$

3. If we imagine a sphere, whose centre is the origin of the co-ordinates and whose radius is equal to unity and draw through the point O and the points of intersection of the axes of z and z' with the surface of this sphere arcs of a great circle, these arcs form a spherical triangle, if we use this term in its most general sense, when its sides as well as angles may be greater than 180 degrees. The three sides OZ, OZ' and $Z'Z$ of this spherical triangle are respectively a, b and c. The spherical angle A at Z' is equal to A', being the angle between the plane passing through the centre and the points O and Z' and the plane passing through the centre and the points Z and Z', while the angle B at Z is generally equal to $180 - B'$. Introducing therefore A and B instead of A' and B' in the equations which we have found in No. 2, we get the following formulae, which are true for every spherical triangle:

$$\begin{aligned} \cos a &= \cos b \cos c + \sin b \sin c \cos A \\ \sin a \sin B &= \sin b \sin A \\ \sin a \cos B &= \cos b \sin c - \sin b \cos c \cos A. \end{aligned}$$

These are the three principal formulae of spherical trigonometry and express but a simple transformation of co-ordinates.

As we may consider each vertex of the spherical triangle as the projection of the point O on the surface of the sphere and the two others as the points of intersection of the two axes z and z' with this surface, it follows, that the above formulae are true also for any other side and the adjacent angle, if we change the other sides and angles correspondingly. Hence we obtain, embracing all possible cases:

$$\begin{aligned}\cos a &= \cos b \cos c + \sin b \sin c \cos A\\ \cos b &= \cos a \cos c + \sin a \sin c \cos B\\ \cos c &= \cos a \cos b + \sin a \sin b \cos C\end{aligned} \qquad (2)$$

$$\begin{aligned}\sin a \sin B &= \sin b \sin A\\ \sin a \sin C &= \sin c \sin A\\ \sin b \sin C &= \sin c \sin B\end{aligned} \qquad (3)$$

$$\begin{aligned}\sin a \cos B &= \cos b \sin c - \sin b \cos c \cos A\\ \sin a \cos C &= \cos c \sin b - \sin c \cos b \cos A\\ \sin b \cos A &= \cos a \sin c - \sin a \cos c \cos B\\ \sin b \cos C &= \cos c \sin a - \sin c \cos a \cos B\\ \sin c \cos A &= \cos a \sin b - \sin a \cos b \cos C\\ \sin c \cos B &= \cos b \sin a - \sin b \cos a \cos C.\end{aligned} \qquad (4)$$

4. We can easily deduce from these formulae all the other formulae of spherical trigonometry. Dividing the formulae (4) by the corresponding formulae (3), we find:

$$\begin{aligned}\sin A \operatorname{cotang} B &= \operatorname{cotang} b \sin c - \cos c \cos A\\ \sin A \operatorname{cotang} C &= \operatorname{cotang} c \sin b - \cos b \cos A\\ \sin B \operatorname{cotang} A &= \operatorname{cotang} a \sin c - \cos c \cos B\\ \sin B \operatorname{cotang} C &= \operatorname{cotang} c \sin a - \cos a \cos B\\ \sin C \operatorname{cotang} A &= \operatorname{cotang} a \sin b - \cos b \cos C\\ \sin C \operatorname{cotang} B &= \operatorname{cotang} b \sin a - \cos a \cos C.\end{aligned} \qquad (5)$$

If we write the last of these formulae thus:

$$\sin C \cos B = \frac{\cos b (\sin a \sin B)}{\sin b} - \cos a \sin B \cos C,$$

we find:

$$\sin C \cos B = \cos b \sin A - \cos a \sin B \cos C,$$

or:

$$\sin A \cos b = \cos B \sin C + \sin B \cos C \cos a$$

an equation, which corresponds to the first of the formulae (4), but contains angles instead of sides and vice versâ. By changing the letters, we find the following six equations:

$$\begin{aligned}\sin A \cos b &= \cos B \sin C + \sin B \cos C \cos a\\ \sin A \cos c &= \cos C \sin B + \sin C \cos B \cos a\\ \sin B \cos a &= \cos A \sin C + \sin A \cos C \cos b\\ \sin B \cos c &= \cos C \sin A + \sin C \cos A \cos b\\ \sin C \cos a &= \cos A \sin B + \sin A \cos B \cos c\\ \sin C \cos b &= \cos B \sin A + \sin B \cos A \cos c\end{aligned} \qquad (6)$$

and dividing these equations by the corresponding equations (3), we have:

$$\begin{aligned}\sin a \operatorname{cotang} b &= \operatorname{cotang} B \sin C + \cos C \cos a\\ \sin a \operatorname{cotang} c &= \operatorname{cotang} C \sin B + \cos B \cos a\\ \sin b \operatorname{cotang} a &= \operatorname{cotang} A \sin C + \cos C \cos b\\ \sin b \operatorname{cotang} c &= \operatorname{cotang} C \sin A + \cos A \cos b\\ \sin c \operatorname{cotang} a &= \operatorname{cotang} A \sin B + \cos B \cos c\\ \sin c \operatorname{cotang} b &= \operatorname{cotang} B \sin A + \cos A \cos c.\end{aligned} \qquad (7)$$

From the equations (6) we easily deduce the following:

$$\begin{aligned}\cos A \sin C &= \sin B \cos a - \sin A \cos C \cos b\\ \cos B \sin C &= \sin A \cos b - \sin B \cos C \cos a.\end{aligned}$$

Multiplying these equations by sin C and substituting the value of sin A sin C cos b taken from the second equation into the first, we find:

$$\cos A = \sin B \sin C \cos a - \cos B \cos C$$

and changing the letters we get the following three equations, which correspond to the formulae (2), but again contain angles instead of sides and vice versâ:

$$\begin{aligned}\cos A &= \sin B \sin C \cos a - \cos B \cos C\\ \cos B &= \sin A \sin C \cos b - \cos A \cos C\\ \cos C &= \sin A \sin B \cos c - \cos A \cos B.\end{aligned} \qquad (8)$$

5. If we add the two first of the formulae (3), we find:

$$\sin a\,[\sin B + \sin C] = \sin A\,[\sin b + \sin c],$$

or:

$$\sin \tfrac{1}{2} a \cos \frac{B-C}{2} . \cos \tfrac{1}{2} a \sin \frac{B+C}{2} = \sin \tfrac{1}{2} A \sin \frac{b+c}{2} . \cos \tfrac{1}{2} A \cos \frac{b-c}{2}$$

and if we subtract the same equations, we get:

$$\sin \tfrac{1}{2} a \sin \frac{B-C}{2} . \cos \tfrac{1}{2} a \cos \frac{B+C}{2} = \sin \tfrac{1}{2} A \cos \frac{b+c}{2} . \cos \tfrac{1}{2} A \sin \frac{b-c}{2} .$$

Likewise we find by adding and subtracting the two first of the formulae (4):

$$\sin \tfrac{1}{2} a \cos \frac{B-C}{2} . \cos \tfrac{1}{2} a \cos \frac{B+C}{2} = \sin \tfrac{1}{2} A \sin \frac{b+c}{2} . \sin \tfrac{1}{2} A \cos \frac{b+c}{2}$$

$$\sin \tfrac{1}{2} a \sin \frac{B-C}{2} . \cos \tfrac{1}{2} a \sin \frac{B+C}{2} = \cos \tfrac{1}{2} A \sin \frac{b-c}{2} . \cos \tfrac{1}{2} A \cos \frac{b-c}{2} .$$

Each of these formulae is the product of two of Gauss's equations; but in order to derive from these formulae Gauss's equations, we must find another formula, in which a different combination of equations occurs. We may use for this purpose either of the following equations:

$$\cos \tfrac{1}{2} a \cos \frac{B+C}{2} . \cos \tfrac{1}{2} a \sin \frac{B+C}{2} = \sin \tfrac{1}{2} A \cos \frac{b+c}{2} . \cos \tfrac{1}{2} A \cos \frac{b-c}{2}$$

$$\sin \tfrac{1}{2} a \cos \frac{B-C}{2} . \sin \tfrac{1}{2} a \sin \frac{B-C}{2} = \sin \tfrac{1}{2} A \sin \frac{b+c}{2} . \cos \tfrac{1}{2} A \sin \frac{b-c}{2} ,$$

which we find by adding or subtracting the first two of the equations (6).

If we take now:

$$\sin\tfrac{1}{2}A\sin\frac{b+c}{2}=\alpha$$

$$\sin\tfrac{1}{2}A\cos\frac{b+c}{2}=\beta$$

$$\cos\tfrac{1}{2}A\sin\frac{b-c}{2}=\gamma$$

$$\cos\tfrac{1}{2}A\cos\frac{b-c}{2}=\delta$$

and:

$$\sin\tfrac{1}{2}a\cos\frac{B-C}{2}=\alpha'$$

$$\cos\tfrac{1}{2}a\cos\frac{B+C}{2}=\beta'$$

$$\sin\tfrac{1}{2}a\sin\frac{B-C}{2}=\gamma'$$

$$\cos\tfrac{1}{2}a\sin\frac{B+C}{2}=\delta',$$

we find the following six equations:

$$\alpha'\delta'=\alpha\delta,\ \gamma'\beta'=\gamma\beta,\ \alpha'\beta'=\alpha\beta,\ \gamma'\delta'=\gamma\delta,\ \beta'\delta'=\beta\delta,\ \alpha'\gamma'=\alpha\gamma,$$

from which we deduce the following:

$$\alpha'=\alpha,\ \beta'=\beta,\ \gamma'=\gamma,\ \delta'=\delta,$$

or:

$$\alpha'=-\alpha,\ \beta'=-\beta,\ \gamma'=-\gamma,\ \delta'=-\delta.$$

Hence we find the following relations between the angles and sides of a spherical triangle:

$$\begin{aligned}
\sin\tfrac{1}{2}A\sin\frac{b+c}{2}&=\sin\tfrac{1}{2}a\cos\frac{B-C}{2}\\
\sin\tfrac{1}{2}A\cos\frac{b+c}{2}&=\cos\tfrac{1}{2}a\cos\frac{B+C}{2}\\
\cos\tfrac{1}{2}A\sin\frac{b-c}{2}&=\sin\tfrac{1}{2}a\sin\frac{B-C}{2}\\
\cos\tfrac{1}{2}A\cos\frac{b-c}{2}&=\cos\tfrac{1}{2}a\sin\frac{B+C}{2}
\end{aligned}\qquad(9)$$

or:

$$\sin\tfrac{1}{2}A\sin\frac{b+c}{2}=-\sin\tfrac{1}{2}a\cos\frac{B-C}{2}$$

$$\sin\tfrac{1}{2}A\cos\frac{b+c}{2}=-\cos\tfrac{1}{2}a\cos\frac{B+C}{2}$$

$$\cos\tfrac{1}{2}A\sin\frac{b-c}{2}=-\sin\tfrac{1}{2}a\sin\frac{B-C}{2}$$

$$\cos\tfrac{1}{2}A\cos\frac{b-c}{2}=-\cos\tfrac{1}{2}a\sin\frac{B+C}{2}.$$

Both systems give us for the unknown quantities, which may be either two sides and the included angle or two angles and the interjacent side, the same value or at least values differing by 360 degrees. If we wish to find for instance A, b and c, we should get from the second system of formulae either for $\frac{b+c}{2}$ and $\frac{b-c}{2}$ the same values as from the first, but for $\frac{1}{2}A$ a value which differs 180^0, or we should find for $\frac{b+c}{2}$ and $\frac{b-c}{2}$ values which differ 180^0 from those derived from the first system, but for $\frac{1}{2}A$ the same value. In each case therefore the values of A, b and c as found from the two systems would differ only by 360^0. The four formulae (9) are therefore generally true and it is indifferent, whether we use for the computation of A, b and c the quantities a, B, C themselves or add to or subtract from any of them 360^0 *).

The four equations (9) are known as „Gauss's equations“ and are used, if either one side and the two adjacent angles of a spherical triangle or two sides and the included angle are given and it is required to find the other parts. The best way of computing them is the following. If a, B and C are the given parts, we find first the logarithms of the following quantities:

(1) $\cos\frac{B-C}{2}$	(4) $\cos\frac{B+C}{2}$
(2) $\sin\frac{1}{2}a$	(5) $\cos\frac{1}{2}a$
(3) $\sin\frac{B-C}{2}$	(6) $\sin\frac{B+C}{2}$

and from these:

(7) $\sin\frac{1}{2}a\cos\frac{B-C}{2}$	(9) $\sin\frac{1}{2}a\sin\frac{B-C}{2}$
(8) $\cos\frac{1}{2}a\cos\frac{B+C}{2}$	(10) $\cos\frac{1}{2}a\sin\frac{B+C}{2}$.

Subtracting the logarithm of (8) from that of (7) and the logarithm of (10) from that of (9), we find log. tang $\frac{1}{2}(b+c)$ and lg. tg. $\frac{1}{2}(b-c)$, from which we get b and c. Then we take either $\log\cos\frac{1}{2}(b+c)$ or $\log\sin\frac{1}{2}(b+c)$ and $\log\cos\frac{1}{2}(b-c)$ or $\log\sin\frac{1}{2}(b-c)$, whichever is the greater one

*) Gauss, Theoria motus corporum coelestium pag. 50 seq.

of the two and subtract the first from the greater one of the logarithms (7) or (8), the other from the greater one of the logarithms (9) or (10) and thus find log sin $\frac{1}{2}A$ and log cos $\frac{1}{2}A$. Subtracting the latter from the first, we get log tang $\frac{1}{2}A$, from which we find A. As sin $\frac{1}{2}A$ as well as cos $\frac{1}{2}A$ must necessarily give the same angle as tang $\frac{1}{2}A$, we may use this as a check for our computation.

If for instance we have the following parts given:

$$a = 11^\circ\ 25'\ 56.''3$$
$$B = 184\ \ 6\ \ 55.\ 4$$
$$C = 11\ \ 18\ \ 40.\ 3$$

we have:

$\frac{1}{2}(B-C) =$	$86^\circ\ 24'\ 7.''55$	$\frac{1}{2}(B+C) =$	$97^\circ\ 42'\ 47.''85$
$\cos\frac{1}{2}(B-C) =$	8.7976413	$\cos\frac{1}{2}(B+C)$	9.1278046_n
$\sin\frac{1}{2}a =$	8.9982605	$\cos\frac{1}{2}a$	9.9978351
$\sin\frac{1}{2}(B-C) =$	9.9991432	$\sin\frac{1}{2}(B+C)$	9.9960526
$\sin\frac{1}{2}a\cos\frac{1}{2}(B-C)$	7.7959018	$\sin\frac{1}{2}a\sin\frac{1}{2}(B-C)$	8.9974037
$\cos\frac{1}{2}a\cos\frac{1}{2}(B+C)$	9.1256397_n	$\cos\frac{1}{2}a\sin\frac{1}{2}(B+C)$	9.9938877
$\frac{1}{2}(b+c)$	177 19 13.49	$\frac{1}{2}(b-c)$	5 45 24.13
$\cos\frac{1}{2}(b+c)$	9.9995248_n	$\cos\frac{1}{2}(b-c)$	9.9978042
$\sin\frac{1}{2}A$	9.1261149	$b =$	$183^\circ\ 4'\ 37.''62$
$\cos\frac{1}{2}A$	9.9960835	$c =$	171 33 49. 36
$\frac{1}{2}A$	$7^\circ\ 40'\ 59.''38$	$A =$	15 21 58. 76.

If we had taken $B = -175^\circ\ 53'\ 4.''6$, hence:

$$\tfrac{1}{2}(B+C) = -82^\circ\ 17'\ 12.''15$$
$$\tfrac{1}{2}(B-C) = -93\ \ 35\ \ 52.\ 45$$

we should have found:

$$\tfrac{1}{2}(b+c) = -\ 2^\circ\ 40'\ 46.''51$$
$$\tfrac{1}{2}(b-c) = 185\ \ 45\ \ 24.\ 13$$

hence $b = 183^\circ\ 4'\ 37.''62$ and $c = -188^\circ\ 26'\ 10.''64$.

Dividing Gauss's equations by each other, we find Napier's equations. Writing A, B, C in place of B, C, A and a, b, c in place of b, c, a, we find from the equations (9):

$$\text{tang}\frac{A+B}{2} = \frac{\cos\frac{a-b}{2}}{\cos\frac{a+b}{2}}\,\text{cotang}\frac{C}{2}$$

$$\text{tang}\frac{A-B}{2} = \frac{\sin\frac{a-b}{2}}{\sin\frac{a+b}{2}}\,\text{cotang}\frac{C}{2} \qquad (9a)$$

$$\left.\begin{aligned}\operatorname{tang}\frac{a+b}{2}&=\frac{\cos\frac{A-B}{2}}{\cos\frac{A+B}{2}}\operatorname{tang}\frac{c}{2}\\ \operatorname{tang}\frac{a-b}{2}&=\frac{\sin\frac{A-B}{2}}{\sin\frac{A+B}{2}}\operatorname{tang}\frac{c}{2}.\end{aligned}\right\}\quad(9\,a)$$

6. As nearly all the formulae in No. 3 and 4 are under a form not convenient for logarithmic computation, their second members consisting of two terms, we must convert them by the introduction of auxiliary angles into others, which are free from this inconvenience. Now as any two real, positive or negative quantities x and y may be taken proportional to a sine or cosine of an angle we may assume:

$$x = m \sin M \text{ and } y = m \cos M$$

for we find immediately:

$$\operatorname{tang} M = \frac{x}{y} \text{ and } m = \sqrt{x^2 + y^2},$$

hence M and m expressed by real quantities. Therefore as all the above formulas, which consist of several terms, contain in each of these terms the sine and cosine of the same angle, we can take their factors proportional to the sine and cosine of an angle and, applying the formulae for the sine or cosine of a binomial, we can convert the formulae into a form convenient for logarithmic computation.

For instance, if we have to compute the three formulae:

$$\begin{aligned}\cos a &= \cos b \cos c + \sin b \sin c \cos A\\ \sin a \sin B &= \sin b \sin A\\ \sin a \cos B &= \cos b \sin c - \sin b \cos c \cos A,\end{aligned}$$

we may put:

$$\begin{aligned}\sin b \cos A &= m \sin M\\ \cos b &= m \cos M.\end{aligned}$$

and find:

$$\begin{aligned}\cos a &= m \cos (c - M)\\ \sin a \sin B &= \sin b \sin A\\ \sin a \cos B &= m \sin (c - M).\end{aligned}$$

If we know the quadrant, in which B is situated, we can also write the formulae in the following manner, substituting for m its value $\frac{\sin b \cos A}{\sin M}$. We compute first:

$$\operatorname{tang} M = \operatorname{tang} b \cos A$$

and then find:

$$\operatorname{tang} B = \frac{\operatorname{tang} A \sin M}{\sin (c - M)}$$

$$\operatorname{tang} a = \frac{\operatorname{tang} (c - M)}{\cos B}$$

If we have logarithmic tables, by which we can find immediately the logarithms of the sum or the difference of two numbers from the logarithms of the numbers themselves, it is easier and at the same time more accurate, to use the three equations in their original form without introducing the auxiliary angle. Such tables have been computed for seven decimals by Zech in Tübingen. (J. Zech, Tafeln für die Additions- und Subtractions-Logarithmen für sieben Stellen.)

Köhler's edition of Lalande's logarithmic tables contains similar tables for five decimals.

7. It is always best, to find angles by their tangents; for as their variation is more rapid than that of the sines or cosines, we can find the angles more accurately than by the other functions.

If Δx denotes a small increment of an angle, we have:

$$\Delta (\log \operatorname{tang} x) = \frac{2 \Delta x}{\sin 2x}.$$

Now it is customary to express the increments of angles in seconds of arc; but as the unit of the tangent is the radius, we must express the increment Δx also in parts of the radius, hence we must divide it by the number 206264,8 *). Moreover the logarithms used in the formula are hyperbolic logarithms; therefore if we wish to introduce common logarithms, we must multiply by the modulus $0.4342945 = M$. Finally if we wish to find $\Delta (\log \operatorname{tang} x)$ expressed in units

*) The number 206264.8, whose logarithm is 5.3144251, is always used in order to convert quantities, which are expressed in parts of the radius, into seconds of arc and conversely. The number of seconds in the whole circumference is 1296000, while this circumference if we take the radius as unit is 2π or 6.2831853. These numbers are in the ratio of 206264,8 to 1. Hence, if we wish to convert quantities, expressed in parts of the radius into seconds of arc, we must multiply them by this number; but if we wish to convert quantities, which are expressed in seconds of arc, into parts of the the radius, we must divide them by this number, which is also equal to the number of seconds contained in an arc equal to the radius, while its complement is equal to the sine or the tangent of one second.

of the last decimal of the logarithms used, we must multiply by 10000000 if we employ logarithms of seven decimals. We find therefore:

$$\Delta\,(\log \text{tang}\, x) = \frac{2\,M}{\sin 2\,x} \cdot \frac{\Delta x''}{206264.8}\, 10000000$$

$$= \frac{42.1}{\sin 2\,x}\, \Delta x'',$$

or:

$$\Delta x'' = \frac{\sin 2\,x}{42.1}\, \Delta\,(\log \text{tang}\, x).$$

This equation shows, with what accuracy we may find an angle by its tangent.

Using logarithms of five decimals we may expect our computation to be exact within two units of the last decimal. Hence in this case Δ (log tang x) being equal to 200, the error of the angle would be:

$$\Delta x'' = \frac{200''}{42.1} \sin 2\,x = 5'' \sin 2\,x.$$

Therefore if we use logarithms of five decimals, the error cannot be greater than $5''$ sin $2x$ or as the maximum value of sin $2x$ is unity, not greater than 5 seconds and an error of that magnitude can occur only if the angle is near 45^0. If we use logarithms of seven decimals, the error must needs be a hundred times less; hence in that case the greatest error of an angle found by the tangent will be $0.''05$.

If we find an angle by the sine or cosine, we should have in the formula for Δ (log sin x) or Δ (log cos x) instead of sin $2x$ the factor tang x or cotang x which may have any value up to infinity. Hence as small errors in the logarithm of the sine or cosine of an angle may produce very great errors in the angle itself, it is always preferable, to find the angles by their tangents.

8. Taking one of the angles in the formulae for oblique triangles equal to 90^0, we find the formulae for right-angled triangles. If we denote then the hypothenuse by h, the two sides by c and c' and the two opposite angles by C and C', we get from the first of the formulae (2), taking $A = 90^0$:

$$\cos h = \cos c \cos c',$$

and by the same supposition from the first of the formulae (3):

$$\sin h \sin C = \sin c$$

and from the first of the formulae (4):

$$\sin h \cos C = \cos c \sin c'$$

or dividing this by $\cos h$:

$$\operatorname{tang} h \cos C = \operatorname{tang} c'.$$

Dividing the same formula by $\sin h \sin C$, we find:

$$\operatorname{cotang} C = \operatorname{cotang} c \sin c',$$

or:

$$\operatorname{tang} c = \operatorname{tang} C \sin c'.$$

Combining with this the following formula:

$$\operatorname{tang} c' = \operatorname{tang} C' \sin c,$$

we obtain

$$\cos h = \operatorname{cotg} C \operatorname{cotg} C'.$$

At last from the combination of the two equations:

$$\sin h \sin C' = \sin c'$$
$$\text{and } \sin h \cos C = \cos c \sin c',$$

we find:

$$\cos C = \sin C' \cos c.$$

We have therefore for a right-angled triangle the following six formulae, which embrace all combinations of the five parts:

$$\begin{aligned} \cos h &= \cos c \cos c' \\ \sin c &= \sin h \sin C \\ \operatorname{tang} c &= \operatorname{tang} h \cos C' \\ \operatorname{tang} c &= \operatorname{tang} C \sin c' \\ \cos h &= \operatorname{cotang} C \operatorname{cotang} C' \\ \cos C &= \cos c \sin C', \end{aligned} \qquad (10)$$

and these formulae enable us to find all parts of a right-angled triangle if two of them are given.

Comparing these formulas with those in No. 6, we easily see, that by the introduction of the auxiliary quantities m and M, we substitute two right-angled triangles for the oblique triangle. For if we let fall an arc of a great circle from the vertex C of the oblique triangle vertical to the side c, it is plain, that m is the cosine of this arc and M the part of the side c between the vertex A and the point, where it is intersected by the vertical arc.

9. For the numerical computation of any quantities in astronomy we must always take certain data from observations. But as we are not sure of the absolute accuracy of any of these, on the contrary as we must suppose all of them to be somewhat erroneous, it is necessary in solving a problem to investigate, whether a small error of the observed quantity may not produce a large error of the quantity which is to be found. Now in order to be able easily to make such an estimate, we must differentiate the formulae of spherical trigonometry and in order to embrace all cases we will take all quantities as variable.

Differentiating thus the first of the equations (2), we get:

$$\begin{aligned} -\sin a\, da = & \, db\,[-\sin b \cos c + \cos b \sin c \cos A] \\ & + dc\,[-\cos b \sin c + \sin b \cos c \cos A] \\ & - \sin b \sin c \sin A\,.\,dA. \end{aligned}$$

Here the factor of db is equal to $-\sin a \cos C$ and the factor of dc equal to $-\sin a \cos B$; if we write also $-\sin a \sin c \sin B$ instead of the factor of A, we find the differential-formula:

$$da = \cos C db + \cos B dc + \sin c \sin B dA.$$

Writing the first of the equations (3) in a logarithmic form, we find:

$$\log \sin a + \log \sin B = \log \sin b + \log \sin A$$

and by differentiating it:

$$\text{cotang}\, a da + \text{cotang}\, B dB = \text{cotang}\, b db + \text{cotang}\, A dA.$$

Instead of the first of the formulae (4), we will differentiate the first of the formulae (5), which were found by the combination of the formulae (3) and (4). Thus we find:

$$\begin{aligned} & -\frac{\sin A}{\sin B^2} dB + dA\,[\text{cotang}\, B \cos A - \sin A \cos c] \\ & = -\frac{\sin c}{\sin b^2} db + dc\,[\text{cotang}\, b \cos c + \cos A \sin c] \end{aligned}$$

or:

$$-\frac{\sin A}{\sin B^2} dB - \frac{\cos C}{\sin B} dA = -\frac{\sin c}{\sin b^2} db + \frac{\cos a}{\sin b} dc.$$

Multiplying this equation by $\sin B$, we find:

$$-\frac{\sin a}{\sin b} dB - \cos C dA = -\frac{\sin C}{\sin b} db + \frac{\cos a \sin B}{\sin b} dc,$$

or finally:

$$\sin a dB = \sin C db - \sin B \cos a dc - \sin b \cos C dA.$$

From the first of the formulae (8) we find by similar reductions as those used for formula (2):

$$dA = -\cos c dB - \cos b dC + \sin b \sin C da.$$

Hence we have the following differential formulae of trigonometry:

$$\left.\begin{aligned} da &= \cos C db + \cos B dc + \sin b \sin C dA \\ \text{cotang}\, a da + \text{cotang}\, B dB &= \text{cotang}\, b db + \text{cotang}\, A dA \\ \sin a dB &= \sin C db - \sin B \cos a dc - \sin b \cos C dA \\ dA &= -\cos c dB - \cos b dC + \sin b \sin C da. \end{aligned}\right\} \quad (11)$$

10. As long as the angles are small, we may take their cosines equal to unity and their sines or tangents equal to the arcs themselves, or if we wish to have the arc expressed in seconds we may take 206265 a instead of sin a or tang a. If the angles are not so small that we can neglect already the second term of the sine, we may proceed in the following way.

We have:

$$\frac{\sin a}{a} = 1 - \frac{1}{6}a^2 + \frac{1}{120}a^4 - \ldots.$$

and:

$$\cos a = 1 - \frac{1}{2}a^2 + \frac{1}{24}a^4 - \ldots.$$

hence:

$$\sqrt[3]{\cos a} = 1 - \frac{1}{6}a^2 + \ldots.$$

We have therefore, neglecting only the terms higher than the third power:

$$\frac{\sin a}{a} = \sqrt[3]{\cos a}$$

or:

$$a = \sin a \sqrt[3]{\sec a}$$

This formula is so accurate that using it for an angle of 10^0 we commit only an error less than a second. For we have:

$$\log \sin 10^0 \sqrt[3]{\sec 10^0} = 9.2418864$$

and adding to this the logarithm 5.3144251 and finding the number corresponding to it, we get 36000.″74 or:

$$10^0\ 0'\ 0.''74.$$

11. As we make frequent use in spherical astronomy of the developement of formulae in series, we will deduce those, which are the most important.

If we have an expression of the following form:

$$\operatorname{tang} y = \frac{a \sin x}{1 - a \cos x},$$

we can easily develop y in a series, progressing according to the sines of the multiples of x. For if we have tang $z = \frac{m}{n}$, we find $dz = \frac{n\,dm - m\,dn}{m^2 + n^2}$. If we take thus in the formula for tang y a and y as variable, we find:

$$\frac{dy}{da}=\frac{\sin x}{1-2a\cos x+a^2}$$

and if we develop this expression by the method of indeterminate coefficients in a series progressing according to the powers of a, we find:

$$\frac{dy}{da}=\sin x+a\sin 2x+a^2\sin 3x+\ldots\text{ *)}$$

Integrating this equation and observing that we have $y=0$ when $x=0$, we find the following series for y:

$$y=a\sin x+\tfrac{1}{2}a^2\sin 2x+\tfrac{1}{3}a^3\sin 3x+\ldots \qquad (12)$$

Often we have two equations of the following form:

$$A\sin B=a\sin x$$
$$A\cos B=1-a\cos x,$$

and wish to develop B and log A in a series progressing according to the sines or cosines of the multiples of x. As in this case we have:

$$\text{tang } B=\frac{a\sin x}{1-a\cos x},$$

we find for B a series progressing according to the sines of the multiples of x from the above formula (12). But in order to develop log A in a similar series, we have:

$$A=\sqrt{1-2a\cos x+a^2}.$$

Now we find the following series by the method of indeterminate coefficients:

$$\frac{a\cos x-a^2}{1-2a\cos x+a^2}=a\cos x+a^2\cos 2x+a^3\cos 3x+\ldots\text{ **)}$$

Multiplying this by $-\frac{da}{a}$ and integrating with respect to a, we find for the left side:

$$\tfrac{1}{2}\frac{d\log(1-2a\cos x+a^2)}{da}$$

and as we have log $A=0$ when $a=0$, we get:

$$\log\sqrt{1-2a\cos x+a^2}=\log A=-[a\cos x+\tfrac{1}{2}a^2\cos 2x+\tfrac{1}{3}a^3\cos 3x+\ldots] \quad (13)$$

---

*) It is easily seen, that te first term is $\sin x$, and that the coefficient of a^n is found by the equation:

$$A_n=2A_{n-1}\cos x-A_{n-2}$$

**) It is again evident, that the coefficient of a is $\cos x$, while the coefficient of a_n is found by the equation:

$$A_n=2A_{n-1}\cos x-A_{n-2}.$$

If we have the two equations:

$$A \sin B = a \sin x$$
$$A \cos B = 1 + a \cos x$$

we find by substituting $180 - x$ instead of x in the equations (12) and (13):

$$B = a \sin x - \tfrac{1}{2} a^2 \sin 2x + \tfrac{1}{3} a^3 \sin 3x - \dots \quad (14)$$
$$\log \sqrt{1 + 2a \cos x + a^2} = \log A = a \cos x - \tfrac{1}{2} a^2 \cos 2x + \tfrac{1}{3} a^3 \cos 3x - \dots \quad (15)$$

If we have an expression of the following form:

$$\operatorname{tang} y = n \operatorname{tang} x,$$

we can easily reduce it to the form $\operatorname{tang} y = \dfrac{a \sin x}{1 - a \cos x}$.

For we have:

$$\operatorname{tang}(y - x) = \frac{\operatorname{tang} y - \operatorname{tang} x}{1 + \operatorname{tang} y \operatorname{tang} x} = \frac{(n-1) \operatorname{tang} x}{1 + n \operatorname{tang} x^2}$$
$$= \frac{(n-1) \sin x \cos x}{\cos x^2 + n \sin x^2} = \frac{(n-1) \sin x \cos x}{\frac{1}{2} + \frac{1}{2} \cos 2x + \frac{n}{2} - \frac{n}{2} \cos 2x}$$
$$= \frac{(n-1) \sin 2x}{(n+1) - (n-1) \cos 2x} = \frac{\frac{n-1}{n+1} \sin 2x}{1 - \frac{n-1}{n+1} \cos 2x}.$$

Hence, if we have the equation $\operatorname{tang} y = n \operatorname{tang} x$, we find:

$$y = x + \frac{n-1}{n+1} \sin 2x + \tfrac{1}{2} \left(\frac{n-1}{n+1}\right)^2 \sin 4x + \tfrac{1}{3} \left(\frac{n-1}{n+1}\right)^3 \sin 6x + \dots \quad (16)$$

If we take here:

$$n = \cos \alpha,$$

we have:

$$\frac{n-1}{n+1} = - \operatorname{tang} \tfrac{1}{2} \alpha^2.$$

Hence from the equation:

$$\operatorname{tang} y = \cos \alpha \operatorname{tang} x$$

we get

$$y = x - \operatorname{tang} \tfrac{1}{2} \alpha^2 \sin 2x + \tfrac{1}{2} \operatorname{tang} \tfrac{1}{2} \alpha^4 \sin 4x - \tfrac{1}{3} \operatorname{tang} \tfrac{1}{2} \alpha^6 \sin 6x + \dots \quad (17)$$

If we have: $n = \sec \alpha,$

we find:

$$\frac{n-1}{n+1} = \operatorname{tang} \tfrac{1}{2} \alpha^2.$$

Hence from the equation:

$$\operatorname{tang} y = \sec \alpha \operatorname{tang} x \quad \text{or } \operatorname{tang} x = \cos \alpha \operatorname{tang} y,$$

we obtain for y:

$$y = x + \operatorname{tang} \tfrac{1}{2} \alpha^2 \sin 2x + \tfrac{1}{2} \operatorname{tang} \tfrac{1}{2} \alpha^4 \sin 4x + \tfrac{1}{3} \operatorname{tang} \tfrac{1}{2} \alpha^6 \sin 6x + \dots \quad (18)$$

As we have:

$$\frac{\cos \alpha - \cos \beta}{\cos \alpha + \cos \beta} = \operatorname{tang} \tfrac{1}{2} (\beta - \alpha) \operatorname{tang} \tfrac{1}{2} (\beta + \alpha)$$

and

$$\frac{\sin \alpha - \sin \beta}{\sin \alpha + \sin \beta} = \operatorname{tang} \tfrac{1}{2} (\alpha - \beta) \operatorname{cotang} \tfrac{1}{2} (\alpha + \beta),$$

we find also from the equation:

$$\operatorname{tang} y = \frac{\cos \alpha}{\cos \beta} \operatorname{tang} x,$$

$$y = x - \operatorname{tang} \tfrac{1}{2}(\alpha - \beta) \operatorname{tang} \tfrac{1}{2}(\alpha + \beta) \sin 2x$$
$$+ \tfrac{1}{2} \operatorname{tang} \tfrac{1}{2}(\alpha - \beta)^2 \operatorname{tang} \tfrac{1}{2}(\alpha + \beta)^2 \sin 4x - \ldots$$

and from:

$$\operatorname{tang} y = \frac{\sin \alpha}{\sin \beta} \operatorname{tang} x,$$

$$y = x + \operatorname{tang} \tfrac{1}{2}(\alpha - \beta) \operatorname{cotang} \tfrac{1}{2}(\alpha + \beta) \sin 2x$$
$$+ \tfrac{1}{2} \operatorname{tang} \tfrac{1}{2}(\alpha - \beta)^2 \operatorname{cotang} \tfrac{1}{2}(\alpha + \beta)^2 \sin 4x + \ldots$$

By the aid of the two last formulae we can develop Napier's formulae into a series. For from the equation:

$$\operatorname{tang} \frac{a-b}{2} = \frac{\sin \frac{A-B}{2}}{\sin \frac{A+B}{2}} \operatorname{tang} \frac{c}{2}$$

we find:

$$\frac{a-b}{2} = \frac{c}{2} - \operatorname{tang} \frac{B}{2} \operatorname{cotang} \frac{A}{2} \sin c + \tfrac{1}{2} \operatorname{tang} \frac{B^2}{2} \operatorname{cotang} \frac{A^2}{2} \sin 2c - \ldots.$$

or:

$$\frac{c}{2} = \frac{a-b}{2} + \operatorname{tang} \frac{B}{2} \operatorname{cotang} \frac{A}{2} \sin(a-b) + \tfrac{1}{2} \operatorname{tang} \frac{B^2}{2} \operatorname{cotang} \frac{A^2}{2} \sin 2(a-b) + \ldots$$

and also in the same way from the equation:

$$\operatorname{tang} \frac{a+b}{2} = \frac{\cos \frac{A-B}{2}}{\cos \frac{A+B}{2}} \operatorname{tang} \frac{c}{2}$$

we find the following two series:

$$\frac{a+b}{2} = \frac{c}{2} + \operatorname{tang} \frac{A}{2} \operatorname{tang} \frac{B}{2} \sin c + \tfrac{1}{2} \operatorname{tang} \frac{A^2}{2} \operatorname{tang} \frac{B^2}{2} \sin 2c + \ldots,$$

$$\frac{c}{2} = \frac{a+b}{2} - \operatorname{tang} \frac{A}{2} \operatorname{tang} \frac{B}{2} \sin(a+b) + \tfrac{1}{2} \operatorname{tang} \frac{A^2}{2} \operatorname{tang} \frac{B^2}{2} \sin 2(a+b) - \ldots$$

Quite similar series may be obtained from the two other equations:

$$\operatorname{tang} \frac{A-B}{2} = \frac{\sin \frac{a-b}{2}}{\sin \frac{a+b}{2}} \operatorname{tang} \frac{180-C}{2},$$

$$\operatorname{tang} \frac{A+B}{2} = \frac{\cos \frac{a-b}{2}}{\cos \frac{a+b}{2}} \operatorname{tang} \frac{180-C}{2}.$$

It often happens, that we meet with an equation of the following form: $\cos y = \cos x + b$

from which we wish to develop y into a series progressing according to the powers of b. We obtain this by applying Taylor's theorem to the equation:

$$y = \text{arc}\cos[\cos x + b]$$

For if we put:

$$\cos x = z \text{ and } y = f(z + b),$$

we get:

$$y = f(z) + \frac{df}{dz} b + \tfrac{1}{2} \frac{d^2 f}{dz^2} b^2 + \tfrac{1}{6} \frac{d^3 f}{dz^3} b^3 + \ldots,$$

or as:

$$f(z) = x, \quad \frac{df}{dz} = \frac{dx}{d.\cos x} = -\frac{1}{\sin x},$$

$$\frac{d^2 f}{dz^2} = \frac{d.-\dfrac{1}{\sin x}}{dx} \cdot \frac{dx}{d.\cos x} = -\frac{\cos x}{\sin x^3},$$

$$\frac{d^3 f}{dz^3} = \frac{d.-\dfrac{\cos x}{\sin x^3}}{dx} \cdot \frac{dx}{d.\cos x} = -\frac{[1 + 3\,\text{cotang}\, x^2]}{\sin x^3},$$

$$y = x - \frac{b}{\sin x} - \tfrac{1}{2}\,\text{cotang}\, x \frac{b^2}{\sin x^2} - \tfrac{1}{6}[1 + 3\,\text{cotang}\, x^2] \frac{b^3}{\sin x^3} \ldots \quad (19)$$

In the same way we find from the equation:

$$\sin y = \sin x + b$$

$$y = x + \frac{b}{\cos x} + \tfrac{1}{2}\,\text{tang}\, x \frac{b^2}{\cos x^2} + \tfrac{1}{6}[1 + 3\,\text{tang}\, x^2] \frac{b^3}{\cos x^3} + \ldots \text{*)} \quad (20)$$

B. THE THEORY OF INTERPOLATION.

12. We continually use in astronomy tables, in which the numerical values of a function are given for certain numerical values of the variable quantity. But as we often want to know the value of the function for such values of the variable quantity as are not given in the tables, we must have means, by which we may be able to compute from certain numerical values of a function its value for any other value of the variable quantity or the argument. This is the object of interpolation. By it we substitute for a function, whose analytical expression is either entirely unknown or at least inconvenient for numerical computation, another, which

*) Encke, einige Reihenentwickelungen aus der sphärischen Astronomie. Schumacher's astronomische Nachrichten No. 562.

is derived merely from certain numerical values, but which may be used instead of the former within certain limits.

We can develop any function by Taylor's theorem into a series, progressing according to the powers of the variable quantity. The only case, which forms an exception, is that, in which for a certain numerical value of the variable quantity the value of one of the differential coefficients is infinity, so that the function ceases to be continuous in the neighbourhood of this value. The theory of interpolation being derived from the development of functions into series, which are progressing according to the integral powers of the variable quantity, assumes therefore, that the function is continuous between the limits within which it comes into consideration and can be applied only if this condition is fulfilled.

If we call w the interval or the difference of two following arguments (which we shall consider as constant), we may denote any argument by $a + nw$, where n is the variable quantity, and the function corresponding to that argument by $f(a + nw)$. We will denote further the difference of two consecutive functions $f(a + nw)$ and $f(a + (n + 1)w)$ by $f'(a+n+\frac{1}{2})$, writing within the parenthesis the arithmetical mean of the two arguments, to which the difference belongs, but omitting the factor w *). Thus $f'(a + \frac{1}{2})$ denotes the difference of $f(a + w)$ and $f(a)$, $f'(a + \frac{3}{2})$ the difference of $f(a+2w)$ and $f(a+w)$. In a similar manner we will denote the higher differences, indicating their order by the accent. Thus for instance $f''(a+1)$ is the difference of the two first differences $f'(a+\frac{3}{2})$ and $f'(a+\frac{1}{2})$.

The schedule of the arguments and the corresponding functions with their differences in thus as follows:

Argument	Function	I. Diff.	II. Diff.	III. Diff.	IV. Diff.	V. Diff.
$a - 3w$	$f(a - 3w)$					
		$f'(a - \frac{5}{2})$				
$a - 2w$	$f(a - 2w)$		$f''(a - 2)$			
		$f'(a - \frac{3}{2})$		$f'''(a - \frac{3}{2})$		
$a - w$	$f(a - w)$		$f''(a - 1)$		$f^{IV}(a - 1)$	
		$f'(a - \frac{1}{2})$		$f'''(a - \frac{1}{2})$		$f^{V}(a - \frac{1}{2})$
a	$f(a)$		$f''(a)$		$f^{IV}(a)$	
		$f'(a + \frac{1}{2})$		$f'''(a + \frac{1}{2})$		$f^{V}(a + \frac{1}{2})$
$a + w$	$f(a + w)$		$f''(a + 1)$		$f^{IV}(a + 1)$	
		$f'(a + \frac{3}{2})$		$f'''(a + \frac{3}{2})$		
$a + 2w$	$f(a + 2w)$		$f''(a + 2)$			
		$f'(a + \frac{5}{2})$				
$a + 3w$	$f(a + 3w)$					

*) This convenient notation was introduced by Encke in his paper on mechanical quadrature in the Berliner Jahrbuch für 1837.

All differences which have the same quantity as the argument of the function, are placed on the same horizontal line. In differences of an odd order the argument of the function consists of $a+$ a fraction whose denominator is 2.

13. As we may develop any function by Taylor's theorem into a series progressing according to the integral powers of the variable quantity, we can assume:

$$f(a+nw)=\alpha+\beta\,.\,nw+\gamma\,.\,n^2w^2+\delta\,.\,n^3w^3+\ldots$$

If the analytical expression of the function $f(a)$ were known, we might find the coefficients α, β, γ, δ etc., as we have $\alpha=f(a)$ $\beta=\frac{d\,.\,f(a)}{da}$ etc. We will suppose however, that the analytical expression is not given, or at least that we will not make use of it, even if it is known, but that we know the numerical values of the function $f(a+nw)$ for certain values of the argument $a+nw$. Then substituting those different values of the variable n successively in the equation above, we get as many equations as we know values of the function and we may therefore find the values of the coefficients α, β, γ, δ etc. from them. It is easily seen, that we have $\alpha=f(a)$ and that βw, γw^2 etc. are linear functions of differences, which all may be reduced to a certain series of differences, so that we may assume $f(a+nw)$ to be of the following form:

$$f(a+nw)=f(a)+A\,.\,f'(a+\tfrac{1}{2})+B\,.\,f''(a+1)+C\,.\,f'''(a+\tfrac{3}{2})+\ldots.$$

where A, B, $C\ldots$ are functions of n, which may be determined by the introduction of certain values of n. But when n is an integral number, any function $f(a+nw)$ is derived from $f(a)$ and the above differences by merely adding them successively, if we take the higher differences as constant or if we consider the different values of the function as forming an arithmetical series of a higher order. If already the first differences are constant, we have simply $f(a+nw)=f(a)+n\,f'(a+\frac{1}{2})$, if the second differences are constant, we must add to the above value $f''(a+1)$ multiplied by the sum of the numbers from 1 to $n-1$ or by $\frac{n(n-1)}{1.2}$; and if only the third differences are constant, we have to add still $f''(a+\frac{3}{2})$ multiplied by the sum of the numbers 1, $1+2$, $1+2+3$ etc. to

$1+2+\ldots+n-2$ or by $\frac{n(n-1)(n-2)}{1.2.3}$. We have therefore in general $A=n$, $B=\frac{n(n-1)}{1.2}$, $C=\frac{n(n-1)(n-2)}{1.2.3}$ etc. hence:

$$f(a+nw)=f(a)+nf'(a+\tfrac{1}{2})+\frac{n(n-1)}{1.2}f''(a+1)$$
$$+\frac{n(n-1)(n-2)}{1.2.3}f'''(a+\tfrac{3}{2})+\ldots, \quad (1)$$

where the law of progression is obvious *).

This formula is known as Newton's formula for interpolation. The coefficient of the difference of the order n is equal to the coefficient of x^n in the development of $(1+x)^n$.

Example. According to the Berlin Almanac for 1850 we have the following heliocentric longitudes of Mercury for mean noon:

		I. Diff.	II. Diff.	III. Diff.	
Jan. 0	303° 25′ 1″.5				
		+6° 41′ 50″.0			
2	310 6 51 .5		+18′ 48″.0		
		7 0 38 .0		+2′ 44″.4	
4	317 7 29 .5		21 32 .4		+10″.1
		7 22 10 .4		2 54 .5	
6	324 29 39 .9		24 26 .9		4 .7
		7 46 37 .3		2 59 .2	
8	332 16 17 .2		27 26 .1		
		8 14 3 .4			
10	340 30 20 .6				

If we wish to find now the longitude of Mercury for Jan. 1 at mean noon, we have:

$$f(a)=303^\circ\ 25'\ 1''.5 \text{ and } n=\tfrac{1}{2},$$

further:

			Product:
$f'(a+\frac{1}{2})=$	$+6^\circ\ 41'\ 50''.0$,	$n=\frac{1}{2}$	$+3^\circ\ 20'\ 55''.0$
$f''(a+1)=$	$+18\ 48.0$,	$\frac{n(n-1)}{1.2}=-\frac{1}{8}$	$-2\ 21.0$
$f'''(a+\frac{3}{2})=$	$+2\ 44.4$,	$\frac{n(n-1)(n-2)}{1.2.3}=+\frac{1}{16}$	$+10.3$
$f^{IV}(a+2)=$	$+10.1$,	$\frac{n(n-1)(n-2)(n-3)}{1.2.3.4}=-\frac{5}{128}$	-0.4

*) We can see this easily by the manner in which the successive functions are formed by the differences. For if we denote these for the sake of brevity by f', f'', f''' etc. we have the following table:

	I. Diff.	II. Diff.	III. Diff.
$f(a)$			
	f'		
$f(a)+f'$		f''	
	$f'+f''$		f'''
$f(a)+2f'+f''$		$f''+f'''$	
	$f'+2f''+f'''$		f'''
$f(a)+3f'+3f''+f'''$		$f''+2f'''$	
	$f'+3f''+3f'''$		f'''
$f(a)+4f'+6f''+4f'''$		$f''+3f'''$	
	$f'+4f''+6f'''$		f'''
$f(a)+5f'+10f''+10f'''$		$f''+4f'''$	
	$f'+5f''+10f'''$		f'''
$f(a)+6f'+15f''+20f'''$		$f''+5f'''$	
	$f'+6f''+15f'''$		
$f(a)+7f'+21f''+35f'''$			

Hence we have to add to $f(a)$

$$+3^0\ 18'\ 43''.9$$

and we find the longitude of Mercury for Jan. 1 0^h

$$306^0\ 43'\ 45''.4.$$

We may write Newton's formula in the following more convenient form, by which we gain the advantage of using more simple fractions as factors:

$$f(a+nw)=f(a)+n\left[f'(a+\tfrac{1}{2})+\frac{n-1}{2}\left[f''(a+1)+\frac{n-2}{3}\times\right.\right.$$
$$\left.\left.\times\left[f'''(a+\tfrac{3}{2})+\frac{n-3}{4}\left[f^{IV}(a+2)\right]\right.\right.\right] \quad (1\,a)$$

If n is again equal to $\frac{1}{2}$, we have $\frac{n-3}{4}=-\frac{5}{8}$, hence $\frac{n-3}{4}f^{IV}(a+2)=-6''.3$. Adding this to $f'''(a+\frac{3}{2})$ and multiplying the sum by $\frac{n-2}{3}=-\frac{1}{2}$, we find $-1'\ 19''.0$. Adding this again to $f''(a+1)$ and multiplying the sum by $\frac{n-1}{2}=-\frac{1}{4}$, we get $-4'\ 22''.2$ and if we finally add this to $f'(a+\frac{1}{2})$ and multiply by $n=\frac{1}{2}$, we have to add $3^0\ 18'\ 43''.9$ to $f(a)$ and thus we find the same value as before, namely $306^0\ 43'\ 45''.4$.

14. We can find more convenient formulae of interpolation, if we transform Newton's formula so, that it contains only such differences as are found on the same horizontal line and that for instance starting from $f(a)$ we have to use only the differences $f(a+\frac{1}{2})$, $f''(a)$ and $f'''(a+\frac{1}{2})$. The two first terms of Newton's formula may therefore be retained.

Now we have:

$$\begin{aligned}
f''(a+1) &= f''(a)+f'''(a+\tfrac{1}{2}),\\
f'''(a+\tfrac{3}{2}) &= f'''(a+\tfrac{1}{2})+f^{IV}(a+1)\\
&= f'''(a+\tfrac{1}{2})+f^{IV}(a)+f^{V}(a+\tfrac{1}{2}),\\
f^{IV}(a+2) &= f^{IV}(a+1)+f^{V}(a+\tfrac{3}{2})\\
&= f^{IV}(a)+2f^{V}(a+\tfrac{1}{2})+f^{VI}(a+1),\\
f^{V}(a+\tfrac{5}{2}) &= f^{V}(a+\tfrac{3}{2})+f^{VI}(a+2)\\
&= f^{V}(a+\tfrac{1}{2})+f^{VI}(a+1)+f^{VI}(a+2),
\end{aligned}$$

etc.

We obtain thus as coefficient of $f''(a)$:

$$\frac{n(n-1)}{1.2},$$

as coefficient of $f'''(a+\frac{1}{2})$:

$$\frac{n(n-1)}{1.2}+\frac{n(n-1)(n-2)}{1.2.3}=\frac{(n+1)n(n-1)}{1.2.3},$$

as coefficient of $f^{\text{IV}}(a)$:

$$\frac{n(n-1)(n-2)}{1.2.3}+\frac{n(n-1)(n-2)(n-3)}{1.2.3.4}=\frac{(n+1)n(n-1)(n-2)}{1.2.3.4},$$

at last as coefficient of $f^{\text{V}}(a+\frac{1}{2})$:

$$\frac{n(n-1)(n-2)}{1.2.3}+2.\frac{n(n-1)(n-2)(n-3)}{1.2.3.4}+\frac{n(n-1)(n-2)(n-3)(n-4)}{1.2.3.4.5}$$
$$=\frac{(n+2)(n+1)n(n-1)(n-2)}{1.2.3.4.5},$$

where the law of progression is obvious. Hence we have:

$$f(a+nw)=f(a)+nf'(a+\tfrac{1}{2})+\frac{n(n-1)}{1.2}f''(a)+\frac{(n+1)n(n-1)}{1.2.3}f'''(a+\tfrac{1}{2})$$
$$+\frac{(n+1)n(n-1)(n-2)}{1.2.3.4}f^{\text{IV}}(a)+\frac{(n+2)(n+1)n(n-1)(n-2)}{1.2.3.4.5}f^{\text{V}}(a+\tfrac{1}{2})+\ldots \quad (2)$$

If we introduce instead of the differences, whose argument is $a+\frac{1}{2}$, those whose argument is $a-\frac{1}{2}$, we find:

$$f'(a+\tfrac{1}{2})=f'(a-\tfrac{1}{2})+f''(a),$$
$$f'''(a+\tfrac{1}{2})=f'''(a-\tfrac{1}{2})+f^{\text{IV}}(a),$$
$$f^{\text{V}}(a+\tfrac{1}{2})=f^{\text{V}}(a-\tfrac{1}{2})+f^{\text{VI}}(a).$$

Therefore in this case the differences of an odd order remain the same, but the coefficient of $f''(a)$ is:

$$n+\frac{n(n-1)}{1.2}=\frac{n(n+1)}{1.2}$$

and that of $f^{\text{IV}}(a)$:

$$\frac{(n+1)n(n-1)}{1.2.3}+\frac{(n+1)n(n-1)(n-2)}{1.2.3.4}=\frac{(n-1)n(n+1)(n+2)}{1.2.3.4}.$$

We find therefore:

$$f(a+nw)=f(a)+nf'(a-\tfrac{1}{2})+\frac{n(n+1)}{1.2}f''(a)+\frac{(n-1)n(n+1)}{1.2.3}f'''(a-\tfrac{1}{2})$$
$$+\frac{(n-1)n(n+1)(n+2)}{1.2.3.4}f^{\text{IV}}(a)+\frac{(n-2)(n-1)n(n+1)(n+2)}{1.2.3.4.5}f^{\text{V}}(a-\tfrac{1}{2})+\ldots,$$

where again the law of progression is obvious.

Supposing now, that we have to interpolate for a value, whose argument lies between a and $a-w$, n will be negative. But if n shall denote a positive number, we must introduce $-n$ instead of n in the above formula, which therefore is changed into the following:

$$f(a-nw)=f(a)-nf'(a-\tfrac{1}{2})+\frac{n(n-1)}{1.2}f''(a)$$
$$-\frac{(n-1)n(n+1)}{1.2.3}f'''(a-\tfrac{1}{2})+\frac{(n+1)n(n-1)(n-2)}{1.2.3.4}f^{IV}(a) \qquad (3)$$
$$-\frac{(n+2)(n+1)n(n-1)(n-2)}{1.2.3.4.5}f^{V}(a-\tfrac{1}{2})+\ldots$$

This formula we use therefore if we interpolate backwards. Making the same change with the formulae (2) and (3) as before made with Newton's formula, we find:

$$f(a+nw)=f(a)+n\left[f'(a+\tfrac{1}{2})+\frac{n-1}{2}\left[f''(a)+\frac{n+1}{3}\times\right.\right.$$
$$\times\left[f'''(a+\tfrac{1}{2})+\frac{n-2}{4}\left[f^{IV}(a)+\ldots\right.\right. \qquad (2a)$$

$$f(a-nw)=f(a)-n\left[f'(a-\tfrac{1}{2})-\frac{n-1}{2}\left[f''(a)-\frac{n+1}{3}\times\right.\right.$$
$$\times\left[f'''(a-\tfrac{1}{2})-\frac{n-2}{4}\left[f^{IV}(a)-\ldots\right.\right. \qquad (3a)$$

If we imagine therefore a horizontal line drawn through the table of the functions and differences near the place which the value of the function, which we seek, would occupy and if we use the first formula, when $a+nw$ is nearer to a than to $a+w$, and the second one, when $a-nw$ is nearer to a than to $a-w$, we have to use always those differences, which are situated next to the horizontal line on both sides. It is then not at all necessary, to pay any attention to the sign of the differences, but we have only to correct each difference so that it comes nearer to the difference on the other side of the horizontal line. For instance if we apply the first formula, the argument being between a and $a+\frac{1}{2}w$, the horizontal line would lie between $f''(a)$ and $f''(a+1)$. Then we have to add to $f''(a)$:

$$+\frac{n+1}{3}f'''(a+\tfrac{1}{2})=+\frac{n+1}{3}\left[f''(a+1)-f''(a)\right].$$

Therefore if $f''(a)$ is $\binom{\text{smaller}}{\text{greater}}$ than $f''(a+1)$, the corrected $f''(a)$ will be $\binom{\text{greater}}{\text{smaller}}$ and hence come nearer $f''(a+1)$.

A little greater accuracy may be obtained by using instead of the highest difference the arithmetical mean of the two differences next to the horizontal line on both sides of it. We shall denote the arithmetical mean of two differences by the sign of the differences, adopted before, but using as the argument the arithmetical mean of the arguments of the two differences, so that we have for instance:

$$f'(a+n)=\frac{f'(a+n-\frac{1}{2})+f'(a+n+\frac{1}{2})}{2}$$

As in this case the quantities within the parenthesis are fractions for differences of an even order and integral numbers for those of an odd order, while in the case of simple differences they are just the reverse, this notation cannot give rise to any ambiguity. If we stop for instance at the second differences, we must use when we interpolate in a forward direction the arithmetical mean of $f''(a)$ and $f''(a+1)$ or $f''(a+\frac{1}{2})$, so that we take now instead of the term

$$\frac{n(n-1)}{1.2}f''(a)$$

the term:

$$\frac{n(n-1)}{1.2}f''(a+\tfrac{1}{2}) \text{ or } \frac{n(n-1)}{1.2}[f''(a)+\tfrac{1}{2}f'''(a+\tfrac{1}{2})].$$

Hence while using merely $f''(a)$ we commit an error equal to the whole third term, the error which we now commit, is only:

$$\left(\frac{n(n-1)(n+1)}{1.2.3}-\frac{n(n-1)}{1.2.2}\right)f'''(a+\tfrac{1}{2})=\frac{n(n-1)(n-\frac{1}{2})}{1.2.3}f'''(a+\tfrac{1}{2}).$$

If we have $n=\frac{1}{2}$, this error, depending on the third differences, is therefore reduced to nothing, and as it is in this case indifferent, which of the two formulae (2) or (3) we use, as we can either start from the argument a and interpolate in a forward direction or starting from the argument $a+w$ interpolate in a backward direction, we get the most convenient formula by the combination of the two. Now for $n=\frac{1}{2}$ formula (2) becomes:

$$f(a+\tfrac{1}{2}w)=f(a)+\tfrac{1}{2}f'(a+\tfrac{1}{2})+\frac{\frac{1}{2}\cdot-\frac{1}{2}}{1.2}f''(a)+\frac{\frac{3}{2}\cdot\frac{1}{2}\cdot-\frac{1}{2}}{1.2.3}f'''(a+\tfrac{1}{2})$$
$$+\frac{\frac{3}{2}\cdot\frac{1}{2}\cdot-\frac{1}{2}\cdot-\frac{3}{2}}{1.2.3.4}f^{\mathrm{IV}}(a)+\ldots$$

while formula (3) becomes, if the argument $(a+w)$ is made the starting point:

$$f(a+\tfrac{1}{2}w)=f(a+w)-\tfrac{1}{2}f'(a+\tfrac{1}{2})+\frac{\frac{1}{2}\cdot-\frac{1}{2}}{1.2}f''(a+1)$$
$$-\frac{-\frac{1}{2}\cdot\frac{1}{2}\cdot\frac{3}{2}}{1.2.3}f'''(a+\tfrac{1}{2})+\frac{\frac{3}{2}\cdot\frac{1}{2}\cdot-\frac{1}{2}\cdot-\frac{3}{2}}{1.2.3.4}f^{\mathrm{IV}}(a+1)-\ldots$$

If we take the arithmetical mean of these two formulae, all terms containing differences of an odd order disappear and we obtain thus for interpolating a value, which lies exactly in the middle between two arguments, the following very convenient formula, which contains only the arithmetical mean of even differences:

$$f(a+\tfrac{1}{2}w)=f(a+\tfrac{1}{2})-\frac{1}{8}f''(a+\tfrac{1}{2})+\frac{3}{128}f^{\mathrm{IV}}(a+\tfrac{1}{2})-\frac{5}{1024}f^{\mathrm{VI}}(a+\tfrac{1}{2})+\ldots (4)$$

or:

$$f(a+\tfrac{1}{2}w)=f(a+\tfrac{1}{2})-\frac{1}{8}[f''(a+\tfrac{1}{2})-\frac{3}{16}[f^{\mathrm{IV}}(a+\tfrac{1}{2})-\frac{5}{24}[f^{\mathrm{VI}}(a+\tfrac{1}{2})-\ldots, \quad (4a)$$

where the law of progression is obvious.

Example. If we wish to find the longitude of Mercury for Jan. 4 12^h, we apply formula (2*a*). The differences, which we have to use, are the following:

		I. Diff.	II. Diff.	III. Diff.	IV. Diff.
		+ 7° 0′ 38″. 0		+ 2′ 44″. 3	
Jan. 4	317° 7′ 29″. 5		+ 21′ 32″. 4		+ 10″. 1
		7 22 10 . 4		2 54 . 5	
6	324 29 39 . 9		24 26 . 9		4 . 7

In this case we have $n=\frac{1}{4}$, hence:

$$\frac{n-1}{2}=\frac{3}{8},\quad \frac{n+1}{3}=\frac{5}{12},\quad \frac{n-2}{4}=\frac{7}{16},$$

taking no account of the signs and we get:

arithmetical mean of the 4th differences	$\times \frac{7}{16} =$		3″. 2
corrected third difference	2′ 51″. 3	$\times \frac{5}{12} =$	1′ 11″. 4
corrected second difference	22′ 43″. 8	$\times \frac{3}{8} =$	8′ 31″. 4
corrected first difference	7° 13′ 39″. 0	$\times \frac{1}{4} =$	1° 48′ 24″. 7,

hence the longitude for Jan. 4 . 5

318° 55′ 54″. 2.

If we wish to find the longitude for Jan. 5.5, we have to apply formula (3*a*) and to use the differences, which are on both sides of the lower one of the two horizontal lines. Then we find the longitude for Jan. 5 . 5

322° 36′ 56″. 7.

In order to make an application of formula (4*a*) we will now find the longitude for Jan. 5 . 0, and get:

arithmetical mean of the 4th differences	$\times - \frac{3}{16} =$	— 1″. 4
arithmetical mean of the 2d differences	$\times - \frac{1}{8} =$	— 2′ 52″. 3
arithmetical mean of the functions	$=$	320° 48′ 34″. 7

hence the longitude for Jan. 5.0

320° 45′ 42″. 4.

Computing now the differences of the values found by interpolation we obtain:

		I. Diff.	II. Diff.	III. Diff.
Jan. 4.0	317° 7′29″.5			
		+ 1° 48′24″.7		
4.5	318 55 54 .2		+ 1′23″.5	
		1 49 48 .2		+ 2″.6
5.0	320 45 42 .4		1 26 .1	
		1 51 14 .3		+ 2″.8
5.5	322 36 56 .7		1 28 .9	
		1 52 43 .2		
6.0	324 29 39 .9			

The regular progression of the differences shows us, that the interpolation was accurately made. This check by forming the differences we can always employ, when we have computed a series of values of a function at equal intervals of the argument. For supposing that an error x has been made in computing the value of $f(a)$, the table of the differences will now be as follows:

$f(a-3w)$				
	$f'(a-\frac{5}{2})$			
$f(a-2w)$		$f''(a-2)$		
	$f'(a-\frac{3}{2})$		$f'''(a-\frac{3}{2})+x$	
$f(a-w)$		$f''(a-1)+x$		$f^{IV}(a-1)-4x$
	$f'(a-\frac{1}{2})+x$		$f'''(a-\frac{1}{2})-3x$	
$f(a)+x$		$f''(a)-2x$		$f^{IV}(a)+6x$
	$f'(a+\frac{1}{2})-x$		$f'''(a+\frac{1}{2})+3x$	
$f(a+w)$		$f''(a+1)+x$		$f^{IV}(a+1)-4x$
	$f'(a+\frac{3}{2})$		$f'''(a+\frac{3}{2})-x$	
$f(a+2w)$		$f''(a+2)$		
	$f'(a+\frac{5}{2})$			
$f(a+3w)$				

Hence an error in the value of a function shows itself very much increased in the higher differences and the greatest irregularities occur on the same horizontal line with the erroneous value of the function.

15. We often have occasion to find the numerical value of the differential coefficient of a function, whose analytical expression in not known and of which only a series of numerical values at equal intervals from each other is given. In this case we must use the formulae for interpolation in order to compute these numerical values of the differential coefficients.

If we develop Newton's formula for interpolation according to the powers of n, we find:

$$f(a+nw)=f(a)+n\left[f'(a+\tfrac{1}{2})-\tfrac{1}{2}f''(a+1)+\tfrac{1}{3}f'''(a+\tfrac{3}{2})-\ldots\right.$$
$$+\frac{n^2}{1.2}\left[f''(a+1)-f'''(a+\tfrac{3}{2})+\ldots\right]$$
$$+\frac{n^3}{1.2.3}\left[f'''(a+\tfrac{3}{2})-\ldots\right.$$

but as we have also according to Taylor's theorem:

$$f(a+nw)=f(a)+\frac{df(a)}{da}nw+\frac{d^2f(a)}{da^2}\frac{n^2w^2}{1.2}+\frac{d^3f(a)}{da^3}\frac{n^3w^3}{1.2.3}+\ldots$$

we find by comparing the two series:

$$\frac{df(a)}{da}=\frac{1}{w}\left[f'(a+\tfrac{1}{2})-\tfrac{1}{2}f''(a+1)+\tfrac{1}{3}f'''(a+\tfrac{3}{2})-\ldots\right]$$

$$\frac{d^2f(a)}{da^2}=\frac{1}{w^2}\left[f''(a+1)-f'''(a+\tfrac{3}{2})+\ldots\right].$$

More convenient values of the differential coefficients may be deduced from formula (2) in No. 14. Introducing the arithmetical mean of the odd differences by the equations:

$$f'(a+\tfrac{1}{2})=f'(a)+\tfrac{1}{2}f''(a)$$
$$f'''(a+\tfrac{1}{2})=f'''(a)+\tfrac{1}{2}f^{IV}(a)$$

etc.

we find:

$$f(a+nw)=f(a)+nf'(a)+\frac{n^2}{1.2}f''(a)+\frac{(n+1)n(n-1)}{1.2.3}f'''(a)$$
$$+\frac{(n+1)n^2(n-1)}{1.2.3.4}f^{IV}(a)+\ldots$$

This formula contains the even differences which are on the same horizontal line with $f(a)$, and the arithmetical mean of the odd differences, which are on both sides of the horizontal line. Developing it according to the powers of n we obtain:

$$f(a+nw)=f(a)+n\left[f'(a)-\tfrac{1}{6}f'''(a)+\tfrac{1}{30}f^{V}(a)-\tfrac{1}{140}f^{VII}(a)+\ldots\right]$$
$$+\frac{n^2}{1.2}\left[f''(a)-\tfrac{1}{12}f^{IV}(a)+\tfrac{1}{90}f^{VI}(a)-\ldots\right]$$
$$+\frac{n^3}{1.2.3}\left[f'''(a)-\tfrac{1}{4}f^{V}(a)+\tfrac{7}{120}f^{VII}(a)-\ldots\right]$$
$$+\frac{n^4}{1.2.3.4}\left[f^{IV}(a)-\tfrac{1}{6}f^{VI}(a)+\ldots\right]$$
$$+\frac{n^5}{1.2.3.4.5}\left[f^{V}(a)-\tfrac{1}{3}f^{VII}(a)+\ldots\right]$$

and from this we find:

$$\begin{aligned}\frac{df(a)}{da}&=\frac{1}{w}\left[f'(a)-\tfrac{1}{6}f'''(a)+\tfrac{1}{30}f^{V}(a)-\tfrac{1}{140}f^{VII}(a)+\ldots\right],\\ \frac{d^2f(a)}{da^2}&=\frac{1}{w^2}\left[f''(a)-\tfrac{1}{12}f^{IV}(a)+\tfrac{1}{90}f^{VI}(a)-\ldots\right],\\ \frac{d^3f(a)}{da^3}&=\frac{1}{w^3}\left[f'''(a)-\tfrac{1}{4}f^{V}(a)+\tfrac{7}{120}f^{VII}(a)-\ldots\right],\end{aligned}\tag{5}$$

etc.

If we wish to find the differential coefficient of a function, which is not given itself, for instance of $f(a+nw)$, we must substitute in these formulae $a+n$ instead of a, so that we have:

$$\frac{df(a+nw)}{da} = \frac{1}{w}\left[f'(a+n) - \tfrac{1}{6}f'''(a+n) + \tfrac{1}{30}f^{V}(a+n) - \ldots\right],$$
$$\frac{d^2f(a+nw)}{da^2} = \frac{1}{w^2}\left[f''(a+n) - \tfrac{1}{12}f^{IV}(a+n) + \ldots\right], \tag{6}$$
etc.

The differences which are to be used now do not occur in the table of the differences, but must be computed. For the even differences such as $f''(a+n)$ for instance this computation is simple, as we find these by the ordinary formulae of interpolation, considering merely now $f''(a)$, $f''(a+n)$ etc. as the functions, the third differences as their first ones etc. But the odd differences are arithmetical means, hence we must find a formula for the interpolation of arithmetical means. But we have:

$$f'(a+n) = \frac{f'(a+n-\frac{1}{2}) + f'(a+n+\frac{1}{2})}{2}$$

and according to formula (2) in No. 14:

$$f'(a-\tfrac{1}{2}+n) = f'(a-\tfrac{1}{2}) + nf''(a) + \frac{n(n-1)}{1.2}f'''(a-\tfrac{1}{2}) + \frac{(n+1)n(n-1)}{1.2.3}f^{IV}(a) + \ldots,$$

$$f'(a+\tfrac{1}{2}+n) = f'(a+\tfrac{1}{2}) + nf''(a) + \frac{n(n+1)}{1.2}f'''(a+\tfrac{1}{2}) + \frac{(n+1)n(n-1)}{1.2.3}f^{IV}(a) + \ldots,$$

therefore taking the arithmetical mean of both formulae we find the following formula for the interpolation of an arithmetical mean:

$$f'(a+n) = f'(a) + nf''(a) + \frac{n^2}{1.2}f'''(a) + \tfrac{1}{4}nf^{IV}(a) + \frac{(n+1)n(n-1)}{1.2.3}f^{IV}(a) + \ldots$$

The two terms:

$$\frac{n^2}{1.2}f'''(a) + \tfrac{1}{4}nf^{IV}(a)$$

arise from the arithmetical mean of the terms:

$$\frac{n(n-1)}{1.2}f'''(a-\tfrac{1}{2})$$

and

$$\frac{n(n+1)}{1.2}f'''(a+\tfrac{1}{2})$$

which gives:

$$\frac{n^2}{1.2}f'''(a) + \frac{n}{4}\left[f'''(a+\tfrac{1}{2}) - f'''(a-\tfrac{1}{2})\right].$$

Combining the two terms, which contain $f^{IV}(a)$, we may write the above formula thus:

$$f'(a+n) = f'(a) + nf''(a) + \frac{n^2}{2} f'''(a) + \frac{2n^3+n}{12} f^{IV}(a) + \dots \qquad (7)$$

The formulae 5, 6 and 7 may be used to find the numerical values of the differential coefficients of a function for any argument by using the even differences and the arithmetical means of the odd differences, whenever a series of numerical values of the function at equal intervals is given.

We can also deduce other formulae for the differential coefficients, which contain the simple odd differences and the arithmetical means of the even differences. For if we introduce in formula (3) in No. 14 the arithmetical means of the even differences by the aid of the equations:

$$f(a) = f(a+\tfrac{1}{2}) - \tfrac{1}{2} f'(a+\tfrac{1}{2})$$
$$f''(a) = f''(a+\tfrac{1}{2}) - \tfrac{1}{2} f'''(a+\tfrac{1}{2})$$
$$f^{IV}(a) = f^{IV}(a+\tfrac{1}{2}) - \tfrac{1}{2} f^{V}(a+\tfrac{1}{2})$$
etc.

we find, as we have:

$$\frac{(n+1)\,n\,(n-1)}{1.2.3} - \tfrac{1}{2}\frac{n(n-1)}{1.2} = \frac{n(n-1)(n-\tfrac{1}{2})}{1.2.3}$$
etc.

$$f(a+nw) = f(a+\tfrac{1}{2}) + (n-\tfrac{1}{2}) f'(a+\tfrac{1}{2}) + \frac{n(n-1)}{1.2} f''(a+\tfrac{1}{2})$$
$$+ \frac{n(n-1)(n-\tfrac{1}{2})}{1.2.3} f'''(a+\tfrac{1}{2}) + \frac{(n+1)\,n\,(n-1)(n-2)}{1.2.3.4} f^{IV}(a+\tfrac{1}{2}) + \dots$$

If we write here $n+\frac{1}{2}$ instead of n, the law of the coefficients becomes more obvious, as we get:

$$f[a+(n+\tfrac{1}{2})w] = f(a+\tfrac{1}{2}) + nf'(a+\tfrac{1}{2}) + \frac{(n+\tfrac{1}{2})(n-\tfrac{1}{2})}{1.2} f''(a+\tfrac{1}{2})$$
$$+ \frac{(n+\tfrac{1}{2})\,n\,(n-\tfrac{1}{2})}{1.2.3} f'''(a+\tfrac{1}{2}) + \frac{(n+\tfrac{3}{2})(n+\tfrac{1}{2})(n-\tfrac{1}{2})(n-\tfrac{3}{2})}{1.2.3.4} f^{IV}(a+\tfrac{1}{2}) + \dots$$

Developing this formula according to the powers of n, we find the terms independent of n:

$$f(a+\tfrac{1}{2}) - \frac{1}{8} f''(a+\tfrac{1}{2}) + \frac{3}{8.16} f^{IV}(a+\tfrac{1}{2}) - \dots = f(a+\tfrac{1}{2}w)$$

hence:

$$\begin{aligned} f[a+(n+\tfrac{1}{2})w] &= f(a+\tfrac{1}{2}w) \\ &+ n\,[f'(a+\tfrac{1}{2}) - \tfrac{1}{24}f'''(a+\tfrac{1}{2}) + \tfrac{3}{640}f^{V}(a+\tfrac{1}{2}) - \ldots] \\ &+ \frac{n^2}{1.2}[f''(a+\tfrac{1}{2}) - \tfrac{5}{24}f^{IV}(a+\tfrac{1}{2}) + \tfrac{259}{5760}f^{VI}(a+\tfrac{1}{2}) - \ldots] \\ &+ \frac{n^3}{1.2.3}[f'''(a+\tfrac{1}{2}) - \tfrac{1}{8}f^{V}(a+\tfrac{1}{2}) + \tfrac{37}{1920}f^{VII}(a+\tfrac{1}{2}) - \ldots] \\ &+ \frac{n^4}{1.2.3.4}[f^{IV}(a+\tfrac{1}{2}) - \tfrac{7}{24}f^{VI}(a+\tfrac{1}{2}) + \ldots] \end{aligned}$$

Comparing this formula with the development of $f(a+\frac{1}{2}w+nw)$ according to Taylor's theorem, we find:

$$\begin{aligned} \frac{df(a+\frac{1}{2}w)}{da} &= \frac{1}{w}[f'(a+\tfrac{1}{2}) - \tfrac{1}{24}f'''(a+\tfrac{1}{2}) + \tfrac{3}{640}f^{V}(a+\tfrac{1}{2}) - \ldots] \\ \frac{d^2f(a+\frac{1}{2}w)}{da^2} &= \frac{1}{w^2}[f''(a+\tfrac{1}{2}) - \tfrac{5}{24}f^{IV}(a+\tfrac{1}{2}) + \tfrac{259}{5760}f^{VI}(a+\tfrac{1}{2}) - \ldots] \end{aligned} \tag{8}$$

etc.

These formulae will be the most convenient in case that we have to find the differential coefficients of a function for an argument, which is the arithmetical mean of two successive given arguments. For other arguments, for instance $a+(n+\frac{1}{2})w$ we have again:

$$\begin{aligned} w\,\frac{df[a+(n+\frac{1}{2})w]}{da} &= f'(a+\tfrac{1}{2}+n) - \tfrac{1}{24}f'''(a+\tfrac{1}{2}+n) \\ &+ \tfrac{3}{640}f^{V}(a+\tfrac{1}{2}+n) - .. \end{aligned} \tag{9}$$

etc.

Here we can compute the difference $f'(a+\frac{1}{2}+n)$ as well as all odd differences by the ordinary formulae of interpolation. But as the even differences are arithmetical means, we must use a different formula, which we may deduce from the formula (7) for interpolating an arithmetical mean of odd differences by substuting $a+\frac{1}{2}$ instead of a and increasing all accents by one, so that we have for instance:

$$\begin{aligned} f''(a+\tfrac{1}{2}+n) &= f''(a+\tfrac{1}{2}) + nf'''(a+\tfrac{1}{2}) + \frac{n^2}{2}f^{IV}(a+\tfrac{1}{2}) \\ &+ \frac{2n^3+n}{12}f^{V}(a+\tfrac{1}{2}) + \ldots. \end{aligned}$$

Example. According to the Berlin Almanac for 1848 we have the following right-ascensions of the moon.

		I. Diff.	II. Diff.	III. Diff.	IV. Diff.
Juli 12 0^h	$16^h 14^m 26^s.33$				
		$+25^m 3^s.99$			
12^h	39 30 .32		$+23^s.75$		
		25 27 .74		$-1^s.39$	
13 0^h	17 4 58 .06		22 .36		$-0^s.85$
		25 50 .10		2 .24	
12^h	30 48 .16		20 .12		0 .79
		26 10 .22		3 .03	
14 0^h	56 58 .38		17 .09		0 .67
		26 27 .31		3 .70	
12^h	18 23 25 .69		13 .39		
		26 40 .70			
15 0^h	50 6 .39				

If we wish to find the first differential coefficients for July 13 10^h, 11^h and 12^h and use formula (9), we must first compute the first and third differences for 10^h, 11^h and 12^h. The third of the first differences corresponds to the argument July 13 6^h and is $f'(a+\frac{1}{2})$, we have therefore for 10^h, 11^h and 12^h n respectively equal to $\frac{1}{3}$, $\frac{5}{12}$ and $\frac{1}{2}$. Then interpolating in the ordinary way, we find:

	$f'(a+\frac{1}{2}+n)$	$f'''(a+\frac{1}{2}+n)$
10^h	$+25^m 57^s.11$	$-2^s.51$
11^h	25 58 .81	2 .58
12^h	26 0 .49	2 .64

and from this the differential coefficients:

for 10^h	$+25^m 57^s.21$
11^h	25 58 .92
12^h	26 0 .60

where the unit is an interval of 12 hours. If we wish to find them so that one hour is the unit, we must divide by 12 and find thus the following values:

10^h	$2^m 9^s.77$
11^h	9 .91
12^h	10 .05,

which are the hourly velocities of the moon in right-ascension.

If we had employed formula (6), where the arithmetical means of odd differences are used, taking $a =$ Juli 13 12^h, we would have found for instance for 10^h, where n is $-\frac{1}{6}$, according to formula (7):

$$f'(a-\tfrac{1}{6}) = +25^m 56^s.77 \text{ and } f'''(a-\tfrac{1}{6}) = -2^s.51$$

and from these the differential coefficient according to formula (6) equal to $+2^m 9^s.77$.

The second differences are the following:

for 10^h	$+20^s.55$
11^h	20 .34
12^h	20 .12.

If we add to these the fourth differences multiplied by $-\frac{1}{12}$ and divide by 144, we find the second differential coefficients

for	10^h	$+0^s.1432$
	11^h	0.1417
	12^h	$0.1402.$

where again the unit of time is one hour *).

C. THEORY OF SEVERAL DEFINITE INTEGRALS USED IN SPHERICAL ASTRONOMY.

16. As the integral $\int e^{-t^2} dt$, either taken between the limits 0 and ∞ or between the limits o and T or T and ∞, is often used in astronomy, the most important theorems regarding it and the formulas used for its numerical computation shall be briefly deduced.

The definite integral $\int_0^\infty e^{-t^2} dt$ is a transformation of one of the first class of Euler's integrals known as the Gamma functions. For this class the following notation has been adopted:

$$\int_0^\infty e^{-x} \cdot x^{a-1}\, dx = \Gamma(a), \tag{1}$$

where a always is a positive quantity, and as we may easily deduce the following formula:

$$\int e^{-x} \cdot x^{a-1}\, dx = \int e^{-x}\, d\left(\frac{x^a}{a}\right) = e^{-x} \cdot \frac{x^a}{a} + \frac{1}{a}\int x^a e^{-x}\, dx$$

and as the term without the integral sign becomes equal to zero after the substitution of the limits, we find:

$$\int_0^\infty e^{-x} \cdot x^{a-1}\, dx = \frac{1}{a}\int_0^\infty e^{-x} \cdot x^a\, dx$$

or:

$$a\Gamma(a) = \Gamma(a+1) \tag{2}$$

But as we have also:

$$\int_0^\infty e^{-x}\, dx = \Gamma(1) = 1$$

---

*) Encke on interpolation and on mechanical quadrature in „Berliner Jahrbuch für 1830 und 1837".

it follows, that when n is an integral number, we have:

$$\Gamma(n) = (n-1)(n-2)(n-3)\ldots.1.$$

If we take in the equation (1) $x = t^2$, we find:

$$2\int_0^\infty e^{-t^2}.\, t^{2(a-1)+1}.\, dt = \Gamma(a);$$

hence for $a = \frac{1}{2}$:

$$\int_0^\infty e^{-t^2}.\, dt = \tfrac{1}{2}\,\Gamma(\tfrac{1}{2})$$

In order to find this integral, we will multiply it by a similar one $\int_0^\infty e^{-y^2} dy$, so that we get:

$$\left(\int_0^\infty e^{-t^2} dt\right)^2 = \int_0^\infty e^{-t^2} dt \int_0^\infty e^{-y^2} dy = \int_0^\infty\int_0^\infty e^{-(t^2+y^2)}\, dt\,.\,dy.$$

Taking here $y = xt$, hence $dy = t.dx$, we find:

$$\left(\int_0^\infty e^{-t^2} dt\right)^2 = \int_0^\infty dx \int_0^\infty e^{-(1+x^2)t^2}.\, t\,dt,$$

or as:

$$\int_0^\infty e^{-(1+x^2)t^2}\, t\,dt = \frac{1}{2(1+x^2)},$$

we find:

$$\left(\int_0^\infty e^{-t^2} dt\right)^2 = \tfrac{1}{2}\int_0^\infty \frac{dx}{1+x^2} = \tfrac{1}{2}\,(\text{arc tang}\,\infty - \text{arc tang}\,0) = \frac{\pi}{4},$$

hence:

$$\int_0^\infty e^{-t^2} dt = \tfrac{1}{2}\,\Gamma(\tfrac{1}{2}) = \frac{\sqrt{\pi}}{2}. \tag{3}$$

From this follows $\Gamma(\frac{1}{2}) = \sqrt{\pi}$, hence from equation (2):

$$\Gamma(\tfrac{3}{2}) = \tfrac{1}{2}\sqrt{\pi},\quad \Gamma(\tfrac{5}{2}) = \tfrac{3}{4}\sqrt{\pi} \text{ etc.}$$

If we introduce in equation (1) a new constant quantity by taking $x = ky$, where k shall be positive in order that the limits of the integral may remain unchanged, we find:

$$\int_0^\infty e^{-ky}\, k^{a-1}\, y^{a-1}\, k\,dy = \Gamma(a),$$

hence:

$$\int_0^\infty e^{-ky}\, y^{a-1}\, dy = \frac{\Gamma(a)}{k^a}. \tag{4}$$

17. To find the integral $\int_0^T e^{-t^2} dt$, various methods are used. While T is small, we easily obtain by developing e^{-t^2} into a series:

$$\int_0^T e^{-t^2} dt = T - \frac{T^3}{3} + \frac{1}{2}\frac{T^5}{5} - \frac{1}{2.3}\frac{T^7}{7} + \dots \quad (5)$$

and as we have $\int_0^\infty e^{-t^2} dt = \frac{\sqrt{\pi}}{2}$, we also find from the above formula the integral $\int_0^\infty e^{-t^2} dt$.

This series must always converge, as the numerators increase only at the ratio of T^2, while the denominators are constantly increasing; but only while T is small, does it converge with sufficient rapidity. When therefore T is large, another series is used for computing this integral, which is obtained by integrating by parts. Although this series is divergent if continued indefinitely, yet we can find from it the value of the integral with sufficient accuracy, as it has the property, that the sum of all the terms following a certain term is not greater than this term itself.

We have:

$$\int e^{-t^2} dt = \int \frac{d\left(-\frac{1}{2}e^{-t^2}\right)}{dt} \cdot \frac{dt}{t}$$

or integrating by parts:

$$= -\frac{1}{2}\frac{e^{-t^2}}{t} - \frac{1}{2}\int e^{-t^2}\frac{dt}{t^2}.$$

By the same process we find:

$$-\frac{1}{2}\int e^{-t^2}\frac{dt}{t^2} = -\frac{1}{2}\int \frac{d\left(-\frac{1}{2}e^{-t^2}\right)}{dt}\frac{dt}{t^3} = +\frac{1}{2}\cdot\frac{1}{2}\cdot\frac{e^{-t^2}}{t^3} + \frac{1}{2}\cdot\frac{3}{2}\int e^{-t^2}\frac{dt}{t^4}$$

$$\frac{3}{4}\int e^{-t^2}\frac{dt}{t^4} = \frac{3}{4}\int \frac{d\left(-\frac{1}{2}e^{-t^2}\right)}{dt}\cdot\frac{dt}{t^5} = -\frac{3}{4}\cdot\frac{1}{2}\frac{e^{-t^2}}{t^5} - \dots,$$

or finally:

$$\int e^{-t^2} dt = -\frac{e^{-t^2}}{2t}\left[1 - \frac{1}{2t^2} + \frac{1.3}{(2t^2)^2} - \frac{1.3.5}{(2t^2)^3} + \dots \pm \frac{1.3.5\dots(2n-1)}{(2t^2)^n} \mp \frac{1.3.5\dots(2n+1)}{2^{n+1}}\int e^{-t^2}\frac{dt}{t^{2n+2}}\right],$$

or after substituting the limits:

$$\int_T^\infty e^{-t^2}\,dt = \frac{e^{-T^2}}{2T}\left[1 - \frac{1}{2T^2} + \frac{1.3}{(2T^2)^2} - \frac{1.3.5}{(2T^2)^3} + \ldots \right.$$

$$\left. \pm \frac{1.3.5\ldots.(2n-1)}{(2T^2)^n} \mp \frac{1.3.5\ldots.(2n+1)}{2^{n+1}} \int e^{-t^2}\frac{dt}{t^{2n+2}}\right]. \quad (6)$$

The factors in the numerator are constantly increasing, hence they will become greater than $2T^2$; when this happens, the terms must indefinitely increase, as the numerators increase more than the denominators. But if we consider the remainder:

$$\mp \frac{1.3.5\ldots.(2n+1)}{2^{n+1}} \int_T^\infty e^{-t^2}\frac{dt}{t^{2n+2}},$$

we can easily prove that it is smaller than the last preceding term. For the value of the integral is less than

$$\int_T^\infty \frac{dt}{t^{2n+2}}$$

multiplied by the greatest value of e^{-t^2} between the limits T and ∞ which is e^{-T^2}, and as we have:

$$\int_T^\infty \frac{dt}{t^{2n+2}} = \frac{1}{2n+1}\,\frac{1}{T^{2n+1}},$$

the remainder must always be less than:

$$\mp \frac{1.3.5\ldots 2n-1}{2^{n+1}\,T^{2n+1}}\,e^{-T^2}.$$

Now this expression is that of the last preceding term with opposite sign, so that if the last term is positive, the remainder is negative and less than it. In order therefore to find a very accurate value of the integral, we have only to see, that the last term which we compute is a very small one, as the error committed by neglecting the remaining terms is less than this very small term.

Another method for computing this integral, given by Laplace, consists in converting it into a continued fraction.

If we put:

$$e^{t^2}\int_t^\infty e^{-x^2}\,dx = U, \qquad (a)$$

we find:

$$\frac{dU}{dt} = 2te^{t^2}\int_t^\infty e^{-x^2}dx - e^{t^2}e^{-t^2}$$
$$= 2tU - 1. \qquad (\beta)$$

Now the nth differential coefficient of a product is:

$$\frac{d^n.xy}{dt^n} = \frac{d^n.x}{dt^n}y + n\cdot\frac{d^{n-1}x}{dt^{n-1}}\cdot\frac{dy}{dt} + \frac{n(n-1)}{1.2}\frac{d^{n-2}x}{dt^{n-2}}\cdot\frac{d^2y}{dt^2} + \ldots,$$

hence we have:

$$\frac{d^{n+1}U}{dt^{n+1}} = 2t.\frac{d^nU}{dt^n} + 2n.\frac{d^{n-1}U}{dt^{n-1}},$$

If we denote the product $1.2.3\ldots.n$ by $n!$, we may write this equation thus:

$$\frac{(n+1)}{(n+1)!}\frac{d^{n+1}.U}{dt^{n+1}} = 2t\frac{d^nU}{n!dt^n} + 2\frac{d^{n-1}U}{(n-1)!dt^{n-1}}$$

or denoting $\frac{d^nU}{n!dt^n}$ by U_n:

$$(n+1)U_{n+1} = 2tU_n + 2U_{n-1}.$$

This equation is true for all values of n from $n = 1$, when U_0 is equal to the function U itself. We find from it:

$$-2\frac{U_{n-1}}{U_n} = 2t - (n+1)\frac{U_{n+1}}{U_n},$$

hence:

$$-\frac{1}{2}\frac{U_n}{U_{n-1}} = \frac{1}{2t - (n+1)\frac{U_{n+1}}{U_n}} = \frac{\frac{1}{2t}}{1 - (n+1)\frac{1}{2t}\frac{U_{n+1}}{U_n}}$$

or:

$$-\frac{U_n}{2tU_{n-1}} = \frac{\frac{1}{2t^2}}{1 - (n+1)\frac{1}{2t}\frac{U_{n+1}}{U_n}}. \qquad (\gamma)$$

But we have from equation (β):

$$\frac{U_{\prime}}{U} = 2t - \frac{1}{U},$$

hence:

$$U = \frac{1}{2t - \frac{U_{\prime}}{U}} = \frac{\frac{1}{2t}}{1 - \frac{1}{2t}\frac{U_{\prime}}{U}},$$

and from equation (γ) follows:

$$-\frac{1}{2t}\frac{U_{\prime}}{U} = \frac{\frac{1}{2t^2}}{1 - 2\frac{1}{2t}\frac{U_2}{U_{\prime}}}.$$

If we substitute this value in the former equation and continue the development, we find:

$$U = \cfrac{\frac{1}{2t}}{1 + \cfrac{\frac{1}{2t^2}}{1 + 2\cfrac{\frac{1}{2t^2}}{1 + 3\cfrac{\frac{1}{2t^2}}{1 + \text{etc.},}}}}$$

therefore, taking $\frac{1}{2T^2} = q$

$$2Te^{T^2}\int_T^\infty e^{-t^2}dt = \cfrac{1}{1 + \cfrac{q}{1 + \cfrac{2q}{1 + \cfrac{3q}{1 + \cfrac{4q}{1 + \text{etc.}}}}}} \tag{7}$$

By one of the three formulae (5), (6) or (7) we can always find the value of the integral $\int_0^T e^{-t^2}dt$ or $\int_T^\infty e^{-t^2}dt$, but on account of the frequent use of this transcendental function tables have been constructed for it. One of such tables is given in Bessel's Fundamenta Astronomiae for the function:

$$e^{T^2}\int_T^\infty e^{-t^2}dt,$$

from which the other forms are easily deduced. The first part of this table has the argument T and extends from $T=0$ to $T=1$, the interval of the arguments being one hundreth. But as according to formula (6) the function is the more nearly inversely proportional to its argument, the greater T becomes, the common logarithms of T are used as arguments for values of T greater than 1. This second part of the table extends from the logarithm $T = 0.000$ to log. $T = 1.000$, which for most purposes is sufficient. For still greater arguments the computation by formula (6) is very easy.

18. The integral

$$\int_0^\infty \frac{e^{-r\beta x}\sin\zeta}{\sqrt{\cos\zeta^2 + 2x\sin\zeta^2}}dx$$

can be easily reduced to the one treated above. For if we introduce another variable quantity, given by the equation:

$$\tfrac{1}{2} \operatorname{cotg} \zeta^2 + x = \frac{1}{\beta r} t^2,$$

from which we have $\qquad dx = \frac{2t}{\beta r} dt,$

the above integral is transformed into:

$$\sqrt{\frac{2}{\beta r}}\, e^{T^2} \int_T^\infty e^{-t^2} dt,$$

if we take: $\qquad T = \operatorname{cotang} \zeta \sqrt{\frac{\beta r}{2}}.$

If now we introduce the following notation:

$$e^{T^2} \int_T^\infty e^{-t^2} dt = \Psi(r),$$

we have: $$\int_0^\infty \frac{e^{-r\beta x} \sin \zeta}{\sqrt{\cos \zeta^2 + 2x \sin \zeta^2}} dx = \sqrt{\frac{2}{\beta r}}\, \Psi(r), \tag{8}$$

and also:

$$\int_0^\infty \frac{e^{-rx} \sin \zeta}{\sqrt{\cos \zeta^2 + \frac{2x \sin \zeta^2}{\beta}}} dx = \sqrt{\frac{2\beta}{r}}\, \Psi(r). \tag{9}$$

If we differentiate the expression $e^{-x} \sqrt{\cos \zeta^2 + \frac{2 \sin \zeta^2}{\beta} x}$ with respect to x and then integrate the resulting equation with respect to x between the limits 0 and ∞, we easily find:

$$\int_0^\infty \frac{x e^{-x} \sin \zeta}{\sqrt{\cos \zeta^2 + \frac{2 \sin \zeta^2}{\beta} x}} dx = \sqrt{2\beta} \left\{ (\tfrac{1}{2} - T^2)\, \Psi(1) + \frac{T}{2} \right\}$$

where $T = \operatorname{cotang} \zeta \sqrt{\frac{\beta}{2}}$.

And as we have by formula (9)

$$\int_0^\infty \frac{e^{-x} \sin \zeta}{\sqrt{\cos \zeta^2 + \frac{2 \sin \zeta^2}{\beta} x}} dx = \sqrt{2\beta}\, .\, \Psi(1)$$

we find:

$$\int_0^\infty \frac{(1-x) e^{-x} \sin \zeta}{\sqrt{\cos \zeta^2 + \frac{2 \sin \zeta^2}{\beta} x}} dx = \sqrt{2\beta} \left\{ (\tfrac{1}{2} + T^2)\, \Psi(1) - \frac{T}{2} \right\}, \tag{10}$$

of which formulae we shall also make use hereafter.

D. THE METHOD OF LEAST SQUARES.

19. In astronomy we continually determine quantities by observations. But when we observe any phenomenon repeatedly, we generally find different results by different observations, as the imperfection of the instruments as well as that of our organs of sense, also other accidental external causes produce errors in the observations, which render the result incorrect. It is therefore very important to have a method, by which notwithstanding the errors of single observations we may obtain a result, which is as nearly correct as possible.

The errors committed in making an observation are of two kinds, either constant or accidental. The former are such errors which are the same in all observations and which may be caused either by a peculiarity of the instrument used or by the idiosyncrasy of the observer, which produces the same error in all observations. On the contrary accidental errors are such which as well in sign as in quantity differ for different observations and therefore are not produced by causes which act always in the same sense. These errors may be eliminated by repeating the observations as often as possible, as we may expect, that among a very great number of observations there are as many which give the result too great as there are such which give it too small. But the final result must necessarily remain affected by constant errors, if there are any, when for instance the same observer is observing with the same instrument. In order to eliminate also these errors, it is therefore necessary, to vary as much as possible the methods of observation as well as the instruments and observers themselves, for then also these errors will for the most part destroy each other in the final result, deduced from the single results of each method. Here we shall consider all errors as accidental, supposing, that the methods have been so multiplied as to justify this hypothesis. But if this is not the case the results deduced according to the method given hereafter, may still be affected by constant errors.

If we determine a quantity by immediate measurement, it is natural to adopt the arithmetical mean of all single observations as the most plausible value. But often we do not determine a single quantity by direct observations, but only find values, which give us certain relations between several unknown quantities; we may however always assume, that these relations between the observed and the unknown quantities have the form of linear equations. For although in general the function $f(\xi, \eta, \zeta$ etc.) which expresses this relation between the observed quantities and the unknown quantities ξ, η, ζ, will not be a linear function, we can always procure approximate values of the unknown quantities from the observations and denoting these by ξ_0, η_0, and ζ_0 and assuming that the correct values are $\xi_0 + x$, $\eta_0 + y$, $\zeta_0 + z$ etc., we find from each observation an equation of the following form:

$$f(\xi, \eta, \zeta \ldots) = f(\xi_0, \eta_0, \zeta_0) + \frac{df}{d\xi} x + \frac{df}{d\eta} y + \frac{df}{d\zeta} z,$$

provided that the assumed values are sufficiently approximate as to allow us to neglect the higher powers of x, y, z etc. Here $f(\xi, \eta, \zeta \ldots)$ is the observed value, $f(\xi_0, \eta_0, \zeta_0 \ldots)$ the value computed from the approximate values, hence $f(\xi_0, \eta_0, \zeta_0 \ldots) - f(\xi, \eta, \zeta \ldots) = n$ is a known quantity. Denoting then $\frac{df}{d\xi}$ by a, $\frac{df}{d\eta}$ by b, $\frac{df}{d\zeta}$ by c etc. and distinguishing these quantities for different observations by different accents, we shall find from the single observations equations of the following form:

$$0 = n + ax + by + cz + \ldots,$$
$$0 = n' + a'x + b'y + c'z + \ldots,$$
etc.,

where x, y, z ... are unknown values, which we wish to determine, while n is equal to the computed value of the function of these unknown quantities minus its observed value. There must necessarily be as many such equations as there are observations and their number must be as great as possible, in order to deduce from them values of x, y, z etc. which are as free as possible from the errors of observation. We easily see also, that the coefficients a, b, c .... in the different equations must have different values; for if two of these coefficients in all the different equations were nearly equal or proportional, we should not be able to separate the unknown quantities by which they are multiplied.

In order to find from a large number of such equations the best possible values of the unknown quantities, the following method was formerly employed. First the signs of all equations were changed so as to give the same sign to all the terms containing x. Then adding all equations, another equation resulted, in which the factor of x was the largest possible. In the same way equations were deduced, in which the coefficient of y and z etc. was the largest possible and thus as many equations were found as there were unknown quantities, whose solution furnished pretty correct values of them. But as this method is a little arbitrary, it is better to solve such equations according to the method of least squares, which allows also an idea to be formed of the accuracy of the values obtained. If the observations were perfectly right and the number of the unknown quantities three, to which number we will confine ourselves hereafter, three such equations would be sufficient, in order to find their true values. But as each of the values n found by observations is generally a little erroneous, none of these equations would be satisfied, even if we should substitute the exact values of x, y and z; therefore denoting the residual error by Δ, we ought to write these equations thus:

$$\begin{aligned} \Delta &= n + ax + by + cz, \\ \Delta' &= n' + a'x + b'y + c'z, \end{aligned} \quad (1)$$
$$\text{etc.,}$$

and the problem is this: to find from a large number of such equations those values of x, y and z, which according to those equations are the most probable.

20. We have a right to assume, that small errors are more probable than large ones and that observations, which are nearly correct, occur more frequently than others, also that errors, surpassing a certain limit, will never occur. There must exist therefore a certain law depending on the magnitude of the error, which expresses how often any error occurs. If the number of observations is m, and an error of the magnitude Δ occurs according to this law p times, $\frac{p}{m}$

expresses the probability of the error Δ, and shall be denoted by $\varphi(\Delta)$. This function $\varphi(\Delta)$ must be therefore zero, if Δ surpasses a certain limit and have a maximum for $\Delta = 0$, besides it must have equal values for equal, positive or negative values of Δ. As we have $p = m\varphi(\Delta)$, there will be among m observations $m\varphi(\Delta)$ errors of the magnitude Δ, likewise $m\varphi(\Delta')$ errors of the magnitude Δ' etc.; but as the number of all errors must be equal to the number of all observations, we have:

$$m\varphi(\Delta) + m\varphi(\Delta') + \ldots = m,$$

or:

$$\Sigma\varphi(\Delta) = 1.$$

This sum being that of all errors must be taken between certain limits $-k$ and $+k$, but as according to our hypothesis $\varphi(\Delta)$ is zero beyond this limit, it will make no difference, if we take instead of the limits $-k$ and $+k$ the limits $-\infty$ and $+\infty$. But as any Δ between these limits are possible, as we cannot assign any quantity between the limits $-k$ and $+k$, which may not possibly be equal to an error, as therefore the number of possible errors, hence also the number of the functions $\varphi(\Delta)$ is infinite, each $\varphi(\Delta)$ must be an infinitely small quantity. The probability that an error lies between certain limits, is equal to the sum of all values $\varphi(\Delta)$ which lie between these limits. If these limits are infinitely near to each other, the value $\varphi(\Delta)$ may be considered constant, hence $\varphi(\Delta).d\Delta$ expresses the chance, that an error lies between the limit Δ and $\Delta + d\Delta$. The probability that an error lies between the limits a and b, is therefore expressed by the definite integral

$$\int_a^b \varphi(\Delta) \,.\, d\Delta$$

and we have according to the formula found before:

$$\int_{-\infty}^{+\infty} \varphi(\Delta) \,.\, d\Delta = 1.$$

According to the theory of probabilities we know, that when $\varphi(\Delta)$, $\varphi(\Delta')$ etc. express the probability of the errors Δ, Δ' etc. the probability, that these errors occur together, is equal to the product of the probabilities of the separate errors. If therefore W denotes the probability, that in a series of observations the errors Δ, Δ', Δ'' etc. occur, we have:

$$W = \varphi(\Delta) \cdot \varphi(\Delta') \cdot \varphi(\Delta'') \dots \qquad (2)$$

Therefore if for certain assumed values of x, y, z the errors Δ, Δ', Δ'' etc. express the residual errors of the equations (1), W is the probability that just these errors have been made and may therefore be used for measuring the probability of these values of x, y and z. Any other system of values of x, y and z will give also another system of residual errors and the most plausible values of x, y and z must evidently be those, which make the probability that just these errors have been committed a maximum, for which therefore the function W itself is a maximum. But in order to determine, when $\varphi(\Delta)$ is a maximum, it is necessary to know the form of this function.

Now in the case that there is only one unknown quantity, for which the m values n, n', n'' etc. have been found by observations, it is always the rule, to take the mean of all observation as the most probable value of x. We have therefore:

$$x = \frac{n + n' + n'' + \dots}{m}$$

or:

$$n - x + n' - x + n'' - x \dots = 0, \qquad (a)$$

where $n - x$, $n' - x$ etc. correspond to the errors Δ, so that we have $n - x = \Delta$, $n' - x = \Delta'$ etc. But as W is a maximum for the most probable value of x, we find differentiating equation (2) in a logarithmic form:

$$\frac{d \cdot \log \varphi(\Delta)}{d\Delta} \cdot \frac{d\Delta}{dx} + \frac{d \cdot \log \varphi(\Delta')}{d\Delta'} \cdot \frac{d\Delta'}{dx} + \dots = 0,$$

and as in this case we have $\frac{d\Delta}{dx} = \frac{d\Delta'}{dx} = \text{etc.} = -1$, we find:

$$\frac{d \cdot \log \varphi(n-x)}{d(n-x)} + \frac{d \cdot \log \varphi(n'-x)}{d(n'-x)} + \dots = 0$$

or:

$$(n-x)\frac{d \cdot \log \varphi(n-x)}{(n-x)\, d \cdot (n-x)} + (n'-x)\frac{d \cdot \log \varphi(n'-x)}{(n'-x)\, d \cdot (n'-x)} + \dots = 0. \qquad (b)$$

But as according to the hypothesis the arithmetical mean gives the most probable value of x, the two equations (a) and (b) must give the same value for x, hence we have:

$$\frac{1}{n-x} \cdot \frac{d \cdot \log \varphi(n-x)}{d(n-x)} = \frac{1}{n'-x} \cdot \frac{d \cdot \log \varphi(n'-x)}{d(n'-x)} = \text{etc.} = k$$

where k is a constant quantity. We have therefore the following equation for determining the function $\varphi(\Delta)$:

$$\frac{d \, . \log \varphi(\Delta)}{\Delta \, . \, d\Delta} = k,$$

hence

$$\log \varphi(\Delta) = \tfrac{1}{2} k \Delta^2 + \log C$$

and

$$\varphi(\Delta) = C \, . \, e^{\frac{1}{2} k \Delta^2}.$$

The sign of k can easily be determined, for as $\varphi(\Delta)$ decreases when Δ is increasing, k must be negative; we may therefore put $\frac{1}{2} k = -h^2$, so that we have $\varphi(\Delta) = C e^{-h^2 \Delta^2}$. In order to determine C we use the equation:

$$\int_{-\infty}^{+\infty} \varphi(\Delta) \, . \, d\Delta = C \int_{-\infty}^{+\infty} e^{-h^2 \Delta^2} \, d\Delta = 1,$$

and as we have $\int_{-\infty}^{+\infty} e^{-x^2} \, dx = \sqrt{\pi}$, we get $\int_{-\infty}^{+\infty} e^{-h^2 \Delta^2} \, d\Delta = \frac{\sqrt{\pi}}{h}$, hence $\frac{C\sqrt{\pi}}{h} = 1$ or $C = \frac{h}{\sqrt{\pi}}$ and finally:

$$\varphi(\Delta) = \frac{h}{\sqrt{\pi}} \, e^{-h^2 \Delta^2}. \qquad (3)$$

The constant quantity h remains the same for a system of observations, which are all equally good or for which the probability of a certain error Δ is the same. For such a system the probability that an error lies between the limits $-\delta$ and $+\delta$ is:

$$\frac{h}{\sqrt{\pi}} \int_{-\delta}^{+\delta} e^{-h^2 \Delta^2} \, d\Delta = \frac{1}{\sqrt{\pi}} \int_{-h\delta}^{+h\delta} e^{-x^2} \, dx$$

Now if in another system of observations the probability of an error Δ is expressed by $\frac{h'}{\sqrt{\pi}} e^{-h' h' \Delta \Delta}$, in this system the probability that an error lies between the limits $-\delta'$ and $+\delta'$, is:

$$\frac{h'}{\sqrt{\pi}} \int_{-\delta'}^{+\delta'} e^{-h' h' \Delta \Delta} \, d\Delta = \frac{1}{\sqrt{\pi}} \int_{-h'\delta'}^{+h'\delta'} e^{-x^2} \, dx.$$

Both integrals become equal when $h\delta = h'\delta'$. Therefore if we have $h = 2h'$, it is obvious, that in the second system an error $2x$ is as probable as an error x in the first system.

The accuracy of the first system is therefore twice as great as that of the second and hence the constant quantity h may be considered as the *measure of precision* of the observations.

21. Usually instead of this measure of precision of observations their probable error is used. In any series of errors written in the order of their absolute magnitude and each written as often as it actually occurs, we call that error which stands exactly in the middle, *the probable error.* If we denote it by r, the probability that an error lies between the limits $-r$ and $+r$, must be equal to $\frac{1}{2}$. Hence we have the equation:

$$\frac{h}{\sqrt{\pi}}\int_{-r}^{+r} e^{-h^2\Delta^2}\,d\Delta = \tfrac{1}{2},$$

or taking $h\Delta = t$

$$\frac{2}{\sqrt{\pi}}\int_0^{hr} e^{-t^2}\,dt = \tfrac{1}{2}, \text{ therefore } \int_0^{hr} e^{-t^2}\,dt = \frac{\sqrt{\pi}}{4}.$$

But as the value of this integral is $\frac{\sqrt{\pi}}{4} = 0.44311$, when $hr = 0.47694$ *), we find the following relation between r and h:

$$r = \frac{0.47694}{h}.$$

The integral $\frac{2}{\sqrt{\pi}}\int_0^{nhr} e^{-t^2}dt$ gives the probability of an error, which is less than n times the probable error and if we compute for instance the value of this integral for $n = \frac{1}{2}$, taking therefore $nhr = 0.23847$, we find the probability of an error, which is less than one half of the probable error equal to 0.264, or among 1000 observations there ought to be 264 errors, which are smaller than one half the probable error. In the same way we find, taking n successively equal to $\frac{3}{2}$, 2, $\frac{5}{2}$, 3, $\frac{7}{2}$, 4, $\frac{9}{2}$, 5, that among 1000 observations there ought to occur:

---

*) On the computation of this integral see No. 17 of the introduction.

688,	where	the	error	in	less	than	$\frac{3}{2}r$
823,	"	"	"	"	"	"	$2r$
908,	"	"	"	"	"	"	$\frac{5}{2}r$
956,	"	"	"	"	"	"	$3r$
982,	"	"	"	"	"	"	$\frac{7}{2}r$
993,	"	"	"	"	"	"	$4r$
998,	"	"	"	"	"	"	$\frac{9}{2}r$
999,	"	"	"	"	"	"	$5r$,

and comparing with this a large number of errors of observations, which actually have been made, we may convince ourselves, that the number of times which errors of a certain magnitude are met with agrees very nearly with the number given by this theory.

We will find now the value of h. Suppose we have a number of m actual errors of observation, which we denote by Δ, Δ' etc., the probability that these occur together is:

$$W = \frac{h^m}{\pi^{\frac{1}{2}m}} e^{-hh[\Delta\Delta + \Delta'\Delta' + \Delta''\Delta'' + \dots]},$$

and if we further suppose, that these errors were actually committed and hence cannot be altered, the maximum of W will depend merely on h and that value of h, which gives the maximum, will be the most probable value of h for these observations. Denoting now for the sake of brevity the sum of the squares of the errors Δ, Δ' etc. by $[\Delta\Delta]$, we have:

$$W = \frac{h^m}{\pi^{\frac{1}{2}m}} e^{-hh[\Delta\Delta]},$$

and we easily find the following conditional equation for the maximum:

$$0 = \frac{mh^{m-1}}{\pi^{\frac{1}{2}m}} e^{-hh[\Delta\Delta]} - \frac{2h^{m+1}}{\pi^{\frac{1}{2}m}} e^{-hh[\Delta\Delta]} [\Delta\Delta]$$

or:

$$0 = m - 2h^2[\Delta\Delta],$$

hence follows:

$$\frac{1}{h\sqrt{2}} = \sqrt{\frac{[\Delta\Delta]}{m}}.$$

This square root of the sum of the squares of real errors of observations divided by their number, is called the *mean error* of these observations. If this error had been made in each observation, it would give the same sum of the squares as that of the actual errors. If we denote it by ε, or put:

$$\varepsilon = \sqrt{\frac{[\Delta\Delta]}{m}},$$

we have:

$$\frac{1}{h\sqrt{2}} = \varepsilon$$

and:

$$r = 0.47694\sqrt{2}\,\varepsilon$$
$$r = 0.674489\,\varepsilon.$$

22. We will now solve the real problem: To find from a system of equations (1), resulting from actual observations, the most probable values of the unknown quantities x, y and z and at the same time their probable error as well as that of the single observations.

If we substitute in the equation (2) instead of $\varphi(\Delta)$, $\varphi(\Delta')$ etc. their expressions according to equation (3), we find:

$$W = \frac{h^m}{(\sqrt{\pi})^m} e^{-h^2[\Delta^2+\Delta'^2+\Delta''^2+\ldots]},$$

if we suppose that all observations can be considered as equally good. Here Δ, Δ', Δ'' etc. are not the pure errors of observations, but depend still on the values of x, y and z. But as for the most probable values of x, y and z the probability that the then remaining errors have occurred together, must be as great as possible, as they become as near as possible equal to the actual errors of observations, which must be expected among a certain number of observations, we see that the values of the unknown quantities must be derived from the equation:

$$\Delta^2 + \Delta'^2 + \Delta''^2 + \ldots = \text{minimum}$$

or the sum of the squares of the residual errors in the equations (1) must be a minimum. Hence this method to find the most probable values of the unknown quantities from such equations is called the method of least squares.

If we first consider the most simple case, that the values of one unknown quantity are found by direct observations, the arithmetical mean of all observations is the most probable value. This of course follows also from the condition of the minimum given above. For the residual errors for any certain value of x are:

$$\Delta = x - n,\ \Delta' = x' - n',\ \Delta'' = x'' - n'', \text{ etc.}$$

We get therefore for the sum of the squares of the residual errors, if we denote

the sum of $n + n' + n'' + \ldots$ by $[n]$
the sum of $n^2 + n'^2 + n''^2 + \ldots$ by $[nn]$

and the number of observations by m:

$$\Sigma (x - n)^2 = m x^2 - 2x[n] + [nn]$$
$$= [nn] - \frac{[n]^2}{m} + m\left(x - \frac{[n]}{m}\right)^2.$$

As all terms of the second member are positive, the sum of the squares will become a minimum, when:

$$x = \frac{[n]}{m},$$

and the sum of the squares of the residual errors will be:

$$[nn] - \frac{[n]^2}{m} = [nn_1].$$

In order to find the probable error of this result from the known probable error of a single observation, we must solve a problem, which on account of an application to be made hereafter we will state in a more general form, namely: To find the probable error of a linear function of several quantities x, x' etc., if the probable errors of the single quantities x, x' etc. are known.

If r is the probable error of x and we have the simple function of x:

$$X = \alpha x,$$

it is evident, that αr is the probable error of X. For if x_0 is the most probable value of x, αx_0 is the most probable value of X and the number of cases, when x lies between the limits $x_0 - r$ and $x_0 + r$ is equal to the number of cases in which X lies between $\alpha x_0 - \alpha r$ and $\alpha x_0 + \alpha r$.

Let X now represent a linear function of two variables or take:

$$X = x + x'$$

and let a and a' represent the most probable values and r and r' the probable errors of x and x'. As we must take then for the errors x and x' respectively $h = \frac{c}{r}$ and $h' = \frac{c}{r'}$, where c is equal to 0.47694, we have the probability of any value of x:

$$= \frac{c}{r\sqrt{\pi}} e^{-\frac{c^2}{r^2}(x-a)^2},$$

and the probability of any value of x':

$$=\frac{c^2}{r'\sqrt{\pi}}\,e^{-\frac{c^2}{r'^2}(x'-a')^2},$$

hence we have the probability that any two values x and x' occur together:

$$=\frac{c^2}{rr'\pi}\,e^{-\left[\frac{c^2}{r^2}(x-a)^2+\frac{c^2}{r'^2}(x'-a')^2\right]}.$$

We shall find therefore the probability of two errors x and x' which satisfy the equation $X=x+x'$, if we substitute $X-x$ for x' in the above expression and denoting this probability by W, we get:

$$W=\frac{c^2}{rr'\pi}\,e^{-\left[\frac{c^2}{r^2}(x-a)^2+\frac{c^2}{r'^2}(X-x-a')^2\right]}.$$

If we perform now the summation of all cases, in which an x may unite with an x' to produce X, where of course we must assign to x all values between the limits $-\infty$ and $+\infty$, or in other words if we integrate W between these limits, we shall embrace all cases, in which X can be produced or we shall determine the probability of X.

Uniting all terms containing x and giving them the form of a square, we easily reduce the integral to the following form:

$$\frac{c^2}{rr'\pi}\int_{-\infty}^{+\infty} e^{-c^2\frac{r^2+r'^2}{r^2r'^2}\left[x-\frac{r^2(X-a')+r'^2a}{r^2+r'^2}\right]^2+\frac{c^2}{r^2+r'^2}(X-a'-a)^2}.\,dx$$

$$=\frac{c}{\sqrt{r^2+r'^2}\sqrt{\pi}}\,e^{-\frac{c^2}{r^2+r'^2}(X-a'-a)^2}\times\frac{2}{\sqrt{\pi}}\int_0^{\infty}e^{-u^2}\,du,$$

if we put:

$$u=\frac{c\sqrt{r^2+r'^2}}{rr'}\left(x-\frac{r^2(X-a')+r'^2a}{r^2+r'^2}\right),$$

and as we have

$$\int_0^{\infty}e^{-u^2}\,du=\frac{\sqrt{\pi}}{2},$$

we find the probability of any value of X:

$$\frac{c}{\sqrt{r^2+r'^2}\sqrt{\pi}}\,e^{-\frac{c^2}{r^2+r'^2}(X-a'-a)^2}.$$

But this expression becomes a maximum, when $X = a + a'$, hence the most probable value of X is equal to the sum of the most probable values of x and x' and the measure of accuracy for X is $\frac{c}{\sqrt{r^2 + r'^2}}$, hence the probable error of X is $\sqrt{r^2 + r'^2}$. From this follows in connection with the formula proved before, that when:

$$X = ax + a'x'$$

the probable error of X is equal to $\sqrt{a^2 r^2 + a'^2 r'^2}$.

We may easily extend this theorem to any number of terms, as in case we have three terms, we can first combine two of them, afterwards these with the third one and so on. Hence if we have any linear function:

$$X = ax + a'x' + a''x'' + \ldots,$$

and if r, r', r'' etc. are the probable errors of x, x', x'' etc. the probable error of X is equal to:

$$\sqrt{a^2 r^2 + a'^2 r'^2 + a''^2 r''^2 + \ldots}$$

From this we find immediately the probable error of the arithmetical mean of m observations, each of which has the probable error r; for as:

$$x = \frac{n + n' + n'' + n''' + \ldots}{m},$$

we have the probable error of the mean equal to $\sqrt{m \cdot \frac{r^2}{m^2}}$ or $\frac{r}{\sqrt{m}}$.

The probable error of the arithmetical mean of m observations is therefore to the probable error of a single observation as $\frac{1}{\sqrt{m}} : 1$ or its measure of precision to the measure of a single observation as $h\sqrt{m} : h$. Often the relative accuracy of two quantities is expressed by their ***weights***, which mean the number of equally accurate observations necessary in order to find from their arithmetical mean a value of the same accuracy as that of the given quantity. Therefore if the weight of a single observation is 1, the arithmetical mean of m observations has the weight m. Hence the weights of two quantities are to each other directly as the squares of their measures of precision and inversely as the squares of the probable errors *).

It remains still to find the probable error r of a single observation. If the residual errors $x-n=\Delta$ of the original equations after substituting the most probable value of x were the real errors of observation, the sum of their squares divided by m would give the square of the mean error of an observation according to No. 20, or this error itself would be $\sqrt{\frac{[nn_1]}{m}}$. But as the arithmetical mean of the observations is not the true value, but only the one which according to the observations made is the most probable, except in case that the number of observations is infinitely great, the residual errors will not be the real errors of observation and differ more or less from them. Now let x_0 be the most probable value of x as given by the arithmetical mean, while $x_0+\xi$ may be the true value which is unknown. By substituting the first value in the equations we get the residual errors x_0-n, x_0-n' etc. which shall be denoted by Δ, Δ' etc. while the substitution of the true value would give the errors $x_0+\xi-n=\delta$ etc. We have therefore the following equations:

$$\Delta+\xi=\delta,$$
$$\Delta'+\xi=\delta',$$
$$\text{etc.,}$$

and if we take the sum of their squares observing that the sum of all Δ is equal to zero, we find according to the adopted notation of sums:

$$[\Delta\Delta]+m\xi^2=[\delta\delta],$$

which equation shows that the sum of the squares of the residual errors belonging to the arithmetical mean is always too small.

As we have $[\delta\delta]=m\varepsilon^2$, when ε denotes the mean error of an observation and further $[\Delta\Delta]=[nn_1]$, we can write the equation also in the following form:

$$[nn_1]+m\xi^2=m\varepsilon^2.$$

---

*) If therefore two quantities have the weights $p=\frac{1}{r^2}$ and $p'=\frac{1}{r'^2}$, the weight of their sum is $\frac{1}{r^2+r'^2}=\frac{pp'}{p+p'}$.

Although we cannot compute from this equation the value of ε, as ξ is unknown, still we shall get this value as near as possible, if we substitute instead of ξ the mean error of x and as we have found this to be equal to $\frac{\varepsilon}{\sqrt{m}}$, we find thus:

$$\varepsilon = \sqrt{\frac{[n n_1]}{m-1}}$$

for the mean error of an observation and hence the probable error:

$$r = 0.674489 \sqrt{\frac{[n n_1]}{m-1}}.$$

Furthermore we find the mean error of the arithmetical mean:

$$\varepsilon(x) = \frac{1}{\sqrt{m}} \sqrt{\frac{[n n_1]}{m-1}}$$

and the probable error:

$$r(x) = \frac{0.674489}{\sqrt{m}} \sqrt{\frac{[n n_1]}{m-1}}.$$

Example. On May 21 1861 the difference of longitude between the observatory at Ann Arbor and the Lake Survey Station at Detroit was determined by means of the electric telegraph, and from 31 stars observed at both stations the following values were obtained:

	Difference of longitude.	Deviation from the mean.		Difference of longitude.	Deviation from the mean.
Star 1	$2^m 43^s$. 60	− 0.11	Star 16	$2^m 43^s$. 50	− 0.01
2	43 . 49	− 0.00	17	43 . 44	+ 0.05
3	43 . 63	− 0.14	18	43 . 37	+ 0.12
4	43 . 52	− 0.03	19	43 . 32	+ 0.17
5	43 . 31	+ 0.18	20	43 . 12	+ 0.37
6	43 . 67	− 0.18	21	43 . 30	+ 0.19
7	43 . 98	− 0.49	22	43 . 72	− 0.23
8	43 . 63	− 0.14	23	43 . 25	+ 0.24
9	43 . 83	− 0.34	24	43 . 13	+ 0.36
10	43 . 79	− 0.30	25	43 . 27	+ 0.22
11	43 . 54	− 0.05	26	43 . 34	+ 0.15
12	43 . 18	+ 0.31	27	43 . 15	+ 0.34
13	43 . 45	+ 0.04	28	43 . 86	− 0.37
14	43 . 68	− 0.19	29	43 . 29	+ 0.20
15	43 . 32	+ 0.17	30	43 . 40	+ 0.09
			31	43 . 95	− 0.46
			Mean	$2^m 43^s$. 49	

Here we find the sum of the squares of the residual errors $[n n_1] = 1.77$, and as the number of observations is 31, we find:

the probable error of a single observation $= \pm 0^s.164$
hence the probable error of the mean of all observations $= \pm 0^s.029$.

Although we cannot expect that in this case the errors of observations, the number of observations being so small, will be distributed according to the law given in No. 21, yet we shall find, that this is approximately the case. According to the theory, the number of observations being 31, the number of errors

smaller than $\frac{1}{2}r$, r, $\frac{3}{2}r$, $2r$, $\frac{5}{2}r$, $3r$
ought to be 8, 15, 21, 25, 28, 30
while it actually is according to the above table:
6, 12, 22, 24, 29, 30.

The error which stands exactly in the middle of all errors written in the order of their magnitude and which ought to be equal to the probable error is 0.18.

23. In the general case, when the equations (1) derived from the observations contain several unknown quantities, the number of which we will limit here to three, the most probable values of these quantities are again those, which give the least sum of the squares of the residual errors. As this sum must necessarily be a minimum with respect to x as well as to y and z, this condition furnishes as many equations as there are unknown quantities, which therefore can be determined by their solution.

The equation of the minimum with respect to x is as follows:

$$\Delta \frac{d\Delta}{dx} + \Delta' \frac{d\Delta'}{dx} + \Delta'' \frac{d\Delta''}{dx} + \ldots = 0,$$

or as we have according to equations (1) $\frac{d\Delta}{dx} = a$, $\frac{d\Delta'}{dx} = a'$ etc. we get:

$$\Delta a + \Delta' a' + \Delta'' a'' + \ldots = 0.$$

If we substitute in this for Δ, Δ' etc. their expressions from (1) and if we adopt a similar notation of the sums as before, taking:

$$aa + a'a' + a''a'' + \ldots = [aa]$$
and $ab + a'b' + a''b'' + \ldots = [ab]$ etc.
we get the equation:

$$[aa]\,x + [ab]\,y + [ac]\,z + [an] = 0; \qquad (A)$$

and likewise $[ab]\,x + [bb]\,y + [bc]\,z + [bn] = 0 \qquad (B)$

and $[ac]\,x + [bc]\,y + [cc]\,z + [cn] = 0 \qquad (C)$

from the two equations of the minimum with respect to y and z. The solution of these tree equations gives the most probable values of x, y and z.

In order to solve them we multiply the first by $\frac{[ab]}{[aa]}$ and subtract it from the second, likewise we multiply the first by $\frac{[ac]}{[aa]}$ and subtract it from the third. Thus we obtain two equations without x, which have the form:

$$[bb_1]\,y + [bc_1]\,z + [bn_1] = 0 \qquad (D)$$

and $[bc_1]\,y + [cc_1]\,z + [cn_1] = 0, \qquad (E)$

when we take

$$[bb_1] = [bb] - \frac{[ab]\,[ab]}{[aa]}, \quad [bc_1] = [bc] - \frac{[ab]\,[ac]}{[aa]}$$

which equations explain the adopted notation.

If we multiply now the equation (D) by $\frac{[bc_1]}{[bb_1]}$ and subtract it from (E), we find:

$$[cc_2]\,z + [cn_2] = 0 \qquad (F),$$

where we have now:

$$[cc_2] = [cc_1] - \frac{[bc_1]\,[bc_1]}{[bb_1]}, \quad [cn_2] = [cn_1] - \frac{[bc_1][bn_1]}{[bb_1]}.$$

From equation (F) we find the value of z, while the equations (D) and (A) give the values of y and x.

If we deduce $[\Delta^2]$ from the equations (1) we find with the aid of equations (A), (B) and (C) for the sum of the squares of the residual errors:

$$[\Delta^2] = [nn] + [an]\,x + [bn]\,y + [cn]\,z.$$

In order to eliminate here x, y and z, we multiply equation (A) by $\frac{[an]}{[aa]}$ and subtract it from the above equation, which gives:

$$[\Delta\Delta] = [nn] - \frac{[an]^2}{[aa]} + [bn_1]\,y + [cn_1]\,z.$$

If we then multiply the equation (D) by $\frac{[bn_1]}{[bb_1]}$ and subtract it from the last equation, we get:

$$[\Delta\Delta] = [nn] - \frac{[an]^2}{[aa]} - \frac{[bn_1]^2}{[bb_1]} + [cn_2]\,z,$$

and if we here substitute the value of z from (F) we find at last for the minimum of the squares of the errors:

$$[\Delta\Delta] = [nn] - \frac{[an]^2}{[aa]} - \frac{[bn_1]^2}{[bb_1]} - \frac{[cn_2]^2}{[cc_2]} = [nn_3].$$

We can find the equations for the minimum of the squares of the errors also without the differential calculus. For if we multiply each of the original equations (1) respectively by ax, by, cz and n and add them, we find:

$$[\Delta\Delta] = [a\Delta]\,x + [b\Delta]\,y + [c\Delta]\,z + [n\Delta] \qquad (a),$$

where

$$[a\Delta] = [aa]\,x + [ab]\,y + [ac]\,z + [an] \qquad (b)$$

etc.

If we now substitute in (a) instead of x its value taken from (b), we find:

$$[\Delta\Delta] = \frac{[a\Delta]^2}{[aa]} + [b\Delta_1]\,y + [c\Delta_1]\,z + [n\Delta_1] \qquad (c)$$

where

$$\left.\begin{aligned} [b\Delta_1] &= [bb_1]\,y + [bc_1]\,z + [bn_1] \\ [n\Delta_1] &= [bn_1]\,y + [cn_1]\,z + [nn_1]. \end{aligned}\right\} \qquad (d)$$

Then substituting in (c) for y its value taken from the first of the equations (d), we find:

$$[\Delta\Delta] = \frac{[a\Delta]^2}{[aa]} + \frac{[b\Delta_1]^2}{[bb_1]} + [c\Delta_2] + [n\Delta_2], \qquad (e)$$

where now

$$\left.\begin{aligned} [c\Delta_2] &= [cc_2]\,z + [cn_2], \\ [n\Delta_2] &= [cn_2]\,z + [nn_2], \end{aligned}\right\} \qquad (f)$$

and if we finally substitute in (e) for z its value taken from the first of these last equations, we have:

$$[\Delta\Delta] = \frac{[a\Delta]^2}{[aa]} + \frac{[b\Delta_1]^2}{[bb_1]} + \frac{[c\Delta_2]^2}{[cc_2]} + [n\Delta_3], \qquad (g)$$

and we easily see that we have $[n\Delta_3] = [nn_3]$.

As the first three terms on the right side of equation (g), which alone contain x, y, and z, have the form of squares, we see, that in order to obtain the minimum of the squares of the errors, we must satisfy the following equations $[a\Delta] = 0$, $[b\Delta_1] = 0$ and $[c\Delta_2] = 0$, which are identical with those we found before. We see also, that $[nn_3]$ is the minimum of the squares of the errors.

24. The theorem for the probable error proved in No. 22 will serve us again to find the probable errors of the unknown quantities, as we easily see by the equations A, D and F that the most probable values of x, y and z can be expressed by linear functions of n, n', n'' etc.

For in order to find x from these three equations, we must multiply each by such a coefficient that taking the sum of the three equations the coefficients of y and z in the resulting equation become equal to zero. Therefore if we multiply (A) by $\frac{1}{[aa]}$, (D) by $\frac{A'}{[bb_1]}$, (F) by $\frac{A''}{[cc_2]}$ and add the three equations, we get the following two equations for determining A' and A'':

$$\frac{[ab]}{[aa]} + A' = 0, \qquad (\alpha)$$

$$\frac{[ac]}{[aa]} + A'\frac{[bc_1]}{[bb_1]} + A'' = 0, \qquad (\beta)$$

and we have:

$$x = -\frac{[an]}{[aa]} - A'\frac{[bn_1]}{[bb_1]} - A''\frac{[cn_2]}{[cc_2]}. \qquad (\gamma)$$

In order to find y we multiply (D) by $\frac{1}{[bb_1]}$, (F) by $\frac{B'}{[cc_2]}$ and adding them we get:

$$\frac{[bc_1]}{[bb_1]} + B' = 0 \qquad (\delta)$$

and

$$y = -\frac{[bn_1]}{[bb_1]} - B'\frac{[cn_2]}{[cc_2]}. \qquad (\varepsilon)$$

At last we have:

$$z = -\frac{[cn_2]}{[cc_2]}. \qquad (\zeta)$$

Developing the quantities $[bn_1]$ and $[cn_2]$, we easily find:

$$[bn_1] = A'[an] + [bn] \qquad (\eta),$$

$$[cn_2] = A''[an] + B'[bn] + [cn] \qquad (\vartheta),$$

and as we may change the letters, the quantities in parenthesis being of a symmetrical form, we find also:

$$[bb_1] = A'[ab] + [bb] \qquad (\iota),$$

$$[cc_2] = A''[ac] + B'[bc] + [cc] \qquad (\varkappa),$$

$$[bc_2] = A''[ab] + B'[bb] + [bc] = 0 \qquad (\lambda),$$

$$[ac_2] = A''[aa] + B'[ab] + [ac] = 0 \qquad (\mu). \text{*)}$$

*) The two last equations we may easily verify with the aid of the equations (α), (β) and (δ).

Now as $[an]$ as well as $[bn_1]$ and $[cn_2]$ are linear functions of n, we can easily compute their probable errors. First we have $[an] = an + a'n' + a''n'' + \ldots.$ If therefore r denotes the probable error of one observation, that of $[an]$ must be:

$$r([an]) = r\sqrt{aa + a'a' + a''a'' + \ldots} = r\sqrt{[aa]}.$$

Every term in $[bn_1]$ is of the following form $(A'a + b)n$. In order to find the square of this, we multiply it successively by $A'an$ and bn and find for the coefficient of n^2:

$$A'(A'aa + ab) + A'ab + bb.$$

This therefore must also be the form of the coefficients of each r^2 in the expression for the square of the probable error of $[bn_1]$ or we have:

$$(r[bn_1])^2 = [A'(A'[aa] + [ab]) + A'[ab] + [bb]]\, r^2,$$

or:

$$r([bn_1]) = r.\sqrt{[bb_1]},$$

as we find immediately by the equations (α) and (ι).

At last the coefficient of each n in the expression of $[cn_2]$ is:

$$A''a + B'b + c.$$

Taking the square of this we find:

$$\begin{aligned} &A''(A''aa + B'ab + ac) \\ &+ B'(A''ab + B'bb + bc) \\ &+ A''ac + B'bc + cc. \end{aligned}$$

Now taking the sum of all single squares, we find the coefficient of r^2 in the expression of $(r[cn_2])^2$:

$$\begin{aligned} &A''(A''[aa] + B'[ab] + [ac]) \\ &+ B'(A''[ab] + B'[bb] + [bc]) \\ &+ A''[ac] + B'[bc] + [cc], \end{aligned}$$

which according to the equations ($\varkappa$), (λ) and (μ) is simply $[cc_2]$; hence we have:

$$r[cn_2] = r.\sqrt{[cc_2]}$$

We can now find the probable errors of x, y and z without any difficulty. For according to equation (γ) we have for the square of the probable error of x the following expression:

$$[r(x)]^2 = \frac{[r(an)]^2}{[aa]^2} + \frac{A'A'}{[bb_1]^2}(r[bn_1])^2 + \frac{A''A''}{[cc_2]^2}(r[cn_2])^2$$

$$= r^2\left\{\frac{1}{[aa]} + \frac{A'A'}{[bb_1]} + \frac{A''A''}{[cc_2]}\right\}.$$

Likewise we find:

$$[r(y)]^2 = r^2 \left\{ \frac{1}{[b b_1]} + \frac{B'' B''}{[c c_2]} \right\}$$

and

$$[r(z)]^2 = r^2 \frac{1}{[c c_2]}.$$

It remains still to find the probable error of a single observation. If we put for x, y and z in the original equations (1) any determinate values, we may give to the sum of the squares of the residual errors the following form:

$$[\Delta\Delta] = \frac{[a\Delta]^2}{[a a]} + \frac{[b\Delta_1]^2}{[b b_1]} + \frac{[c\Delta_2]^2}{[c c_2]} + [n n_3].$$

In case that we substitute here for x, y and z the most probable values resulting from this system of equations, the quantities $[a\Delta]$, $[b\Delta_1]$ and $[c\Delta_2]$ become equal to zero and the sum of the squares of the residual errors resulting from these values of x, y and z is equal to $[n n_3]$. But these values will be the true values only in case that the number of observations is infinitely great. Supposing now, that these true values were known and were substituted in the above equations, $[\Delta\Delta]$ would be the sum of the squares of the real errors of observation and we should have the following equation:

$$m\varepsilon^2 = \frac{[a\Delta]^2}{[aa]} + \frac{[b\Delta_1]^2}{[b b_1]} + \frac{[c\Delta_2]^2}{[c c_2]} + [n n_3],$$

where now the quantities $[a\Delta]$, $[b\Delta_1]$ and $[c\Delta_2]$ would be a little different from zero. As all these terms are squares, we see that the sum of the squares as found from the most probable values is to small and in order to come a little nearer the true value we may substitute for $[a\Delta]$ etc. their mean errors. But as in the equations:

$$a x_0 + b y_0 + c z_0 + n = \Delta$$

etc.

no quantity on the left side is affected by errors except n, Δ must be affected by the same errors and the mean errors of $[a\Delta]$, $[b\Delta_1]$ and $[c\Delta_2]$ are equal to those we found for $[an]$, $[b n_1]$ and $[c n_2]$. Substituting these in the above equation we find:

$$m\varepsilon^2 = \varepsilon^2 + \varepsilon^2 + \varepsilon^2 + [n n_3]$$

or:

$$\varepsilon = \sqrt{\frac{[n n_3]}{m-3}}.$$

Hence the mean error of an observation is derived from a finite number of equations between several unknown quantities by dividing the sum of the squares of the residual errors, resulting from the condition of the minimum, by the number of all observations minus the number of unknown quantities and extracting the square root.

Likewise we find for the probable error of an observation:

$$r = 0.674489 \sqrt{\frac{[n n_3]}{m-3}}.$$

Note 1. We have hitherto always supposed, that all observations, which we use for the determination of the unknown quantities, may be considered as equally good. If this is not the case and if h, h', h'' etc. are the measures of precision for the single observations, the probability of the errors Δ, Δ' etc. of single observations is expressed by:

$$\frac{h}{\sqrt{\pi}} e^{-h^2 \Delta^2}, \quad \frac{h'}{\sqrt{\pi}} e^{-h'^2 \Delta'^2}, \text{ etc.}$$

Hence the function W becomes in this case:

$$W = \frac{h . h' . h'' \ldots}{(\sqrt{\pi})^m} e^{-(h^2 \Delta^2 + h' \Delta'^2 + h''^2 \Delta''^2 + \ldots)}$$

and the most probable values of x, y and z will be those, which make the sum

$$h^2 \Delta^2 + h'^2 \Delta'^2 + h''^2 \Delta''^2 + \ldots.$$

a minimum. In order therefore to find these, we must multiply the original equations respectively by h, h', h'' etc. and then computing the sums with these new coefficients perform the same operations as before.

Note 2. If we have only one unknown quantity and the original equations have the following form:

$$0 = n + a x,$$
$$0 = n' + a' x,$$
$$0 = n'' + a'' x, \text{ etc.},$$

we find $x = -\frac{[an]}{[aa]}$ with the probable error $r_x = \frac{r}{\sqrt{[aa]}}$, where r denotes the probable error of one observation.

25. This method may be illustrated by the following example, which is taken from Bessel's determination of the constant quantity of refraction, in the seventh volume of the „Koenigsberger Beobachtungen" pag. XXIII etc. But of the 52 equations given there only the following 20 have been selected, whose weights have been taken as equal and in which the numerical term is a quantity resulting from the observations of the stars, while y denotes the correction of the constant quantity of refraction and x a constant error which may be assumed in each observation.

The general form of the equations of condition in this case is $n = x + b\,y$, as the factor denoted before by a is equal to 1, and the equations derived from the single stars are:

		Residual errors.
α Urs. min.	$0 = +0''.02 + x + 0.2\,y$	$-0''.03$
β Urs. min.	$0 = +0\ .45 + x + 8.2\,y$	$+0\ .43$
β Cephei	$0 = +0\ .10 + x + 20.1\,y$	$+0\ .14$
α Urs. maj.	$0 = -0\ .14 + x + 36.0\,y$	$-0\ .03$
α Cephei	$0 = -0\ .62 + x + 43.9\,y$	$-0\ .47$
δ Cephei	$0 = -0\ .25 + x + 65.9\,y$	$0\ .00$
ε Cephei	$0 = -0\ .03 + x + 74.9\,y$	$+0\ .26$
μ Cephei	$0 = -1\ .24 + x + 77.8\,y$	$-0\ .94$
α Cassiop.	$0 = +0\ .59 + x + 75.5\,y$	$+0\ .88$
γ Urs. maj.	$0 = -0\ .47 + x + 79.6\,y$	$-0\ .16$
β Draconis	$0 = 0\ .00 + x + 104.5\,y$	$+0\ .42$
γ Draconis	$0 = -0\ .51 + x + 114.3\,y$	$-0\ .04$
η Urs. maj.	$0 = -1\ .20 + x + 125.6\,y$	$-0\ .68$
α Persei	$0 = +0\ .12 + x + 142.1\,y$	$+0\ .72$
α Aurigae	$0 = -1\ .31 + x + 216.8\,y$	$-0\ .37$
α Cygni	$0 = -1\ .64 + x + 254.8\,y$	$-0\ .53$
ε Aurigae	$0 = -1\ .39 + x + 280.2\,y$	$-0\ .16$
γ Androm.	$0 = -1\ .24 + x + 393.5\,y$	$+0\ .51$
η Aurigae	$0 = -1\ .80 + x + 419.6\,y$	$+0\ .06$
β Persei	$0 = -2\ .16 + x + 481.2\,y$	$-0\ .01$

In order now to find from these the equations for the most probable values of x and y (equations (*A*) and (*B*) in No. 23), we must first compute all the different sums $[aa]$, $[ab]$, $[an]$, $[bb]$ and $[bn]$. In this case, where the number of unknown quantities is so small, besides one of the coefficients is constant and equal to one, this computation is very easy; but if there are more unknown quantities, whose coefficients may be for instance a, b, c, d it is advisable, to take also the algebraic sum of the coefficients of each equation, which shall be denoted by s and to compute with these the sums $[as]$, $[bs]$, $[cs]$ etc., as then the following equations may be used as checks for the correctness of the computations:

$$[ns] = [an] + [bn] + [cn] + [dn],$$
$$[as] = [aa] + [ab] + [ac] + [ad],$$

etc.

If we compute now the sums for our example, we find the following two equations for determining the most probable values of x and y:

$$+20.000\,x + 3014.80\,y - 12.72 = 0,$$
$$+3014.80\,x + 844586.1\,y - 3700.65 = 0.$$

The solution of these equations can be made in the following form, which may easily be extended to more unknown quantities:

	$[aa]$	$[ab]$	$[an]$	$[nn]$
	$+20.000$	$+3014.80$	-12.72	20.28
	1.301030	3.479259	1.104487_n	$\frac{[an]^2}{[aa]}$ 8.09
$[an] = -12.72$		$[bb]$	$[bn]$	12.19
$[ab]\,x = +13.78$		$+844586.1$	-3700.65	$\frac{[bn_1]^2}{[bb_1]}$ 8.15
$+1.06$		$+454452.0$	-1917.41	$[nn_2] = 4.04$
0.025306_n		$[bb_1] = +390134.1$	$[bn_1] = -1783.24$	
1.301030			$\log\,[bn_1]\ 3.251210$	
$\log x = 8.724276_n$			$\log\,[bb_1]\ 5.591214$	
$x = -0''.053$			$\log y = 7.659996$	
			$y = +0.0045708$	

In case that we have computed the quantities $[as]$, $[bs]$ etc. we may compute also $[bs_1]$ and use the equation $[bb_1] = [bs_1]$ as a check. In the case of 3 unknown quantities we should use $[bb_1] + [bc_1] = [bs_1]$ and $[cc_2] = [cs_2]$ and similar equations for a greater number of unknown quantities.

In order to compute the probable errors of x and y, we use besides $[bb_1]$ also the quantity

$$[aa_1] = [aa] - \frac{[ab]\,[ab]}{[bb]} = +9.2384.$$

Then we find the probable error of the quantity n for a single star:

$$r = 0.67449\sqrt{\frac{[nn_2]}{18}} = \pm 0.3195,$$

hence the probable errors of x and y:

$$r(x) = \frac{0''.3195}{\sqrt{[aa_1]}} = \pm 0''.105,$$
$$r(y) = \frac{0''.3195}{\sqrt{[bb_1]}} = \pm 0''.0005116.$$

We see therefore, that the determination of x from the above equations is very inaccurate, as the probable error is greater than the resulting value of x; but the probable error of the correction of the constant quantity of refraction is only $\frac{1}{9}$ of the correction itself.

If we substitute the most probable values of x and y in the above equations, we find the residual errors of the several equations, which have been placed in the table above at the side of each equation. Computing the sum of the squares of these residual errors, we find 4.04 in accordance with $[nn_2]$, thus proving the accuracy of the computation by another check.

Note. On the method of least squares consult: Gauss, Theoria motus corporum coelestium, pag. 205 et seq. Gauss, Theoria combinationis observationum erroribus minimis obnoxiae. Encke in the appendix to the „Berliner Jahrbücher für 1834, 1835 und 1836."

E. THE DEVELOPMENT OF PERIODICAL FUNCTIONS FROM GIVEN NUMERICAL VALUES.

26. Periodical functions are frequently used in astronomy, as the problem, to find periods in which certain phenomena return, often occurs; but as these are always comprised within certain limits without becoming infinite, only such periodical functions will come under consideration as contain the sines and cosines of the variable quantities. Therefore if X denotes such a function, we may assume the following form for it:

$$X = a_0 + a_1 \cos x + a_2 \cos 2x + a_3 \cos 3x + \ldots$$
$$+ b_1 \sin x + b_2 \sin 2x + b_3 \sin 3x + \ldots$$

Now the case usually occurring is this, that the numerical values of X are given for certain values of x, from which we must find the coefficients, a problem whose solution is especially convenient, if the circumference is divided in n equal parts and the values of X are given for $x = 0$, $x = \frac{2\pi}{n}$, $x = 2\frac{2\pi}{n}$ etc. to $x = (n-1)\frac{2\pi}{n}$, as in that case we can make use of several lemmas, which greatly facilitate the solution. These lemmas are the following.

If A is an aliquot part of the circumference, nA being equal to 2π, the sum of the series

$$\sin A + \sin 2A + \sin 3A + \ldots + \sin (n-1) A$$

is always equal to zero; likewise also the sum of the series

$$\cos A + \cos 2A + \cos 3A + \ldots + \cos (n-1) A,$$

is zero except when A is equal either to 2π or to a multiple of 2π, in which case this sum is equal to n.

The latter case is obvious, as the series then consists of n terms, each of which is equal to 1. We have therefore to prove only the two other theorems. If we now put:

$$\cos r \frac{2\pi}{n} + i \sin r \frac{2\pi}{n} = T^r,$$

where we take $i = \sqrt{-1}$ and $T = e^{i\frac{2\pi}{n}}$, we have:

$$\sum_{r=0}^{r=n-1} \cos r \frac{2\pi}{n} + i \sum_{r=0}^{r=n-1} \sin r \frac{2\pi}{n} = \sum_{r=0}^{r=n-1} T^r = \frac{T^n - 1}{T-1}.$$

As we have now $T^n = \cos 2\pi + i \sin 2\pi = 1$, it follows that:

$$\sum_{r=0}^{r=n-1} \cos r \frac{2\pi}{n} + i \sum_{r=0}^{r=n-1} \sin r \frac{2\pi}{n} = 0,$$

hence:

$$\sum_{r=0}^{r=n-1} \sin r \frac{2\pi}{n} = 0 \qquad (1)$$

and this equation is true without any exception, as there is nothing imaginary on the right side. It follows also, that we have in general:

$$\sum_{r=0}^{r=n-1} \cos r \frac{2\pi}{n} = 0. \qquad (2)$$

Only when $n=0$, the expression $\frac{T^n - 1}{T-1}$ takes the form $\frac{0}{0}$ and has the value n, as we can easily see by differentiating it.

From the equations (1) and (2) several others, which we shall make use of, can be easily deduced. For we find:

$$\sum_{r=0}^{r=n-1} \sin r \frac{2\pi}{n} \cos r \frac{2\pi}{n} = \tfrac{1}{2} \sum_{r=0}^{r=n-1} \sin 2r \frac{2\pi}{n} = 0, \qquad (3)$$

$$\sum_{r=0}^{r=n-1} \left(\cos r \frac{2\pi}{n}\right)^2 = \tfrac{1}{2} n + \tfrac{1}{2} \sum_{r=0}^{r=n-1} \cos 2r \frac{2\pi}{n} = \tfrac{1}{2} n \text{ in general} \qquad (4)$$

$$= n \text{ in the exceptional case,}$$

finally:

$$\sum_{r=0}^{r=n-1}\left(\sin r\frac{2\pi}{n}\right)^2=\tfrac{1}{2}n-\tfrac{1}{2}\sum_{r=0}^{r=n-1}\cos 2r\frac{2\pi}{n}=\tfrac{1}{2}n \text{ in general} \qquad (5)$$

$$=0 \text{ in the exceptional case.}$$

27. We will assume now:

$$X=a_p\cos px+b_p\sin px,$$

in which equation all integral numbers beginning with zero must be successively put for p. If now q denotes a certain number, we have:

$$X\cos qx=\tfrac{1}{2}a_p\cos(p+q)x+\tfrac{1}{2}a_p\cos(p-q)x$$
$$+\tfrac{1}{2}b_p\sin(p+q)x+\tfrac{1}{2}b_p\sin(p-q)x,$$

and if we assign x successively the values 0, A, $2A$ .... to $(n-1)A$, where $A=\frac{2\pi}{n}$, and add the several resulting equations, all terms on the right side will be zero according to the equations (1) and (2) with the exception of the sum of the terms of the cosine, in which $(p+q)A$ is equal to $2k\pi$, which will receive the factor n. But as $A=\frac{2\pi}{n}$, we have for the remaining terms $p+q=kn$ or $p-q=kn$, hence $p=-q+kn$ or $=+q+kn$. Therefore denoting the value of X, which corresponds to the value rA of x by X_{rA}, we have:

$$\sum_{r=0}^{r=n-1}X_{rA}\cos qA=\frac{n}{2}a_{-q+kn}+\frac{n}{2}a_{q+kn}$$

$$=\frac{n}{2}[a_{-q}+a_q+a_{n-q}+a_{n+q}+a_{2n-q}+a_{2n+q}+\ldots].$$

But as X does not contain any coefficients whose index is negative, we must take $a_{-q}=0$ and get:

$$\sum_{r=0}^{r=n-1}X_{rA}\cos qA=\frac{n}{2}[a_q+a_{n-q}+a_{n+q}+a_{2n-q}+a_{2n+q}+\ldots]. \qquad (6)$$

Here we have to consider two particular cases. For when $q=0$, we have $a_{-q}=a_q$, $a_{n-q}=a_{n+q}$ etc. hence:

$$\sum_{r=0}^{r=n-1}X_{rA}=n[a_0+a_n+a_{2n}+\ldots], \qquad (7)$$

and when n is an even number and $q=\tfrac{1}{2}n$, a_{-q} is to be omitted and a_q unites with a_{n-q} etc., hence we have also in this case:

$$\sum_{r=0}^{r=n-1} X_{rA} \cos \tfrac{1}{2} n A = n\,[a_{\frac{1}{2}n} + a_{\frac{3}{2}n} + \ldots], \tag{8}$$

As:
$$X \sin q x = \tfrac{1}{2} a_p \sin (p+q)\,x - \tfrac{1}{2} a_p \sin (p-q)\,x$$
$$+ \tfrac{1}{2} b_p \cos (p-q)\,x - \tfrac{1}{2} b_p \cos (p+q)\,x,$$

we find in a similar way:

$$\sum_{r=0}^{r=n-1} X_{rA} \sin q A = \frac{n}{2}\,[b_q - b_{n-q} + b_{n+q} - b_{2n-q} + b_{2n+q} - \ldots]. \tag{9}$$

If we take now for n a sufficiently large number in proportion to the convergence of the series, so that we can neglect on the right side of the equations (6) to (9) all terms except the first, we may determine by these equations the coefficients of the cosines from $q=0$ to $q=\frac{1}{2}n$ and the coefficients of the sines to $q=\frac{1}{2}n-1$, as a larger q gives only a repetition of the former equations. The larger we take n, the more accurate shall we find the values of the coefficients whose index is small, while those of a high index remain always inaccurate. For instance when $n=12$ and $q=4$, we have the equation:

$$\Sigma X \cos 4x = 6\,(a_4 + a_8 + \ldots),$$

hence the value of a_4 will be incorrect by the quantity a_8; but if we had taken $n=24$, this coefficient would be only incorrect by a_{20}.

From the above we find then the following equations:

$$a_p = \frac{2}{n} \sum_{r=0}^{r=n-1} X_{rA} \cos r p A,$$

$$b_p = \frac{2}{n} \sum_{r=0}^{r=n-1} X_{rA} \sin r p A,$$

with these exceptions, that for $p=0$ and $p=\frac{1}{2}n$ we must take $\frac{1}{n}$ instead of the factor $\frac{2}{n}$.

It is always of some advantage to take for n a number divisible by 4, as in this case each quadrant is divided into a certain number of parts and therefore the same values of the sines and cosines return only with different signs. As the cosines of angles, which are the complements to 360^0, are the same, we can then take the sum of the terms, whose indices are the complements to 360^0 and multiply it by the cosine; but the terms of the sine, whose indices are the complements to 360° must be subtracted from each other. If we denote then the sum of two such quantities, for instance $X_A + X_{(n-1)A}$ by $\underset{+}{X_A}$, and the difference $X_A - X_{(n-1)A}$ by $\underset{-}{X_A}$, we have:

$$a_p = \frac{2}{n} \sum_{r=0}^{r=\frac{1}{2}n} \underset{+}{X_{rA}} \cos rpA,$$

$$b_p = \frac{2}{n} \sum_{r=1}^{r=(\frac{1}{2}n-1)} \underset{-}{X_{rA}} \sin rpA.$$

Again denoting here the sum or the difference of two terms of the cosine, whose indices are the complements to 180°, by $\underset{++}{X_{rA}}$ and $\underset{+-}{X_{rA}}$, and the sum or difference of two terms of sines, whose indices are the complements to 180°, by $\underset{-+}{X_{rA}}$ and $\underset{--}{X_{rA}}$, we have:

$$a_p = \frac{2}{n} \sum_{r=0}^{r=\frac{1}{4}n} \underset{++}{X_{rA}} \cos rpA, \quad \text{when } p \text{ is an even number,} \qquad (10)$$

with the two exceptional cases mentioned before:

$$a_p = \frac{2}{n} \sum_{r=0}^{r=\frac{1}{4}n} \underset{+-}{X_{rA}} \cos rpA, \quad \text{when } p \text{ is an odd number,} \qquad (11)$$

$$b_p = \frac{2}{n} \sum_{r=1}^{r=\frac{1}{4}n-1} \underset{--}{X_{rA}} \sin rpA, \quad \text{when } p \text{ is an even number,} \qquad (12)$$

$$b_p = \frac{2}{n} \sum_{r=1}^{r=\frac{1}{4}n-1} \underset{-+}{X_{rA}} \sin rpA, \quad \text{when } p \text{ is an odd number.} \qquad (13)$$

If for instance n is equal to 12, we find:

$$a_0 = \tfrac{1}{12} \left\{ \underset{++}{X_0} + \underset{++}{X_{30}} + \underset{++}{X_{60}} + \underset{++}{X_{90}} \right\},$$

$$a_1 = \tfrac{1}{6} \left\{ \underset{+-}{X_0} + \underset{+-}{X_{30}} \cos 30 + \underset{+-}{X_{60}} \cos 60 \right\},$$

$$a_2 = \tfrac{1}{6} \left\{ \underset{++}{X_0} + \underset{++}{X_{30}} \cos 60 - \underset{++}{X_{60}} \cos 60 - \underset{++}{X_{90}} \right\},$$

etc.

$$b_1 = \tfrac{1}{6} \left\{ \underset{-+}{X_{30}} \sin 30 + \underset{-+}{X_{60}} \sin 60 + \underset{-+}{X_{90}} \right\},$$

$$b_2 = \tfrac{1}{6} \left\{ \underset{--}{X_{30}} \sin 60 + \underset{--}{X_{60}} \sin 60 \right\},$$

etc.

28. If we wish to develop a periodical function up to a certain multiple of the angle, it is necessary that as many numerical values are known as we wish to determine coefficients. If then the given values are perfectly correct, we shall find these coefficients as correct as theory admits, only the less correct, the higher the index of the coefficient is compared to the given number of values. But in case that the values of the function are the result of observations, it is advisable in order to eliminate the errors of observation to use as many observations as possible, therefore to use many more observations than are necessary for determining the coefficients. In this case these equations should be treated according to the method of least squares; but one can easily see, that this method furnishes the same equations for determining the coefficients as those given in No. 27. We see therefore that the values obtained by this method are indeed the most probable values.

For if the n values X_0, X_A, $X_{2A} \ldots X_{(n-1)A}$ are given, we should have the following equations, supposing that the function contains only the sines and cosines of the angle itself:

$$\begin{aligned} 0 &= -X_0 + a_0 + a_1, \\ 0 &= -X_A + a_0 + a_1 \cos A + b_1 \sin A, \\ 0 &= -X_{2A} + a_0 + a_1 \cos 2A + b_1 \sin 2A, \\ &\vdots \\ 0 &= -X_{(n-1)A} + a_0 + a_1 \cos(n-1)A + b_1 \sin(n-1)A, \end{aligned}$$

and according to the method of least squares we should find for the equations of the minimum, when $[\cos A]$ again denotes the sum of all the cosines of A, from $A = 0$ to $A = n - 1$, the following:

$$\begin{aligned} n a_0 + [\cos A]\, a_1 + [\sin A]\, b_1 - [X_A] &= 0, \\ [\cos A]\, a_0 + [\cos A^2]\, a_1 + [\sin A . \cos A]\, b_1 - [X_A \cos A] &= 0, \qquad (14) \\ [\sin A]\, a_0 + [\cos A \sin A]\, a_1 + [\sin A^2]\, b_1 - [X_A \sin A] &= 0. \end{aligned}$$

But if we take into consideration the equations (3), (4) and (5) in No. 26 we see, that these equations are reduced to the following:

$$a_0 = \frac{1}{n}[X_A],$$

$$a_1 = \frac{2}{n}[X_A \cos A],$$

$$b_1 = \frac{2}{n}[X_A \sin A],$$

which entirely agree with those found in No. 27. What is shown here for the three first coefficients, is of course true for any number of them.

We can also find the probable error of an observation and of a coefficient. For if $[\nu\nu]$ is the sum of the squares of the residual errors, which remain after substituting the most probable values in the equations of condition, the probable error of one observation is

$$r = 0.67449 \sqrt{\frac{[\nu\nu]}{n-3}},$$

and that of $a_0 = \frac{r}{\sqrt{n}}$,

$$a_1 = \frac{r}{\sqrt{[\cos A^2]}} = \frac{r\sqrt{2}}{\sqrt{n}},$$

$$a_2 = \frac{r}{\sqrt{[\sin A^2]}} = \frac{r\sqrt{2}}{\sqrt{n}}.$$

An example will be found in No. 6 of the seventh section.

Note. Consult Encke's Berliner Jahrbuch für 1857 pag. 334 and seq. Leverrier gives in the Annales de l'Observatoire Impérial, Tome I. another method for determining the coefficients, which is also given by Encke in the Jahrbuch for 1860 in a different form.

SPHERICAL ASTRONOMY.

FIRST SECTION.

THE CELESTIAL SPHERE AND ITS DIURNAL MOTION.

In spherical astronomy we consider the positions of the stars projected on the celestial sphere, referring them by spherical co-ordinates to certain great circles of the sphere. Spherical astronomy teaches then the means, to determine the positions of the stars with respect to these great circles and the positions of these circles themselves with respect to each other. We must therefore first make ourselves acquainted with these great circles, whose planes are the fundamental planes of the several systems of co-ordinates and with the means, by which we may reduce the place of a heavenly body given for one of these fundamental planes to another system of co-ordinates.

Some of these co-ordinates are independent of the diurnal motion of the sphere, but others are referred to planes which do not participate in this motion. The places of the stars therefore, when referred to one of the latter planes, must continually change and it will be important to study these changes and the phenomena produced by them. As the stars besides the diurnal motion common to all have also other, though more slow motions, on account of which they change also their positions with respect to those systems of co-ordinates, which are independent of the diurnal motion, it is never sufficient, to know merely the place of a heavenly body but it is also necessary to know the time, to which these places correspond. We must therefore show, how the daily motion either alone or combined with the motion of the sun is used as a measure of time.

I. THE SEVERAL SYSTEMS OF GREAT CIRCLES OF THE CELESTIAL SPHERE.

1. The stars appear projected on the concave surface of a sphere, which on account of the rotatory motion of the earth on her axis appears to revolve around us in the opposite direction namely from east to west. If we imagine at any place on the surface of the earth a line drawn parallel to the axis of the earth, it will generate on account of the rotatory motion of the earth the surface of a cylinder, whose base is the parallel-circle of the place. But as the distance of the stars may be regarded as infinite compared to the diameter of the earth, this line remaining parallel to itself will appear to pierce the celestial sphere always in the same points as the axis of the earth. These points which appear immoveable in the celestial sphere are called the ***Poles*** of the celestial sphere or the Poles of the heavens, and the one corresponding to the *North-Pole* of the earth, being therefore visible in the northern hemisphere of the earth is called the North-Pole of the celestial sphere, while the opposite is called the *South-Pole*. If we now imagine a line parallel to the equator of the earth, hence vertical to the former, it will on account of the diurnal motion describe a plane, whose intersection with the celestial sphere coincides with the great circle, whose poles are the Poles of the heavens and which is called the *Equator*. Any straight line making an angle different from 90^{0} with the axis of the earth generates the surface of a cone, which intersects the celestial sphere in two small circles, parallel to the equator, whose distance from the poles is equal to the angle between the generating line and the axis. Such small circles are called *Parallel-circles*.

A plane tangent to the surface of the earth at any place intersects the celestial sphere in a great circle, which separates the visible from the invisible hemisphere and is called the *Horizon*. The inclination of the axis to this plane is equal to the latitude of the place. The straight line tangent to the meridian of a place generates by the rotation of the earth the surface of a cone, which intersects the celestial sphere in two parallel circles, whose distance from the nearest pole is equal to the latitude of the place and as the plane of the horizon is revolved in such a manner, that it remains always tangent to this cone, these two parallel circles must include two zones, of which the one around the visible pole remains always above the horizon of the place, while the other never rises above it. All other stars outside of these zones rise or set and move from east to west in a parallel circle making in general an oblique angle with the horizon. A line vertical to the plane of the horizon points to the highest point of the visible hemisphere, which is called the ***Zenith***, while the point directly opposite below the horizon is called ***the Nadir***. The point of intersection of this line with the celestial sphere describes on account of the rotation a small circle, whose distance from the pole is equal to the co-latitude of the place; hence all stars which are at this distance from the pole pass through the zenith of the place. As the line vertical to the horizon as well as the one drawn parallel to the axis of the earth are in the plane of the meridian of the place, this plane intersects the celestial sphere in a great circle, passing through the poles of the heavens and through the zenith and nadir, which is also called the *Meridian*. Every star passes through this plane twice during a revolution of the sphere. The part of the meridian from the visible pole through the zenith to the invisible pole corresponds to the meridian of the place on the terrestrial sphere, while the other half corresponds to the meridian of a place, whose longitude differs 180^{0} or 12 hours from that of the former. When a star passes over the first part of the Meridian, it is said to be in its *upper culmination*, while when it passes over the second part it is in its *lower culmination*. Hence only those stars are visible at their upper culmination, whose distance from the invisible pole is greater than the latitude of the place, while only those can be seen at their lower culmination, whose distance from the visible pole is less than the latitude. The arc of the meridian between the pole and the horizon is called the *altitude of the pole* and is equal to the latitude of the place, while the arc between the equator and the horizon is called the *altitude of the equator*. One is the complement of the other to 90 degrees.

2. In order to define the position of a star on the celestial sphere, we make use of spherical co-ordinates. We imagine a great circle drawn through the star and the zenith and hence vertical to the horizon. If we now take the point of intersection of this great circle with the horizon and count the number of degrees from this point upwards to the star and also the number of degrees of the horizon from this point to the meridian, the position of the star is defined. The great circle passing through the star and the zenith is called the *vertical circle* of the star; the arc of this circle between the horizon and the star is called the *altitude,* while the arc between the vertical-circle and the meridian is the *azimuth* of the star. The latter angle is reckoned from the point South through West, North etc. from 0^0 to 360^0. Instead of the altitude of a star its zenith-distance is often used, which is the arc of the vertical circle between the star and the zenith, hence equal to the complement of the altitude. Small circles whose plane is parallel to the horizon are called *almucantars*.

Instead of using spherical co-ordinates we may also define the position of a star by rectangular co-ordinates, referred to a system of axes, of which that of z is vertical to the plane of the horizon, while the axes of y and x are situated in its plane, the axis of x being directed to the origin of the azimuths, and the positive axis of y towards the azimuth 90^0 or the point West. Denoting the azimuth by A, the altitude by h, we have:

$$x = \cos h \cos A\,, \quad y = \cos h \sin A\,, \quad z = \sin h.$$

Note. For observing these spherical co-ordinates an instrument perfectly corresponding to them is used, the altitude- and azimuth-instrument. This consists in its essential parts of a horizontal divided circle, resting on three screws, by which it can be levelled with the aid of a spirit-level. This circle represents the plane of the horizon. In its centre stands a vertical column, which therefore points to the zenith, supporting another circle, which is parallel to the column and hence vertical to the horizon. Round the centre of this second circle a telescope is moving connected with an index, by which the direction of the telescope can be measured. The vertical column, which moves with the vertical circle and the telescope, carries around with it another index, by which one can read its position on the horizontal circle. If then the points of the two circles, corresponding to the zenith and the point South, are known, the azimuth and zenith-distance of any star towards which the instrument is directed, may be determined.

Besides this instrument there are others by which one can observe only altitudes. These are called altimeters, while instruments, by which azimuths alone are measured, are called theodolites.

3. The azimuth and the altitude of a star change on account of the rotation of the earth and are also at the same instant different for different places on the earth. But as it is necessary for certain purposes to give the places of the stars by co-ordinates which are the same for different places and do not depend on the diurnal motion, we must refer the stars to some great circles, which remain fixed in the celestial sphere. If we lay a great circle through the pole and the star, the arc contained between the star and the equator is called the *declination* and the arc between the star and the pole the *polar-distance* of the star. The great circle itself is called the *declination-circle* of the star. The declination is positive, when the star is north of the equator and negative, when it is south of the equator. The declination and the polar-distance are the complements of each other. They correspond to the altitude and the zenith-distance in the first system of co-ordinates.

The arc of the equator between the declination-circle of the star and the meridian, or the angle at the pole measured by it, is called the *hour-angle* of the star. It is used as the second co-ordinate and is reckoned in the direction of the apparent motion of the sphere from east to west from 0^0 to 360^0.

The declination-circles correspond to the meridians on the terrestrial globe and it is evident, that when a star is on the meridian of a place, it has at the same moment at a place, whose longitude east is equal to k, the hour-angle k and in general, when at a certain place a star has the hour-angle t, it has at the same instant at another place, whose longitude is k (positive when east, negative when west) the hour-angle $t + k$.

Instead of using the two spherical co-ordinates, the declination and the hour-angle, we may again introduce rectangular co-ordinates if we refer the place of the star to three axes, of which the positive axis of z is directed to the North-pole, while the axes of x and y are situated in the plane of the equator, the positive axis of x being directed to the meridian or the origin of the hour-angles while the positive axis of y is directed towards the hour-angle 90^0. Denoting then the declination by δ, the hour-angle by t, we have:

$$x' = \cos\delta\cos t,\quad y' = \cos\delta\sin t,\quad z' = \sin\delta.$$

Note. Corresponding to this system of co-ordinates we have a second class of instruments, which are called parallactic instruments or equatorials. Here the circle, which in the first class of instruments is parallel to the horizon, is parallel to the equator, so that the vertical column is parallel to the axis of the earth. The circle parallel to this column represents therefore a declination circle. If the points of the circles, corresponding to the meridian, being the origin of the hour-angles, and the pole, are known, the hour-angle and the declination of a star may be determined by such an instrument.

4. In this latter system of co-ordinates one of them, the declination, does not change while the hour-angle increases proportional to the time and differs in the same moment at different places on the earth according to the difference of longitude. In order to have also the second coordinate invariable, one has chosen a fixed point of the equator as origin, namely the point in which the equator is intersected by the great circle, which the centre of the sun seen from the centre of the earth appears to describe among the stars. This great circle is called the ***ecliptic*** and its inclination to the equator, which is about $23\frac{1}{2}$ degrees, the ***obliquity of the ecliptic***. The points of intersection between equator and ecliptic are called the points of the ***equinoxes***, one that of the vernal the other that of the autumnal equinox, because day and night are of equal length all over the earth, when the sun on the 21st of March and on the 23d of September reaches those points *). The points of the ecliptic at the distance of 90 degrees from the points of the equinoxes are called ***solstitial points***.

The new co-ordinate, which is reckoned in the equator from the point of the vernal equinox, is called the ***right-ascension*** of the star. It is reckoned from 0^0 to 360^0 from

*) For as the sun is then on the equator, and as equator and horizon divide each other into equal parts, the sun must remain as long below as above the horizon.

west to east or opposite to the direction of the diurnal motion. Instead of using the spherical co-ordinates, declination and right-ascension, we can again introduce rectangular co-ordinates, referring the place of the star to three vertical axes, of which the positive axis of z is directed towards the North-pole, while the axes of x and y are situated in the plane of the equator, the positive axis of x being directed towards the origin of the right-ascensions, the positive axis of y to the point, whose right-ascension is 90^0. Denoting then the right-ascension by α, we have:

$$x'' = \cos\delta\cos\alpha,\quad y'' = \cos\delta\sin\alpha,\quad z'' = \sin\delta.$$

The co-ordinates α and δ are constant for any star. In order to find from them the place of a star on the apparent celestial sphere at any moment, it is necessary to know the position of the point of the vernal equinox with regard to the meridian of the place at that moment, or the hour-angle of the point of the equinox, which is called the ***sidereal time***, while the time of the revolution of the celestial sphere is called a ***sidereal day*** and is divided into 24 sidereal hours. It is 0^h sidereal time at any place or the sidereal day commences when the point of the vernal equinox crosses the meridian, it is 1^h when its hour-angle is 15^0 or 1^h etc. For this reason the equator is divided not only in 360^0 but also into 24 hours. Denoting the sidereal time by Θ, we have always:

$$\Theta - t = \alpha,$$

hence

$$t = \Theta - \alpha.$$

If therefore for instance the right-ascension of a star is $190^0\ 20'$ and the sidereal time is 4^h, we find $t = 229^0\ 40'$ or $130^0\ 20'$ east.

From the equation for t follows $\Theta = \alpha$ when $t = 0$. Therefore every star comes in the meridian or is culminating at the sidereal time equal to its right-ascension expressed in time. Hence when the right-ascension of a star which is culminating, is known, the sidereal time at that instant is also known by it *).

---

*) The problem to convert an arc into time occurs very often.

If we have to convert an arc into time, we must multiply by 15 and multiply the remainder of the degrees, minutes and seconds by 4, in order to convert them into minutes and seconds of time.

If the sidereal time at any place is Θ, at the same instant the sidereal time at another place, whose difference of longitude is k, must be $\Theta + k$, where k is to be taken positive or negative if the second place is East or West of the first place.

Note. The co-ordinates of the third system can be found by instruments of the second class, if the sidereal time is known. In one case these co-ordinates may be even found by instruments of the first class, namely when the star is crossing the meridian, for then the right-ascension is determined by the time of the meridian-passage and the declination by observing the meridian-altitude of the star, if the latitude of the place is known. For such observations a meridian-circle is used. If such an instrument is not used for measuring altitudes but merely for observing the times of the meridian-passages of the stars, if it is therefore a mere azimuth-instrument mounted in the meridian, it is called a transit-instrument. If we observe by such an instrument and a good sidereal clock the times of the meridian-passages we get thus the differences of the right-ascensions of the stars. But as the point from which the right-ascensions are reckoned cannot be observed itself, it is more difficult, to find the absolute right-ascensions of the stars.

5. Besides these systems of co-ordinates a fourth is used, whose fundamental plane is the ecliptic. Great circles which pass through the poles of the ecliptic and therefore are vertical to it, are called *circles of latitude* and the arc of such a circle between the star and the ecliptic is called the *latitude* of the star. It is positive or negative if the star is North or South of the ecliptic. The other co-ordinate, the *longitude*, is reckoned in the ecliptic and is the arc between the circle of latitude of the star and the point of the vernal equinox. It is reckoned from 0^0 to 360^0 in the same direction as the right-ascension or contrary to the diurnal

---

Thus we have $239^0\, 18'\, 46''.75$

$= 15^h, 4 \times 14 + 1$ minutes, $4 \times 3 + 3$ seconds and $0^s.117$

$= 15^h\, 57^m\, 15^s.117$.

If on the contrary we have to convert a quantity expressed in time into an arc, we must multiply the hours by 15, but divide the minutes and seconds by 4 in order to convert them into degrees and minutes of arc. The remainders must again be multiplied by 15.

Thus we have $15^h\, 57^m\, 15^s.117$

$= 225 + 14$ degrees, $15 + 3$ minutes and 46.75 seconds

$= 239^0\, 18'\, 46''.75$.

motion of the celestial sphere*). The circle of latitude whose longitude is zero, is called the *colure of the equinoxes* and that, whose longitude is 90^0, is the *colure of the solstices.* The arc of this colure between the equator and the ecliptic, likewise the arc between the pole of the equator and that of the ecliptic is equal to the obliquity of the ecliptic.

The longitude shall always be denoted by λ, the latitude by β and the obliquity of the ecliptic by ε.

If we express again the spherical co-ordinates β and λ by rectangular co-ordinates, referred to three axes vertical to each other, of which the positive axis of z is vertical to the ecliptic and directed to the north-pole of it, while the axes of x and y are situated in the plane of the ecliptic, the positive axis of x being directed to the point of the vernal equinox, the positive axis of y to the 90th degree of longitude, we have:

$$x''' = \cos\beta\cos\lambda\,,\quad y''' = \cos\beta\sin\lambda\,,\quad z''' = \sin\beta.$$

These co-ordinates are never found by direct observations, but are only deduced by computation from the other systems of co-ordinates.

Note. As the motion of the sun is merely apparent and the earth really moving round the sun, it is expedient, to define the meaning of the circles introduced above also for this case. The centre of the earth moves round the sun in a plane, which passes through the centre of the sun and intersects the celestial sphere in a great circle called the ecliptic. Hence the longitude of the earth seen from the sun differs always 180^0 from that of the sun seen from the earth. The axis of the earth makes an angle of $66\frac{1}{2}{}^0$ with this plane and as it remains parallel while the earth is revolving round the sun it describes in the course of a year the surface of an oblique cylinder, whose base is the orbit of the earth. But on account of the infinite distance of the celestial sphere the axis appears in these different positions to intersect the sphere in the same two points, whose distance from the poles of the ecliptic is $23\frac{1}{2}{}^0$. Likewise the equator is carried around the sun parallel to itself and the line of intersection between the equator and the plane of the ecliptic, although remaining always parallel, changes its position in the course of the year by the entire diameter of the earth's orbit. But the intersections of the equator of the earth with the celestial sphere in all the different positions to which it is carried appear to coincide on account of the

---

*) The longitudes of the stars are often given in signs, each of which has 30^0. Thus the longitude 6 signs 15 degrees is $= 195^0$.

infinite distance of the stars with the great circle, whose poles are the poles of the heavens and all the lines of intersections between the plane of the equator and that of the ecliptic are directed towards the point of intersection between the two great circles of the equator and the ecliptic.

II. THE TRANSFORMATION OF THE DIFFERENT SYSTEMS OF CO-ORDINATES.

6. In order to find from the azimuth and altitude of a star its declination and hour-angle, we must revolve the axis of z in the first system of co-ordinates in the plane of x and z from the positive side of the axis of x to the positive side of the axis of z through the angle $90-\varphi$ (where φ designates the latitude), as the axes of y of both systems coincide. We have therefore according to formula (1 a) for the transformation of co-ordinates, or according to the formulae of spherical trigonometry in the triangle formed by the zenith, the pole and the star *):

$$\sin\delta = \sin\varphi \sin h - \cos\varphi \cos h \cos A$$
$$\cos\delta \sin t = \cos h \sin A$$
$$\cos\delta \cos t = \sin h \cos\varphi + \cos h \sin\varphi \cos A.$$

In order to render the formulae more convenient for logarithmic computation, we will put:

$$\sin h = m \cos M$$
$$\cos h \cos A = m \sin M,$$

and find then:

$$\sin\delta = m \sin(\varphi - M)$$
$$\cos\delta \sin t = \cos h \sin A$$
$$\cos\delta \cos t = m \cos(\varphi - M).$$

These formulae give the unknown quantities without any ambiguity. For as all parts are found by the sine and cosine, there can be no doubt about the quadrant, in which they lie, if proper attention is paid to the signs. The auxiliary angles, which are introduced for the transformation of such formulae, have always a geometrical meaning, which in each case may be easily discovered. For the geometrical construction amounts to this, that the oblique spherical triangle

*) The three sides of this triangle are respectively $90^\circ - h$, $90^\circ - \delta$ and $90^\circ - \varphi$ and the opposite angles t, $180 - A$ and the angle at the star.

is either divided into two right-angled triangles or by the addition of a right-angled triangle is transformed into one. In the present case we must draw an arc of a great circle from the star perpendicular to the opposite side $90 - \varphi$, and as we have:

$$\operatorname{tang} h = \cos A \operatorname{cotang} M,$$

it follows from the third of the formulae (10) in No. 8 of the introduction, that *M* is the arc between the zenith and the perpendicular arc, while *m* according to the first of the formulae (10) is the cosine of this perpendicular arc itself, since we have:

$$\sin h = \cos P \cos M,$$

if we denote the perpendicular arc by *P*.

We will suppose, that we have given:

$$\varphi = 52^\circ\, 30'\, 16''.0, \quad h = 16^\circ\, 11'\, 44''.0 \text{ and } A = 202^\circ\, 4'\, 15''.5.$$

Then we have to make the following computation:

$\cos A$ 9.9669481$_n$	$m \sin M$ 9.9493620$_n$
$\cos h$ 9.9824139	$m \cos M$ 9.4454744
$\sin A$ 9.5749045$_n$	$M = -72^\circ 35' 54''.61$
	$\sin M$ 9.9796542$_n$

$$\varphi - M = 125^\circ\, 6'\, 10''.61$$

$\sin(\varphi - M)$ 9.9128171	$\cos\delta \sin t$ 9.5573184$_n$	$\sin\delta$ 9.8825249
m 9.9697078	$\cos\delta \cos t$ 9.7294114$_n$	$\cos\delta$ 9.8104999
$\cos(\varphi - M)$ 9.7597036$_n$	$t = 213\ 56\ 2.22$	$\delta = +49\ 43\ 46.00$
	$\cos t$ 9.9189115$_n$.	

7. More frequently occurs the reverse problem, to convert the hour-angle and declination of a star into its azimuth and altitude. In this case we have again according to formula (1) for the transformation of co-ordinates:

$$\begin{aligned} \sin h &= \sin\varphi \sin\delta + \cos\varphi \cos\delta \cos t \\ \cos h \sin A &= \cos\delta \sin t \\ \cos h \cos A &= -\cos\varphi \sin\delta + \sin\varphi \cos\delta \cos t, \end{aligned}$$

which may be reduced to a more convenient form by introducing an auxiliary angle. For if we take:

$$\begin{aligned} \cos\delta \cos t &= m \cos M \\ \sin\delta &= m \sin M \end{aligned}$$

we have:

$$\begin{aligned} \sin h &= m \cos(\varphi - M) \\ \cos h \sin A &= \cos\delta \sin t \\ \cos h \cos A &= m \sin(\varphi - M) \end{aligned}$$

or:
$$\operatorname{tang} A = \frac{\cos M \operatorname{tang} t}{\sin(\varphi - M)}$$
$$\operatorname{tang} h = \frac{\cos A}{\operatorname{tang}(\varphi - M)}\ ^{*}).$$

When the zenith distance alone is to be found, the following formulae are convenient. From the first formula for $\sin h$ we find:
$$\cos z = \cos(\varphi - \delta) - 2\cos\varphi\cos\delta\sin\tfrac{1}{2}t^2,$$
or:
$$\sin\tfrac{1}{2}z^2 = \sin\tfrac{1}{2}(\varphi - \delta)^2 + \cos\varphi\cos\delta\sin\tfrac{1}{2}t^2.$$

If we take now:
$$n = \sin\tfrac{1}{2}(\varphi - \delta)$$
$$m = \sqrt{\cos\varphi\cos\delta},$$
we have:
$$\sin\tfrac{1}{2}z^2 = n^2\left(1 + \frac{m^2}{n^2}\sin\tfrac{1}{2}t^2\right),$$
or taking
$$\frac{m}{n}\sin\tfrac{1}{2}t = \operatorname{tang}\lambda$$
$$\sin\tfrac{1}{2}z = \frac{n}{\cos\lambda}.$$

If $\sin\lambda$ should be greater than $\cos\lambda$, it is more convenient to use the following formula:
$$\sin\tfrac{1}{2}z = \frac{m}{\sin\lambda}\sin\tfrac{1}{2}t.$$

In the formula by which n is found, we must use $\varphi - \delta$, if the star culminates south of the zenith, but $\delta - \varphi$ if the star culminates north of the zenith, as will be afterwards shown.

Applying Gauss's formulae to the triangle between the star, the zenith and the pole, and designating the angle at the star by p, we find:
$$\cos\tfrac{1}{2}z \,.\, \sin\tfrac{1}{2}(A - p) = \sin\tfrac{1}{2}t \,.\, \sin\tfrac{1}{2}(\varphi + \delta)$$
$$\cos\tfrac{1}{2}z \,.\, \cos\tfrac{1}{2}(A - p) = \cos\tfrac{1}{2}t \,.\, \cos\tfrac{1}{2}(\varphi - \delta)$$
$$\sin\tfrac{1}{2}z \,.\, \sin\tfrac{1}{2}(A + p) = \sin\tfrac{1}{2}t \,.\, \cos\tfrac{1}{2}(\varphi + \delta)$$
$$\sin\tfrac{1}{2}z \,.\, \cos\tfrac{1}{2}(A + p) = \cos\tfrac{1}{2}t \,.\, \sin\tfrac{1}{2}(\varphi - \delta).$$

If the azimuth should be reckoned from the point North, as it is done sometimes for the polar star, we must introduce $180 - A$ instead of A in these formulae and obtain now:
$$\cos\tfrac{1}{2}z \,.\, \sin\tfrac{1}{2}(p + A) = \cos\tfrac{1}{2}t \,.\, \cos\tfrac{1}{2}(\delta - \varphi)$$
$$\cos\tfrac{1}{2}z \,.\, \cos\tfrac{1}{2}(p + A) = \sin\tfrac{1}{2}t \,.\, \sin\tfrac{1}{2}(\delta + \varphi)$$
$$\sin\tfrac{1}{2}z \,.\, \sin\tfrac{1}{2}(p - A) = \cos\tfrac{1}{2}t \,.\, \sin\tfrac{1}{2}(\delta - \varphi)$$
$$\sin\tfrac{1}{2}z \,.\, \cos\tfrac{1}{2}(p - A) = \sin\tfrac{1}{2}t \,.\, \cos\tfrac{1}{2}(\delta + \varphi).$$

---

*) As the azimuth is always on the same side of the meridian with the hour angle, these last formulae leave no doubt as to the quadrant in which it lies.

Frequently the case occurs, that these computations must be made very often for the same latitude, when it is desirable to construct tables for facilitating these computations *). In this case the following transformation may be used. We had:

$$(a) \qquad \sin h = \sin \varphi \sin \delta + \cos \varphi \cos \delta \cos t$$
$$(b) \qquad \cos h \sin A = \cos \delta \sin t$$
$$(c) \qquad \cos h \cos A = - \cos \varphi \sin \delta + \sin \varphi \cos \delta \cos t.$$

If we designate now by A_0 and δ_0 those values of A and δ, which substituted in the above equation make h equal to zero, we have:

$$(d) \qquad 0 = \sin \varphi \sin \delta_0 + \cos \varphi \cos \delta_0 \cos t$$
$$(e) \qquad \sin A_0 = \cos \delta_0 \sin t$$
$$(f) \qquad \cos A_0 = - \cos \varphi \sin \delta_0 + \sin \varphi \cos \delta_0 \cos t.$$

Multiplying now (f) by $\cos \varphi$ and subtracting from it equation (d) after having multiplied it by $\sin \varphi$, further multiplying equation (f) by $\sin \varphi$ and adding to it equation (d), after multiplying it by $\cos \varphi$, we find:

$$\cos A_0 \cos \varphi = - \sin \delta_0$$
$$\cos A_0 \sin \varphi = \cos \delta_0 \cos t$$
$$\sin A_0 = \cos \delta_0 \sin t.$$

Taking then:

$$\sin \varphi = \sin \gamma \cos B$$
$$\cos \varphi \cos t = \sin \gamma \sin B$$
$$\cos \varphi \sin t = \cos \gamma,$$

we find from the equation (d) the following:

$$0 = \sin \gamma \sin (\delta_0 + B)$$

or:

$$\delta_0 = - B$$

and from (a):

$$\sin h = \sin \gamma \sin (\delta + B).$$

Then subtracting from the product of equations (b) and (f) the product of the equations (c) and (e) we get:

$$\cos h \sin (A - A_0) = \cos \varphi \sin t \sin (\delta - \delta_0) = \cos \gamma \sin (\delta + B)$$

and likewise adding to the product of the equations (c) and (f) the product of the equations (b) and (e) and that of the equations (a) and (d):

$$\cos h \cos (A - A_0) = \cos \delta \cos \delta_0 \sin t^2 + \sin \delta \sin \delta_0 + \cos \delta \cos \delta_0 \cos t^2$$
$$= \cos (\delta - \delta_0) = \cos (\delta + B).$$

*) For instance if one has to set an altitude- and azimuth instrument at objects, whose place is given by their right ascension and declination. Then one must first compute the hour angle from the right ascension and the sidereal time.

Hence the complete system of formulae is as follows:

$$\left.\begin{array}{r} \sin\varphi = \sin\gamma\cos B \\ \cos\varphi\cos t = \sin\gamma\sin B \\ \cos\varphi\sin t = \cos\gamma \end{array}\right\} \quad (1)$$

$$\left.\begin{array}{r} \sin B = \cos A_0\cos\varphi \\ \cos B\cos t = \cos A_0\sin\varphi \\ \cos B\sin t = \sin A_0 \end{array}\right\} \quad (2)$$

$$\left.\begin{array}{r} \sin h = \sin\gamma\sin(\delta + B) \\ \cos h\cos(A - A_0) = \cos(\delta + B) \\ \cos h\sin(A - A_0) = \cos\gamma\sin(\delta + B) \end{array}\right\} \quad (3).$$

These formulae by taking $D = \sin\gamma$, $C = \cos\gamma$ and $A - A_0 = u$ are changed into the following:

$$\begin{array}{r} \operatorname{tang} B = \operatorname{cotg}\varphi\cos t \\ \operatorname{tang} A_0 = \sin\varphi\operatorname{tang} t \\ \sin h = D\sin(B + \delta) \\ \operatorname{tang} u = C\operatorname{tang}(B + \delta) \\ A = A_0 + u \end{array}$$

where D and C are the sine and cosine of an angle γ, which is found from the following equation *):

$$\operatorname{cotang}\gamma = \sin B\operatorname{tang} t = \operatorname{cotang}\varphi\sin A_0.$$

These are the formulae given by Gauss in „Schumacher's Hülfstafeln herausgegeben von Warnstorff pag. 135." If now the quantities D, C, B and A_0 are brought into tables whose argument is t, the computation of the altitude and the azimuth from the hour angle and the declination is reduced to the computation of the following simple formulae:

$$\begin{array}{r} \sin h = D\sin(B + \delta) \\ \operatorname{tang} u = C\operatorname{tang}(B + \delta) \\ A = A_0 + u. \end{array}$$

Such tables for the latitude of the observatory at Altona have been published in Warnstorff's collection of tables quoted above. It is of course only necessary to extend these tables from $t = 0$ to $t = 6^h$. For it follows from the equation $\operatorname{tang} A_0 = \sin\varphi\operatorname{tang} t$, that A_0 lies always in the same quadrant as t, that therefore to the hour angle $12^h - t$ belongs the azimuth $180^0 - A$. Furthermore it follows from the equations for B, that this angle becomes negative, when $t > 6^h$ or $> 90^0$, that therefore if the hour angle is $12^h - t$ the value $-B$ must be used. The quantities

*) For we have according to the formulae (2)

$$\operatorname{cotang}\varphi\sin A_0 = \sin B\operatorname{tang} t.$$

6*

$$C = \cos\varphi \sin t \quad \text{and} \quad D = \sqrt{\sin\varphi^2 + \cos\varphi^2 \cos t^2}$$

are not changed if $180^0 - t$ instead of t is substituted in these expressions. When t lies between 12^h and 24^h, the computation must be carried through with the complement of t to 24^h and afterwards instead of the resulting value of A its complement to 360^0 must be taken.

It is easy to find the geometrical meaning of the auxiliary angles. As δ_0 represents that value of δ, which substituted in the first of the original equations makes it equal to zero, δ_0 is the declination of that point, in which the declination circle of the star intersects the horizon; likewise is A_0 the azimuth of this point. Furthermore as we have $B = -\delta_0$, $B + \delta$ is the arc SF Fig. 1 *) of the declination circle extended to the horizon. In the right angled triangle FOK, which is formed by the horizon, the equator and the side $FK = B$, we have according to the sixth of the formulae (10) of the introduction, because the angle at O is equal to $90^0 - \varphi$:

Fig. 1.

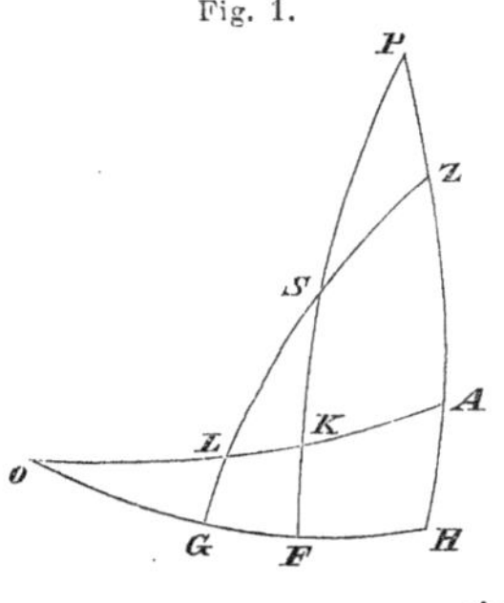

$$\sin\varphi = \cos B \sin OFK.$$

But as we have also $\sin\varphi = D\cos B$, we see, that D is the sine of the angle OFK, therefore C its cosine. At last we easily see that FH is equal to A_0 and FG equal to u.

We can find therefore the above formulae from the three right angled triangles PFH, OFK and SFG. The first triangle gives:

$$\operatorname{tang} A_0 = \operatorname{tang} t \sin\varphi,$$

the second:

$$\operatorname{tang} B = \operatorname{cotang}\varphi \cos t$$
$$\operatorname{cotang}\gamma = \sin B \operatorname{tang} t = \operatorname{cotg}\varphi \sin A_0,$$

and the third:

$$\sin h = \sin\gamma \sin(B + \delta)$$
$$\operatorname{tang} u = \cos\gamma \operatorname{tang}(B + \delta).$$

The same auxiliary quantities may be used for solving the inverse problem, given in No. 6, to find the hour angle

---

*) In this figure P is the pole, Z the zenith, OH the horizon, OA the equator, and S the star.

and the declination of a star from its altitude and azimuth. For we have in the right angled triangle SKL, designating LG by B, LK by u, AL by A_0 and the cosine and sine of the angle SLK by C and D:

$$C \operatorname{tang}(h - B) = \operatorname{tang} u$$
$$D \sin (h - B) = \sin \delta$$
$$\text{and} \qquad t = A_0 - u,$$

where now:

$$\operatorname{tang} B = \operatorname{cotang} \varphi \cos A$$
$$\operatorname{tang} A_0 = \sin \varphi \operatorname{tang} A$$

and where D and C are the sine and cosine of an angle γ, which is found by the equation:

$$\operatorname{cotang} \gamma = \sin B \operatorname{tang} A.$$

We use therefore for computing the auxiliary quantities the same formulae as before only with this difference, that in these A occurs in the place of t; we can use therefore also the same tables as before, taking as argument the azimuth converted into time.

8. The cotangent of the angle γ, which Gauss denotes by E, can be used to compute the angle at the star in the triangle between the pole, the zenith and the star. This angle between the vertical circle and the declination circle, which is called the *parallactic angle* is often made use of. If we have tables, such as spoken of before, which give also the angle E, we find the parallactic angle, which shall be denoted by p, from the following simple formula:

$$\operatorname{tang} p = \frac{E}{\cos (B + \delta)},$$

as is easily seen, if the fifth of the formulae (10) in No. 8 of the introduction is applied to the right angled triangle SGF Fig. 1. But if one has no such tables, the following formulae which are easily deduced from the triangle SPZ can be used:

$$\cos h \sin p = \cos \varphi \sin t$$
$$\cos h \cos p = \cos \delta \sin \varphi - \sin \delta \cos \varphi \cos t,$$

or taking:

$$\cos \varphi \cos t = n \sin N$$
$$\sin \varphi = n \cos N,$$

the following formulae, which are more convenient for logarithmic computation:

$$\cos h \sin p = \cos \varphi \sin t$$
$$\cos h \cos p = n \cos (\delta + N).$$

The parallactic angle is used, if we wish to compute the effect which small increments of the azimuth and altitude produce in the declination and the hour angle. For we have, applying to the triangle between the pole, the zenith and the star the first and third of the formulae (9) in No. 11 of the introduction:

$$d\delta = \cos p\, dh + \cos t\, d\varphi + \cos h \sin p\,.\, dA$$
$$\cos\delta\, dt = -\sin p\, dh + \sin t \sin\delta\,.\, d\varphi + \cos h \cos p\,.\, dA$$

and likewise:

$$dh = \cos p\, d\delta - \cos A\, d\varphi - \cos\delta \sin p\,.\, dt$$
$$\cos h\, dA = \sin p\, d\delta - \sin A \sin h\, d\varphi + \cos\delta \cos p\, dt.$$

9. In order to convert the right ascension and declination of a star into its latitude and longitude, we must revolve the axis of z'' *) in the plane of $y''z''$ through the angle ε equal to the obliquity of the ecliptic in the direction from the positive axis of y'' towards the positive axis of z''. As the axes of x'' and x''' of the two systems coincide, we find according to the formulae (1 a) in No. 1 of the introduction:

$$\cos\beta \cos\lambda = \cos\delta \cos\alpha$$
$$\cos\beta \sin\lambda = \cos\delta \sin\alpha \cos\varepsilon + \sin\delta \sin\varepsilon$$
$$\sin\beta = -\cos\delta \sin\alpha \sin\varepsilon + \sin\delta \cos\varepsilon.$$

These formulae may be also derived from the triangle between the pole of the equator, the pole of the ecliptic and the star, whose three sides are $90^0 - \delta$, $90^0 - \beta$ and ε and the opposite angles respectively $90^0 - \lambda$, $90^0 + \alpha$ and the angle at the star.

In order to render these formulae convenient for logarithmic computation, we introduce the following auxiliary quantities:

$$M \sin N = \sin\delta$$
$$M \cos N = \cos\delta \sin\alpha, \qquad (a)$$

by which the three original equations are changed into the following:

$$\cos\beta \cos\lambda = \cos\delta \cos\alpha$$
$$\cos\beta \sin\lambda = M \cos(N - \varepsilon)$$
$$\sin\beta = M \sin(N - \varepsilon),$$

or if we find all quantities by their tangents and substitute for M its value $\dfrac{\cos\delta \sin\alpha}{\cos N}$

*) See No. 4 of this Section.

we get as final equations:

$$\left.\begin{aligned} \operatorname{tang} N &= \frac{\operatorname{tang}\delta}{\sin\alpha} \\ \operatorname{tang}\lambda &= \frac{\cos(N-\varepsilon)}{\cos N}\operatorname{tang}\alpha \\ \operatorname{tang}\beta &= \operatorname{tang}(N-\varepsilon)\sin\lambda \end{aligned}\right\} \quad (b).$$

The original formulae give us α and δ without any ambiguity; but if we use the formulae (b) we may be in doubt as to the quadrant in which we must take λ. However it follows from the equation:

$$\cos\beta\cos\lambda = \cos\delta\cos\alpha$$

that λ must be taken in that quadrant, which corresponds to the sign of tang λ and at the same time satisfies the condition, that $\cos\alpha$ and $\cos\lambda$ must have the same sign.

As a check of the computation the following equation may be used:

$$\frac{\cos(N-\varepsilon)}{\cos N} = \frac{\cos\beta\sin\lambda}{\cos\delta\sin\alpha}, \quad (c)$$

which we find by dividing the two equations:

$$\begin{aligned} \cos\beta\sin\lambda &= M\cos(N-\varepsilon) \\ \cos\delta\sin\alpha &= M\cos N. \end{aligned}$$

The geometrical meaning of the auxiliary angles is easily found. N is the angle which the great circle passing through the star and the point of the vernal equinox makes with the equator, and M is the sine of this arc.

Example. If we have:

$$\alpha = 6^\circ\, 33'\, 29''.30 \quad \delta = -16^\circ\, 22'\, 35''.45$$
$$\varepsilon = 23^\circ\, 27'\, 31''.72,$$

the computation of the formulae (b) and (c) stands as follows:

$$\begin{array}{rl} \cos\delta & 9.9820131 \\ \operatorname{tang}\delta & 9.4681562_n \\ \sin\alpha & 9.0577093 \\ \hline N = & -68^\circ\, 45'\, 41''.88 \\ \varepsilon = & +23\;\; 27\;\; 31\;.72 \\ \hline N-\varepsilon = & -92\;\; 13\;\; 13\;.60 \\ \cos(N-\varepsilon) & 8.5882086_n \\ \cos N & 9.5590069 \end{array} \qquad \begin{array}{rl} \operatorname{tang}\alpha & 9.0605604 \\ \frac{\cos(N-\varepsilon)}{\cos N} & 9.0292017_n \\ \hline \lambda = & 359^\circ\, 17'\, 43''.91 \\ \operatorname{tang}(N-\varepsilon) & 1.4114653 \\ \sin\lambda & 8.0897293_n \\ \hline \beta = & -17^\circ\, 35'\, 37''.53 \\ \cos\beta = & 9.9791948 \end{array}$$

$$\begin{array}{rl} \cos\beta\sin\lambda = & 8.0689241_n \\ \cos\delta\sin\alpha = & 9.0397224 \\ \hline & 9.0292017_n \end{array}$$

If we apply Gauss's formulae to the triangle between the pole of the equator, the pole of the ecliptic and the star and denote the angle at the star by $90^0 - E$, we find:

$$\begin{aligned}
\sin(45^0 - \tfrac{1}{2}\beta)\sin\tfrac{1}{2}(E-\lambda) &= \cos(45^0 + \tfrac{1}{2}\alpha)\sin[45^0 - \tfrac{1}{2}(\varepsilon+\delta)]\\
\sin(45 - \tfrac{1}{2}\beta)\cos\tfrac{1}{2}(E-\lambda) &= \sin(45 + \tfrac{1}{2}\alpha)\cos[45 - \tfrac{1}{2}(\varepsilon-\delta)]\\
\cos(45 - \tfrac{1}{2}\beta)\sin\tfrac{1}{2}(E+\lambda) &= \sin(45 + \tfrac{1}{2}\alpha)\sin[45 - \tfrac{1}{2}(\varepsilon-\delta)]\\
\cos(45 - \tfrac{1}{2}\beta)\cos\tfrac{1}{2}(E+\lambda) &= \cos(45 + \tfrac{1}{2}\alpha)\cos[45 - \tfrac{1}{2}(\varepsilon+\delta)].
\end{aligned}$$

These formulae are especially convenient, if we wish to find besides β and λ also the angle $90^0 - E$.

Note. Encke has given in the Berlin Jahrbuch for 1831 tables, which are very convenient for an approximate computation of the longitude and latitude from the right ascension and declination. The formulae on which they are based are deduced by the same transformation of the three fundamental equations in No. 9 as that used in No. 7 of this section for equations of a similar form. More accurate tables have been given in the Jahrbuch for 1856.

10. The formulae for the inverse problem, to convert the longitude and latitude of a star into its right ascension and declination, are similar. We get in this case from the formulae (1) for the transformation of co-ordinates or also from the same spherical triangle as before:

$$\begin{aligned}
\cos\delta\cos\alpha &= \cos\beta\cos\lambda\\
\cos\delta\sin\alpha &= \cos\beta\sin\lambda\cos\varepsilon - \sin\beta\sin\varepsilon\\
\sin\delta &= \cos\beta\sin\lambda\sin\varepsilon + \sin\beta\cos\varepsilon.
\end{aligned}$$

We can find these equations also by exchanging in the three original equations in No. 9 β and λ for δ and α and conversely and taking the angle ε negative. In the same way we can deduce from the formulae (b) the following:

$$\begin{aligned}
\operatorname{tang} N &= \frac{\operatorname{tang}\beta}{\sin\lambda}\\
\operatorname{tang}\alpha &= \frac{\cos(N+\varepsilon)}{\cos N}\operatorname{tang}\lambda\\
\operatorname{tang}\delta &= \operatorname{tang}(N+\varepsilon)\sin\alpha
\end{aligned}$$

and from (c) the following formula, which may be used as a check:

$$\frac{\cos(N+\varepsilon)}{\cos N} = \frac{\cos\delta\sin\alpha}{\cos\beta\sin\lambda}.$$

Here is N the angle, which the great circle passing through the star and the point of the vernal equinox makes with the ecliptic.

Finally Gauss's equations give in this case:

$$\sin(45^0 - \tfrac{1}{2}\delta)\sin\tfrac{1}{2}(E+\alpha) = \sin(45^0 + \tfrac{1}{2}\lambda)\sin[45^0 - \tfrac{1}{2}(\varepsilon+\beta)]$$
$$\sin(45 - \tfrac{1}{2}\delta)\cos\tfrac{1}{2}(E+\alpha) = \cos(45 + \tfrac{1}{2}\lambda)\cos[45 - \tfrac{1}{2}(\varepsilon-\beta)]$$
$$\cos(45 - \tfrac{1}{2}\delta)\sin\tfrac{1}{2}(E-\alpha) = \cos(45 + \tfrac{1}{2}\lambda)\sin[45 - \tfrac{1}{2}(\varepsilon-\beta)]$$
$$\cos(45 - \tfrac{1}{2}\delta)\cos\tfrac{1}{2}(E-\alpha) = \sin(45 + \tfrac{1}{2}\lambda)\cos[45 - \tfrac{1}{2}(\varepsilon+\beta)].$$

Note. As the sun is always in the ecliptic, the formulae become more simple in this case. If we designate the longitude of the sun by L, its right ascension and declination by A and D, we find:

$$\text{tang}\, A = \text{tang}\, L \cos\varepsilon$$
$$\sin D = \sin L \sin\varepsilon$$

or:

$$\text{tang}\, D = \text{tang}\,\varepsilon \sin A.$$

11. The angle at the star in the triangle between the pole of the equator, the pole of the ecliptic and the star, or the angle at the star between its circle of declination and its circle of latitude, is found at the same time with λ and β, if Gauss's equations are used for computing them, as, denoting this angle by η, we have $\eta = 90 - E$. But if we wish to find this angle without computing those formulae, we can obtain it from the following equations:

$$\cos\beta\sin\eta = \cos\alpha\sin\varepsilon$$
$$\cos\beta\cos\eta = \cos\varepsilon\cos\delta + \sin\varepsilon\sin\delta\sin\alpha$$

or:

$$\cos\delta\sin\eta = \cos\lambda\sin\varepsilon$$
$$\cos\delta\cos\eta = \cos\varepsilon\cos\beta - \sin\varepsilon\sin\beta\sin\lambda,$$

or taking:

$$\cos\varepsilon = m\cos M$$
$$\sin\varepsilon\sin\alpha = m\sin M$$

or:

$$\cos\varepsilon = n\cos N$$
$$\sin\varepsilon\sin\lambda = n\sin N$$

we may find it from the equations:

$$\cos\beta\sin\eta = \cos\alpha\sin\varepsilon$$
$$\cos\beta\cos\eta = m\cos(M - \delta)$$

or:

$$\cos\delta\sin\eta = \cos\lambda\sin\varepsilon$$
$$\cos\delta\cos\eta = n\cos(N + \beta).$$

The angle η is used to find the effect, which small increments of λ and β have on α and δ and conversely. For we get by applying the first and third of the formulae (11) in No. 9 of the introduction to the triangle used before:

$$d\beta = \cos\eta\, d\delta - \cos\delta\sin\eta\, .\, d\alpha - \sin\lambda\, d\varepsilon$$
$$\cos\beta\, d\lambda = \sin\eta\, d\delta + \cos\delta\cos\eta\, .\, d\alpha + \cos\lambda\sin\beta\, d\varepsilon,$$

and also:

$$d\delta = \cos\eta\, d\beta + \cos\beta\sin\eta\, .\, d\lambda + \sin\alpha\, d\varepsilon$$
$$\cos\delta\, d\alpha = -\sin\eta\, d\beta + \cos\beta\cos\eta\, .\, d\lambda - \cos\alpha\sin\delta\, .\, d\varepsilon.$$

Note. The supposition made above that the centre of the sun is always moving in the ecliptic is not rigidly true, as the sun on account of the perturbations produced by the planets has generally a small latitude either north or south, which however never exceeds one second of arc. Having therefore computed right ascension and declination by the formulae given in the note to No. 10, we must correct them still for this latitude. If we designate it by dB, we have the differential formulae:

$$dA = -\frac{\sin\eta}{\cos D} \cdot dB,$$

$$dD = \cos\eta \cdot dB,$$

or if we substitute the values of $\sin\eta$ and $\cos\eta$ from the formulae for $\cos\beta\cos\eta$ and $\cos\delta\cos\eta$ after having taken $\beta = 0$, we find:

$$\cos D\, dA = -\cos A \sin\varepsilon \cdot dB,$$

$$dD = \frac{\cos\varepsilon}{\cos D} \cdot dB.$$

12. The formulae for converting altitudes and azimuths into longitudes and latitudes may be briefly stated, as they are not made use of.

We have first the co-ordinates with respect to the plane of the horizon:

$$x = \cos A \cos h,$$
$$y = \sin A \cos h,$$
$$z = \sin h.$$

If we revolve the axis of x in the plane of x and z through the angle $90^0 - \varphi$ in the direction towards the positive side of the axis of z, we find the new co-ordinates:

$$x' = x \sin\varphi + z \cos\varphi,$$
$$y' = y,$$
$$z' = z \sin\varphi - x \cos\varphi.$$

If we then revolve the axis of x' in the plane of x' and y', which is the plane of the equator, through the angle Θ, so that the axis of x'' is directed towards the point of the vernal equinox, we find the following formulae, observing that the positive side of y'' must be directed towards a point whose right ascension is 90^0 and that the right ascensions and hour angles are reckoned in an opposite direction:

$$x'' = x' \cos\Theta + y' \sin\Theta$$
$$-y'' = y' \cos\Theta - x' \sin\Theta$$
$$z'' = z'.$$

If we finally revolve the axis of y'' in the plane of y'' and z'' through the angle ε in the direction towards the positive side of the axis of z'', we find:

$$x''' = x''$$
$$y''' = y'' \cos\varepsilon + z'' \sin\varepsilon$$
$$z''' = -y'' \sin\varepsilon + z'' \cos\varepsilon,$$

and as we also have:

$$x''' = \cos\beta \cos\lambda$$
$$y''' = \cos\beta \sin\lambda$$
$$z''' = \sin\beta,$$

we can express λ and β directly by A, h, φ, Θ and ε by eliminating x', y', z' as well as x'', y'', z''.

III. THE DIURNAL MOTION AS A MEASURE OF TIME. SIDEREAL, APPARENT AND MEAN SOLAR TIME.

13. The diurnal revolution of the celestial sphere or rather that of the earth on her axis being perfectly uniform, it serves as a measure of time. The time of an entire revolution of the earth on its axis or the time between two successive culminations of the same fixed point of the celestial sphere, is called a ***sidereal day***. It is reckoned from the moment the point of the vernal equinox is crossing the meridian, when it is 0^h sidereal time. Likewise it is 1^h, 2^h, 3^h etc. sidereal time, when the hour angle of the point of the equinox is 1^h, 2^h, 3^h etc. or when the point of the equator whose right ascension is 1^h, 2^h, 3^h etc. or 15^0, 30^0, 45^0 etc. is on the meridian.

We shall see hereafter, that the two points of the equinoxes are not fixed points of the celestial sphere, but that they are moving though slowly on the ecliptic. This motion is rather the result of two motions, of which one is proportional to the time and therefore unites with the diurnal motion of the sphere, while the other is periodical. This latter motion has the effect, that the hour angle of the point of the vernal equinox does not increase uniformly, hence that sidereal time is not strictly uniform. But this want of uniformity is exceedingly small as it amounts during a period of nineteen years only to $\pm 1^s$.

14. The sun being on the 21th of March at the vernal equinox it crosses the meridian on that day at nearly 0^h sidereal time. But at it moves in the ecliptic and is at the point of the autumnal equinox on the 23^{d} of September, having the right ascension 12^{h}, it culminates on this day at nearly 12^{h} sidereal time. Thus the time of the culmination of the sun moves in the course of a year through all hours of a sidereal day and on account of this inconvenience the sidereal time would not suit the purposes of society, hence the motion of the sun is used as the measure of civil time. The hour angle of the sun is called the *apparent solar time* and the time between two successive culminations of the sun an *apparent solar day*. It is 0^{h} apparent time when the centre of the sun passes over the meridian. But as the right ascension of the sun does not increase uniformly, this time is also not uniform. There are two causes which produce this variable increase of the sun's right ascension, namely the obliquity of the ecliptic and the variable motion of the sun in the ecliptic. This annual motion of the sun is only apparent and produced by the motion of the earth, which according to Kepler's laws moves in an ellipse, whose focus is occupied by the sun, and in such a manner that the line joining the centre of the earth and that of the sun (the radius vector of the earth) describes equal areas in equal times. If we denote the length of the sidereal year, in which the earth performs an entire revolution in her orbit, by τ we find for the areal velocity F of the earth $\frac{a^2\pi\sqrt{1-e^2}}{\tau}$, as the area of the ellipse is equal to $a^2\pi\sqrt{1-e^2}$, or if we take the semi-major axis of the ellipse equal to unity and introduce instead of e the angle of excentricity φ, given by the equation $e=\sin\varphi$, we find:

$$F=\frac{\pi\cos\varphi}{\tau}.$$

If we call the time, when the earth is nearest to the sun or at the perihelion T, we find for any other time t the sector, which the radius vector has described since the time of the perihelion passage equal to $F(t-T)$. But this sector is also expressed by the definite integral $\frac{1}{2}\int_0^{v} r^2\,dv$, where r designates the radius vector and v the angle, which the radius vector makes with the major axis, or the ***true anomaly*** of the earth. We have therefore the following equation:

$$2F(t-T)=\int_0^{\nu} r^2\,d\nu.$$

As we have for the ellipse $r=\frac{a\,(1-e^2)}{1+e\cos\nu}=\frac{a\cos\varphi^2}{1+e\cos\nu}$, this integral would become complicated. We can however introduce another angle for ν; for as the radius vector at the perihelion is $=a-ae$, at the aphelion $=a+ae$, we may assume $r=a\,(1-e\cos E)$ where E is an angle which is equal to zero at the same time as ν. For we get the following equation for determining E from the two expressions of r:

$$\cos E=\frac{\cos\nu+e}{1+e.\cos\nu},$$

from which we see, that E has always a real value, as the right side is always less than ∓ 1.

By a simple transformation we get also:

$$\frac{\cos E-e}{1-e\cos E}=\cos\nu \text{ and } \frac{\cos\varphi\sin E}{1-e\cos E}=\sin\nu$$

and differentiating the two expressions for r, we find:

$$\frac{d\nu}{dE}=\frac{a\cos\varphi}{r}.$$

Introducing now the variable E into the above definite integral, we find:

$$2F(t-T)=a^2\cos\varphi\int_0^{E}(1-e\cos E)\,dE=a^2\cos\varphi\,(E-e\sin E),$$

hence taking again the semi-major axis equal to unity and substituting for F its value found before we obtain:

$$\frac{2\pi}{\tau}(t-T)=E-e\sin E,$$

where $\frac{2\pi}{\tau}$ is the mean sidereal daily motion of the earth, that is the daily motion the earth would have if it were performing the whole revolution with uniform velocity in the time τ. The first member of the above equation expresses therefore the angle, which such a fictitious earth, moving with uniform velocity, would describe in the time $t-T$. This angle is called the ***mean anomaly*** and denoting it by M, we can write the above equation also thus:

$$M = E - e \sin E,$$

and having found from this the auxiliary angle E, we get the true anomaly from the equation:

$$\text{tang}\, v = \frac{\cos\varphi \sin E}{\cos E - e}.$$

But in case that the excentricity is small it is more convenient, to develop the difference between the true and mean anomaly into a series. Several elegant methods have been given for this, whose explanation would lead us too far, but as we need only a few terms for our present purpose, we can easily find them in the following way. As we have $v = M$ when $e = 0$, we can take:

$$v = M + v'_0 \,.\, e + \tfrac{1}{2} v''_0 \,.\, e^2 + \tfrac{1}{6} v'''_0 \,.\, e^3 + \ldots,$$

where v'_0, v''_0 etc. designate the first, second etc. differential coefficient of v with respect to e in case that we take $e = 0$.

If we differentiate the equation $\sin v = \frac{\cos\varphi \sin E}{1 - \cos E}$ written logarithmically, we find:

$$\frac{\cos v}{\sin v} dv = \frac{dE}{\sin E} \cdot \frac{\cos E - e}{1 - e\cos E} + \frac{d\varphi}{\cos\varphi} \cdot \frac{\cos E - e}{1 - e\cos E},$$

or:
$$dv = \frac{\sin v}{\sin E} \cdot dE + \frac{\sin v}{\cos\varphi} d\varphi = \frac{a\cos\varphi}{r} dE + \frac{\sin v}{\cos\varphi} d\varphi,$$

and if we differentiate also the equation for M, considering only E and e as variable, we find:

$$dE = \sin v \, d\varphi$$

$$\frac{dv}{d\varphi} = \frac{\sin v}{\cos\varphi}(2 + e\cos v) \text{ and } \frac{dv}{de} = \frac{\sin v}{\cos\varphi^2}(2 + e\cos v).$$

Taking here $e = 0$, we get $v'_0 = 2\sin M$.

In order to find also the higher differential coefficients we will put $P = \frac{\sin v}{\cos\varphi^2}$ and $Q = 2 + e\cos v$. We find then easily, denoting the differential coefficients of P and Q after having taken $e = 0$ by P'_0, Q'_0 etc.

$$P'_0 = \cos M \,.\, v'_0 = \sin 2M,$$
$$Q'_0 = \cos M,$$
$$v''_0 = \sin M \,.\, Q'_0 + 2P'_0 = \tfrac{5}{2}\sin 2M,$$
$$P''_0 = \cos M \,.\, v''_0 - \sin M \,.\, v'^2_0 + 2\sin M = \tfrac{9}{4}\sin 3M + \tfrac{1}{4}\sin M,$$
$$Q''_0 = -2\sin M \,.\, v'_0 = -4\sin M^2,$$
$$v'''_0 = \sin M \,.\, Q''_0 + 2Q'_0 \,.\, P'_0 + 2P''_0 = \tfrac{13}{2}\sin 3M - \tfrac{3}{2}\sin M.$$

Hence we get:

$$v = M + e \,.\, 2\sin M + e^2 \,.\, \tfrac{5}{4}\sin 2M + e^3 \left(\tfrac{13}{12}\sin 3M - \tfrac{1}{4}\sin M\right)$$
$$= M + \left(2e - \tfrac{1}{4}e^3\right)\sin M + \tfrac{5}{4}e^2 \sin 2M + \tfrac{13}{12}e^3 \sin 3M + \ldots$$

The excentricity of the earth's orbit for the year 1850 is 0.0167712. If we substitute this value for e and multiply all terms by 206265 in order to get $\nu - M$ expressed in seconds of arc, we find:

$$\nu = M + 6918''.37 \sin M + 72''.52 \sin 2M + 1''.05 \sin 3M,$$

where the periodical part, which is always to be added to the mean anomaly in order to get the true anomaly, is called the *equation of the centre.*

As the apparent angular motion of the sun is equal to the angular motion of the earth around the sun, we obtain the true longitude of the sun by adding to ν the longitude π which the sun has when the earth is at the perihelion and $M + \pi$ is the longitude of the fictitious mean sun, which is supposed to move with uniform velocity in the ecliptic, or the *mean longitude* of the sun. Denoting the first by λ, the other by L, we have the following expression for the true longitude of the sun:

$$\lambda = L + 6918''.37 \sin M + 72''.52 \sin 2M + 1''.05 \sin 3M\text{*)},$$

or if we introduce L instead of M, as we have $M = L - \pi$ and $\pi = 280^0\ 21'\ 41''.0$:

$$\begin{aligned} \lambda = L &+ 1244''.31 \sin L &&+ 6805''.56 \cos L \\ &- 67\ .82 \sin 2L &&+ 25\ .66 \cos 2L \\ &- 0\ .54 \sin 3L &&- 0\ .90 \cos 3L. \end{aligned}$$

In order to deduce the right ascension of the sun from its longitude, we use the formula:

$$\operatorname{tang} A = \operatorname{tang} \lambda \,.\, \cos \varepsilon,$$

which by applying formula (17) in No. 11 of the introduction is changed into:

$$A = \lambda - \operatorname{tang} \tfrac{1}{2} \varepsilon^2 \sin 2\lambda + \tfrac{1}{2} \operatorname{tang} \tfrac{1}{2} \varepsilon^4 \sin 4\lambda - \ldots$$

where the periodical part taken with the opposite sign is called the *reduction to the ecliptic.*

If we substitute in this formula the last formula found for λ and develop the sines and cosines of the complex terms we find after the necessary reductions and after dividing by 15 in order to get the right ascension expressed in seconds of time:

---

*) To this the perturbations of the longitude produced by the planets must be added as well as the small motions of the point of the equinox.

$$\begin{aligned} A = L &+ 86^s.53 \sin L &&+ 434^s.15 \cos L \\ &- 596.64 \sin 2L &&+ 1.69 \cos 2L \\ &- 3.77 \sin 3L &&- 18.77 \cos 3L \\ &+ 13.23 \sin 4L &&- 0.19 \cos 4L \\ &+ 0.16 \sin 5L &&+ 0.82 \cos 5L \\ &- 0.36 \sin 6L &&+ 0.02 \cos 6L \\ &- 0.01 \sin 7L &&- 0.04 \cos 7L. \end{aligned}$$

15. As the right ascension of the sun does not increase at a uniform rate, the apparent solar time, being equal to the hour angle of the sun, cannot be uniform. Another uniform time has therefore been introduced, the ***mean solar time***, which is regulated by the motion of another fictitious sun, supposed to move with uniform velocity in the equator while the fictitious sun used before was moving in the ecliptic. The right ascension of this mean sun is therefore equal to the longitude L of the first mean sun. It is mean noon at any place, when this mean sun is on the meridian, hence when the sidereal time is equal to the mean longitude of the sun and the hour angle of this mean sun is the mean time which for astronomical purposes is reckoned from one noon to the next from 0^h to 24^h.

According to Hansen the mean right ascension L of the sun is for 1850 Jan. 0 0^h Paris mean time:

$$18^h\,39^m\,9^s.261,$$

and as the length of the tropical year that is the time in which the sun makes an entire revolution with respect to the vernal equinox is 365.2422008, the mean daily tropical motion of the sun is:

$$\frac{360^0}{365.2422008} = 59'\,8''.33 \text{ or } = 3^m\,56^s.555 \text{ in time,}$$

$$\text{its motion in 365 days} = 23^h 59^m\,2^s.706 = -57^s.294,$$

$$\text{its motion in 366 days} = 24\quad 2\quad 59\;.261 = +2^m\,59^s\,261.$$

By this we are enabled to compute the sidereal time for any other time. In order to find the sidereal time at noon for any other meridian, we have the sidereal time at noon for Jan. 0 1850 equal to:

$$18^h\,39^m\,9^s.261 + \frac{k}{24} \times 3^m\,56^s.555,$$

where k denotes the difference of longitude from Paris, taken positive when West, negative when East *).

---

*) Here again the small motion of the vernal equinox must be added.

The relation between mean and apparent time follows from the formula for A. The mean sun is sometimes ahead of the real sun, sometimes behind according to the sign of the periodical part of the formula for A.

If we compute L for mean noon at a certain place, the value of $L-A$ given by the above formula is the hour angle of the sun at mean noon, as L is the sidereal time at mean noon*). Now we call *equation of time* the quantity, which must be added to the apparent time in order to get the mean time. In order therefore to find from the expression for $L-A$ the equation of time x for apparent noon, we must convert the hour angle $L-A$ into mean time and take it with the opposite sign. But if n is the mean daily motion of the sun in time and $n+w$ the true daily motion on that certain day, 24 hours of mean time are equal to $24-w$ hours of apparent time, hence we have:

$$x : A - L = 24^{\mathrm{h}} : 24^{\mathrm{h}} - w,$$

$$\text{or } x = (A - L)\frac{24^{\mathrm{h}}}{24^{\mathrm{h}} - w}.$$

From the equation for A we can easily see how the equation of time changes in the course of a year. For if we take $A-L=0$, retaining merely the three principal terms, we have the equation:

$$0 = 86.5 \sin L - 596.6 \sin 2L + 434.1 \cos L,$$

from which we can find the values of L, for which the equation of time is equal to zero, namely $L=23^{0}\,16'$, $L=83^{0}\,26'$, $L=160^{0}\,15'$, $L=273^{0}\,3'$, which correspond to the 15th of April, the 14th of June, the 31st of August and the 24th of December. Likewise we find the dates, when the equation of time is a maximum, from the differential equation and we get the 4 maxima:

	$+14^{\mathrm{m}}\,31^{\mathrm{s}}$,	$-3^{\mathrm{m}}\,53^{\mathrm{s}}$,	$+6^{\mathrm{m}}\,12^{\mathrm{s}}$,	$-16^{\mathrm{m}}\,18^{\mathrm{s}}$
on	Febr. 12,	May 14,	July 26,	Nov. 18.

The apparent solar day is the longest, when the variation

*) The above expression for $L-A$ is only approximate. The true value must be found from the solar tables and is equal to the mean longitude minus the true right ascension of the sun. The latest solar tables are those of Hansen and Olufsen (Tables du soleil. Copenhagen 1853.) and Leverrier's tables in Annales de l'Observatoire Impérial Tome IV.

of the equation of time in one day is at its maximum and positive. This occurs about Dec. 23, when the variation is 30^s hence the length of a solar day $24^h\,0^m\,30^s$. On the contrary the apparent day is the shortest, when the variation of the equation of time is negative and again at its maximum. This happens about the middle of September, when the variation is -21^s, hence the length of the apparent day $23^h\,59^m\,39^s$.

The transformation of these three different times can now be performed without any difficulty, but it will be useful, to treat the several problems separately.

16. *To convert mean solar time into sidereal time and conversely sidereal into mean time.* As the sun on account of its motion from West to East from one vernal equinox to the next loses an entire diurnal revolution compared with the fixed stars, the tropical year must contain exactly one more sidereal day than there are mean days. We have therefore:

$$\text{a sidereal day} = \frac{365.242201}{366.242201} \text{ mean day,}$$
$$= \text{a mean day} - 3^m\,55^s.909 \text{ mean time,}$$
$$\text{and a mean day} = \frac{366.242201}{365.242201} \text{ sidereal day,}$$
$$= \text{a sidereal day} + 3^m\,56^s.555 \text{ sidereal time.}$$

Hence if Θ designates the sidereal time, M the mean time and Θ_0 the sidereal time at mean noon, we have:

$$M = (\Theta - \Theta_0)\,\frac{24^h - 3^m\,55^s.909}{24^h}$$

and

$$\Theta = \Theta_0 + M\,\frac{24^h + 3^m\,56^s.555}{24^h}.$$

The sidereal time at mean noon can be computed by the formulae given before, or it can be taken from the astronomical almanacs, where it is given for every mean noon.

To facilitate the computation tables have been constructed, which give the values of

$$\frac{24^h - 3^m\,55^s.909}{24^h}\,.\,t$$

and

$$\frac{24^h + 3^m\,56^s.555}{24^h}\,.\,t$$

for any value of t. Such tables are published also in the almanacs and in all collections of astronomical tables.

Example. Given 1849 Juny 9 $14^h\ 16^m\ 36^s.35$ Berlin sidereal time. To convert it into mean time.

According to the Berlin Almanac for 1849 the sidereal time at mean noon on that day is

$$5^h\ 10^m\ 48^s.30,$$

hence $9^h\ 5^m\ 48^s.05$ sidereal time have elapsed between noon and the given time and this according to the tables or if we perform the multiplication by

$$\frac{24^h - 3^m\ 55^s.909}{24^h}$$

is equal to $9^h\ 4^m\ 18^s.63$ mean time. If the mean time had been given, we should convert it into sidereal hours, minutes and seconds and add the result to the sidereal time at mean noon in order to find the sidereal time which corresponds to the given mean time.

17. ***To convert apparent solar time into mean time and mean time into apparent time.*** In order to convert apparent time into mean time, we take simply the equation of time corresponding to this apparent time from an almanac and add it algebraically to the given time. According to the Berlin Almanac we have for the equation of time at the apparent noon the following values:

		I. Diff.	II. Diff.
1849 June 8	$-1^m\ 20^s.73$		
		$+11^s.36$	
9	$1\ \ 9\ .37$		$+0^s.27.$
		$11\ .63$	
10	$0\ 57\ .74$		

Therefore if the apparent time given is June 9 $9^h\ 5^m\ 23^s.60$, we find the equation of time equal to $-1^m.4^s.98$, hence the mean time equal to $9^h\ 4^m\ 18^s.62$.

In order to convert mean time into apparent time, the same equation of time is used. But as this sometimes is given for apparent time, we ought to know already the apparent time in order to interpolate the equation of time. But on account of its small variation, it is sufficient, to take first an approximate value of the equation of time, find with this the approximate apparent time and then interpolate with this a new value of the equation of time. For instance if $9^h\ 4^m\ 18^s.62$ mean time is given, we may take first the equation of time equal to -1^m and then find for $9^h 5^m 18^s.6$ apparent time the equation of time $-1^m 4^s.98$, hence the exact apparent time equal to $9^h 5^m 23^s.60$.

In the Nautical Almanac we find besides the equation of time for every apparent noon also the quantity $L-A$ for every mean noon given, which must be added to the mean time in order to find the apparent time. Using then this quantity, if we have to convert mean time into apparent time, we perform a similar computation as in the first case.

18. *To convert apparent time into sidereal time and conversely sidereal into apparent time.* As the apparent time is equal to the hour angle of the sun, we have only to add the right ascension of the sun in order to find the sidereal time.

According to the Berlin Almanac we have the following right ascensions of the sun for the mean noon:

		I. Diff.	
1849 June 8	$5^h 5^m 30^s.79$		
		$+4^m 7^s.96$	
9	9 38 .75		$+0^s.27.$
		4 8 .23	
10	13 46 .98		

Now if $9^h 5^m 23^s.60$ apparent time on June 9 is to be converted into sidereal time, we find the right ascension of the sun for this time equal to $5^h 11^m 12^s.75$, hence the sidereal time equal to $14^h 16^m 36^s.35$.

In order to convert sidereal time into apparent time we must know the apparent time approximately for interpolating the right ascension of the sun. But if we subtract from the sidereal time the right ascension at noon, we get the number of sidereal hours, minutes, etc. which have elapsed since noon. These sidereal hours, minutes, etc. ought to be converted into apparent time. But it is sufficient, to convert them into mean time and to interpolate the right ascension of the sun for this time. Subtracting this from the given sidereal time we find the apparent time.

On June 9 we have the right ascension of the sun at noon equal to $5^h 9^m 38^s.75$, hence $9^h 6^m 57^s.60$ sidereal time or $9^h 5^m 28^s.00$ mean time have elapsed between noon and the given sidereal time $14^h 16^m 36^s.35$. If we interpolate for this time the right ascension of the sun, we find again $5^h 11^m 12^s.75$, hence the corresponding apparent time $9^h 5^m 23^s.60$.

Instead of this we might find from the sidereal time the corresponding mean time and from this with the aid of the equation of time the apparent time.

Note. In order to make these computations for the time t of a meridian, whose difference of longitude from the meridian of the almanac is k, positive if West, negative if East, we must interpolate the quantities from the almanac, namely the sidereal time at noon, the equation of time and the right ascension of the sun for the time $t + k$.

IV. PROBLEMS ARISING FROM THE DIURNAL MOTION.

19. In consequence of the diurnal motion every star comes twice on a meridian of a place, namely in its upper culmination, when the sidereal time is equal to its right ascension and in its lower culmination, when the sidereal time is greater by 12 hours than its right ascension. The time of the culmination of a fixed star is therefore immediately known. But if the body has a proper motion, we ought to know already the time of culmination in order to be able to compute the right ascension for that moment.

By the equation of time at the apparent noon, as given in the almanacs, we find the mean time of the culmination of the sun for the meridian, for which the ephemeris is published, and the equation of time interpolated for the time k gives the time of culmination for another meridian, whose difference of longitude is equal to k.

The places of the sun, the moon and the planets are given in the almanacs for the mean noon of a certain meridian. Now let $f(a)$ denote the right ascension of the body at noon, expressed in time, and t the time of culmination, we find the right ascension at the time of culmination by Newton's formula of interpolation, neglecting the third differences, as follows:

$$f(a) + tf'(a + \tfrac{1}{2}) + \frac{t(t-1)}{1 \,.\, 2} f''(a),$$

or a little more exact:

$$f(a) + tf'(a + \tfrac{1}{2}) + \frac{t(t-1)}{1 \,.\, 2} f''(a + \tfrac{1}{2}).$$

As this must be equal to the sidereal time at that moment, we obtain the following equation, where Θ_0 designates the sidereal time at mean noon and where the interval of the arguments of $f(a)$ is assumed to be 24 hours:

$$\Theta_0 + t\,(24^h 3^m 56^s.56) = f(a) + tf'(a+\tfrac{1}{2}) + \frac{t(t-1)}{1.2} f''(a+\tfrac{1}{2}),$$

hence:

$$t = \frac{f(a) - \Theta_0}{[24^h\,3^m\,56^s.56 - f'(a+\tfrac{1}{2})] - \frac{t-1}{2} f''(a+\tfrac{1}{2})}.$$

The second member of this equation contains it is true t, but as the second differences are always small, we can in computing t from this formula use for t in the second member the approximate value $\frac{f(a) - \Theta_0}{24^h\,3^m\,56^s.56 - f'(a+\frac{1}{2})}$ *).

The quantity $\Theta_0 - f(a)$ is the hour angle of the body at noon for the meridian for which the ephemeris has been computed; if k is the longitude of another place, again taken positive if West, the hour angle at this place would be $\Theta_0 - f(a) - k$, hence the time of culmination for this place but in time of the first meridian is

$$t' = \frac{f(a) - \Theta_0 + k}{24^h\,3^m\,56^s.56 - f'(a+\frac{1}{2}) - \frac{t'-1}{2} f''(a+\frac{1}{2})}$$

and the local time of culmination $t = t' - k$.

Example. The following right ascensions of the moon are given for Berlin mean time:

	$f(a)$		
1861 July 14.5	$13^h\ 7^m\ 5^s.3$		
		+27 17.6	
15.0	13 34 22 .9		+41.2
		27 58.8	
15.5	14 2 21 .7		43.5,
		28 42.3	
16.0	14 31 4 .0		

and the sidereal time at mean noon on July 15 $\Theta_0 = 7^h\,33^m\,7^s.9$. To find the time of the culmination of the moon for Greenwich.

As the difference of longitude in this case is $k = 53^m\,34^s.9$, the numerator of the formula for t' becomes $6^h 54^m 49^s.9$,

*) If the interval of the arguments of $f(a)$ were 12 hours instead of 24 hours, the first term of the denominator in the above formula would be $12^h\,1^m\,58^s.28$, and if we start from a value $f(a)$, whose argument is midnight, we would have to use $\Theta_0 + 12^h 1^m 58^s.28$ instead of Θ_0.

the first terms of the denominator become $11^h\ 33^m\ 59^s.5$, hence the approximate value of t' is 0.59775; with this we find the correction of the denominator $+\ 8^s.5$ and the corrected value of t' equal to 0.59762 or $7^h\ 10^m\ 17^s.0$, hence the local time of the culmination equal to $6^h\ 16^m\ 42^s.1$.

For the lower culmination we have the following equation, where a again designates the argument nearest to the lower culmination:

$$\Theta_0 + t\,(24^h\,3^m\,56^s.6) = 12^h + f(a) + tf'(a+\tfrac{1}{2}) + \frac{t(t-1)}{1.2} f''(a+\tfrac{1}{2}),$$

hence the formula for a place whose longitude is k, is:

$$t' = \frac{12^h + f'(a) - \Theta_0 + k}{24^h\,3^m\,56^s.56 - f'(a+\tfrac{1}{2}) - \dfrac{t'-1}{2} f''(a+\tfrac{1}{2})},$$

or in case the interval of the arguments is 12 hours:

$$t' = \frac{12^h + f(a) - \Theta_0 + k}{12^h\,1^m\,58^s.3 - f'(a+\tfrac{1}{2}) - \dfrac{t'-1}{2} f''(a+\tfrac{1}{2})}.$$

Example. If we wish to find the time of the lower culmination at Greenwich on July 15, we start from July 15.5. Hence the numerator becomes $7^h\ 20^m\ 50^s.4$, the first terms of the denominator become $11^h\ 33^m\ 16^s.0$, hence the aproximate value of t' is equal to 0.6359 and the corrected value 0.63577 or $7^h\ 37^m\ 45^s.1$. The lower culmination occurs therefore at $19^h\ 37^m\ 45^s.1$ Berlin mean time or at $18^h\ 44^m\ 10^s.2$ Greenwich time.

20. In No. 7 we found the following equation:

$$\sin h = \sin\varphi \sin\delta + \cos\varphi \cos\delta \cos t.$$

If the star is in the horizon, therefore h equal to zero, we have:

$$0 = \sin\varphi \sin\delta + \cos\varphi \cos\delta \cos t_0.$$

hence:

$$\cos t_0 = -\operatorname{tang}\varphi \operatorname{tang}\delta.$$

By this formula we find for any latitude the hour angle at rising or setting of a star, whose declination in δ. This hour angle taken absolute is called the semi-upper diurnal arc of the star. If we know the sidereal time at which the star passes the meridian or its right ascension, we find the time of the rising or setting of the star, by subtracting the absolute value of t_0 from or adding it to the right ascension.

From the sidereal time we can find the mean time by the method given before.

Example. To find the time when Arcturus rises and sets at Berlin. For the beginning of the year 1861 we have the following place of Arcturus:

$$\alpha = 14^h\, 9^m\, 19^s.3 \qquad \delta = +19^\circ\, 54'\, 29''.$$

and further we have:

$$\varphi = 52^\circ\, 30'\, 16''.$$

With this we find the semi-diurnal arc:

$$t_0 = 118^\circ\, 10'\, 1''.3 = 7^h\, 52^m\, 40^s.$$

Hence Arcturus rises at $6^h\, 16^m\, 39^s$ and sets at $22^h\, 1^m\, 39^s$ sidereal time.

In order to find the time of the rising and setting of a moveable body, we must know its declination at the time of rising and setting and therefore we have to make the computation twice. In the case of the sun this is simple. We first take an approximate value of the declination and compute with it an approximate value of the hour angle of the sun or of the apparent time of the rising or setting. As the declination of the sun is given in the almanacs for every apparent noon, one can easily find by interpolation the declination for the time of the rising or setting and repeat the computation with this.

In the case of the moon the computation is a little longer. If we compute the mean time of the upper and lower culminations of the moon, we can find the mean time corresponding to any hour angle of the moon. We then find with an approximate value of the declination the hour angle at the time of the rising or setting, find from it an approximate value of the mean time and after having interpolated the declination of the moon for this time repeat the computation. An example is found in No. 14 of the third section.

Note. The equation for the hour angle at the time of the rising or setting may be put into another form. For if we subtract it from and add it to unity, we find by dividing the new equations:

$$\operatorname{tang}^2 \tfrac{1}{2} t = \frac{\cos(\varphi - \delta)}{\cos(\varphi + \delta)}.$$

21. The above formula for $\cos t_0$ embraces all the various phenomena, which the rising and setting of stars according to their positions with respect to the equator present at any place on the surface of the earth.

If δ is positive or the star is north of the equator, cos t_0 is negative for all places which have a northern latitude; t_0 therefore in this case is greater than 90^0 and the star remains a longer time above than below the horizon. On the contrary for stars, whose declination is south, t_0 becomes less than 90^0, therefore these remain a longer time below than above the horizon of places in the northern hemisphere. In the southern hemisphere of the earth, where φ is negative, it is the reverse, as there the upper diurnal arc of the southern stars is greater than 12 hours. If we have $\varphi = 0$, t_0 is 90^0 for any value of δ; therefore at the equator of the earth all stars remain as long above as below the horizon. If we have $\delta = 0$, t_0 is also equal to 90^0 for any value of t, hence stars on the equator remain as long above the horizon of any place on the earth as below.

Therefore while the sun is north of the equator, the days are longer than the nights in the northern hemisphere of the earth, and the reverse takes place while the sun is south of the equator. But when the sun is in the equator, days and night are equal at all places on the earth. At places on the equator this is always the case.

It is obvious that a value of t_0 is only possible while we have tang φ tang $\delta < 1$. Therefore if a star rises or sets at a place whose latitude is φ, tang δ must be less than cotang φ or $\delta < 90 - \varphi$. If $\delta = 90 - \varphi$, we find $t = 180^0$ and the star grazes the horizon at the lower culmination. If we have $\delta > 90 - \varphi$, the star never sets, and if the south declination is greater than $90 - \varphi$, the star never rises.

As the declination of the sun lies always between the limits $-\varepsilon$ and $+\varepsilon$, those places on the earth, where the sun does not rise or set at least once during the year, have a latitude north or south equal to $90 - \varepsilon$ or $66\frac{1}{2}{}^0$. These places are situated on the *polar circles*. The places within these circles have the sun at midsummer the longer above and in winter the longer below the horizon, the nearer they are to the pole.

Note. A point of the equator rises when its hour angle is 6^h. Hence if we call the right ascension of this point α, we find the stars, which rise at the same time, if we lay a great circle through this point and the points of the sphere, whose right ascensions are $\alpha - 6^h$ and $\alpha + 6^h$ and whose declinations are respectively $-(90^0 - \varphi)$ and $+(90^0 - \varphi)$. Likewise we find the stars, which set at the same time as this point of the equator, if we lay the great circle through the points, whose right ascensions are $\alpha + 6^h$ and $\alpha - 6^h$ and whose declinations are respectively $-(90^0 - \varphi)$ and $90^0 - \varphi$. The point, which at the time of the rising of the point α was in the horizon in its lower culmination, is therefore now in its upper culmination at an altitude equal to 2φ. Hence at the latitude of 45^0 the constellations make a turn of 90^0 with respect to the horizon from the time of their rising to the time of setting, as the great circle which is rising at the same time with a certain point of the equator, is vertical to the horizon, when this point is setting. On the equator the stars, which rise at the same time, set also at the same instant.

22. In order to find the point of the horizon, where a star rises or sets, we must make in the equation:

$$\sin\delta = \sin\varphi \sin h - \cos\varphi \cos h \cos A,$$

which was found in No. 6, h equal to zero and obtain:

$$\cos A_0 = -\frac{\sin\delta}{\cos\varphi} \qquad (b).$$

The negative value of A_0 is the azimuth of the star at its rising, the positive value that at the time of setting. The distance of the star, when rising or setting, from the east and west points of the horizon is called the amplitude of the star. Denoting it by $A_{,}$, we have:

$$A_0 = 90 + A_{,}$$

hence:

$$\sin A_{,} = \frac{\sin\delta}{\cos\varphi} \qquad (c),$$

where $A_{,}$ is positive, when the point where the star rises or sets, lies on the north of the east or west points, negative when it lies towards south.

The formula (c) for the amplitude may be written in a different shape. For as we have:

$$\frac{1 + \sin A_{,}}{1 - \sin A_{,}} = \frac{\sin\psi + \sin\delta}{\sin\psi - \sin\delta},$$

when $\psi = 90 - \varphi$, we find:

$$\operatorname{tang}\left(45 - \frac{A_{,}}{2}\right)^2 = \frac{\operatorname{tang}\frac{\psi - \delta}{2}}{\operatorname{tang}\frac{\psi + \delta}{2}}.$$

For Arcturus we find with the values of δ and φ, given before:

$$A_{\prime} = 34^{0}\ 0'.9.$$

23. If we write in the equation:

$$\sin h = \sin\varphi \sin\delta + \cos\varphi \cos\delta \cos t$$

$1 - 2\sin\frac{1}{2}t^2$ instead of $\cos t$, we get:

$$\sin h = \cos(\varphi - \delta) - 2\cos\varphi\cos\delta\sin\tfrac{1}{2}t^2.$$

From this we see, that equal altitudes correspond to equal hour angles on both sides of the meridian. As the second term of the second member is always negative, h has its maximum value for $t = 0$ and the maximum itself is found from the equation:

$$\cos z = \cos(\varphi - \delta) \qquad (d),$$

from which we get:

$$z = \varphi - \delta \text{ or } = \delta - \varphi.$$

If we take therefore in general:

$$z = \delta - \varphi,$$

we must take the zenith distances towards south as negative, because for those star, which culminate south of the zenith, δ is less than φ.

On the contrary h is a minimum at the lower culmination or when $t = 180^0$, as is seen, when we introduce $180 + t'$ instead of t, reckoning therefore t' from that part of the meridian, which is below the pole. For then we have:

$$\sin h = \sin\varphi\sin\delta - \cos\varphi\cos\delta\cos t'.$$

or introducing again $1 - 2\sin\frac{1}{2}t'^2$ instead of $\cos t'$:

$$\sin h = \cos[180^0 \mp (\varphi + \delta)] + 2\cos\varphi\cos\delta\sin\tfrac{1}{2}t'^2.$$

As the second term of the second member is always positive, h is a minimum when t' equals zero or at the lower culmination, when we have:

$$\cos z = \cos[180^0 \mp (\varphi + \delta)].$$

As z is always less than 90^0, when the star is visible in its lower culmination, we must use the upper sign, when φ and δ are positive, and the lower sign for the southern hemisphere, so that we have:

$$z = 180^0 - (\varphi + \delta),$$

for places in the northern hemisphere, and:

$$z = -(180^0 + \varphi + \delta)$$

for places in the southern hemisphere.

The declination of α Lyrae is $38^0\,39'$, hence we have for the latitude of Berlin $\delta - \varphi = -13^0\,51'$. The star α Lyrae is therefore at its upper culmination at Berlin $13^0\,51'$ south of the zenith, and its zenith distance at the lower culmination equal to $180^0 - \varphi - \delta$ is $88^0\,51'$.

24. A body reaches its greatest altitude at the time of its culmination only if its declination does not change, and in case that this is variable, its altitude is a maximum a little before or after the culmination. If we differentiate the formula:

$$\cos z = \sin \varphi \sin \delta + \cos \varphi \cos \delta \cos t,$$

taking z, δ and t as variable, we find:

$$-\sin z\, dz = [\sin \varphi \cos \delta - \cos \varphi \sin \delta \cos t]\, d\delta - \cos \varphi \cos \delta \sin t\, dt$$

and from this we obtain in the case that z is a maximum or $dz = 0$:

$$\sin t = \frac{d\delta}{dt}\,[\text{tang}\,\varphi - \text{tang}\,\delta \cos t].$$

This equation gives the hour angle at the time of the greatest altitude. $\frac{d\delta}{dt}$ is the ratio of the change of the declination to the change of the hour angle, or if dt denotes a second of arc, it is the change of the declination in $\frac{1}{15}$ of a second of time. As this quantity is small for all heavenly bodies, and as we may take the arc itself instead of $\sin t$ and take $\cos t$ equal to unity, we get for the hour angle corresponding to the greatest altitude:

$$t = \frac{d\delta}{dt}\,[\text{tang}\,\varphi - \text{tang}\,\delta]\,\frac{206265}{15} \qquad (g),$$

where $\frac{d\delta}{dt}$ is the change of the declination in one second of time and t is found in seconds of time. This hour angle must be added algebraically to the time of the culmination, in order to find the time of the greatest altitude.

If the body is culminating south of the zenith and approaching the north pole, so that $\frac{d\delta}{dt}$ is positive, the greatest altitude occurs after the culmination if φ is positive; but if the declination is decreasing, the greatest altitude occurs before the culmination. The reverse takes place, if the body culminates between the zenith and the pole.

25. If we differentiate the formulae:

$$\cos h \sin A = \cos \delta \sin t,$$
$$\cos h \cos A = -\cos \varphi \sin \delta + \sin \varphi \cos \delta \cos t,$$

we find:

$$\sin h \frac{dh}{dt} = \cos \delta [\sin \varphi \cos A \sin t - \cos t \sin A],$$
$$\cos h \frac{dA}{dt} = \cos \delta [\cos A \cos t + \sin \varphi \sin t \sin A],$$

or:

$$\frac{dh}{dt} = -\cos \delta \sin p = -\cos \varphi \sin A,$$
$$\cos h \frac{dA}{dt} = +\cos \delta \cos p. \qquad (h)$$

Frequently we make use also of the second differential coefficient. For this we find:

$$\frac{d^2 h}{dt^2} = -\cos \varphi \cos A \,.\, \frac{dA}{dt},$$
$$= -\frac{\cos \varphi \cos \delta \cos A \cos p}{\cos h}. \qquad (i)$$

Likewise we have:

$$\frac{dz}{dt} = \cos \delta \sin p = \cos \varphi \sin A,$$
$$\frac{d^2 z}{dt^2} = \frac{\cos \varphi \cos \delta \cos A \cos p}{\cos h} \qquad (k)$$

Furthermore we find from the second of the formulae (h):

$$\cos h^2 \frac{d^2 A}{dt^2} = -\cos h \cos \delta \sin p \frac{dp}{dt} + \cos \delta \cos p \sin h \frac{dh}{dt}.$$

But we get also, differentiating the formula:

$$\sin \varphi = \sin h \sin \delta + \cos h \cos \delta \cos p,$$
$$\cos h \cos \delta \sin p \frac{dp}{dt} = [\cos h \sin \delta - \sin h \cos \delta \cos p] \frac{dh}{dt}.$$

Hence we have:

$$\cos h^2 \frac{d^2 A}{dt^2} = +[\cos h \sin \delta - 2 \cos \delta \sin h \cos p] \cos \delta \sin p,$$

or, if we introduce A instead of p:

$$\cos h^2 \frac{d^2 A}{dt^2} = -\cos \varphi \sin A [\cos h \sin \delta + 2 \cos \varphi \cos A].$$

26. As we have:

$$\frac{dh}{dt} = -\cos \varphi \sin A,$$

we find $\frac{dh}{dt} = 0$, or h is a maximum or minimum, when we have $\sin A = 0$ or when the star is on the meridian.

We find also that $\frac{dh}{dt}$ is a maximum, when $\sin A = \pm 1$, hence when $A = 90$ or $= 270^0$.

The altitude of a star changes therefore most rapidly, when it crosses the vertical circle, whose azimuth is 90^0 or 270^0. This vertical circle is called the *prime vertical.*

In order to find the time of the passage of the star across the prime vertical as well as its altitude at that time, we take in the formulae found in No. 6 $A = 90^0$ or we consider the right angled triangle between the star, the zenith and the pole and find:

$$\cos t = \frac{\operatorname{tang} \delta}{\operatorname{tang} \varphi} \qquad (l).$$
$$\sin h = \frac{\sin \delta}{\sin \varphi}$$

Finally we have:

$$\sin p = \frac{\cos \varphi}{\cos \delta}.$$

If we have $\delta > \varphi$, $\cos t$ would be greater than unity, therefore the star cannot come then in the prime vertical but culminates between the zenith and the pole. If δ is negative, $\cos t$ become negative; but as in northern latitudes the hour angles of the southern stars while above the horizon are always less than 90^0, those stars cross the prime vertical below the horizon.

For Arcturus and the latitude of Berlin we find:

$$t = 73^0\, 52'.1 = 4^h\, 55^m\, 28^s$$
$$h = 25^0\, 24'.9.$$

Arcturus reaches therefore the prime vertical before its culmination at $9^h\, 13^m\, 51^s$ and after the culmination at $19^h\, 4^m\, 47^s$.

If the hour angle is near zero, we do not find t very accurate by its cosine nor h by its sine. But we easily get from the formula for $\cos t$ the following:

$$\operatorname{tang} \tfrac{1}{2} t^2 = \frac{\sin (\varphi - \delta)}{\sin (\varphi + \delta)}$$

and for computing the altitude we may use the formula:

$$\operatorname{cotang} h = \operatorname{tang} t \cos \varphi.$$

27. As we have:

$$\frac{dA}{dt} = \frac{\cos \delta \cos p}{\cos h},$$

we see that this differential coefficient becomes equal to zero, or that the star does not change its azimuth for an instant, when we have $\cos p = o$, or when the vertical circle is vertical to the declination circle. But as we have:

$$\cos p = \frac{\sin \varphi - \sin h \sin \delta}{\cos h \cos \delta}$$

this must occur when $\sin \varphi = \frac{\sin \varphi}{\sin \delta}$. It happens therefore only to circumpolar stars, whose declination is greater than the latitude, at the point where the vertical circle is tangent to the parallel circle. The star is then at its greatest distance from the meridian and the azimuth at that time is given by the equation:

$$\sin A = \frac{\cos \delta}{\cos \varphi}$$

and the hour angle by the equation:

$$\cos t = \frac{\operatorname{tang} \varphi}{\operatorname{tang} \delta}.$$

For the polar star, whose declination for 1861 is $88^0\ 34'\ 6''$ and for the latitude of Berlin, we find:

$t = \pm 88^\circ\ 8'\ 0'' = 5^h\ 52^m\ 32^s$,

$A = 2^\circ\ 21'\ 9''$ reckoned from the north point, $h = 52^\circ\ 31'.7$.

28. Finally we will find the time, in which the discs of the sun and moon move over a certain great circle.

If $\Delta\alpha$ is the increment of the right ascension between two consecutive culminations expressed in seconds of time, we find the number of sidereal seconds x, in which the body moves through the hour angle t from the following proportion:

$$x : t = 86400 + \Delta\alpha : 86400$$

as we may consider the motion of the sun and moon during the small intervals of time which we here consider, as uniform; hence we have:

$$x = t \frac{1}{1 - \dfrac{\Delta\alpha}{86400 + \Delta\alpha}}$$

or denoting the second term of the denominator, which is equal to the increment of the right ascension expressed in time in one second of sidereal time, by λ:

$$x = t \cdot \frac{1}{1 - \lambda}.$$

When the western limb of the body is on the meridian, the hour angle of the centre, is found from the equation:

$$\cos R = \sin \delta^2 + \cos \delta^2 \cos t$$

where R designates the apparent radius, or from:

$$\sin \tfrac{1}{2} R = \cos \delta \sin \tfrac{1}{2} t.$$

Hence, as t is small, this hour angle expressed in time is:

$$t = \frac{R}{15 \cos \delta}$$

therefore the sidereal time of the semi-diameter passing the meridian:

$$2x = \frac{2R}{15.\cos \delta} \cdot \frac{1}{1-\lambda}.$$

When the upper limb of the body is in the horizon, the depression of the lower limb is equal to $2R$, and as we have: $\frac{dz}{dt} = \cos \delta \sin p$, the difference of the hour angles of the upper and lower limb in time is:

$$\frac{2R}{15.\cos \delta \sin p}$$

hence the sidereal time of the diameter rising or setting:

$$\frac{2R}{15.\cos \delta \sin p} \cdot \frac{1}{1-\lambda},$$

where p is found from the equation:

$$\cos p = \frac{\sin \varphi}{\cos \delta}.$$

If we imagine two vertical circles one through the centre, the other tangent to the limb, the difference of their azimuths is found from the equation:

$$\sin \tfrac{1}{2} R = \cos h \sin \tfrac{1}{2} a$$

or, as R is small, from the equation:

$$R = \cos h \,.\, a.$$

But as we have $dt = \frac{\cos h \, dA}{\cos \delta \cos p}$, we find for the sidereal time in which the diameter passes over a vertical circle:

$$\frac{2R}{15 \cos \delta . \cos p} \cdot \frac{1}{1-\lambda},$$

$$\text{where } p = \frac{\cos \delta \sin \varphi - \sin \delta \cos \varphi \cos t}{\cos h}.$$

SECOND SECTION.

ON THE CHANGES OF THE FUNDAMENTAL PLANES, TO WHICH THE PLACES OF THE STARS ARE REFERRED.

As the two poles do not change their place at the surface of the earth, the angle between the plane of the horizon of a place and the axis of the earth or the plane of the equator remains constant. Likewise therefore the pole and the equator of the celestial sphere remain in the same position with respect to the horizon. But as the position of the axis of the earth in space is changed by the attraction of the sun and moon, the great circle of the equator and the poles coincide at different times with different stars, or the latter appear to change their position with respect to the equator. Furthermore as the attractions of the planets change the plane of the orbit of the earth, the apparent orbit of the sun among the stars must coincide in the course of years with different stars. Hence the motion of these two planes, namely that of the earth's equator and that of the earth's orbit produce a change of the angle between them or of the obliquity of the ecliptic as well as a change of the points of intersection of the two corresponding great circles. The longitudes and latitudes as well as the right ascensions and declinations of the stars are therefore variable and it is most important to know the changes of these co-ordinates.

In order to form a clear idea of the mutual motions of the equator and ecliptic, we must refer them to a fixed place, for which we take according to Laplace that great circle, with which the ecliptic coincided at the beginning of the year 1750. Now Physical Astronomy teaches, that the attraction of the sun and moon on the excess of matter near the equator of the spheroid of the earth, creates a motion of the axis of the earth and hence a motion of the equator of the earth with respect to the fixed ecliptic, by which the points of intersection have a slow, uniform and retrograde motion on this fixed plane and at the same time a periodical motion, depending on the places of the sun and moon and on the position of the moon's nodes viz. of the points in which the orbit of the moon intersects the ecliptic. The uniform motion of the equinoxes is called ***Lunisolar Precession***, the other periodical motion is called the *Nutation* or the *Equation of the equinoxes in longitude.* Besides this attraction creates a periodical change of the inclination of the equator to the fixed plane, dependent on the same quantities, which is called the *Nutation of obliquity.*

As the mutual attractions of the planets change the inclinations of the orbits with respect to the fixed ecliptic as well as the position of the line of the nodes, the plane of the orbit of the earth must change its position with respect to the plane, with which it coincided in the year 1750 or the fixed ecliptic. This change produces therefore a change of the ecliptic with respect to the equator, which is called the ***Secular variation of the obliquity of the ecliptic*** and the motion of the point of the intersection of the equator with the apparent ecliptic on the latter, which is called the *General Precession* differs from the motion of the equator on the fixed ecliptic, which is called the luni-solar precession *).

But this change of the orbit of the earth has still another effect. For as by it the position of the orbit of the sun and the moon with respect to the equator of the earth is changed, though slowly, this must produce a motion of the equator similar to the nutation only of a period of great length, by which the inclination of the equator with respect to the ecliptic as well as the position of the points of intersection is changed. These changes on account of their long period can be united with the secular variation of the obliquity of the ecliptic and with the precession. Hence the

---

*) The periodical terms, the nutation, are the same for the fixed and moveable ecliptic.

motion of the equator, indirectly produced by the perturbations of the planets, changes a little the lunisolar precession as well as the general precession and the angle, which the fixed and the true ecliptic make with the equator *).

I. THE PRECESSION.

1. Laplace has given in §. 44 of the sixth chapter of the Mécanique Céleste the expressions for these several slow motions of the equator and the ecliptic, which can be applied to a time of 1200 years before and after the epoch of 1750, as the secular perturbations of the earth's orbit are taken into consideration so as to be sufficient for such a space of time. Bessel has developed these expressions according to the powers of the time which elapsed since 1750 and has given in the preface to his Tabulae Regiomontanae these expressions to the second power. According to this the annual lunisolar precession at the time $1750 + t$ is:

$$\frac{dl_{\prime}}{dt} = 50''.37572 - 0''.000243589\, t$$

or the amount of the precession in the interval of time from 1750 to $1750 + t$:

$$l_{\prime} = t\,.\,50''.37572 - t^2\, 0''.0001217945.$$

This therefore is the arc of the fixed ecliptic between the points of intersection with the equator at the beginning of the year 1750 and at the time $1750 + t$.

Furthermore the annual general precession is:

$$\frac{dl}{dt} = 50''.21129 + 0''.0002442966\, t$$

and the general precession in the interval of time from 1750 to $1750 + t$:

$$l = t\, 50''.21129 + t^2\, 0''.0001221483,$$

and this is the arc of the apparent ecliptic between the points of intersection with the equator at the beginning of the year 1750 and at the time $1750 + t$.

---

*) In the expressions developed in series they change only the terms dependent on t^2.

Finally the angle between the equator and the fixed ecliptic is at the time $1750+t$:

$$\varepsilon_0 = 23^0\ 28'\ 18''.0 + t^2\ 0''.0000098423$$

and the angle between the equator and the ecliptic at the time $1750+t$ (if we neglect as before the periodical terms of nutation), which is called the *mean obliquity of the ecliptic,* is:

$$\varepsilon = 23^0\ 28'\ 18''.0 - t\ 0''.48368 - t^2\ 0''.00000272295\ ^{*}),$$

so that we have:

$$\frac{d\varepsilon_0}{dt} = +\ 0''.00001968466\ t,$$

$$\frac{d\varepsilon}{dt} = -\ 0''.48368 - 0''.0000054459\ t.$$

Now let AA_0 Fig. 2 represent the equator and EE_0 the ecliptic both for the beginning of the year 1750, and let $A'A''$ and EE' represent the equator and the obliquity of the ecliptic for $1750+t$; then the arc BD of the ecliptic, through which the equator has retrograded on it, is the lunisolar precession in t years, equal to $l_{\prime}$. Further are BCE and $A'BE$ respectively the inclination of the true ecliptic and of the fixed ecliptic of 1750 against the equator, equal to ε and ε_0. If

---

*) Bessel has changed a little the numerical values of the expressions given in the Mécanique Céleste, as he recomputed the secular perturbations of the earth with a more correct value of the mass of Venus and determined the term of the lunisolar precession $l_{\prime}$, which is multiplied by t, from more recent observations. The secular variation of the obliquity of the ecliptic as deduced from the latest observations differs from the value given above, as it is $0''.4645$. But the above value is retained for the computation of the quantities π and Π, which determine the position of the ecliptic with respect to the fixed plane, as it must be combined for this purpose with the value of $\frac{dl}{dt}$, based on the same values of the masses. The terms multiplied by t^2, which depend on the perturbations produced by the planets, are based on the values of the masses adopted by Laplace and need a more accurate determination.

Peters gives in his work „Numerus constans nutationis" other values computed with the latest values of the masses. These are, reduced to the year 1750 and to Bessel's value of the lunisolar precession as follows:

$$l_{\prime} = t\ 50''.37572 - t^2\ 0''.0001084$$
$$l = t\ 50''.21484 + t^2\ 0''.0001134$$
$$\varepsilon_0 = 23^0\ 28'\ 17''.9 + 0''.00000735\ t^2$$
$$\varepsilon = 23^0\ 28'\ 17''.9 - 0''.4738\ t - 0''.00000140\ t^2.$$

But as Bessel's values are generally used, they have been retained.

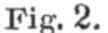

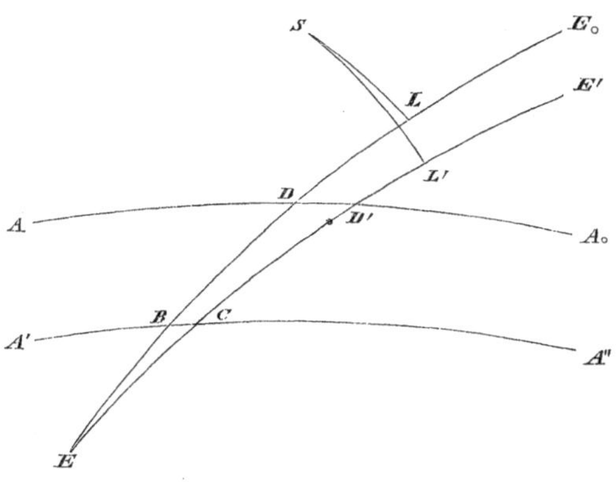

then S represents a star and SL and SL' are drawn vertical to the fixed and to the true ecliptic, DL is the longitude of the star for 1750 and CL' the longitude of the star for $1750+t$. If further D' denotes the same point of the true ecliptic which in the fixed ecliptic was denoted by D, the arc CD' is the general precession, being the arc of the true ecliptic between the equinox of 1750 and that of $1750+t$. This portion of the precession is the same for all stars, and in order to find the complete precession in longitude, we must add to it $D'L'-DL$; which portion on account of the slow change of the obliquity is much less than the other. For computing this portion we must know the position of the true ecliptic with respect to the fixed ecliptic, which is given by the secular perturbations and may also be deduced from the expressions given before. For if we denote by Π the longitude of the ascending node of the true ecliptic on the fixed ecliptic (or that point of intersection of the two great circles setting out from which the true ecliptic has a north latitude) and if we reckon this angle from the fixed equinox of the year 1750, we have $BE = 180^0 - \Pi - l_{,}$ and $CE = 180^0 - \Pi - l$, as the longitudes are reckoned in the direction from B towards D and as E is the descending node of the true ecliptic, hence $DE = 180^0 - \Pi$. If we denote the inclination of the true ecliptic or the angle BEC by π, we have according to Napier's formulae:

$$\text{tang}\ \tfrac{1}{2}\pi\ .\ \sin\left\{\Pi + \frac{l_{,}+l}{2}\right\} = \sin\frac{l_{,}-l}{2}\ \text{tang}\ \frac{\varepsilon+\varepsilon_0}{2},$$

$$\text{tang}\ \tfrac{1}{2}\pi\ .\ \cos\left\{\Pi + \frac{l_{,}+l}{2}\right\} = \cos\frac{l_{,}-l}{2}\ \text{tang}\ \frac{\varepsilon-\varepsilon_0}{2},$$

As B is the same point of the equator which in the year 1750 was at D, BC is the arc of the equator, through which the point of intersection with the ecliptic has moved on the equator from west to east during the time t. If we denote this arc, which is the *Planetary Precession* during the time t, by a, we find from the same triangle:

$$\text{tang}\ \tfrac{1}{2}a\ .\ \cos\frac{\varepsilon+\varepsilon_0}{2} = \text{tang}\ \tfrac{1}{2}(l_{,}-l)\cos\frac{\varepsilon-\varepsilon_0}{2}.$$

From these equations we can develop a, as well as π and Π into a series progressing according to the powers of t. From the last equation, after introducing:

$$\varepsilon_0 + \tfrac{1}{2}(\varepsilon-\varepsilon_0)\ \text{instead of}\ \frac{\varepsilon+\varepsilon_0}{2}$$

and taking instead of the sines and tangents of the small angles $l_{,}-l$, a and $\varepsilon-\varepsilon_0$ the arcs themselves, we find:

$$a = \frac{l_{,}-l}{\cos\varepsilon_0} + \tfrac{1}{2}\frac{(l_{,}-l)}{\cos\varepsilon_0^{\,2}}\sin\varepsilon_0\ .\ \frac{\varepsilon-\varepsilon_0}{206265},$$

or if we substitute for $l_{,}$, l and $\varepsilon-\varepsilon_0$ their expressions, which are of the following form $\lambda_{,}t+\lambda'_{,}t^2$, $\lambda t+\lambda' t^2$ and $\eta t+\eta' t^2$, we obtain:

$$a = t\ .\ \frac{\lambda_{,}-\lambda}{\cos\varepsilon_0} + t^2\left\{\frac{\lambda'_{,}-\lambda'}{\cos\varepsilon_0} + \tfrac{1}{2}\frac{(\lambda_{,}-\lambda)\eta}{206265}\cdot\frac{\sin\varepsilon_0}{\cos\varepsilon_0^{\,2}}\right\}$$

or if we substitute the numerical values:

$$a = t\ .\ 0.17926 - t^2\ 0''.0002660393,$$

$$\frac{da}{dt} = 0.17926 - t\ .\ 0''.0005320786.$$

In addition we have:

$$\text{tang}\left\{\Pi + \frac{l_{,}+l}{2}\right\} = \text{tang}\frac{a}{2}\cdot\frac{\sin\frac{\varepsilon+\varepsilon_0}{2}}{\sin\frac{\varepsilon-\varepsilon_0}{2}},$$

and

$$\text{tang}\ \tfrac{1}{2}\pi^2 = \left\{\text{tang}\ \frac{l_{,}-l^2}{2}\ \text{tang}\ \frac{\varepsilon+\varepsilon_0{}^2}{2} + \text{tang}\ \frac{\varepsilon-\varepsilon_0{}^2}{2}\right\}\cos\frac{l_{,}-l^2}{2},$$

or proceeding in a similar way as before:

$$\text{tang}\left\{\Pi + \tfrac{1}{2}(l_{,}+l)\right\} = \frac{a\sin\varepsilon_0}{\varepsilon-\varepsilon_0} + \frac{\tfrac{1}{2}a\cos\varepsilon_0}{206265}$$

$$\pi^2 = a^2\sin\varepsilon_0{}^2 + (\varepsilon-\varepsilon_0)^2 + \frac{a^2\sin\varepsilon_0\cos\varepsilon_0(\varepsilon-\varepsilon_0)}{206265}.$$

Substituting here also for $\varepsilon - \varepsilon_0$ and a the expressions $\eta t + \eta' t^2$ and $\alpha t + \alpha' t^2$, we find:

$$\Pi + \tfrac{1}{2}(l + l_{\prime}) = \text{arc tang} \frac{\alpha \sin \varepsilon_0}{\eta}$$
$$+ t \left\{ \frac{\alpha' \eta \sin \varepsilon_0 - \alpha \eta' \sin \varepsilon_0}{\eta^2} 206265 + \tfrac{1}{2} a \cos \varepsilon_0 \right\} \cos \Pi^2$$
$$\pi = t \sqrt{\alpha^2 \sin \varepsilon_0{}^2 + \eta^2} + \frac{t^2}{\pi} \left\{ \alpha \alpha' \sin \varepsilon_0{}^2 + \eta \eta' + \frac{\tfrac{1}{2} \alpha^2 \eta \sin \varepsilon_0 \cos \varepsilon_0}{206265} \right\},$$

or substituting the numerical values:

$$\Pi = 171^0\, 36'\, 10' - t\,.\,5''.21$$
$$\pi = t\,.\,0''.48892 - t^2\, 0''.0000030715$$
$$\frac{d\pi}{dt} = 0''.48892 - t\,.\,0''.0000061430.$$

2. The mutual changes of the planes, to which the positions of the stars are referred, having thus been determined, we can easily find the resulting changes of the places of the stars themselves. If λ and β denote the longitude and latitude of a star referred to the ecliptic of $1750 + t$, the co-ordinates of the star with respect to this plane, if we take the ascending node of the ecliptic on the fixed ecliptic of 1750 as origin of the longitudes, are as follows:

$$\cos \beta \cos (\lambda - \Pi - l), \quad \cos \beta \sin (\lambda - \Pi - l), \quad \sin \beta.$$

If further L and B are the longitude and latitude of the star referred to the fixed ecliptic of 1750, the three co-ordinates with respect to this plane and the same origin as before are:

$$\cos B \cos (L - \Pi), \quad \cos B \sin (L - \Pi), \quad \sin B.$$

As the fundamental planes of these two systems of coordinates make the angle π with each other, we find by the formulae (1 a) of the introduction the following equations:

$$\begin{aligned} \cos \beta \cos (\lambda - \Pi - l) &= \cos B \cos (L - \Pi) \\ \cos \beta \sin (\lambda - \Pi - l) &= \cos B \sin (L - \Pi) \cos \pi + \sin B \sin \pi \qquad (A) \\ \sin \beta &= -\cos B \sin (L - \Pi) \sin \pi + \sin B \cos \pi. \end{aligned}$$

If we differentiate these equations, taking L and B as constant, we find by the differential formulae (11) in No. 9 of the introduction, as we have in this case $a = 90^0 - \beta$, $b = 90^0 - B$, $c = \pi$, $A = 90^0 + L - \Pi$, $B = 90^0 - (\lambda - \Pi - l)$:

$$\begin{aligned} d(\lambda - \Pi - l) &= -d\Pi + \pi \tang \beta \sin (\lambda - \Pi - l)\, d\Pi \\ &\quad + \tang \beta \cos (\lambda - \Pi - l)\, d\pi \\ d\beta &= +\pi \cos (\lambda - \Pi - l)\, d\Pi - \sin (\lambda - \Pi - l)\, d\pi. \end{aligned}$$

Dividing by dt and substituting $t\frac{d\pi}{dt}$ instead of π in the coefficient of $d\Pi$, we obtain from these the following formulae for the annual changes of the longitudes and latitudes of the stars:

$$\frac{d\lambda}{dt}=\frac{dl}{dt}+\operatorname{tang}\beta\cos\left(\lambda-\Pi-l-\frac{d\Pi}{dt}t\right)\frac{d\pi}{dt}$$

$$\frac{d\beta}{dt}=-\sin\left(\lambda-\Pi-l-\frac{d\Pi}{dt}t\right)\frac{d\pi}{dt}$$

or, as we have $\Pi+\frac{d\Pi}{dt}t=171^{0}\,36'\,10''-t.10''.42$, taking:

$$\Pi+t\frac{d\Pi}{dt}+l=171^{0}\,36'\,10''+t\,39''.79=M,$$

$$\left.\begin{aligned}\frac{d\lambda}{dt}&=\frac{dl}{dt}+\operatorname{tang}\beta\cos(\lambda-M)\frac{d\pi}{dt}\\ \frac{d\beta}{dt}&=-\sin(\lambda-M)\frac{d\pi}{dt},\end{aligned}\right\}\quad(B)$$

where the numerical values for $\frac{dl}{dt}$ and $\frac{d\pi}{dt}$ as given in the preceding No. must be substituted.

Let L and B again denote the longitude and latitude of a star, referred to the fixed ecliptic and the equinox of 1750, then the longitude reckoned from the point of intersection of the equator of $1750+t$ with the fixed ecliptic, is equal to $L+l_{,}$, when $l_{,}$ is the lunisolar precession during the interval from 1750 to $1750+t$. Hence the co-ordinates of the star with respect to the plane of the fixed ecliptic and the origin of the longitudes adopted last are:

$$\cos B\cos(L+l_{,}),\ \cos B\sin(L+l_{,})\ \text{and}\ \sin B.$$

If now α and δ denote the right ascension and declination of the star, referred to the equator and the true equinox at the time $1750+t$, the right ascension reckoned from the origin adopted before, is equal to $\alpha+a$. We have therefore the co-ordinates of the star with respect to the plane of the equator and this origin as follows:

$$\cos\delta\cos(\alpha+a),\ \cos\delta\sin(\alpha+a)\ \text{and}\ \sin\delta.$$

As the angle between the two planes of co-ordinates is ε_0, we find from the formulae (1) of the introduction:

$$\begin{aligned}\cos\delta\cos(\alpha+a)&=\cos B\cos(L+l_{,})\\ \cos\delta\sin(\alpha+a)&=\cos B\sin(L+l_{,})\cos\varepsilon_0-\sin B\sin\varepsilon_0\\ \sin\delta&=\cos B\sin(L+l_{,})\sin\varepsilon_0+\sin B\cos\varepsilon_0.\end{aligned}\quad(C)$$

If we differentiate these equations, taking L and B as constant, we find from the differential formulae (11) of the introduction, as we have in the triangle between the pole of the ecliptic, that of the equator and the star $a = 90^0 - \delta$, $b = 90^0 - B$, $c = \varepsilon_0$, $A = 90^0 - (L + l_{,})$, $B = 90 + (\alpha + a)$:

$$d(\alpha + a) = [\cos\varepsilon_0 + \sin\varepsilon_0 \operatorname{tang}\delta \sin(\alpha + a)]\, dl_{,} - \cos(\alpha + a) \operatorname{tang}\delta\, d\varepsilon_0$$
$$d\delta = \cos(\alpha + a) \sin\varepsilon_0\, dl_{,} + \sin(\alpha + a)\, d\varepsilon_0.$$

We find therefore for the annual variations of the right ascensions and declinations of the stars the following formulae:

$$\frac{d\alpha}{dt} = -\frac{da}{dt} + [\cos\varepsilon_0 + \sin\varepsilon_0 \operatorname{tang}\delta \sin\alpha]\frac{dl_{,}}{dt}$$
$$+ \left\{ a \sin\varepsilon_0 \frac{dl_{,}}{dt} - \frac{d\varepsilon_0}{dt} \right\} \operatorname{tang}.\delta \cos\alpha,$$
$$\frac{d\delta}{dt} = \cos\alpha \sin\varepsilon_0 \frac{dl_{,}}{dt} - \left\{ a \sin\varepsilon_0 \frac{dl_{,}}{dt} - \frac{d\varepsilon_0}{dt} \right\} \sin\alpha,$$

or neglecting the last term of each equation on account of its being very small *):

$$\frac{d\alpha}{dt} = -\frac{da}{dt} + [\cos\varepsilon_0 + \sin\varepsilon_0 \operatorname{tang}\delta \sin\alpha]\frac{dl_{,}}{dt},$$
$$\frac{d\delta}{dt} = \cos\alpha \sin\varepsilon_0 \cdot \frac{dl_{,}}{dt}.$$

If we take here:

$$\cos\varepsilon_0 \frac{dl_{,}}{dt} - \frac{da}{dt} = m,$$
$$\sin\varepsilon_0 \frac{dl_{,}}{dt} = n,$$

we find simply:

$$\frac{d\alpha}{dt} = m + n \operatorname{tang}\delta \sin\alpha,$$
$$\frac{d\delta}{dt} = n \cos\alpha, \qquad (D)$$

where the numerical values of m and n, obtained by substituting the numerical values of ε_0, $\frac{dl_{,}}{dt}$ and $\frac{da}{dt}$, are:

$$m = 46''.02824 + 0''.0003086450\, t$$
$$n = 20''.06442 - 0''.0000970204\, t.$$

In order to find the precession in longitude and latitude or in right ascension and declination in the interval from

*) The numerical value of the coefficient $a \sin\varepsilon_0 \frac{dl_{,}}{dt} - \frac{d\varepsilon_0}{dt}$ is only $- 0.0000022471\, t$.

$1750+t$ to $1750+t'$, it would be necessary to take the integral of the equations (B) or (D) between the limits t and t'. We can find however this quantity to the terms of the second order inclusively from the differential coefficient at the time $\frac{t+t'}{2}$ and from the interval of time. For if $f(t)$ and $f(t')$ are two functions, whose difference $f(t')-f(t)$ is required, (in our case therefore the precession during the time $t'-t$), we take:

$$\tfrac{1}{2}(t'+t)=x,$$
$$\tfrac{1}{2}(t'-t)=\Delta x.$$

Then we have:

$$f(t)=f(x-\Delta x)=f(x)-\Delta x f'(x)+\tfrac{1}{2}\Delta x^2 f''(x),$$
$$f(t')=f(x+\Delta x)=f(x)+\Delta x f'(x)+\tfrac{1}{2}\Delta x^2 f''(x),$$

where $f'(x)$ and $f''(x)$ denote the first and second differential coefficient of $f(x)$. From this we find:

$$f(t')-f(t)=2\Delta x f'(x)=(t'-t)f'\left(\frac{t+t'}{2}\right).$$

Hence in order to find the precession during the interval of time $t'-t$, it is only necessary to compute the differential coefficient for the time exactly at the middle and to multiply it by the interval of time. By this process only terms of the third order are neglected.

For instance if we wish to find the precession in longitude and latitude in the time from 1750 to 1850 for a star, whose place for the year 1750 is:

$$\lambda=210^\circ\,0',\ \beta=+34^\circ\,0'$$

we find the following values of $\frac{dl}{dt}$, $\frac{d\pi}{dt}$ and M for 1800:

$$\frac{dl}{dt}=50''.22350,\ \frac{d\pi}{dt}=0''.48861,\ M=172^\circ\,9'\,20''.$$

With these we find the following place for 1800, computing the precession from 1750 to 1800 only approximately:

$$\lambda=210^\circ\,42'.1,\ \beta=+33^\circ\,59'.8$$

from the formulae (B) we find then the annual variations for 1800:

$$\frac{d\lambda}{dt}=+50''.48122,\ \frac{d\beta}{dt}=-0''.30447,$$

hence the precession in the interval from 1750 to 1850:

in longitude $+1^\circ\,24'\,8''.12$ and in latitude $-30''.45$.

If we wish to find the precession in right ascension and declination from 1750 to 1850 for a star, whose right ascension and declination for 1750 is:

$$\alpha = 220^0\ 1'\ 24'',\quad \delta = +\ 20^0\ 21'\ 15''$$

we have for 1800:

$$m = 46''.04367,\quad n = 20''.05957,$$

and the approximate place of the star at that time:

$$\alpha = 220^0\ 35'.8,\quad \delta = +\ 20^0\ 8'.6$$

hence we have according to formulae (*D*):

$\text{tang}\,\delta\ 9.56444$	$n\ \text{tang}\,\delta \sin\alpha = -\ \ 4.78806$
$\sin\alpha\ 9.81340_n$	$m = +\ 46.04367$
$\text{tang}\,\delta \sin\alpha = 9.37784_n$	$\frac{d\alpha}{dt} = +\ 41.25561$
$n = 1.30232$	
$\cos\alpha = 9.88042_n,$	$\frac{d\delta}{dt} = -\ 15.2314$

therefore the precession in the interval of time from 1750 to 1850

in right ascension $1^0\ 8'\ 45''.56$ and in declination $-\ 25'\ 23''.14$.

In the catalogues of stars we find usually for every star its annual precession in right ascension and declination (variatio annua) given for the epoch of the catalogue and besides this its variation in one hundred years (variatio saecularis). If then t_0 denotes the epoch of the catalogue, the precession of a star according to the above rules equals:

$$\left\{\text{variatio annua} + \frac{t - t_0}{200}\ \text{variatio saecularis}\right\}(t - t_0).$$

If we differentiate the two formulae:

$$\frac{d\alpha}{dt} = m + n\ \text{tang}\,\delta \sin\alpha,$$

$$\frac{d\delta}{dt} = n \cos\alpha,$$

taking all quantities as variable and denoting the annual variations of m and n by m' and n', we find:

$$\frac{d^2\alpha}{dt^2} = \frac{n^2}{w}\sin 2\alpha\left[\tfrac{1}{2} + \text{tang}\,\delta^2\right] + \frac{mn}{w}\text{tang}\,\delta\cos\alpha + m' + n'\ \text{tang}\,\delta\sin\alpha,$$

$$\frac{d^2\delta}{dt^2} = -\frac{n^2}{w}\sin\alpha^2\ \text{tang}\,\delta - \frac{mn}{w}\sin\alpha + n'\cos\alpha,$$

where w signifies the number 206265, and multiplying these equations by 100 we find the secular variation in right ascension and declination. For the star used before we find from this the secular variation:

$$\text{in right ascension} = +0''.0286,$$
$$\text{in declination} = +0''.2654.$$

3. The differential formulae given above cannot be used if we wish to compute the precession of stars near the pole. In this case the exact formulae must be employed.

Let λ and β denote the longitude and the latitude of a star, referred to the ecliptic and the equinox of $1750+t$, we find from these the longitude and latitude L and B, referred to the fixed ecliptic of 1750, from the following equations, which easily follow from the equations (A) in No. 2:

$$\begin{aligned}\cos B\cos(L-\Pi) &= \cos\beta\cos(\lambda-\Pi-l)\\ \cos B\sin(L-\Pi) &= \cos\beta\sin(\lambda-\Pi-l)\cos\pi-\sin\beta\sin\pi\\ \sin B &= \cos\beta\sin(\lambda-\Pi-l)\sin\pi+\sin\beta\cos\pi.\end{aligned}$$

If we wish to find now the longitude and latitude λ' and β', referred to the ecliptic and the equinox of $1750+t'$, we get these from L and B by the following equations, in which Π', π' and l' denote the values of Π, π and l for the time t':

$$\begin{aligned}\cos\beta'\cos(\lambda'-\Pi'-l') &= \cos B\cos(L-\Pi')\\ \cos\beta'\sin(\lambda'-\Pi'-l') &= \cos B\sin(L-\Pi')\cos\pi'+\sin B'\sin\pi'\\ \sin\beta' &= -\cos B\sin(L-\Pi')\sin\pi'+\sin B'\cos\pi'.\end{aligned}$$

If we eliminate L and B from these equations, we can find λ' and β' expressed directly by λ and β and the values of l, Π and π for the times t and t'.

The exact formulae for the right ascension and declination are similar. If α and δ are the right ascension and declination of a star for $1750+t$, we find from them the longitude and latitude L and B, referred to the fixed ecliptic of 1750, by the following equations *):

$$\begin{aligned}\cos B\cos(L+l_{,}) &= \cos\delta\cos(\alpha+a)\\ \cos B\sin(L+l_{,}) &= \cos\delta\sin(\alpha+a)\cos\varepsilon_0+\sin\delta\sin\varepsilon_0\\ \sin B &= -\cos\delta\sin(\alpha+a)\sin\varepsilon_0+\sin\delta\cos\varepsilon_0.\end{aligned}$$

If we wish to know now the right ascension and declination α' and δ' for $1750+t'$, we find these from L and B

---

*) These equations are easily deduced from the equations (C) in No. 2.

by the following equations, in which $l_{\prime}$, a' and ε'_0 denote the values of $l_{\prime}$, a and ε_0 for the time t':

$$\cos\delta'\cos(\alpha'+a') = \cos B\cos(L+l'_{\prime})$$
$$\cos\delta'\sin(\alpha'+a') = \cos B\sin(L+l'_{\prime})\cos\varepsilon'_0 - \sin B\sin\varepsilon'_0$$
$$\sin\delta' = \cos B\sin(L+l'_{\prime})\sin\varepsilon'_0 + \sin B\cos\varepsilon'_0.$$

If we eliminate L and B from the two systems of equations and observe that we have:

$$\cos B\sin L = -\cos\delta\cos(\alpha+a)\sin l_{\prime} + \cos\delta\sin(\alpha+a)\cos\varepsilon\cos l_{\prime}$$
$$+ \sin\delta\sin\varepsilon\cos l_{\prime}$$
$$\cos B\cos L = \cos\delta\cos(\alpha+a)\cos l_{\prime} + \cos\delta\sin(\alpha+a)\cos\varepsilon\sin l_{\prime}$$
$$+ \sin\delta\sin\varepsilon\sin l_{\prime}$$
$$\sin B = -\cos\delta\cos(\alpha+a)\sin\varepsilon + \sin\delta\cos\varepsilon,$$

we easily find the following equations:

$$\cos\delta'\cos(\alpha'+a') = \cos\delta\cos(\alpha+a)\cos(l'_{\prime}-l_{\prime})$$
$$-\cos\delta\sin(\alpha+a)\sin(l'_{\prime}-l_{\prime})\cos\varepsilon_0$$
$$-\sin\delta\sin(l'_{\prime}-l_{\prime})\sin\varepsilon_0$$
$$\cos\delta'\sin(\alpha'+a') = \cos\delta\cos(\alpha+a)\sin(l'_{\prime}-l_{\prime})\cos\varepsilon'_0$$
$$+\cos\delta\sin(\alpha+a)[\cos(l'_{\prime}-l_{\prime})\cos\varepsilon_0\cos\varepsilon'_0+\sin\varepsilon_0\sin\varepsilon'_0]$$
$$+\sin\delta[\cos(l'_{\prime}-l_{\prime})\sin\varepsilon_0\cos\varepsilon'_0-\cos\varepsilon_0\sin\varepsilon'_0]$$
$$\sin\delta' = \cos\delta\cos(\alpha+a)\sin(l_{\prime}'-l_{\prime})\sin\varepsilon'_0$$
$$+\cos\delta\sin(\alpha+a)[\cos(l'_{\prime}-l_{\prime})\cos\varepsilon_0\sin\varepsilon'_0-\sin\varepsilon_0\cos\varepsilon'_0]$$
$$+\sin\delta[\cos(l'_{\prime}-l_{\prime})\sin\varepsilon_0\sin\varepsilon'_0+\cos\varepsilon_0\cos\varepsilon'_0].$$

If we imagine a spherical triangle, whose three sides are $l'_{\prime}-l_{\prime}$, 90^0-z and $90^0+z'$ whilst the angles opposite those sides are respectively Θ, ε'_0 and $180^0-\varepsilon_0$, we can express the coefficients of the above equations, containing $l'_{\prime}-l$, ε_0 and ε'_0 by Θ, z and z' and we find:

$$\cos\delta'\cos(\alpha'+a') = \cos\delta\cos(\alpha+a)[\cos\Theta\cos z\cos z' - \sin z\sin z']$$
$$-\cos\delta\sin(\alpha+a)[\cos\Theta\sin z\cos z' + \cos z\sin z']$$
$$-\sin\delta\sin\Theta\cos z'$$
$$\cos\delta'\sin(\alpha'+a') = \cos\delta\cos(\alpha+a)[\cos\Theta\cos z\sin z' + \sin z\cos z']$$
$$-\cos\delta\sin(\alpha+a)[\cos\Theta\sin z\sin z' - \cos z\cos z']$$
$$-\sin\delta\sin\Theta\sin z'$$
$$\sin\delta' = \cos\delta\cos(\alpha+a)\sin\Theta\cos z$$
$$-\cos\delta\sin(\alpha+a)\sin\Theta\sin z$$
$$+\sin\delta\cos\Theta.$$

Multiplying the first of these equations by $\sin z'$, the second by $\cos z'$ and subtracting the first, then multiplying the first by $\cos z'$, the second by $\sin z'$ and adding the products we get:

$$\cos\delta'\sin(\alpha'+a'-z') = \cos\delta\sin(\alpha+a+z)$$
$$\cos\delta'\cos(\alpha'+a'-z') = \cos\delta\cos(\alpha+a+z)\cos\Theta - \sin\delta\sin\Theta \quad (a).$$
$$\sin\delta' = \cos\delta\cos(\alpha+a+z)\sin\Theta + \sin\delta\cos\Theta.$$

These formulae give α' and δ' expressed by α, δ, a, a' and the auxiliary quantities z, z' and Θ. These latter quantities may be found by applying Gauss's formulae to the spherical triangle considered before, as we have:

$$\begin{aligned}
\sin \tfrac{1}{2} \Theta \cos \tfrac{1}{2} (z' - z) &= \sin \tfrac{1}{2} (l'_{,} - l_{,}) \sin \tfrac{1}{2} (\varepsilon'_0 + \varepsilon_0) \\
\sin \tfrac{1}{2} \Theta \sin \tfrac{1}{2} (z' - z) &= \cos \tfrac{1}{2} (l'_{,} - l_{,}) \sin \tfrac{1}{2} (\varepsilon'_0 - \varepsilon_0) \\
\cos \tfrac{1}{2} \Theta \sin \tfrac{1}{2} (z' + z) &= \sin \tfrac{1}{2} (l_{,}' - l_{,}) \cos \tfrac{1}{2} (\varepsilon'_0 + \varepsilon_0) \\
\cos \tfrac{1}{2} \Theta \cos \tfrac{1}{2} (z' + z) &= \cos \tfrac{1}{2} (l_{,}' - l_{,}) \cos \tfrac{1}{2} (\varepsilon'_0 - \varepsilon_0)
\end{aligned}$$

As we may always take here instead of $\sin \frac{1}{2} (z' - z)$ and $\sin \frac{1}{2} (\varepsilon'_0 - \varepsilon_0)$ the arc itself and the corresponding cosines equal to unity, we find the following simple formulae for computing these three auxiliary quantities:

$$\begin{aligned}
\operatorname{tang} \tfrac{1}{2} (z' + z) &= \cos \tfrac{1}{2} (\varepsilon'_0 + \varepsilon_0) \operatorname{tang} \tfrac{1}{2} (l'_{,} - l_{,}) \\
\tfrac{1}{2} (z' - z) &= \tfrac{1}{2} (\varepsilon'_0 - \varepsilon_0) \frac{\operatorname{cotang} \frac{1}{2} (l'_{,} - l_{,})}{\sin \frac{1}{2} (\varepsilon'_0 + \varepsilon_0)} \qquad (A). \\
\operatorname{tang} \tfrac{1}{2} \Theta &= \operatorname{tang} \tfrac{1}{2} (\varepsilon'_0 + \varepsilon_0) \sin \tfrac{1}{2} (z' + z).
\end{aligned}$$

The formulae (a) can be rendered more convenient for computation by the introduction of an auxiliary angle or we may use instead of them a different system of formulae derived from Gauss's equations. For we arrive at the formulae (a) if we apply the three fundamental formulae of spherical trigonometry to a triangle, whose sides are $90^0 - \delta'$, $90^0 - \delta$ and Θ, whilst the angles opposite the two first sides are respectively $\alpha' + a + z$ and $180^0 - \alpha' - a' + z'$. If we now apply to the same triangle Gauss's formulae and denote the third angle by c, $\alpha + a + z$ by A and $\alpha' + a' - z'$ by A, we find:

$$\begin{aligned}
\cos \tfrac{1}{2} (90^0 + \delta') \cos \tfrac{1}{2} (A' + c) &= \cos \tfrac{1}{2} [90^0 + \delta + \Theta] \cos \tfrac{1}{2} A \\
\cos \tfrac{1}{2} (90 + \delta') \sin \tfrac{1}{2} (A' + c) &= \cos \tfrac{1}{2} [90 + \delta - \Theta] \sin \tfrac{1}{2} A \\
\sin \tfrac{1}{2} (90 + \delta') \cos \tfrac{1}{2} (A' - c) &= \sin \tfrac{1}{2} [90 + \delta + \Theta] \cos \tfrac{1}{2} A \\
\sin \tfrac{1}{2} (90 + \delta') \sin \tfrac{1}{2} (A' - c) &= \sin \tfrac{1}{2} [90 + \delta - \Theta] \sin \tfrac{1}{2} A.
\end{aligned} \qquad (b)$$

As it is even more accurate to find the difference $A' - A$ instead of the quantity A' itself, we multiply the first of the equations (a) by $\cos A$, the second by $\sin A$ and subtract them, then we multiply the first equation by $\sin A$, the second by $\cos A$ and add the products. We find thus:

$$\begin{aligned}
\cos \delta' \sin (A' - A) &= \cos \delta \sin A \sin \Theta [\operatorname{tang} \delta + \operatorname{tang} \tfrac{1}{2} \Theta \cos A] \\
\cos \delta' \cos (A' - A) &= \cos \delta - \cos \delta \cos A \sin \Theta [\operatorname{tang} \delta + \operatorname{tang} \tfrac{1}{2} \Theta \cos A],
\end{aligned}$$

hence:

$$\operatorname{tang} (A' - A) = \frac{\sin A \sin \Theta [\operatorname{tang} \delta + \operatorname{tang} \frac{1}{2} \Theta \cos A]}{1 - \cos A \sin \Theta [\operatorname{tang} \delta + \operatorname{tang} \frac{1}{2} \Theta \cos A]}$$

and from Gauss's equations we find:

$$\cos \tfrac{1}{2} c \,.\, \sin \tfrac{1}{2} (\delta' - \delta) = \sin \tfrac{1}{2} \Theta \cos \tfrac{1}{2} (A' + A)$$
$$\cos \tfrac{1}{2} c \,.\, \cos \tfrac{1}{2} (\delta' - \delta) = \cos \tfrac{1}{2} \Theta \cos \tfrac{1}{2} (A' - A).$$

If we put therefore:

$$p = \sin \Theta \, [\operatorname{tang} \delta + \operatorname{tang} \tfrac{1}{2} \Theta \cos A] \qquad (B),$$

we have:

$$\operatorname{tang} (A' - A) = \frac{p \sin A}{1 - p \cos A}$$

and:
$$\qquad (C).$$

$$\operatorname{tang} \tfrac{1}{2} (\delta' - \delta) = \operatorname{tang} \tfrac{1}{2} \Theta \frac{\cos \tfrac{1}{2} (A' + A)}{\cos \tfrac{1}{2} (A' - A)}$$

By the formulae (*A*), (*B*) and (*C*) we are enabled to compute rigorously the right ascension and declination of a star for the time $1750 + t'$, when the right ascension and declination for the time $1750 + t$ are given.

Example. The right ascension and declination of α Ursae minoris at the beginning of the year 1755 is:

$$\alpha = 10^\circ\, 55'\, 44''.\, 955$$
and
$$\delta = 87^\circ\, 59'\, 41''.\, 12.$$

If we wish to compute from this the place referred to the equator and the equinox of 1850, we have first:

$$l_{\prime} = 4'\, 11''.\, 8756 \qquad l'_{\prime} = 1^\circ\, 23'\, 56''.\, 3541$$
$$a = 0''.\, 8897 \qquad a' = 15''.\, 2656$$
$$\varepsilon_0 = 23^\circ\, 28'\, 18''.\, 0002 \qquad \varepsilon'_0 = 23^\circ\, 28'\, 18''.\, 0984.$$

With this we find from the formulae (*A*):

$$\tfrac{1}{2} (z' + z) = 0^\circ\, 36'\, 34''.\, 314 \qquad \tfrac{1}{2} (z' - z) = 10''.\, 6286$$

hence:

$$z = 0^\circ\, 36'\, 23''.\, 685$$
$$z' = 0^\circ\, 36'\, 44''.\, 943$$

and:

$$\Theta = 0^\circ\, 31'\, 45''.\, 600$$

therefore:

$$A = \alpha + a + z = 11^\circ\, 32'\, 9''.\, 530.$$

If we compute then the values of $A' - A$ and $\delta' - \delta$ from the formulae (*B*) and (*C*), we find:

$$\log p = 9{,}4214471$$

and:

$$A' - A = 4^\circ\, 4'\, 17''.\, 710, \quad \tfrac{1}{2} (\delta' - \delta) = 0^\circ\, 15'\, 26''.\, 780$$

hence:

$$A' = 15^\circ\, 36'\, 27''.\, 240$$

and at last:

$$\alpha' = 16^\circ\, 12'\, 56''.\, 917$$
$$\delta' = 88 \quad 30 \quad 34 \;.\, 680.$$

4. As the point of intersection of the equator and the ecliptic has an annual retrograde motion of 50″.2 on the latter, the pole of the ecliptic describes in the course of time a small circle around the pole of the ecliptic, whose radius is equal to the obliquity of the ecliptic*). The pole of the equator coincides therefore with different points of the celestial sphere or different stars will be in its neigbourhood at different times. At present the extreme star in the tail of the Lesser Bear (α Ursae minoris) is of all the bright stars nearest to the north-pole and is called therefore the pole-star. This star, whose declination is at present $88\frac{1}{2}^0$, will approach still nearer to te pole, until its right ascension, which at present is 17^0, has increased to 90^0. Then the declination will reach its maximum $89^0\,32'$ and begin to decrease, because the precession in declination of stars whose right ascension lies in the second quadrant, is negative.

In order to find the place of the pole for any time t, we must consider the spherical triangle between the pole of the ecliptic at a certain time t_0 and the poles of the equator P and P' at the times t_0 and t. If we denote the right ascension and declination of the pole at the time t referred to the equator and the equinox at the time t_0, by α and δ, and the obliquity of the ecliptic at the times t_0 and t by ε_0 and ε, we have the sides $PP' = 90^0 - \delta$, $EP = \varepsilon_0$, $EP' = \varepsilon$, the angle at $P = 90^0 + \alpha$ and the angle at E equal to the general precession in the interval of time $t - t_0$; we have therefore according to the fundamental formulae of spherical trigonometry:

$$\cos\delta\sin\alpha = \sin\varepsilon\cos\varepsilon_0\cos l - \cos\varepsilon\sin\varepsilon_0$$
$$\cos\delta\cos\alpha = \sin\varepsilon\sin l$$
$$\sin\delta = \sin\varepsilon\sin\varepsilon_0\cos l + \cos\varepsilon\cos\varepsilon_0.$$

This computation does not require any great accuracy, as we wish to find the place of the pole only approximately and although the variation of the obliquity of the ecliptic for short intervals of time is proportional to the time, we may take $\varepsilon = \varepsilon_0$ and get simply:

$$\tang\alpha = -\cos\varepsilon_0 \tang\tfrac{1}{2} l$$

*) This radius is strictly speaking not constant, but equal to the actually existing obliquity of the ecliptic.

and:

$$\cos\delta = \frac{\sin\varepsilon_0 \sin l}{\cos\alpha}.$$

Though α is found by means of a tangent, we find nevertheless the value of α without ambiguity, as it must satisfy the condition, that cos α and cos λ have the same sign.

If we wish to find for instance the place of the pole for the year 14000 but referred to the equinox of 1850, we have the general precession for 12150 years equal to about 174°, hence we have:

$$\alpha = 273^\circ\ 16' \text{ and } \delta = +43^\circ\ 7'.$$

This agrees nearly with the place of α Lyrae, whose right ascension and declination for 1850 is:

$$\alpha = 277^\circ\ 58' \text{ and } \delta = +38^\circ\ 39'.$$

Hence about the year 14000 this star will be the pole-star.

On account of the change of the declination by the precession stars will rise above the horizon of a place, which before were always invisible, while other stars now for instance visible at a place in the northern hemisphere, will move so far south of the equator that they will no longer rise at this place. Likewise stars, which now always remain above the horizon of the place, will begin to rise and set, while other stars will move so far north of the equator that they become circumpolar stars. The precession changes therefore essentially the aspect of the celestial sphere at any place on the earth after long intervals of time.

The latest tables of the sun give the length of the sidereal year, that is, the time, in which the sun describes exactly 360° of the celestial sphere or in which it returns to same fixed star, equal to 365 days 6 hours 9 minutes and $9^s.35$ or to 365.2563582 mean days. As the points of the equinoxes have a retrograde motion, opposite to the direction in which the sun is moving, the time in which the sun returns to the same equinox or the tropical year must be shorter than the sidereal year by the time in which the sun moves through the small arc equal to the annual precession. But we have for 1850 $l = 50''.2235$ and as the mean motion of the sun is $59'8''.33$, we find for this time 0.014154 of a day, hence the length of the tropical year equal to 365.242204 days. As the precession is variable and the annual increase amounts to $0''.0002442966$, the tropical year is also variable and the annual change equal to 0.000000068848 of a day. If we express the decimals in hours, minutes and seconds, we find the length of the tropical year equal to:

$$365 \text{ days } 5^h\, 48^m\, 46^s.42 - 0^s.00595\,(t - 1800).$$

II. THE NUTATION.

5. Thus far we have neglected the periodical change of the equator with respect to the ecliptic, which, as was stated before, consists of a periodical motion of the point of intersection of the equator and the ecliptic on the latter as well as in a periodical change of the obliquity of the ecliptic. The point in which the equator would intersect the ecliptic, if there were no nutation, but only the slow changes considered before were taking place, is called the *mean equinox* and the obliquity of the ecliptic, which would then occur, the mean obliquity of the ecliptic. The point however, in which the equator really intersects the ecliptic at any time is called the *apparent equinox* while the actual angle between the equator and the ecliptic at any time is called the *apparent obliquity of the ecliptic.*

The expressions for the equation of the points of the equinoxes and the nutation of the obliquity are according to the latest determinations of Peters in his work entitled „Numerus constans nutationis“:

$$\begin{aligned}
\Delta\lambda = & -17''.2405 \sin \Omega + 0''.2073 \sin 2\Omega \\
& - 1''.2692 \sin 2\odot - 0''.2041 \sin 2☾ \\
& + 0''.1279 \sin(\odot - P) - 0''.0213 \sin(\odot + P) \\
& + 0''.0677 \sin(☾ - P') \qquad (A) \\
\Delta\varepsilon = & + 9''.2231 \cos \Omega - 0''.0897 \cos 2\Omega \\
& + 0''.5509 \cos 2\odot + 0''.0886 \cos 2☾ \\
& + 0''.0093 \cos(\odot + P),
\end{aligned}$$

where Ω is the longitude of the ascending node of the moon's orbit, $\odot$ and ☾ are the longitudes of the sun and of the moon and P and P' are the longitudes of the perihelion of the sun and of the perigee of the moon. The expressions given above are true for 1800, but the coefficients are a little variable with the time and we have for 1900:

$$\begin{aligned}\Delta\lambda = & -17''.2577 \sin \Omega + 0''.2073 \sin 2\,\Omega \\ & -\ 1''.2693 \sin 2\,\odot - 0''.2041 \sin 2\,☾ \\ & +\ 0''.1275 \sin(\odot - P) - 0''.0213 \sin(\odot + P) \\ & +\ 0''.0677 \sin(☾ - P') \qquad (A_1)\\ \Delta\varepsilon = & +\ 9''.2240 \cos \Omega - 0''.0896 \cos 2\,\Omega \\ & +\ 0''.5506 \cos 2\,\odot + 0''.0885 \cos 2\,☾ \\ & +\ 0''.0092 \cos(\odot + P).\end{aligned}$$

In order to find the changes of the right ascensions and declinations of the stars, arising from this, we must observe, that we have:

$$\alpha' - \alpha = \frac{d\alpha}{d\lambda}\Delta\lambda + \frac{d\alpha}{d\varepsilon}\Delta\varepsilon + \tfrac{1}{2}\left(\frac{d^2\alpha}{d\lambda^2}\right)\Delta\lambda^2 + \left(\frac{d^2\alpha}{d\lambda . d\varepsilon}\right)\Delta\lambda\Delta\varepsilon + \tfrac{1}{2}\left(\frac{d^2\alpha}{d\varepsilon^2}\right)\Delta\varepsilon^2 + ..$$

and: (a)

$$\delta' - \delta = \frac{d\delta}{d\lambda}\Delta\lambda + \frac{d\delta}{d\varepsilon}\Delta\varepsilon + \tfrac{1}{2}\left(\frac{d^2\delta}{d\lambda^2}\right)\Delta\lambda^2 + \left(\frac{d^2\delta}{d\lambda . d\varepsilon}\right)\Delta\lambda\Delta\varepsilon + \tfrac{1}{2}\left(\frac{d^2\delta}{d\varepsilon^2}\right)\Delta\varepsilon^2 + ..$$

But we have according to the differential formulae in No. 11 of Section I, if we substitute instead of $\cos\beta \sin\eta$ and $\cos\beta\cos\eta$ their expressions in terms of α, δ and ε:

$$\frac{d\alpha}{d\lambda} = \cos\varepsilon + \sin\varepsilon \operatorname{tang}\delta \sin\alpha \qquad \frac{d\delta}{d\lambda} = \cos\alpha \sin\varepsilon$$

$$\frac{d\alpha}{d\varepsilon} = -\cos\alpha \operatorname{tang}\delta \qquad \frac{d\delta}{d\varepsilon} = \sin\alpha,$$

from which we find by differentiating:

$$\left(\frac{d^2\alpha}{d\lambda^2}\right) = \sin\varepsilon^2\,[\tfrac{1}{2}\sin 2\alpha + \operatorname{cotang}\varepsilon \cos\alpha \operatorname{tang}\delta + \sin 2\alpha \operatorname{tang}\delta^2]$$

$$\left(\frac{d^2\alpha}{d\lambda . d\varepsilon}\right) = -\sin\varepsilon\,[\cos\alpha^2 - \operatorname{cotang}\varepsilon \operatorname{tang}\delta \sin\alpha + \operatorname{tang}\delta^2 \cos 2\alpha]$$

$$\left(\frac{d^2\alpha}{d\varepsilon^2}\right) = -[\tfrac{1}{2}\sin 2\alpha + \sin 2\alpha \operatorname{tang}\delta^2]$$

$$\left(\frac{d^2\delta}{d\lambda^2}\right) = -\sin\varepsilon^2 \sin\alpha\,[\operatorname{cotang}\varepsilon + \operatorname{tang}\delta \sin\alpha]$$

$$\left(\frac{d^2\delta}{d\lambda . d\varepsilon}\right) = \sin\varepsilon\cos\alpha\,[\operatorname{cotang}\varepsilon + \sin\alpha \operatorname{tang}\delta]$$

$$\left(\frac{d^2\delta}{d\varepsilon^2}\right) = -\cos\alpha^2 \operatorname{tang}\delta.$$

If we substitute these expressions in the equations (a) and introduce instead of $\Delta\lambda$ and $\Delta\varepsilon$ their values given before by the equations (A) and take for ε the mean obliquity of the ecliptic at the beginning of the year 1800 = $23^0\,27'\,54''.2$, we find the terms of the first order as follows:

$$\begin{aligned}
\alpha'-\alpha = & -15''.8148\sin\Omega-[6''.8650\sin\Omega\sin\alpha+9''.2231\cos\Omega\cos\alpha]\operatorname{tang}\delta \\
& +\ 0''.1902\sin 2\Omega+[0''.0825\sin 2\Omega\sin\alpha+0''.0897\cos 2\Omega\cos\alpha]\operatorname{tang}\delta \\
& -\ 1''.1642\sin 2\odot-[0''.5054\sin 2\odot\sin\alpha+0''.5509\cos 2\odot\cos\alpha]\operatorname{tang}\delta \\
& -\ 0''.1872\sin 2☾-[0''.0813\sin 2☾\sin\alpha+0''.0886\cos 2☾\cos\alpha]\operatorname{tang}\delta \\
& -\ 0''.0195\sin(\odot+P) \\
& -\ [0''.0085\sin(\odot+P)\sin\alpha+0''.0093\cos(\odot+P)\cos\alpha]\operatorname{tang}\delta \qquad (B) \\
& +\ [0''.0621+0''.0270\sin\alpha\operatorname{tang}\delta]\sin(☾-P') \\
& +\ [0''.1173+0''.0509\sin\alpha\operatorname{tang}\delta]\sin(\odot-P),
\end{aligned}$$

$$\begin{aligned}
\delta'-\delta = & -\ 6''.8650\sin\Omega\cos\alpha+9''.2231\cos\Omega\sin\alpha \\
& +\ 0''.0825\sin 2\Omega\cos\alpha-0''.0897\cos 2\Omega\sin\alpha \\
& -\ 0''.5054\sin 2\odot\cos\alpha+0''.5509\cos 2\odot\sin\alpha \qquad (C) \\
& -\ 0''.0813\sin 2☾\cos\alpha+0''.0886\cos 2☾\sin\alpha \\
& -\ 0''.0085\sin(\odot+P)\cos\alpha+0''.0093\cos(\odot+P)\sin\alpha \\
& +\ 0''.0270\cos\alpha\sin(☾-P') \\
& +\ 0''.0509\cos\alpha\sin(\odot-P).
\end{aligned}$$

These expressions are true for 1800: for 1900 they are a little different, but the change is only of some amount for the first terms depending on the moon's node. These are for 1900:

in $\alpha'-\alpha$: $\quad -15''.8321\sin\Omega-[6''.8683\sin\Omega\sin\alpha+9''.2240\cos\Omega\cos\alpha]\operatorname{tang}\delta$
in $\delta'-\delta$: $\quad -\ 6''.8683\sin\Omega\cos\alpha+9''.2240\cos\Omega\sin\alpha.$

Of the terms of the second order only those are of any amount, which arise from the greatest terms in $\Delta\lambda$ and $\Delta\varepsilon$. If we put for the sake of brevity:

$$\Delta\varepsilon = 9''.2231\cos\Omega = a\cos\Omega$$

and $\quad -\sin\varepsilon\,\Delta\lambda = 6''.8650\sin\Omega = b\sin\Omega,$

these terms give in right ascension:

$$\begin{aligned}
\alpha'-\alpha = & \frac{b^2-a^2}{4}\sin 2\alpha\,[\operatorname{tang}\delta^2+\tfrac{1}{2}]+\frac{b^2}{4}\operatorname{tang}\delta\cos\alpha\operatorname{cotang}\varepsilon \\
& +[\tfrac{1}{2}-\operatorname{cotang}\varepsilon\sin\alpha\operatorname{tang}\delta+\operatorname{tang}\delta^2\cos 2\alpha+\tfrac{1}{2}\cos 2\alpha]\frac{ab}{2}\sin 2\Omega \\
& -\left\{\frac{b^2+a^2}{4}\operatorname{tang}\delta^2\sin 2\alpha+\frac{b^2}{4}\operatorname{tang}\delta\cos\alpha\operatorname{cotg}\varepsilon+\frac{b^2+a^2}{8}\sin 2\alpha\right\}\cos 2\Omega
\end{aligned}$$

and in declination:

$$\begin{aligned}
\delta'-\delta = & -\left\{\frac{a^2+b^2}{8}+\frac{a^2-b^2}{8}\cos 2\alpha\right\}\operatorname{tang}\delta-\frac{b^2}{4}\sin\alpha\operatorname{cotang}\varepsilon \\
& -[\operatorname{tang}\delta\sin 2\alpha+2\operatorname{cotang}\varepsilon\cos\alpha]\frac{ab}{4}\sin 2\Omega \\
& -\left\{\left(\frac{a^2-b^2}{8}+\frac{a^2+b^2}{8}\cos 2\alpha\right)\operatorname{tang}\delta-\frac{b^2}{4}\sin\alpha\operatorname{cotang}\varepsilon\right\}\cos 2\Omega.
\end{aligned}$$

Those terms which are independent of Ω change merely

the mean place of the stars and therefore may be neglected. Another part, namely:

$$\frac{ab}{4}\sin 2☊ - \left(\frac{ab}{2}\text{cotang}\,\varepsilon\sin\alpha\sin 2☊ + \frac{b^2}{4}\text{cotang}\,\varepsilon\cos\alpha\cos 2☊\right)\text{tang}\,\delta$$

and

$$-\frac{ab}{2}\text{cotang}\,\varepsilon\sin 2☊\cos\alpha + \frac{b^2}{4}\text{cotang}\,\varepsilon\sin\alpha\cos 2☊$$

can be united with the similar terms multiplied by sin 2☊ and cos 2☊ of the first order, which then become equal to:

in right ascension

$$+0''.1902\sin 2☊ + [0''.0822\sin 2☊\sin\alpha + 0''.0896\cos 2☊\cos\alpha]\,\text{tang}\,\delta$$

and in declination (D)

$$+0''.0822\sin 2☊\cos\alpha - 0''.0896\cos 2☊\sin\alpha.$$

The remaining terms of the second order are as follows:

in right ascension

$$+0''.0001535\,[\text{tang}\,\delta^2 + \tfrac{1}{2}]\sin 2☊\cos 2\alpha$$
$$-0''.000160\,[\text{tang}\,\delta^2 + \tfrac{1}{2}]\cos 2☊\sin 2\alpha$$

and in declination (E)

$$-0''.0000768\,\text{tang}\,\delta\sin 2\alpha\sin 2☊$$
$$-[0''.000023 + 0''.000080\cos 2\alpha]\,\text{tang}\,\delta\cos 2☊.$$

But as the first terms amount to $0^s.01$ only when the declination is $88^0\,10'$ and as the others equal $0''.01$ only when the declination is $89^0\,26'$, they are even in the immediate neighbourhood of the pole of little influence and can be neglected except for stars very near the pole.

6. We shall hereafter use the changes of the expressions (*B*) and (*C*) produced by a change of the constant of nutation, that is, of the coefficient of cos ☊ in the nutation of obliquity. These are different for the terms of the lunar and solar nutation. For in the formula of the nutation as given by theory all terms of the lunar nutation are multiplied by a factor N' which depends on the moments of inertia of the earth as well as on the mass and the mean motion of the moon, while the terms of the solar nutation are multiplied by a similar factor, which is the same function of the moments of inertia of the earth and of the mass and mean motion of the sun. But as it is impossible to compute the moments of inertia of the earth, the numerical values of N and N' must be determined from observations. Now the coefficient of the term of the nutation of obliquity, which is multiplied by $\sin \Omega$, is equal to $0.765428\,N'$. If we take this equal to $9''.2231\,(1+i)$, where $9''.2231$ is the value of the constant of nutation as it follows from the observations, while $9''.2231\,i$ is its correction, we have therefore:

$$0.765428\,N' = 9''.2231\,(1+i).$$

But the lunisolar precession depends on the same quantities N and N' and the value determined from observations ($50''.36354$ for 1800) gives the following equation between N and N':

$$17.469345 = N + 0.991988\,N',$$

from which we get in connection with the former equation:

$$N = 5.516287\,(1 - 2\ 16687\,i).$$

Therefore if we take the constant of nutation equal to $9''.2231\,(1+i)$ we must multiply all terms of the lunar nutation by $1+i$ and all terms of the solar nutation by $1-2.16687\,i$. Taking therefore $9''.2235\,i = d\nu$, we have:

$$d\Delta\lambda = \left\{\begin{array}{l} -1.8702\sin\Omega + 0.0225\sin 2\Omega - 0.0221\sin 2\text{☾} + 0.0073\sin(\text{☾} - P') \\ +0.2981\sin 2\odot - 0.0300\sin(\odot - P) + 0.0050\sin(\odot + P) \end{array}\right\} d\nu$$

$$\begin{array}{l} d\Delta\varepsilon = [\cos\Omega - 0.0097\cos 2\Omega + 0.0096\cos 2\text{☾} - 0.1294\cos 2\odot \\ \qquad\qquad - 0.0022\cos(\odot + P)]\,d\nu \end{array}$$

and from this we find in the same way as in No. 5:

$$\begin{array}{rl} \dfrac{d(\alpha' - \alpha)}{d\nu} = & -1.7156\sin\Omega - [0.7445\sin\Omega\sin\alpha + 1.0000\cos\Omega\cos\alpha]\tan\delta \\ & +0.0206\sin 2\Omega + [0.0090\sin 2\Omega\sin\alpha + 0.0097\cos 2\Omega\cos\alpha]\tan\delta \\ & -0.0203\sin 2\text{☾} - [0.0088\sin 2\text{☾}\sin\alpha + 0.0096\cos 2\text{☾}\cos\alpha]\tan\delta \\ & +0.0067\sin(\text{☾} - P') + [0.0029\sin(\text{☾} - P')\sin\alpha]\tan\delta \\ & +0.2735\sin 2\odot + [0.1187\sin 2\odot\sin\alpha + 0.1294\cos 2\odot\cos\alpha]\tan\delta \\ & -0.0275\sin(\odot - P) - [0.0119\sin(\odot - P)\sin\alpha]\tan\delta \\ & +0.0046\sin(\odot + P) + [0.0020\sin(\odot + P)\sin\alpha + \\ & \qquad\qquad + 0.0022\cos(\odot + P)\cos\alpha]\tan\delta \end{array}$$

$$\begin{array}{rl} \dfrac{d(\delta' - \delta)}{d\nu} = & -0.7445\sin\Omega\cos\alpha + 1.0000\cos\Omega\sin\alpha \\ & +0.0090\sin 2\Omega\cos\alpha - 0.0097\cos 2\Omega\sin\alpha \\ & -0.0088\sin 2\text{☾}\cos\alpha + 0.0096\cos 2\text{☾}\sin\alpha \\ & +0.0029\sin(\text{☾} - P')\cos\alpha \\ & +0.1187\sin 2\odot\cos\alpha - 0.1294\cos 2\odot\sin\alpha \\ & -0.0119\sin(\odot - P)\cos\alpha \\ & +0.0020\sin(\odot + P)\sin\alpha - 0.0022\cos(\odot + P)\sin\alpha. \end{array}$$

7. In order to compute the nutation in right ascension and declination it is most convenient to find the values of $\Delta\lambda$ and $\Delta\varepsilon$ from the formulae (A) and (A_1) and to compute the numerical values of the differential coefficients $\frac{d\alpha}{d\lambda}$, $\frac{d\alpha}{d\varepsilon}$, etc. But the labor of computing formulae (*B*) and (*C*) has been greatly reduced by the construction of tables. First the terms:

$$-15''.82 \sin \Omega = c \text{ and } -1''.16 \sin 2 \odot = g$$

have been brought in tables whose arguments are Ω and $2\odot$.

The several terms of the nutation in right ascension multiplied by tang δ are of the following form:

$$a \cos\beta \cos\alpha + b \sin\beta \sin\alpha = A\,[h \cos\beta \cos\alpha + \sin\beta \sin\alpha].$$

Now any expression of this form may be reduced to the following form:

$$x \cos\,[\beta - \alpha + y],$$

For if we develop the latter expression and compare it with the former, we find the following equations for determining x and y:

$$\left.\begin{aligned} A\,h \cos\beta &= x\,[\cos\beta \cos y - \sin\beta \sin y] \\ A \sin\beta &= x\,[\sin\beta \cos y + \cos\beta \sin y] \end{aligned}\right\} \quad (b),$$

from which we find:

$$x^2 = A^2\,[1 - (1 - h^2) \cos\beta^2]$$

and:

$$\text{tang}\, y = \frac{(1 - h) \sin\beta \cos\beta}{1 - (1 - h) \cos\beta^2},$$

where x and y are always real. If we have now tables for x and y, whose argument is β, we find the term of the nutation in right ascension, multiplied by tang δ by computing:

$$x \cos\,[\beta + y - \alpha]$$

while: (*c*),

$$x \sin\,[\beta + y - \alpha]$$

gives the term of the nutation in declination depending cos β. For as these terms have the form:

$$A\,[- h \cos\beta \sin\alpha + \sin\beta \cos\alpha],$$

we find taking it equal to $x \sin(\beta + y - \alpha)$ the same equations (*b*) for determining x and y.

Such tables have been computed by Nicolai and are given in the collection of tables by Warnstorff, mentioned before. These give besides the quantity c the quantities log b and B with the argument Ω, and with these we find the terms of the right ascension depending on cos Ω and sin Ω by computing:

$$c - b \,\text{tang}\, \delta \cos(\Omega + B - \alpha)$$

and the corresponding terms of the declination by computing:

$$-b\sin(\Omega+B-\alpha) \qquad (d)$$

This part of the nutation together with the small terms depending on 2Ω, $2☾$ and $☾-P'$, is the lunar nutation.

A second table gives the quantities g, $\log f$ and F with the argument $2\odot$, by which we find the terms depending on $2\odot$, which for right ascension are:

$$g-f\tang\delta\cos[2\odot+F-\alpha]$$

and for declination: (e)

$$-f\sin[2\odot+F-\alpha]$$

This part of the nutation together with the small terms depending on $\odot+P$ and $\odot-P$ is the solar nutation.

No separate tables have been computed for the small terms depending on $2☾$, 2Ω and $\odot+P$. For these may be found from the tables of the solar nutation, using instead of $2\odot$ as argument successively $2☾$, $180+2\Omega$ (because these terms have the opposite sign) and $\odot+P$, and multiplying the values obtained according to the equations (e) respectively by $\frac{1}{6}$, $\frac{6}{37}$ and $\frac{1}{60}$, as these fractions express approximately the ratio of the coefficients of these terms to that of the solar nutation.

The form of the terms multiplied by $☾-P'$ and $\odot-P$ is different, but analogous to the annual precession in right ascension and declination; they are therefore obtained by multiplying the annual precession in right ascension and declination by $\frac{1}{472}\sin(☾-P')$ and $\frac{1}{394}\sin(\odot-P)$.

8. If we consider only the largest term of the nutation we can render its effect very plain. We have then:

$$\Delta\lambda=-17''.25\sin\Omega,$$
$$\Delta\varepsilon=+\ \ 9''.22\cos\Omega,$$

or rather according to theory:

$$\sin\varepsilon\,\Delta\lambda=-10''.05\cos2\varepsilon.\sin\Omega,$$
$$\Delta\varepsilon=-10''.05\cos\varepsilon.\cos\Omega.$$

Now the pole of the equator on account of the lunisolar precession describes a small circle, whose radius is ε, about the pole of the ecliptic. If we imagine now a plane tangent to the mean pole at any time and in it a system of axes at right angles to each other so that the axis of x is tangent to the circle of latitude, we find the co-ordinates of the apparent pole (affected by nutation) $y = \sin \varepsilon \Delta \lambda$, $x = \Delta \varepsilon$ and we have therefore according to the expressions given above the following equation:

$$y^2 = C^2 . \cos 2 \varepsilon^2 - \frac{\cos 2 \varepsilon^2}{\cos \varepsilon^2} x^2, \quad \text{where } C = 10''.05.$$

The apparent pole describes therefore an ellipse around the mean pole, whose semi-major axis is $C \cos \varepsilon = 9''.22$, and whose semi-conjugate axis is $C \cos 2 \varepsilon = 6''.86$. This ellipse is called the ***ellipse of nutation.*** In order to find the place of the pole on the circumference of this ellipse, we imagine a circle described about its centre with the semi-major axis as radius. Then it is obvious, that a radius of this circle must move through it in a time equal to the period of the revolution of the moon's nodes with uniform and retrograde motion *), so that it coincides with the side of the major axis nearest to the ecliptic, when the ascending node of the moon's orbit coincides with the vernal equinox. If we now let fall from the extremity of this radius a line perpendicular to the major axis, the point, in which this line intersects the circumference of the ellipse, gives us the place of the pole.

---

*) As the motion of the moon's nodes on the ecliptic is retrograde.

THIRD SECTION.

CORRECTIONS OF THE OBSERVATIONS ARISING FROM THE POSITION OF THE OBSERVER ON THE SURFACE OF THE EARTH AND FROM CERTAIN PROPERTIES OF THE LIGHT.

The astronomical tables and ephemerides give always the places of the heavenly bodies as they appear from the centre of the earth. For stars at an infinite distance this place agrees with the place observed from any point on the surface of the earth. But when the distance of the body has a finite ratio to the radius of the earth, the place of the body seen from the centre must differ from the place seen from any point on the surface. If we wish therefore to compare any observed place with such tables, we must have means by which we can reduce the observed place to the place which we should have seen from the centre of the earth. And conversely if we wish to employ the observed place with respect to the horizon in connection for instance with its known position with respect to the equator for the computation of other quantities, we must use the apparent place seen from the place of observation, and hence we must convert the place seen from the centre, which is taken from the ephemeris, into the apparent place.

The angle at the object between the two lines drawn from the centre of the earth to the body and to the place at the surface is called the *parallax* of the body. We need therefore means, by which we can find the parallax of a body at any time and at any place on the surface of the earth.

Our earth is surrounded by an atmosphere, which has the property of refracting the light. We therefore do not see the heavenly bodies in their true places but in the direction which the ray of light after being refracted in the atmosphere has at the moment, when it reaches the eye of the observer. The angle between this direction and that, in which the star would be seen if there was no atmosphere, is called the *refraction*. In order therefore to find from observations the true places of the heavenly bodies, we must have means to determine the refraction for any part of the sphere and any state of the atmosphere.

If the earth had no proper motion or if the velocity of light were infinitely greater than that of the earth, the latter would have no effect upon the apparent place of a star. But as the velocity of the light has a finite ratio to the velocity of the earth, an observer on the earth sees all stars a little ahead of their true places in the direction in which the earth is moving. This small change of the places of the stars caused by the velocities of the earth and of light, is called the *aberration*. In order therefore to find the true places of the heavenly bodies from observations, we must have means, to correct the observed places for aberration.

I. THE PARALLAX.

1. The earth is no perfect sphere, but an oblate spheroid that is a spheroid generated by the revolution of an ellipse on its conjugate axis. If a denotes the semi-major axis, b the semi-minor axis of such a spheroid, and α is their difference expressed in parts of the semi-major axis, we have:

$$\alpha = \frac{a-b}{a} = 1 - \frac{b}{a}.$$

If then ε is the excentricity of the generating ellipse or of the ellipse, in which a plane passing through the minor axis intersects the surface of the spheroid, also expressed in parts of the semi-major axis, we have:

$$\varepsilon^2 = 1 - \frac{b^2}{a^2}$$

therefore:

$$\frac{b}{a} = \sqrt{1-\varepsilon^2}$$

and

$$\alpha = 1 - \sqrt{1-\varepsilon^2}$$

likewise:

$$\varepsilon = \sqrt{2\alpha - \alpha^2}.$$

The ratio $\frac{b}{a}$ is for the earth according to Bessel's investigations: $\frac{298.1528}{299.1528}$

or we have: $$\alpha = \frac{1}{299.1528}$$

and expressed in toises:

$$a = 3272077.14 \quad \log a = 6.5148235$$
$$b = 3261139.33 \quad \log b = 6.5133693.$$

However in astronomy we de not use the toise as unit but the semi-major axis of the earth's orbit. If we denote then by π the angle at the sun subtended by the equatoreal radius of the earth and by R the semi-major axis of the earth's orbit or the mean distance of the earth from the sun, we have:

$$a = R \sin \pi$$

or: $$a = \frac{R.\pi}{206265}.$$

The angle π or the equatoreal horizontal parallax of the sun is according to Encke equal to:

$$8''.57116.$$

It is the angle at the sun subtended by the radius of a place on the equator of the earth when the sun at this place is rising or setting.

2. In order to compute the parallax of a body for any place at the surface of the earth, we must refer the place on the spheroidal earth to the centre by co-ordinates. As the first co-ordinate we use the sidereal time or the angle, which a plane passing through the place of observation and the minor axis *) makes with the plane passing through the the same axis and the point of the vernal equinox. If then OAC Fig. 3 represents the plane through

Fig. 3.

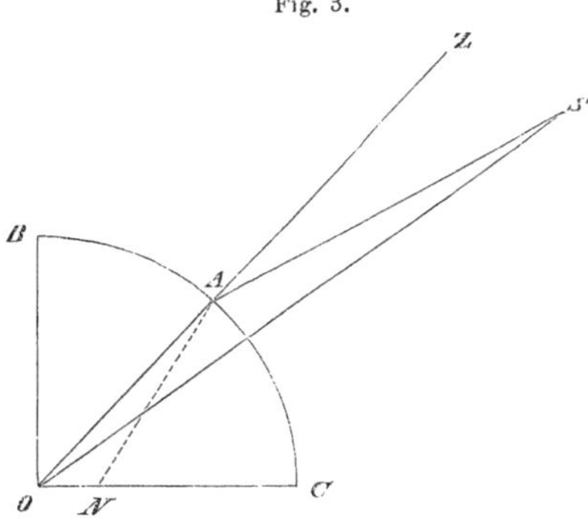

*) This plane is the plane of the meridian, as it passes through the poles and the zenith of the place of observation.

the axis and the place of observation, we must further know the distance $AO = \varrho$ from the centre of the earth and the angle AOC, which is called the *geocentric latitude.* But these quantities can always be computed from the latitude ANC (or the angle which the horizon of A makes with the axis of the earth or which the normal line AN at the place of observation makes with the equator) and from the two axes of the spheroid.

For if x and y are the co-ordinates of A with respect to the centre O, the axes of the abscissae and ordinates being OC and OB, we have the following equation, as A is a point of an ellipse, whose semi-major and semi-minor axes are a and b:

$$a^2 y^2 + b^2 x^2 = a^2 b^2.$$

Now we have also, if we denote the geocentric latitude by φ':

$$\operatorname{tang} \varphi' = \frac{y}{x}$$

and also:

$$\operatorname{tang} \varphi = -\frac{dx}{dy}$$

because the latitude φ is the angle between the normal line at A and the axis of the abscissae. As we have then from the differential equation of the ellipse:

$$\frac{y}{x} = -\frac{b^2}{a^2}\frac{dx}{dy}$$

we find the following equation between φ and φ':

$$\operatorname{tang} \varphi' = \frac{b^2}{a^2} \operatorname{tang} \varphi \qquad (a).$$

In order to compute ϱ we have:

$$\varrho = \sqrt{x^2 + y^2} = \frac{x}{\cos \varphi'},$$

and as we obtain from the equation of the ellipse:

$$x = \frac{a}{\sqrt{1 + \frac{a^2}{b^2} \operatorname{tang} \varphi'^2}} = \frac{a}{\sqrt{1 + \operatorname{tang} \varphi \,.\, \operatorname{tang} \varphi'}}$$

we find:

$$\varrho = \frac{a \sec \varphi'}{\sqrt{1 + \operatorname{tang} \varphi \operatorname{tang} \varphi'}} = a \sqrt{\frac{\cos \varphi}{\cos \varphi' \cos(\varphi' - \varphi)}} \qquad (b).$$

If therefore the latitude φ of a place is given, we can compute by these formulae the geocentric latitude φ' and the radius ϱ.

For the co-ordinates x and y we easily get the following formulae, which will be used afterwards:

$$x = \frac{a \cos \varphi}{\sqrt{\cos \varphi^2 + (1 - \varepsilon^2) \sin \varphi^2}}$$

$$= \frac{a \cos \varphi}{\sqrt{1 - \varepsilon^2 \sin \varphi^2}} \qquad (c)$$

and

$$y = x \operatorname{tang} \varphi' = x \frac{b^2}{a^2} \operatorname{tang} \varphi = x (1 - \varepsilon^2) \operatorname{tang} \varphi$$

$$= \frac{a (1 - \varepsilon^2) \sin \varphi}{\sqrt{1 - \varepsilon^2 \sin \varphi^2}} \qquad (d).$$

From the formula (a) we can develop φ' in a series progressing according to the sines of the multiples of φ, for we obtain by the formula (16) in No. 11 of the introduction:

$$\varphi' = \varphi - \frac{a^2 - b^2}{a^2 + b^2} \sin 2 \varphi + \tfrac{1}{2} \left(\frac{a^2 - b^2}{a^2 + b^2}\right)^2 \sin 4 \varphi - \text{etc.} \qquad (A)$$

or taking

$$\frac{a - b}{a + b} = n$$

we find:

$$\varphi' = \varphi - \frac{2n}{1 + n^2} \sin 2 \varphi + \tfrac{1}{2} \left(\frac{2n}{1 + n^2}\right)^2 \sin 4 \varphi - \text{etc.} \qquad (B).$$

If we compute the numerical values of the coefficients from the values of the two axes given above and multiply them by 206265 in order to find them in seconds, we get:

$$\varphi' = \varphi - 11' \, 30''.65 \sin 2 \varphi + 1''.16 \sin 4 \varphi - \ldots \qquad (C),$$

from which we find for instance for the latitude of Berlin $\varphi = 52^0 \, 30' \, 16''.0$

$$\varphi' = 52^\circ \, 19' \, 8''.3.$$

Although ϱ itself cannot be developed into an equally elegant series, we can find one for $\log \varrho$ *). For we get from formula (b):

$$\varrho^2 = \frac{a^2}{\cos \varphi'^2 \left[1 + \frac{b^2}{a^2} \operatorname{tang} \varphi^2\right]}.$$

If we substitute here for $\cos \varphi'^2$ its value

$$\frac{a^4}{a^4 + b^4 \operatorname{tang} \varphi^2},$$

---

*) Encke in the Berliner Jahrbuch für 1852 pag. 326. He gives also tables, from which the values of φ' and $\log \varrho$ may be found for any latitude.

we find:

$$\varrho^2 = \frac{a^4 \cos\varphi^2 + b^4 \sin\varphi^2}{a^2 \cos\varphi^2 + b^2 \sin\varphi^2}$$

$$= \frac{a^4 + b^4 + (a^4 - b^4)\cos 2\varphi}{a^2 + b^2 + (a^2 - b^2)\cos 2\varphi}$$

$$= \frac{(a^2+b^2)^2 + (a^2-b^2)^2 + 2(a^2+b^2)(a^2-b^2)\cos 2\varphi}{(a+b)^2 + (a-b)^2 + 2(a+b)(a-b)\cos 2\varphi}$$

hence:

$$\varrho = \frac{(a^2+b^2)}{(a+b)} \frac{\left[1 + \left(\frac{a^2-b^2}{a^2+b^2}\right)^2 + 2\frac{a^2-b^2}{a^2+b^2}\cos 2\varphi\right]^{\frac{1}{2}}}{\left[1 + \left(\frac{a-b}{a+b}\right)^2 + 2\frac{a-b}{a+b}\cos 2\varphi\right]^{\frac{1}{2}}}.$$

If we write this formula in a logarithmic form and develop the logarithms of the square roots according to formula (15) in No. 11 of the introduction into series progressing according to the cosines of the multiples of 2φ, we find:

$$\begin{aligned}\log\text{hyp}\,\varrho = \log\text{hyp}\,\frac{a^2+b^2}{a+b} &+ \left\{\frac{a^2-b^2}{a^2+b^2} - \frac{a-b}{a+b}\right\}\cos 2\varphi \\ &- \tfrac{1}{2}\left\{\left(\frac{a^2-b^2}{a^2+b^2}\right)^2 - \left(\frac{a-b}{a+b}\right)^2\right\}\cos 4\varphi \qquad (D) \\ &+ \tfrac{1}{3}\left\{\left(\frac{a^2-b^2}{a^2+b^2}\right)^3 - \left(\frac{a-b}{a+b}\right)^3\right\}\cos 6\varphi \\ &- \text{etc.}\end{aligned}$$

or using common logarithms and denoting the quantity

$$\frac{a-b}{a+b}$$

by n, we get:

$$\begin{aligned}\log\varrho = \log\left(a\frac{1+n^2}{1+n}\right) + M\Big\{&\left(\frac{2n}{1+n^2} - n\right)\cos 2\varphi \\ &- \tfrac{1}{2}\left[\left(\frac{2n}{1+n^2}\right)^2 - n^2\right]\cos 4\varphi \qquad (E) \\ &+ \tfrac{1}{3}\left[\left(\frac{2n}{1+n^2}\right)^3 - n^3\right]\cos 6\varphi \\ &- \text{etc.}\Big\},\end{aligned}$$

where M denotes the modulus of the common logarithms, hence:

$$\log M = 9.6377843.$$

If we compute again the numerical values of the coefficients and take $a = 1$, we find:

$$\log\varrho = 9.9992747 + 0.0007271\cos 2\varphi - 0.0000018\cos 4\varphi \qquad (F)$$

and from this we get for instance for the latitude of Berlin:

$$\log\varrho = 9.9990880.$$

If we know therefore the latitude of a place, we can compute from the two series (C) and (F) the geocentric latitude and the distance of the place from the centre of the earth and these two quantities in connection with the sidereal time define the position of the place with respect to the centre of the earth at any moment. If we now imagine a system of rectangular axes passing through the centre of the earth, the axis of z being vertical to the plane of the equator, whilst the axes of x and y are situated in the plane of the equator so that the positive axis of x is directed towards the point of the vernal equinox, the positive axis of y to the point whose right ascension is 90^0, we can express the position of the place with respect to the centre by the following three co-ordinates:

$$\begin{aligned} x &= \varrho \cos\varphi' \cos\Theta \\ y &= \varrho \cos\varphi' \sin\Theta \qquad (G). \\ z &= \varrho \sin\varphi' \end{aligned}$$

3. The plane in which the lines drawn from the centre of the earth and from the place of observation to the centre of the heavenly body are situated, passes through the zenith of the place, if we consider the earth as spherical, and intersects therefore the celestial sphere in a vertical circle. Hence it follows that the parallax affects only the altitude of the heavenly bodies while their azimuth remains unchanged. If A (Fig. 3) then represents the place of observation, Z its zenith, S the heavenly body and O the centre of the earth, ZOS is the true zenith distance z as seen from the centre of the earth and ZAS the apparent zenith distance z' seen from the place at the surface. Denoting then the parallax or the angle at S equal to $z' - z$ by p' we have:

$$\sin p' = \frac{\varrho}{\Delta} \sin z',$$

where Δ denotes the distance of the body from the earth, and as p' is always a very small angle except in the case of the moon, we can always take the arc itself instead of the sine and have:

$$p' = \frac{\varrho}{\Delta} \sin z' . 206265.$$

Hence the parallax is proportional to the sine of the apparent zenith distance. It is zero at the zenith, has its maximum in the horizon and has always the effect to decrease the altitude of the object. The maximum value for $z' = 90^0$

$$p = \frac{\varrho}{\Delta} 206265$$

is called the ***horizontal parallax*** and the quantity

$$p = \frac{a}{\Delta} 206265,$$

where a is the radius of the earth's equator, is called the *horizontal equatoreal parallax.*

Here the earth has been supposed to be a sphere; but as it really is a spheroid, the plane of the lines drawn from the centre of the earth and from the place of observation to the object does not pass through the zenith of the place, but through the point, in which the line from the centre of the earth to the place intersects the celestial sphere. Hence the parallax changes a little the azimuth of an object and the rigorous expression of the parallax in altitude differs a little from the expression given before.

If we imagine three axes of co-ordinates at right angles with each other, of which the positive axis of z is directed towards the zenith of the place, whilst the axes of x and y are situated in the horizon, so that the positive axis of x is directed towards the south, the positive axis of y towards the west, the co-ordinates of the body with respect to these axes are:

$$\Delta' \sin z' \cos A', \ \Delta' \sin z' \sin A' \text{ and } \Delta' \cos z',$$

where Δ' denotes the distance of the object from the place and z' and A are the zenith distance and azimuth seen from the place.

The co-ordinates of the same object with respect to a system of axes parallel to the others but passing through the centre of the earth are:

$$\Delta \sin z \cos A, \ \Delta \sin z \sin A \text{ and } \Delta \cos z,$$

where Δ denotes the distance of the object from the centre and z and A are the zenith distance and the azimuth seen from the centre. Now as the co-ordinates of the centre of the earth with respect to the first system are:

$$-\varrho \sin(\varphi - \varphi'), \ 0 \text{ and } -\varrho \cos(\varphi - \varphi')$$

we have the following three equations:

$$\Delta' \sin z' \cos A' = \Delta \sin z \cos A - \varrho \sin(\varphi - \varphi')$$
$$\Delta' \sin z' \sin A' = \Delta \sin z \sin A$$
$$\Delta' \cos z' \qquad = \Delta \cos z - \varrho \cos(\varphi - \varphi'),$$

or:

$$\Delta' \sin z' \sin(A' - A) = \varrho \sin(\varphi - \varphi') \sin A$$
$$\Delta' \sin z' \cos(A' - A) = \Delta \sin z - \varrho \sin(\varphi - \varphi') \cos A \qquad (a)$$
$$\Delta' \cos z' \qquad = \Delta \cos z - \varrho \cos(\varphi - \varphi').$$

If we multiply the first equation by $\sin \frac{1}{2}(A' - A)$, the second by $\cos \frac{1}{2}(A' - A)$ and add the two products, we find:

$$\Delta' \sin z' = \Delta \sin z - \varrho \sin(\varphi - \varphi') \frac{\cos \frac{1}{2}(A' + A)}{\cos \frac{1}{2}(A' - A)}$$
$$\Delta' \cos z' = \Delta \cos z - \varrho \cos(\varphi - \varphi').$$

Then putting:

$$\operatorname{tang} \gamma = \frac{\cos \frac{1}{2}(A' + A)}{\cos \frac{1}{2}(A' - A)} \operatorname{tang}(\varphi - \varphi'), \qquad (b)$$

we find:

$$\Delta' \sin z' = \Delta \sin z - \varrho \cos(\varphi - \varphi') \operatorname{tang} \gamma$$
$$\Delta' \cos z' = \Delta \cos z - \varrho \cos(\varphi - \varphi'),$$

or:

$$\left.\begin{aligned} \Delta' \sin(z' - z) &= \varrho \cos(\varphi - \varphi') \frac{\sin(z - \gamma)}{\cos \gamma} \\ \Delta' \cos(z' - z) &= \Delta - \varrho \cos(\varphi - \varphi') \frac{\cos(z - \gamma)}{\cos \gamma} \end{aligned}\right\} \qquad (c)$$

and besides if we multiply the first equation by $\sin \frac{1}{2}(z' - z)$, the second by $\cos \frac{1}{2}(z' - z)$ and add the products:

$$\Delta' = \Delta - \varrho \frac{\cos(\varphi - \varphi') \cos[\frac{1}{2}(z' + z) - \gamma]}{\cos \gamma}.$$

If we divide the equations (a), (b) and (c) by Δ and put:

$$\frac{1}{\Delta} = \sin p,$$

taking the radius of the earth's equator equal to unity, so that p is the horizontal equatoreal parallax, we obtain by the aid of formulae (12) and (13) in No. 11 of the introduction:

$$A' - A = \frac{\varrho \sin p \sin(\varphi - \varphi')}{\sin z} \sin A + \frac{1}{2}\left(\frac{\varrho \sin p \sin(\varphi - \varphi')}{\sin z}\right)^2 \sin 2A + \ldots$$
$$\gamma = \cos A(\varphi - \varphi') - \sin A \operatorname{tang} \frac{1}{2}(A' - A)(\varphi - \varphi')$$
$$+ \frac{1}{3} \frac{\sin A \sin A' \cos \frac{1}{2}(A' + A)}{\cos \frac{1}{2}(A' - A)^3} (\varphi - \varphi')^3 \ldots . \text{*)}$$

---

*) We have:

$$\gamma = \frac{\cos \frac{1}{2}(A' + A)}{\cos \frac{1}{2}(A' - A)} \operatorname{tang}(\varphi - \varphi') - \frac{1}{3} \frac{\cos \frac{1}{2}(A' + A)^3}{\cos \frac{1}{2}(A' - A)^3} \operatorname{tang}(\varphi - \varphi')^3 + \ldots$$

Substituting here for $\operatorname{tang}(\varphi - \varphi')$ the series

$$(\varphi - \varphi') + \frac{1}{3}(\varphi - \varphi')^3 + \ldots,$$

we can easily deduce the expression given above.

$$z' - z = \frac{\varrho \sin p \cos(\varphi - \varphi')}{\cos \gamma} \sin(z - \gamma)$$
$$+ \tfrac{1}{2} \left(\frac{\varrho \sin p \cos(\varphi - \varphi')}{\cos \gamma} \right)^2 \sin 2(z - \gamma) + \ldots .$$
$$\log \text{hyp}\, \Delta' = \log \text{hyp}\, \Delta - \frac{\varrho \sin p \cos(\varphi - \varphi')}{\cos \gamma} \cos(z - \gamma)$$
$$- \tfrac{1}{2} \left(\frac{\varrho \sin p \cos(\varphi - \varphi')}{\cos \gamma} \right)^2 \cos 2(z - \gamma) - \ldots$$

We have therefore neglecting quantities of the order of $\sin p\,(\varphi - \varphi')$ which have little influence on the quantity γ:
$$\gamma = (\varphi - \varphi') \cos A$$
hence the parallax in azimuth is:
$$A' - A = \frac{\varrho \sin p \sin(\varphi - \varphi')}{\sin z} \sin A,$$
or its rigorous expression, which must be used when z is very small:
$$\operatorname{tang}(A' - A) = \frac{\frac{\varrho \sin p \sin(\varphi - \varphi')}{\sin z} \sin A}{1 - \frac{\varrho \sin p \sin(\varphi - \varphi')}{\sin z} \cos A}$$

Furthermore as:
$$\frac{\cos(\varphi - \varphi')}{\cos \gamma} = \frac{\cos \frac{1}{2}(A' + A) \sin(\varphi - \varphi')}{\cos \frac{1}{2}(A' - A) \sin \gamma},$$
is always nearly equal to unity, the parallax in zenith distance is:
$$z' - z = \varrho \sin p \sin[z - (\varphi - \varphi') \cos A],$$
and the rigorous equations for it are:
$$\frac{\Delta'}{\Delta} \sin(z' - z) = \varrho \sin p \sin[z - (\varphi - \varphi') \cos A]$$
$$\frac{\Delta'}{\Delta} \cos(z' - z) = 1 - \varrho \sin p \cos[z - (\varphi - \varphi') \cos A].$$

Hence if the object is on the meridian, the parallax in azimuth is zero and the parallax in zenith distance is:
$$z' - z = \varrho \sin p \sin[z - (\varphi - \varphi')].$$

4. In a similar way we obtain the expressions for the parallax in right ascension and declination. The co-ordinates of a body with respect to the earth's centre and the plane of the equator are:
$$\Delta \cos \delta \cos \alpha, \quad \Delta \cos \delta \sin \alpha \quad \text{and} \quad \Delta \sin \delta.$$

The apparent co-ordinates as they appear from the place at the surface with respect to the same plane are:
$$\Delta' \cos \delta' \cos \alpha', \quad \Delta' \cos \delta' \sin \alpha' \quad \text{and} \quad \Delta' \sin \delta'.$$

Since the co-ordinates of the place at the surface with respect to the centre referred to the same fundamental plane are:

$$\varrho \cos\varphi' \cos\Theta,\ \varrho\cos\varphi'\sin\Theta \text{ and } \varrho\sin\varphi'$$

we have the following three equations for determining Δ', α' and δ':

$$\begin{aligned}\Delta'\cos\delta'\cos\alpha' &= \Delta\cos\delta\cos\alpha - \varrho\cos\varphi'\cos\Theta\\ \Delta'\cos\delta'\sin\alpha' &= \Delta\cos\delta\sin\alpha - \varrho\cos\varphi'\sin\Theta\\ \Delta'\sin\delta' &= \Delta\sin\delta - \varrho\sin\varphi'.\end{aligned} \qquad (a)$$

If we multiply the first equation by $\sin\alpha$, the second by $\cos\alpha$ and subtract one from the other, we find:

$$\Delta'\cos\delta'\sin(\alpha'-\alpha) = -\varrho\cos\varphi'\sin(\Theta-\alpha).$$

But if we multiply the first equation by $\cos\alpha$, the second by $\sin\alpha$ and add them, we find:

$$\Delta'\cos\delta'\cos(\alpha'-\alpha) = \Delta\cos\delta - \varrho\cos\varphi'\cos(\Theta-\alpha).$$

We have therefore:

$$\operatorname{tang}(\alpha'-\alpha) = \frac{\varrho\cos\varphi'\sin(\alpha-\Theta)}{\Delta\cos\delta - \varrho\cos\varphi'\cos(\alpha-\Theta)} = \frac{\dfrac{\varrho\cos\varphi'}{\Delta\cos\delta}\sin(\alpha-\Theta)}{1-\dfrac{\varrho\cos\varphi'}{\Delta\cos\delta}\cos(\alpha-\Theta)},$$

or developing $\alpha'-\alpha$ in a series, we find:

$$\alpha'-\alpha = \frac{\varrho\cos\varphi'}{\Delta\cos\delta}\sin(\alpha-\Theta) + \tfrac{1}{2}\left(\frac{\varrho\cos\varphi'}{\Delta\cos\delta}\right)^2\sin 2(\alpha-\Theta) + \tfrac{1}{3}\left(\frac{\varrho\cos\varphi'}{\Delta\cos\delta}\right)^3\sin 3(\alpha-\Theta)+\dots \qquad (A)$$

In all cases excepting the moon it is sufficiently accurate to take only the first term of the series. Taking then the radius of the earth's equator as the unit of ϱ and writing in the numerator $\sin\pi$ as factor (where π is the equatoreal parallax of the sun) in order to use the same unit in the numerator as in the denominator, namely the semi-major axis of the earth's orbit, we get:

$$\alpha'-\alpha = \frac{\varrho\sin\pi\cos\varphi'}{\Delta}\cdot\frac{\sin(\alpha-\Theta)}{\cos\delta}. \qquad (B)$$

where $\alpha-\Theta$ is the east hour angle of the object. The parallax therefore increases the right ascensions of the stars when east of the meridian and diminishes them on the west side of the meridian. If the object is on the meridian, its parallax in right ascension is zero.

In order to find a similar formula for $\delta' - \delta$, we will write in the formula for:

$$\Delta' \cos \delta' \cos (\alpha' - \alpha)$$

now

$$1 - 2 \sin \tfrac{1}{2} (\alpha' - \alpha)^2$$

instead of

$$\cos (\alpha' - \alpha),$$

and obtain:

$$\Delta' \cos \delta' = \Delta \cos \delta - \varrho \cos \varphi' \cos (\Theta - \alpha) + 2\, \Delta' \cos \delta' \sin \tfrac{1}{2} (\alpha' - \alpha)^2.$$

If we here multiply and divide the last term by $\cos \frac{1}{2} (\alpha' - \alpha)$ and make use of the formula:

$$\Delta' \cos \delta' \sin (\alpha' - \alpha) = - \varrho \cos \varphi' \sin (\Theta - \alpha)$$

we easily find:

$$\Delta' \cos \delta' = \Delta \cos \delta - \varrho \cos \varphi' \frac{\cos [\Theta - \frac{1}{2} (\alpha' + \alpha)]}{\cos \frac{1}{2} (\alpha' - \alpha)}. \qquad (b)$$

Introducing now the auxiliary quantities β and γ given by the following equations:

$$\begin{aligned} \beta \sin \gamma &= \sin \varphi' \\ \beta \cos \gamma &= \frac{\cos \varphi' \cos [\Theta - \frac{1}{2} (\alpha' + \alpha)]}{\cos \frac{1}{2} (\alpha' - \alpha)}, \end{aligned} \qquad (c)$$

we find from (b):

$$\Delta' \cos \delta' = \Delta \cos \delta - \varrho \beta \cos \gamma$$

and from the third of the equations (a):

$$\Delta' \sin \delta' = \Delta \sin \delta - \varrho \beta \sin \gamma.$$

From these two equations we easily deduce the following:

$$\begin{aligned} \Delta' \sin (\delta' - \delta) &= - \varrho \beta \sin (\gamma - \delta) \\ \Delta' \cos (\delta' - \delta) &= \Delta - \varrho \beta \cos (\gamma - \delta), \end{aligned}$$

or:

$$\operatorname{tang} (\delta' - \delta) = - \frac{\frac{\varrho \beta}{\Delta} \sin (\gamma - \delta)}{1 - \frac{\varrho \beta}{\Delta} \cos (\gamma - \delta)},$$

or according to formula (12) in No. 11 of the introduction:

$$\delta' - \delta = - \frac{\varrho \beta}{\Delta} \sin (\gamma - \delta) - \tfrac{1}{2} \frac{\varrho^2 \beta^2}{\Delta^2} \sin 2 (\gamma - \delta) - \text{etc.} \qquad (C)$$

If we introduce here instead of β its value $\frac{\sin \varphi'}{\sin \gamma}$ and write again $\varrho \sin \pi$ instead of ϱ in order to have the same unit in the numerator as in the denominator, we find, taking only the first term of the series:

$$\delta' - \delta = - \frac{\varrho \sin \pi \sin \varphi'}{\Delta} \cdot \frac{\sin (\gamma - \delta)}{\sin \gamma}.$$

If we further take in the second of the formulae (c) $\cos\frac{1}{2}(\alpha' - \alpha)$ equal to unity and write α instead of $\frac{1}{2}(\alpha' + \alpha)$, we have the following approximate formulae for computing the parallax in right ascension and declination:

$$\alpha' - \alpha = -\frac{\pi\varrho\cos\varphi'}{\Delta}\cdot\frac{\sin(\Theta - \alpha)}{\cos\delta}$$

$$\operatorname{tang}\gamma = \frac{\operatorname{tang}\varphi'}{\cos(\Theta - \alpha)}$$

$$\delta' - \delta = -\frac{\pi\varrho\sin\varphi'}{\Delta}\frac{\sin(\gamma - \delta)}{\sin\gamma}\ ^{*)}$$

If the object has a visible disc, its apparent diameter must change with the distance. But we have:

$$\Delta'\sin(\delta' - \gamma) = \Delta\sin(\delta - \gamma)$$

$$\Delta' = \Delta\frac{\sin(\delta - \gamma)}{\sin(\delta' - \gamma)}$$

and as the semi-diameters, as long as they are small, vary inversely as the distances, we have:

$$R' = R\,.\,\frac{\sin(\delta' - \gamma)}{\sin(\delta - \gamma)}\,.$$

Example. 1844 Sept. 3 De Vico's comet was observed at Rome at $20^h\,41^m\,38^s$ sidereal time and its right ascension and declination were found as follows:

$$\alpha = 2^\circ\,35'\,55''.5$$
$$\delta = -18\ \ 43\ \ 21\ .6.$$

The logarithm of its distance from the earth was at that time 9.27969 and we have for Rome:

$$\varphi' = 41^\circ\,42'.5$$

and

$$\log\varrho = 9.99936.$$

The computation of the parallax is then performed as follows:

---

*) If the object is on the meridian, we find:

$$\delta' - \delta = -\frac{\pi\varrho}{\Delta}\sin(\varphi' - \delta) = \varrho\,\frac{\pi}{\Delta}\sin[z - (\varphi - \varphi')],$$

hence the parallax in declination is equal to the parallax in altitude.

Θ in arc	$310^{\circ}\,24'.5$		
α	$2\;\;35\,.9$		
$\Theta-\alpha$	$-52^{\circ}\,11'.4$		
$\operatorname{tang}\varphi'$	9.94999	$\gamma=$	$55^{\circ}\,28'.6$
$\cos(\Theta-\alpha)$	9.78749	$\delta=$	$-\;18\;\;43\,.4$
$\sin(\Theta-\alpha)$	9.89765_n	$\gamma-\delta=$	$+\;74\;\;12\,.0$
$-\dfrac{\pi\varrho\cos\varphi'}{\Delta}$	1.52576_n	$\sin(\gamma-\delta)$	9.98327
$\sec\delta$	0.02362	$-\dfrac{\pi\varrho\sin\varphi'}{\Delta}$	1.47576_n
		$\operatorname{cosec}\gamma$	0.08413
$\log(\alpha'-\alpha)$	1.44703	$\log\delta'-\delta=$	1.54316_n
$\alpha'-\alpha=$	$+27''.99$	$\delta'-\delta=$	$-34''.93$

Thus the parallax increases the geocentric right ascension of the comet $28''.0$ and diminishes the geocentric declination $34''.9$. Hence the place of the comet corrected for parallax is:

$$\alpha = 2^{\circ}\,35'\,27''.5$$
$$\delta = -18\;\;42\;\;46\;.7.$$

In order to find the parallax of a body for co-ordinates referred to the plane of the ecliptic, it is necessary to know the co-ordinates of the place of observation with respect to the earth's centre referred to the same fundamental plane. But if we convert Θ and φ' into longitude and latitude according to No. 9 of the first section and if the values thus found are l and b, these co-ordinates are:

$$\varrho\cos b\cos l$$
$$\varrho\cos b\sin l$$
$$\varrho\sin b$$

and we have the following three equations, where λ', β', Δ' are the apparent, λ, β, Δ the true longitude and latitude:

$$\Delta'\cos\beta'\cos\lambda' = \Delta\cos\beta\cos\lambda - \varrho\cos b\cos l$$
$$\Delta'\cos\beta'\sin\lambda' = \Delta\cos\beta\sin\lambda - \varrho\cos b\sin l$$
$$\Delta'\sin\beta' = \Delta\sin\beta - \varrho\sin b,$$

from which we finally obtain similar equations as before, namely:

$$\lambda'-\lambda = -\frac{\pi\varrho\cos b}{\Delta}\,\frac{\sin(l-\lambda)}{\cos\beta}$$
$$\operatorname{tang}\gamma = \frac{\operatorname{tang} b}{\cos(l-\lambda)}$$
$$\beta'-\beta = -\frac{\pi\varrho\sin b}{\Delta}\,\frac{\sin(\gamma-\beta)}{\sin\gamma},$$

Θ and φ' are the right ascension and declination of that point, in which the radius of the earth intersects the celestial sphere,

l and b are therefore the longitude and latitude of the same point. If we consider the earth as a sphere, this point is the zenith and the longitude of the point of the ecliptic which is at the zenith is also called the *nonagesimal*, since its distance from the points of the ecliptic which are rising and setting is 90^0.

5. As the horizontal equatoreal parallax of the moon or the angle whose sine is $\frac{1}{\Delta}$, Δ being the distance of the moon from the earth, is always between 54 and 61 minutes, it is not sufficiently accurate to use only the first term of the series found for the parallax in right ascension and declination and we must either compute some of the higher terms or use the rigorous formulae.

If we wish to find the parallax of the moon in right ascension and declination for Greenwich for 1848 April 10 10^h mean time, we have for this time:

$$\alpha = 7^h\,43^m\,20^s.25 = 115^0\,50'\,3''.75$$
$$\delta = +16^0\,27'\,22''.9$$
$$\Theta = 11^h\,17^m\,0^s.02 = 169^0\,15'\,0''.30$$

and the horizontal equatoreal parallax and the radius of the moon:

$$p = 56'\,57''.5$$
$$R = 15'\,31''.3.$$

We have further for Greenwich:

$$\varphi' = 51^0\,17'\,25''.4$$
$$\log \varrho = 9.9991134.$$

If we introduce the horizontal parallax p of the moon into the two series found for $\alpha' - \alpha$ and $\delta' - \delta$ in No. 4, as we have $\sin p = \frac{1}{\Delta}$, we find:

$$\alpha' - \alpha = -206265 \left\{ \frac{\varrho \cos\varphi' \sin p}{\cos\delta} \sin(\Theta - \alpha) + \tfrac{1}{2}\left(\frac{\varrho\cos\varphi'\sin p}{\cos\delta}\right)^2 \sin 2(\Theta - \alpha) + \tfrac{1}{3}\left(\frac{\varrho\cos\varphi'\sin p}{\cos\delta}\right)^3 \sin 3(\Theta - \alpha) + \ldots \right\}$$

and:

$$\delta' - \delta = -206265 \left\{ \frac{\varrho \sin\varphi' \sin p}{\sin\gamma} \sin(\gamma - \delta) + \tfrac{1}{2}\left(\frac{\varrho\sin\varphi'\sin p}{\sin\gamma}\right)^2 \sin 2(\gamma - \delta) + \tfrac{1}{3}\left(\frac{\varrho\sin\varphi'\sin p}{\sin\gamma}\right)^3 \sin 3(\gamma - \delta) + \ldots \right\},$$

where we must use the rigorous formula for computing the auxiliary angle γ:

$$\operatorname{tang}\gamma = \operatorname{tang}\varphi' \frac{\cos\frac{1}{2}(\alpha' - \alpha)}{\cos[\Theta - \frac{1}{2}(\alpha' + \alpha)]}.$$

If we compute these formulae, we find for $\alpha' - \alpha$:

from the first term:	$-29'\,45''.71$
„ „ second „	$-11\,.47$
„ „ third „	$-\;0\,.03$
hence $\alpha' - \alpha =$	$-29'\,57''.21$

and for $\delta' - \delta$:

from the first term:	$-36'\,34''.21$
„ „ second „	$-20\,.91$
„ „ third „	$-\;0\,.12$
hence $\delta' - \delta$	$-36'\,55''.24.$

The apparent right ascension and declination of the moon is therefore:

$$\alpha' = 115^{0}\,20'\,6''.54 \qquad \delta' = 15^{0}\,50'\,27''.66.$$

Finally we find the apparent semi-diameter:

$$R' = 15'\,40''.20.$$

If we prefer to compute the parallax from the rigorous formulae, we must render them more convenient for logarithmic computation. We had the rigorous formula for tang $(\alpha' - \alpha)$:

$$\operatorname{tang}(\alpha' - \alpha) = \frac{\varrho\cos\varphi'\sin p\sin(\alpha - \Theta)\sec\delta}{1 - \varrho\cos\varphi'\sin p\cos(\alpha - \Theta)\sec\delta} \qquad (a).$$

Further from the two equations:

$$\Delta'\sin\delta' = \Delta[\sin\delta - \varrho\sin\varphi'\sin p]$$

and:

$$\Delta'\cos\delta'\cos(\alpha' - \alpha) = \Delta[\cos\delta - \varrho\cos\varphi'\sin p\cos(\alpha - \Theta)]$$

we find:

$$\operatorname{tang}\delta' = \frac{[\sin\delta - \varrho\sin\varphi'\sin p]\cos(\alpha' - \alpha)\sec\delta}{1 - \varrho\cos\varphi'\sin p\sec\delta\cos(\alpha - \Theta)} \qquad (b).$$

Since we have:

$$\frac{\Delta}{\Delta'} = \frac{\cos\delta'\cos(\alpha' - \alpha)}{\cos\delta - \varrho\cos\varphi'\sin p\cos(\alpha - \Theta)},$$

we find in addition:

$$\sin R' = \frac{\cos\delta'\cos(\alpha' - \alpha)\sec\delta}{1 - \varrho\cos\varphi'\sin p\sec\delta\cos(\alpha - \Theta)}\sin R \qquad (c).$$

If we introduce in (a), (b) and (c) the following auxiliary quantities:

$$\cos A = \frac{\varrho\sin p\cos\varphi'\cos(\alpha - \Theta)}{\cos\delta}$$

and:

$$\sin C = \varrho\sin p\sin\varphi',$$

we find the following formulae which are convenient for logarithmic computation:

$$\operatorname{tang}(\alpha' - \alpha) = \frac{\frac{1}{2}\varrho \cos\varphi' \sin p \,.\, \sin(\alpha - \Theta)}{\cos\delta \sin\frac{1}{2}A^2}$$

$$\operatorname{tang}\delta' = \frac{\sin\frac{1}{2}(\delta - C)\cos\frac{1}{2}(\delta + C)\cos(\alpha' - \alpha)}{\cos\delta\sin\frac{1}{2}A^2}$$

and:

$$R' = \frac{\frac{1}{2}\cos\delta'\cos(\alpha' - \alpha)}{\cos\delta\sin\frac{1}{2}A^2} \,.\, R.$$

If we compute the values $\alpha' - \alpha$, δ' and R' with the data used before, we find almost exactly as before:

$$\alpha' - \alpha = -29'\,57''.21$$
$$\delta' = +15^0\,50'\,27''.68$$
$$R' = 15'\,40''.21.$$

We can find similar formulae for the exact computation of the parallax in longitude and latitude and we can deduce them immediately from the above formulae by substituting λ', λ, β', β, l and b in place of α', α, δ', δ, Θ and φ'.

II. THE REFRACTION.

6. The rays of light from the stars do not come to us through a vacuum but through the atmosphere of the earth. While in a medium of uniform density, the light moves in a straight line, but when it enters a medium of a different density, the ray is bent from its original direction. If the medium, like our atmosphere, consists of an infinite number of strata of different density, the ray describes a curve. But an observer at the surface of the earth sees the object in the direction of the tangent of this curve at the point where it meets the eye and from this observed direction or the apparent place of the star he must find the true place or the direction, which the ray of light would have, if it had undergone no refraction. The angle between these two directions is called the *refraction* and as the curve of the ray of light turns its concave side to the observer, the stars appear too high on account of refraction.

We will consider the earth as a sphere, as the effect of the spheroidal form of the earth upon the refraction is exceedingly small. The atmosphere we shall consider as consisting of concentric strata of an infinitely small thickness, within which the density and hence the refractive power is taken as uniform. In order to determine then the change of the direction of the ray of light on account of the refraction at the surface of each stratum, we must know the laws governing the refraction of the light. These laws are as follows:

1) If a ray of light meets the surface separating two media of different density, and we imagine a tangent plane at the point where the ray meets the surface, and if we draw the normal and lay a plane through it and through the ray of light, the ray after its refraction will continue to move on in the same plane.

2) If we imagine the normal produced beyond the surface, the sine of the angle between this part of the normal and the ray of light before entering the medium (the angle of incidence) has always a constant ratio to the sine of the angle between the normal and the refracted ray of light (the angle of refraction), as long as the density of the two media is the same. This ratio is called the *index of refraction* or *refractive index.*

3) If the index of refraction is given for two media A and B and also that for two media B and C, the index of refraction for the two media A and C is the compound ratio of the indices between A and B and between B and C.

4) If μ is the index of refraction for two media if the light passes from the medium A into the medium B, the index for the same media if the light passes from the medium B into the medium A is $\frac{1}{\mu}$.

Now let O Fig. 4 be a place at the surface of the earth, C the centre of the earth, S the real place of a star, CJ the normal at the point J where the ray of light SJ meets the first stratum of the atmosphere. If we know then the density of this first stratum, we find the direction of the ray of light after the refraction according to the laws of refraction and thus find a new angle of incidence for the second stratum. If we now consider the nth stratum taking

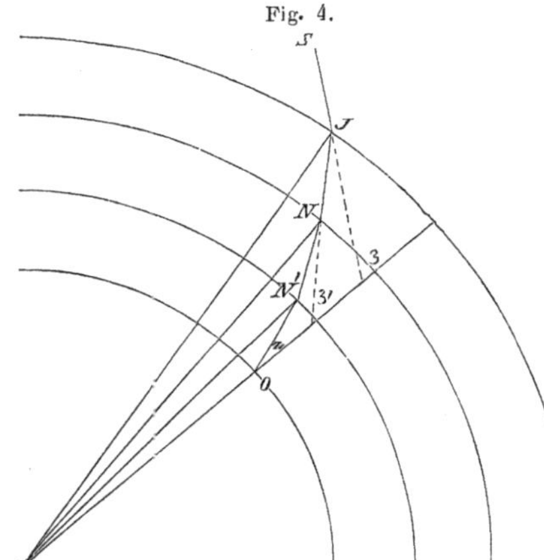

CN as the line from the centre of the earth to the point in which the ray of light meets this stratum, and denoting the angle of incidence by i_n, the angle of refraction by f_n, the index of refraction for the vacuum and the $(n-1)^{\text{th}}$ stratum by μ_n, the same for the nth stratum by μ_{n+1}, we have *):

$$\sin i_n : \sin f_n = \mu_{n+1} : \mu_n.$$

If further N' is the point in which the ray of light meets the $n+1^{\text{th}}$ stratum, we have in the triangle NCN', denoting the lines NC and $N'C$ by r_n and r_{n+1}:

$$\sin f_n : \sin i_{n+1} = r_{n+1} : r_n,$$

and combining this formula with the one found before we get:

$$r_n \sin i_n \, \mu_n = r_{n+1} \sin i_{n+1} \, \mu_{n+1}.$$

Therefore as the product of the distance from the centre into the index of refraction and the sine of the angle of incidence is constant for all strata of the atmosphere, we may denote this product by γ and we have therefore as the general law of refraction:

$$r \,.\, \mu \,.\, \sin i = \gamma, \qquad (a)$$

where r, μ and i belong to the same point of the atmosphere. For the stratum nearest to the surface of the earth the angle i or the angle between the last tangent at the curve of the ray of light and the normal is equal to the apparent zenith distance z of the star. If we therefore denote the radius of the earth by a, and the index of refraction for the stratum nearest to the surface of the earth by μ_0, we can determine γ from the following equation:

$$a \mu_0 \sin z = \gamma. \qquad (b)$$

---

*) These indices are fractions whose numerators are greater than the denominators. For a stratum at the surface of the earth for instance we have $\mu = 1.000294$ or nearly equal to $\frac{3400}{3399}$.

If we now assume, that the thickness of the strata, within which the density is uniform, is infinitely small, the path of the light through the atmosphere will be a curve whose equation we can find. Using polar co-ordinates and denoting the angle, which any r makes with the radius CO by v, we easily find:

$$r\frac{dv}{dr} = \text{tang}\, i. \qquad (c)$$

The direction of the last tangent at the point where the curve meets the eye is the apparent zenith distance, but the true zenith distance ζ is the angle, which the original direction SJ of the ray of light produced makes with the normal. This ζ, it is true, has its vertex at a point different from the one occupied by the eye of the observer; but as the height of the atmosphere is small compared with the distance of the heavenly bodies and the refraction itself is a small angle, the angle ζ differs very little from the true zenith distance seen from the point O. Even in the case of the moon, where this difference is the greatest, it does not amount to a second of arc, when the moon is in the horizon. We may therefore consider the angle ζ as the true zenith distance.

If we now draw a tangent to the ray at the point N, to which the variable quantities i, r and μ belong and if we denote the angle between it and the normal CO by ζ', we have:

$$\zeta' = i + v. \qquad (d)$$

Differentiating the general equation (a) written in a logarithmic form, we find:

$$\frac{dr}{r} + \text{cotang}\, i \,.\, di + \frac{d\mu}{\mu} = 0$$

and from this formula in connection with the equations (c) and (d) we get:

$$d\zeta' = -\text{tang}\, i \frac{d\mu}{\mu},$$

or eliminating tang i by the equation:

$$\text{tang}\, i = \frac{\sin i}{\sqrt{1-\sin i^2}} = \frac{\gamma}{\sqrt{r^2\mu^2-\gamma^2}}$$

and substituting for γ its value $a\,\mu_0 \sin z$; we find:

$$d\zeta' = -\frac{\frac{a}{r}\mu_0 \sin z\, d\mu}{\mu\sqrt{\mu^2 - \frac{a^2}{r^2}\mu_0{}^2 \sin z^2}}.$$

The integral of this equation taken between the limits $\zeta' = \zeta$ and $\zeta' = z$ gives then the refraction. If we put:

$$\frac{a}{r} = 1 - s,$$

we can write the equation in the following form:

$$d\zeta' = -\frac{(1-s)\sin z\, d\mu}{\mu\sqrt{\cos z^2 - \left(1 - \frac{\mu^2}{\mu_0^{\,2}}\right) + (2s - s^2)\sin z^2}}. \qquad (e)$$

In order to integrate this formula we must know how s depends upon μ. The latter quantity depends on the density and we know from Physics, that the quantity $\mu^2 - 1$, which is called the refractive power, is proportional to the density. If we introduce now as a new variable quantity the density ϱ, given by the equation:

$$\mu^2 - 1 = c\varrho,$$

where c is a constant quantity, we obtain:

$$d\zeta' = -\frac{\frac{1}{2}(1-s)\sin z \,.\, c \,.\, \frac{d\varrho}{1 + c\varrho_0}}{\frac{1 + c\varrho}{1 + c\varrho_0}\sqrt{\cos z^2 - \left(1 - \frac{1 + c\varrho}{1 + c\varrho_0}\right) + (2s - s^2)\sin z^2}},$$

or taking:

$$\frac{c\varrho_0}{1 + c\varrho_0} = \frac{\mu_0^{\,2} - 1}{\mu_0^{\,2}} = 2\alpha, \text{ hence } \frac{c\varrho_0 - c\varrho}{1 + c\varrho_0} = 2\alpha\left(1 - \frac{\varrho}{\varrho_0}\right),$$

$$d\zeta' = -\frac{\alpha(1-s)\sin z\,\frac{d\varrho}{\varrho_0}}{\left[1 - 2\alpha\left(1 - \frac{\varrho}{\varrho_0}\right)\right]\sqrt{\cos z^2 - 2\alpha\left(1 - \frac{\varrho}{\varrho_0}\right) + (2s - s^2)\sin z^2}}. \quad (f$$

The coefficient

$$1 - 2\alpha\left(1 - \frac{\varrho}{\varrho_0}\right)$$

is the square of the ratio of the index of refraction for a stratum whose radius is r to the index for the stratum at the surface of the earth. But as we have $\mu = 1$ at the limits of the atmosphere, and the index of the stratum at the surface is $\mu_0 = \frac{3400}{3399}$, the ratio $\frac{\mu}{\mu_0}$ is always contained between narrow limits. Hence as α is always a small quantity, we may take instead of the variable factor

$$1 - 2\alpha\left(1 - \frac{\varrho}{\varrho_0}\right)$$

its mean value between the two extreme limits 1 and $1-2\alpha$ or the constant value $1-\alpha$.

If we put for brevity $1-\frac{\varrho}{\varrho_0}=w$, where w is a function of s, to be defined hereafter, and if we change the sign of $d\zeta'$, in order that the formula will give afterwards the quantity, which is to be added to the apparent place in order to find the true place, we get:

$$d\zeta' = \frac{\alpha}{1-\alpha}\,\frac{(1-s)\sin z\,dw}{\sqrt{\cos z^2 - 2\alpha w + (2s - s^2)\sin z^2}}$$

or as s is always a small quantity, since the greatest value of s supposing the height of the atmosphere to be 46 miles is only 0.0115:

$$d\zeta = \frac{\alpha}{1-\alpha}\cdot\frac{\sin z\,dw}{\sqrt{\cos z^2 - 2\alpha w + 2s\sin z^2}} - \frac{\alpha}{1-\alpha}\cdot\frac{s\sin z\,[\cos z^2 - 2\alpha w] + s^2\sin z^2}{[\cos z^2 - 2\alpha w + 2s\sin z^2]^{\frac{3}{2}}} \qquad (g),$$

where already the second term, as we shall see afterwards, is so small, that it can always be neglected. In order to find the refraction from the above equation we must integrate it with respect to s between the limits $s=0$ and $s=H$, where H denotes the height of the atmosphere.

If we now put:

$$w = F(s)$$

and introduce the new variable quantity x, given by the following equation:

$$-\frac{\alpha F(s)}{\sin z^2} + s = x$$

or taking:

$$\frac{\alpha F(s)}{\sin z^2} = \varphi(s),$$

$$s = x + \varphi(s),$$

we have according to Lagrange's theorem:

$$F(s) = F(x) + \varphi(x)\frac{dF(x)}{dx} + \frac{1}{1.2}\,\frac{d\left[\varphi(x)^2\,\frac{dF(x)}{dx}\right]}{dx} + \frac{1}{1.2.3}\,\frac{d^2\left[\varphi(x)^3\,\frac{dF(x)}{dx}\right]}{dx^2} + \ldots$$

hence

$$dF(s) = dF(x) + d\left[\varphi(x)\frac{dF(x)}{dx}\right] + \frac{1}{1.2}\,\frac{d^2\left[\varphi(x)^2\frac{dF(x)}{dx}\right]}{dx^2}$$
$$+ \frac{1}{1.2.3}\,\frac{d^3\left[\varphi(x)^3\frac{dF(x)}{dx}\right]}{dx^3} + \ldots \qquad (h).$$

In order to find from this the refraction, we must multiply each term by $\frac{\alpha}{1-\alpha}\cdot\frac{\sin z}{\sqrt{\cos z^2 + 2x\sin z^2}}$ and integrate between the limits given above. But in order to perform these integrations, it is necessary to express w as a function of s or to find the law, according to which the density of the atmosphere decreases with the elevation above the surface.

7. Let p_0 and τ_0 be the atmospheric pressure and the temperature at the surface of the earth, p and τ the same quantities at the elevation x above the surface, m the expansion of atmospheric air for one degree of Fahrenheit's thermometer; then we have the following equation:

$$p = \frac{1+m\tau}{1+m\tau_0}\cdot\frac{\varrho}{\varrho_0}\cdot p_0. \qquad (\alpha)$$

For if we take first a volume of air under the pressure p_0 at the temperature τ_0, and of the density ϱ_0 and change the pressure to p, while the temperature remains the same, the density according to Mariotte's law will change to $\frac{p}{p_0}\varrho_0$. If then also the temperature increases to τ, the resulting density will be:

$$\varrho = \frac{p}{p_0}\cdot\frac{1+m\tau_0}{1+m\tau}\varrho_0,$$

from which we get the equation above. Hence the quantity $\frac{p}{\varrho(1+m\tau)}$ or the quotient: the atmospheric pressure divided by the density and reduced to a certain fixed temperature, is always a constant quantity. Now if we denote by l_0 the height of a column of air of the uniform density ϱ_0 and of the temperature τ_0, which corresponds to the atmospheric pressure p_0, we have, denoting the force of gravity at the surface of the earth by g_0:

$$p_0 = (1+m\tau_0)\varrho_0 g_0 . l_0, \qquad (\beta)$$

l_0 is the height which the atmosphere would have if the density and temperature were uniformly the same at any elevation as at the surface of the earth, and if we take for τ_0 the temperature of 8^0 Réaumur $= 10^0$ Celsius $= 50^0$ Fahrenheit, we have according to Bessel:

$$l_0 = 4226.05 \text{ toises},$$

equal to the mean height of the barometer at the surface of the sea multiplied by the density of mercury relatively to that of air.

If we ascend now in the atmosphere through dr, the decrease of the pressure is equal to the small column of air $\varrho\, dr$ multiplied by the force of gravity at the distance r, hence we have:

$$dp = -g_0 \frac{a^2}{r^2} \cdot \varrho \cdot dr,$$

and dividing this equation by the equation (β) and putting

$$\frac{a}{r} = 1 - s$$

also reckoning the temperature from the temperature τ_0, so that τ means the temperature minus 50^0 Fahrenheit we find:

$$\frac{dp}{p_0} = -\frac{a\,ds}{l_0}(1 - w) \qquad (\gamma)$$

and from the equation (α) we have:

$$\frac{p}{p_0} = (1 + m\tau)(1 - w).$$

If we eliminate p from these two equations, we find $1 - w$ and hence the density expressed by s and $1 + m\tau$. The latter quantity is itself a function of s; but as we do not know the law according to which the temperature decreases with the elevation, we are obliged to adopt an hypothesis and to try whether the refractions computed according to it are in conformity with the observations. Thus the various theories of refraction differ from each other by the hypothesis made in regard to the decrease of the temperature in the atmosphere.

If we take the temperature as constant, we have:

$$\frac{p}{p_0} = 1 - w, \quad \text{hence} \quad \frac{dp}{p_0} = d(1 - w),$$

and we find, combining this with the first of the equation (γ):

$$\frac{d(1 - w)}{1 - w} = -\frac{a}{l_0}\, ds,$$

$$\text{hence} \qquad 1 - w = e^{-\frac{a}{l_0} s},$$

as the constant quantity which ought to be added to the integral is in this case equal to zero. This hypothesis was adopted by Newton, but is represents so little the true state of the atmosphere that the refractions computed according to it differ considerably from the observed refractions.

If we take for $1+m\tau$ an exponential expression $e^{-\frac{as}{h}}$ we arrive at Bessel's form. We find then by the combination of the two equations (γ):

$$\frac{d(1-w)}{1-w}=\left[\frac{a}{h}-\frac{a}{l_0}e^{\frac{as}{h}}\right]ds,$$

and integrating and determining the constant quantity so that $1-w$ is equal to unity when $s=0$, we find:

$$1-w=e^{-\frac{h}{l_0}\left[e^{\frac{as}{h}}-1\right]+\frac{a}{h}s},$$

instead of which we can use the approximate expression:

$$1-w=e^{-\frac{h-l_0}{hl_0}as} \qquad (\delta).$$

Bessel determines the constant quantity h is such a manner that the computed refractions agree as nearly as possible with the values derived from observations. But the decrease of the temperature resulting from the formula $1+m\tau=e^{-\frac{as}{h}}$ for this value of h do not at all agree with the decrease as observed near the surface of the earth. For we find $\frac{d\tau}{ds}=-\frac{a}{hm}$ for $s=0$, and as we have also $\frac{dr}{ds}=\frac{1}{a}$ for $s=0$, we find:

$$\frac{d\tau}{dr}=-\frac{1}{hm}$$

at the surface of the earth. Now as m for one degree of Fahrenheit's thermometer is 0.0020243 and as h according to Bessel is 116865.8 toises, we find $\frac{d\tau}{dr}=-\frac{1}{237}$. There would be therefore a decrease of the temperature equal to 1^0 Fahrenheit if we ascend 237 toises, whilst the observations show that a decrease of 1^0 takes place already for a change of elevation equal to 47 toises.

Ivory therefore in his theory assumes also an exponential expression for $1+m\tau$, but determines it so that it represents the observed decrease of the temperature at the surface of the earth. He takes:

$$1 - w = e^{-u},$$

where u is a function of s, and further:

$$1 + m\tau = 1 - f(1 - e^{-u}).$$

Then we easily get from the equations (γ):

$$\frac{a}{l_0} ds = (1 - f)\, du + 2fe^{-u} du,$$

$$\text{and} \quad \frac{a}{l_0} s = (1 - f)\, u + 2f(1 - e^{-u}). \qquad (\varepsilon)$$

Taking $r = a$ we find from these two equations:

$$\frac{d\tau}{dr} = -\frac{1}{l_0 m} \cdot \frac{f}{1+f}$$

and we see that we must take f equal to $\frac{2}{9}$ in order to make $\frac{d\tau}{dr}$ equal to $-\frac{1}{47}$ which value represents the observations at the surface of the earth.

Several other hypotheses have been adopted by Laplace, Young, Lubbock and others. Here however we shall confine ourselves to those of Bessel and Ivory, as the refractions computed from their theories are more frequently used, and the other theories may be treated in a similar manner.

8. If we put in equation (δ):

$$\frac{h - l_0}{h\, l_0}\, a = \beta,$$

we have for Bessel's hypothesis:

$$w = F(s) = 1 - e^{-\beta s},$$

we have therefore:

$$F(x) = 1 - e^{-\beta x}$$

$$\varphi(x) = -\frac{\alpha}{\sin z^2}(e^{-\beta x} - 1).$$

and we find:

$$d\,F(x) \varphi(x)^n = (-1)^n \frac{\alpha^n}{\sin z^{2n}} \left\{ e^{-(n+1)\beta x} - n \,.\, e^{-n\beta x} + \frac{n(n-1)}{1\,.\,2} e^{-(n-1)\beta x} - \ldots \right\},$$

hence as:

$$\frac{d^n e^{-px}}{dx^n} = (-1)^n p^n e^{-px},$$

$$\frac{d^n [d F(x)\, \varphi(x)^n]}{dx} = \frac{\alpha^n \beta^{n+1}}{\sin z^{2n}} \left\{ (n+1)^n e^{-(n+1)\beta x} - n \,.\, n^n e^{-n\beta x} \right.$$
$$\left. + \frac{n(n-1)}{1\,.\,2}(n-1)^n e^{-(n-1)\beta x} - \ldots \right\}$$

and the general term of the differential $d\zeta'$ becomes:

$$\frac{\alpha}{1-\alpha}\cdot\frac{1}{1\ldots.n}\frac{\alpha^n\beta^{n+1}}{\sin z^{2n}}\frac{\sin z}{\sqrt{\cos z^2+2x\sin z^2}}\cdot\Big\{(n+1)^n e^{-(n+1)\beta x}$$
$$-n.n^n e^{-n\beta x}+\frac{n(n-1)}{1.2}(n-1)^n e^{-(n-1)\beta x}-\ldots\Big\},$$

where we have to put for n successively all integral numbers beginning with zero. All these terms must then be integrated between the limits $s=0$ and $s=H$, instead of which we can use also without any sensible error the limits 0 and ∞, as $e^{-\beta s}$ is exceedingly small for $s=H$. As we have $x=0$ when $s=0$ and $x=\infty$ when $s=\infty$ we must integrate the different terms with respect to x between the limits 0 and ∞. All the integrals which here occur can be reduced to the functions denoted by ψ in No. 18 of the introduction and if we apply formula (8) of that No., we find the general term of the expression for the refraction:

$$\frac{\alpha}{1-\alpha}\sqrt{2\beta}\cdot\frac{1}{1.2\ldots n}\frac{\alpha^n\beta^n}{\sin z^{2n}}\Big\{(n+1)^{\frac{2n-1}{2}}\psi(n+1)-n.n^{\frac{2n-1}{2}}\psi(n)$$
$$+\frac{n(n-1)}{1.2}(n-1)^{\frac{2n-1}{2}}\psi(n-1)-\ldots\Big\},$$

or denoting the refraction by $\delta\zeta$, we find:

$$\delta\zeta=\frac{\alpha}{1-\alpha}\sqrt{2\beta}\left\{\begin{array}{l}\psi(1)\\ +\frac{\alpha\beta}{\sin z^2}\left[2^{\frac{1}{2}}\psi(2)-\psi(1)\right]\\ +\frac{\alpha^2\beta^2}{1.2.\sin z^4}\left[3^{\frac{3}{2}}\psi(3)-2.2^{\frac{3}{2}}\psi(2)+\psi(1)\right]\\ \text{etc.}\end{array}\right\} \quad (i)$$

and as we have:

$$1-x+\frac{x^2}{1.2}-\frac{x^3}{1.2.3}+\ldots=e^{-x}$$

we can write this in the following form:

$$\delta\zeta=\frac{\alpha}{1-\alpha}\sqrt{2\beta}\left\{\begin{array}{l}e^{-\frac{\alpha\beta}{\sin z^2}}\psi(1)\\ +\frac{\alpha\beta}{\sin z^2}2^{\frac{1}{2}}e^{-\frac{2\alpha\beta}{\sin z^2}}\psi(2)\\ +\frac{\alpha^2\beta^2}{1.2.\sin z^4}3^{\frac{3}{2}}e^{-\frac{3\alpha\beta}{\sin z^2}}\psi(3)\\ +\ldots.\end{array}\right\} \quad (k)$$

9. In Ivory's hypothesis we have:

$$w=F(u)=1-e^{-u},$$

and taking $\frac{l_0}{\alpha} = \frac{1}{\beta}$:

$$s = \frac{1-f}{\beta} u + \frac{2f}{\beta}(1 - e^{-u}).$$

If we introduce here the new variable x, given by the equation:

$$-\frac{\alpha w}{\sin z^2} + s = \frac{x}{\beta},$$

the differential expression for the refraction according to equation (g) in No. 6 becomes:

$$d\zeta' = \frac{\alpha}{1-\alpha} \frac{\sin z \,.\, dF(u)}{\sqrt{\cos z^2 + \frac{2\sin z^2}{\beta} x}},$$

$$\text{where} \quad x = u - \frac{\alpha\beta}{\sin z^2}(1 - e^{-u}) - fu + 2f(1 - e^{-u}).$$

Taking again:

$$F(x) = 1 - e^{-x}$$

$$\varphi(x) = \frac{\alpha\beta}{\sin z^2}(1 - e^{-x}) + fx - 2f(1 - e^{-x}),$$

we find from the formula (h):

$$dF(u) = e^{-x} + \frac{d[\varphi(x)\, e^{-x}]}{dx} + \frac{1}{1\,.\,2} \frac{d^2[\varphi(x)^2\, e^{-x}]}{dx^2} + \ldots$$

As the third term may be already neglected, we have:

$$e^{-x} + \frac{d[\varphi(x)\, e^{-x}]}{dx} = e^{-x} + \frac{\alpha\beta}{\sin z^2}[2e^{-2x} - e^{-x}] + f(1-x)\, e^{-x} - 2f[2e^{-2x} - e^{-x}].$$

If we multiply these terms by $\frac{\alpha}{1-\alpha} \frac{\sin z}{\sqrt{\cos z^2 + \frac{2\sin z^2}{\beta} x}}$ and integrate them with respect to x between the limits 0 and ∞, we find again according to the formulae (9) and 10) in No. 8 of the introduction:

$$\delta\zeta = \frac{\alpha}{1-\alpha}\sqrt{2\beta} \left\{ \begin{aligned} &\psi(1) \\ &+ \frac{\alpha\beta}{\sin z^2}\left[2^{\frac{1}{2}}\psi(2) - \psi(1)\right] - 2f\left[2^{\frac{1}{2}}\psi(2) - \psi(1)\right] \\ &\qquad + f\left[(\tfrac{1}{2} + T^2)\,\psi(1) - \frac{T}{2}\right] \end{aligned} \right\} \quad (l)$$

$$\text{where} \quad T = \text{cotang}\, z \sqrt{\frac{\beta}{2}}\,.$$

The higher terms are complicated, but already the next term is so small on account of the numerical values of $\alpha\beta$

and f that it can be neglected. For we have for the horizon, where the term is the greatest, putting $2f - \alpha\beta = g$

$$\frac{d^2\,(\varphi(x)^2\,e^{-x})}{dx} = f^2 x^2 e^{-x} - (4f^2 + 2fg) x e^{-x} + 8fg x e^{-2x} + (2f^2 + g^2 + 4fg) e^{-x}$$
$$- (8fg + 8g^2) e^{-2x} + 9g^2 e^{-3x}.$$

If we divide each term by $\sqrt{\frac{2x}{\beta}}$ and integrate it between the limits s and ∞ we find, applying the formulae for $\Gamma(\frac{1}{2})$, $\Gamma(\frac{3}{2})$ etc. given in No. 16 of the introduction:

$$\frac{\alpha}{1-\alpha}\frac{\sqrt{\pi}}{2}\sqrt{\frac{\beta}{2}}\,[\tfrac{3}{4}f^2 - 3fg\,(\sqrt{2}-1) + g^2\,(1 - 2\sqrt{2} + 3\sqrt{3})]$$

and if we substitute here the numerical values, which are given in No. 10, we find that the greatest value of this term, which occurs in the horizon, is 2″.11. The next term gives only 0″.18. In the differential equation (g) in No. 6 we have also neglected the second term, as it is small and amounts to about half a second in the horizon. As the sign of the latter term is negative, we shall not commit an error greater than 1″.5 if we compute the horizontal refraction from formula (l).

10. The numerical computation of the refraction from formula (k) or (l) can be made without any difficulty, as the values of the functions ψ can be taken from the tables or can be computed by the methods given in No. 17 of the introduction.

According to Bessel the constant quantity α at the temperature of 50^0 Fahrenheit and for the height of the barometer of 29.6 English inches, reduced to the normal temperature, is

$$\alpha = 57''.4994, \text{ hence } \log\frac{\alpha}{1-\alpha} = 1.759785$$

and $h = 116865.8$ toises.

As we have $l_0 = 4226.05$ toises, we find, if we take according to Bessel for a the radius of curvature for Greenwich to 3269805 toises:

$$\beta = 745.747, \text{ hence } \log\frac{\alpha}{1-\alpha}\sqrt{2\beta} = 3.347295$$

If we wish to compute for instance the refraction for the zenith distance 80^0, we have in this case $\log T_1 = 0.53210$ etc. and we find:

	$\log n^{\frac{1}{2}(2n-3)}$	$\log \frac{1}{(n-1)!}\left(\frac{\alpha\beta}{\sin z^2}\right)^{n-1}$	$\log \psi(n)$	$\log e^{-n\frac{\alpha\beta}{\sin z^2}}$
$n=1$	0.00000	0.00000	9.14983	9.90691
$n=2$	0.15051	9.33113	9.00745	9.81382
$n=3$	0.71568	8.36122	8.92228	9.72073
$n=4$	1.50515	7.21523	8.86128	9.62763
$n=5$	2.44640	5.94430	8,81372	9.53454
$n=6$	3.5017	4.57645	8.77473	9.44145
$n=7$	4.6480	3.12943	8.74168	9.34836
$n=8$	5.8701	1.6155	8.7130	9.2553
$n=9$	7.157	0.043	8.688	9.162
$n=10$	8.500	8.420	8.665	9.069

The horizontal rows give the terms within the parenthesis in formula (k) and if we multiply their sum by the constant quantity $\frac{\alpha}{1-\alpha}\sqrt{2\beta}$, we find 314″.91 exactly in confoımity with Bessel's tables.

Far more simple is the computation of Ivory's formula. In this case we have:

$$\log \alpha\beta = 9.333826, \quad \log \frac{\alpha}{1-\alpha}\sqrt{2\beta} = 3.354594, \ f = \tfrac{2}{9}.$$

If we now compute the refraction according to formula (l), we have:

$$\log T_1 = 0.540098 \qquad \log T_2 = 0.690613$$
$$\log \psi(1) = 9.142394 \quad \log \psi(2) = 8.999757$$

and with this the terms independent of f give 315″.32, whilst the terms multiplied by f give — 0″.12. The refraction is therefore 315″.20 or nearly the same as Bessel's value. The refractions according to the two formulae continue to agree about as far as 86° and represent the observed refractions well. But nearer to the horizon Bessel's refractions are too great, while those computed by Ivory's theory are too small. It is therefore best, to determine the refraction for such great zenith distances from observations and to compute tables from those observed values, as Bessel has done.

We find the horizontal refraction according to Bessel, as we have in this case:

$$\psi(r) = \int_0^\infty e^{-t^2}\,dt = \tfrac{1}{2}\sqrt{\pi}$$

$$\delta z = \frac{\alpha}{1-\alpha}\sqrt{\frac{\beta}{2}}\sqrt{\pi}\left[e^{-\alpha\beta} + \alpha\beta\,.\,2^{\frac{1}{2}}\,.\,e^{-2\alpha\beta} + \frac{\alpha^2\beta^2}{1.2}3^{\frac{3}{2}}\,e^{-3\alpha\beta} + \ldots\right]$$

and substituting here the numerical values we get 36′ 5″.

According to Ivory we find the horizontal refraction:

$$\delta z = \frac{\alpha}{1-\alpha} \sqrt{\pi} \, . \sqrt{\frac{\beta}{2}} \, [1 + \alpha\beta(\sqrt{2} - 1) - f(2\sqrt{2} - \tfrac{5}{2})]$$
$$= 33' \, 58'',$$

whilst the observations give 34′ 50″, a value which is nearly the mean of the two.

As long as the zenith distance is not too great, it is not necessary to use the rigorous formulae (k) and (l), but it is more convenient, to develop them into series. If we substitute in formula (l) for $\psi(1)$ and $\psi(2)$ the series found in No. 17 of the introduction and observe that $\frac{1}{\sin z^2} = 1 + \operatorname{cotg} z^2$, we find: *)

$$\delta z = \frac{\alpha}{1-\alpha}\Big[(1+\tfrac{1}{2}\alpha)\operatorname{tang} z - \Big(\frac{1}{\beta} - \tfrac{1}{2}\alpha + \tfrac{9}{4}\frac{\alpha}{\beta}\Big)\operatorname{tang} z^3 + \Big(\frac{3}{\beta^2} - \tfrac{9}{4}\frac{\alpha}{\beta}$$
$$+ \frac{105}{8}\frac{\alpha}{\beta^2}\Big)\operatorname{tang} z^5 - \Big(\frac{15}{\beta^3} - \frac{105}{8}\frac{\alpha}{\beta^2} + \frac{1575}{16}\frac{\alpha}{\beta^3}\Big)\operatorname{tang} z^7 + \ldots\Big] \quad (l_1)$$

or if we substitute the numerical values:

$$\delta z = [1.759845] \operatorname{tang} z - [8.821943] \operatorname{tang} z^3 + [6.383727] \operatorname{tang} z^5 - [4.180257] \operatorname{tang} z^7,$$

where the figures enclosed in brackets are logarithms.

Furthermore the terms multiplied by f give:

$$-\frac{\alpha}{1-\alpha} f \Big\{\frac{3}{2\beta^2}\operatorname{tang} z^5 - \frac{75}{4\beta^3}\operatorname{tang} z^7 - \frac{1785}{8\beta^4}\operatorname{tang} z^9 - \frac{46305}{16\beta^5}\operatorname{tang} z^{11}\Big\}$$

or (l_2)

$$-\Big\{[5.506187] \operatorname{tang} z^5 - [3.714510] \operatorname{tang} z^7 + [1.901468] \operatorname{tang} z^9 - [9.018568] \operatorname{tang} z^{11}\Big\}$$

For 75° we find from the series $\delta z = 211''.39$ and the part depending on f equal to $-0''.02$, hence the refraction equal to 211″.37 in conformity with the rigorous formula.

---

*) For we get:

$$\sqrt{2\beta}\,\psi(1) = \operatorname{tang} z - \frac{1}{\beta}\operatorname{tang} z^3 + \frac{3}{\beta^2}\operatorname{tang} z^5 - \frac{15}{\beta^3}\operatorname{tang} z^7 + \frac{105}{\beta^4}\operatorname{tang} z^9 - \ldots$$

$$2^{\frac{1}{2}}\sqrt{2\beta}\,\psi(2) = \operatorname{tang} z - \frac{1}{2\beta}\operatorname{tang} z^3 + \frac{3}{4\beta^2}\operatorname{tang} z^5 - \frac{15}{8\beta^3}\operatorname{tang} z^7 + \frac{105}{16\beta^4}\operatorname{tang} z^9 - \ldots$$

Ivory gives in the Phil. Transactions for 1823 another series, which can be used for all zenith distances.

11. The above formulae give the refraction for any zenith distance but only for a certain density of the air, namely that, which occurs when the temperature is 50^0 Fahrenheit and the height of the barometer 29.6 English inches. The refraction which belongs to this normal state of the atmosphere is called the *mean refraction.* In order to find from this the refraction for any other temperature τ and height of the barometer b, we must examine, how the refraction is changed, when the density of the atmosphere or the stand of the meteorological instruments, upon which it depends, changes. Let ε be the expansion of air for one degree of Fahrenheit's thermometer, for which Bessel deduced the following value:

$$\varepsilon = 0.0020243$$

from astronomical observations. If we take now a volume of air at the temperature of 50^0 as unit, the same volume at the temperature τ will be $1 + \varepsilon(\tau - 50)$, hence the density of the air when the thermometer is τ is to the density when the thermometer is 50 as $1 : 1 + \varepsilon(\tau - 50)$. We know further from Mariotte's law, that the density of the air when the barometer is b is to the density when the barometer is 29.6 as $b : 29.6$. If we therefore denote the density of the air when the thermometer is τ and the barometer is b by ϱ, and the density in the normal state of the atmosphere by ϱ_0, we have:

$$\varrho = \frac{\varrho_0 \dfrac{b}{29.6}}{1 + \varepsilon(\tau - 50)}$$

and as the quantity α which occurs in the formulae for the refraction may be considered as being proportional to the density, at least for so small changes of the density as we take into consideration, we should deduce also the true refraction from the mean refraction by the formula:

$$\delta z' = \frac{\delta z \, . \dfrac{b}{29.6}}{1 + \varepsilon(\tau - 50)}$$

if α did occur only as a factor, as the quantity $1 - \alpha$ in the divisor can be considered as constant on account of the smallness of α. But α occurs also in the factor of $\frac{\alpha}{1 - \alpha}$, which

shall be denoted by Z and the quantity β varies also with the temperature, as it depends on l_0 or when the temperature is τ upon
$$l = l_0\,[1 + \varepsilon\,(\tau - 50)]$$
if we denote the height of an atmosphere of uniform density at the temperature τ by l. We find therefore the true refraction from the following formula:

$$\delta z' = \frac{\delta z}{1+\varepsilon(\tau - 50)} \cdot \frac{b}{29.6} + \frac{\alpha}{1-\alpha} \cdot \frac{dZ}{d\tau}(\tau - 50) + \frac{\alpha}{1-\alpha}\,\frac{dZ}{db}(b - 29.6), \quad (m)$$

but as the influence of the last two terms is small we may take for the sake of convenience:

$$\delta z' = \frac{\delta z}{[1+\varepsilon\,(\tau - 50)]^{1+p}} \cdot \left(\frac{b}{29.6}\right)^{1+q}. \quad (m_1)$$

But if we develop this we find, neglecting the squares and higher powers as well as the products of p and q:

$$\delta z' = \frac{\delta z \,.\, \frac{b}{29.6}}{1+\varepsilon\,(\tau - 50)} \left\{1 - \varepsilon p\,(\tau - 50) + q\left(\frac{b}{29.6} - 1\right)\right\}, \quad (n)$$

Thus we obtain from the formulae (m) and (n) the following equations for determining p and q:

$$p = -\frac{\alpha}{1-\alpha} \cdot \frac{dZ}{d\tau} \cdot \frac{1}{\varepsilon\,.\,\delta z}$$
$$q = +\frac{\alpha}{1-\alpha} \cdot \frac{dZ}{db} \cdot \frac{29.6}{\delta z}, \quad (o)$$

if we take in the second member δz instead of $\delta z \,.\, \frac{\frac{b}{29.6}}{1+\varepsilon\,(\tau - 50)}$.

The moisture diminishes also the density of the atmosphere and hence the refractive power, but, as Laplace has observed first, this decrease is almost entirely compensated by the greater refractive power of aqueous vapour. The quantity α therefore is hardly changed by the moisture and as the effect upon the quantities p and q is very small, we shall pay no regard to the moisture in computing the refraction.

In order to obtain the expressions for p and q, we must find the differential coefficients $\frac{dZ}{dt}$ and $\frac{dZ}{db}$, but we shall deduce these values only for Ivory's theory, as the deduction from Bessel's formula is very similar. According to formula (l) we have:

$$Z = \sqrt{2\beta}\,[(1-\lambda)\,\psi(1) + \lambda\sqrt{2}\,\psi(2) + f\,Q],$$

taking $\frac{\alpha\beta}{\sin z^2} = \lambda$. From this we obtain:

$$dZ = \tfrac{1}{2} \cdot \frac{\delta z\,(1-\alpha)}{\alpha} \frac{d\beta}{\beta} + \sqrt{2\beta}\,\lambda\,[\sqrt{2}\,\psi(2) - \psi(1)] \frac{d\lambda}{\lambda}$$
$$+ d\beta\sqrt{2\beta}\left\{(1-\lambda)\frac{d\psi(1)}{d\beta} + \lambda\sqrt{2}\frac{d\psi(2)}{d\beta}\right\} + f\frac{dQ}{d\beta}, \qquad (p)$$

as f does not change with the temperature and the stand of the barometer.

Now we have $\psi(1) = e^{-T_1^2}\int_{T_1}^{\infty} e^{-t^2}\,dt$, where $T_1 = \operatorname{cotg} z \sqrt{\frac{\beta}{2}}$,

$$\psi(2) = e^{-T_2^2}\int_{T_2}^{\infty} e^{-t^2}\,dt, \text{ where } T_2 = \operatorname{cotg} z \sqrt{\beta},$$

and as $\frac{d\psi(1)}{dT_1} = 2\,T_1\psi(1) - 1$ and $\frac{d\psi(2)}{dT_2} = 2T_2\psi(2) - 1$,

the last but one term in (p) becomes:

$$+\frac{d\beta}{\beta} \cdot \sqrt{2\beta}\,[(1-\lambda)(T_1^{\,2}\,\psi(1) - \tfrac{1}{2}\,T_1) + \lambda\sqrt{2}\,.\,(T_2^{\,2}\,\psi(2) - \tfrac{1}{2}\,T_2)].$$

The factor Q consists of two terms, the first of which having the factor -2 is equal to the factor of λ in the expression of δz. We therefore embrace this in the latter term by writing $\lambda - 2f$ instead of λ. There remains then only the following term

$$+f\sqrt{2\beta}\,[(\tfrac{1}{2} + T_1^{\,2})\,\psi(1) - \tfrac{1}{2}\,T_1]$$

and as we find differentiating it:

$$\frac{d\beta}{\beta}\sqrt{2\beta}\,.\,f\left\{\frac{T_1}{4} + (\tfrac{3}{2} + T_1^{\,2})(T_1^{\,2}\,\psi(1) - \tfrac{1}{2}\,T_1)\right\},$$

the complete expression for dZ becomes:

$$dZ = \tfrac{1}{2}\frac{d\beta}{\beta} \cdot \frac{\delta z(1-\alpha)}{\alpha} + \frac{d\lambda}{\lambda}\sqrt{2\beta}\,.\,\lambda\,[\sqrt{2}\,\psi(2) - \psi(1)]$$
$$+\frac{d\beta}{\beta}\sqrt{2\beta}\left\{f\frac{T_1}{4} + (1-\lambda+\tfrac{7}{2}f+fT_1^{\,2})(T_1^{\,2}\psi(1) - 1)\right.$$
$$\left.+\sqrt{2}\,(\lambda - 2f)(T_2^{\,2}\,\psi(2) - \tfrac{1}{2}\,T_2)\right\}.$$

As we have:

$$\alpha + d\alpha = \frac{\alpha\frac{b}{29.6}}{1+\varepsilon\,(\tau-50)}, \text{ hence } 1 + \frac{d\alpha}{\alpha} = \left(1 - \frac{29.6 - b}{29.6}\right)[1 - \varepsilon\,(\tau - 50)],$$

$$\text{we find: } \frac{d\alpha}{\alpha} = \frac{b - 29.6}{29.6} - \varepsilon\,(\tau - 50),$$

and likewise:

$$\beta + d\beta = \frac{a}{l_0} - \frac{a}{l_0}\,\varepsilon\,(\tau - 50), \quad \text{hence } \frac{d\beta}{\beta} = -\,\varepsilon\,(\tau - 50);$$

finally we have:

$$\lambda = \frac{\alpha\beta}{\sin z^2}, \quad \text{hence } \frac{d\lambda}{\lambda} = \frac{d\alpha}{\alpha} + \frac{d\beta}{\beta} = \frac{b - 29.6}{29.6} - 2\,\varepsilon\,(\tau - 50).$$

We find therefore:

$$\delta z\,.\,q = \frac{\alpha}{1-\alpha}\sqrt{2\beta}\,.\,\lambda\,[\sqrt{2}\,\psi(2) - \psi(1)]$$

$$\delta z\,.\,p = \tfrac{1}{2}\,\delta z + \frac{\alpha}{1-\alpha}\sqrt{2\beta}\,.\,2\,\lambda\,[\sqrt{2}\,\psi(2) - \psi(1)] \qquad (q)$$

$$+ \frac{\alpha}{1-\alpha}\sqrt{2\beta}\left\{\frac{T_1}{18} + (\tfrac{16}{9} - \lambda + \tfrac{2}{9}\,T_1{}^2)\,(T_1{}^2\,\psi(1) - \tfrac{1}{2}\,T_1)\right.$$

$$\left. + (\lambda - \tfrac{4}{9})\,(T_2{}^2\,\psi(2) - \tfrac{1}{2}\,T_2)\sqrt{2}\right\},$$

where instead of f its value $\frac{2}{9}$ has been substituted.

If we compute from this p and q for $z = 87^0$, δz being $852''.79$ we find:

$\log T_1 = 0.013175$, $\log[\sqrt{2}\,\psi(2) - \psi(1)] = 8.605021$,
$\log(T_1{}^2\,\psi(1) - \frac{1}{2}\,T_1) = 9.081168_n$, $\log T_2 = 0.163690$,
$\log(T_2{}^2\,\psi(2) - \frac{1}{2}\,T_2)\sqrt{2} = 9.191771_n$ and with this
$\delta z\,.\,q = 19''.71$, $\delta z\,.\,p = 185''.36$,

hence:

$$q = 0.0231,$$
$$p = 0.2173.$$

When the zenith distance is not too great, we can find p and q also by the series given in No. 10. For differentiating the coefficients of $\frac{\alpha}{1-\alpha}$ in (l_1) and (l_2) with respect to α and β, we easily find the following series:

$$q\,\delta z = +\,[7.90399]\,\text{tang}\,z + [7.90146]\,\text{tang}\,z^3 - [5.66533]\,\text{tang}\,z^5 + [3.54172]\,\text{tang}\,z^7 - \ldots$$

$$p\,\delta z = +\,[7.90399]\,\text{tang}\,z + [8.91567]\,\text{tang}\,z^3 - [6.70990]\,\text{tang}\,z^5 + [4.56712]\,\text{tang}\,z^7 - \ldots,$$

where the coefficients are again logarithms.

For $z = 75^0$ for instance we find from this $q = 0.0020$ and $p = 0.0188$.

12. For the complete computation of the true refraction from formula (m_1), we must know the height of the barometer reduced to the normal temperature. If we take the length of the column of mercury at the temperature 50^0 as unit and denote the expansion of mercury from the freezing to the boiling point equal to $\frac{1}{55.5}$ by q, the stand of the barometer observed at the temperature t*) is to the stand, which would have been observed if the temperature had been 50^0 as $1 + \frac{q}{180}(t - 50) : 1$, or the length of the column of mercury reduced to the temperature 50 is:

$$b_{50} = b_t \frac{180}{180 + q(t - 50)}.$$

If further s is the expansion of the scale of the barometer from the freezing to the boiling point, s being 0.0018782 if the scale is of brass, we have taking again the length of the scale at the temperature 50^0 as unit:

$$b_t : b_{50} = 1 : 1 + \frac{s}{180}(t - 50).$$

Hence the height b_t of the barometer observed at the temperature t, is reduced to 50^0, taking account of the expansion of the mercury and the scale, by the formula:

$$b_{50} = b_t \frac{180 + s(t - 50)}{180 + q(t - 50)}.$$

The normal length of an English inch is however not referred to the temperature 50^0 but to the temperature 62^0; hence the stand of the barometer observed at the temperature 50^0 is measured on a scale which is too small, we must therefore divide the value b_{50} by $1 + \frac{12s}{180}$, so that finally we get:

$$b_{50} = b_t \frac{180 + s(t - 50)}{180 + q(t - 50)} \cdot \frac{180}{180 + 12s}.$$

If the scale is divided according to Paris lines and the thermometer is one of Réaumur, we should get, as the normal temperature of the French inch is 13^0 R. and we have 50^0 Fahr. $= 8^0$ Réaum.:

$$b_8 = b_t \frac{80 + s(t - 8)}{80 + q(t - 8)} \cdot \frac{80}{80 + 5s}.$$

This embraces every thing necessary for computing formula (m_1). If we denote by f the temperature according to

---

*) The temperature t is observed at a thermometer attached to the barometer, which is called the interior thermometer, whilst the other thermometer used for observing the temperature of the atmosphere is called the exterior thermometer.

Fahrenheit's thermometer, by r the same according to Réaumur's thermometer, by $b^{(e)}$ and $b^{(l)}$ the height of the barometer expressed in English inches and Paris lines and if we put:

$$B = \frac{b^{(e)}}{29.6} \frac{180}{180+12s} = \frac{b^{(l)}}{333.28} \cdot \frac{80}{80+5s}$$

$$T = \frac{180+s(f-50)}{180+q(f-50)} = \frac{80+s(r-8)}{80+q(r-8)}$$

$$\gamma = \frac{1}{1+\varepsilon\,.\,(f-50)} = \frac{1}{1+\frac{9}{4}\varepsilon(r-8)},$$

and give to the mean refraction the form $\delta z = a \operatorname{tang} z$, we have:

$$\delta z' = a \operatorname{tang} z \,.\, \gamma^{1+p} (B\,.\,T)^{1+q} \qquad (A)$$

hence $\log \delta z' = \log a + \log \operatorname{tang} z + (1+p) \log \gamma + (1+q)(\log B + \log T)$.

If we have then tables, from which we take $\log a$, $1+p$ and $1+q$ for any zenith distance, and $\log B$, $\log T$ and $\log \gamma$ for any stand of the barometer and any height of the interior and exterior thermometer, the computation of the true refraction for any zenith distance is rendered very easy. This form, which perhaps is the most convenient, has been adopted by Bessel for his tables of refraction in his work Tabulae Regiomontanae.

13. The hypothesis which we have made in deducing the formulae of refraction, namely that the atmosphere consists of concentric strata, whose density diminishes with the elevation above the surface according to a certain law, can never represent the true state of the atmosphere on account of several causes which continually disturb the state of equilibrium. The values of the refraction as found by theory must therefore generally deviate from the observed values and represent only the mean of a large number of them, as they are true only for a mean state of the atmosphere. Bessel has compared the refractions given by his tables with the observations and has thus determined the probable error of the refraction for observations made at different zenith distances. According to the table given in the introduction to the Tab. Reg. pag. LXIII these probable errors are at $45^0 \pm 0''.27$, at $81^0 \pm 1''$, at $85^0 \pm 1''.7$, at $89^0\,30' \pm 20''$. We thus see, that especially in the neighbourhood of the horizon we can only expect, that a mean obtained from a great many observations made at very different states of the atmosphere may be considered as free from the effect of refraction.

For zenith distances not exceeding 80^0 it is almost indifferent, what hypothesis we adopt for the decrease of the density of the atmosphere with the elevation above the surface of the earth and the real advantage of a theory which is founded upon the true law consists only in this, that the refractions very near the horizon as well as the coefficients $1+p$ and $1+q$ are found with greater accuracy, hence the reduction of the mean refraction to the true refraction can be made more accurately. Even the simple hypothesis, adopted by Cassini, of an atmosphere of uniform density, when the light is refracted once at the upper limit, represents the mean refractions for zenith distances not exceeding 80^0 quite well. In this case we have simply according to the formulae in No. 6:

$$\sin i = \mu_0 \sin f,$$

or as we have now $i = f + \delta z$:

$$\delta z = (\mu_0 - 1) \operatorname{tang} f,$$

and since we have also, as is easily seen, $\sin f = \frac{a}{a+l} \sin z$, where l is the height of the atmosphere, we get:

$$\delta z = (\mu_0 - 1) \frac{\sin z}{\sqrt{\cos z^2 + \frac{2l}{a}}} = (\mu_0 - 1) \operatorname{tang} z \left(1 - \frac{l}{a} \frac{1}{\cos z^2}\right).$$

If we take now for $\mu_0 - 1$ the value 57″.717, we find for the refraction at the zenith distances 45^0, 75^0 and 80^0 the values 57″.57, 211″.37, 314″.14, whilst according to Ivory they are 57″.45, 211″.37 and 315″.20. But beyond this the error increases very rapidly and the horizontal refraction is only about 19′.

The equation (*f*) in No. 6 can be integrated very easily, if we adopt the following relation between s and r:

$$1 - s = \left[1 - 2\alpha\left(1 - \frac{\varrho}{\varrho_0}\right)\right]^m.$$

For if we introduce a new variable, given by the equation:

$$\left[1 - 2\alpha\left(1 - \frac{\varrho}{\varrho_0}\right)\right]^{\frac{2m-1}{2}} \sin z = w,$$

the equation (f) becomes simply:

$$d\zeta' = -\frac{dw}{(2m-1)\sqrt{1-w^2}}:$$

therefore if we integrate and substitute the limits $w = \sin z$ and $w = (1-2\alpha)^{\frac{2m-1}{2}} \sin z$, we find:

$$\delta z = \frac{1}{2m-1}\left[z - \text{arc} \sin (1-2\alpha)^{\frac{2m-1}{2}} \sin z\right],$$

or:

$$\sin [z-(2m-1)\,\delta z] = (1-2\alpha)^{\frac{2m-1}{2}} \sin z,$$

for which we may write for brevity:

$$M \sin z = \sin [z - N\delta z].$$

This is Simpson's formula for refraction by which the refractions for zenith distances not exceeding 85^0 may be represented very well, if the coefficients M and N are suitably determined.

If we add to the last equation the identical equation $\sin z = \sin z$ and also subtract it, we easily find two equations from which we obtain dividing one by the other:

$$\text{tang}\left(\frac{N}{2}\,\delta z\right) = \frac{1-M}{1+M} \text{tang}\left[z - \frac{N}{2}\,\delta z\right],$$

or $$\text{tang}\,(A\,.\,\delta z) = B\;\text{tang}\,[z - A\,.\,\delta z],$$

which is Bradley's formula for refraction.

14. As the altitude of the stars is increased by the refraction, we can see them on account of it, when they really are beneath the horizon. The stars rise therefore earlier and set later on account of the refraction.

We have in general:

$$\cos z = \sin \varphi \sin \delta + \cos \varphi \cos \delta \cos t \qquad (r)$$

from which follows:

$$\sin z\, dz = \cos \varphi \cos \delta \sin t\,.\,dt$$

hence if the object is in the horizon:

$$dt = \frac{dz}{\cos \varphi \cos \delta \sin t}.$$

As in this case dz is the horizontal refraction or equal to $35'$, we find for the variation of the hour angle at the rising or setting:

$$dt = \frac{140^s}{\cos \varphi \cos \delta \sin t}.$$

In No. 20 of the first section we found for Arcturus and the latitude of Berlin:

$$t_0 = 7^h\ 42^m\ 40^s$$

and as we have $\delta = 19^0\ 54'.5$, $\varphi = 52^0\ 30'.3$, we find:

$$\Delta t_0 = 4^m\ 37^s.$$

Arcturus rises therefore so much earlier and sets so much later. We can compute also directly the hour angle at the rising or setting with regard to refraction, if we take in the last formula (r) $z = 90^0\ 35'$. We have then:

$$\cos t = \frac{\cos z - \sin \varphi \sin \delta}{\cos \varphi \cos \delta}$$

and adding 1 to both members, we find the following convenient formula:

$$\cos \tfrac{1}{2} t = \sqrt{\frac{\cos \frac{1}{2}(\varphi + \delta + z) \cos \frac{1}{2}(\varphi + \delta - z)}{\cos \varphi \cos \delta}}.$$

If we subtract both members from 1, we obtain a similar formula:

$$\sin \tfrac{1}{2} t = \sqrt{\frac{\sin \frac{1}{2}(z + \varphi - \delta) \sin \frac{1}{2}(z + \delta - \varphi)}{\cos \varphi \cos \delta}}.$$

In the case of the moon we must take into account besides the refraction her parallax, which increases the zenith distance and hence makes the time of rising later, that of setting earlier. The method of computing them has been given already in No. 20 of the first section and shall here only be explained by an example.

For 1861 July 15 we have the following declinations and horizontal parallaxes of the moon for Greenwich mean time.

	δ		p
July 15 0^h	-15^0 32.1		59 13
		2 19.4	
12^h	17 51.5		59 15
		2 4.1	
16 0^h	19 55.6		59 14
		1 46.4	
12^h	21 42.0		59 13

It is required to find the time of setting for Greenwich. According to No. 19 of the first section, where the mean time of the upper and lower culmination was found, we have:

Lunar time	Mean time	
0^h	$6^h\ 16^m.7$	
		12 27.5.
12^h	$18^h\ 44^m.2$	

If we take now an approximate value of the declination $-17^0\,51'.5$ we find with $\varphi = 51^0\,28'.6$ and $z = 89^0\,35'.8$, $t = 4^h\,21^m.5$ and the mean time corresponding to this lunar time $10^h\,48^m$. If we interpolate for this time the declination of the moon, we find $-17^0\,38'.2$ and repeating with this the former computation, we find the hour angle equal to $4^h\,22^m.9$, hence the mean time of setting $10^h\,49^m.6$.

15. The effect of the atmosphere on the light produces besides the refraction the twilight. For as the sun sets later for the higher strata of the atmosphere than for an observer at the surface of the earth, these strata are still illuminated after sunset and the light reflected from them causes the twilight. According to the observations the sun ceases to illuminate any portions of the atmosphere which are above the horizon when he is about 18^0 below the horizon. Thus the moment, when the sun reaches the zenith distance 108^0 is the beginning of the morning or the end of the evening twilight.

If we denote the zenith distance of the sun at the beginning or end of twilight by $90^0 + c$, by t_0 the hour angle at the time of rising or setting and by τ the duration of twilight, we have:

$$-\sin c = \sin\varphi \sin\delta + \cos\varphi \cos\delta \cos(t_0 + \tau)$$

hence:

$$\cos(t_0 + \tau) = -\frac{\sin\varphi \sin\delta + \sin c}{\cos\varphi \cos\delta}$$

or putting $H = 90^0 - \varphi + \delta$

$$\sin\tfrac{1}{2}(t_0 + \tau) = \sqrt{\frac{\sin\frac{1}{2}(H + c)\cos\frac{1}{2}(H - c)}{\cos\varphi\cos\delta}}$$

from which we can find τ after having computed t_0.

If we call Z' the point of the heavenly sphere, which at the time of sunset was at the zenith and by Z that point which is at the zenith at the end of twilight, we easily see that in the triangle between these two points and the pole the angle at the pole is equal to τ and we have:

$$\cos ZZ' = \sin\varphi^2 + \cos\varphi^2 \cos\tau.$$

But as we have in the triangle between those two points and the sun S, $ZS = 90 + c$, $Z'S = 90^0$, we have also calling the angle at the sun S:

$$\cos ZZ' = \cos c \cos S$$

and thus we find:

$$\sin \tfrac{1}{2} \tau^2 = \frac{1 - \cos c \,.\, \cos S}{2 \cos \varphi^2},$$

where S, as is easily seen, is the difference of the parallactic angles of the sun at the time of sunset and at the end of twilight. The equation shows, that τ is a minimum, when the angle S is zero, or when at the end of twilight the point, which was at the zenith at sunset, lies in the vertical circle of the sun. The two parallactic angles are therefore in that case equal.

The duration of the shortest twilight is thus given by the equation:

$$\sin \tfrac{1}{2} \tau = \frac{\sin \tfrac{1}{2} c}{\cos \varphi}$$

and as we have:

$$\cos p = \frac{\sin \varphi}{\sin \delta}, \quad \cos p' = \frac{\sin \varphi + \sin c \sin \delta}{\cos c \cos \delta},$$

we find:

$$\sin \delta = - \operatorname{tang} \tfrac{1}{2} c \sin \varphi,$$

from which equation we find the declination which the sun has on the day when the shortest twilight occurs.

If we denote the two azimuths of the sun at the time of sunset and when it reaches the zenith distance $90 + c$ by A and A', we have:

$$\cos \varphi \sin A = \cos \delta \sin p$$
$$\cos \varphi \sin A' = \cos \delta \sin p'.$$

Hence we have at the time of the shortest twilight $\sin A = \sin A'$ or the two azimuths are then the supplements of each other to 180^0.

From the two equations:

$$- \sin c = \sin \varphi \sin \delta + \cos \varphi \cos \delta \cos (t_0 + \tau)$$

and

$$0 = \sin \varphi \sin \delta + \cos \varphi \cos \delta \cos t_0$$

follows also:

$$\sin (t_0 + \tfrac{1}{2} \tau) \sin \tfrac{1}{2} \tau = \frac{\cos \tfrac{1}{2} c}{\cos \delta} \cdot \frac{\sin \tfrac{1}{2} c}{\cos \varphi},$$

If we take $c = 18^0$ we find for the latitude $\varphi = 81^0$ $\sin \frac{1}{2} \tau = 1$, hence the duration of the shortest twilight for that latitude is 12 hours. This occurs, when the declination of the sun is -9^0, the sun therefore is then in the horizon at noon and 18^0 below at midnight. But we cannot speak any more of the shortest twilight, as the sun only when it has this certain declination fulfills the two conditions, that it comes in the horizon and reaches also a depression of 18^0 below the horizon; for if the south declination is greater the sun remains below the horizon and if the south declination is less it never descends 18^0 below the horizon.

At still greater latitudes there is no case when we can speak of the shortest twilight in the above sense and hence the formula for $\sin \frac{1}{2} \tau$ becomes impossible.

Note. Consult: on refraction: Laplace Mécanique Céleste Livre X. — Bessel Fundamenta Astronomiae pag. 26 et seq. — Ivory in Philosophical Transactions for 1823 and 1838. — Bruhns in his work: Die Astronomische Strahlenbrechung has given a compilation of all the different theories.

III. THE ABERRATION.

16. As the velocity of the earth in her orbit round the sun has a finite ratio to the velocity of light, we do not see the stars on account of the motion of the earth in the direction, in which they really are, but we see them a little displaced in the direction, towards which the earth is moving. We will distinguish two moments of time t and t' at which the ray of light coming from an unmoveable object (fixed star) strikes in succession the object-glass and the eye-piece of a telescope (or the lense and the nerve of the eye). The positions of the object-glass and of the eye-piece in space at the time t shall be a and b, and at the time t' a' and b' Fig. 5. Then the line ab' represents the real direction of the ray of light, whilst ab or $a'b'$, both being parallel on account of the infinite distance of the fixed stars, gives us the direction of the apparent place, which is observed. The angle between the two directions $b'a$ and ba is called the *annual aberration* of the fixed stars.

Fig. 5.

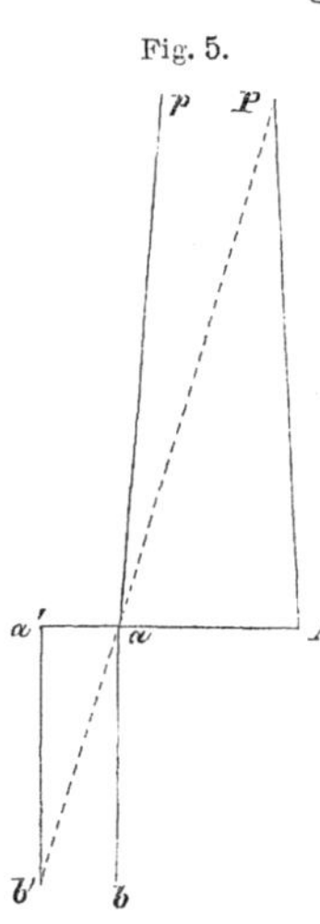

Let x, y, z be the rectangular co-ordinates of the eye-piece b at the time t, referred to a certain unmoveable point in space; then:

$$x + \frac{dx}{dt}(t' - t),\quad y + \frac{dy}{dt}(t' - t) \text{ and } z + \frac{dz}{dt}(t' - t)$$

are the co-ordinates of the eye-piece at the time t', since during the interval $t' - t$ we may consider the motion of the earth to be linear. If the relative co-ordinates of the object-glass with respect to the eye-piece are denoted by ξ, η and ζ, the co-ordinates of the object-glass at the time t, when the light enters it, are $x + \xi$, $y + \eta$, $z + \zeta$.

If we now take as the plane of the x and y the plane of the equator and the other two planes vertical to it, so that the plane of the x, z passes through the equinoctial, the plane of y, z through the solstitial points; if we further denote by α and δ the right ascension and declination of that point in which the real direction of the ray of light intersects the celestial sphere and by μ the velocity of light, then will the latter in the time $t' - t$ describe a space whose projections on the three co-ordinate axes are:

$$\mu(t' - t)\cos\delta\cos\alpha,\quad \mu(t' - t)\cos\delta\sin\alpha,\quad \mu(t' - t)\sin\delta.$$

Denoting further the length of the telescope by l and by α' and δ' the right ascension and declination of the point towards which the telescope is directed, we have for the co-ordinates of the object-glass with respect to the eye-piece, which are observed:

$$\xi = l\cos\delta'\cos\alpha',\quad \eta = l\cos\delta'\sin\alpha',\quad \zeta = l\sin\delta'.$$

Now the true direction of the ray of light is given by the co-ordinates of the object-glass at the time t:

$$\begin{aligned} &l\cos\delta'\cos\alpha' + x,\\ &l\cos\delta'\sin\alpha' + y,\\ &l\sin\delta' \qquad\quad + z, \end{aligned}$$

and by the co-ordinates of the eye-piece at the time t':

$$\begin{aligned} &x + \frac{dx}{dt}(t' - t),\\ &y + \frac{dy}{dt}(t' - t),\\ &z + \frac{dz}{dt}(t' - t). \end{aligned}$$

We have therefore the following equation if we denote $\frac{l}{t'-t}$ by L:

$$\mu \cos\delta \cos\alpha = L \cos\delta' \cos\alpha' - \frac{dx}{dt},$$
$$\mu \cos\delta \sin\alpha = L \cos\delta' \sin\alpha' - \frac{dy}{dt},$$
$$\mu \sin\delta = L \sin\delta' \qquad - \frac{dz}{dt}.$$

We easily derive from these equations the following:

$$\frac{L}{\mu} \cos\delta' \cos(\alpha' - \alpha) = \cos\delta + \frac{1}{\mu}\left\{\frac{dy}{dt}\sin\alpha + \frac{dx}{dt}\cos\alpha\right\},$$
$$\frac{L}{\mu} \cos\delta' \sin(\alpha' - \alpha) = \frac{1}{\mu}\left\{\frac{dy}{dt}\cos\alpha - \frac{dx}{dt}\sin\alpha\right\},$$

or:

$$\operatorname{tang}(\alpha' - \alpha) = \frac{\frac{1}{\mu}\sec\delta\left\{\frac{dy}{dt}\cos\alpha - \frac{dx}{dt}\sin\alpha\right\}}{1 + \frac{1}{\mu}\sec\delta\left\{\frac{dy}{dt}\sin\alpha + \frac{dx}{dt}\cos\alpha\right\}}.$$

We find a similar equation for $\operatorname{tang}(\delta' - \delta)$. If we develop both equations into series applying formula (14) in No. 11 of the introduction, we find, if we substitute in the formula for $\operatorname{tang}(\delta' - \delta)$ instead of $\operatorname{tang}\frac{1}{2}(\alpha' - \alpha)$ the value derived from $\alpha' - \alpha$ and omit the terms of the third order:

$$\alpha' - \alpha = -\frac{1}{\mu}\left\{\frac{dx}{dt}\sin\alpha - \frac{dy}{dt}\cos\alpha\right\}\sec\delta$$
$$+ \frac{1}{\mu^2}\left\{\frac{dx}{dt}\sin\alpha - \frac{dy}{dt}\cos\alpha\right\}\left\{\frac{dx}{dt}\cos\alpha + \frac{dy}{dt}\sin\alpha\right\}\sec\delta^2,$$

$$\delta' - \delta = -\frac{1}{\mu}\left\{\frac{dx}{dt}\sin\delta\cos\alpha + \frac{dy}{dt}\sin\delta\sin\alpha - \frac{dz}{dt}\cos\delta\right\}$$
$$- \frac{1}{2\mu^2}\left\{\frac{dx}{dt}\sin\alpha - \frac{dy}{dt}\cos\alpha\right\}^2 \operatorname{tang}\delta \qquad (a)$$
$$+ \frac{1}{\mu^2}\left\{\frac{dx}{dt}\cos\delta\cos\alpha + \frac{dy}{dt}\cos\delta\sin\alpha + \frac{dz}{dt}\sin\delta\right\}$$
$$\times\left\{\frac{dx}{dt}\sin\delta\cos\alpha + \frac{dy}{dt}\sin\delta\sin\alpha - \frac{dz}{dt}\cos\delta\right\}.$$

If we now refer the place of the earth to the centre of the sun by co-ordinates x, y in the plane of the ecliptic, taking the line from the centre of the sun to the point of the vernal equinox as the positive axis of x, and the positive axis of y perpendicular to it or directed to the point of the summer solstice and denoting the geocentric longitude of the sun by $\odot$, its distance from the earth by R, we have *):

$$x = -R\cos\odot,$$
$$y = -R\sin\odot.$$

If we refer these co-ordinates to the plane of the equator, retaining as the axis of x the line towards the point of the vernal equinox and imagining the axis of y in the plane of yz to be turned through the angle ε, equal to the obliquity of the ecliptic, we get:

$$x = -R\cos\odot,$$
$$y = -R\sin\odot\cos\varepsilon,$$
$$z = -R\sin\odot\sin\varepsilon,$$

and from this we find, since according to the formulae in No. 14 of the first section we have the longitude of the sun $\odot = \nu + \pi$ or equal to the true anomaly *plus* the longitude of the perihelion:

$$\frac{dx}{dt} = -\cos\odot\frac{dR}{dt} + R\sin\odot\frac{d\nu}{dt}$$
$$\frac{dy}{dt} = -\sin\odot\cos\varepsilon\frac{dR}{dt} - R\cos\odot\cos\varepsilon\frac{d\nu}{dt}$$
$$\frac{dz}{dt} = -\sin\odot\sin\varepsilon\frac{dR}{dt} - R\cos\odot\sin\varepsilon\frac{d\nu}{dt}.$$

But we have also according to the formulae in No. 14 of the first section:

$$d\nu = \frac{a\cos\varphi}{R}dE \text{ and as we have also } dE = \frac{a}{R}dM$$

we find:
$$\frac{d\nu}{dt} = \frac{a^2\cos\varphi}{R^2}\frac{dM}{dt}.$$

Further follows from the equation $R = \frac{p}{1+e\cos\nu}$ in connection with the last:

$$\frac{dR}{dt} = a\,\text{tang}\,\varphi\sin\nu\frac{dM}{dt}$$

and from this we get:

$$\frac{dx}{dt} = \frac{a}{\cos\varphi}\frac{dM}{dt}\left\{\sin\odot\frac{a^2\cos\varphi}{R} - \sin\varphi\sin\nu\cos\odot\right\}$$

hence observing that:

$$\frac{a^2\cos\varphi}{R} = 1 + \sin\varphi\cos\nu \text{ and } \odot - \nu = \pi,$$
$$\frac{dx}{dt} = \frac{a}{\cos\varphi}\frac{dM}{dt}[\sin\odot + \sin\varphi\sin\pi] \qquad (b)$$

---

*) As the heliocentric longitude of the earth is $180^0 + \odot$.

and
$$\frac{dy}{dt} = -\frac{a}{\cos\varphi}\cos\varepsilon\frac{dM}{dt}[\cos\odot + \sin\varphi\cos\pi] \qquad (b)$$
$$\frac{dz}{dt} = -\frac{a}{\cos\varphi}\sin\varepsilon\frac{dM}{dt}[\cos\odot + \sin\varphi\cos\pi].$$

If we substitute these expressions in the formulae (a), the constant terms dependent on π give in the expressions for the aberration also constant terms which change merely the mean places of the stars and therefore can be neglected. If we introduce also instead of μ the number k of seconds, in which the light traverses the semi-major axis of the earth's orbit, so that we have:

$$\frac{1}{\mu} = \frac{k}{a},$$

we find, taking only the terms of the first order:

$$\alpha' - \alpha = -\frac{k}{\cos\varphi}\frac{dM}{dt}[\cos\odot\cos\varepsilon\cos\alpha + \sin\odot\sin\alpha]\sec\delta$$
$$\delta' - \delta = +\frac{k}{\cos\varphi}\frac{dM}{dt}[\cos\odot(\sin\alpha\sin\delta\cos\varepsilon - \cos\delta\sin\varepsilon) - \cos\alpha\sin\delta\sin\odot].$$

The constant quantity $\frac{k}{\cos\varphi}\frac{dM}{dt}$ is called the constant of aberration, and since $\frac{dM}{dt}$ denotes the mean sidereal motion of the sun in a second of time, which is the unit of k, we are able to compute it, if besides the time in which the light traverses the semi-major axis of the earth's orbit is known. Delambre determined this time from the eclipses of Jupiter's satellites and thus found for the constant of aberration the value $20''.255$. Struve determined this constant latterly from the observations of the apparent places of the fixed stars and found $20''.4451$ and as we have $\frac{dM}{dt} = \frac{59'\,8''.19}{86400} = 0.0410670$ and $\cos\varphi = 9.999939$ we find from this for the time in which the light traverses the semi-major axis of the earth's orbit $497^s.78$ *).

We have therefore the following formulae for the annual aberration of the fixed stars in right ascension and declination:

---

*) According to Hansen the length of the sidereal year is 365 days 6 hours 9 minutes and 9,35 seconds or 365.2563582 days, hence the mean daily sidereal motion of the sun is $59'\,8''.193$.

$$\alpha' - \alpha = -20''.4451 \,[\cos \odot \cos \varepsilon \cos \alpha + \sin \odot \sin \alpha] \sec \delta$$
$$\delta' - \delta = +20''.4451 \cos \odot \,[\sin \alpha \sin \delta \cos \varepsilon - \cos \delta \sin \varepsilon] \qquad (A)$$
$$-20''.4451 \sin \odot \cos \alpha \sin \delta.$$

The terms of the second order are so small, that they can be neglected nearly in every case. We find these terms of the right ascension by introducing the values of the differential coefficients (*b*) into the second term of the formulae (*a*), as follows:

$$-\tfrac{1}{4} \frac{k^2}{\cos \varphi^2} \left(\frac{dM}{dt}\right)^2 \sec \delta^2 \,[\cos 2 \odot \sin 2 \alpha (1 + \cos \varepsilon^2) - 2 \sin 2 \odot \cos 2 \alpha \cos \varepsilon],$$

where the small term multiplied by $\sin 2 \alpha \sin \varepsilon^2$ has been omitted. For we find setting aside the constant factor:

$$2 \sin 2 \alpha \,[\cos \odot^2 \cos \varepsilon^2 - \sin \odot^2] - 2 \sin 2 \odot \cos \varepsilon \,[\cos \alpha^2 - \sin \alpha^2]$$

from which the above expression can be easily deduced. If we substitute the numerical values taking $\varepsilon = 23^0\, 28'$, we obtain:

$$\begin{aligned} &-0''.0009329 \sec \delta^2 \sin 2 \alpha \cos 2 \odot \\ &+0''.0009295 \sec \delta^2 \cos 2 \alpha \sin 2 \odot \end{aligned} \qquad (c).$$

As these terms amount to $\frac{1}{100}$ of a second of time only if the declination of the star is $85\frac{1}{2}{}^0$, they can always be neglected except for stars very near the pole.

The terms of the second order in declination, if we neglect all terms not multiplied by tang δ, are:

$$-\tfrac{1}{8} \frac{k^2}{\cos \varphi^2} \left(\frac{dM}{dt}\right)^2 \operatorname{tang} \delta \,[\cos 2 \odot (\cos 2 \alpha (1 + \cos \varepsilon^2) - \sin \varepsilon^2)$$
$$+ 2 \sin 2 \odot \sin 2 \alpha \cos \varepsilon].$$

For we find the term multiplied by tang δ, setting aside the constant factor:

$$\sin \odot^2 \sin \alpha^2 + \cos \odot^2 \cos \varepsilon^2 \cos \alpha^2 + \tfrac{1}{2} \sin 2 \odot \sin 2 \alpha \cos \varepsilon$$

and if we express here the squares of the sines and cosines by the sines and cosines of twice the angle and omit the constant terms $1 + \cos \varepsilon^2$ as well as the term $\cos 2 \alpha \sin \varepsilon^2$ we easily deduce the above expression. Substituting again the numerical values we find:

$$\begin{aligned} &+[0''.0000402 - 0''.0004665 \cos 2 \alpha] \operatorname{tang} \delta \cos 2 \odot \\ &-0''.0004648 \operatorname{tang} \delta \sin 2 \alpha \sin 2 \odot. \end{aligned} \qquad (d)$$

As these terms also do not amount to $\frac{1}{100}$ of a second of arc while the declination is less than $87^0\, 6'$, they are taken into account only for stars very near the pole.

In the formulae (*A*) for the aberration it is assumed, that α, δ and $\odot$ be referred to the apparent equinox and that ε is the apparent obliquity of the ecliptic. But in computing the aberration of a star for any long period it is convenient, to neglect the nutation and to refer α, δ and $\odot$ to the mean equinox and to take for ε the mean obliquity. In this case however the values of the aberration found in that way must be corrected. We find the expressions of these corrections by differentiating the formulae (A) with respect to α, δ, $\odot$ and ε and taking $d\alpha$, $d\delta$, $d\odot$ and $d\varepsilon$ equal to the nutation for these quantities. Of course it is only necessary to take the largest terms of the nutation and omitting in the correction of the right ascension all terms, which are not multiplied by $\sec\delta \,.\, \operatorname{tang}\delta$ and in declination all terms which are not multiplied by $\sin\delta \,.\, \operatorname{tang}\delta$, we easily see, since the increments $d\odot$ and $d\varepsilon$ do not produce any such terms, that we need only take the following:

$$d\alpha = -[6''.867 \sin \Omega \sin \alpha + 9''.223 \cos \Omega \cos \alpha] \operatorname{tang} \delta,$$
$$d\delta = -[6''.867 \sin \Omega \cos \alpha + 9''.223 \cos \Omega \sin \alpha].$$

Taking here $6''.867 = b$ and $9''.223 = a$, we find, if we substitute these quantities into the differentials of the equations (A):

$$\alpha' - \alpha = \operatorname{tang}\delta \sec\delta\, 10''.2225 \left\{ \begin{array}{l} -(b + a\cos\varepsilon) \sin 2\alpha \cos(\odot + \Omega) \\ +(b\cos\varepsilon + a) \cos 2\alpha \sin(\odot + \Omega) \\ +(b - a\cos\varepsilon) \sin 2\alpha \cos(\odot - \Omega) \\ -(b\cos\varepsilon - a) \cos 2\alpha \sin(\odot - \Omega) \end{array} \right\}$$

$$\delta' - \delta = \operatorname{tang}\delta \sin\delta\, 5''.1112 \left\{ \begin{array}{l} -(b + a\cos\varepsilon) \cos 2\alpha \cos(\odot + \Omega) \\ -(b\cos\varepsilon + a) \sin 2\alpha \sin(\odot + \Omega) \\ +(b - a\cos\varepsilon) \cos 2\alpha \cos(\odot - \Omega) \\ +(b\cos\varepsilon - a) \sin 2\alpha \sin(\odot - \Omega) \\ +(b - a\cos\varepsilon) \cos(\odot + \Omega) \\ -(b + a\cos\varepsilon) \cos(\odot - \Omega) \end{array} \right\}$$

or if we substitute the numerical values:

$$\alpha' - \alpha = \operatorname{tang}\delta \sec\delta \,. \left\{ \begin{array}{l} -0''.0007597 \sin 2\alpha \cos(\odot + \Omega) \\ +0''.0007693 \cos 2\alpha \sin(\odot + \Omega) \\ -0''.0000790 \sin 2\alpha \cos(\odot - \Omega) \\ +0''.0001449 \cos 2\alpha \sin(\odot - \Omega) \end{array} \right\} \quad (e)$$

$$\delta' - \delta = \operatorname{tang}\delta \sin\delta \,. \left\{ \begin{array}{l} -0''.0003798 \cos 2\alpha \cos(\odot + \Omega) \\ -0''.0003847 \sin 2\alpha \sin(\odot + \Omega) \\ -0''.0000395 \cos 2\alpha \cos(\odot - \Omega) \\ -0''.0000725 \sin 2\alpha \sin(\odot - \Omega) \\ -0''.0000395 \cos(\odot + \Omega) \\ -0''.0003798 \cos(\odot - \Omega) \end{array} \right\}$$

While the declination is less than $85\frac{1}{2}{}^{0}$, $\alpha' - \alpha$ is less than $\frac{1}{100}$ of a second of time and $\delta' - \delta$ is greater than $\frac{1}{100}$ of a second of arc only for declinations exceeding $85^{0}\,6'$. Hence these terms as well as those given by the equations (c) and (d) can be neglected except in the case of stars very the pole.

The equations for the aberration are much more simple, if we take the ecliptic instead of the equator as the fundamental plane. For then neglecting again the constant terms we find:

$$\frac{dx}{dt} = +\frac{a}{\cos\varphi}\sin\odot\frac{dM}{dt},$$
$$\frac{dy}{dt} = -\frac{a}{\cos\varphi}\cos\odot\frac{dM}{dt},$$
$$\frac{dz}{dt} = 0.$$

and if we substitute these expressions in the formulae (a) and write λ and β in place of α and δ, we find for the aberration of the fixed stars in longitude and latitude:

$$\begin{aligned}\lambda' - \lambda &= -20''.4451\cos(\lambda - \odot)\sec\beta,\\ \beta' - \beta &= +20''.4451\sin(\lambda - \odot)\sin\beta,\end{aligned} \qquad (B)$$

which formulae are not changed if we use the apparent instead of the mean equinox.

The terms of the second order are:

$$\begin{aligned}&\text{in longitude:} = +0''.0010133\sin 2(\odot - \lambda)\sec\beta^2,\\ &\text{in latitude:} \;\;= -0''.0005067\cos 2(\odot - \lambda)\operatorname{tang}\beta,\end{aligned}$$

where the numerical factor 0.0010133 is equal to $\frac{1}{2}\cdot\frac{(20''.4451)^2}{206265}$.

Example. On the first of April 1849 we have for Arcturus:

$$\alpha = 14^h\,8^m\,48^s = 212^0\,12'.0,\ \delta = +19^0\,58'.1,\ \odot = 11^0\,37'.2$$
$$\varepsilon = 23^0\,27'.4.$$

With this we find:

$$\begin{aligned}\alpha' - \alpha &= +18''.88,\\ \delta' - \delta &= -\ \ 9''.65,\end{aligned}$$

and as

$$\lambda = 202^0\,8',\ \beta = +30^0\,50',$$

we find also:

$$\begin{aligned}\lambda' - \lambda &= +23''.41,\\ \beta' - \beta &= -\ \ 1''.91.\end{aligned}$$

17. In order to simplify the computation of the aberration in right ascension and declination, tables have been constructed, the most convenient of which are those given by Gauss. He takes:

$$20''.445 \sin \odot = a \sin (\odot + A),$$
$$20''.445 \cos \odot \cos \varepsilon = a \cos (\odot + A),$$

and thus has simply:

$$\alpha' - \alpha = - a \sec \delta \cos (\odot + A - \alpha),$$
$$\delta' - \delta = - a \sin \delta \sin (\odot + A - \alpha) - 20''.445 \cos \odot \cos \delta \sin \varepsilon$$
$$= - a \sin \delta \sin (\odot + A - \alpha) - 10''.222 \sin \varepsilon \cos (\odot + \delta)$$
$$- 10''.222 \sin \varepsilon \cos (\odot - \delta).$$

From these formulae the tables have been computed. The first table gives A and $\log a$, the argument being the longitude of the sun, and with these values the aberration in right ascension and the first part of the aberration in declination is easily computed. The second and third part is found from another table, the angles $\odot + \delta$ and $\odot - \delta$ being successively used as arguments. Such tables were first published by Gauss in the Monatliche Correspondenz Band XVII pag. 312, but the constant there used was that of Delambre $20''.255$. Latterly they have been recomputed by Nicolai with the value $20''.4451$ and have been published in Warnstorff's collection of tables.

For the preceding example we find from those tables:

$$A = 1^\circ\, 1', \quad \log a = 1.2748$$

and with this

$$\alpha' - \alpha = + 18''.88$$

and the first part of the aberration in declination $-2''.15$. For the second and third part we find $-3''.47$ and $-4''.03$, if we enter the second table with the arguments $31^\circ 35'$ and $-8^\circ 21$. We have therefore:

$$\delta' - \delta = - 9''.65.$$

18. The maximum and minimum of aberration in longitude takes place, when the longitude of the star is either equal to the longitude of the sun or greater by 180°, while the maximum and minimum in latitude occurs, when the star is 90° ahead of the sun or follows 90° after. Very similar to the formulae for the annual aberration are those for the annual parallax of the stars (that is for the angle which lines drawn from the sun and from the earth subtend at the fixed star) only the maxima and minima in this case occur at different times. For if Δ be the distance of the fixed star from the sun, λ and β its longitude and latitude as seen from the sun, the co-ordinates of the star with respect to the sun are:

$$x = \Delta \cos\beta \cos\lambda,\ y = \Delta \cos\beta \sin\lambda,\ z = \Delta \sin\beta.$$

But the co-ordinates of the star referred to the centre of the earth are:

$$x' = \Delta' \cos\beta' \cos\lambda',\ y' = \Delta' \cos\beta' \sin\lambda',\ z' = \Delta' \sin\beta'$$

and as the co-ordinates of the sun with respect to the earth are:

$$X = R \cos \odot \quad \text{and} \quad Y = R \sin \odot$$

where the semi-major axis of the earth's orbit is the unit, we have:

$$\begin{aligned} \Delta' \cos\beta' \cos\lambda' &= \Delta \cos\beta \cos\lambda + R \cos\odot \\ \Delta' \cos\beta' \sin\lambda' &= \Delta \cos\beta \sin\lambda + R \sin\odot \\ \Delta' \sin\beta' &= \Delta \sin\beta, \end{aligned}$$

from which we easily deduce:

$$\lambda' - \lambda = -\frac{R}{\Delta'} \sin(\lambda - \odot) \sec\beta \,.\, 206265,$$

$$\beta' - \beta = -\frac{R}{\Delta'} \cos(\lambda - \odot) \sin\beta \,.\, 206265.$$

or as $\frac{1}{\Delta'}$ 206265 is equal to the annual parallax π:

$$\begin{aligned} \lambda' - \lambda &= -\pi R \sin(\lambda - \odot) \sec\beta \\ \beta' - \beta &= -\pi R \cos(\lambda - \odot) \sin\beta. \end{aligned} \qquad (C)$$

Hence we see that the formulae are similar to those of the aberration, only the maximum and minimum of the parallax in longitude occurs, when the star is 90° ahead of the sun or follows 90° after it, while the maximum and minimum in latitude occurs, when the longitude is equal to that of the sun or is greater by 180°.

For the right ascensions and declinations we have the following equations:

$$\begin{aligned} \Delta' \cos\delta' \cos\alpha' &= \Delta \cos\delta \cos\alpha + R \cos\odot \\ \Delta' \cos\delta' \sin\alpha' &= \Delta \cos\delta \sin\alpha + R \sin\odot \cos\varepsilon \\ \Delta' \sin\delta' &= \Delta \sin\delta \qquad + R \sin\odot \sin\varepsilon, \end{aligned}$$

from which we find in a similar way as before:

$$\begin{aligned} \alpha' - \alpha &= -\pi R [\cos\odot \sin\alpha - \sin\odot \cos\varepsilon \cos\alpha] \sec\delta \\ \delta' - \delta &= -\pi R [\cos\varepsilon \sin\alpha \sin\delta - \sin\varepsilon \cos\delta] \sin\odot \\ &\quad - \pi R \cos\odot \sin\delta \cos\alpha. \end{aligned} \qquad (D)$$

19. The rotation of the earth on her axis produces likewise an aberration which is called the ***diurnal aberration.*** But this is much smaller than the annual aberration, since the velocity of the rotation of the earth on the axis is much smaller than the velocity of her orbital motion.

If we imagine three rectangular axes, one of which coincides with the axis of rotation, whilst the two others are situated in the plane of the equator so that the positive axis of x is directed from the centre towards the point of the vernal equinox and the axis of y towards the 90th degree of right ascension, the co-ordinates of a place at the surface of the earth are according to No. 2 of this section as follows:

$$x = \varrho \cos \varphi' \cos \Theta,$$
$$y = \varrho \cos \varphi' \sin \Theta,$$
$$z = \varrho \sin \varphi'.$$

We have therefore:

$$\frac{dx}{dt} = - \varrho \cos \varphi' \sin \Theta \,.\, \frac{d\Theta}{dt},$$
$$\frac{dy}{dt} = + \varrho \cos \varphi' \cos \Theta \,.\, \frac{d\Theta}{dt},$$
$$\frac{dz}{dt} = 0.$$

If we substitute these expressions in formula (a) in No. 16, we easily find omitting the terms of the second order:

$$\alpha' - \alpha = \frac{1}{\mu} \frac{d\Theta}{dt} \varrho \cos \varphi' \cos (\Theta - \alpha) \sec \delta,$$
$$\delta' - \delta = \frac{1}{\mu} \frac{d\Theta}{dt} \varrho \cos \varphi' \sin (\Theta - \alpha) \sin \delta.$$

If now T be the number of sidereal days in a sidereal year, the angular motion of a point caused by the rotation on the axis is T times faster than the angular motion of the earth in its orbit and we have:

$$\frac{d\Theta}{dt} = T \frac{dM}{dt}.$$

Thus as we have:

$$\frac{1}{\mu} \varrho = k \frac{\varrho}{a} = k \sin \pi$$

where π is the parallax of the sun, k the number of seconds in which the light traverses the semi-major axis of the earth's orbit, the constant of diurnal aberration is:

$$k \,.\, \frac{dM}{dt} \,.\, \sin \pi \,.\, T,$$

or as we have:

$$k \cdot \frac{dM}{dt} = 20''.445, \ \pi = 8''.5712 \text{ and } T = 366.26 \text{ is,}$$

$$0''.3113.$$

Hence if we take instead of the geocentric latitude φ' simply the latitude φ, we find the diurnal aberration in right ascension and declination as follows:

$$\begin{aligned} \alpha' - \alpha &= 0''.3113 \cos\varphi \cos(\Theta - \alpha) \sec\delta, \\ \delta' - \delta &= 0''.3113 \cos\varphi \sin(\Theta - \alpha) \sin\delta. \end{aligned} \qquad (E)$$

The diurnal aberration in declination is therefore zero, when the stars are on the meridian, whilst the aberration in right ascension is then at its maximum and equals:

$$0''.3113 \,.\, \cos\varphi \sec\delta.$$

20. We have found the following formulae for the annual aberration of the fixed stars in longitude and latitude:

$$\begin{aligned} \lambda' - \lambda &= -k \cos(\lambda - \odot) \sec\beta, \\ \beta' - \beta &= +k \sin(\lambda - \odot) \sin\beta, \end{aligned}$$

where now k denotes the constant $20''.445$. If we now imagine a tangent plane to the celestial sphere at the mean place of the star and in it two rectangular axes of co-ordinates, the axes of x and y being the lines of intersection of the parallel circle and of the circle of latitude with the plane and if we refer the apparent place of the star affected with aberration to the mean place by the co-ordinates:

$$x = (\lambda' - \lambda)\cos\beta \text{ and } y = \beta' - \beta \ ^{*}),$$

we easily find by squaring the above equations:

$$y^2 = k^2 \sin\beta^2 - x^2 \sin\beta^2.$$

This is the equation of an ellipse, whose semi-major axis is k and whose semi-minor axis is $k \sin\beta$. We see therefore that the stars on account of the annual aberration describe round their mean place an ellipse, whose semi-major axis is $20''.445$ and whose semi-minor axis is equal to the maximum of the aberration in latitude. Now if the star is in the ecliptic, β and hence the minor axis is zero. Such stars describe therefore in the course of a year a straight line, moving $20''.445$ on each side of the mean place. If the star is at the pole of the ecliptic, β equals 90^0 and the mi-

---

*) For as the distances from the origin are very small we can suppose that the tangent plane coincides with that small part of the celestial sphere.

nor axis is equal to the major axis. Such a star describes therefore in the course of a year about its mean place a circle whose radius is 20″.445.

In order to find the place which the star occupies at any time in this ellipse, we imagine round the centre of the ellipse a circle, whose diameter is the major axis of the ellipse. Then it is obvious, that the radius must move in the course of a year over the area of the circle with uniform velocity so that it coincides with the west side of the major axis, when the longitude of the sun is equal to the longitude of the star, and with the south part of the minor axis, when the longitude of the sun exceeds the longitude of the star by 90°. If we draw then the radius corresponding to any time and let fall a perpendicular line from the extremity of the radius on the major axis, the point, in which this intersects the ellipse, will be the place of the star.

If the star has also a parallax π, the expressions for the two rectangular co-ordinates become:

$$x = -k\cos(\lambda - \odot) - \pi\sin(\lambda - \odot)$$
$$y = +k\sin(\lambda - \odot)\sin\beta - \pi\cos(\lambda - \odot)\sin\beta$$

or, taking:

$$k = a\cos A$$
$$\pi = a\sin A$$
$$x = -a\cos(\lambda - \odot - A)$$
$$y = +a\sin(\lambda - \odot - A)\sin\beta.$$

Hence also in this case the star describes round its mean place an ellipse, whose semi-major axis is $\sqrt{k^2 + \pi^2}$ and whose semi-minor axis is $\sin\beta\sqrt{k^2 + \pi^2}$.

The effect of the diurnal aberration is similar. The stars describe on account of it in the course of a sidereal day round their mean places an ellipse, whose sem-imajor axis is 0″.3113 $\cos\varphi$ and whose semi-minor axis is 0″.3113 $\cos\varphi\sin\delta$. If the star is in the equator, this ellipse is changed into a straight line, while a star exactly at the pole of the heavens describes a circle.

21. If the body have a proper motion like the sun, the moon and the planets, then for such the aberration of the fixed stars is not the complete aberration. For as such a body changes its place during the time in which a ray of light travels from it to the earth, the observed direction of the ray, even if corrected for the aberration of the fixed stars, does not give the true geocentric place of the object at the time of observation. We will suppose, that the light, which reaches the object-glass of the telescope at the time t, has left the planet at the time T. Let then P Fig. 5 be the place of the planet at the time T, p its place at the time t, A the place of the object-glass at the time T, a and b the places of the object-glass and the eye-piece at the time t and finally a' and b' their places at the time t', when the light reaches the eye-piece. Then is:

1) AP the direction towards the place of the body at the time T, ap that towards the true place at the time t,
2) ab and $a'b'$ the direction towards the apparent place at the time t or t', the difference of the two being indefinitely small,
3) $b'a$ the direction towards the same apparent place corrected for the aberration of the fixed stars.

Now as P, a, b' are situated in a straight line, we have:

$$Pa : ab' = t - T : t' - t.$$

Furthermore as the interval $t' - T$ is always so small, that we can suppose, that the earth during the same is moving in a straight line and with a uniform velocity, the points A, a, a' are also situated in a straight line, so that Aa and aa' are also proportional to the times $t - T$ and $t' - t$. Hence it follows that AP is parallel to $b'a'$ or that the apparent place of the planet at the time t is equal to the true place at the time T. But the interval between these two times is the time, in which the light from the planet reaches the eye or is equal to the distance of the planet multiplied by $497^s.8$, that is, by the time in which the light traverses the semi-major axis of the earth's orbit, which is taken as the unit.

It follows then that we can use three methods, for computing the true place of a planet from its apparent place at any time t.

I. We subtract from the observed time the time in which the light from the planet reaches the earth; thus we find the time T and the true place at the time T is identical with the apparent place at the time t.

II. We can compute from the distance of the planet the reduction of time $t - T$ and from the daily motion of the planet in right ascension and declination compute the reduction of the observed apparent place to the time T.

III. We can consider the observed place corrected for the aberration of the fixed stars as the true place at the time T, but as seen from the place which the earth occupies at the time t. This last method is used when the distance of the body is not known, for instance in computing the orbit of a newly discovered planet or comet.

Since the time in which the light traverses the semi-major axis of the earth's orbit is $497^s.8$ and the mean daily motion of the sun is $59' \, 8''.19$, we find the aberration of the sun in longitude according to rule II. equal to $20''.45$, by which quantity we observe the longitude always too small. On account of the change of the distance and the velocity of the sun this value varies a little in the course of a year but only by some tenths of a second.

22. The aberration for a moveable body, being in fact the general case, may also be deduced from the fundamental equations (a) in No. 16. For it is evident, that in this case we need only substitute instead of the absolute velocity of the earth its relative velocity with respect to the moveable body, since this combined with the motion of the light again determines the angle by which the telescope must be inclined to the real direction of the rays of light emanating from the body in order that the latter always appear in the axis of the telescope nothwithstanding the motion of the earth and the proper motion of the body. If therefore ξ, η and ζ be the co-ordinates of the body with respect to the system of axes used there, we must substitute in (a) $\frac{dx}{dt} - \frac{d\xi}{dt}$, $\frac{dy}{dt} - \frac{d\eta}{dt}$, $\frac{dz}{dt} - \frac{d\zeta}{dt}$ instead of $\frac{dx}{dt}$, $\frac{dy}{dt}$ and $\frac{dz}{dt}$. But if Δ is the distance of the body from the earth, we find the heliocentric co-ordinates ξ, η, ζ, since the geocentric co-ordinates are $\Delta \cos\delta \cos\alpha$ etc., from the formulae:

$$\begin{aligned} \xi &= \Delta \cos\delta \cos\alpha + x, \\ \eta &= \Delta \cos\delta \sin\alpha + y, \\ \zeta &= \Delta \sin\delta \qquad\quad + z, \end{aligned} \qquad (f)$$

from which we easily deduce the following:

$$\left(\frac{dx}{dt}-\frac{d\xi}{dt}\right)\sin\alpha-\left(\frac{dy}{dt}-\frac{d\eta}{dt}\right)\cos\alpha=\Delta\cos\delta\,\frac{d\alpha}{dt}$$

$$\left(\frac{dx}{dt}-\frac{d\xi}{dt}\right)\sin\delta\cos\alpha+\left(\frac{dy}{dt}-\frac{d\eta}{dt}\right)\sin\delta\sin\alpha+\left(\frac{dz}{dt}-\frac{d\zeta}{dt}\right)\cos\delta=\Delta\frac{d\delta}{dt}.$$

Hence the formulae (a) change into:

$$\alpha'-\alpha=-\frac{\Delta}{\mu}\frac{d\alpha}{dt},$$

$$\delta'-\delta=-\frac{\Delta}{\mu}\frac{d\delta}{dt},$$

or as $\frac{\Delta}{\mu}$ equals the time in which the light traverses the distance Δ, we find, if we denote this by $t-T$:

$$\alpha'=\alpha-(t-T)\frac{d\alpha}{dt},$$

$$\delta'=\delta-(t-T)\frac{d\delta}{dt},$$

which formulae show, that the apparent place is equal to the true place at the time T and therefore correspond to the rules I and II of the preceding number.

But we also find the aberration for this case by adding to the second member of the first formula (a) the term $\frac{1}{\mu}\left[\frac{d\xi}{dt}\sin\alpha-\frac{d\eta}{dt}\cos\alpha\right]\sec\delta$ and a similar term to the second member of the second equation. We get therefore, if we denote the aberration of the fixed stars by $D\alpha$ and $D\delta$:

$$\alpha'-\alpha=D\alpha+\frac{1}{\mu}\left[\frac{d\xi}{dt}\sin\alpha-\frac{d\eta}{dt}\cos\alpha\right]\sec\delta,$$

$$\delta'-\delta=D\delta+\frac{1}{\mu}\left[\frac{d\xi}{dt}\sin\delta\cos\alpha+\frac{d\eta}{dt}\sin\delta\sin\alpha+\frac{d\zeta}{dt}\cos\delta\right].$$

But differentiating the equations (f), taking in the second member only the geocentric quantities Δ, α, δ as variable and the co-ordinates of the earth as constant, and denoting the partial differential coefficients by $\left(\frac{d\alpha}{dt}\right)$ and $\left(\frac{d\delta}{dt}\right)$, we find the second members of the above equations respectively equal to:

$$-\frac{\Delta}{\mu}\left(\frac{d\alpha}{dt}\right)\text{ and }-\frac{\Delta}{\mu}\left(\frac{d\delta}{dt}\right).$$

We therefore have:

$$\alpha'-D\alpha=\alpha-(t-T).\left(\frac{d\alpha}{dt}\right)$$

$$\text{and }\delta'-D\delta=\delta-(t-T).\left(\frac{d\delta}{dt}\right),$$

which formulae correspond to the third rule of the preceding No. For since $\left(\frac{d\alpha}{dt}\right)$ and $\left(\frac{d\delta}{dt}\right)$ are the differential coefficients of α and δ, if the heliocentric place of the planet is changed whilst the place of the earth remains the same, the second members of the two equations give the places of the planet at the time T, but as seen from the place which the earth occupies at the time t.

Note. The motion of the earth round the sun and the rotation on the axis are not the only causes which produce a motion of the points on the surface of the earth in space, as the sun itself has a motion, of which the earth as well as the whole solar system participates. This motion consists of a progressive motion, as we shall see hereafter, and also of a periodical one caused by the attractions of the planets. For if we consider the sun and one planet, they both describe round their common centre of gravity ellipses, which are inversely as the masses of the two bodies. The first motion which at present and undoubtedly for long ages may be considered as going on in a straight line, produces only a permanent and hence imperceptible change of the places of the stars and the aberration caused by the second motion is so small that it always can be neglected. For if a and a' are the radii of the orbits of two planets which are here considered as circular, τ and τ' their times of revolution, then the angular velocities of the two will be as $\frac{1}{\tau}:\frac{1}{\tau'}$, hence their linear velocities as $a\tau' : a'\tau$ or as $\sqrt{a'} : \sqrt{a}$, since according to the third law of Kepler the squares of the periodic times of two planets are as the cubes of their semi-major axes. The constant of aberration for a planet, the semi-major axis of whose orbit is a, taking the radius of the earth's orbit as unit, is therefore $\frac{20''.45}{\sqrt{a}}$ and hence the constant of aberration caused by the motion of the sun round their common centre of gravity is equal to $m \cdot \frac{20''.45}{\sqrt{a}}$, where m is the mass of the planet expressed in parts of the mass of the sun. In the case of Jupiter we have $m = \frac{1}{1050}$ and $a = 5.20$, hence the constant of aberration caused by the attraction of Jupiter is only $0''.0086$.

The perturbations of the earth caused by the planets produce also changes of the aberration, which however are so small, that they can be neglected.

Compare on aberration: The introduction to Bessel's Tabulae Regiomontanae p. XVII et seq.; also Wolfers, Tabulae Reductionum p. XVIII etc. Gauss, Theoria motus pag. 68 etc.

FOURTH SECTION.

ON THE METHODS BY WHICH THE PLACES OF THE STARS AND THE VALUES OF THE CONSTANT QUANTITIES NECESSARY FOR THEIR REDUCTION ARE DETERMINED BY OBSERVATIONS.

The chief problem of spherical astronomy is the determination of the places of the stars with respect to the fundamental planes and especially the equator, as their longitudes and latitudes are never determined by observations, but, the obliquity of the ecliptic being known, are computed from their right ascensions and declinations. When the observations are made in such a way as to give immediately the places of the stars with respect to the equator and the vernal equinox, they are called ***absolute determinations***, whilst ***relative determinations*** are such, which give merely the differences of the right ascensions and declinations of stars from those of other stars, which have been determined before.

The observations give us the apparent places of the stars, that is, the places affected with refraction *) and aberration and referred to the equator and the apparent equinox at the time of observation. It is therefore necessary to reduce these places to mean places by adding the corrections which have been treated in the two last sections. But the expressions of each of these corrections contain a constant quantity, whose numerical value must at the same time be determined by similar observations as those by which we find the places of the stars. The values of these constant quantities given in the last two chapters are those derived from the latest determinations, but they are still liable to small corrections by future observations.

---

*) In the case of observations of the sun, the moon and the planets these places are affected also with parallax.

If we observe the places of the fixed stars at different times we ought to find only such differences as can be ascribed to any such errors of the constant quantities and to errors of observation. However, comparing the places determined at different epochs we find greater or less differences which cannot be explained by such errors and must be the effect of proper motions of the stars. These motions are partly without any law and peculiar to the different stars, partly they are merely of a parallactic character and caused by the progressive motion of the solar system, that is, by a proper motion of the sun itself. So far these proper motions with a few exceptions can be considered as uniform and as going on in a great circle. They must necessarily be taken into account in order to reduce the mean places of the stars from one epoch to the other.

The methods for computing the various corrections which must be applied to the places of the stars have been given in the two last sections; but as these computations must be made so very frequently for the reductions of stars, still other methods are used, which make the reduction of the apparent places of stars to their mean places at the beginning of the year as short and easy as possible and which shall be given now.

I. ON THE REDUCTION OF THE MEAN PLACES OF STARS TO APPARENT PLACES AND VICE VERSÂ.

1. If we know the mean place of a star for the beginning of a certain year and we wish to find the apparent place for any given day of another year, we must first reduce the given place to the mean place at the beginning of this other year by applying the precession and if necessary the proper motion and then add the precession and the proper motion from the beginning of the year to the given day as well as the nutation and aberration for this day. Now in order to make the computation of these three last corrections easy, tables have been constructed for all of them, which have for argument the day of the year. Such tables have been given by Bessel in his work „Tabulae Regiomontanae" *).

Let α and δ be the mean right ascension and declination of a star at the beginning of a year, whilst α' and δ' designate the apparent right ascension and declination at the time τ, reckoned from the beginning of the year and expressed in parts of a Julian year. If then μ und μ' designate the proper motion of the star in right ascension and declination, which is considered to be proportional to the time, we have according to the formulae (D) in No. 2, (B) and (C) in No. 5 of the second section and (A) in No. 16 of the third section the following expression:

$$\begin{aligned}\alpha' - \alpha = & + \tau\,[m + n \operatorname{tang}\delta \sin\alpha] + \tau\mu \\ & - [15''.8148 + 6''.8650 \operatorname{tang}\delta \sin\alpha] \sin \Omega \\ & - 9''.2231 \operatorname{tang}\delta \cos\alpha \cos\Omega \\ & + [0''.1902 + 0''.0822 \operatorname{tang}\delta \sin\alpha] \sin 2\Omega \\ & + 0''.0896 \operatorname{tang}\delta \cos\alpha \cos 2\Omega \\ & - [1''.1642 + 0''.5054 \operatorname{tang}\delta \sin\alpha] \sin 2\odot \\ & - 0''.5509 \operatorname{tang}\delta \cos\alpha \cos 2\odot \\ & + [0''.1173 + 0''.0509 \operatorname{tang}\delta \sin\alpha] \sin(\odot - P) \\ & - [0''.0195 + 0''.0085 \operatorname{tang}\delta \sin\alpha] \sin(\odot + P) \\ & - 0''.0093 \operatorname{tang}\delta \cos\alpha \cos(\odot + P) \\ & - 20''.4451 \cos\varepsilon \sec\delta \cos\alpha \cos\odot \\ & - 20''.4451 \sec\delta \sin\alpha \sin\odot\end{aligned}$$

and:

$$\begin{aligned}\delta' - \delta = & + \tau n \cos\alpha + \tau\mu' \\ & - 6''.8650 \cos\alpha \sin\Omega + 9''.2231 \sin\alpha \cos\Omega \\ & + 0''.0822 \cos\alpha \sin 2\Omega - 0''.0896 \sin\alpha \cos 2\Omega \\ & - 0''.5054 \cos\alpha \sin 2\odot + 0''.5509 \sin\alpha \cos 2\odot \\ & + 0''.0509 \cos\alpha \sin(\odot - P) \\ & - 0''.0085 \cos\alpha \sin(\odot + P) + 0''.0093 \sin\alpha \cos(\odot + P) \\ & + 20''.4451 [\sin\alpha \sin\delta \cos\varepsilon - \cos\delta \sin\varepsilon] \cos\odot \\ & - 20''.4451 \cos\alpha \sin\delta \sin\odot.\end{aligned}$$

The terms of the nutation, which depend on twice the longitude of the moon 2☾ and on the anomaly ☾ — P' of the moon have been omitted here, as they have a short period on account of the rapid motion of the moon and therefore are better tabulated separately. Moreover these terms are only small and on account of their short period are nearly eliminated in the mean of many observations of a star. Hence

*) For a few stars it is necessary to add also the annual parallax, for which the most convenient formulae shall be given hereafter.

they are only taken into account for stars in the neighbourhood of the pole, for which also the terms depending on the square and the product of nutation and aberration *) become significant. These terms are brought in tables, whose arguments are ☾, ☉, ☉ + ☊ and ☉ − ☊.

Now in order to construct tables for the above expressions for $\alpha' - \alpha$ and $\delta' - \delta$, we put:

$$6''.8650 = ni \qquad 15''.8148 - mi = h$$
$$0''.0822 = ni_1 \qquad 0''.1902 - mi_1 = h_1$$
$$0''.5054 = ni_2 \qquad 1''.1642 - mi_2 = h_2$$
$$0''.0509 = ni_3 \qquad 0''.1173 - mi_3 = h_3$$
$$0''.0085 = ni_4 \qquad 0''.0195 - mi_4 = h_4.$$

Then we can write the formulae also in this way:

$$\begin{aligned}\alpha' - \alpha = &[\tau - i \sin \Omega + i_1 \sin 2\Omega - i_2 \sin 2\odot + i_3 \sin(\odot - P) \\ &\qquad - i_4 \sin(\odot + P)] [m + n \operatorname{tang} \delta \sin \alpha] \\ &- [9''.2231 \cos \Omega - 0''.0896 \cos 2\Omega + 0''.5509 \cos 2\odot \\ &\qquad + 0''.0093 \cos(\odot + P)] \operatorname{tang} \delta \cos \alpha \\ &- 20''.4451 \cos \varepsilon \cos \odot \,.\, \cos \alpha \sec \delta \\ &- 20''.4451 \sin \odot \,.\, \sin \alpha \sec \delta \\ &+ \tau \mu \\ &- h \sin \Omega + h_1 \sin 2\Omega - h_2 \sin 2\odot + h_3 \sin(\odot - P) - h_4 \sin(\odot + P)\end{aligned}$$

and:

$$\begin{aligned}\delta' - \delta = &[\tau - i \sin \Omega + i_1 \sin 2\Omega - i_2 \sin 2\odot + i_3 \sin(\odot - P) \\ &\qquad - i_4 \sin(\odot + P)] n \cos \alpha \\ &+ [9''.2231 \cos \Omega - 0''.0896 \cos 2\Omega + 0''.5509 \cos 2\odot \\ &\qquad + 0''.0093 \cos(\odot + P)] \sin \alpha \\ &- 20''.4451 \cos \varepsilon \cos \odot [\operatorname{tang} \varepsilon \cos \delta - \sin \delta \sin \alpha] \\ &- 20''.4451 \sin \odot \,.\, \sin \delta \cos \alpha \\ &+ \tau \mu'.\end{aligned}$$

If we introduce therefore the following notation:

$$A = \tau - i \sin \Omega + i_1 \sin 2\Omega - i_2 \sin 2\odot + i_3 \sin(\odot - P) - i_4 \sin(\odot + P)$$
$$B = -9''.2231 \cos \Omega + 0''.0896 \cos 2\Omega - 0''.5509 \cos 2\odot - 0''.0093 \cos(\odot + P)$$
$$C = -20''.4451 \cos \varepsilon \cos \odot$$
$$D = -20''.4451 \sin \odot$$
$$E = -h \sin \Omega + h_1 \sin 2\Omega - h_2 \sin 2\odot + h_3 \sin(\odot - P) - h_4 \sin(\odot + P)$$

$$a = m + n \operatorname{tang} \delta \sin \alpha \qquad a' = n \cos \alpha$$
$$b = \operatorname{tang} \delta \cos \alpha \qquad b' = - \sin \alpha$$
$$c = \sec \delta \cos \alpha \qquad c' = \operatorname{tang} \varepsilon \cos \delta - \sin \delta \sin \alpha$$
$$d = \sec \delta \sin \alpha \qquad d' = \sin \delta \cos \alpha,$$

---

*) These terms are given by the formulae (*E*) in No. 5 of the second section and (*c*), (*d*) and (*e*) in No. 16 of the third section

we have simply:

$$\begin{aligned} \alpha' - \alpha &= Aa + Bb + Cc + Dd + \tau\mu + E \\ \delta' - \delta &= Aa' + Bb' + Cc' + Dd' + \tau\mu', \end{aligned} \qquad (A)$$

where the quantities a, b, c, d, a', b', c', d' depend only on the place of the star and the obliquity of the ecliptic, while A, B, C, D depend only on ☉ and ☊ and thus being mere functions of the time may be tabulated with the time for argument.

The numerical values given in the above formulae are those for 1800 and we have for this epoch:

$$\begin{array}{lllll} i=0.34223 & i_1=0.00410 & i_2=0.02519 & i_3=0.00254 & i_4=0.00042 \\ h=0.0572 & h_1=0.0016 & h_2=0.0041 & h_3=0.0005 & h_4=0.0000. \end{array}$$

We see therefore that the quantity E never amounts to more than a small part of a second, hence it may always be neglected except when the greatest accuracy should be required. As several of the coefficients in the above formulae for $\alpha'-\alpha$ and $\delta'-\delta$ are variable (according to No. 5 of the second section) and likewise the values of m and n, we have for the year 1900:

$$\begin{array}{lllll} i=0.34256 & i_1=0.00410 & i_2=0.02520 & i_3=0.00253 & i_4=0.00042 \\ h=0.0488 & h_1=0.0014 & h_2=0.0035 & h_3=0.0005. & \end{array}$$

The values of the quantities A, B, C, D, E from the year 1750 to 1850 have been published by Bessel in his work „Tabulae Regiomontanae". But as he has used there a different value of the constants of nutation and of aberration and also neglected the terms multiplied by $☉ - P$ and $☉ + P$, the values given by him require the following corrections in order to make them correspond to the formulae given above:

For 1750:

$$\begin{aligned} dA &= -0.0090 \sin ☊ + 0.0001 \sin 2☊ + 0.0013 \sin 2☉ \\ &\qquad + 0.0025 \sin(☉ - P) - 0.0004 \sin(☉ + P) \\ dB &= -0.2456 \cos ☊ + 0.0019 \cos 2☊ + 0.0290 \cos 2☉ \\ &\qquad - 0.0093 \cos(☉ + P) \\ dC &= -0.1744 \cos ☉ \\ dD &= -0.1901 \sin ☉ \\ dE &= -0.006 \sin ☊ + 0.001 \sin 2☊ \end{aligned}$$

For 1850 the value of dB becomes:

$$dB = -0.2465 \cos ☊ + 0.0019 \cos 2☊ + 0.0291 \cos 2☉ - 0.0093 \cos(☉ + P).$$

The values of the quantities A, B etc. for the years 1850 to 1860 have been computed by Zech according to Bessel's formulae, and for the years 1860 to 1880 they have been given by Wolfers in his work „Tabulae Reductionum Observationum Astronomicarum“, where they have been computed from the formulae given above. The values for each year are published in all astronomical almanacs.

2. The arguments of all these tables are the days of the year, the beginning of which is taken at the time, when the mean longitude of the sun is equal to 280^{0}. Hence the tables are referred to that meridian, for which the beginning of the civil year occurs when the sun has that mean longitude. But as the sun performs an entire revolution in 365 days and a fraction of a day, it is evident, that in every year the tables are referred to a different meridian.

Therefore if we denote the difference of longitude between Paris and that place, for which at the beginning of the year the mean longitude of the sun is 280^{0}, by k, which we take positive, when the place is east of Paris, and if further we denote by d the difference of longitude between any other place and Paris, taking it positive, when this place is west of Paris and if we suppose both k and d to be expressed in time, we must add to the time of the second place for which we wish to find the quantities A, B, C, D, E from the tables, the quantity $k+d$ and for the time thus corrected we must take the values from the tables. The quantity k is found from:

$$k=\frac{L-280^{0}}{\mu},$$

where L is the mean longitude of the sun at the beginning of the year for the meridian of Paris, while μ is the mean tropical motion of the sun or $59' 8''.33$. This quantity is given in the „Tabulae Regiomontanae“ and in Wolfers' Tables for every year and expressed in parts of a day and the constant quantities A, B, C, D, E are given for the beginning of the fictitious year or for $18^{h} 40^{m}$ sidereal time of that meridian, for which the sun at the beginning of the year has the longitude 280^{0} and then for the same time of every tenth sidereal day*). If now we wish to have these values for any other sidereal time, for instance for the time of culmination of a star whose right ascension is α, we must add to the argument $k+d$ the quantity:

$$\alpha' = \frac{\alpha - 18^h\,40^m}{24^h} = \frac{\alpha}{24} - 0.778.$$

Furthermore as on that day, on which the right ascension of the sun is equal to the right ascension of the star, two culminations of the star occur, we must after this day add a unit to the datum of the day, so that the complete argument is always the datum *plus* the quantity:

$$k + d + \alpha' + i,$$

where we have $i = 0$ from the beginning of the year to the time, when the right ascension of the sun is equal to α, while afterwards we take $i = 1$.

Now the day, denoted in the tables by Jan. 0, is that, at the sidereal time $18^h\,40^m$ of which the year begins, the commencement of the days being always reckoned from noon. Hence the culmination of stars, whose right ascension is $< 18^h\,40^m$ does not fall on that day, which in the tables is denoted by 0, but already on the day preceding and therefore for such stars we must add 1 to the datum of the day reckoned from noon or we must take $i = 1$ from the beginning of the year to the day when the right ascension of the sun is equal to α and afterwards $i = 2$.

We will find for instance the correction of the mean place of α Lyrae for April 1861 and for the time of culmination for Berlin. We have for the beginning of the year:

$\alpha = 278^\circ\,3'30''$ $\delta = +38^\circ\,39'23''$ $\varepsilon = 23''27'22''$ $m = 46''.062$ $\log n = 1.30220$

and from this we find:

*) We have therefore to use for computing the tables:

$$\tau = \frac{10\,n}{366.242201}.$$

$$\text{Mean longitude of the sun} = 280^\circ + \frac{10\,n\,.\,360^\circ}{366.242201},$$

where n must be taken in succession equal to all integral numbers from 0 to 37. With this we find the true longitude according to I. No. 14. We have also:

$$\Omega = 33^\circ\,15'25''.9 - 19^\circ\,20'29''\,53\,(t - 1800) - \frac{10\,n}{366.242201}\,19^\circ\,20'29''.53.$$

$\log a = 1.47971$ $\log a' = 0.44889$
$\log b = 9.04973$ $\log b' = 9.99569$
$\log c = 9.25409$ $\log c' = 9.98106$
$\log d = 0.10309_n$ $\log d' = 8.94233$

and besides we have:

$\log \mu = 9.4425$ $\log \mu' = 9.4564.$

Further we have according to Wolfers' Tabulae Reductionum:

	$\log A$	$\log B$	$\log C$	$\log D$	$\log \tau$	E
March 31	9.7494	0.5497_n	1.2660_n	0.5668_n	9.3905	+ 0.05
April 10	9.7653	0.5279_n	1.2456_n	0.8488_n	9.4362	+ 0.05
20	9.7819	0.4982_n	1.2109_n	1.0089_n	9.4776	+ 0.05
30	9.7995	0.4620_n	1.1596_n	1.1155_n	9.5154	+ 0.05

and we get according to the formulae (*A*):

	$\alpha' - \alpha$	$\delta' - \delta$
March 31	$+ 1^s.203$	$- 19''.85$
April 10	+ 1 .541	− 19 .09
20	+ 1 .871	− 17 .79
30	+ 2 .185	− 15 .97.

Now we have $k = + 0.124$, $d = - 0.031$, $\frac{\alpha - 18^h 40^m}{24^h} = - 0.005$, and as here i is equal to 1, because α is less than $18^h 40^m$ and in March and April the right ascension of the sun is less than $18^h 40^m$, the argument in this case is

the datum + 1.088.

We find therefore at the time of culmination for Berlin:

March 31	$+ 1^s.239$	$- 19''.79$
April 10	+ 1 .577	18 .98
20	+ 1 .906	17 .62
30	+ 2 .219	15 .76.

If we subtract these corrections from the apparent place, we find the mean place at the beginning of the year.

3. This method of reducing the mean place to the apparent place and *vice versâ* is especially convenient in case, that we wish to compute an ephemeris for any greater length of time, for instance if we have to reduce many observations of the same star. But in case that the reduction for only one day is wanted, the following method may be used with greater convenience, as it does not require the computation of the constant quantities *a*, *b*, *c*, etc.

The precession and nutation in right ascension are equal to:

$$Am + An \sin\alpha \operatorname{tang}\delta + B \operatorname{tang}\delta \cos\alpha + E$$

and in declination: $An \cos\alpha - B \sin\alpha.$

Therefore if we put:
$$An = g \cos G$$
$$B = g \sin G$$
$$Am + E = f,$$
the terms for the right ascension become:
$$f + g \sin (G + \alpha) \operatorname{tang} \delta$$
and those for the declination:
$$g \cos (G + \alpha).$$

Further the aberration in right ascension is:
$$C \sec \delta \cos \alpha + D \sec \delta \sin \alpha$$
and in declination:
$$- C \sin \delta \sin \alpha + D \sin \delta \cos \alpha + C \operatorname{tang} \varepsilon \cos \delta.$$

Hence if we put:
$$C = h \sin H \qquad D = h \cos H \qquad i = C \operatorname{tang} \varepsilon,$$
the aberration in right ascension becomes:
$$h \sin (H + \alpha) \sec \delta$$
and in declination:
$$h \cos (H + \alpha) \sin \delta + i \cos \delta.$$

Therefore the complete formulae for the reduction to the apparent place are:
$$\begin{aligned} \alpha' - \alpha &= f + g \sin (G + \alpha) \operatorname{tang} \delta + h \sin (H + \alpha) \sec \delta + \tau \mu \\ \delta' - \delta &= \phantom{f +{}} g \cos (G + \alpha) + h \cos (H + \alpha) \sin \delta + i \cos \delta + \tau \mu'. \end{aligned} \qquad (B)$$

Here again for the quantities f, g, h, i, G and H tables may be computed, whose argument is the time. They are always published in all almanacs for every tenth day and for mean noon.

If we wish to find for instance the reduction of α Lyrae for 1861 April 10 at $17^h 15^m$ mean time, this being the time of culmination of α Lyrae on that day, we take from the Berlin Jahrbuch for this time:

$f = +26''.98$ $g = +12''.20$ $G = 344^\circ 3'$ $h = +18''.98$ $H = 247^\circ 3'$ $i = -7''.58$

hence $\qquad G + \alpha = 262^\circ 6' \qquad H + \alpha = 165^\circ 6'$

$\cos (G + \alpha)$	9.13813_n	$g \sin (G + \alpha)$	1.08222_n
g	1.08636	$\operatorname{tang} \delta$	9.90304
$\sin (G + \alpha)$	9.99586_n	$h \sin (H + \alpha)$	0.68846
$\cos (H + \alpha)$	9.98515_n	$\cos \delta$	9.89260
h	1.27830	i	0.87967_n
$\sin (H + \alpha)$	9.41016	$h \cos (H + \alpha)$	1.26345
		$\sin \delta$	9.79564

$f =$	$+ 26''.98$	$i \cos \delta =$	$- 5''.92$
$g \sin (G + \alpha) \operatorname{tang} \delta =$	$- 9''.67$	$g \cos (G + \alpha) =$	$- 1''.68$
$h \sin (H + \alpha) \sec \delta =$	$+ 6''.25$	$h \cos (H + \alpha) \sin \delta =$	$- 11''.46$
$\tau \mu =$	$+ 0''.08$	$\tau \mu' =$	$+ 0''.08$
$\alpha' - \alpha =$	$+ 23''.64 = + 1^s.576$	$\delta' - \delta =$	$- 18''.98.$

4. The formulae (A) and (B) for the reduction to the apparent place do not contain the daily aberration nor the annual parallax. For as the daily aberration depends upon the latitude of the place, it cannot be included in general tables; however for meridian observations the daily aberration in declination is equal to zero and the expression for the aberration in right ascension being of the same form as that of the correction for the error of collimation, which must be added to the observations, as we shall see hereafter, it may in that case always be united with the latter correction.

The annual parallax has been determined only for very few stars, but for those it must be computed, when the greatest accuracy is required. Now the formulae for the annual parallax are according to No. 18 of the third chapter:

$$\alpha' - \alpha = -\pi\,[\cos\odot \sin\alpha - \sin\odot \cos\varepsilon \cos\alpha]\sec\delta$$
$$\delta' - \delta = -\pi\,[\cos\varepsilon \sin\alpha \sin\delta - \sin\varepsilon \cos\delta]\sin\odot - \pi \cos\odot \sin\delta \cos\alpha.$$

Therefore if we put:

$$\begin{aligned} -\cos\varepsilon\cos\alpha &= k\sin K \\ -\sin\alpha &= k\cos K \\ \sin\alpha\sin\delta\cos\varepsilon - \cos\delta\sin\varepsilon &= l\sin L \\ -\cos\alpha\sin\delta &= l\cos L, \end{aligned}$$

we have simply:

$$\alpha' - \alpha = \pi k \cos(K + \odot)\sec\delta$$
$$\delta' - \delta = \pi l \cos(L + \odot).$$

But the cases in which this correction must be applied are rare, for instance when observations of α Centauri whose parallax amounts to nearly $1''$ or those of Polaris are to be reduced.

II. DETERMINATION OF THE RIGHT ASCENSIONS AND DECLINATIONS OF THE STARS AND OF THE OBLIQUITY OF THE ECLIPTIC.

5. If we observe the difference of the time of culmination of the stars, these are equal to the difference of their apparent right ascensions expressed in time. We need therefore for these observations only a good clock, that is, one which for equal arcs of the equator passing across the meridian gives always an equal number of seconds *) and an altitude instrument, mounted firmly in the plane of the meridian, that is, a meridian-circle. This in its essential parts consists of a horizontal axis, lying on two firm Y-pieces, which carries a vertical circle and a telescope. Attached to the Y-pieces are verniers or microscopes, which give the arc passed over by the telescope by means of the simultaneous motion of the telescope and the circle round the horizontal axis.

In order to examine the uniform rate of the clock without knowing the places of the stars themselves, the interval of time is observed in which different stars return to the meridian or to a wire stretched in the focus of the telescope so that it is always in the plane of the meridian when the telescope is turned round the axis **). Now the time between two successive culminations of the same star is equal to $24^h + \Delta\alpha$, where $\Delta\alpha$ is the variation of the apparent place during those 24 hours. Therefore if the observations were right and the instrument at both times exactly in the plane of the meridian, a condition which we here always assume to be fulfilled, the intervals between two culminations measured by a perfectly regulated clock would also be found equal to $24^h + \Delta\alpha$. But on account of the errors of single observations, we can only assume, that the arithmetical mean of the interval found from several stars *minus* the mean of all $\Delta\alpha$ is equal to 24 hours. On the contrary if we find, that this arithmetical mean is not equal to 24 hours but to $24^h - a$, we call a the daily rate of the clock and we must correct all observations on account of it. In case that for a certain time all the different stars give so nearly the same difference $24^h - a$, that we can ascribe the deviations to possible errors of observation, we take the rate of the clock during this time as constant and equal to the arithmetical mean

*) It is not necessary to know the error of the clock, as only intervals of time are observed.

**) Usually there is a cross of wires, one wire being placed parallel to the daily motion of the stars. This is effected by letting a star near the equator run along the wire and by turning the cross by a screw attached to the apparatus for this purpose, until the star during its passage through the field does not leave the wire.

of all single a and we multiply the observed differences of right ascensions by $\frac{24}{24-a}=\frac{1}{1-\frac{a}{24}}$, in order to correct them for the rate of the clock. But if we see that the rate of the clock is increasing or decreasing with the time and the observations are sufficiently numerous, we may assume the hourly rate of the clock at the time t as being of the form $a+b(t-T)$, where a is the rate at the time T. Multiplying this by dt and integrating it between the limits t and $24+t$, we find the rate between two successive culminations of a star, whose time of culmination is t, equal to:

$$24a+24b(12+t-T)=u.$$

If we compute therefore the coefficient of b for every star and then take u equal to the rate found from the several stars, we obtain a number of equations, from which we can find the values of a and b by the method of least squares. The rate during the time $t''-t'$ we find then by means of the formula:

$$a(t''-t')+b(t''-t')\left\{\frac{t'+t''}{2}-T\right\},$$

and we must correct every interval of time $t''-t'$ according to this.

In case that already the differences of the right ascensions of a number of stars are known, the difference of the apparent place of each star and of the time U observed by the clock, gives the error of the clock ΔU, which ought to be found the same (at least within the limits of the errors of observation) from all the different stars, if the clock is exactly regulated. But if it has a rate equal to a at the time T, each star gives an equation of the following form:

$$0=U-\alpha+\Delta U+a(t-T)+\frac{b}{2}(t-T)^2$$

and from a great number of stars we may find ΔU, a and b*).

Now in order to observe the time of culmination of the stars, it is necessary to rectify the meridian circle in such

---

*) As we suppose that the right ascensions themselves are not known yet, at least not with accuracy, the error of the clock U would also be erroneous.

a way, that the intersection of the cross wires is in the plane of the meridian in every position of the telescope or that at least the deviation from the meridian is known*). If the line of collimation, that is, the line from the centre of the object-glass to the wire-cross is vertical to the axis of the pivots (the axis of revolution of the instrument), it describes when the telescope is turned a plane, which intersects the celestial sphere in a great circle. If besides the axis of the pivots is horizontal, this great circle is at the same time a vertical circle and if the axis is directed also to the West and East points, the line of collimation must always move in the plane of the meridian. Hence the instrument requires those three adjustments.

As will be shown in No. 1 of the last section, we can always examine with the aid of a spirit-level, whether the axis of the pivots is horizontal and we may also correct any error of this kind, since one of the Y-pieces can be raised or lowered by adjusting screws. The position of the line of collimation with respect to the axis can be examined by reversing the whole instrument and directing the telescope in each position of the instrument to a distant terrestrial object or still better to a small telescope (collimator) placed for this purpose in front of the telescope of the meridian circle so that its line of collimation coincides with that of the meridian circle. For if there is a wire-cross at the focus of this small telescope, it can be seen in the telescope of the meridian circle like any object at an infinitely great distance, since the rays coming from the focus of the collimator after their refraction by its object glass are parallel. Now if the angle, which the line of collimation makes with the axis of the meridian circle, differs by x from a right angle, the angles which the lines of collimation of the two telescopes make with each other in both positions of the meridian circle, will differ by $2x$ or the wire of the collimator as seen in the

*) The complete methods for rectifying the meridian circle and for determining its errors as well as for correcting the observations on account of them, are given in the seventh section. Here it is only shown, that these determinations can be made without the knowledge of the places of the stars.

telescope of the meridian circle will appear to have moved through an angle equal to $2x$. Therefore if we move the wires of the meridian telescope by the adjusting screws in a plane vertical to the line of collimation through the angle x, the line of collimation will be vertical to the axis and the wire of the collimator will remain unchanged with respect to the wires of the telescope in both positions of the instrument or to speak more correctly it will in both positions be at the same distance from the middle wire of the telescope. If this should not be exactly the case, the operation of reversing the instrument and moving the wires of the telescope must be repeated.

When these corrections have been made, the line of collimation describes a vertical circle. At last in order to direct the horizontal axis exactly from East to West, we must make use of the observations of stars, but a knowledge of their place is not required. The circumpolar stars, for instance the pole-star, describe an entire circle above the horizon, except at places near the equator. Therefore if the telescope moves in a vertical circle which is at least near the meridian, the line of collimation intersects the parallel circle twice, and the star can therefore be seen in the telescope twice during one entire revolution. If we observe now the time of the passage of the star over the wire at first above and then below the pole and the telescope is accurately in the plane of the meridian, the interval between the two observations will be $12^h + \Delta\alpha$, where $\Delta\alpha$ designates the variation of the apparent right ascension of the star in 12 hours; on the contrary, the interval will be greater or less than $12^h + \Delta\alpha$, if the plane of the telescope is East or West of the meridian. Now as one of the Y-pieces admits always of a motion in the direction from North to South, we can move this until the interval between two observations is exactly $12^h + \Delta\alpha$ and when this has been accomplished the telescope is exactly in the plane of the meridian or the axis is directed from East to West *).

*) As the complete adjustment of an instrument would be impracticable on account of the continuous change of the errors, it is always only approx-

We can also compare the intervals between three successive culminations with each other, as these must be equal if the instrument is accurately in the plane of the meridian. If the intervals are unequal, the telescope is on that side of the meridian, on which the star remains the shortest time.

If now we observe with an instrument thus adjusted the times of transit of stars, we find the differences of the apparent right ascensions and we must apply to these the reductions to the apparent place with the opposite sign in order to find the differences of the mean right ascensions referred to the beginning of the year. But the computation of the formulae for these corrections requires already an approximate knowledge of the right ascension and declination, which however can always be taken from former catalogues.

If the observed object has a visible disc, we can only observe one limb and as such objects have also a proper motion, we must compute the time of its semi-diameter passing across the meridian according to No. 28 of the first section, and we must add this time to the observed time if we have observed the first limb or substract it from it, if we have observed the second limb. In case of the sun having been observed, where both limbs are usually taken, we can simply take the arithmetical mean of both times of observation.

The time of culmination of a star may be determined still by another method, namely by observing the time, at which the star arrives at equal altitudes on both sides of the meridian. For these observations a circle is required, which is attached to a vertical column admitting of a motion round its axis in order that the circle may be brought into the plane of any vertical circle. If we observe with such an instrument the time, when a star arrives at equal altitudes on both sides of the meridian, the arithmetical mean of both times is the clock-time of the culmination of the star. It is evident, that it is not necessary to know the altitude

imately adjusted and the observations are corrected for the remaining errors, which have been determined by the above methods or by similar ones, which will be given in the last section.

of the star itself, but it is essential, that the telescope in both observations has exactly the same inclination to the horizon. If there is a difference of the two inclinations and this is known, we can easily compute the error of the clock-time of culmination produced by it; for if the zenith distance on the West side has been observed too great, the star has been observed in an hour angle which is too great by $\frac{\Delta z}{\cos\varphi \sin A}$, hence we must subtract from the arithmetical mean of both times the correction $\frac{1}{30}\frac{\Delta z}{\cos\varphi\sin A}$. Such a correction is always required on account of refraction; for although the mean refraction is the same for both observations, yet the different state of the atmosphere, as indicated by the thermometer and barometer, will produce a slight difference of the refraction, whose effect can be computed by the above formula. In case of the sun being observed the change of the declination during the interval of both observations will also make a correction necessary.

We see from the formula $\frac{dz}{dt} = \cos\varphi \sin A$, that it is best to observe the zenith distances of the stars in the neighbourhood of the prime vertical, because their changes are then the most rapid. It is also desirable, to make these observations at a place not too far from the equator, because then $\cos\varphi$ is also equal to 1, and to observe stars near the equator. As the determination of absolute right ascensions depends upon such observations, it may be made with advantage by this method at a place near the equator.

6. If we bring the stars at the time, when they cross the vertical wire of the meridian circle, on the horizontal wire and read the circle by a vernier or a microscope, the differences of these readings for different stars give us the differences of their apparent meridian altitudes*), and if we know the zenith point of the circle and subtract this from

*) In the seventh section the corrections will be given, which must be applied to these readings in order to free them from the errors of the instrument, for instance the errors of division of the circle, or errors produced by the action of the force of gravity upon different parts of the instrument.

all readings, we find the apparent zenith distances of the stars. This point can be easily determined by observing the images of the wires reflected from an artificial horizon. For if we turn the telescope towards the nadir, and place a basin with mercury under the object glas and reflect light from the outside of the eye-piece towards the mercury, we see in the light field besides the wires also their reflected images. Therefore if we turn the telescope until the reflected image of the horizontal wire coincides with the wire itself, the line of collimation must be directed exactly to the nadir, hence we find by the reading of the circle the nadir point or by adding 180^0 the zenith point of the circle.

The apparent zenith distances must first be corrected for refraction and if the sun, the moon or the planets have been observed, also for parallax by adding to them the refraction computed according to formula A in No. 12 of the third section and by subtracting $p \sin z$, where p is the horizontal parallax *). If the object has a visible disc, we must add to or substract from the zenith distance of the limb, corrected for refraction and parallax, the radius of the disc or if in case of observations of the sun, the lower as well as the upper limb has been observed, we must take the arithmetical mean of both corrected observations. Since in this case these observations are made at a little distance from the meridian, it is still necessary to apply a small correction (whose expression will be given in the seventh section) because the horizontal wire represents a great circle on the celestial sphere and therefore differs from the parallel of the sun.

When the zenith distances at the time of culmination are known, the declinations are found according to No. 23 of the first section, if the latitude of the place of observation is known. But the latter can always easily be determined by observing the zenith distances of any circumpolar star in its upper and lower culmination, as the arithmetical mean of these zenith distances corrected for refraction $+\frac{1}{2}\Delta\delta$ is equal to the co-latitude of the place, where $\Delta\delta$

---

*) In the case of the moon the rigorous formula must be used.

denotes the variation of the apparent declination during the interval of time. We may also determine the latitude by observing any circumpolar star in its upper and lower culmination as well direct as reflected from an artificial horizon. For then the arithmetical mean of the corrected altitudes *minus* $\frac{1}{2}\Delta\delta$ is equal to the latitude. But as the reflected observations cannot be made at the same time as the direct observations, usually also several observations are taken before and after the time of culmination, we must reduce first each observation to the meridian by the method given in the seventh section.

If the place of observation is in the neighbourhood of the equator, the method of determining the latitude by circumpolar stars cannot be used. At such a place we must determine it by observations of the sun as will be shown in the next number.

When the latitude has been determined we find from the zenith distances corrected for refraction the apparent declinations of the stars, which are converted into mean declinations for the beginning of the year by applying the reduction to the apparent declination with the opposite sign.

7. If A and D be the right ascension and declination of the sun, we have:

$$\sin A \operatorname{tang} \varepsilon = \operatorname{tang} D,$$

hence the observation of the declination of the sun gives us either the obliquity of the ecliptic, when the right ascension is known, or the right ascension, when the obliquity of the ecliptic is known from other observations. But the differential equation (which we get by differentiating the above equation written in a logarithmic form)

$$\operatorname{cotang} A \,.\, dA + \frac{2\,d\varepsilon}{\sin 2\,\varepsilon} = \frac{2\,dD}{\sin 2D}$$

shows, that it is best, to determine the obliquity of the ecliptic by observations in the neighbourhood of the solstices and the right ascension by observations in the neighbourhood of the equinoxes. If we determine the declination of the sun exactly at the time, when the right ascension is equal to 90^0 or 270^0 we find immediately by subtracting the latitude of the sun the obliquity of the ecliptic. But even if we only observe the declination in the neighbourhood of the solstice and know approximately the position of the equinox, we can compute the obliquity of the ecliptic either by the above formula or better by developing it in a series.

If we denote by D' the observed declination, by B the latitude of the sun, the declination of the sun corrected for the latitude, which would have been observed, if the centre of the sun had been in the ecliptic, will be according to the formulae in the Note to No. 11 of the first Section:

$$D' - \frac{\cos \varepsilon}{\cos D} B = D.$$

Moreover if x is the distance of the sun from the solstitial point expressed in right ascension or equal to $90 - A$, we have the following equation:

$$\cos x \operatorname{tang} \varepsilon = \operatorname{tang} D,$$

and as x is a small quantity, we can develop ε into a rapidly converging series, for we find according to formula (18) in No. 11 of the introduction:

$$\varepsilon = D + \operatorname{tang} \tfrac{1}{2} x^2 \,.\, \sin 2D + \tfrac{1}{2} \operatorname{tang} \tfrac{1}{2} x^4 \sin 4D + \ldots \qquad (A)$$

Thus we can easily find the obliquity of the ecliptic from an observation of the sun in the neighbourhood of the solstitial points. It is evident, that the aberration, as it affects merely the apparent place in the ecliptic, has no influence whatever upon the result, nor is the value of ε changed, if A and D are reduced to another equinox by applying the precession. But if A and D are the apparent places, affected with nutation, the value of ε, which we deduce from them, will be also the apparent obliquity of the ecliptic, affected with nutation.

On the 19th of June 1843 the declination of the sun was observed at Koenigsberg and after being corrected for refraction and parallax was found equal to $+23^\circ\, 26'\, 8''.57$. At the same time the right ascension of the sun was $5^h\, 48^m\, 50^s.54$. Hence we have in this case $x = 0^h\, 11^m\, 9^s.46 = 2^\circ 47' 21''.90$ and as the latitude of the sun was equal to $+0''.70$, we have:

$$\begin{array}{rr} D = & +23^\circ\, 26'\ \ 7''.87 \\ \text{I. term of the series} = & +1\ 29\ .23 \\ \text{II. term of the series} = & +0\ .04 \\ \hline \varepsilon = & 23^\circ\, 27' 37''.14. \end{array}$$

This is the apparent obliquity of the ecliptic on the 19th of June 1843, as deduced from this one observation. If we compute now the nutation according to the formulae in No. 5 of the second section, taking $\Omega = 272^{\circ}\, 37'.4$, $\odot = 87^{\circ}\, 0'$, $☾ = 350^{\circ}\, 17'$ and $P = 280^{\circ}\, 14'$, we find $\Delta\varepsilon = +0''.05$, hence the mean obliquity on that day according to that one observation is $23^{\circ}\, 27'\, 37''.09$.

We should find the same value only in a more circuitous way by correcting A and D for nutation according to the formulae in No. 5 and 7 of the second section and computing the formula (A) with these corrected values. As the nutation in longitude is equal to $+17''.18$, we find $\Delta\alpha = +1^{s}.25$, $\Delta\delta = +0''.39$, therefore:

Corrected $D =$	$23^{\circ}\, 26'\;\; 7''.48$
I. term	$+1\;\, 29\;.\,57$
II. term	$+0\;.\,04$
Mean obliquity $=$	$23^{\circ}\, 27' 37''.09.$

In order to free the result from accidental errors of observation, the declination of the sun is observed on as many days as possible in the neighbourhood of the solstices and the arithmetical mean taken of all single observations. But any constant errors, with which x and D are affected, will not be eliminated in this way. If we denote the value of the obliquity of the ecliptic which has been computed from x and D according to the above method by ε', its true value by ε, the errors of x and D by dx and dD, each observation gives an equation of the following form:

$$\varepsilon = \varepsilon' + \tfrac{15}{2} \operatorname{tang} x \sin 2\varepsilon\, dx + \frac{\sin 2\varepsilon}{\sin 2D}\, dD,$$

which is easily deduced from the differential equation given before and in which dx is expressed in seconds of time. We have for instance for the above example:

$$\varepsilon = 23^{\circ}\, 27'\, 37''.09 + 0.212\, dx + 1.001\, dD,$$

from which we see, that an error in x, equal to a second of time, produces only an error of $0''.21$ in the obliquity of the ecliptic. If we assume then a certain value ε_0, taking $\varepsilon = \varepsilon_0 + d\varepsilon$ and $\varepsilon_0 - \varepsilon' = n$, we find from each observation an equation of the following form:

$$0 = n + d\varepsilon - \tfrac{15}{2} \operatorname{tang} x \sin \varepsilon\, dx - \frac{\sin 2\varepsilon}{\sin 2D}\, dD.$$

By applying to them the method of least squares, we can find $d\varepsilon$ as a function of dx and dD, hence if we should afterwards be obliged to alter the right ascensions or the declinations of the sun by the constant quantities $dA = -dx$ and dD, we can easily compute the effect, which these alterations have upon the value of the obliquity of the ecliptic. Hence we may assume, that the most probable value of the obliquity of the ecliptic, deduced from observations in the neighbourhood of a certain solstice, is of the following form:

$$\varepsilon' + a\,dD + b\,dx,$$

where the coefficient of dD is always nearly equal to unity. Now if there are no constant errors in D and x, or if dD and dx are equal to zero, we ought to find from observations made in the neighbourhood of the next solstice nearly the same value of ε, the difference being equal to the secular variation during the interval of time, which amounts to 0''. 23. But since accidental errors committed in taking the single zenith distances or accidental errors of the refraction are not entirely eliminated in the arithmetical mean of all observations made in the neighbourhood of the same solstice, we can only expect to arrive at an accurate value of the mean obliquity of the ecliptic by reducing the values derived from a great many solstices to the same epoch and in this case we may determine at the same time the secular variation. If we have found from observations the mean obliquity of the ecliptic at the time t equal to ε and if we suppose, that the true value of the obliquity at the time t_0 is equal to $\varepsilon_0 + d\varepsilon$ and that the annual variation is $\Delta\varepsilon + x$, we should have the equation:

$$\varepsilon = \varepsilon_0 + d\varepsilon - (\Delta e + x)(t - t_0)$$

in case that the observed value were right. Hence if we take:

$$\varepsilon_0 - \Delta\varepsilon(t - t_0) - \varepsilon = n,$$

every determination of the mean obliquity of the ecliptic at the time of a solstice gives an equation of the following form:

$$0 = n + d\varepsilon + x(t - t_0)$$

and if there have been several such determinations made, we can find from all equations the most probable values of $d\varepsilon$ and x according to the method of least squares. In this way Bessel found from his own observations and those of Bradley the mean obliquity of the ecliptic for the beginning of the year 1800 equal to $23^0\,27'\,54''.80$ and the annual variation $0''.457$. Peters comparing Struve's observations with those of Bradley found:

$$23^0\,27'\,54''.22 - 0''.4645\,(t - 1800)$$

a value which now generally is considered as more exact.

If a constant error has been committed in observing the declinations, if for instance the altitude of the pole is only approximately known, the values of the obliquity derived from summer or winter solstices will show constant differences. Since we have $D = z + \varphi$ and if we denote by $d\varphi$ the correction which must be applied to the altitude of the pole, by ε the true value of the obliquity of the ecliptic, by ε' the value deduced from observations, we have the following equation from a summer solstice:

$$\varepsilon = \varepsilon' + a\,d\varphi,$$

and for a winter solstice:

$$\varepsilon_{,} = \varepsilon'' - a'\,d\varphi$$

hence we have:

$$d\varphi = \frac{\varepsilon'' - \varepsilon' + \varepsilon - \varepsilon_{,}}{a + a'},$$

where $\varepsilon - \varepsilon_{,}$ is the secular variation during the interval of time. This is the correction which must be applied to the latitude, if a constant error has been committed in observing the zenith distances. We can find in this way an approximate value of the latitude by observing the zenith distance of the sun on the days of the summer and winter solstice. For if z' and z'' are those zenith distances corrected for refraction, parallax and nutation, taken negative if the sun culminates on the north side of the zenith, we have:

$$\varphi = \frac{z' + z''}{2}.$$

8. If then the obliquity of the ecliptic be known, the absolute right ascension of a star and hence from the differences of right ascensions that of all stars may be found with the utmost accuracy. For this purpose a bright star is selected, which can be observed in the daylight as well as by night and which is in the neighbourhood of the equator, for instance α Canis minoris (Procyon) or α Aquilae (Altair).

If then the transit of the star is observed at the time t, that of the sun at the time T, the interval $t - T$, corrected for the rate of the clock, is equal to the difference of the right ascensions of the star and the sun at the time of culmination of the latter. If now also the true declination of the sun has been determined at the time of culmination, we find the right ascension of the sun from the following equation:

$$\sin A \operatorname{tang} \varepsilon = \operatorname{tang} D,$$

and we have therefore:

$$\alpha = \operatorname{arc} \sin \frac{\operatorname{tang} D}{\operatorname{tang} \varepsilon} + t - T,$$

where strictly the time T must also be corrected for the latitude of the sun by adding $+ \cos A \sec \delta \sin \varepsilon \frac{B}{15}$.

If now D and ε be in error, we shall on this account also obtain an erroneous value of $t - T$, independently of errors of observation in $t - T$. In order to estimate the effect of any such errors, we use the differential equation found in the preceding No.:

$$dA = - \frac{2 \operatorname{tang} A}{\sin 2 \varepsilon} d\varepsilon + \frac{2 \operatorname{tang} A}{\sin 2 D} dD,$$

and consequently we obtain from each observation an equation of the following form:

$$\alpha = \operatorname{arc} \sin \frac{\operatorname{tang} D}{\operatorname{tang} \varepsilon} + t - T - \frac{2 \operatorname{tang} A}{\sin 2 \varepsilon} d\varepsilon + \frac{2 \operatorname{tang} A}{\sin 2 D} dD. \qquad (A)$$

We easily see from this equation, that it is best to make these observations in the neighbourhood of the equinox, because then the coefficients of $d\varepsilon$ and dD arrive at their minimum, that of $d\varepsilon$ being zero and that of dD being cotang ε or 2.3. Moreover we see that it is possible to combine several observations in such a way, that the effect of an error in ε as well as of any constant error in D is eliminated. For if in the equation $\sin A = \frac{\operatorname{tang} D}{\operatorname{tang} \varepsilon}$ we take the angle A always acute, we have, when the right ascension of the sun is $180 - A'$, the following equation:

$$\alpha = 180 - \operatorname{arc} \sin \frac{\operatorname{tang} D'}{\operatorname{tang} \varepsilon} + t' - T' + \frac{2 \operatorname{tang} A'}{\sin 2 \varepsilon'} d\varepsilon - \frac{2 \operatorname{tang} A'}{\sin 2 D'} dD,$$

where t' and T' are again the times of transit of the star and the sun, and if we combine this equation with the former, we find:

$$\alpha = \tfrac{1}{2}[(t-T)+(t'-T')] + \tfrac{1}{2}\left[\text{arc sin}\frac{\text{tang}\, D}{\text{tang}\, \varepsilon} - \text{arc sin}\frac{\text{tang}\, D'}{\text{tang}\, \varepsilon} + 180^{0}\right]$$

$$+ \left[\frac{\text{tang}\, A}{\sin 2D} - \frac{\text{tang}\, A'}{\sin 2D'}\right] dD - \frac{\text{tang}\, A - \text{tang}\, A'}{\sin 2\varepsilon}\, d\varepsilon. \qquad (B)$$

If now the acute angle $A' = A$, then we have also $D' = D$. If therefore the difference of right ascensions of the sun and the star be observed at the times when the sun has the right ascensions A and $180^{0} - A$, the coefficients of dD and $d\varepsilon$ in equation (B) will be equal to zero and the constant errors in the declination and the obliquity will thus have no effect on the right ascension of the star. This it is true will never be attained with the utmost rigour, as it will never exactly happen, that, when the sun at one culmination has the right ascension A, the right ascension $180 - A$ shall exactly correspond to another culmination. But if A' be only nearly equal to $180^{0} - A$, the remaining errors dependent on dD and $d\varepsilon$ will be always exceedingly small.

Therefore for the determination of the absolute right ascension of a star, the difference of right ascensions of the sun and the star should be observed in the neighbourhood of the vernal and autumnal equinoxes. But if one observation has been made after the vernal equinox, the second must be made as much before the autumnal equinox and *vice versâ*. If we combine any two such observations, the effect of any constant errors in D and ε is eliminated and the result is only affected with casual errors, which may have been committed in observing the times of transit or the declinations. These can only be got rid of in a mass of observations and hence it is necessary to combine not only two such observations but as great a number as possible of observations taken before and after the vernal and autumnal equinox, in which case it is not necessary to confine the observations to the immediate neighbourhood of the equinox. Let α_0 be an approximate value and $\alpha = \alpha_0 + d\alpha$ the true value of the right ascension and put:

$$\alpha_0 - \text{arc sin}\frac{\text{tang}\, D}{\text{tang}\, \varepsilon} - (t - T) = n.$$

Then each observation gives an equation of the following form:

$$0 = n + d\alpha + \frac{2 \operatorname{tang} A}{\sin 2\varepsilon} d\varepsilon - \frac{2 \operatorname{tang} A}{\sin 2D} dD.$$

If we treat then all those equations according to the method of least squares, we can find the most probable values of $d\alpha$, $d\varepsilon$ and dD or at least $d\alpha$ as a function of $d\varepsilon$ and dD, so that, if these should be found from other observations and their values be substituted in the expression for $d\alpha$, we get that correction $d\alpha$ which in connection with these determinate values of $d\varepsilon$ and dD makes the sum of the residual errors a minimum. In case that the number of observations is very great and the observations are well distributed about the equinoxes, the coefficients of $d\varepsilon$ and dD in the final equation for $d\alpha$ will always be very small.

If the observations extend to a great distance from the equinoxes and the observed declinations lie between the limits $\mp D$, it may not be accurate to take dD for the entire range $2D$ as constant, for instance, in case that the circle-readings are affected with errors dependent on the zenith distance, or if the constant of refraction should need a correction. Although even in this case these errors have no effect upon the result, if the observations are distributed symmetrically around the equinoxes, yet the resulting value of dD or the term dependent on dD in the final expression of $d\alpha$ would have no meaning. In this case it is necessary to divide the observations according to the zenith distance into groups, within which it is allowable to consider the error dD as constant and to treat those several groups according to the method of least squares. Since we have $D = \varphi - z - \varrho$, if the object is south of the zenith, we may take instead of dD in the above equation $d\varphi - dk \operatorname{tang} z - \beta f(z)$, where dk denotes the correction of the constant of refraction and $\beta f(z)$ the correction which must be applied to the circle-readings. But for determining the values of these quantities, there are generally other and better methods used.

Bessel observed in 1828 March 24 at Koenigsberg the declination of the sun's centre, corrected for refraction and parallax:

$$D' = +1^\circ\, 15'\, 27''.24$$

and the interval between the transit of the sun and the star α Canis minoris, corrected for the rate of the clock:

$$t - T = 7^h\, 19^m\, 29^s.86.$$

As the latitude of the sun was $+0''.21$, the correction of the declination is $-0''.19$, whilst that of the time is nothing. Now the values D and T referring to the sun, need not be corrected for aberration, since this merely changes the place of the sun in the ecliptic, but for the star we find according to formula (A) in No. 16 of the third section, as the longitude of the sun is $3^0\, 10'$ and the approximate place of the star $\alpha = 112^0\, 46'$ and $\delta = +5^0\, 37'$:

$$\alpha' - \alpha = 0^s.42.$$

This being subtracted from the time t, we find:

$$t - T = 7^h\, 19^m\, 29^s.44$$
$$D = +1^0\, 15'\, 27''.05,$$

both being referred to the apparent equinox at the time of the observation. If we take now for the mean obliquity on that day $23^0\, 27'\, 35''.05$, we must add to it the nutation in order to find the apparent obliquity at the time of observation. But as:

$$\Omega = 277^0\, 13'.8, \quad \odot = 1^0\, 14', \quad ☾ = 283^0\, 56', \quad P = 280^0\, 14'$$

we find by the formula in No. 5 of the second section $\Delta\varepsilon = +1''.72$, hence:

$$\varepsilon = 23^0\, 27'\, 36''.77.$$

and with this we find:

$$A = \text{arc sin}\,\frac{\text{tang}\, D}{\text{tang}\, \varepsilon} = 2^0\, 53'\, 57''.44 = 0^h\, 11^m\, 35^s.83.$$

Hence the right ascension referred to the apparent equinox is:

$$\alpha = 7^h\, 31^m\, 5^s.27$$

and adding the nutation in right ascension $+1^s.10$ and subtracting the precession and proper motion from the beginning of the year to March 24 equal to $+0^s.71$ (since the annual variation is $+3^s.146$) and computing the coefficients of dD and $d\varepsilon$, we find according to this observation the mean right ascension of α Canis minoris for 1843.0

$$\alpha = 7^h\, 31^m\, 3^s.46 + 0.1539\, dD - 0.0092\, d\varepsilon,$$

where dD and $d\varepsilon$ are expressed in seconds of arc.

On the 20th of September of the same year Bessel observed:

$$D' = +1^\circ\, 16'\, 29''.22$$
$$t' - T' = -4^h\, 17^m\, 5^s.82.$$

As on that day the latitude of the sun was $B = -0''.56$, and $\Omega = 267^\circ\, 41'.9$, $\odot = 178^\circ\, 39'$, ☾ $= 135^\circ\, 41'$, $P = 280^\circ\, 14'$, we find the corrections dependent on B equal to $-0''.51$ and $+0^s.01$; furthermore the aberration is $= -0^s.56$, the nutation of the obliquity is $+0''.27$, hence, as the mean obliquity was on that day $23^\circ\, 27'\, 34''.82$, we find:

$$D = +1^\circ\, 16'\, 29''.73$$
$$t' - T' = -4^h\, 17^m\, 5^s.27$$
$$\varepsilon = 23^\circ\, 27'\, 35''.09.$$

From this we get $A = 2^\circ\, 56'\, 22''.36 = 0^h\, 11^m\, 45^s.49$, hence the right ascension of the sun equal to $11^h\, 48^m\, 14^s.51$, therefore $\alpha = 7^h\, 31^m\, 9^s.24$ and as the nutation was $+1^s.11$, the precession and proper motion equal to $+2^s.27$, we find according to this observation the mean right ascension for 1843.0

$$\alpha = 7^h\, 31^m\, 5^s.86 - 0.1539\, dD + 0.0094\, d\varepsilon.$$

Taking the arithmetical mean of both determinations we find:

$$\alpha = 7^h\, 31^m\, 4^s.66\ ^{*)}.$$

a result which is free from the constant errors in D and ε.

We might have deduced the mean right ascension by subtracting from D, T and t the reductions to the apparent place, neglecting for the sun the terms dependent on aberration. Then using the mean obliquity for each day, we would have found immediately the right ascension referred to the mean equinox for the beginning of the year.

9. When the right ascension of one star has been thus determined, the right ascensions of all stars, whose differences of right ascension have been observed, are known also and can be collected in a catalogue together with the decli-

---

*) According to Bessel's Tabulae Regiomontanae is $\alpha = 7^h\, 31^m\, 4^s.81$. As the arithmetical mean of both observations agrees so nearly with this, the casual errors on both days must have been also nearly equal. If we compare the two observed declinations with the solar tables we find the errors of the declinations equal to $+7''.67$ and $8''.24$.

nations. Thus the right ascensions given in the catalogues of different observers can have a constant difference on account of the errors committed in the determination of the absolute right ascension. This can be determined by comparing a large number of stars, contained in the several catalogues, after reducing them to the same epoch. Similar differences may occur in the declinations and can be determined in the same way. But since these errors may be variable, as was stated before, one must form zones of a certain number of degrees and determine the difference for these several zones.

In order to facilitate the relative determination of the places of stars as well as of planets and comets, the apparent places of some stars, which have been determined with great accuracy and are therefore called ***standard stars***, are given in the astronomical almanacs for the time of culmination for every tenth day of the year. Thus in order to find the right ascension and declination of an unknown object, one compares it with one or several of these standard stars, determining according to the methods given before the difference of right ascension and declination. In case that the declination of the unknown object differs little from the standard star, any errors of the instrument will have nearly the same effect upon both observations and hence their difference will be nearly free from those errors.

If the unknown object whose difference of right ascension and declination is to be determined, should be very near the star, one can use for the observation instead of a meridian instrument a telescope furnished with a micrometer (which will be described in the seventh section). This method has this advantage, that the observation can be repeated as often as one pleases and that it is not necessary to wait for the culmination of the object, which moreover might happen at daylight and thus frustrate the observation of a faint object. This method is therefore always used, if one wishes to observe the relative places of stars very near each other or the places of new planets and comets. For this purpose it is necessary to have a large number of stars determined, so as to be able to find under all circumstances stars, by which the object can be micrometrically determined. Therefore on this account as well as in general for an extensive knowledge of the fixed stars, large collections of observations of stars down to the ninth and tenth magnitude have been made and are still added to. In order to seize as many stars as possible and at the same time to facilitate the reduction of the stars to their mean places, the observer takes every day only such stars, which form a narrow zone of a few degrees in declination and observes the clock-times of transit and the circle-readings for every star. Such observations are called therefore *observations of zones*. A table is then computed for every zone, by which the mean place of every star for a certain epoch can be easily deduced from the observed place and since such tables can be easily recomputed, whenever more accurate means for their computation, for instance more accurate places of the stars, on which they are based, are available, the arangement of these observations in zones is of great advantage.

If now t be the observed transit of a star over the wire of the instrument, z the circle-reading, it is necessary to apply corrections to both in order to find the mean right ascension and declination of the star for a certain epoch. We must apply to t the error of the clock, the deviation of the wire from the meridian, the reduction to the apparent place with opposite sign, and the precession in the interval between the time of observation and the epoch, whilst we must apply to z the polar point of the circle, the errors of flexure and division, the refraction and, as before, the reduction to the apparent place with opposite sign and the precession. Bessel has introduced a very convenient form for tabulating these corrections. First a table is constructed, which gives for every tenth minute of the clock-time t occurring in the zone the values k and d of these corrections for the declination D corresponding to the middle of the zone, and besides another table, which gives the variations of these corrections for a variation of the declination equal to 100 minutes. The mean right ascension and declination of any star for the assumed epoch is then found by the formulae:

$$\alpha = t + k + k' \frac{z - Z}{100},$$

$$\delta = z + d + d' \frac{z - Z}{100}.$$

where Z denotes the circle-reading corresponding to the middle of the zone.

If we denote by u and u' the error of the clock and its variation in one hour, by e and e' the deviation of the wire from the meridian corresponding to the position Z and its variation for 100 minutes, by P the polar point, by ϱ and s the refraction and the errors of division and flexure, by ϱ' and s' their variations for 100 minutes, at last by $\Delta\alpha$ and $\Delta\delta$ the reductions to the apparent place and if we assume, that the divisions increase in the direction of declination and that we take as epoch the beginning of the year, we have:

$$\alpha = t + u + e + u'(t - T) + e' \frac{(z - Z)}{100} - \Delta\alpha,$$

$$\delta = z - P + 90^0 \mp \varrho \mp \varrho' \frac{z - Z}{100} + s + s' \frac{z - Z}{100} - \Delta\delta.$$

But according to the formulae in No. 3 we have:

$$\Delta\alpha = \frac{f}{15} + \frac{g}{15} \sin(G + \alpha) \operatorname{tang} D + \frac{h}{15} \sin(H + \alpha) \sec D,$$
$$+ \left[\frac{g}{15} \frac{(\sin G + \alpha)}{\cos D^2} 100' + \frac{h}{15} \sin(H + \alpha) \frac{\operatorname{tang} D}{\operatorname{ccs} D} 100'\right] \frac{z - Z}{100},$$
$$\Delta\delta = g \cos(G + \alpha) + h \cos(H + \alpha) \sin D + i \cos D$$
$$+ \left[h \cos(H + \alpha) \cos D\, 100' - i \sin D\, 100'\right] \frac{z - Z}{100},$$

hence we find:

$$k = u + e + u'(t - T) - \frac{f}{15} - \frac{g}{15} \sin(G + \alpha) \operatorname{tg} D - \frac{h}{15} \sin(H + \alpha) \sec D,$$
$$k' = e' - \frac{g}{15} \frac{\sin(G + \alpha)}{\cos D^2} 100' + \frac{h}{15} \sin(H + \alpha) \frac{\operatorname{tang} D}{\cos D} 100',$$
$$d = - P + 90^0 \mp \varrho + s - g \cos(G + \alpha) - h \cos(H + \alpha) \sin D - i \cos D,$$
$$d' = \mp \varrho' + s' - [h \cos(H + \alpha) \cos D\, 100' + i \sin D\, 100'].$$

The error of the clock and the polar point of the circle are determined by any known stars, which occur in the zone, or by the standard stars, if any of them have been observed before and after observing the zone-stars and if the errors of the instrument, as well as the polar point and the rate of the clock can either be considered as constant or be interpolated from those observations. The values of k,

k', d and d' are then tabulated for every tenth minute of the clock time t and may thus be easily interpolated for any other value of t.

III. ON THE METHODS OF DETERMINING THE MOST PROBABLE VALUES OF THE CONSTANTS USED FOR THE REDUCTION OF THE PLACES OF THE STARS.

A. Determination of the constant of refraction.

10. It was shown in No. 6, how the apparent zenith distances of stars are determined by observations which first must be cleared from refraction, in order to obtain the true zenith distances. If the zenith distance of a circumpolar star be observed at its upper and lower culmination and corrected for refraction as well as for the small variations of the aberration, nutation and precession in the interval between the two observations, the arithmetical mean of the two corrected zenith distances is equal to the complement of the latitude. Now if a set of such observations of different stars is made, all should give the same value for the latitude or at least only such differences as may be attributed to errors of observation and casual errors of the refraction as mentioned in No. 13 of the third section, provided that the adopted formula for the refraction and especially the adopted value of the constant of refraction is true. Hence if there are any differences, they must enable us to correct the constants on which the tables of refraction, which are used for the reduction, are based.

Denoting by z and ζ the observed zenith distances at the upper and lower culmination, by r and ϱ the refraction, we have for any north latitude the equations:

$$\delta - \varphi = z \pm r$$
$$180^0 - \delta - \varphi = \zeta + \varrho,$$

where south zenith distances must be taken negative and where the upper or lower sign must be used, if the star at its upper culmination be north or south of the zenith. From these equations we find:

$$90^0 - \varphi = \frac{\zeta + z}{2} + \frac{\varrho \pm r}{2}. \qquad (a)$$

If another star be observed at both culminations and the zenith distances ζ' and z' be found, we should be able, to find from the following two equations:

$$90^{0}-\varphi=\frac{\zeta+z}{2}+\frac{\varrho\pm r}{2}$$

$$\text{and}\quad 90^{0}-\varphi=\frac{\zeta'+z'}{2}+\frac{\varrho'\pm r'}{2}$$

the values of φ and of that constant which in ϱ, ϱ', r and r' occurs as factor. But the values thus found would be only approximate on account of the errors of observation; besides equation (l) in No. 9 of the third section shows, that the refraction is not strictly proportional to the constant α but that it contains some other constants, the correct values of which it is desirable to determine from observations. Ivory's formula contains besides α the constant f, which depends on the decrease of temperature with the elevation above the surface of the earth, which however shall here be neglected, since its influence, which is always small, is felt only in the immediate neighbourhood of the horizon; but besides this, like all other formulae for the refraction, it contains the coefficient ε for the expansion of air by heat, which it is also best to determine in this case by astronomical observations. For since the atmosphere has always a certain degree of moisture and the expansion of the air depends on its state of moisture, therefore if we determine this coefficient from a large number of observed refractions, we shall obtain a value, which corresponds to a mean state of the atmosphere, and the refractions computed with this value will give in the mean of a great many observations as near as possible that value which would have been obtained, if the actual moisture of the atmosphere at the time of each observation had been taken into account. Now denoting the mean and the true refraction by R and R', we have according to the formula (12) of the third section:

$$R'=R\,[B\,.\,T]^{A}\,[1+\varepsilon\,(\tau-50)]^{-\lambda},$$

where $A=1+q$ and $\lambda=1+p$. From this we get:

$$dR'=\frac{dR'}{d\alpha}\,d\alpha-\frac{\lambda\,(\tau-50)}{1+\varepsilon\,(\tau-50)}\,R'd\varepsilon,$$

or taking:

$$\alpha + d\alpha = \alpha(1+k), \quad \varepsilon + d\varepsilon = \varepsilon(1+i)$$

$$dR' = \alpha \frac{dR'}{d\alpha} k - \frac{\lambda\varepsilon(\tau-50)}{1+\varepsilon(\tau-50)} R' i.$$

But according to the formula (l) in No. 9 of the third section we have:

$$\alpha \frac{dR}{d\alpha} = R + \frac{\alpha^2 \beta \sqrt{2\beta}}{(1-\alpha)\sin z^2} [2^{\frac{1}{2}} \psi(2) - \psi(1)].$$

The second term of the second member of this equation becomes significant only for zenith distances greater than 80° and if we put:

$$\alpha \frac{dR}{d\alpha} = R\left(1 + \frac{1}{y}\right),$$

we can take the values of y from the following table:

z	y	z	y
80°	246	86°	60.5
81°	205	87°	43.2
82°	168	88°	29.5
83°	135	89°	19.0
84°	106	89° 30′	14.8
85°	82		

We have therefore:

$$dR' = R'\left(1 + \frac{1}{y}\right) k - \frac{\lambda\varepsilon(\tau-50)}{1+\varepsilon(\tau-50)} R' i.$$

If we assume therefore, that the values of the refraction, which have been used for computing formula (a), are erroneous and that the corrections are $d\varrho$ and dr, we get:

$$90^0 - \varphi = \frac{\zeta + z}{2} + \frac{\varrho \pm r}{2} + \frac{\varrho\left(1+\frac{1}{y}\right) \pm r}{2} k - \frac{\mu\varrho \pm mr}{2} i,$$

if we denote by m and μ the values of $\frac{\lambda\varepsilon(\tau-50)}{1+\varepsilon(\tau-50)}$ for the upper and lower culmination. If we also assume an approximate value φ_0 for φ, the true value being $\varphi = \varphi_0 + d\varphi$ and take:

$$\frac{\zeta + z}{2} + \frac{\varrho \pm r}{2} + \varphi_0 - 90^0 = n,$$

we obtain, combining the result of the upper and lower culmination of each star, an equation of the following form:

$$0 = n + d\varphi + \frac{\varrho\left(1+\frac{1}{y}\right) \pm r}{2} k - \frac{\mu\varrho \pm mr}{2} i. \qquad (b).$$

Now the observations of the several stars will not have the same weight, since the accidental errors of observation are the greater the nearer the star is to the horizon. Hence the probable error of an observation will generally increase with the zenith distance of the star. In case that the values of $d\varphi$, k and i were already known and were substituted in the equations, the quantities n would be the real errors of observation and hence the probable error of one observation might be determined. But since these values are unknown, this can only approximately be found from the deviations of the single observations from their arithmetical mean. If then w and w' are the probable errors of an observation at the upper and lower culmination, all equations of the same star must be divided by $\sqrt{w^2 + w'^2}$ in order to give to the equations of the several stars their true weight. In case that the probable errors should be found very different when the equations have been solved, the whole calculation may be repeated.

Also stars culminating south of the zenith can be used for determining the correction i of the coefficient ε for the expansion of air. For such stars we have according to the notation which we used before, taking the zenith distances positive:

$$\varphi_0 - \delta_0 + d(\varphi - \delta) = z + r + r\left(1 + \frac{1}{y}\right)k - mri,$$

or taking:

$$n = z + r + \delta_0 - \varphi_0,$$

$$0 = n + d(\delta - \varphi) + r\left(1 + \frac{1}{y}\right)k - mri. \qquad (c)$$

If also in this case we multiply the equations of the several stars by their corresponding weights and deduce the equations for the minimum from all equations of the same star, we can eliminate the unknown quantities $d(\delta - \varphi)$ and k, so that each star gives finally an equation of the form:

$$0 = N - Mi. \qquad (d)$$

But a similar equation can be deduced from every circumpolar star observed at the times of both culminations, if the equations (b) are treated in a similar way. Hence we find a number of equations of the form (d) equal to the number of observed stars, from which the most probable value of i can be deduced *). By this method Bessel determined the quantity i and thus the coefficient of the expansion of air for a mean state of the moisture of the atmosphere from observations made at Koenigsberg. (Consult Bessel, Astronomische Beobachtungen, Siebente Abtheilung, pag. X) and the value found by him is the one which was given before namely 0.0020243 for one degree Fahrenheit.

If we substitute the most probable value of i in the equations (b) or rather in the equations of the minimum, deduced for each star, we find from the combination of these equations corresponding to the several stars, the most probable values of $d\varphi$ and k **).

If it should be desirable, to take the correction of the quantity f into account, it would be necessary to add to dR' the term $\frac{dR'}{df}\,df$ or, taking $f + df = f(1+h)$, the term $f\frac{dR'}{df}\,h = \frac{R'}{x}\,h$, where the values of x can be taken from the following table:

z	x	z	x
85°	338	88°	59.3
86°	196	89°	29.8
87°	111	89° 30′	20.6.

B. Determination of the constants of aberration and nutation and of the annual parallaxes of stars.

11. The aberration, nutation and annual parallax are the periodical terms contained in the expression for the apparent places of the stars, hence their constants must be determined by observing the apparent places of the stars at different times. Aberration and parallax have the period of

---

*) As a change of temperature has the greatest effect upon low stars, it is not necessary to take for this purpose stars whose meridian altitude is greater than 60°.

**) The equations given in the example in No. 25 of the introduction are those, which would have been obtained by giving all observations the same weight and taking the arithmetical mean of all equations of the same star. For the form of the equations after the correction of i has been applied, is $0 = n + d\varphi + ak$. But Bessel has referred all observations to the polar point not, as has been assumed here, to the zenith point of the circle, hence the coefficient a differs from the coefficient of k in the above equations.

a year and therefore may be determined from observations made during one year. But the principal term of nutation has a period of 18 years and 219 days, the time in which the moon's nodes perform an entire revolution. Hence the constant of nutation can be determined only by observations distribued over a long series of years.

Since the apparent right ascensions of the pole-star are very much changed by aberration and nutation on account of the large factors sec δ and tang δ, their observations afford the best means for determining these constants; for the same reason the parallax of the pole-star can be determined in this way with great advantage. Putting:

$$-\cos\varepsilon\cos\alpha = a\sin A$$
$$-\sin\alpha = a\cos A,$$

the formulae for aberration and parallax in right ascension in No. 16 and 18 of the third section, can be thus written:

$$\alpha' - \alpha = +ka\sin(\odot + A)\sec\delta + \pi a\cos(\odot + A)\sec\delta + \varphi(k^2),$$

where k and π are the constant of aberration and the parallax and $\varphi(k^2)$ denotes the terms of the second order. If several observations are taken at the times when $\sin(\odot + A) = \pm 1$ and hence the maximum of aberration occurs, an approximate value of k can be found by comparing the right ascensions observed at both times after reducing them to the same mean equinox. But in order to obtain a more accurate value, the most probable value must be determined from a great many observations. Now the mean right ascension α and the assumed value of the constant k be erroneous by $\Delta\alpha$ and Δk, the true values being $\alpha + \Delta\alpha$ and $k + \Delta k$. If then α_0 denotes that value of the apparent right ascension, which has been computed from α with the value k of the constant of aberration (the computed precession and nutation being supposed to be the true values) and to which the small terms dependent on the square of k and on the product of aberration and nutation have also been added, since the effect of a change of k upon them is very small, and if further α' denotes the observed apparent right ascension, we have:

$$\alpha' = \alpha_0 + \Delta\alpha + \Delta k\, a\sin(\odot + A)\sec\delta + \pi a\cos(\odot + A)\sec\delta,$$

hence, taking:

$$\alpha_0 - \alpha' = n,$$

every observation of the right ascension of Polaris leads to an equation of the following form:

$$0 = n + \Delta\alpha + \Delta k \,.\, a \sin(\odot + A) \sec\delta + \pi\, a \cos(\odot + A) \sec\delta,$$

and from all these equations the most probable values of $\Delta\alpha$, Δk and π can be determined according to the method of least squares.

Should these observations embrace a long period of years, the constant of nutation, that is, the coefficient of $\cos\Omega$ in the expression for the nutation of the obliquity can be determined at the same time. If we denote by $\Delta\nu$ the correction of this coefficient, we must add to the above equation the term $\frac{d\alpha_0}{d\nu}\Delta\nu$, where the expression for $\frac{d\alpha_0}{d\nu}$ has been given in No. 6 of the second section. The complete equation for determining the aberration, parallax and nutation from the observation of an apparent right ascension is therefore:

$$0 = n + \Delta\alpha + \Delta k\, a \sin(\odot + A) \sec\delta + \pi\, a \cos(\odot + A) \sec\delta + \frac{d\alpha_0}{d\nu}\Delta\nu.$$

If for this purpose the observations made at different observatories are used, the probable errors of the observations of the several observers must be determined and the corresponding weight be given to the different equations. In this case also the correction $\Delta\alpha$ may not be the same for the observations of the several observatories, as the observed right ascensions may have a constant difference. Hence this difference must be determined and be applied to the observations or the unknown quantities $\Delta\alpha$, $\Delta\alpha'$ etc. must be eliminated separately by the observations of each observatory.

In this way von Lindenau determined the following values of the constants from right ascensions of Polaris observed by Bradley, Maskelyne, Pond, Bessel and himself in the course of 60 years:

$$k = 20''.4486 \qquad \nu = 8''.97707 \qquad \pi = 0''.1444,$$

Peters found later from observations made by Struve and Preuss at Dorpat during the years 1822 to 1838 the following values:

$$k = 20''.4255 \qquad \nu = 9''.2361 \qquad \pi = 0''.1724.$$

For the determination of these constants by declinations those of Polaris are also very suitable, as their accuracy can be greatly increased by taking several zenith distances at every culmination of the star. If we introduce in this case the following auxiliary quantities:

$$\sin\alpha \sin\delta \cos\varepsilon - \cos\delta \sin\varepsilon = b \sin B$$
$$- \cos\alpha \sin\delta = b \cos B,$$

the aberration in declination is equal to $kb \sin(\odot + B)$, the parallax equal to $\pi b \cos(\odot + B)$. Then denoting by δ_0 that value of the apparent declination which has been computed from the mean declination with the constants of aberration and nutation k and ν (the computed precession being taken as accurate) and to which the small terms dependent on the square of k and on the product of aberration and nutation have also been added; further denoting the observed apparent declination by δ' and taking $\delta_0 - \delta' = n$, every observation of a declination leads to an equation of the following form:

$$0 = n + \Delta\delta + \Delta k b \sin(\odot + B) + \pi b \cos(\odot + B) + \frac{d\delta_0}{d\nu} \Delta\nu,$$

and in case that the observations embrace a sufficiently long period, the most probable values of $\Delta\delta$, Δk, π and $\Delta\nu$ can be determined according to the method of least squares *). It was by such observations that Bradley discovered the aberration. He observed at Kew since the year 1725 principally the star γ Draconis besides 22 other stars, passing nearly through the zenith of the place, and discovered a periodical change of the zenith distance, which could not be explained as being the effect of parallax, for the determination of which these observations were really intended. The true explanation of this change as the effect of the motion of the earth combined with that of light was not given by him until later. The instrument, which he used for these observations, was a zenith sector, that is, a sector of very large radius, with which he could observe the zenith distances of stars a little over 12 degrees on each side of the zenith. The star γ Draconis, being near the north pole of the ecliptic, was especially suitable for determining the parallax and thus also the

*) If the stars have also proper motions, the terms $p(t - t_0)$ and $q(t - t_0)$ must be added to the equations for right ascensions and declinations, where p and q are the proper motions in right ascension and declination.

aberration, as for this pole we have $\alpha = 270^0$, $\delta = 90^0 - \varepsilon$, hence $b = 1$ and $B = 90^0$ and the maximum and minimum of the aberration and parallax in declination are equal to $\pm k$ and $\pm \pi$.

By similar observations he discovered also the nutation. The observations embrace the time from the 19th of August 1727 to the 3d of September 1747, hence an entire period of the nutation. Busch found from their discussion the constant of aberration equal to 20″.23. Lundahl found the following values from the declinations of Polaris observed at Dorpat by Struve and Preuss:

$$k = 20''.5508 \qquad \nu = 9''.2164 \qquad \pi = 0''.1473.$$

The value of the constant of nutation given in No. 5 of the second section is taken from Peters's pamphlet „Numerus Constans Nutationis". It was derived from the three determinations made by Peters, Busch and Lundahl, the probable errors of the single results being taken into account.

But the value of the constant of aberration given in No. 16 of the third section has not been deduced from the values given above, but has been determined by Struve from the transits of stars across the prime vertical. For if an instrument is placed exactly in the plane of the prime vertical and a star is observed on the wire on the east and west side *), the interval of time divided by 2 is equal to the hour angle of the star at the transit across the prime vertical. If we denote this by t, we get from the right angled triangle between the zenith, the pole and the star:

$$\operatorname{tang} \delta = \operatorname{tang} \varphi \cos t,$$

hence we see that the declinations of the stars can be determined by such observations. Differentiating the formula in a logarithmic form, we find:

$$d\delta = \frac{\sin 2\delta}{\sin 2\varphi} d\varphi - \tfrac{1}{2} \sin 2\delta \operatorname{tang} t\, dt,$$

and thus we see that an error in t has the less influence the smaller t is or the nearer to the zenith the star passes across the prime vertical. Hence if the zenith distance is very small, the declination of such a star can be determined by this

*) See No. 26 of the seventh section.

method very accurately. The equations for each star are in this case quite similar to those given before and it is again preferable to select for these observations stars near the pole of the ecliptic. By this method Struve found the constant of aberration equal to $20''.4451$, a value which undoubtedly is very exact. But his observations embrace too short a period for determining the constant of nutation, which however as well as the parallax might also be found by this method with a great degree of accuracy.

The constant of aberration may also be computed from the velocity of light and that of the earth according to No. 16 of the third section. The mean daily motion of the earth has been determined with great accuracy and is equal to $59' 8''.193$. The time in which the light moves through a distance equal to the semi-diameter of the earth's orbit, was first determined by Olav Roemer from the eclipses of the satellites of Jupiter. For he found in the year 1675, that those eclipses which took place about opposition were observed $8^m 13^s$ earlier and those about conjunction as much later than an average occurrence *). Now as the difference of the distances of Jupiter from the earth at both times is equal to the diameter of the earth's orbit, Römer soon found the true explanation, that the light does not move with an infinite velocity and traverses the diameter of the earth's orbit in $16^m 26^s$. If therefore T be the time of the beginning or the end of an eclipse computed from the tables, then must be added to it in order to render it conformable to the observations, the term

$$+ K\Delta$$

where K is the number of seconds, in which the light traverses the semi-diameter of the earth's orbit and Δ is the distance of the satellite from the earth, the semi-major axis of the earth's orbit being taken as the unit. If then T_0 is the time of the eclipse thus corrected, T' the observed time, every eclipse gives an equation of the form:

$$0 = T_0 - T' + \Delta dK$$

---

*) At the opposition the earth stands between Jupiter and the sun, whilst at conjunction the sun it between Jupiter and the earth.

and from a large number of such equations the most probable value of dK can be determined. However the observations of the beginning and the end of an eclipse are always a little uncertain, since the satellites lose their light only gradually and as thus the errors of observation greatly depend upon the quality of the telescope, it is best, to combine only such observations which have been made with the same instrument and also to treat the observations of the beginning and of the end separately. Delambre found by a careful discussion of a large number of observed eclipses the constant of aberration equal to $20''.255$, a value which according to Struve's determination is too small.

12. The annual parallax of a star can be determined still by another method, if the change of the place of the star relatively to that of another star, which has no parallax, be observed. This method is even preferable to the former, because the relative places of two stars near each other can be measured with great accuracy by means of a micrometer (as will be shown in the seventh section) and because the effect of the small corrections upon the places of both stars is so nearly equal, that any errors in the adopted values of the constants can have no influence on the difference of the mean places *). It is true, this method gives strictly only the difference of the parallaxes of both stars. But since is may be taken for granted, that very faint stars are at a great distance, the parallaxes thus found, when one or several such faint stars have been chosen as comparison stars, can be considered as nearly correct.

If the difference of right ascension and declination of both stars has been observed, each observation freed from the small corrections gives two equations of the following form, taking the differences at the time t_0 equal to $\alpha'_0 - \alpha_0$ and $\delta'_0 - \delta$ and denoting $\alpha'_0 - \alpha_0 - (\alpha' - \alpha)$ and $\delta'_0 - \delta_0 -$

*) In this case, when the stars are near each other, it is preferable, not to compute the mean place of each star, but to free only the difference of the apparent places from refraction, aberration, precession and nutation. The formulae necessary for this purpose will be given in VIII and IX of the seventh section.

$(\delta' - \delta)$ by n and n' and the errors of the adopted place by $\Delta\alpha$ and $\Delta\delta$:

$$0 = n + \Delta\alpha + \pi a \cos(\odot + A) \sec\delta + p(t - t_0)$$
$$0 = n' + \Delta\delta + \pi b \cos(\odot + B) \qquad + q(t - t_0).$$

Usually however instead of the difference of the right ascensions and declinations of both stars their distance is observed and besides the angle of position, that is, the angle which the declination circle of one star makes with the great circle passing through both stars. If then α and δ be the true right ascension and declination of one star, α' and δ' their values not freed from parallax, α'' and δ'' the right ascension and declination of the comparison star, we find the changes of the differences of the right ascensions and declinations produced by parallax as follows:

$$d(\alpha'' - \alpha) = \alpha - \alpha' = \pi R[\cos\odot \sin\alpha - \sin\odot \cos\varepsilon \cos\alpha] \sec\delta$$
$$d(\delta'' - \delta) = \delta - \delta' = \pi R[\cos\varepsilon \sin\alpha \sin\delta - \sin\varepsilon \cos\delta] \sin\odot$$
$$+ \pi R \sin\delta \cos\alpha \cos\odot.$$

If then the true distance and the true angle of position be denoted by Δ and P, we have:

$$\Delta \sin P = \cos\delta(\alpha'' - \alpha)$$
$$\Delta \cos P = \delta'' - \delta$$

hence:

$$d\Delta = \sin P \cos\delta\, d(\alpha'' - \alpha) + \cos P\, d(\delta'' - \delta)$$
$$\Delta dP = \cos P \cos\delta\, d(\alpha'' - \alpha) - \sin P\, d(\delta'' - \delta).$$

If we substitute here the expressions given before and take:

$$m \cos M = \sin\alpha \sin P + \sin\delta \cos\alpha \cos P,$$
$$m \sin M = [-\cos\alpha \sin P + \sin\delta \sin\alpha \cos P] \cos\varepsilon - \cos\delta \cos P \sin\varepsilon,$$
$$m' \cos M' = \frac{1}{\Delta}[\sin\alpha \cos P - \sin\delta \cos\alpha \sin P],$$
$$m' \sin M' = \frac{1}{\Delta}[-(\cos\alpha \cos P + \sin\delta \sin\alpha \sin P) \cos\varepsilon + \cos\delta \sin P \sin\varepsilon],$$

we easily find:

$$d\Delta = \pi R m \cos(\odot - M)$$
$$dP = \pi R m' \cos(\odot - M').$$

Therefore if $d\Delta_0$ denotes the correction of the adopted distance at the time t_0, dq the correction of the adopted value of the proper motion in the direction towards the other star, we find from the observed distances equations of the form:

$$0 = \nu + d\Delta_0 + (t - t_0)\, dq + \pi R m \cos(\odot - M)$$

and from the angles of position equations of the form:

$$0 = \nu' + dP_0 + (t - t_0)\,dq' + \pi R m' \cos(\odot - M'),$$

which must be solved according to the method of least squares. By this method Bessel first determined the parallax of 61 Cygni.

C. Determination of the constant of precession and of the proper motions of the stars.

13. We find the change of the right ascension and declination of a star by the precession during the interval $t' - t$, if we compute the annual variations:

$$\frac{d\alpha}{dt} = m + n \operatorname{tg}\delta \sin\alpha = \cos\varepsilon_0 \frac{dl_{\prime}}{dt} - \frac{da}{dt} + \sin\varepsilon_0 \frac{dl_{\prime}}{dt} \operatorname{tg}\delta \sin\alpha$$

$$\frac{d\delta}{dt} = n \cos\alpha = \sin\varepsilon_0 \frac{dl_{\prime}}{dt} \cos\alpha$$

for the time $\frac{t+t'}{2}$ and then multiply them by $t' - t$. Now since the numerical value of $\frac{da}{dt}$ is known from the theory of the secular perturbations of the planets, we may determine the lunisolar precession $\frac{dl_{\prime}}{dt}$ either from the right ascensions or from the declinations, comparing the difference of the values found by observations at the time t' and t with the above formula. Then if the places of the stars were fixed we should find nearly the same value of the precession from different stars and the more exactly, the greater the interval is between the observations, as any errors of observation would have the less influence. But since not only different stars but also the right ascensions and declinations of the same star give different values for the constant of precession, we must attribute these differences to proper motions of the stars. As they are like the precession proportional to the time, they cannot be separated from it and the difficulty is still increased by the fact, that the proper motions, partly at least, follow a certain law depending on the places of the stars. Hence we can eliminate the proper motions only by comparing a large number of stars distributed over all parts of the heavens and excluding all those, which on account of their large proper motion give a very different value for the precession. The large number will compensate any errors of observation entirely and the effect of the proper motions as much as possible. As the proper motions are proportional to the time, the uncertainty of the value of the precession arising from them remains the same, however great the interval between the two compared catalogues of stars may be, but it will be most important, that the catalogues are very correct and contain a large number of stars in common and that the interval is long enough so as to make any uncertainty arising from errors of observation sufficiently small. If then m_0 and n_0 are the two values of m and n employed in comparing the two catalogues, if further α, δ and α' and δ' are the mean places of a star for the times t and t', given in the two catalogues, and $\Delta\alpha$ and $\Delta\delta$ the constant differences of the catalogues for α and δ and if we take:

$$\alpha + (m_0 + n_0 \operatorname{tg} \delta_0 \sin \alpha_0)(t' - t) - \alpha' = \nu (t' - t)$$

and

$$\delta + n_0 \cos \alpha_0 (t' - t) \qquad\qquad - \delta' = \nu' (t' - t)$$

every star gives two equations of the form:

$$0 = \nu + \frac{\Delta\alpha}{t' - t} + dm_0 + dn_0 \operatorname{tg} \delta_0 \sin \alpha_0$$

and

$$0 = \nu' + \frac{\Delta\delta}{t' - t} + dn_0 \cos \alpha_0 .$$

Therefore if we consider the proper motions embraced in ν and ν' like casual errors of observation, we may find the most probable values of the unknown quantities from a large number of equations by the method of least squares. This supposition would be justified, if the proper motions were not following a law depending on the places of the stars. But as it is very difficult, if not impossible, to introduce in the above equations a term expressing this law, a matter which shall be more fully considered afterwards, hardly anything better can be substituted in place of that supposition, provided that a large number of stars distributed over all parts of the heavens be used. We then get from the right ascensions a determination of m and n, from the declinations a determination of n; but it is evident, that an error of the absolute right ascensions, which is constant for every catalogue, remains united with dm and as $\frac{dm}{dt} = \cos \varepsilon_0 \frac{dl_1}{dt} - \frac{da}{dt}$

there remains also in it any error of the value of $\frac{da}{dt}$ arising from incorrect values of the masses of the planets. But the determination of $dn = dl_{,} \sin \varepsilon_0$ from the right ascensions is independent of any such constant error, and besides the constant difference of the declination may be determined. But since the supposition, that the latter is constant for all declinations, is not allowable, it is better to divide the stars in zones of several degrees for instance of 10^0 of declination and to solve the equations for the stars of each zone separately, and hence to determine the mean difference $\Delta\delta$ for each zone. In this way Bessel in his work Fundamenta Astronomiae determined the value of this constant from more than 2000 stars, whose places had been deduced for 1755 and 1800 from Bradley's and Piazzi's observations. He found for 1750 the value 50″.340499, which he afterwards changed according to the observations made at Koenigsberg into 50″.37572. (Compare Astron. Nachr. No. 92.)

14. The differences of the places of the stars observed at two different epochs and the precession in the same interval of time, which has been computed with the value of the constant determined as before, are then taken as the proper motions of the stars. In general they may be accounted for within the limits of possible errors of observation by the supposition, that the single stars are moving on a great circle with uniform velocity. Halley first discovered in the year 1713 the proper motion of the stars Sirius, Aldebaran and Arcturus*). Since then the proper motions of a great many stars have been recognized with certainty and it is inferred, that all stars are subject to such, although for most stars these motions have not yet been determined, since they are small and are still confounded with errors of observation. The greatest proper motions have 61 Cygni (whose annual change in right ascension and declination amounts to 5″.1 and 3″.2), α Centauri (whose annual motion in the direction of the two

*) The last mentioned star has a proper motion of 2″ in declination and has therefore changed its place since the time of Hipparchus more than one degree.

co-ordinates is $7''.0$ and $0''.8$) and 1830 Groombridge (which moves $5''.2$ in right ascension and $5''.7$ in declination).

The elder Herschel first discovered a law in the direction of the proper motions of the stars, when comparing a great many of them he observed, that in general the stars move from a point in the neighbourhood of the star λ Herculis. Hence he suggested the hypothesis that the proper motions of the stars are partly at least only apparent and caused by a motion of the entire solar system towards that point of the heavens, a hypothesis, which is well confirmed by later investigations on this subject. The proper motions of the fixed stars are therefore the result of two motions, first of the motion peculiar to each star, by which they really change their place according to a law hitherto unknown, and secondly of the apparent or parallactic motion which is the effect of the motion of the solar system. Now on account of the motion peculiar to each star, stars in the same region of the celestial sphere may change their places in any direction whatever, but the direction of the parallactic motion is at once determined by the place of the star relatively to that towards which the solar system is moving, and can be easily calculated, if the right ascension and declination A and D of that point are known. If we compare the direction, computed for any star, with the direction, which is really observed, we can etablish for each star the equation between the difference of the computed and the observed direction and changes of the right ascension and declination A and D; and since those portions of these differences, which are caused by the peculiar motions of the stars, follow no law and can therefore be treated like casual errors of observation, we can find from a large number of such equations the most probable values of dA and dD by the method of least squares.

It is evident that the direction of the parallactic portion of the proper motion of a star coincides with the great circle, drawn through the star and the point towards which the solar system is moving, because the star, supposing of course that the sun is moving in a straight line, is always seen in the plane passing through it and the straight line described by the sun. Now if we denote the motion of the sun during the time $t'-t$ divided by the distance of the star by a, and then denote the right ascension and declination of the star at the two epochs t and t' by α, δ and α', δ', and finally the ratio of the distances of the star from the sun at the same epochs by ϱ, we have the following equations:

$$\varrho \cos \delta' \cos \alpha' = \cos \delta \cos \alpha - a \cos A \cos D$$
$$\varrho \cos \delta' \sin \alpha' = \cos \delta \sin \alpha - a \sin A \cos D$$
$$\varrho \sin \delta' = \sin \delta - a \sin D,$$

from which we easily deduce:

$$\cos \delta' = \cos \delta - a \cos D \cos (\alpha - A),$$

therefore:

$$\begin{aligned} \cos \delta' (\alpha' - \alpha) &= a \cos D \sin (\alpha - A) \\ \delta' - \delta &= - a [\cos \delta \sin D - \sin \delta \cos D \cos (\alpha - A)]. \end{aligned} \quad (A)$$

But we have also in the spherical triangle between the pole of the equator, the star and the point, whose right ascension and declination are **A** and **D**, denoting the distance of the star from that point by Δ and the angle at the star by **P**:

$$\begin{aligned} \sin \Delta \sin P &= \cos D \sin (\alpha - A) \\ \sin \Delta \cos P &= \sin D \cos \delta - \cos D \sin \delta \cos (\alpha - A). \end{aligned} \quad (B)$$

Now if we denote the angle, which the direction of the proper motion of the star makes with the declination circle, by p, we have:

$$\operatorname{tang} p = \frac{\cos \delta' (\alpha' - \alpha)}{\delta' - \delta}$$

hence we see, that $p = 180^0 - P$ or that the star is moving on a great circle passing through it and the point whose right ascension and declination is **A** and **D**, so that it is moving from the latter point.

From the third of the differential formulae (11) in No. 9 of the introduction, we have:

$$\begin{aligned} dP = &- \frac{\cos \delta \sin (\alpha - A)}{\sin \Delta^2} dD \\ &+ \frac{\cos D}{\sin \Delta^2} [\sin \delta \cos D - \cos \delta \sin D \cos (\alpha - A)] dA, \end{aligned}$$

hence:

$$\begin{aligned} dp = &+ \frac{\cos \delta \sin (\alpha - A)}{\sin \Delta^2} dD \\ &- \frac{\cos D}{\sin \Delta^2} [\sin \delta \cos D - \cos \delta \sin D \cos (\alpha - A)] dA. \end{aligned}$$

Therefore if p' be the observed angle, which the direction of the proper motion makes with the declination circle, reckoned from the north part of it through east from 0^0 to 360^0 so that:

$$\text{tang}\, p' = \frac{\cos\delta' (\alpha' - \alpha)}{\delta' - \delta}$$

and if further p be the value of $180 - P$ computed according to the formulae (*B*) with the approximate values A and D, we have for each star an equation of the form:

$$0 = p - p' + \frac{\cos\delta \sin(\alpha - A)}{\sin\Delta^2} dD$$
$$- \frac{\cos D}{\sin\Delta^2} [\sin\delta \cos D - \cos\delta \sin D \cos(\alpha - A)]\, dA,$$

or:

$$0 = (p - p') \sin\Delta + \frac{\cos\delta \sin(\alpha - A)}{\sin\Delta} dD$$
$$- \frac{\cos D}{\sin\Delta} [\sin\delta \cos D - \cos\delta \sin D \cos(\alpha - A)]\, dA,$$

and from a large number of such equations the most probable values of dA and dD can be deduced.

In this way Argelander determined the direction of the motion of the solar system *). Bessel in his work „Fundamenta Astronomiae“ had already derived the proper motions of a large number of stars by comparing Bradley's observations with those of Piazzi. Argelander selected from those all stars, which in the interval of 45 years from 1755 and 1800 exhibited a proper motion greater than 5″ and determined their proper motions more accurately by comparing Bradley's observations with his own made at the observatory at Åbo **). For determining the direction of the motion of the solar system he used then 390 stars, whose annual proper motion amounted to more than 0″.1. These were divided into three classes according to the magnitude of the proper motions and the corrections dA and dD determined separately from each class. From those three results, which well agreed with each other, he finally deduced the following values of A and D, referred to the equator and the equinox of 1800:

$$A = 259^0\, 51'.8 \text{ and } D = +32^0\, 29'.1,$$

*) Compare Astronom. Nachrichten No. 363.

**) Argelander, DLX stellarum fixarum positiones mediae ineunte anno 1830. Helsingforsiae 1835.

and these agree well with the values adopted by Herschel. Lundahl determined the position of this point from 147 other stars, by comparing Bradley's places with Pond's Catalogue of 1112 stars and found:

$$A = 252^\circ\ 24'.4 \text{ and } D = +\ 14^\circ\ 26'.1.$$

From the mean of both determinations, taking into account their probable errors, Argelander found:

$$A = 257^\circ\ 59'.7 \text{ and } D = +\ 28^\circ\ 49'.7.$$

Similar investigations were made by O. v. Struve and more recently by Galloway. Struve comparing 400 stars which had been observed at Dorpat with Bradley's catalogue, found:

$$A = 261^\circ\ 23' \text{ and } D = +\ 37^\circ\ 36'.$$

Galloway used for his investigations the southern stars, and comparing the observations made by Johnson on St. Helena and by Henderson at the Cape of Good Hope with those of Lacaille, found:

$$A = 260^\circ\ 1' \text{ and } D = +\ 34^\circ\ 23'.$$

Another extensive investigation was made by Mädler, who found from a very large number of stars:

$$A = 261^\circ\ 38'.8 \text{ and } D = +\ 39^\circ\ 53'.9$$

Since all these values agree well with each other, it seems that the point towards which the solar system is moving, is now known with great accuracy, at least as far as it is attainable considering the difficulties of the problem.

15. We may therefore assume, that the direction of the parallactic proper motion of a star, computed by means of the formula:

$$\operatorname{tang} P = \frac{\cos D \sin (\alpha - A)}{\sin D \cos \delta - \cos D \sin \delta \cos (\alpha - A)}$$

with a mean value of A and D, is nearly correct. If now, besides, the amount of this portion of the proper motion were known for every star, we should be able to compute for every star the annual change of the right ascension and declination, caused by this parallactic motion, and could add this to the equations given in No. 13 for determining the constant of precession. The amount of this parallactic motion must necessarily depend on the distance of the star, hence if the latter were known, we could determine the parallactic motion corresponding to a certain distance. For since those equations are transformed into the following:

$$0 = \nu + dm_0 + dn_0 \operatorname{tg} \delta_0 \sin \alpha_0 + \frac{k}{\Delta} \frac{\cos D_0}{\cos \delta_0} \sin (\alpha_0 - A)$$

and $$0 = \nu' + dn_0 \cos \alpha_0 + \frac{k}{\Delta} g \sin (G - D_0)$$

where $\delta_0 = g \cos G$,

$\sin \delta_0 \cos (\alpha_0 - A) = g \sin G$,

we could find, if Δ were known, from these equations k, that is, the motion of the sun as seen from a distance equal to the adopted unit and expressed in seconds, and besides we should find the values of dm_0 and dn_0 free from this parallactic proper motion of the stars. Now since the distances of the stars are unknown, O. v. Struve substituted for Δ hypothetical values of the mean distances of the different classes of stars, which had been deduced by W. v. Struve in his work, Etudes de l'Astronomie stellaire from the number of stars in the several classes *). Struve then compared 400 stars which had been observed by W. v. Struve and Preuss at Dorpat with Bradley's observations and, at first neglecting the motion of the solar system, he found for the corrections of the constant of precession from the right ascensions and declinations two contradicting results, one being positive, the other negative. But taking the proper motion of the sun into account he found the corrections $+1''.16$ from the right ascensions and $+0''.66$ from the declinations and hence, taking into account their probable errors, he found the value of the constant of precession for 1790 equal to $50''.23449$ or greater than Bessel had found it by 0.01343. Further he found for the motion of the sun, as seen from a point at the distance of the stars of the first magnitude, $0''.321$ from the right ascensions and $0''.357$ from the declinations. But although these values of the constant of precession and of the motion of the solar system are apparently of great weight, it must not be overlooked, that they are based on the hypothetical ratio of the distances of stars of

---

*) According to this, the distance of a star of the first magnitude being 1, that of the stars of the second magnitude is 1.71, that of the third 2.57, the fourth 3.76, the fifth 5.44, the sixth 7.86 and the seventh 11.34.

different magnitudes. Besides it cannot be entirely approved of, that the number of stars used for this determination, which are nearly all double stars, is so very small.

If it should be desirable for a more correct determination of the constant of precession, to take the motion of the solar system into account, it may be better, not to introduce the ratios of the distances of stars of different magnitude according to any adopted hypothesis, but rather to divide the stars into classes according to their magnitude or their proper motions, and to determine for each class a value of $\frac{k}{\Delta}$ and the correction of the constant of precession. The values of $\frac{k}{\Delta}$ thus found can be considered as mean values for these different classes and the values of m and n will then be independent at least of a portion of the parallactic motion, which will be the greater, the more nearly equal the distances of the stars of the same class are*). Even the corrections of A and D might be found in this way, since the equations in this case would be, taking $\frac{k}{\Delta} = a$:

$$0 = \nu + dm_0 + dn_0 \operatorname{tang} \delta_0 \sin \alpha_0 - \frac{\cos D}{\cos \delta_0} \cos(\alpha_0 - A)\, a\, dA + [\cos D - \sin D\, dD] \frac{\sin(\alpha_0 - A)}{\cos \delta_0} a$$

$$0 = \nu' + dn_0 \cos \alpha_0 - g \cos(G - D)\, a\, dD + \cos D \sin \delta_0 \sin(\alpha_0 - A)\, a\, dA + a g \sin(G - D)$$

from which the most probable values of a, $a\,dA$, $a\,dD$, dm_0 and dn_0 can be determined for each class. In case, that Struve's ratio of the distances be adopted, the unknown quantity a after multiplying the factor by $\frac{1}{\Delta}$ would

---

*) The author has undertaken this investigation already many years ago without being able to finish it. The proper motions were deduced from a comparison of Henderson's observations made at Edinborough with those of Bradley. The following mean values were found for the annual parallactic motions of stars of several classes:

for	32 stars of magnitude	4.3.	0″.068985 ± 0.010964
„	75 „ „ „	4.	0″.069715 ± 0.006584
„	71 „ „ „	4.5.	0″.046811 ± 0.006925
„	284 „ „ „	5.	0″.029043 ± 0.002446.

Stars, whose annual proper motion exceeds 0″.3 of arc, were excluded in making this investigation.

be the same for all classes. (Compare on this subject also Airy's pamphlet in the Memoirs of the Royal Astronomical Society Vol. XXVIII.)

16. At present we always assume that the proper motions of the stars are proportional to the time and take place on a fixed great circle. But the proper motions in right ascension and declination are variable on account of the change of the fundamental plane to which they are referred, and it is necessary to take this into account, at least for stars very near the pole.

The formulae, which express the polar co-ordinates referred to the equinox at the time t' by means of the co-ordinates referred to another equinox at the time t, are according to No. 3 of the second section:

$$\cos\delta' \sin(\alpha' + a' - z') = \cos\delta \sin(\alpha + a + z)$$
$$\cos\delta' \cos(\alpha' + a' - z') = \cos\delta \cos(\alpha + a + z) \cos\Theta - \sin\delta \sin\Theta$$
$$\sin\delta' = \cos\delta \cos(\alpha + a + z) \sin\Theta + \sin\delta \cos\Theta,$$

where a denotes the precession produced by the planets during the time $t' - t$, and z, z' and Θ are auxiliary quantities obtained by means of the formulae (A) of the same No. Since the proper motions are so small, that their squares and products may be neglected, we obtain by the first and third formulae (11) in No. 9 of the introduction, remembering that the formulae above are derived from a triangle the sides of which are $90^0 - \delta'$, $90^0 - \delta$ and Θ and the angles of which are $\alpha + a + z$, $180^0 - \alpha' - a' + z'$ and c:

$$\Delta\delta' = \cos c\,\Delta\delta - \sin\Theta \sin(\alpha' + a' - z')\,\Delta\alpha$$
$$\cos\delta'\,\Delta\alpha' = \sin c\,\Delta\delta + \cos\delta \cos c\,\Delta\alpha$$

or if $\sin c$ and $\cos c$ be expressed in terms of the other parts of the triangle:

$$\Delta\alpha' = \Delta\alpha\,[\cos\Theta + \sin\Theta \operatorname{tang}\delta' \cos(\alpha' + a' - z')] + \frac{\Delta\delta}{\cos\delta} \sin\Theta \frac{\sin(\alpha' + a' - z')}{\cos\delta'}$$
$$\Delta\delta' = -\Delta\alpha \sin\Theta \sin(\alpha' + a' - z') + \frac{\Delta\delta}{\cos\delta} \cos\delta' [\cos\Theta + \sin\Theta \operatorname{tang}\delta' \cos(\alpha' + a' - z')] \quad (a)$$

and in the same manner:

$$\Delta\alpha = \Delta\alpha'\,[\cos\Theta - \sin\Theta \operatorname{tang}\delta \cos(\alpha + a + z)] - \frac{\Delta\delta'}{\cos\delta'} \sin\Theta \frac{\sin(\alpha + a + z)}{\cos\delta}$$
$$\Delta\delta = \Delta\alpha' \sin\Theta \sin(\alpha + a + z) + \frac{\Delta\delta'}{\cos\delta'} \cos\delta\,[\cos\Theta - \sin\Theta \operatorname{tang}\delta \cos(\alpha + a + z)]. \quad (b)$$

Example. The mean right ascension and declination of Polaris for the beginning of the year 1755 is:

$$\alpha = 10^{0}\,55'\,44''.955 \qquad \delta = +\,87^{0}\,59'\,41''.12.$$

By application of the precession the place of Polaris was computed in No. 3 of the second section for 1850 Jan. 1, and found to be:

$$\alpha' = 16^{0}\,12'\,56''.917 \qquad \delta' = +\,88^{0}\,30'\,34''.680.$$

But in Bessel's Tabulae Regiomontanae this place is:

$$\alpha' = 16^{0}\,15'\,19''.530 \qquad \delta' = +\,88^{0}\,30'\,34''.898.$$

The difference between these two values of α' and δ' arises from the proper motion of Polaris, which thus amounts to $+\,2'\,22''.613$ in right ascension and to $+\,0''.218$ in declination in the interval from 1755 to 1850. The annual proper motion of Polaris referred to the equator of 1850 is therefore:

$$\Delta\alpha' = +\,1''.501189 \qquad \Delta\delta' = +\,0''.002295.$$

If we wish to find from this, for example, the proper motion of Polaris referred to the equator of 1755, it must be computed by means of the formulae (*b*). But we have:

$$\Theta = 0^{0}\,31'\,45''.600$$
$$\alpha + a + z = 11^{0}\,32'\,9''.530$$

and with this we obtain:

$$\Delta\alpha = +\,1''.10836 \qquad \Delta\delta = +\,0''.005063.$$

In the case of a few stars the assumption of an uniform proper motion does not satisfy the observations made at different epochs, since there would remain greater errors, than can be attributed to errors of observation. Bessel first discovered this variability of the proper motions in the case of Sirius and Procyon, comparing their places with those of stars in their neighbourhood, and he accounted for it by the attraction of large but invisible bodies of great masses in the neighbourhood of those stars. Basing his investigations on this hypothesis, Peters at Altona has determined by means of the right ascensions of Sirius its orbit round such a central body and has deduced the following formula, which expresses the correction to be applied to the right ascension of this star:

$$q = 0^{s}.127 + 0^{s}.00050\,(t - 1800) + 0^{s}.171 \sin\,(u + 77^{0}\,44'),$$

where the angle u is found by means of the equation:

$$M = 7^{\circ}.1865\,(t - 1791.431) = u - 0.7994 \sin u$$

and where** $7^{\circ}.1865$ is the mean motion of Sirius round the central body. By the application of the correction computed according to this formula the observed right ascensions of Sirius agree well with each other. Safford at Cambridge has recently shown, that the declinations of Sirius exhibit the same periodical change, and that the following correction must be applied to the observed declination:

$$q' = +0''.56 + 0''.0202\,(t - 1800) + 1''.47 \sin u + 0''.51 \cos u,$$

where u is the same as in the formula above *).

*) Of great interest in regard to this matter is the discovery, made recently by A. Clarke of Boston, of a faint companion of Sirius at a distance of about 8 seconds.

** Corresponding period is 50.094 years.

FIFTH SECTION.

DETERMINATION OF THE POSITION OF THE FIXED GREAT CIRCLES OF THE CELESTIAL SPHERE WITH RESPECT TO THE HORIZON OF A PLACE.

It has been already shown in No. 5 and 6 of the preceding section, how the position of the fixed great circles of the celestial sphere can be determined by means of a meridian instrument. For if the instrument has been adjusted so that the line of collimation describes a vertical circle, it is brought in the plane of the meridian (i. e. the vertical circle of the pole of the equator is determined) by observing the circumpolar stars above and below the pole, since the interval between the observations must be equal to 12^h of sidereal time $+\Delta\alpha$, where $\Delta\alpha$ is the variation of the apparent place in the interval of time. Further the observation of the zenith distances of a star at both culminations gives the co-latitude, since this is equal to the arithmetical mean of the two zenith distances corrected for refraction $+\frac{1}{2}\Delta\delta$, where $\Delta\delta$ is the variation of the apparent declination during the interval between the observations. If the culmination of a star, whose right ascension is known, be observed, the apparent right ascension of the star is equal to the hour angle of the vernal equinox or to the sidereal time at that moment. If a similar observation is made at another place at the same instant, the difference of both times is equal to the difference of the hour angles of the vernal equinox at both places or to their difference of longitude, and it remains only to be shown, by what means the determinations of the time at both places are made simultaneously or by which at least the difference of the time of observation at both places becomes known.

These methods, which are the most accurate as well as the most simple, are used, when the observer can employ a firmly mounted meridian instrument. But the position of the zenith with respect to the pole and the vernal equinox may also be determined by observing the co-ordinates of stars, whose places are known, with respect to the horizon, and thus various methods have been invented, by which travellers or seamen can make these determinations with more or less advantage according to circumstances and which may be used on all occasions, when the means necessary for employing the methods given before are not at hand.

We have the following formulae expressing the relations between the altitude and azimuth of a star, its right ascension and declination and the sidereal time and the latitude:

$$\sin h = \sin \varphi \sin \delta + \cos \varphi \cos \delta \cos (\Theta - \alpha)$$

$$\operatorname{cotang} A = -\frac{\cos \varphi \operatorname{tang} \delta}{\sin (\Theta - \alpha)} + \sin \delta \operatorname{cotg} (\Theta - \alpha).$$

These equations show, that if the latitude is known, the time may be determined by the observation of an altitude or azimuth of a star, whose right ascension and declination are known, and conversely the latitude can be determined, if the time is known, therefore by the observations of two altitudes or azimuths both the latitude and the time can be determined.

The observations used for this purpose must be freed from refraction and diurnal parallax (if the observed object is not a fixed star) and the places of the stars must be apparent places. The instruments used for these observations are altitude and azimuth instruments, which must be corrected so that the line of collimation, when the telescope is turned round the axis, describes a vertical circle (see No. 12 of the seventh section), or, if only altitudes are taken, reflecting circles are used, by which the angle between the star and its image reflected from an artificial horizon, one half of which is equal to the altitude, can be measured. When an altitude and azimuth instrument is used, the zenith point of the circle is determined by means of an artificial horizon, or the star is observed first in one position of the instrument, and again after it has been turned 180^0 round its vertical axis. For if ζ and ζ' are the circle-readings in those two positions, corresponding to the times Θ and Θ', and if $\frac{dz}{d\Theta}$ and $\frac{d^2 z}{d\Theta^2}$ are the differential coefficients of the zenith distance (I, 25) corresponding to the time $\Theta_0 = \frac{\Theta + \Theta'}{2}$, assuming that in the first position the divisions increase in the direction of zenith distance and denoting the zenith point by Z, then the circle-readings reduced to the arithmetical mean of both times are:

$$z_0 + Z = \zeta + \frac{dz}{d\Theta_0}(\Theta_0 - \Theta) - \tfrac{1}{2}\frac{d^2 z}{d\Theta_0^{\,2}}(\Theta - \Theta_0)^2$$

$$Z - z_0 = \zeta' + \frac{dz}{d\Theta_0}(\Theta' - \Theta_0) + \tfrac{1}{2}\frac{d^2 z}{d\Theta_0^{\,2}}(\Theta' - \Theta_0)^2.$$

Hence the zenith distance z_0 corresponding to the arithmetical mean of the times is:

$$z_0 = \tfrac{1}{2}(\zeta - \zeta') - \tfrac{1}{8}\frac{d^2 z}{d\Theta_0^{\,2}}(\Theta' - \Theta)^2.$$

Finally in case that the object is observed direct and reflected from an artificial horizon, we have, since the first member of the second equation is then $180^0 - z_0 + Z$:

$$90^0 - z_0 = \tfrac{1}{2}(\zeta' - \zeta) + \tfrac{1}{8}\frac{d^2 z}{d\Theta_0^{\,2}}(\Theta' - \Theta)^2 \text{ *)}.$$

In order to observe the azimuth by such an instrument, the reading of the circle corresponding to the meridian or the zero of the azimuth must be determined, and this be subtracted from or added to all circle-readings, if the divisions increase or decrease in the direction of the azimuth.

I. METHODS OF FINDING THE ZERO OF THE AZIMUTH AND THE TRUE BEARING OF AN OBJECT.

1. The simplest method of finding the zero of the azimuth consists in observing the time, when a star arrives at its greatest altitude above the horizon, and for this purpose one observes the sun with an altitude and azimuth instrument,

*) It is supposed here, that exactly the same point of the circle corresponds to the zenith in both positions. For the sake of examining this, a spirit level is fastened to the circle, whose bubble changes its position, as soon as any fixed line of the circle changes its position with respect to the vertical line. Such a level indicates therefore any change of the zenith point and affords at the same time a means for measuring it. (See No. 13 of the seventh section.)

and assumes that the sun is on the meridian as soon as it ceases to change its altitude. This method is used at sea to find approximately the moment of apparent noon, but necessarily it is very uncertain, because the altitude of the sun, being at its maximum, changes very slowly.

Another method is that of observing the greatest distance of the circumpolar stars from the meridian. According to No. 27 of the first section we have for the hour angle of the star at that time:

$$\cos t = \frac{\operatorname{tang} \varphi}{\operatorname{tang} \delta} \text{ or } \operatorname{tang} \tfrac{1}{2} t^2 = \frac{\sin(\delta - \varphi)}{\sin(\delta + \varphi)},$$

and the motion of the star is then vertical to the horizon, since the vertical circle is tangent to the parallel circle. Therefore if one observes such a star with an azimuth instrument, whose line of collimation describes a vertical circle, the telescope must in general be moved in a horizontal as well as a vertical direction in order to keep the star on the wire-cross, and only at the time of the greatest distance the vertical motion alone will be sufficient. If the reading of the azimuth circle is a in this position of the instrument and a', when the same observation is made on the other side of the meridian, $\frac{a+a'}{2}$ is the reading of the circle corresponding to the zero of the azimuth. It is best to use the pole-star for these observations on account of its slow motion.

A third method for determining the zero of the azimuth is that of taking corresponding altitudes. For as equal hour angles on both sides of the meridian belong to equal altitudes, it follows, that if a star has been observed at two different times at the same altitude, then two vertical circles equally distant from the meridian are determined by this. Therefore if we observe a star at the wire-cross of an azimuth instrument, read the circle and then wait, until the star after the culmination is seen again at the wire-cross, then if the altitude of the telescope has not been changed but merely its azimuth, the arithmetical mean of the two readings of the circle is the zero of the azimuth. If the sun, whose declination changes in the time between the two observations, is observed, a correction must be applied to the arithmetical mean of the two readings. For, differentiating the equation:

$$\sin\delta = \sin\varphi \sin h - \cos\varphi \cos h \cos A,$$

taking only A and δ as variable, we have:

$$dA = \frac{\cos\delta\, d\delta}{\cos\varphi \cos h \sin A} = \frac{d\delta}{\cos\varphi \sin t}.$$

Therefore if $\Delta\delta$ denotes the change of the declination in the time between the two observations, we must subtract from the arithmetical mean of the two readings:

$$\frac{\Delta\delta \cos\delta}{2\cos\varphi \cos h \sin A} = \frac{\Delta\delta}{2\cos\varphi\ \sin t}$$

if the divisions increase in the direction of the azimuth.

The fourth method is identical with that given in No. 5 of the fourth section for adjusting a meridian circle. For if we observe the times at which a circumpolar star arrives at the same azimuth above and below the pole, the plane of the telescope coincides with the meridian, if the interval between the observations is 12^h of sidereal time $+\Delta\alpha$, where $\Delta\alpha$ is the change of the apparent place in the interval of the two times. But if this is not the case, the azimuth of the telescope is found in the following way. If the azimuth be reckoned from the north point instead of the south point, we have for the first observation:

$$\begin{aligned}\cos h \sin A &= \cos\delta \sin t\\ \cos h \cos A &= \cos\varphi \sin\delta - \sin\varphi \cos\delta \cos t,\end{aligned}$$

and for the second observation below the pole:

$$\begin{aligned}\cos h' \sin A &= \cos\delta \sin t'\\ \cos h' \cos A &= \cos\varphi \sin\delta - \sin\varphi \cos\delta \cos t'.\end{aligned}$$

Adding the first equation to the third and subtracting the second equation from the fourth, and then dividing the two resulting equations we easily find:

$$\operatorname{tang} A = \operatorname{cotang} \tfrac{1}{2}(t' - t)\, \frac{\operatorname{tang} \frac{1}{2}(h + h') \operatorname{tang} \frac{1}{2}(h - h')}{\sin\varphi}.$$

In case that $t' - t$ is nearly equal to 12 hours of sidereal time, A as well as $90^0 - \frac{1}{2}(t' - t)$ are small angles, and since then $\frac{1}{2}(h + h')$ and $\frac{1}{2}(h - h')$ are nearly equal to φ and $90^0 - \delta$, we get:

$$A = \frac{90^0 - \frac{1}{2}(t' - t)}{\cos\varphi \operatorname{tang}\delta}.$$

2. It is not necessary for applying any of these methods to know the latitude of the place or the time, or at least they need be only very approximately known. But in case they are correctly known, any observation of a star, whose place is known, with an azimuth instrument, gives the zero of the azimuth, if the circle-reading is compared with the azimuth computed from the two equations:

$$\begin{aligned} \cos h \sin A &= \cos \delta \sin t \\ \cos h \cos A &= -\cos \varphi \sin \delta + \sin \varphi \cos \delta \cos t \end{aligned} \qquad (a)$$

In case that a set of such observations has been made, it is not necessary to compute the azimuth for each observation by means of these formulae, but we can arrive at the same result by a shorter method. Let Θ, Θ', Θ'' etc., be the several times of observation, whose number is n, let Θ_0 be the arithmetical mean of all times and A_0 the azimuth corresponding to the time Θ_0, then we have:

$$A = A_0 + \frac{dA}{dt}(\Theta - \Theta_0) + \tfrac{1}{2}\frac{d^2A}{dt^2}(\Theta - \Theta_0)^2,$$

$$A' = A_0 + \frac{dA}{dt}(\Theta' - \Theta_0) + \tfrac{1}{2}\frac{d^2A}{dt^2}(\Theta' - \Theta_0)^2,$$

etc.

and since $\Theta - \Theta_0 + \Theta' - \Theta_0 + \text{etc.} = 0$, we find:

$$A_0 = \frac{A + A' + A'' + \ldots}{n} - \tfrac{1}{2}\frac{d^2A}{dt^2}\left[\frac{(\Theta - \Theta_0)^2 + (\Theta' - \Theta_0)^2 + \ldots}{n}\right]$$

$$= \frac{A + A' + A'' + \ldots}{n} - \frac{d^2A}{dt^2}\,\frac{\Sigma\, 2 \sin \frac{1}{2}(\Theta - \Theta_0)^2}{n},$$

where $\Sigma\, 2 \sin \frac{1}{2}(\Theta - \Theta_0)^2$ denotes the sum of all the quantities $2 \sin \frac{1}{2}(\Theta - \Theta_0)^2$. These have been introduced instead of $\frac{1}{2}(\Theta - \Theta_0)^2$ on account of the small difference and because in all collections of astronomical tables, for instance in „Warnstorff's Hülfstafeln", convenient tables are given, from which we can take the quantity $2 \sin^2 \frac{1}{2} t$ expressed in seconds of arc, the argument being t expressed in time. Now we have according to No. 25 of the first section:

$$\frac{d^2A}{dt^2} = -\frac{\cos \varphi \sin A_0}{\cos h_0{}^2}\left[\cos h_0 \sin \delta + 2 \cos \varphi \cos A_0\right].$$

Therefore if we add to the arithmetical mean of all readings of the circle the correction:

$$\frac{\cos \varphi \sin A_0}{\cos h_0{}^2}\left[\cos h_0 \sin \delta + 2 \cos \varphi \cos A_0\right] \frac{\Sigma\, 2 \sin \frac{1}{2}(\Theta - \Theta_0)^2}{n},$$

we find the value A_1, which we must compare with the azimuth computed by means of the formulae (a) for $t = \Theta_0 - \alpha$.

Differentiating the equation (a) or using the differential formulae given in No. 8 of the first section, we find:

$$dA = \frac{\cos\delta\cos p}{\cos h}\,dt - \operatorname{tang} h \sin A\, d\varphi + \frac{\sin p}{\cos h}\,d\delta,$$

hence we see, that it is especially advisable to observe the pole-star near the time of its greatest distance from the meridian, because we have then $p = 90^0$ and A is nearly 180^0, except in very high latitudes. Then an error of the time has no influence and an error of the assumed latitude only a very small influence on the computed azimuth and hence on the determination of the zero of the azimuth.

3. If the zero of the azimuth has been determined, we can find the bearing of any terrestrial object *). This can also be determined, though with less accuracy, by measuring the distance of the object from any celestial body, if the time, the latitude and the altitude of the object above the horizon are known.

For if the hour angle of the star at the time of the observation is known, we can compute according to No. 7 of the first section its altitude h and azimuth a, and we have then in the triangle formed by the star, the zenith and the terrestrial object:

$$\cos\Delta = \sin h \sin H + \cos h \cos H \cos(a - A)$$

where H and A are the altitude and the azimuth of the object and Δ is the observed distance**). We find therefore $a - A$ from the equation

$$\cos(a - A) = \frac{\cos\Delta - \sin h \sin H}{\cos h \cos H}, \qquad (A)$$

hence also the azimuth of the object A, since a is known.

The equation (A) may be changed into another form more convenient for logarithmic computation. For we have:

---

*) For this a correction is necessary, dependent on the distance of the object, if the telescope is fastened to one end of the axis. See No. 12 of the seventh section.

**) To the computed value of h the refraction must be added, and if the sun is observed, the parallax must be subtracted from it. Likewise is H the apparent altitude of the object, which is found by observation.

$$1 + \cos(a - A) = \frac{\cos(H + h) + \cos\Delta}{\cos h \cos H}$$

and:

$$1 - \cos(a - A) = \frac{\cos(H - h) - \cos\Delta}{\cos h \cos H}$$

hence:

$$\operatorname{tang}\tfrac{1}{2}(a - A)^2 = \frac{\sin\frac{1}{2}(\Delta - H + h)\sin\frac{1}{2}(\Delta + H - h)}{\cos\frac{1}{2}(\Delta + H + h]\cos\frac{1}{2}(H + h - \Delta)}$$

or taking:

$$S = \tfrac{1}{2}(\Delta + H + h),$$

$$\operatorname{tang}\tfrac{1}{2}(a - A)^2 = \frac{\sin(S - H)\sin(S - h)}{\cos S\cos(S - \Delta)} \qquad (B).$$

If the terrestrial object is in the horizon, therefore $H = 0$, we have simply:

$$\operatorname{tang}\tfrac{1}{2}(a - A)^2 = \operatorname{tang}\tfrac{1}{2}(\Delta + h)\operatorname{tang}\tfrac{1}{2}(\Delta - h).$$

Differentiating the formula for $\cos\Delta$, taking $a - A$ and Δ as variable, we get:

$$d(a - A) = \frac{\sin\Delta}{\cos h\cos H\sin(a - A)}\,d\Delta.$$

and from I. No. 8:

$$da = \frac{\cos\delta\cos p}{\cos h}\,dt.$$

Hence we see, that the star must not be taken too far from the horizon, in order that $\cos h$ may not be too small and errors of the time and distance may not have too great an influence on A.

If two distances of a star from a terrestrial object have been observed, the hour angle and declination of the latter can be determined and also its altitude and azimuth.

For if we denote the hour angle and the declination of the object by T and D, the same for the star by t and δ, we have in the spherical triangle formed by the pole, the star and the terrestrial object:

$$\cos\Delta = \sin\delta\sin D + \cos\delta\cos D\cos(t - T).$$

Then, if λ is the interval of time between both observations, which in case of the sun being observed must be expressed in apparent time, we have for the second distance Δ' the equation:

$$\cos\Delta' = \sin\delta\sin D + \cos\delta\cos D\cos(t - T + \lambda).$$

From these equations we can find D and $t - T$, as will

be shown for similar equations in No. 14 of this section. If then the hour angle t at the time of the first observation be computed, we can find T and D, and then by means of the formulae in I. No. 7 A and H.

II. METHODS OF FINDING THE TIME OR THE LATITUDE BY AN OBSERVATION OF A SINGLE ALTITUDE.

4. If the altitude of a star, whose place is known, is observed and the latitude of the place is known, we find the hour angle by means of the equation:

$$\cos t = \frac{\sin h - \sin \varphi \sin \delta}{\cos \varphi \cos \delta}.$$

In order to render this formula convenient for logarithmic computation, we proceed in the same way as in the preceding No. and we find, introducing the zenith distance instead of the altitude:

$$\text{tang}\, \tfrac{1}{2} t^2 = \frac{\sin \frac{1}{2}(z - \varphi + \delta) \sin \frac{1}{2}(z + \varphi - \delta)}{\cos \frac{1}{2}(z + \varphi + \delta) \cos \frac{1}{2}(\varphi + \delta - z)}$$

or:

$$\left.\begin{aligned} \text{tang}\, \tfrac{1}{2} t^2 &= \frac{\sin (S - \varphi) \sin (S - \delta)}{\cos S \,.\, \cos (S - z)} \\ \text{where } S &= \tfrac{1}{2}(z + \varphi + \delta) \end{aligned}\right\} \qquad (A).$$

The sign of t is not determined by this formula, but t must be taken positive or negative, accordingly as the altitude is taken on the west or on the east side of the meridian.

If the right ascension of the star is α, we find the sidereal time of the observation from the equation:

$$\Theta = t + \alpha,$$

but if the sun was observed, the computed hour angle is the apparent solar time.

Example. Dr. Westphal observed in 1822, Oct. 29, at Abutidsch in Egypt the altitude of the lower limb of the sun:

$$h = 33^{\circ}\, 42'\, 18''.7$$

at the clock-time $20^{h}\, 16^{m}\, 20^{s}$.

The altitude must first be freed from refraction and parallax; but as the meteorological instruments have not been observed, only the mean refraction equal to $1'\, 26''.4$ can be used, which is to be subtracted from the observed altitude.

Adding also the parallax in altitude 6''.9 and the semi-diameter of the sun 16' 8''.7, we find for the altitude of the centre of the sun:

$$h = 33^\circ\, 57'\, 7''.9.$$

Now the latitude of Abutidsch is 27° 5' 0'' and the declination of the sun was on that day:

$$-13^\circ\, 38'\, 11''.1$$

hence we have:

$$S = \tfrac{1}{2}(z + \varphi + \delta) = +34^\circ\, 44'\, 50''.5$$

$$S - \varphi = +7^\circ\, 39'\, 50''.5,\quad S - \delta = +48^\circ\, 23'\, 1''.6,\quad S - z = -21^\circ\, 18'\, 1''.6$$

and the computation is made as follows:

$\sin(S-\varphi)$	9.1250385	$\cos S$	9.9146991
$\sin(S-\delta)$	9.8736752	$\cos(S-z)$	9.9692707
	8.9987137		
	9.8839698		
$\text{tang}\,\tfrac{1}{2}t^2$	9.1147439	$\text{tang}\,\tfrac{1}{2}t$	9.5573719

$$\tfrac{1}{2}t = -19^\circ\, 50'\, 37''.98$$
$$t = -39\;\; 41\;\; 15\;\; .96$$
$$t = -\;\; 2^s\, 38^m\, 45^s\,.06.$$

Hence the apparent time of the observation is $21^h\, 21^m\, 14^s.9$, and since the equation of time is $-16^m\, 8^s.7$, the mean time is $21^h\, 5^m\, 6^s.2$. The chronometer was therefore $48^m\, 46^s.2$ too fast, or $+48^m\, 46^s.2$ must be added to the time of the chronometer in order to get mean time.

Since the declination and the equation of time are variable, we ought to know already the true time, in order to interpolate, for computing t, the values of the declination, and afterwards the value of the equation of time, corresponding to the true time. But at first we can only use an approximate value for the declination and the equation of time, and when the true time is approximately known, it is necessary, to interpolate these values with greater accuracy and to repeat the computation.

The correction which must be applied to the clock-time, in order to get the true time, is called *the error of the clock*, whilst the difference of the errors of the clock at two different times is called the *rate of the clock* in the interval of time. Its sign is always taken so, that the positive sign designates, that the clock is losing, and the negative sign, that the clock is gaining. If the interval between both times is equal to $24^h - t$ and Δu is the rate of the clock in this time, we find the rate for 24 hours, considering it to be uniform, by means of the formula:

$$\frac{24\,\Delta u}{24-t} = \frac{\Delta u}{1-\frac{t}{24}}$$

Differentiating the original equation:

$$\sin h = \sin\varphi \sin\delta + \cos\varphi \cos\delta \cos t,$$

we find according to I. No. 8:

$$dh = -\cos A\, d\varphi - \cos\delta \sin p\, dt,$$

or since:

$$\cos\delta \sin p = \cos\varphi \sin A$$

we get:

$$dt = -\frac{1}{\cos\varphi \sin A}\, dh - \frac{1}{\cos\varphi \operatorname{tang} A}\, d\varphi.$$

The value of the coefficients of dh and $d\varphi$ is the less, the nearer A is $\pm 90^0$. In this case the value of the tangent is infinity, hence an error of the latitude has no influence on the hour angle and thus on the time found, if the altitude is taken on the prime vertical. Since then also $\sin A$ is a maximum, and hence the coefficient of dh is a minimum, an error of the altitude has then also the least influence on the time. Therefore, in order to find the time by the observation of an altitude, it is always advisable, to take this as near as possible to the prime vertical.

Since the coefficient of dh can also be written $-\frac{1}{\cos\delta \sin p}$, it is evident, that one must avoid taking stars of great declination and that it is best to observe equatoreal stars.

If we compute the values of the differential coefficients for the above example, we find first by means of the formula

$$\sin A = \frac{\cos\delta \sin t}{\cos h}: \quad A = -48^0\ 25'.8$$

and then

$$dt = +1.5013\, dh + 0.9966\, d\varphi$$

or dt expressed in seconds of time:

$$dt = +0.1001\, dh + 0.0664\, d\varphi.$$

Therefore if the error of the altitude be one second of arc, the error of t would be $0^s.10$, whilst an error of the latitude equal to $1''$ produces an error of the time equal to $0^s.07$.

Besides we see from the differential equation, that it is the less advisable to find the time by an altitude, the less the value of $\cos\varphi$, and hence, the less the latitude is. Near the pole, where $\cos\varphi$ is very small, the method cannot be used at all.

5. In case that several altitudes or zenith distances have been taken, it is not necessary, to compute the error of the clock from each observation, unless it is desirable to know how far they agree with each other, but the error of the clock may be found immediately from the arithmetical mean of all zenith distances. However, since the zenith distances do not increase proportionally to the time, it is necessary, either to apply to the arithmetical mean a correction, as was done in No. 2, in order to find from this corrected zenith distance the hour angle corresponding to the arithmetical mean of the clock-times, or to apply a correction to the hour angle computed from the arithmetical mean of all zenith distances.

Let τ, τ', τ'', etc. be the clock-times, at which the zenith distances, whose number be n, are taken; let T be the arithmetical mean of all, and Z the zenith distance belonging to the time T, then we have:

$$z = Z + \frac{dZ}{dt}(\tau - T) + \tfrac{1}{2}\frac{d^2 Z}{dt^2}(\tau - T)^2,$$

$$z' = Z + \frac{dZ}{dt}(\tau' - T) + \tfrac{1}{2}\frac{d^2 Z}{dt^2}(\tau' - T)^2,$$

etc.,

where t is the hour angle corresponding to the time T, or since $\tau - T + \tau' - T + \tau'' - T + \ldots = 0$:

$$Z = \frac{z + z' + z'' + \ldots}{n} - \tfrac{1}{2}\frac{d^2 Z}{dt^2}\,\frac{(\tau - T)^2 + (\tau' - T)^2 + \ldots}{n}$$

$$= \frac{z + z' + z'' + \ldots}{n} - \frac{d^2 Z}{dt^2}\,\frac{\Sigma 2\sin\frac{1}{2}(\tau - T)^2}{n}.$$

If we substitute here the expression for $\frac{d^2 z}{dt^2}$ found in No. 25 of the first section, we finally get:

$$Z = \frac{z + z' + z'' + \ldots}{n} - \frac{\cos\delta\cos\varphi}{\sin Z}\cos A\cos p\,\frac{\Sigma 2\sin\frac{1}{2}(\tau - T)^2}{n}.$$

With this corrected zenith distance we ought to compute the hour angle and from this the true time, which compared with T gives the error of the clock. But if we compute the hour angle with the uncorrected arithmetical mean of the zenith distances, we must apply to it the correction:

$$-\frac{dt}{dz}\,\frac{\cos\delta\cos\varphi}{\sin Z}\cos A\cos p\,\frac{\Sigma\, 2\sin\tfrac{1}{2}(\tau-T)^2}{n},$$

or if we substitute for $\frac{dt}{dz}$ its value according to No. 25 of the first section, we find this correction expressed in time:

$$-\frac{\cos p\cos A}{15\sin t}\,\frac{\Sigma\, 2\sin\tfrac{1}{2}(\tau-T)^2}{n}, \qquad (a)$$

where A and p are found by means of the formulae:

$$\sin A = \frac{\sin t}{\sin Z}\cos\delta$$

and $$\sin p = \frac{\sin t}{\sin Z}\cos\varphi.$$

These, it is true, do not determine the sign of $\cos A$ and $\cos p$; but we can easily establish a rule by which we may always decide about the sign of the correction (a).

If the hour angles are not reckoned in the usual way, but on both sides of the meridian from 0^0 to 180^0, the correction is always to be applied to the absolute value of t, and its sign will depend only upon the sign of the product $\cos A\cos p$, which is positive or negative, if $\cos p$ and $\cos A$ have the same or opposite signs. Now we have:

$$\cos p = \frac{\sin\varphi\left(1-\cos z\,\frac{\sin\delta}{\sin\varphi}\right)}{\sin z\cos\delta} = \frac{\sin\delta\left(\frac{\sin\varphi}{\sin\delta}-\cos z\right)}{\sin z\cos\delta},$$

$$\cos A = \frac{\sin\varphi\left(\cos z-\frac{\sin\delta}{\sin\varphi}\right)}{\sin z\cos\varphi} = \frac{\sin\delta\left(\frac{\cos z\sin\varphi}{\sin\delta}-1\right)}{\sin z\cos\varphi}.$$

Therefore, if $\delta < \varphi$, $\cos p$ is always positive,

and $\cos A$ is positive, if $\cos z > \frac{\sin\delta}{\sin\varphi}$,

negative, if $\cos z < \frac{\sin\delta}{\sin\varphi}$,

and if $\delta > \varphi$, $\cos A$ is always negative,

and $\cos p$ is negative, if $\cos z > \frac{\sin\varphi}{\sin\delta}$,

positive, if $\cos z < \frac{\sin\varphi}{\sin\delta}$.

Therefore if we take the fraction

$$\frac{\sin\delta}{\sin\varphi}, \text{ if } \varphi > \delta$$

and $$\frac{\sin\varphi}{\sin\delta}, \text{ if } \varphi < \delta,$$

the two cosines have the same sign and the correction (a) is negative, if $\cos z$ is greater than this fraction; but they have opposite signs and the correction (a) is positive, if $\cos z$ is less than this fraction. For stars of south declination $\cos A$ and $\cos p$ are always positive, hence the sign of the correction is always negative*).

Dr. Westphal took on the 29th of October not only one zenith distance of the sun but eight in succession, namely:

Chronometer-time	True zenith distance of the centre of the sun	$\tau - T$	$2 \sin \frac{1}{2} (\tau - T)^2$
$20^h 16^m 20^s$	$56^0 \; 2' 52''.1$	$3^m 32^s$	$24''.51$
17 21	55 52 51 . 5	2 31	12 . 43
18 21	42 51 . 0	1 31	4 . 52
19 21	32 50 . 5	0 31	0 . 52
20 21	22 50 . 0	0 29	0 . 46
21 23	12 49 . 4	1 31	4 . 52
22 23	2 48 . 9	2 31	12 . 43
23 25	54 52 48 . 4	3 33	24 . 74
$20^h 19^m 51^s.9$	$55^0 27' 50''.2$		$10''.52.$

Now the arithmetical mean of the zenith distances is $55^0 27' 50''.2$ and the declination of the sun $- 13^0 38' 14''.7$, hence we find the hour angle:

$$2^h 35^m 13^s.18.$$

to which value the correction must be applied. But we have:

$$\sin p = 9.83079, \; \sin A = 9.86881,$$

hence, as the declination is south, the correction is:

$$- 8''.32 \text{ in arc or } - 0^s.55 \text{ in time.}$$

With the corrected hour angle $- 2^h 35^m 12^s.63$ we find the mean time $21^h 8^m 38^s.70$, hence the error of the clock is equal to:

$$+ 48^m 46^s.8.$$

6. If an altitude of a star is taken and the time known, we can find the latitude of the place. For we have again the equation:

$$\sin h = \sin \varphi \sin \delta + \cos \varphi \cos \delta \cos t.$$

*) Warnstorff's Hülfstafeln pag. 122.

Taking now:

$$\begin{aligned} \sin\delta &= M\sin N, \\ \cos\delta\cos t &= M\cos N, \end{aligned} \qquad (A)$$

we find:

$$\sin h = M\cos(\varphi - N),$$

and hence:

$$\cos(\varphi - N) = \frac{\sin h}{M} = \frac{\sin N}{\sin\delta}\sin h. \qquad (B)$$

The formula leaves it doubtful, whether the positive or negative value of $\varphi - N$ must be taken, but it is always easy to decide this in another way. For if in Fig. 6 we draw an arc SQ perpendicular to the meridian, we easily see that $N = 90 - FQ$ or equal to the distance of Q from the equator, hence that $ZQ = \varphi - N$, whilst M is the cosine of the arc SQ. Therefore as long as SQ intersects the meridian south of the zenith, we must take the positive value $\varphi - N$, but $N - \varphi$ is to be taken, when the point of intersection lies north of the zenith. In case that $t > 90^0$, the perpendicular arc is below the pole, hence its distance from the equator is $> 90^0$ and the zenith distance of Q equal to $N - \varphi$. Therefore in this case the negative value $N - \varphi$ of the angle found by the cosine is to be taken.

Fig. 6.

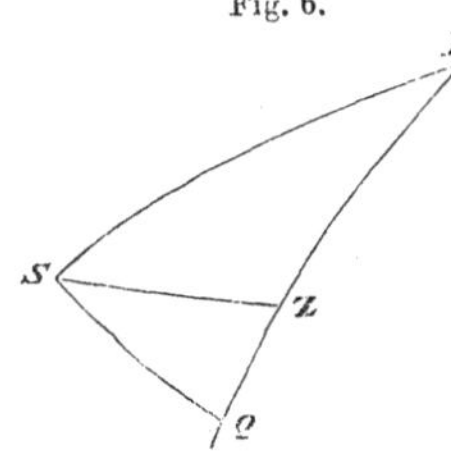

If the altitude is taken on the meridian, we find φ by means of the simple equation

$$\varphi = \delta \pm z,$$

where the upper or lower sign must be taken, if the star passes across the meridian south or north of the zenith. In case that the star culminates below the pole, we have:

$$\varphi = 180 - \delta - z.$$

Dr. Westphal in 1822 October 19 at Benisuef in Egypt took the altitude of the centre of the sun at $23^h\,1^m\,10^s$ mean time and found for it $49^0\,17'\,22''.8$. The declination at that time was $-10^0\,12'\,16''.1$, the equation of time $-15^m\,0^s.0$, hence the hour angle of the sun $23^h 16^m 10^s = -10^0 57' 30''.0$. We find therefore:

$$\begin{aligned}
\operatorname{tang}\delta &= 9.2552942_n \\
\cos t &= 9.9920078 \\
N &= -10^\circ\,23'\,23''.67 \\
\sin N &= 9.2561063_n \\
\sin\delta &= 9.2483695_n \\
& \quad 0.0077368 \\
\sin h & \quad 9.8796788 \\
\varphi - N &= 39^\circ\,29'\,54''.51 \\
\text{hence } \varphi &= 29\quad 6\quad 30\,.84.
\end{aligned}$$

In order to enable us to estimate the effect, which any errors of h and t can have on φ, we differentiate the equation for $\sin h$ and find according to I. No. 8:

$$d\varphi = -\sec A\,dh - \cos\varphi\,\operatorname{tang} A\,.\,dt.$$

Here the coefficients are at a minimum, when $A=0$ or $=180^\circ$. The secant of A is then ± 1, hence errors of the altitude are then at least not increased and since tang A is then equal to zero, errors of the time have no influenze at all. Therefore in order to find the latitude as correct as possible by altitudes, they must be taken on the meridian or at least as near it as possible.

For the example we have $A = -16^\circ\,40'.1$, hence we find:

$$d\varphi = -1.044\,dh + 0.2616\,dt,$$

or if dt be expressed in seconds of time:

$$d\varphi = -1.044\,dh + 3.924\,dt.$$

If several altitudes are taken, we find according to No. 5 the altitude corresponding to the arithmetical mean of the times by means of the formula:

$$H = \frac{h + h' + h'' + \ldots}{n} + \frac{\cos\delta\cos\varphi}{\cos H}\cos A\cos p\,\frac{\Sigma 2\sin\tfrac{1}{2}(\tau - T)^2}{n}.$$

7. If the altitude is taken very near the meridian, we can deduce the latitude from it in an easier way than by solving the triangle. For since the altitudes of the stars arrive at a maximum on the meridian and hence change very slowly in the neighbourhood of the meridian, we have only to add a small correction to an altitude taken near the meridian, in order to find the meridian altitude. But this in connection with the declination gives immediately the latitude.

This method of finding the latitude is called that by *circum-meridian altitudes*.

From:

$$\cos z = \sin \varphi \sin \delta + \cos \varphi \cos \delta \cos t,$$

we get:

$$\cos z = \cos (\varphi - \delta) - 2 \cos \varphi \cos \delta \sin \tfrac{1}{2} t^2$$

and from this according to the formula (19) in No. 11 of the introduction:

$$z = \varphi - \delta + \frac{2 \cos \varphi \cos \delta}{\sin (\varphi - \delta)} \sin \tfrac{1}{2} t^2 - \frac{2 \cos \varphi^2 \cos \delta^2}{\sin (\varphi - \delta)^2} \operatorname{cotang} (\varphi - \delta) \sin \tfrac{1}{2} t^4.$$

or denoting $\frac{\cos \varphi \cos \delta}{\sin (\varphi - \delta)}$ by b:

$$\varphi = z + \delta - b \, . \sin \tfrac{1}{2} t^2 + b^2 \, . \operatorname{cotang} (\varphi - \delta) \, . \, 2 \sin \tfrac{1}{2} t^4. \qquad (A)$$

Therefore if we compute $\varphi - \delta$ and b with an approximate value of φ, and take the values of $2 \sin \frac{1}{2} t^2$ and $2 \sin \frac{1}{2} t^4$ from tables, the computation for the latitude is exceedingly simple. Such tables are given for instance in Warnstorff's Hülfstafeln, where for greater convenience also the logarithms of those quantities are given. If the value of φ should differ considerably from the assumed value, it is necessary, to repeat the computation, at least that of the first term. Stars culminating near the zenith must not be used for this method, since for these the correction becomes large on account of the small divisor $\varphi - \delta$.

Westphal in 1822 October 3 at Cairo took the zenith distance of the centre of the sun at $0^h\, 2^m\, 2^s.7$ mean time and found $34^0\, 1'\, 34''.2$. The declination of the sun being $-3^0\, 48'\, 51''.2$, the equation of time $-10^m\, 48^s.6$, and hence the hour angle $+12^m\, 51^s.3$, we find from the tables:

$$\log 2 \sin \tfrac{1}{2} t^2 = 2.51105 \qquad \log 2 \sin \tfrac{1}{2} t^4 = 9.4060.$$

Taking $\varphi = 30^0\, 4'$, we have $\log b = 0.19006$ and then the first term of the correction is $-8'\, 22''.47$, the second $+0''.91$, therefore we have:

$$\begin{array}{rl} \text{Correction} & -\;\; 8'\, 21''.56 \\ z + \delta = & \underline{30^0\, 12'\, 43''.00} \\ \varphi = & 30^0\;\; 4'\, 21''.44. \end{array}$$

A change of 1' in the assumed value of φ gives in this case only a change of $0''.30$ in the computed value of φ, and the true value, found by repeating the computation, is:

$$\varphi = 30^0\, 4'\, 21''.54.$$

The formula (A) is true, if the star passes the meridian south of the zenith. But if the declination is greater than the latitude and thence the star passes the meridian north of the zenith, we must use $\delta - \varphi$ instead of $\varphi - \delta$, and we get in this case:

$$\varphi = \delta - z + \frac{\cos\varphi \cos\delta}{\sin(\delta - \varphi)} 2 \sin \tfrac{1}{2} t^2 - \frac{\cos\varphi^2 \cos\delta^2}{\sin(\delta - \varphi)^2} \operatorname{cotang}(\delta - \varphi) 2 \sin \tfrac{1}{2} t^4.$$

Finally, if the star be observed near its lower culmination, we have, reckoning t from the lower culmination:

$$\cos z = \cos(180 - \varphi - \delta) + 2 \cos\varphi \cos\delta \sin \tfrac{1}{2} t^2$$

and hence:

$$\varphi = 180 - \delta - z - \frac{\cos\varphi \cos\delta}{\sin(\varphi + \delta)} 2 \sin \tfrac{1}{2} t^2 + \frac{\cos\varphi^2 \cos\delta^2}{\sin(\varphi + \delta)^2} \operatorname{cotang}(\varphi + \delta) 2 \sin \tfrac{1}{2} t^4.$$

If the latitude of a place is determined by this method, of course not only a single zenith distance but a number of them are taken in succession in the neighbourhood of the meridian. Then the values of $2 \sin \frac{1}{2} t^2$ and $2 \sin \frac{1}{2} t^4$ must be found for each t and the arithmetical means of all be multiplied by the constant factors. The correction, found in this way, is to be added to the arithmetical mean of the zenith distances *).

The reduction to the meridian can also be made in another form. For from the equation:

$$\cos z - \cos(\varphi - \delta) = -2 \cos\varphi \cos\delta \sin \tfrac{1}{2} t^2$$

follows:

$$\sin \frac{\varphi - \delta + z}{2} \sin \frac{\varphi - \delta - z}{2} = -\cos\varphi \cos\delta \sin \tfrac{1}{2} t^2.$$

Now if we take the reduction to the meridian:

$$\varphi - \delta - z = -x,$$

we find:

$$\frac{\varphi - \delta + z}{2} = \varphi - \delta + \tfrac{1}{2} x;$$

hence:

$$\sin \tfrac{1}{2} x = \frac{\cos\varphi \cos\delta}{\sin(\varphi - \delta + \frac{1}{2} x)} \sin \tfrac{1}{2} t^2$$

an equation which may be written in this way:

$$\frac{\sin \frac{1}{2} x}{\frac{1}{2} x} \cdot x = \frac{\cos\varphi \cos\delta}{\sin(\varphi - \delta)} 2 \sin \tfrac{1}{2} t^2 \, \frac{\sin(\varphi - \delta)}{\sin(\varphi - \delta + \frac{1}{2} x)}.$$

Now it has been proved in No. 10 of the introduction, that

*) In case that the snn is observed, the change of the declination must be taken into account. See the following No.

$\frac{\sin a}{a} = \sqrt[3]{\cos a}$, neglecting terms of the fourth order. If we apply this and take as a first approximation for x the value ξ from the equation:

$$\xi = \frac{\cos\varphi\cos\delta}{\sin(\varphi-\delta)} 2\sin\tfrac{1}{2}t^2 \qquad (B),$$

we find:

$$x\sqrt[3]{\cos\tfrac{1}{2}x} = \xi\frac{\sin(\varphi-\delta)}{\sin(\varphi-\delta+\tfrac{1}{2}x)},$$

or if we find x from this equation, write in the second number ξ instead of x, and denote the new value of x by ξ':

$$\xi' = \xi\frac{\sin(\varphi-\delta)}{\sin(\varphi-\delta+\tfrac{1}{2}\xi)}\sec\tfrac{1}{2}\xi^{\frac{1}{3}}.$$

This second approximation is in most cases already sufficiently correct. But if this should not be the case, we compute φ from ξ', then ξ by means of (*B*), and find the corrected value:

$$\xi'' = \xi\frac{\sin(\varphi-\delta)}{\sin(\varphi-\delta+\tfrac{1}{2}\xi')}\sec\tfrac{1}{2}\xi'^{\frac{1}{3}}.$$

With the data used before, we find:

$$\begin{aligned} \xi &= 8'\,22''.47 \\ \log\xi &= 2.70111 \\ \sin(\varphi-\delta) &= 9.74620 \\ \operatorname{cosec}(\varphi-\delta+\tfrac{1}{2}\xi) &= 0.25293 \\ \log\xi' &= 2.70024, \end{aligned}$$

hence $\xi' = 8'\,22''.47$ and $\varphi = 30^0\,4'\,21''.53$.

8. If we take circum-meridian altitudes of the sun, we must take the change of its declination into account, hence we ought to make the computation for each hour angle with a different declination. But in order to render the reduction more convenient, we can proceed in the following way:

We have:

$$\varphi = z + \delta - \frac{\cos\varphi\cos\delta}{\sin(\varphi-\delta)} 2\sin\tfrac{1}{2}t^2.$$

Now if D is the declination of the sun at noon, we can express the declination corresponding to any hour angle t by $D+\beta t$, where β is the change of the declination in one hour and t is expressed in parts of an hour. Then we have:

$$\varphi = z + D + \beta t - \frac{\cos\varphi\cos\delta}{\sin(\varphi-\delta)} 2\sin\tfrac{1}{2}t^2. \qquad (a)$$

If we take now:

$$\beta t - \frac{\cos\varphi\cos\delta}{\sin(\varphi-\delta)} 2\sin\tfrac{1}{2}t^2 = - \frac{\cos\varphi\cos\delta}{\sin(\varphi-\delta)} 2\sin\tfrac{1}{2}(t+y)^2, \qquad (b)$$

we must find y from the following equation:

$$2\frac{\cos\varphi\cos\delta}{\sin(\varphi-\delta)}[\sin\tfrac{1}{2}(t+y)^2 - \sin\tfrac{1}{2}t^2] = -\beta t$$

or since:

$$\sin a^2 - \sin b^2 = \sin(a+b)\sin(a-b)$$

$$\sin\tfrac{1}{2}y = -\frac{\beta}{2}\cdot\frac{\sin(\varphi-\delta)}{\cos\varphi\cos\delta}\frac{t}{\sin(t+\frac{1}{2}y)}$$

we have:

$$y = -\beta\cdot\frac{\sin(\varphi-\delta)}{\cos\varphi\cos\delta}\cdot\frac{206265}{3600\times 15},$$

where the numerical factor has been added, because we take $\sin(t+\frac{1}{2}y) = t$, and the unit of t is one hour, whilst the unit of $\sin t$ is the radius or rather unity. If we denote the change of the declination in 48 hours expressed in seconds of arc by μ, we have $\beta = \frac{\mu}{48}$, or if we wish to express y in seconds of time, $\beta = \frac{\mu}{720}$. We have therefore:

$$y = -\frac{\mu}{188.5}[\operatorname{tang}\varphi - \operatorname{tang}\delta] \qquad (A)$$

and then we find the latitude from each single observation by means of the formula:

$$\varphi = z + D - \frac{\cos\varphi\cos\delta}{\sin(\varphi-\delta)} 2\sin\tfrac{1}{2}(t+y)^2 \text{ *)}. \qquad (B)$$

The quantity y is the hour angle of the greatest altitude, taken negative.

For in I. No. 24 we found for this the following expression:

$$t = \frac{d\delta}{dt}[\operatorname{tang}\varphi - \operatorname{tang}\delta]\frac{206265}{15}$$

where t is expressed in seconds of time and $\frac{d\delta}{dt}$ is the change of the declination in one second of time. But this is equal to $\frac{\mu}{48}\cdot\frac{1}{3600}$, hence the hour angle at the time of the greatest altitude, expressed in seconds of time, is:

---

*) To this there ought to be added still the second term dependent on $2\sin\frac{1}{2}t^4$.

$$t_0 = \frac{\mu}{720} [\text{tang}\,\varphi - \text{tang}\,\delta] \frac{206265}{3600 \times 15}$$

$$= \frac{\mu}{188.5} [\text{tang}\,\varphi - \text{tang}\,\delta],$$

which formula is the same as that for y taken with the opposite sign. Hence $t + y$ is the hour angle of the sun, reckoned not from the time of the culmination but from the time of the greatest altitude.

Therefore if circum-meridian altitudes of a heavenly body have been taken, whose declination is variable, it is not necessary to use for their reduction the declination corresponding to each observation, but we can use for all the declination at the time of culmination, if we compute the hour angles so that they are not reckoned from the time of the culmination but from the time of the greatest altitude. Then the computation is as easy as in the former case, when the declination is supposed not to change.

For the observation made at Cairo (No. 7) we have:

$$\log \mu = 3.4458_n \text{ and } D = -3^\circ\, 48'\, 38''.57,$$

with this we get:

$$y = +9^s.6, \text{ hence } t + y = 13^m\, 0^s.9$$

and hence we find for the first term of the reduction to the meridian:

$$= -8'\, 35''.00.$$

On account of the second term multiplied by $\sin \frac{1}{2} t^4$ we must add to this $+0''.91$, and we finally find $\varphi = 30^\circ\, 4'\, 21''.54$.

In case that only one altitude has been observed, it is of course easier to interpolate the declination of the sun for the time of the observation; but if several altitudes have been taken, the method of reduction just given is more convenient.

9. Since the polar distance of the pole-star is very small, it is always in the neighbourhood of the meridian, and hence its altitude taken at any time may be used with advantage for finding the latitude; but the method given in No. 7 is not applicable to this case, as the series given there is converging only as long as the hour angle is small. In this case, the polar distance being small, it is convenient to develop the expression for the correction which is to be applied to the observed altitude according to the powers of this quantity.

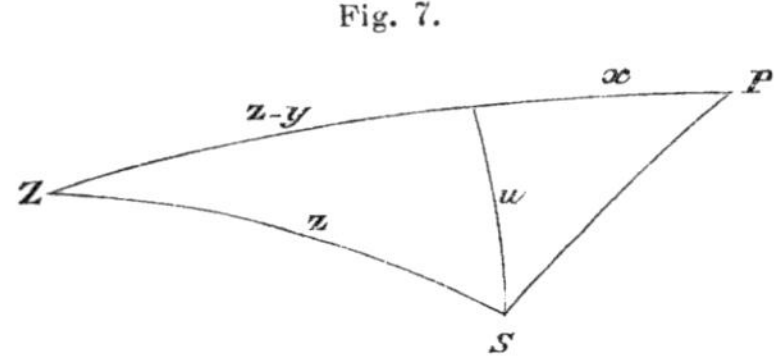

Fig. 7.

If we draw (Fig. 7) an arc of a great circle from the place of the star perpendicular to the meridian, and denote the arc of the meridian between the point of intersection with this arc and the pole by x, the arc between the same point and the zenith by $z - y$, where y is a small quantity, we have:

$$90^0 - \varphi = z - y + x,$$

or

$$\varphi = 90^0 - z + y - x,$$

and we have in the right angled triangle:

$$\text{tang}\, x = \text{tang}\, p \cos t$$

$$\cos(z - y) = \frac{\cos z}{\cos u}. \qquad (a)$$

We get immediately from the first equation:

$$x = \text{tang}\, p \cos t - \tfrac{1}{3} \text{tang}\, p^3 \cos t^3,$$

neglecting the fifth and higher powers of tang p, or neglecting again terms of the same order:

$$x = p \cos t + \tfrac{1}{3} p^3 \cos t \sin t^2. \qquad (b)$$

If we develop the second equation (a), we find:

$$\sin y = \text{cotang}\, z \frac{1 - \cos u}{\cos u} + 2 \sin^2 \tfrac{1}{2} y \,.\, \text{cotang}\, z,$$

or neglecting the fifth and higher powers of u:

$$\sin y = \text{cotang}\, z \left(\tfrac{1}{2} u^2 + \tfrac{5}{24} u^4\right) + 2 \sin^2 \tfrac{1}{2} y \,\text{cotang}\, z.$$

But we get from the equation

$$\sin u = \sin p \sin t:$$

$$u = p \sin t - \tfrac{1}{6} p^3 \sin t \cos t,$$

hence substituting this value in the equation above we find, again neglecting terms of the fifth order:

$$y = \tfrac{1}{2} p^2 \sin t^2 \,\text{cotg}\, z - \tfrac{1}{24} p^4 \sin t^2 (4 \cos t^2 - 5 \sin t^2) \,\text{cotg}\, z + \tfrac{1}{2} \text{cotg}\, z \,.\, y^2. \qquad (c)$$

This formula, it is true, contains still y in the second member, but on account of the term $\frac{1}{2}$ cotang $z \,.\, y^2$ being very small, it is sufficient, to substitute in this term for y the value computed by means of the first term alone. Thus we obtain:

$$\begin{aligned} \varphi = 90^0 - z - p \cos t &+ \tfrac{1}{2} p^2 \sin t^2 \,\text{cotang}\, z - \tfrac{1}{3} p^3 \cos t \sin t^2 \\ &+ \tfrac{1}{24} p^4 \sin t^2 (5 \sin t^2 - 4 \cos t^2) \,\text{cotang}\, z \\ &+ \tfrac{1}{8} p^4 \sin t^4 \,\text{cotang}\, z^3. \qquad (A) \end{aligned}$$

Since it would be very inconvenient to compute this

formula for every observation, tables are every year published in the Nautical Almanac and other astronomical almanacs, which render the computation very easy. They embrace the largest terms of the above expression, which are always sufficient, unless the greatest accuracy should be required. If we neglect the terms dependent on the third and fourth power of p, we have simply: *)

$$\varphi = 90^0 - z - p \cos t + \tfrac{1}{2} p^2 \sin t^2 \operatorname{cotang} z.$$

If we denote thus a certain value of the right ascension and polar distance by α_0 and p_0, the apparent values at the time of the observation being

$$\alpha = \alpha_0 + \Delta\alpha, \qquad p = p_0 + \Delta p$$

we find substituting these values:

$$\varphi = 90^0 - z - p_0 \cos t_0 + \tfrac{1}{2} p_0{}^2 \operatorname{cotang} z \sin t_0{}^2$$
$$- \Delta p \cos t_0 - p \sin t_0 \, \Delta\alpha,$$

where $t_0 = \Theta - \alpha_0$.

We find now in the Almanac three tables. The first gives the term $-p_0 \cos t_0$, the argument being Θ, since this alone is variable. The second table gives the value of the term $\frac{1}{2} p_0{}^2 \operatorname{cotang} z \sin t_0{}^2$, the arguments being z and Θ. Finally the third table gives the term dependent on Θ, $\Delta\alpha$ and Δp

$$- \Delta p \cos t_0 - p \sin t_0 \, \Delta\alpha,$$

the arguments being the sidereal time and the days of the year.

Tables of a different construction have been published by Petersen in Warnstorff's Hülfstafeln pag. 73 and these embrace all terms and can be used while the polar distance of the pole-star is between the limits $1^0\,20'$ and $1^0\,40'$. Let p_0 again be a certain value of p, for which Petersen takes $p_0 = 1^0\,30'$, then the formula (A) can easily be written in this way:

---

*) The term multiplied by p^3 is at its maximum, when $t = 54^0\,44'$ and its value, if we take $p = 1^0\,40'$, is then only $0''.65$. The terms multiplied by p^4 are still less, unless z should be very small. These terms can be easily embraced in the tables, as the first may be united with $p \cos t$, the other with $\frac{1}{2} p^2 \sin t^2 \operatorname{cotang} z$.

$$\varphi = 90^0 - z - \frac{p}{p_0}[p_0 \cos t + \tfrac{1}{3} p_0{}^3 \cos t \sin t^2] - \tfrac{1}{3}\frac{p}{p_0}\left(\frac{p^2}{p_0{}^2} - 1\right) p_0{}^3 \cos t \sin t^2$$
$$+ \frac{p^2}{p_0{}^2} \operatorname{cotang} z\,[\tfrac{1}{2} p_0{}^2 \sin t^2 + \tfrac{1}{24} p_0{}^4 \sin t^2 (5 \sin t^2 - 4 \cos t^2)]$$
$$+ \tfrac{1}{8} \frac{p^4}{p_0{}^4} p_0{}^4 \sin t^4 \operatorname{cotang} z^3.$$

If we put now:

$$\frac{p}{p_0} = A$$
$$p_0 \cos t + \tfrac{1}{3} p_0{}^3 \cos t \sin t^2 = \alpha,$$
$$\tfrac{1}{3} A (A^2 - 1) p_0{}^3 \cos t \sin t^2 = \gamma,$$
$$\tfrac{1}{2} p_0{}^2 \sin t^2 + \tfrac{1}{24} p_0{}^4 \sin t^2 (5 \sin t^2 - 4 \cos t^2) = \beta,$$
$$\tfrac{1}{8} A^4 p_0{}^4 \sin t^4 \operatorname{cotang} z^3 = \tfrac{1}{2} A^4 \beta^2 . \operatorname{cotang} z^3 = \mu,$$

we obtain:

$$\varphi = 90^0 - z - A\alpha - \gamma + A^2 \beta \operatorname{cotang} z + \mu.$$

Now four tables have been constructed, the first two of which give α and β, the argument being t; a third table gives the value of the small quantity γ, the arguments being p and t and finally a fourth table gives the quantity μ, which is likewise very small, the arguments being $y = A^2 \beta \operatorname{cotang} z$ and $90^0 - z$. These tables have been computed from $t = 0^h$ to $t = 6^h$. Therefore if $t > 90^0$, the hour angle must be reckoned from the lower culmination, so that in this case we have:

$$\varphi = 90^0 - z + A\alpha + \gamma + A^2 \beta \operatorname{cotang} z + \mu.$$

Example. In 1847 Oct. 12 the altitude of Polaris was taken with a small altitude and azimuth instrument at the observatory of the late Dr. Hülsmann at Düsseldorf and it was at $18^h\,22^m\,48^s.8$ sidereal time $h = 50^0\,55'\,30''.8$, which is already corrected for refraction.

According to the Berlin Jahrbuch the place of Polaris on that day is:

$$\alpha = 1^h\,5^m\,31^s.7, \qquad \delta = 88^0\,29'\,52''.4.$$

Hence we have:

$$p = 1^0\,30'\,7''.6, \qquad t = 17^h\,17^m\,17^s.1 = 259^0\,19'\,16''.5,$$

and:

$$\log A = 0.0006108$$

and we obtain by means of the tables or the formulae:

$$\alpha = 1000''.85,\ \beta = 68''.28,\ \gamma = 0''.00,\ \mu = 0''.02,$$

therefore:

$$A\alpha = +16' 42''.26$$
$$A^2\beta \operatorname{cotang} z = +\ \ 1\ 24\ .33$$
$$\mu = +\ \ \ \ 0\ .02$$
$$\text{sum} = +18'\ 6''.61$$
$$\text{hence: } \varphi = 51^0 13' 37''.41.$$

10. Gauss has also published a method for finding the latitude from the arithmetical mean of several zenith distances, taken long before or after the culmination, which is especially convenient for the pole-star.

If an approximate value φ_0 of the latitude φ is known, and Θ is the sidereal time, at which the zenith distance z is observed, we can compute from Θ and φ_0 the value of the zenith distance ζ by means of the formulae:

$$\operatorname{tang} x = \cos t \operatorname{cotang} \delta$$
$$\cos \zeta = \frac{\sin \delta}{\cos x} \sin (\varphi_0 + x)$$

and then we obtain:

$$d\varphi . \frac{d\zeta}{d\varphi} = z_1 - \zeta,$$

hence:

$$d\varphi = \frac{\zeta - z_1}{\frac{\sin \delta}{\cos x} . \frac{\cos (\varphi_0 + x)}{\sin \zeta}};$$

x is again the arc between the pole and the point in which an arc drawn through the star and perpendicular to the meridian intersects the latter and since the length of this arc is always between the limits $\pm 90^0 - \delta$, we can take in case of the pole-star $\frac{\sin \delta}{\cos x}$ as well as $\frac{\cos (\varphi + x)}{\sin \zeta}$ equal to unity, if the latitude is known within a few seconds and $d\varphi$ is therefore a small quantity.

If another zenith distance has been taken at the sidereal time θ', we have:

$$\operatorname{tang} x' = \cos t' \operatorname{tang} \delta$$
$$\cos \zeta' = \frac{\sin \delta}{\cos x'} \sin (\varphi_0 + x')$$

and:

$$d\varphi = \frac{z_1' - \zeta'}{\frac{d\zeta'}{d\varphi}},$$

or, if Z denotes the arithmetical mean of both observed zenith distances equal to $\frac{1}{2}(z_1 + z_1')$:

$$d\varphi = \frac{Z - \frac{1}{2}(\zeta' + \zeta)}{\frac{1}{2}\left(\frac{d\zeta}{d\varphi} + \frac{d\zeta'}{d\varphi}\right)}$$

$$= \frac{\frac{1}{2}(\zeta' + \zeta) - Z}{\frac{1}{2}(A + B)}, \qquad (a)$$

where:

$$A = \frac{\sin\delta}{\cos x} \cdot \frac{\cos(\varphi_0 + x)}{\sin\zeta}$$
$$B = \frac{\sin\delta}{\cos x'} \cdot \frac{\cos(\varphi_0 + x')}{\sin\zeta'}, \qquad (b)$$

or:

$$A = \text{cotang}\,\zeta \,.\, \text{cotang}\,(\varphi_0 + x)$$
$$B = \text{cotang}\,\zeta' \,.\, \text{cotang}\,(\varphi_0 + x'), \qquad (c)$$

and finally, if we find $\frac{d\zeta}{d\varphi}$ from the original equation:

$$\cos\zeta = \sin\varphi_0 \sin\delta + \cos\varphi_0 \cos\delta \cos t$$

we obtain also:

$$\tfrac{1}{2}(A + B) = \frac{\cos\varphi \sin\delta}{\sin Z} - \frac{\sin\varphi\cos\delta}{\sin Z}\cos\tfrac{1}{2}(t' + t). \qquad (d)$$

In case of the pole-star we have simply:

$$d\varphi = \tfrac{1}{2}(\zeta + \zeta') - Z. \qquad (e)$$

If several zenith distances have been observed, we ought to compute ζ for each sidereal time separately and we should then obtain:

$$d\varphi = -\frac{\frac{1}{n}[\zeta + \zeta' + \zeta'' + \ldots + \zeta_{n-1}] - Z}{\frac{1}{n}\left(\frac{d\varphi}{d\zeta} + \frac{d\varphi}{d\zeta'} + \ldots\ldots\ldots\right)}, \qquad (f)$$

where Z again denotes the arithmetical mean of all observed zenith distances. But the following way of proceeding is more simple.

If we denote by Θ_0 the arithmetical mean of all sidereal times and put:

$$\theta - \Theta_0 = \tau,\ \theta' - \Theta_0 = \tau' \text{ etc.}$$

and then denote by ζ_0 the zenith distance corresponding to Θ_0, we obtain in the same way as in No. 5 of this section:

$$\frac{\zeta + \zeta' + \zeta'' + \ldots}{n} = \zeta_0 + \frac{d^2\zeta_0}{dt^2} \cdot \frac{\Sigma 2\sin\frac{1}{2}(\theta - \Theta_0)^2}{n}.$$

Now if T is taken from the following equation:

$$2\sin\tfrac{1}{2}T^2 = \frac{\Sigma 2\sin\frac{1}{2}(\theta - \Theta_0)^2}{n},$$

the zenith distances z and z' at the times $\Theta_0 - T$ and $\Theta_0 + T$ are:

$$z = \zeta_0 - \frac{d\zeta_0}{dt} T + \tfrac{1}{2} \frac{d^2\zeta_0}{dt^2} T^2$$

$$z' = \zeta_0 + \frac{d\zeta_0}{dt} T + \tfrac{1}{2} \frac{d^2\zeta_0}{dt^2} T^2$$

hence:

$$\frac{z + z'}{2} = \zeta_0 + \frac{d^2\zeta_0}{dt^2} 2 \sin \tfrac{1}{2} T^2 = \frac{\zeta + \zeta' + \zeta'' + \dots}{n},$$

and we obtain according to the formula (f) simply:

$$d\varphi = \frac{\frac{1}{2}(z' + z) - Z}{\frac{1}{2}(A' + B')},$$

if the values of A and B corresponding to z' are denoted by A' and B'.

Therefore if several zenith distances of a star have been observed, we take the mean of the observed clock-times and subtract from it each clock-time without regard to the sign. These differences converted into sidereal time give the quantities τ, for which we find from the tables the quantities $2 \sin \frac{1}{2} \tau^2$. From the same tables we find the argument T corresponding to the arithmetical mean of all these quantities and compute the hour angles:

$$\Theta_0 - (\alpha + T) = t$$

$$\Theta_0 - (\alpha - T) = t'$$

and then z and z' by means of the formulae:

$$\operatorname{tang} x = \cos t \operatorname{cotang} \delta$$

$$\cos z = \frac{\sin \delta}{\cos x} \sin (\varphi_0 + x)$$

and:

$$\operatorname{tang} x' = \cos t' \operatorname{cotang} \delta$$

$$\cos z' = \frac{\sin \delta}{\cos x'} \sin (\varphi_0 + x').$$

In case of the pole-star we then have immediately:

$$d\varphi = \tfrac{1}{2}(z + z') - Z,$$

where Z is now the arithmetical mean of all observed zenith distances. For other stars the rigorous formula for $d\varphi$ must be computed, namely:

$$d\varphi = \frac{\frac{1}{2}(z + z') - Z}{\frac{1}{2}(A + B)},$$

where A and B are obtained by means of the formulae (b), (c) or (d) after taking $\zeta = z$ and $\zeta' = z'$ *).

*) Warnstorff's Hülfstafeln pag. 127.

Example. In 1847 Oct. 12 the following ten zenith distances of Polaris were taken at the observatory of Dr. Hülsmann:

Sidereal time.	Zenith distance.	τ	$2\sin\frac{1}{2}\tau^2$
$17^h 56^m 21^s.4$	$39^\circ 13' 42''.1$	$13^m 19^s.75$	348.75
59 54 .5	12 17 . 6	9 46 .65	187.69
18 3 29 .7	11 6 . 8	6 11 .45	75.24
6 2 .9	10 3 . 6	3 38 .25	25.98
8 35 .0	9 0 . 6	1 6 .15	2.39
11 5 .1	8 2 . 8	1 23 .95	3.85
13 32 .0	7 7 . 6	3 50 .85	29.06
16 34 .0	6 4 . 8	6 52 .85	92.95
18 28 .1	5 15 . 3	8 46 .95	151.43
22 48 .8	3 42 . 7	13 7 .65	338.28
$\Theta_0 = 18^h\ 9^m 41^s.15$	$39^\circ 8' 38''.39$		125.56
	Refr. $46''.50$		$T = 7^m 59^s.83$
	$Z = 39^\circ 9' 24''.89$		

$$\Theta_0 - (\alpha + T) = 16^h 56^m 9^s.62 = 254^\circ 2' 24''.3 \qquad \Theta_0 - (\alpha - T) = 17^h 12^m 9^s.28 = 258^\circ 2' 19''.2.$$

Now taking:

$$\varphi_0 = 51^\circ 13' 30''.0,$$

we obtain:

$$z = 39^\circ 12' 37''.56 \qquad z' = 39^\circ 6' 34''.54$$
$$\tfrac{1}{2}(z + z') = 39^\circ 9' 36''.05$$
$$\tfrac{1}{2}(z + z') - Z = +11''.16,$$

hence:

$$\varphi = 51^\circ 13' 41''.16.$$

III. METHODS OF FINDING BOTH THE TIME AND THE LATITUDE BY COMBINING SEVERAL ALTITUDES.

11. If we observe two altitudes of stars, we have two equations:

$$\sin h = \sin\varphi \sin\delta + \cos\varphi \cos\delta \cos t,$$
$$\sin h' = \sin\varphi \sin\delta' + \cos\varphi \cos\delta' \cos t'.$$

In these equations, since we always observe stars, whose places are known, δ and δ' are known, and further we have:

$$t' = t + (t' - t) = t + (\Theta' - \Theta) - (\alpha' - \alpha).$$

Now since $\alpha' - \alpha$ and $\Theta' - \Theta$ are likewise known, the latter being equal to the interval of time between the two observations, the two equations contain only two unknown quantities Θ and φ, which therefore can be found by solving them. Thus the latitude and the time can be found by observing two altitudes, but the combination of two altitudes in some cases is also very convenient for finding either the latitude or the time alone.

We have seen before, that if two altitudes of the same star are taken at its upper and lower culmination, their arithmetical mean is equal to the latitude, which thus is determined independently of the declination. This is even found at the same time, since it is equal to half the difference of the altitudes.

Likewise we can find the latitude by the difference of the meridian zenith distances of two stars, one of which culminates south, the other north of the zenith. For if δ is the declination of the first star, its meridian zenith distance is:

$$z = \varphi - \delta,$$

and if δ' is the declination of the other star, north of the zenith, we have:

$$z' = \delta' - \varphi,$$

and therefore we get:

$$\varphi = \tfrac{1}{2}(\delta + \delta') + \tfrac{1}{2}(z - z').$$

12. If two equal altitudes of the same star have been observed, we have:

$$\begin{aligned} \sin h &= \sin\varphi \sin\delta + \cos\varphi \cos\delta \cos t, \\ \sin h &= \sin\varphi \sin\delta + \cos\varphi \cos\delta \cos t', \end{aligned} \qquad (a)$$

from which we find $t = -t'$. The altitudes therefore are then taken at equal hour angles on both sides of the meridian. Now if u is the clock-time of the first, u' that of the second observation, $\tfrac{1}{2}(u + u')$ is the time, when the star was on the meridian and since this must be equal to the known right ascension of the star, we find the error of the clock equal to:

$$\alpha - \tfrac{1}{2}(u' + u).$$

This method of finding the time by *equal altitudes* is the most accurate of all methods of finding the time by altitudes. Since neither the latitude of the place nor the declination of the heavenly body need be known and since for this reason it is also not necessary to know the longitude of the place, this method is well adapted to find the time at a place, whose geographical position is entirely unknown. It is also not all necessary to know the altitude itself, so that it is possible to obtain by this method accurate results, even if the quality of the instrument employed does not admit of any accurate absolute observations. All which is required for this method is a good clock, which in the interval between the two observations keeps a uniform rate, and an altitude instrument, whose circle need not be accurately divided.

We have hitherto supposed, that the declination of the heavenly body does not change. But in case that altitudes of the sun are taken, the arithmetical mean of both times does not give the time of culmination, for, if the declination is increasing, that is, if the sun approaches the north pole, the hour angle corresponding to the same altitude in the afternoon will be greater than that taken in the forenoon and hence the arithmetical mean of both times falls a little later than apparent noon. The reverse takes place if the declination of the sun is decreasing. Therefore in case of the sun a correction dependent on the change of the declination must be applied to the arithmetical of the two times. This is called *the equation of equal altitudes*.

If δ is the declination of the sun at noon, $\Delta\delta$ the change of the declination between noon and the time of each observation, we have:

$$\sin h = \sin\varphi \sin(\delta - \Delta\delta) + \cos\varphi \cos(\delta - \Delta\delta) \cos t$$
$$\sin h = \sin\varphi \sin(\delta + \Delta\delta) + \cos\varphi \cos(\delta + \Delta\delta) \cos t'.$$

Let the clock-time of the observation before noon be denoted by u, the one in the afternoon by u', then $\frac{1}{2}(u' + u) = U$ is the time, at which the sun would have been on the meridian, if the declination had not changed.

Then denoting half the interval between the observations $\frac{1}{2}(u' - u)$ by τ, the equation of equal altitudes by x, the moment of apparent noon is given by $U + x$ and we have:

$$t = \tfrac{1}{2}(u' - u) + x = \tau + x,$$
$$t' = \tfrac{1}{2}(u' - u) - x = \tau - x,$$

and also:

$$\sin h = \sin\varphi \sin(\delta - \Delta\delta) + \cos\varphi \cos(\delta - \Delta\delta) \cos(\tau + x)$$

and:

$$\sin h = \sin\varphi \sin(\delta + \Delta\delta) + \cos\varphi \cos(\delta + \Delta\delta) \cos(\tau - x).$$

From these expressions for sin h we find the following equation for x:

$$0 = \sin\varphi\cos\delta\sin\Delta\delta - \cos\varphi\sin\delta\sin\Delta\delta\cos\tau\cos x + \cos\varphi\cos\Delta\delta\cos\delta\sin\tau\sin x.$$

Now in case of the sun x is always so small, that we can take cos x equal to 1 and sin x equal to x. Then we obtain, taking also $\Delta\delta$ instead of tang $\Delta\delta$:

$$x = -\left(\frac{\operatorname{tang}\varphi}{\sin\tau} - \frac{\operatorname{tang}\delta}{\operatorname{tang}\tau}\right)\Delta\delta \; ^{*}).$$

If we denote now by μ the change of the declination during 48 hours, which may be considered here to be proportional to the time, we have:

$$\Delta\delta = \frac{\mu}{48}\tau \; ^{**}).$$

hence:

$$x = \frac{\mu}{48}\left(-\frac{\tau}{\sin\tau}\operatorname{tang}\varphi + \frac{\tau}{\operatorname{tang}\tau}\operatorname{tang}\delta\right)$$

or if x is expressed in seconds of time:

$$x = \frac{\mu}{720}\left(-\frac{\tau}{\sin\tau}\operatorname{tang}\varphi + \frac{\tau}{\operatorname{tang}\tau}\operatorname{tang}\delta\right).$$

In order to simplify the computation of this formula, tables have been published by Gauss in Zach's monatliche Correspondenz Vol. XXIII, which are also given in Warnstorff's Hülfstafeln. These tables, whose argument is τ, give the quantities:

$$\frac{1}{720}\cdot\frac{\tau}{\sin\tau} = A$$

and:

$$\frac{1}{720}\cdot\frac{\tau}{\operatorname{tang}\tau} = B,$$

and thus the formula for the equation of equal altitudes is simply:

$$x = -A\mu\operatorname{tang}\varphi + B\mu\operatorname{tang}\delta. \qquad (A)$$

Differentiating the two formulae (a), taking δ as constant, we find:

---

*) We find this also, if we differentiate the original equation for sin h, taking δ and t as variable, since we have $x = -\frac{dt}{d\delta}\Delta\delta$.

**) Since the change of the declination at apparent noon is to be used, we ought to take the arithmetical mean of the first differences of the declination, preceding and following the day of observation. Instead of this the almanacs give the quantity μ.

$$dh = -\cos A\, d\varphi - \cos\varphi \sin A\, dt$$
$$dh' = -\cos A' d\varphi - \cos\varphi \sin A' dt.$$

In these equations dt' has been taken equal to dt, since we can suppose, that the error committed in taking the time of the observation is united with the errors of the altitudes. Since we have now $A = -A'$, we obtain:

$$dh = -\cos A' d\varphi + \cos\varphi \sin A' dt,$$
$$dh' = -\cos A' d\varphi - \cos\varphi \sin A' dt,$$

and:

$$dt = \frac{\frac{1}{2}(dh - dh')}{\cos\varphi \sin A'}.$$

Therefore we see, that we must observe the heavenly body at the time, when its azimuth is as nearly as possible $+90^0$ and -90^0.

In 1822 Oct. 8 Dr. Westphal observed at Cairo the following equal altitudes of the sun:

Double the altitude of ☉ (Lower limb)	Chronometer-time forenoon	Chronometer-time afternoon	Mean
73° 0′	$21^h\ 7^m\ 27^s$	$2^h\ 33^m\ 59^s$	$23^h\ 50^m\ 43^s.0$
20	8 24	33 3	43 .5
40	9 23	32 5	44 .0
74 0	10 18	31 9	43 .5
20	11 16	30 12	44 .0
40	12 11	29 14	42 .5
75 0	13 11	28 13	42 .0
20	14 9	27 15	42 .0
40	15 10	26 15	42 .5
76 0	16 6	25 20	43 .0

Hence we find for the arithmetical mean of all observations:

$$23^h\ 50^m\ 43^s.00.$$

Now half the interval between the first observation in the forenoon and the last in the afternoon is $2^h\ 43^m\ 16^s$ and that between the last observation in the forenoon and the first in the afternoon $2^h\ 34^m\ 37^s$, hence we take:

$$\tau = 2^h\ 38^m\ 56^s.5 = 2^h.649.$$

If we compute with this A and B, we find:

$\log \tau$	0.42308		0.42308
cosec τ	0.19435	cotang τ	0.08028
Compl. log 720	7.14267		7.14267
$\log A$	7.7601	$\log B$	7.6460,

and as:

$$\delta = -6^0\ 7',\quad \varphi = 30^0\ 4'$$

and:

$$\log \mu = 3.4391_n,$$

we obtain:

$$x = +10^s.46.$$

Therefore the sun was on the meridian or it was apparent noon at the chronometer-time $23^h\ 50^m\ 53^s.46$. Now since the equation of time was $-12^h\ 33^s.18$, the sun was on the meridian at $23^h\ 47^m\ 26^s.82$ mean time, and hence the error of the chronometer was:

$$-3^m\ 26^s.64.$$

If we compute the differential equation and express dt in seconds of time, we find:

$$dt = -0^s.048\,(dh' - dh),$$

and we see, that if an error of $10''$ was committed in taking an altitude, the value of the error of the clock would be $0^s.48$ wrong.

We can make use of this differential formula in computing the small correction, which must be added to the arithmetical mean of the times, if the altitudes taken before and after noon were not exactly but only nearly equal. For if h and h' are the altitudes taken before and after noon and we take $h' - h = dh'$, we ought to apply to h' the correction $-dh'$, and hence the correction of U is:

$$dU = +\frac{dh'}{30 \cos\varphi \sin A'}$$
$$= +\frac{dh' \cos h'}{30 \cos\varphi \cos\delta \sin t'}.$$

In case that the greatest accuracy is required, such a correction is necessary even if equal altitudes have been taken. For although the mean refraction is the same for equal apparent altitudes, yet this is not the case with the true refraction, unless the indications of the meteorological instruments be accidentally the same. Therefore if ϱ is the refraction for the observation in the forenoon, $\varrho + d\varrho$ that in the afternoon, the heavenly body has been observed in the afternoon at a true altitude which is too small by $d\varrho$, and hence we must add to U the correction:

$$dU = -\frac{d\varrho \cos h}{30 \cos\varphi \cos\delta \sin t}.$$

13. Often the weather does not admit of taking equal altitudes in the forenoon and afternoon. But if we have obtained equal altitudes in the afternoon of one day and in the forenoon of the following day, we can find by them the time of midnight. The expression for the equation of equal altitudes in this case is of course different.

If T is half the interval between the observations, the hour angles are:

$$\tau = 12^h - T$$

and:

$$-\tau = -12^h + T.$$

The case is now the same as before only with this difference, that if $\Delta\delta$ is positive, the sun has the greater declination when the hour angle is $-\tau$, hence the correction μ must be taken with the opposite sign and we have in this case:

$$x = \frac{\mu}{720}\left(\frac{T}{\sin\tau}\operatorname{tang}\varphi - \frac{T}{\operatorname{tang}\tau}\operatorname{tang}\delta\right)$$

$$= \frac{\mu}{720}\left(\frac{12^h - \tau}{\sin\tau}\operatorname{tang}\varphi - \frac{12^h - \tau}{\operatorname{tang}\tau}\operatorname{tang}\delta\right).$$

If we write instead of it:

$$x = \frac{\mu}{720}\cdot\frac{12^h - \tau}{\tau}\left(\frac{\tau}{\sin\tau}\operatorname{tang}\varphi - \frac{\tau}{\operatorname{tang}\tau}\operatorname{tang}\delta\right),$$

we can use the same tables as before; but besides, the quantity $\frac{12^h - \tau}{\tau}$ must be tabulated, the argument being T or half the interval between the observations. This quantity in Warnstorff's Hülfstafeln is denoted by f, hence we have for the correction in this case:

$$x = f\mu\,[A\operatorname{tang}\varphi - B\operatorname{tang}\delta].$$

In 1810 Sept. 17 and 18 v. Zach observed at Marseilles equal altitudes of the sun. Half the interval of time was $10^h\,55^m$ and as:

$$10^h\,55^m,\quad \delta = +2^\circ\,14'\,16'',\quad \varphi = 43^\circ\,17'\,50''$$

and:

$$\log\mu = 3.4453_n.$$

We find:

$$\log A = 7.7305 \quad \log B = 7.7128,$$
$$\log f = 1.0033,$$
$$\mu f A\operatorname{tang}\varphi = -142^s.33$$
$$-\mu f B\operatorname{tang}\delta = +\quad 5.67,$$

hence for the correction:

$$x = -136^s.66.$$

Note 1. The equation for equal altitudes is expressed in apparent solar time. If now for these observations a clock adjusted to mean time is used, we may assume the equation to be expressed in mean time without any further correction. But if we use a chronometer adjusted to sidereal time, we must multiply the correction by $\frac{366}{365}$, a fraction whose logarithm is 0.0012.

Note 2. If the hour angle τ is so small, that we may use the arc instead of the sine and the tangent, the equation of equal altitudes becomes:

$$x = -\frac{\mu}{720}[\text{tang}\,\varphi - \text{tang}\,\delta].$$

But as the unit of τ in the numerator is not the same as in the denominator, being in the first case one hour, in the other the radius or unity, we must multiply the second member of the equation by 206265 and divide it by 15×3600. Thus we obtain:

$$x = -\frac{\mu}{188.5}[\text{tang}\,\varphi - \text{tang}\,\delta],$$

where now x is the equation of time for $\tau = 0$. But in this case the two altitudes are only one, namely the greatest altitude, and hence x is the correction, which must be applied to the time of the greatest altitude in order to find the time of culmination.

The same expression was found already in No. 8 for the reduction of circum-meridian altitudes.

14. If the altitudes of two heavenly bodies have been observed as well as the interval of time between the two observations, we can find the time and the latitude at the same time. In this case we have the two equations:

$$\sin h = \sin\varphi \sin\delta + \cos\varphi \cos\delta \cos t,$$
$$\sin h' = \sin\varphi \sin\delta' + \cos\varphi \cos\delta' \cos t'.$$

If then u and u' are the clock-times of the first and second observation, Δu the error of the clock on sidereal time, we have: *)

$$t = u + \Delta u - \alpha$$
$$t' = u' + \Delta u - \alpha',$$

where Δu has been taken the same for both observations, because the rate of the clock must be known and hence we can suppose one of the observations to be corrected on account of it. Then is

*) If the sun is observed and a mean time clock is used, we have, denoting the equation of time for both observations by w and w':

$$t = u + \Delta u - w,$$
$$t' = u' + \Delta u - w',$$

hence: $\lambda = u' - u - (w' - w)$.

$$u' - u - (\alpha' - \alpha) = \lambda$$

a known quantity and we have $t' = t + \lambda$. Hence the two equations contain only the two unknown quantities φ and t, which can be found by means of them. For this purpose we express the three quantities

$$\sin\varphi,\ \cos\varphi\sin t \text{ and } \cos\varphi\cos t$$

by the parallactic angle, since we have in the triangle between the pole, the zenith and the star:

$$\begin{aligned} \sin\varphi &= \sin h\sin\delta + \cos h\cos\delta\cos p, \\ \cos\varphi\sin t &= \cos h\sin p, \qquad (a) \\ \cos\varphi\cos t &= \sin h\cos\delta - \cos h\sin\delta\cos p. \end{aligned}$$

Substituting these expressions in the equation for $\sin h'$, we find:

$$\begin{aligned} \sin h' = &[\sin\delta\sin\delta' + \cos\delta\cos\delta'\cos\lambda]\sin h \\ &+ [\cos\delta\sin\delta' - \sin\delta\cos\delta'\cos\lambda]\cos h\cos p \\ &- \cos\delta'\sin\lambda\,.\cos h\sin p. \end{aligned}$$

But in the triangle between the two stars and the pole, denoting the distance of the stars by D, and the angles at the stars by s and s', we have:

$$\begin{aligned} \cos D &= \sin\delta\sin\delta' + \cos\delta\cos\delta'\cos\lambda \\ \sin D\cos s &= \cos\delta\sin\delta' - \sin\delta\cos\delta'\cos\lambda \qquad (b) \\ \sin D\sin s &= \cos\delta\sin\lambda, \end{aligned}$$

hence, if we substitute these expressions in the equation for $\sin h'$:

$$\sin h' = \cos D\sin h + \sin D\cos h\cos(s+p),$$

$$\text{hence}\quad \cos(s+p) = \frac{\sin h' - \cos D\sin h}{\sin D\cos h}. \qquad (c)$$

Further if we substitute in

$$\sin h = \sin\varphi\sin\delta + \cos\varphi\cos\delta\cos(t' - \lambda)$$

the expressions for $\sin\varphi$, $\cos\varphi\sin t'$ and $\cos\varphi\cos t'$, which we derive from the triangle between the pole, the zenith and the second star, we easily find:

$$\cos(s' - p') = \frac{\sin h - \cos D\sin h'}{\sin D\cos h'}. \qquad (d)$$

After the angles p and p' have thus been found by means of the equations (b) and (c) or (d), the equations (a) or the corresponding equations for $\sin\varphi$, $\cos\varphi\sin t'$ and $\cos\varphi\cos t'$ give finally φ and t or φ and t'.

The equations (b) give for D and s the sine and cosine, the same is the case with the equations (a) for φ and t, hence there can never be any doubt, in what quadrant these angles lie. But the equations (c) and (d) give only the cosine of $s+p$ and $s'-p'$; however we have in the triangle between the zenith and both stars:

$$\sin D \sin (s+p) = \cos h' \sin (A'-A)$$
$$\text{and } \sin D \sin (s'-p') = \cos h \sin (A'-A),$$

hence we see that $\sin (s+p)$ and $\sin (s'-p')$ have always the same sign as $\sin (A'-A)$, so that also in this case there can never be any doubt as to the quadrant, in which the angles lie.

The formulae (a) and (b) can be made more convenient by introducing auxiliary angles, and the formula for $\cos (s+p)$ can be transformed into another formula for $\operatorname{tang} \frac{1}{2} (s+p)^2$ in the same way as in No. 4 of this section. Thus we obtain the following system of equations:

$$\begin{aligned} \sin \delta' &= \sin f \sin F \\ \cos \delta' \cos \lambda &= \sin f \cos F \\ \cos \delta' \sin \lambda &= \cos f, \end{aligned} \qquad (e)$$

$$\begin{aligned} \cos D &= \sin f \cos (F-\delta) \\ \sin D \cos s &= \sin f \sin (F-\delta) \\ \sin D \sin s &= \cos f, \end{aligned} \qquad (f)$$

$$\operatorname{tang} \tfrac{1}{2} (s+p)^2 = \frac{\cos S \,.\, \sin (S-h')}{\cos (S-D) \sin (S-h)}, \qquad (g)$$
$$\text{where } S = \tfrac{1}{2} (D+h+h'),$$

$$\begin{aligned} \sin g \sin G &= \sin h \\ \sin g \cos G &= \cos h \cos p \\ \cos g &= \cos h \sin p, \end{aligned} \qquad (h)$$

$$\begin{aligned} \sin \varphi &= \sin g \cos (G-\delta) \\ \cos \varphi \sin t &= \cos g \\ \cos \varphi \cos t &= \sin g \sin (G-\delta). \end{aligned} \qquad (i)$$

The Gaussian formulae may also be used in this case. For first we have in the triangle between the pole and the two stars, the sides being D, $90^0-\delta$ and $90^0-\delta'$ and the opposite angles λ, s' and s:

$$\begin{aligned} \sin \tfrac{1}{2} D \,.\, \sin \tfrac{1}{2} (s'-s) &= \sin \tfrac{1}{2} (\delta'-\delta) \cos \tfrac{1}{2} \lambda \\ \sin \tfrac{1}{2} D \,.\, \cos \tfrac{1}{2} (s'-s) &= \cos \tfrac{1}{2} (\delta'+\delta) \sin \tfrac{1}{2} \lambda \\ \cos \tfrac{1}{2} D \,.\, \sin \tfrac{1}{2} (s'+s) &= \cos \tfrac{1}{2} (\delta'-\delta) \cos \tfrac{1}{2} \lambda \\ \cos \tfrac{1}{2} D \,.\, \cos \tfrac{1}{2} (s'+s) &= \sin \tfrac{1}{2} (\delta'+\delta) \sin \tfrac{1}{2} \lambda. \end{aligned} \qquad (A)$$

Then we have as before:

$$\begin{aligned} \operatorname{tang} \tfrac{1}{2} (s+p)^2 &= \frac{\cos S \,.\, \sin (S-h')}{\cos (S-D) \sin (S-h)}, \\ \text{or } \operatorname{tang} \tfrac{1}{2} (s'-p')^2 &= \frac{\cos S \,.\, \sin (S-h)}{\cos (S-D) \sin (S-h')}. \end{aligned} \qquad (B)$$

Finally we have in the triangle between the zenith, the pole and the star:

$$\begin{aligned}
\sin(45^\circ - \tfrac{1}{2}\varphi)\sin\tfrac{1}{2}(A+t) &= \sin\tfrac{1}{2}p\cos\tfrac{1}{2}(h+\delta)\\
\sin(45^\circ - \tfrac{1}{2}\varphi)\cos\tfrac{1}{2}(A+t) &= \cos\tfrac{1}{2}p\sin\tfrac{1}{2}(h-\delta)\\
\cos(45^\circ - \tfrac{1}{2}\varphi)\sin\tfrac{1}{2}(A-t) &= \sin\tfrac{1}{2}p\sin\tfrac{1}{2}(h+\delta)\\
\cos(45^\circ - \tfrac{1}{2}\varphi)\cos\tfrac{1}{2}(A-t) &= \cos\tfrac{1}{2}p\cos\tfrac{1}{2}(h-\delta),
\end{aligned} \qquad (C)$$

In case that the other triangle is used, we have similar equations, in which A', t', p', h' and δ' occur.

Since we find by these formulae also the azimuth, we have this advantage, that in case the observations have been made with an altitude and azimuth instrument and the readings of the azimuth circle have been taken at the same time, the comparison of these readings with the computed values of the azimuths gives the zero of the azimuth, which it may be desirable to know for other observations.

Example. Westphal in 1822 Oct. 29 at Benisuef in Egypt observed the following altitudes of the centre of the sun:

$$u = 20^h 48^m 48^s \qquad h = 37^\circ\, 56'\, 59''.6$$
$$u' = 23 \quad 7 \quad 17 \qquad h' = 50 \quad 40\; 55\,.3,$$

where u' is already corrected for the rate of the clock and h and h' are the true altitudes. The interval of time converted into apparent time gives $\lambda = 2^h\, 18^m\, 28^s.66 = 34^\circ\, 37'\, 9''.90$ and the declination of the sun was for the two observations:

$$\delta = -10^\circ\, 10'\, 50''.1 \text{ and } \delta' = -10^\circ\, 12'\, 57''.8.$$

From these data we find by means of the Gaussian formulae:

$$\begin{aligned}
D &= 34^\circ\; 3'\, 20''.27\\
s &= 93\;\; 12\; 58\,.26\\
s' &= 93\;\;\; 6\;\; 1\,.93\\
\text{Further: } s+p &= 53\;\; 15\; 41\,.26\\
\text{hence: } p &= -39\;\; 57\; 17\,.00\\
\text{and then: } \varphi &= 29\;\;\; 5\; 39\,.80\\
t &= -35\;\; 24\; 59\,.23\\
A &= -46\;\; 19\; 52\,.17.
\end{aligned}$$

It is advisable to compute φ and t' also from the other triangle as a verification of the computation, since the values of φ must be the same and $t' - t = \lambda$.

Now in order to see, what stars we must select so as to find the best results by this method, we must resort to the two differential equations:

$$dh = -\cos A\,d\varphi - \cos\varphi \sin A\,dt$$
$$dh' = -\cos A'd\varphi - \cos\varphi \sin A'dt$$

where dt has been supposed to be the same in both equations, because the difference of dt and dt' may be transferred to the error of the altitude. From these equations we obtain, eliminating either $d\varphi$ or dt:

$$\cos\varphi\,dt = \frac{\cos A'}{\sin(A'-A)}\,dh - \frac{\cos A}{\sin(A'-A)}\,dh'$$
$$d\varphi = -\frac{\sin A'}{\sin(A'-A)}\,dh + \frac{\sin A}{\sin(A'-A)}\,dh'.$$

Hence we see, that if the errors of observation shall have no great influence on the values of φ and t, we must select the stars so that $A'-A$ is as nearly as possible $\pm 90^0$, since, if this condition is fulfilled, we have:

$$\cos\varphi\,dt = \cos A'dh - \cos A\,dh'$$
$$d\varphi = -\sin A'dh + \sin A\,dh'.$$

Then we see, that if A' is $\pm 90^0$ and therefore A is 0^0, the coefficient of dh in the first equation is 0, that of dh' equal to ± 1; hence the accuracy of the time depends principally on the altitude taken near the prime vertical. In the same way we find from the second equation, that the accuracy of the latitude depends principally on the altitude taken near the meridian. For the above example we have, since $A' = -1^0\,15'$:

$$d\varphi = +0.0308\,dh - 1.0215\,dh'$$
$$dt = +0.1077\,dh - 0.0744\,dh'.$$

15. The problem can be greatly simplified, for instance, by observing the same star twice. Then the declination being the same and $s' = s$, the formulae (A) of the preceding No. are changed into:

$$\sin\tfrac{1}{2}D = \cos\delta \sin\tfrac{1}{2}\lambda$$
$$\cos\tfrac{1}{2}D \sin s = \cos\tfrac{1}{2}\lambda$$
$$\cos\tfrac{1}{2}D \cos s = \sin\delta \sin\tfrac{1}{2}\lambda.$$

By means of these we find D and s, and then from the first of the equation (B) and the equations (C) φ and t and, if it should be desirable, A.

In this case we can solve the problem also in the following way. We find from the formulae:

$$\sin h = \sin\varphi \sin\delta + \cos\varphi \cos\delta \cos t$$
$$\sin h' = \sin\varphi \sin\delta + \cos\varphi \cos\delta \cos(t+\lambda)$$

by adding and subtracting them:

$$\cos\delta\sin\tfrac{1}{2}\lambda\,.\cos\varphi\sin(t+\tfrac{1}{2}\lambda)=\cos\tfrac{1}{2}(h+h')\sin\tfrac{1}{2}(h-h')$$
$$\sin\varphi\sin\delta+\cos\delta\cos\tfrac{1}{2}\lambda\,.\cos\varphi\cos(t+\tfrac{1}{2}\lambda)=\sin\tfrac{1}{2}(h+h')\cos\tfrac{1}{2}(h-h'). \qquad (a)$$

Therefore if we put:

$$\begin{aligned}\sin\delta &= \cos b\cos B\\ \cos\delta\cos\tfrac{1}{2}\lambda &= \cos b\sin B \qquad (A)\\ \cos\delta\ \sin\tfrac{1}{2}\lambda &= \sin b,\end{aligned}$$

the second of the equations (a) is changed into:

$$\sin\varphi\cos B+\cos\varphi\cos(t+\tfrac{1}{2}\lambda)\sin B=\frac{\sin\tfrac{1}{2}(h+h')\cos\tfrac{1}{2}(h-h')}{\cos b},$$

and if we finally take:

$$\begin{aligned}\sin\varphi &= \cos F\cos G\\ \cos\varphi\sin(t+\tfrac{1}{2}\lambda) &= \sin G \qquad (B)\\ \cos\varphi\cos(t+\tfrac{1}{2}\lambda) &= \sin F\cos G,\end{aligned}$$

we obtain:

$$\begin{aligned}\sin G &= \frac{\cos\tfrac{1}{2}(h+h')\sin\tfrac{1}{2}(h-h')}{\sin b}\\ \cos G\,.\cos(B-F) &= \frac{\sin\tfrac{1}{2}(h+h')\cos\tfrac{1}{2}(h-h')}{\cos b}.\end{aligned} \qquad (C)$$

Fig. 8.

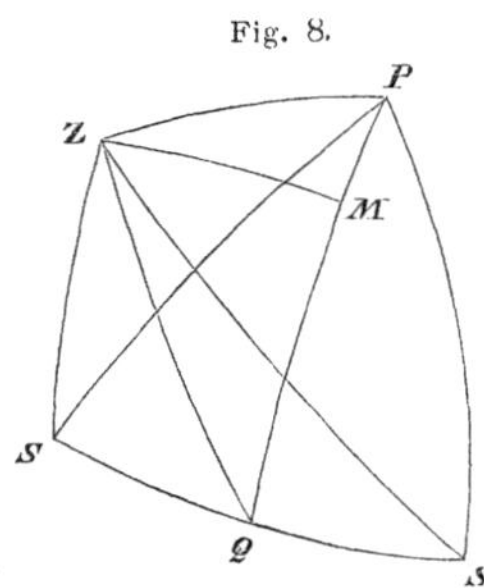

Therefore if we first compute the equations (A), we find G and F by means of the equations (C) and then φ and t from the equations (B). The geometrical signification of the auxiliary angles is easily discovered by means of Fig. 8, where PQ is drawn perpendicular to the great circle joining the two stars, and ZM is perpendicular to PQ. We then see, that $b=QS=\tfrac{1}{2}D$, $B=PQ$, $F=PM$ and $G=ZM$.

If we use the same data as in the preceding example, paying no attention to the change of the declination and taking $\delta=-10^\circ\,12'\,57''.8$, we find:

$B=100^\circ\,41'\,23''.1$ $\quad\sin b=9.466600$ $\quad\cos b=9.980534$
$\sin G=9.432863_n$ $\quad\cos G=9.983445$ $\quad F=41^\circ\,1'\,53''.3$
and hence $t=-35^\circ\,22'\,21''.0$ $\quad\varphi=29^\circ\,5'\,42''.7$.

In case that the two altitudes are equal, the formulae (A) or (e) and (f) in No. 14 remain unchanged, but the formulae (B) are transformed into:

$$\operatorname{tang}\tfrac{1}{2}(s+p)^2=\operatorname{tang}\tfrac{1}{2}(s'-p')^2=\frac{\cos(h+\tfrac{1}{2}D)}{\cos(h-\tfrac{1}{2}D)},$$

and then p being known, φ and t can be computed by means of the formulae (h) and (i), or φ, t and A by means of the formulae (C).

16. A similar problem, though not strictly belonging to the class of problems we have under consideration at present, is the following: To find the time and the latitude and at the same time the altitude and the azimuth of the stars by the differences of their altitudes and azimuths and the interval of time between the observations.

In this case we must compute as before the formulae (A) in No. 14.

Then we have in the triangle between the zenith and both stars, denoting the angles at the two stars by q and q', the third angle being $A' - A$ and the opposite sides $90^0 - h'$, $90^0 - h$ and D:

$$\sin \tfrac{1}{2}(q'+q) = \frac{\cos \tfrac{1}{2}(h'-h) \cos \tfrac{1}{2}(A'-A)}{\cos \tfrac{1}{2} D}$$

$$\sin \tfrac{1}{2}(q'-q) = \frac{\sin \tfrac{1}{2}(h'-h) \cos \tfrac{1}{2}(A'-A)}{\sin \tfrac{1}{2} D} \qquad (B)$$

$$\operatorname{tang} \tfrac{1}{2}(h'+h) = \frac{\cos \tfrac{1}{2}(q'+q)}{\cos \tfrac{1}{2}(q'-q)} \operatorname{cotang} \tfrac{1}{2} D.$$

By means of these equations we find $\frac{1}{2}(h+h')$, thence h and h' and the angles q and q'. But since we have according to No. 14 $q = s + p$ and $q' = s' - p'$, we thus know p and p', hence we can compute φ, t and A by means of the formulae (C) in No. 14 and as a verification of the computation also φ, t' and A'.

In this case the differential equations are according to No. 8 of the first section:

$$dh = -\cos A\, d\varphi - \cos\delta \sin p \,.\, d\frac{t'+t}{2} + \cos\delta \sin p\, d\frac{t'-t}{2}$$

$$dh' = -\cos A' d\varphi - \cos\delta' \sin p' \,.\, d\frac{t'+t}{2} - \cos\delta' \sin p' d\frac{t'-t}{2}$$

$$dA = -\sin A \operatorname{tang} h\, d\varphi + \frac{\cos\delta \cos p}{\cos h} d\frac{t'+t}{2} - \frac{\cos\delta \cos p}{\cos h} d\frac{t'-t}{2}$$

$$dA' = -\sin A' \operatorname{tang} h' d\varphi + \frac{\cos\delta' \cos p'}{\cos h'} d\frac{t'+t}{2} + \frac{\cos\delta' \cos p'}{\cos h'} d\frac{t'-t}{2},$$

where $\frac{t'+t}{2} + \frac{t'-t}{2}$ and $\frac{t'+t}{2} - \frac{t'-t}{2}$ have been put in place of t' and t occurring in the original formulae.

Subtracting the first equation from the second and the third from the fourth, then eliminating first $d\frac{t'+t}{2}$ and then $d\varphi$, and remembering that we have:

$$\cos\delta\sin p = \cos\varphi\sin A$$

$$\frac{\cos\delta\cos p}{\cos h} = \sin\varphi + \cos\varphi\,\mathrm{tang}\,h\cos A$$

we easily find:

$$M d\varphi = [\mathrm{tang}\,h\cos A - \mathrm{tang}\,h'\cos A']\,d(h'-h) + [\sin A - \sin A']\,d(A'-A)$$
$$+\left[\frac{\cos\delta}{\cos h}\cos p\sin A' - \frac{\cos\delta}{\cos h'}\cos p'\sin A\right]d(t'-t),$$

$$M\cos\varphi\, d\frac{t'+t}{2} = [\mathrm{tang}\,h\sin A - \mathrm{tang}\,h'\sin A']\,d(h'-h) - [\cos A - \cos A']\,d(A'-A)$$
$$+[\cos\varphi(\mathrm{tg}\,h - \mathrm{tg}\,h')\sin^2\tfrac{1}{2}(A'+A) + \sin\varphi(\cos A - \cos A')]\,d(t'-t),$$
$$\text{where } M = 2\,[\mathrm{tg}\,h + \mathrm{tg}\,h')\sin^2\tfrac{1}{2}(A'-A).$$

We see from this, that it is necessary to select stars for which the differences of the altitudes and the azimuths are great, in order that M be as great as possible. If $\frac{1}{2}(A'-A) = 90^0$, even the coefficient of $d(h'-h)$ is less than $\frac{1}{2}$.

v. Camphausen has proposed to observe the stars at the time, when their altitude is equal to their declination, because then the triangle between the zenith, the pole and the star is an isosceles triangle and we have $t = 180^0 - A$ and:

$$\mathrm{cotg}\,\delta\cos t = \mathrm{cotg}\,\delta'\cos t' = \mathrm{tg}\,(45 - \tfrac{1}{2}\varphi)$$
$$-\mathrm{cotg}\,\delta\cos A = -\mathrm{cotg}\,\delta'\cos A' = \mathrm{tg}\,(45 - \tfrac{1}{2}\varphi),$$

by means of which we find:

$$\mathrm{tang}\,\tfrac{1}{2}(t'+t) = \frac{\sin(\delta-\delta')}{\sin(\delta+\delta')}\,\mathrm{cotg}\,\tfrac{1}{2}(t'-t)$$

or

$$\mathrm{tang}\,\tfrac{1}{2}(A'+A) = \frac{\sin(\delta-\delta')}{\sin(\delta+\delta')}\,\mathrm{cotg}\,\tfrac{1}{2}(A'-A).$$

From these formulae we obtain $t'+t$ or $A'+A$ and φ. But since the altitudes are hardly ever taken exactly at the moment, when they are equal to the declination, the observed quantities $t'-t$ and $A'-A$ must first be reduced to that moment. (Compare Encke, Ueber die Erweiterung des Douwes'schen Problems in the Berlin Jahrbuch for 1859.)

Example. In 1856 March 30 the following differences of the altitudes and the azimuths of η Ursae majoris and α Aurigae were observed at Cologne.

$$h' - h = -4^0\,10'\,46''.0$$
$$A' - A = 226^0\,28'\;\;9''.9$$

The interval of time between the observations, expressed in sidereal time, was $0^h\,18^m\,8^s.70$.

The apparent places of the stars were on that day:

η Ursae majoris $\alpha = 13^h\,41^m\,54^s.53$ $\delta = +50^0\;1'\,45''.9$
α Aurigae $\alpha' = 5\;\;6\;\;1.69$ $\delta' = +45\;51\;\;1.7$.

Hence we get $\lambda = 133^0\,30'\,23''.1$, and we obtain first by means of the formulae (A) in No. 14:

$$s = +31^0\,22'\,33''.18$$
$$s' = +28^0\,41'\,50''.20 \qquad D = 76^0\,0'\,14''.79.$$

Then we find from the formulae (B) $q' = -28^0\,40'\,53''.44$, $q = -31^0\,21'\,32''.80$, and since $q' = s' - p'$, $q = s + p$, we find $p = -62^0\,44'\,5''.98$, $p' = +57^0\,22'\,43''.64$. Since we find $\frac{1}{2}(h' + h) = 47^0\,56'\,40''.61$, and hence $h = 50^0\,2'\,3''.61$, we get by means of the equations (C) in No. 14: $\varphi = 50^0\,55'\,55''.57$, $t = 295^0\,2'\,56''.70$, $A = 244^0\,57'\,48''.50$.

If we compute also the differential equations we find, if we express all errors in seconds of arc:

$$d\varphi = -0.0342\,d(h' - h) - 0.4892\,d(A' - A) + 0.2438\,d(t' - t)$$
$$d\frac{t' + t}{2} = -0.8621\,d(h' - h) + 0.0244\,d(A' - A) - 0.0188\,d(t' - t).$$

17. The method of finding the latitude and the time by two altitudes it often used at sea. But sailors do not solve the problem in the direct way which was shown before, because the computation is too complicate, but they make use of an indirect method which was proposed by Douwes, a Dutch seaman.

Since the latitude is always approximately known from the log-book, they first find an approximate time by the altitude most distant from the meridian, and with this they find the latitude by the altitude taken near the meridian. Then they repeat with this value of the latitude the computation for finding the time by the first altitude.

Supposing again that the same heavenly body has been observed twice, we have:

$$\begin{aligned}\sin h - \sin h' &= \cos\varphi\cos\delta\,[\cos t - \cos(t + \lambda)]\\ &= 2\cos\varphi\cos\delta\sin(t + \tfrac{1}{2}\lambda)\sin\tfrac{1}{2}\lambda,\end{aligned}$$

hence:

$$2\sin(t + \tfrac{1}{2}\lambda) = \sec\varphi\sec\delta\,\mathrm{cosec}\,\tfrac{1}{2}\lambda\,[\sin h - \sin h']$$

or, if we write the formula logarithmically:

$$\log . 2 \sin (t + \tfrac{1}{2}\lambda) = \log \sec \varphi + \log \sec \delta + \log [\sin h - \sin h'] + \log \operatorname{cosec} \tfrac{1}{2}\lambda. \quad (A)$$

Since an approximate value of φ is known, we find from this equation $t + \frac{1}{2}\lambda$, and hence also t, and then we find a more correct latitude by the altitude taken near the meridian by means of the formula:

$$\cos (\varphi - \delta) = \sin h' + \cos \varphi \cos \delta \,.\, 2 \sin \tfrac{1}{2} (t + \lambda)^2. \qquad (B)$$

If the result differs much from the first value of the latitude, the formulae (A) and (B) must be computed a second time with the new value of φ.

Douwes has constructed tables for simplifying this computation, which have been published in the „Tables requisite to be used with the nautical ephemeris for finding the latitude and longitude at sea“ and in all works on navigation. One table with the heading „log. half elapsed time“ gives the value of log. cosec $\frac{1}{2}\lambda$, the argument being the hour angle expressed in time. Another table with the heading „log. middle time“ gives the value of $\log 2 \sin (t + \frac{1}{2}\lambda)$, and a third table with the heading „log. rising time“ gives that of $\log 2 \sin \frac{1}{2} t^2$. The quantity log. sec φ sec δ is called log. ratio and we have therefore according to the equation (A):

$$\text{Log. middle time} = \text{Log. ratio} + \text{Log} (\sin h - \sin h')$$
$$+ \text{Log. half elapsed time.}$$

By means of the table for middle time we find from this logarithm immediately t. Then we take from the tables log. rising time for the hour angle $t + \lambda$, subtract from it log. ratio and add the number corresponding to it to the sine of the greater one of the altitudes. Thus we obtain the sine of the meridian altitude and hence also the latitude.

If we cannot use these tables, we compute:

$$\sin [t + \tfrac{1}{2}\lambda] = \frac{\cos \frac{1}{2} (h + h') \sin \frac{1}{2} (h - h')}{\cos \varphi \cos \delta \sin \frac{1}{2}\lambda}$$

and:

$$\cos (\varphi - N) = \frac{\sin h'}{M},$$

where:

$$\sin \delta = M \sin N$$
$$\cos \delta \cos t = M \cos N.$$

If we compute the example given in No. 14 according to Douwes's method, we find:

$$\varphi = 29^\circ\ 0'$$

log ratio	0.06512
log (sin h — sin h')	9.20049_n
log half elapsed time	0.52645
log middle time	9.79206_n
$t =$	$-2^h 21^m.4$
hence $t' =$	$-0^h\ 2^m.9$
log rising time	5.90340
log ratio	0.06512
	+0.00007
sin h'	+0.77364
$\cos(\varphi - \delta) =$	9.88858
$\varphi - \delta =$	39° 18'.7
$\varphi =$	29 5.7.

In case that the observations are made at sea, the two altitudes are taken at two different places on account of the motion of the ship during the interval of time between the observations. But since the velocity of the motion is known from the log and the direction of the course from the needle, it is very easy to reduce the altitudes to the same place of observation.

Fig. 9.

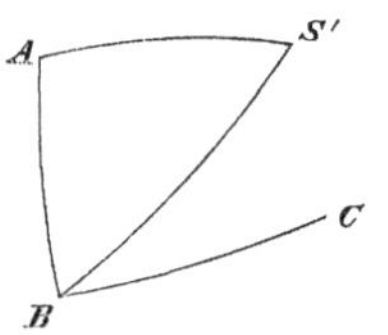

The ship at the time of the first observation shall be in A (Fig. 9) and at the time of the second in B. If we imagine then a straight line drawn from the centre of the earth to the heavenly body, which intersects the surface of the earth in S', then the side BS' in the triangle ABS' will be the zenith distance taken at the place B, and since BA is known, we could find, if the angle $S'BA$ were known, the side AS', that is, the zenith distance which would have been taken at the place A. Therefore at the time of the second observation the azimuth of the object, that is, the angle $S'BC$ must be observed, and since the angle CBA, which the direction of the course of the ship makes with the meridian, is known, the angle $S'BA$ is known also. Denoting this angle by α and the distance between the two places A and B by Δ, we have:

$$\sin h_0 = \sin h \cos \Delta + \sin \Delta \cos h \cos \alpha,$$

where h_0 is the reduced altitude. If we write instead of this:

$$\sin h_0 = \sin h + \sin \Delta \cos h \cos \alpha - 2 \sin \tfrac{1}{2} \Delta^2 \sin h,$$

and take Δ instead of $\sin \Delta$, we obtain by means of the formula (20) of the introduction:

$$h_0 = h + \Delta \cos \alpha - \tfrac{1}{2} \Delta^2 \operatorname{tang} h,$$

where the last term can in most cases be neglected.

18. If three altitudes of the same star have been observed, we have the three equations:

$$\begin{aligned}\sin h &= \sin \varphi \sin \delta + \cos \varphi \cos \delta \cos t \\ \sin h' &= \sin \varphi \sin \delta + \cos \varphi \cos \delta \cos (t + \lambda) \\ \sin h'' &= \sin \varphi \sin \delta + \cos \varphi \cos \delta \cos (t + \lambda'),\end{aligned}$$

from which we can find φ, t and δ. For if we introduce the following auxiliary quantities:

$$\begin{aligned}x &= \cos \varphi \cos \delta \cos t \\ y &= \cos \varphi \cos \delta \sin t \\ z &= \sin \varphi \sin \delta,\end{aligned}$$

those three formulae are transformed into:

$$\begin{aligned}\sin h &= z + x \\ \sin h' &= z + x \cos \lambda - y \sin \lambda \\ \sin h'' &= z + x \cos \lambda' - y \sin \lambda',\end{aligned}$$

from which we can obtain the three unknown quantities x, y and z in the usual way. But when these are known, we find φ and t by the equations:

$$\begin{aligned}\operatorname{tang} t &= \frac{y}{x} \\ \sin \varphi \sin \delta &= z \\ \cos \varphi \cos \delta &= \sqrt{x^2 + y^2}.\end{aligned}$$

This method would be one of the most convenient and useful, since no further data are required for computing the quantities sought*). But it is not practical, since the errors of observation have a very great effect on the unknown quantities. But if we do not consider δ as constant, that is, if we observe three different stars, whose declinations are known, at equal altitudes, the problem is at once very elegant and useful.

19. In this case the three equations are:

$$\begin{aligned}\sin h &= \sin \varphi \sin \delta + \cos \varphi \cos \delta \cos t \\ \sin h &= \sin \varphi \sin \delta' + \cos \varphi \cos \delta' \cos (t + \lambda) \qquad (a) \\ \sin h &= \sin \varphi \sin \delta'' + \cos \varphi \cos \delta'' \cos (t + \lambda'),\end{aligned}$$

$$\text{where } \lambda = (u' - u) - (\alpha' - \alpha)$$
$$\text{and } \lambda' = (u'' - u) - (\alpha'' - \alpha).$$

*) Since three altitudes of the same star have been taken, λ and λ' are not dependent on the right ascension.

If we now introduce in the two first equations $\frac{1}{2}(\delta'+\delta)+\frac{1}{2}(\delta-\delta')$ instead of δ, and $\frac{1}{2}(\delta+\delta')-\frac{1}{2}(\delta-\delta')$ instead of δ', and subtract the second equation from the first, we get:

$$0=2\sin\varphi\sin\tfrac{1}{2}(\delta-\delta')\cos\tfrac{1}{2}(\delta+\delta')+\cos\varphi\cos t\,[\cos\tfrac{1}{2}(\delta+\delta')\cos\tfrac{1}{2}(\delta-\delta')-\sin\tfrac{1}{2}(\delta+\delta')\sin\tfrac{1}{2}(\delta-\delta')]$$
$$-\cos\varphi\cos(t+\lambda)\,[\cos\tfrac{1}{2}(\delta+\delta')\cos\tfrac{1}{2}(\delta-\delta')+\sin\tfrac{1}{2}(\delta+\delta')\sin\tfrac{1}{2}(\delta-\delta')]$$

or:

$$\left.\begin{aligned}0&=\sin\varphi\sin\tfrac{1}{2}(\delta-\delta')\cos\tfrac{1}{2}(\delta+\delta')\\&+\cos\varphi\cos\tfrac{1}{2}(\delta+\delta')\cos\tfrac{1}{2}(\delta-\delta')\sin\tfrac{1}{2}\lambda\sin(t+\tfrac{1}{2}\lambda)\\&-\cos\varphi\sin\tfrac{1}{2}(\delta+\delta')\sin\tfrac{1}{2}(\delta-\delta')\cos\tfrac{1}{2}\lambda\cos(t+\tfrac{1}{2}\lambda).\end{aligned}\right.\qquad(\alpha)$$

From this we find:

$$\begin{aligned}\text{tang}\,\varphi=&-\sin\tfrac{1}{2}\lambda\,.\,\sin(t+\tfrac{1}{2}\lambda)\,\text{cotang}\,\tfrac{1}{2}(\delta-\delta')\\&+\cos\tfrac{1}{2}\lambda\,.\,\cos(t+\tfrac{1}{2}\lambda)\;\;\text{tang}\,\tfrac{1}{2}(\delta+\delta').\end{aligned}$$

Introducing now the auxiliary quantities A' and B', given by the formulae:

$$\begin{aligned}\sin\tfrac{1}{2}\lambda\,.\,\text{cotang}\,\tfrac{1}{2}(\delta-\delta')&=A'\sin B'\\\cos\tfrac{1}{2}\lambda\,.\quad\text{tang}\,\tfrac{1}{2}(\delta+\delta')&=A'\cos B'\\B'+\tfrac{1}{2}\lambda&=C',\end{aligned}\qquad(A)$$

we obtain:

$$\text{tang}\,\varphi=A'\cos(t+C').\qquad(B)$$

From the first and third of the equations (α) we find in the same way similar equations:

$$\left.\begin{aligned}\sin\tfrac{1}{2}\lambda'\,\text{cotang}\,\tfrac{1}{2}(\delta-\delta'')&=A''\sin B''\\\cos\tfrac{1}{2}\lambda'\quad\text{tang}\,\tfrac{1}{2}(\delta+\delta'')&=A''\cos B''\\B''+\tfrac{1}{2}\lambda'\qquad&=C'',\end{aligned}\right\}\qquad(C)$$

$$\text{tang}\,\varphi=A''\cos(t+C'').\qquad(D)$$

Furthermore we find from the two formulae (**B**) and (**D**):

$$A'\cos(t+C')=A''\cos(t+C'').$$

In order to find ***t*** from this equation, we will write it in this way:

$$A'\cos[t+H+C'-H]=A''\cos[t+H+C''-H],$$

where ***H*** is an arbitrary angle, and from this we easily get:

$$\text{tang}\,(t+H)=\frac{A'\cos(C'-H)-A''\cos(C''-H)}{A'\sin(C'-H)-A''\sin(C''-H)}.$$

For ***H*** we can substitute such a value as gives the formula the most convenient form, for instance 0, C' or C''. But we obtain the most elegant form, if we take:

$$H=\tfrac{1}{2}(C'+C'')$$

for then we have:

$$\text{tang}\,[t+\tfrac{1}{2}(C'+C'')]=\frac{A'-A''}{A'+A''}\,\text{cotang}\,\tfrac{1}{2}(C'-C'').$$

Introducing now an auxiliary angle ζ, given by the equation:

$$\operatorname{tang} \zeta = \frac{A''}{A'}, \qquad (E)$$

we find:

$$\frac{A' - A''}{A' + A''} = \frac{1 - \operatorname{tang} \zeta}{1 + \operatorname{tang} \zeta} = \operatorname{tang} (45^\circ - \zeta),$$

hence:

$$\operatorname{tang} [t + \tfrac{1}{2} (C' + C'')] = \operatorname{tang} (45^\circ - \zeta) \operatorname{cotang} \tfrac{1}{2} (C' - C''). \qquad (F)$$

We find therefore first by means of the equations (A) and (C) the values of the auxiliary quantities A', B', C' and A'', B'', C''; then we obtain t by means of the equations (E) and (F), and finally φ by either of the equations (B) or (D). It is not necessary to know the altitude itself, in order to find φ and t, but if we substitute their values in the original equations (a), we find the value of h; hence, if the altitude itself is observed, we can obtain the error of the instrument.

In order to see, how the three stars should be selected so as to give the most accurate result, we must consider the differential equations. Since the three altitudes are equal, we can assume also dh to be the same for the three altitudes, uniting the errors, which may have been committed in taking the altitudes, with those of the times of observation. Now since we have:

$$t = u + \Delta u - \alpha,$$

the error dt will we composed of two errors, first of the error $d(\Delta u)$, thas is, that of the error of the clock, which may be assumed to be the same for the three observations, since we suppose the rate of the clock to be known, and then of the error of the time of observation du which will be different for the three observations. Hence the three differential equations are:

$$\begin{aligned}
dh &= - \cos A \, d\varphi - \cos \varphi \sin A \, du - \cos \varphi \sin A \, d(\Delta u) \\
dh &= - \cos A' d\varphi - \cos \varphi \sin A' du' - \cos \varphi \sin A' d(\Delta u) \\
dh &= - \cos A'' d\varphi - \cos \varphi \sin A'' du'' - \cos \varphi \sin A'' d(\Delta u).
\end{aligned}$$

If we subtract the first two equations from each other, we find by a simple reduction:

$$0 = 2\sin\frac{A+A'}{2}\,d\varphi - 2\cos\frac{A+A'}{2}\cos\varphi\, d(\Delta u) - \frac{\cos\varphi\sin A}{\sin\frac{A-A'}{2}}\,du + \frac{\cos\varphi\sin A'}{\sin\frac{A-A'}{2}}\,du',$$

and in the same way from the first and third equation:

$$0 = 2\sin\frac{A+A''}{2}\,d\varphi - 2\cos\frac{A+A''}{2}\cos\varphi\, d(\Delta u) - \frac{\cos\varphi\sin A}{\sin\frac{A-A''}{2}}\,du + \frac{\cos\varphi\sin A''}{\sin\frac{A-A''}{2}}\,du''.$$

From these two equations we obtain, eliminating first $d(\Delta u)$ and then $d\varphi$:

$$d\varphi = \frac{\cos\varphi\sin A\,.\cos\frac{A'+A''}{2}}{2\sin\frac{A-A'}{2}\sin\frac{A-A''}{2}}\,du + \frac{\cos\varphi\sin A'\cos\frac{A+A''}{2}}{2\sin\frac{A'-A}{2}\sin\frac{A'-A''}{2}}\,du' + \frac{\cos\varphi\sin A''\cos\frac{A+A'}{2}}{2\sin\frac{A''-A}{2}\sin\frac{A''-A'}{2}}\,du''$$

and:

$$d(\Delta u) = \frac{\sin A\,.\sin\frac{A'+A''}{2}}{2\sin\frac{A-A'}{2}\sin\frac{A-A''}{2}}\,du + \frac{\sin A'\sin\frac{A+A''}{2}}{2\sin\frac{A'-A}{2}\sin\frac{A'-A''}{2}}\,du' + \frac{\sin A''\sin\frac{A+A'}{2}}{2\sin\frac{A''-A}{2}\sin\frac{A''-A'}{2}}\,du''.$$

We see from this, that the stars must be selected so, that the differences of the azimuths of any two of them become as great as possible, and hence as nearly as possible equal to 120^0, because in this case the denominators of the differential coefficients are as great as possible *).

Example. In 1822 Oct. 5 Dr. Westphal observed at Cairo the following three stars at equal altitudes:

α Ursae minoris at	$8^h\,28^m$	17^s	
α Herculis	31	21	West of the Meridian
α Arietis	47	30	East of the Meridian.

*) This solution of the problem was given by Gauss in Zach's Monatliche Correspondenz Band XVIII pag. 277.

The places of the stars were on that day:

α Ursae minoris	0^h	58^m	$14^s.10$	$+88^\circ$	$21'$	$54''.3$
α Herculis	17	6	34 .26	14	36	2 .0
α Arietis	1	57	14 .00	22	37	22 .7.

Now we have:

$$u' - u = +3^m\ 4^s.0 \qquad u'' - u = +\ 19^m\ 13^s.0$$

or expressed in sidereal time:

$$\begin{aligned} u' - u &= +\ 0^h\ 3^m\ 4^s.50 & &+0^h\ 19^m\ 16^s.16 \\ \alpha' - \alpha &= -\ 7\ 51\ 39\ .84 & \alpha'' - \alpha &= +0\ 58\ 59\ .90 \\ \lambda &= 7^h\ 54^m\ 44^s.34 & \lambda' &= -0^h\ 39^m\ 43\ .74 \\ &= 118^\circ\ 41'\ 5''.10 & &= -9^\circ\ 55'\ 56''.10. \end{aligned}$$

Then we have:

$$\begin{aligned} \tfrac{1}{2}(\delta - \delta') &= 36^\circ\ 52'\ 56''.15 \\ \tfrac{1}{2}(\delta + \delta') &= 51\ \ 28\ \ 58\ .15 \\ \tfrac{1}{2}(\delta - \delta'') &= 32\ \ 52\ \ 15\ .80 \\ \tfrac{1}{2}(\delta + \delta'') &= 55\ \ 29\ \ 38\ .50, \end{aligned}$$

and from this we obtain:

$$\begin{aligned} \log A' &= 0.1183684 & \log A'' &= 0.1629829 \\ B' &= 60^\circ\ 48'\ 11''.92 & B'' &= -\ 5^\circ\ 16'\ 52''.22 \\ C' &= 120\ \ 8\ \ 44\ .47 & C'' &= -10\ \ 14\ \ 50\ .27 \end{aligned}$$

$$\begin{aligned} \tfrac{1}{2}(C' + C'') &= 54^\circ\ 56'\ 57''.10 \\ \tfrac{1}{2}(C' - C'') &= 65\ \ 11\ \ 47\ .37 \\ \zeta &= 47\ \ 56\ \ 16\ .08 \\ t &= -56^\circ\ 18'\ 28''.09 \\ &= -\ 3^h\ 45^m\ 13^s.87 \\ t + C' &= 63^\circ\ 50'\ 16''.38 \\ t + C'' &= -66\ \ 33\ \ 18\ .36 \end{aligned}$$

and the formulae (*B*) and (*D*) give the same value of φ:

$$\varphi = 30^\circ\ 4'\ 23''.72.$$

From t we find the sidereal time:

$$\Theta = 21^h\ 13^m\ 0^s.23,$$

and since the sidereal time at mean noon was $12^h\ 54^m\ 2^s.04$, we find the mean time $8^h\ 17^m\ 36^s.44$, hence the error of the chronometer:

$$\Delta u = -\ 10^m\ 40^s.56.$$

Computing h from one of the three equations (a) we get:

$$h = 30^\circ\ 58'\ 14''.44,$$

and for the other two hour angles we find:

$$\begin{aligned} t' &= 62^\circ\ 22'\ 37''.01 \\ t'' &= -66\ \ 14\ \ 24\ .19. \end{aligned}$$

We then are able to compute the three azimuths:

$$A = 181^\circ\ 35'.2$$
$$A' = 89\ \ 33\ .2$$
$$A'' = 279\ \ 50\ .4;$$

and finally the three differential equations:

$$d\varphi = -\ 0.329\, du - 5.739\, du' - 6.068\, du'',$$
$$d(\Delta u) = -\ 0.0018\, du + 0.468\, du' - 0.396\, du'',$$

where $d\varphi$ is expressed in seconds of arc, whilst $d(\Delta u)$ and du, du', du'' are expressed in seconds of time.

20. Cagnoli has given in his Trigonometry another solution, not of the problem we have here under consideration, but of a similar one. His formulae can be immediately applied to this case, and if it is required, to find the altitude itself besides the latitude and the time, they are even a little more convenient.

Fig. 10.

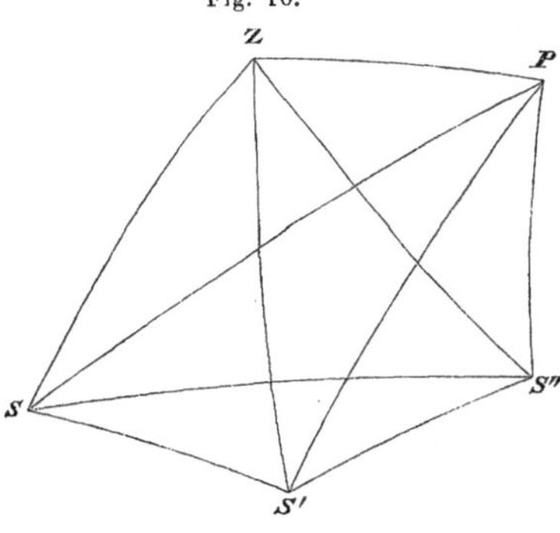

Let S, S' and S'' (Fig. 10) be the three stars which are observed. In the triangle between the zenith, the pole and the star we have then according to Gauss's or Napier's formulae, denoting the parallactic angle by p:

$$\left.\begin{aligned}\text{tang}\,\tfrac{1}{2}(\varphi + h) &= \frac{\cos\frac{1}{2}(t+p)}{\cos\frac{1}{2}(t-p)}\,\text{cotang}\,(45^\circ - \tfrac{1}{2}\delta)\\ &= \frac{\cos\frac{1}{2}(t+p)}{\cos\frac{1}{2}(t-p)}\,\text{tang}\,(45^\circ + \tfrac{1}{2}\delta)\\ \text{and:}\quad \text{tang}\,\tfrac{1}{2}(\varphi - h) &= \frac{\sin\frac{1}{2}(t-p)}{\sin\frac{1}{2}(t+p)}\,\text{tang}\,(45^\circ - \tfrac{1}{2}\delta)\\ &= \frac{\sin\frac{1}{2}(t-p)}{\sin\frac{1}{2}(t+p)}\,\text{cotang}\,(45^\circ + \tfrac{1}{2}\delta).\end{aligned}\right\}\quad (A)$$

But in the triangles PSS', $PS'S''$ and PSS'' we have also according to Napier's formulae, putting for the sake of brevity

$$A = \tfrac{1}{2}[PS''S' - PS'S'']$$
$$A' = \tfrac{1}{2}[PS''S - PSS'']$$
$$A'' = \tfrac{1}{2}[PS'S - PSS']:$$

$$\left.\begin{aligned}\text{tang}\,A &= \frac{\sin\frac{1}{2}(\delta'' - \delta')}{\cos\frac{1}{2}(\delta'' + \delta')}\,\text{cotang}\,\tfrac{1}{2}(\lambda' - \lambda)\\ \text{tang}\,A' &= \frac{\sin\frac{1}{2}(\delta'' - \delta)}{\cos\frac{1}{2}(\delta'' + \delta)}\,\text{cotang}\,\tfrac{1}{2}\lambda'\\ \text{tang}\,A'' &= \frac{\sin\frac{1}{2}(\delta' - \delta)}{\cos\frac{1}{2}(\delta' + \delta)}\,\text{cotang}\,\tfrac{1}{2}\lambda,\end{aligned}\right\}\quad (B)$$

where λ and λ' have the same signification as before. Now since we have:

$$\begin{aligned} p + PSS' &= PS'S - p' \\ p' + PS'S'' &= PS''S' - p'' \\ p + PSS'' &= PS''S - p'', \end{aligned}$$

we easily find, that:

$$\begin{aligned} p &= A' + A'' - A \\ p' &= A + A'' - A' \\ p'' &= A + A' - A''. \end{aligned} \qquad (C)$$

But we also have:

$$\begin{aligned} \sin t : \sin p &= \cos h : \cos \varphi \\ \sin (t + \lambda) : \sin p' &= \cos h : \cos \varphi, \end{aligned}$$

hence:

$$\sin t : \sin (t + \lambda) = \sin p : \sin p'$$

or:

$$\frac{\sin t + \sin (t + \lambda)}{\sin t - \sin (t + \lambda)} = \frac{\sin [A' + A'' - A] + \sin [A + A'' - A']}{\sin [A' + A'' - A] - \sin [A + A'' - A']}.$$

From this follows:

$$\operatorname{tang} [t + \tfrac{1}{2}\lambda] \operatorname{cotang} \tfrac{1}{2}\lambda = \operatorname{tang} A'' \operatorname{cotang} (A - A')$$

or substituting for tang A'' its value taken from the equations (B):

$$\operatorname{tang} [t + \tfrac{1}{2}\lambda] = \frac{\sin \frac{1}{2}(\delta' - \delta)}{\cos \frac{1}{2}(\delta' + \delta)} \operatorname{cotang} (A - A'). \qquad (D)$$

Therefore we first find from the equations (B) the values of A, A' and A'', then we find p and t by means of the equations (C) and (D), and then φ and h by means of the equations (A). An inconvenience connected with these formulae is the doubt in which we are left in regard to the quadrant in which the several angles lie, all being found by tangents. However it is indifferent whether we take the angles 180° wrong, only we must then take $180^\circ + t$ instead of t, if we should find for φ and h such values, that $\cos \varphi$ and $\sin h$ have oppositive signs. Likewise if we find for φ and h values greater than 90° we must take the supplement to 180° or to the nearest multiple of 180°. The latitude is north or south, if $\sin \varphi$ and $\sin h$ have either the same sign or opposite signs.

If we compute the example given in No. 19 by means of these formulae, we have:

$$\begin{aligned} \tfrac{1}{2}\lambda &= 59^\circ\, 20'\, 32''.55 \\ \tfrac{1}{2}\lambda' &= -4\, 57\, 58.05 \end{aligned}$$

$$\tfrac{1}{2}(\delta'' - \delta') = 4^\circ\, 0'\, 40''.35 \quad \tfrac{1}{2}(\delta'' - \delta) = -32^\circ\, 52'\, 15''.80$$

$$\tfrac{1}{2}(\delta' - \delta) = -36^\circ\, 52'\, 56''.15$$

$$\tfrac{1}{2}(\delta'' + \delta') = 18\; 36\; 42.35 \quad \tfrac{1}{2}(\delta'' + \delta) = 55\; 29\; 38.50$$

$$\tfrac{1}{2}(\delta' + \delta) = 51\; 28\; 58.15,$$

and from this we find:

$$A = -2^\circ\ 2'\ 1''.33,\quad A' = 84^\circ\ 49'\ 4''.07,\quad A'' = -29^\circ\ 44'\ 16''.52$$

$$A - A' = -86^\circ\ 51'\ 5''.40$$

$$t + \tfrac{1}{2}\lambda = \quad 3\ \ 2\ \ 4\ .47$$

$$t = -56\ \ 18\ 28\ .08.$$

Then we find φ and h from one of the triangles between the pole, the zenith and one of the stars, and since in the triangle formed by the first star small angles occur, we choose the triangle formed by the second star, using the formulae:

$$\text{tang}\ \tfrac{1}{2}(\varphi + h) = \frac{\cos \frac{1}{2}(t' + p')}{\cos \frac{1}{2}(t' - p')}\ \text{tang}\ (45^\circ + \tfrac{1}{2}\delta')$$

$$\text{tang}\ \tfrac{1}{2}(\varphi - h) = \frac{\sin \frac{1}{2}(t' - p')}{\sin \frac{1}{2}(t' + p')}\ \text{cotang}\ (45^\circ + \tfrac{1}{2}\delta').$$

Now we have:

$$t' = t + \lambda = 62^\circ\ 22'\ 37''.02$$

$$p' = A + A'' - A' = 243^\circ\ 24'\ 38''.08,$$

therefore we find:

$$\varphi = \ \ 30^\circ\ 4'\ 23''.73$$

$$h = 149\ \ 1\ \ 45\ .58$$

or taking for h the supplement to 180°:

$$h = \ \ 30\ 58\ 14\ .42,$$

which values almost entirely agree with those found in the preceding No.

21. We can also find Cagnoli's formulae by an analytical method. According to the fundamental formulae of spherical trigonometry we have for each of the three stars the following three equations:

$$\left.\begin{aligned}\sin h &= \sin\varphi \sin\delta + \cos\varphi \cos\delta \cos t\\ \cos h \sin p &= \cos\varphi \sin t\\ \cos h \cos p &= \sin\varphi \cos\delta - \cos\varphi \sin\delta \cos t\end{aligned}\right\}\ (a)$$

$$\left.\begin{aligned}\sin h &= \sin\varphi \sin\delta' + \cos\varphi \cos\delta' \cos(t+\lambda)\\ \cos h \sin p' &= \cos\varphi \sin(t+\lambda)\\ \cos h \cos p' &= \sin\varphi \cos\delta' - \cos\varphi \sin\delta' \cos(t+\lambda)\end{aligned}\right\}\ (b)$$

$$\left.\begin{aligned}\sin h &= \sin\varphi \sin\delta'' + \cos\varphi \cos\delta'' \cos(t+\lambda')\\ \cos h \sin p'' &= \cos\varphi \sin(t+\lambda')\\ \cos h \cos p'' &= \sin\varphi \cos\delta'' - \cos\varphi \sin\delta'' \cos(t+\lambda')\end{aligned}\right\}\ (c)$$

If we subtract the first of the equations (b) from the first of the equations (a) and introduce $\frac{1}{2}(\delta' + \delta) + \frac{1}{2}(\delta - \delta')$ instead of δ, and $\frac{1}{2}(\delta' + \delta) - \frac{1}{2}(\delta - \delta')$ instead of δ', we find the equation (α) in No. 19. By a similar process we deduce from the third of the equations (a) and (b):

$$\begin{aligned}\cos h \sin \tfrac{1}{2}(p'+p) \sin \tfrac{1}{2}(p'-p) = \sin\varphi \sin \tfrac{1}{2}(\delta'+\delta) \sin \tfrac{1}{2}(\delta'-\delta) \\ - \cos\varphi \sin \tfrac{1}{2}(\delta'+\delta) \cos \tfrac{1}{2}(\delta'-\delta) \sin(t+\tfrac{1}{2}\lambda) \sin \tfrac{1}{2}\lambda \\ + \cos\varphi \cos \tfrac{1}{2}(\delta'+\delta) \sin \tfrac{1}{2}(\delta'-\delta) \cos(t+\tfrac{1}{2}\lambda) \cos \tfrac{1}{2}\lambda,\end{aligned}$$

and if we eliminate $\sin\varphi$ in this equation by means of the equation (α), multiplying the first by $\cos \frac{1}{2}(\delta'+\delta)$, the latter by $\sin \frac{1}{2}(\delta'+\delta)$, we obtain:

$$\cos h \cos \tfrac{1}{2}(\delta'+\delta) \sin \tfrac{1}{2}(p'+p) \sin \tfrac{1}{2}(p'-p) = \cos\varphi \sin \tfrac{1}{2}(\delta'-\delta) \cos(t+\tfrac{1}{2}\lambda) \cos \tfrac{1}{2}\lambda. \quad (d)$$

Now if we subtract the second equations (a) and (b), we find:

$$\cos h \cos \tfrac{1}{2}(p'+p) \sin \tfrac{1}{2}(p'-p) = \cos\varphi \cos(t+\tfrac{1}{2}\lambda) \sin \tfrac{1}{2}\lambda,$$

and hence:

$$\operatorname{tang} \tfrac{1}{2}(p'+p) = \frac{\sin \frac{1}{2}(\delta'-\delta)}{\cos \frac{1}{2}(\delta'+\delta)} \operatorname{cotang} \tfrac{1}{2}\lambda = \operatorname{tang} A''.$$

We can find similar formulae by combining the corresponding equations (a) and (c) and (b) and (c), which we can write down immediately on account of their symmetrical form:

$$\operatorname{tang} \tfrac{1}{2}(p''+p) = \frac{\sin \frac{1}{2}(\delta''-\delta)}{\cos \frac{1}{2}(\delta''+\delta)} \operatorname{cotang} \tfrac{1}{2}\lambda' = \operatorname{tang} A'$$

$$\text{and } \operatorname{tang} \tfrac{1}{2}(p''+p') = \frac{\sin \frac{1}{2}(\delta''-\delta')}{\cos \frac{1}{2}(\delta''+\delta')} \operatorname{cotang} \tfrac{1}{2}(\lambda'-\lambda) = \operatorname{tang} A.$$

If we add finally the second equations (a) and (b), we find:

$$\cos h \sin \tfrac{1}{2}(p'+p) \cos \tfrac{1}{2}(p'-p) = \cos\varphi \sin(t+\tfrac{1}{2}\lambda) \cos \tfrac{1}{2}\lambda,$$

and from this in connection with (d) we obtain:

$$\operatorname{tang}(t+\tfrac{1}{2}\lambda) = \frac{\sin \frac{1}{2}(\delta'-\delta)}{\cos \frac{1}{2}(\delta'+\delta)} \operatorname{cotang} \tfrac{1}{2}(p'-p),$$

$$\text{where } \tfrac{1}{2}(p'-p) = A - A'.$$

When thus p and t for the first star are known, we can compute φ and h by means of the formulae found before, which were derived by Napier's formulae:

$$\operatorname{tang} \tfrac{1}{2}(\varphi+h) = \frac{\cos \frac{1}{2}(t+p)}{\cos \frac{1}{2}(t-p)} \operatorname{cotang}(45^\circ - \tfrac{1}{2}\delta)$$

$$\operatorname{tang} \tfrac{1}{2}(\varphi-h) = \frac{\sin \frac{1}{2}(t-p)}{\sin \frac{1}{2}(t+p)} \operatorname{tang}(45^\circ - \tfrac{1}{2}\delta).$$

IV. METHODS OF FINDING THE LATITUDE AND THE TIME BY AZIMUTHS.

22. If we observe the clock-time, when a star, whose place is known, has a certain azimuth, we can find the error of the clock, if the latitude is known, because we can compute the hour angle of the star from its declination, its azimuth and the latitude. If we take the observation, when the star is on the meridian, it is not necessary to know the declination nor the latitude; at the same time, the change of the azimuth being at its maximum, the observation can be made with greater accuracy than at other times.

If we differentiate the equation:

$$\text{cotang}\, A \sin t = -\cos\varphi \,\text{tang}\,\delta + \sin\varphi\cos t,$$

we obtain according to the third formula (11) in No. 9 of the introduction:

$$\cos h dA = -\sin A \sin h d\varphi + \cos\delta\cos p \,.\, dt.$$

If the star is on the meridian, we have:

$$\sin A = 0,\ \cos p = 1$$

and:

$$h = 90^0 - \varphi + \delta$$

at least if the star is south of the zenith, hence we obtain:

$$dt = \frac{\sin(\varphi - \delta)}{\cos\delta} dA.$$

We see therefore, that in order to find the time by the observation of stars on the meridian, we must select stars which culminate near the zenith, because there an error of the azimuth has no influence upon the time.

If α be the right ascension of the star and u the clock-time of observation, we have the error of the clock equal to $\alpha - u$, if the clock is a sidereal clock. But if a mean-time clock is used, we must convert the sidereal time of the culmination of the star, that is, its right ascension into mean time. If we denote this by m, the error of the clock is equal to $m - u$.

For stars at some distance from the zenith the accuracy of the determination of the time depends upon the accuracy of the azimuth or upon the deviation of the instrument from the meridian. If this error is small, we can easily determine it by observing two stars, one of which culminates near the zenith the other near the horizon, and then we can free the observation from that error. For if dA be the deviation from the meridian, the hour angles $\Theta - \alpha$ and $\Theta' - \alpha'$ which the stars have at the times of the observations are also small and equal to:

$$\frac{\sin(\varphi - \delta)}{\cos \delta} \Delta A$$

and:

$$\frac{\sin(\varphi - \delta')}{\cos \delta'} \Delta A.$$

Hence, since $\Theta = u + \Delta u$, we have the following two equations:

$$\alpha = u + \Delta u - \frac{\sin(\varphi - \delta)}{\cos \delta} \Delta A$$

and:

$$\alpha' = u' + \Delta u - \frac{\sin(\varphi - \delta')}{\cos \delta'} \Delta A,$$

from which we can find both Δu and ΔA. If the instrument is so constructed that we can see stars north of the zenith, we find ΔA still more accurately if we select two stars, one of which is near the equator, the other near the pole, because in this case the coefficient of ΔA in one of the above equations is very large and besides has the opposite sign *).

Example. At the observatory at Bilk the following transits were observed with the transit-instrument, before it was well adjusted:

α Aurigae	$5^h\,6^m\,27^s.72$
β Orionis	$5\quad 8\quad 12\,.71.$

Since the right ascensions of the stars were:

α Aurigae	$5^h\,5^m\,33^s.25$	$+45^\circ\,50'.3$
β Orionis	$5\quad 7\quad 17\,.33$	$-\;8\quad 23.1$

and the latitude is $51^\circ\,12'.5$, we have the two equations:

$$-54^s.47 = \Delta u - 0.13433\,\Delta A$$
$$-55\,.38 = \Delta u - 0.87178\,\Delta A,$$

from which we find:

$$\Delta u = -54^s.30$$

and:

$$\Delta A = +1^s.23.$$

---

*) It is assumed here, that the instrument be so adjusted, that the line of collimation describes a vertical circle. If this is not the case, the observations must be corrected according to the formulae in No. 22 of the seventh section.

23. The time can also be found by a very simple method, proposed by Olbers, namely by observing the time, when any fixed star disappears behind a vertical terrestrial object. This of course must be a high one and at considerable distance from the observer so that it is distinctly seen in a telescope whose focus is adjusted for objects at an infinite distance. The telescope used for these observations must always be placed exactly in the same position, and a low power ought to be chosen.

Now if for a certain day the sidereal time of the disappearance of the star be known by other methods, we find by the observation on any other day immediately the error of the sidereal clock, because the star disappears every day exactly at the same sidereal time, as long as it does not change its place. But if a mean-time clock is used for these observations, the acceleration of the fixed stars must be taken into account, since the star disappears earlier every day by $0^h\,3^m\,55^s.909$ of mean time.

If the right ascension of the star changes, the time of the disappearance of the star is changed by the same quantity, because the star is always observed at the same azimuth and hence at the same hour angle. But if the declination changes, the hour angle of the star, corresponding to this azimuth, is changed and we have according to the differential formulae in No. 8 of the first section, since dA as well as $d\varphi$ are in this case equal to zero:

$$d\delta = \cos p\, dh$$
$$\cos\delta\, dt = -\sin p\, dh,$$

hence:

$$dt = -\frac{d\delta \,.\, \operatorname{tang} p}{\cos\delta},$$

where p denotes the parallactic angle.

Therefore if the change of the star's right ascension and declination is $\Delta\alpha$ and $\Delta\delta$, the change of the sidereal time, at which the star disappears, is:

$$+\frac{\Delta\alpha}{15} - \frac{\Delta\delta}{15}\,\frac{\operatorname{tang} p}{\cos\delta}.$$

Olbers had found from other observations, that in 1800 Sept. 6 the star α Coronae disappeared behind the vertical wall of a distant spire, whose azimuth was $64^0\,56'\,21''.4$, at

$11^h\,23^m\,18^s.3$ mean time, equal to $22^h\,26^m\,21^s.78$ sidereal time. On Sept. 12 he observed the time of the disappearance of the star $10^h 49^m\,21^s.0$. Now since $6 \times 3^m 55^s.909$ is equal to $23^m\,35^s.4$, the star ought to have disappeared at $10^h 59^m 42^s.9$ mean time, hence the error of the clock on mean time was equal to $+\,10^m\,21^s.9$.

In 1801 Sept. 6 was:

$$\Delta\alpha = +\,42''.0$$

and:

$$\Delta\delta = -\,13''.2,$$

and since we have:

$$p = 37^\circ\,31'$$

and:

$$\delta = +\,26^\circ\,41',$$

we find:

$$\Delta\delta\frac{\text{tang}\,p}{\cos\delta} = -\,11''.35,$$

hence the complete correction is $+\,53''.35$ or $3^s.56$. Therefore in 1801 Sept. 6 the star δ Coronae disappeared at $22^h\,26^m\,25^s.34$ sidereal time *).

24. If we know the time, we can find the latitude by observing an azimuth of a star, whose place is known, since we have:

$$\text{cotang}\,A\sin t = -\cos\varphi\,\text{tang}\,\delta + \sin\varphi\cos t.$$

Differentiating this equation we find:

$$\sin A\,d\varphi = -\,\text{cotang}\,h\,dA + \frac{\cos\delta\cos p}{\sin h}\,dt + \frac{\sin p}{\sin h}\,d\delta.$$

Hence in order to find the latitude by an azimuth as accurately as possible, we must observe the star near the prime vertical, because then $\sin A$ is at a maximum. Besides we must select a star which passes near the zenith of the place, since then the coefficients of dA and dt are very small, as we have:

$$\cos\delta\cos p = \sin\varphi\cos h + \cos\varphi\sin h\cos A.$$

Therefore we see that errors of the azimuth and the time have then no influence, whilst an error of the assumed declination of the star produces the same error of the latitude, since we have then $\sin p = 1$.

If we observe only one star, we must observe the azi-

---

*) v. Zach, Monatliche Correspondenz Band III. pag. 124.

muth itself besides the time. But if we suppose, that two stars have been observed, we have the two equations:

$$\begin{aligned} \text{cotang}\, A \sin t &= -\cos\varphi \,\text{tang}\, \delta + \sin\varphi \cos t \\ \text{cotang}\, A' \sin t' &= -\cos\varphi \,\text{tang}\, \delta' + \sin\varphi \cos t'. \end{aligned} \qquad (a)$$

Multiplying the first equation by $\sin t'$, the second by $\sin t$, we find:

$$\sin t \sin t' \frac{\sin (A'-A)}{\sin A \sin A'} = \cos\varphi \,[\text{tang}\, \delta' \sin t - \text{tang}\, \delta \sin t'] + \sin\varphi \sin (t'-t),$$

or as:

$$\cos\delta \sin t = \cos h \sin A,$$

also:

$$\cos h \cos h' \sin (A'-A) = \cos\varphi \,[\cos\delta \sin\delta' \sin t - \sin\delta \cos\delta' \sin t'] + \sin\varphi \sin (t'-t) \cos\delta \cos\delta'. \qquad (b)$$

We will introduce now the following auxiliary quantities:

$$\begin{aligned} \sin (\delta' + \delta) \sin \tfrac{1}{2} (t'-t) &= m \sin M \\ \sin (\delta' - \delta) \cos \tfrac{1}{2} (t'-t) &= m \cos M. \end{aligned} \qquad (A)$$

If we multiply the first of these equations by $\cos \frac{1}{2} (t'+t)$, the other by $\sin \frac{1}{2} (t'+t)$ and subtract the second equation from the first, we get:

$$m \sin [\tfrac{1}{2} (t'+t) - M] = \sin \delta' \cos \delta \sin t - \cos \delta' \sin \delta \sin t'.$$

But if we multiply the first equation by $\cos \frac{1}{2} (t'-t)$, the second by $\sin \frac{1}{2} (t'-t)$, and subtract the first equation from the second, we get:

$$m \sin [\tfrac{1}{2} (t'-t) - M] = -\sin\delta \cos\delta' \sin (t'-t).$$

Hence the equation (b) is transformed into the following:

$$\cos h \cos h' \sin (A'-A) = m \cos\varphi \sin [\tfrac{1}{2} (t'+t) - M] - m \sin\varphi \sin [\tfrac{1}{2} (t'-t) - M] \,\text{cotang}\, \delta.$$

If we assume now, that the two stars were observed either at the same azimuth or at two azimuths, whose difference is 180^0, we have in both cases $\sin (A'-A) = 0$ and hence we find:

$$\text{tang}\, \varphi = \text{tang}\, \delta \frac{\sin [\frac{1}{2} (t'+t) - M]}{\sin [\frac{1}{2} (t'-t) - M]}. \qquad (B)$$

Therefore in this case it is not necessary to know the azimuth itself, but we find the latitude by the times of observation and by the declination of the star by means of the formulae (A) and (B).

If the same star was observed both times, the formulae become still more simple. For since we have in this case $M = 90^0$ according to the second formula (A), we find:

$$\operatorname{tang}\varphi = \operatorname{tang}\delta \cdot \frac{\cos\frac{1}{2}(t'+t)}{\cos\frac{1}{2}(t'-t)}. \qquad (C)$$

For the general case, that two stars have been observed at two different azimuths, the differential equations are:

$$\cos h\, dA = \sin p\, d\delta + \cos\delta\cos p\, dt - \sin h \sin A\, d\varphi$$
$$\cos h' dA' = \sin p' d\delta' + \cos\delta' \cos p' dt' - \sin h' \sin A' d\varphi.$$

If we introduce here also the difference of the azimuths and therefore multiply the first equation by $\cos h'$, the other by $\cos h$, and subtract them, we get:

$$\begin{aligned}\cos h\cos h' d(A'-A) = & -\cos h'\cos\delta\cos p\, dt + \cos h\cos\delta'\cos p' dt' \\ & - [\sin h'\cos h\sin A' - \sin h\cos h'\sin A]\, d\varphi \\ & + \cos h\sin p' d\delta' - \cos h'\sin p\, d\delta.\end{aligned}$$

Now since $dt = du + d(\Delta u)$ and $dt' = du' + d(\Delta u)$, where du and du' are the errors of observation and $d(\Delta u)$ that of the error of the clock, we find, if we substitute these values in place of dt and dt' and take at the same time $A' = 180^0 + A$ *):

$$\begin{aligned}\sin A\, d\varphi - \cos\varphi\cos A\, d(\Delta u) = & \frac{\cos h\cos h'}{\sin(h'+h)}[d(A'-A) - \sin\varphi\, d(u'-u)] \\ & + \frac{\cos\varphi\cos A\sin h\cos h'}{\sin(h'+h)} du + \frac{\cos\varphi\cos A\sin h'\cos h}{\sin(h'+h)} du' \\ & - \frac{\sin p'\cos h}{\sin(h'+h)} d\delta' + \frac{\sin p\cos h'}{\sin(h'+h)} d\delta.\end{aligned}$$

Hence we see again that it is best to make the observations on the prime vertical. For then the coefficient of $d\varphi$ is at a maximum and those of the errors du, du' and $d(\Delta u)$ are equal to zero; and only the difference of the two errors of observation, the errors of the declination and the quantity, by which the difference of the two azimuths was greater or less than 180^0, will have any effect upon the result. In case that the same star was observed on the prime vertical in the east and west, we have $h = h'$ and $\sin p' = -\sin p$, hence:

$$d\varphi = \tfrac{1}{2}\operatorname{cotang} h\, [d(A'-A) - \sin\varphi\, d(u'-u)] + \frac{\sin p}{\sin h} d\delta,$$

---

*) In order to find the equation given above, we must also substitute for $\cos\delta\cos p$ and $\cos\delta'\cos p'$ the following expressions:

$$\cos\delta\cos p = \sin\varphi\cos h + \cos\varphi\sin h\cos A$$
$$\cos\delta'\cos p' = \sin\varphi\cos h' - \cos\varphi\sin h'\cos A.$$

and since according to No. 26 of the first section:

$$\sin h = \frac{\sin \delta}{\sin \varphi} \text{ and } \sin p = \frac{\cos \varphi}{\cos \delta},$$

we have:

$$d\varphi = \tfrac{1}{2} \operatorname{cotang} h\,[d(A' - A) - \sin \varphi\, d(u' - u)] + \frac{\sin 2\varphi}{\sin 2\delta}\, d\delta.$$

We see again from this eqnation, that it is best to observe stars, which pass near the zenith, because then cotang h is very large and hence errors in $A' - A$ and $u' - u$ have only very little influence upon the result. In this case the coefficient of $d\delta$ is equal to 1, since the declination of stars passing through the zenith is equal to φ, and hence the result will be affected with the whole error of the declination. But if the difference of latitude should be determined by this method for two places not far from each other so that the same star can be used at each place, this difference will be entirely free from the error of the declination *).

Example. The star β Draconis passes very near the zenith of Berlin. Therefore this star was observed at the observatory with a prime vertical instrument. The interval between the transits of the star east and west was $34^{m} 43^{s}.5$ hence:

$$\tfrac{1}{2}(t' - t) = 4^{0}\ 20'\ 26''.25$$

and it was

$$\delta = 52^{0}\ 25'\ 26''.77.$$

Now since in case that the observations are taken on the prime vertical we have $\frac{1}{2}(t' + t) = 0$, we find from (C) the following simple formula for finding the latitude:

$$\operatorname{tang} \varphi = \frac{\operatorname{tang} \delta}{\cos \frac{1}{2}(t' - t)}\ \text{**}),$$

and by means of this we obtain:

$$\varphi = 52^{0}\ 30'\ 13''.04.$$

Finally the differential equation is:

$$d\varphi = +\,0.02310\,[d(A' - A) - 0.7934\, d(u' - u)] + 0.99925\, d\delta.$$

---

*) It is again assumed, that the transit instrument is so far adjusted, that the line of collimation describes a vertical circle. Compare No. 26 of the seventh section.

**) This formula is also found simply from the triangle between the pole, the zenith and the star, which in this case is a right angled triangle.

25. If we observe two stars on the same vertical circle, we can find the time, if we know the latitude of the place, since we have:

$$\sin[\tfrac{1}{2}(t'+t)-M]=\frac{\operatorname{tang}\varphi}{\operatorname{tang}\delta}\sin[\tfrac{1}{2}(t'-t)-M], \qquad (A)$$

where:

$$t=u+\Delta u-\alpha$$
$$t'=u'+\Delta u-\alpha'$$

and

$$m\sin M=\sin(\delta'+\delta)\sin\tfrac{1}{2}(t'-t)$$
$$m\cos M=\sin(\delta'-\delta)\cos\tfrac{1}{2}(t'-t).$$

Since $t'-t$, that is, half the interval of time between the observations, expressed in sidereal time, is known, we can find $t'+t$ and hence t and t'.

The differential equation given in No. 22 shows, that for finding the time by azimuths it is best to observe stars near the meridian, because there the coefficient of $d\varphi$ is at a minimum, that of dt at a maximum.

The azimuth itself can also be found by such observations. For we have:

$$\operatorname{tang}A=\frac{\cos\delta\sin t}{-\cos\varphi\sin\delta+\sin\varphi\cos\delta\cos t},$$

and making use of the equation:

$$\operatorname{tang}\varphi=\operatorname{tang}\delta\frac{\sin[\tfrac{1}{2}(t'+t)-M]}{\sin[\tfrac{1}{2}(t'-t)-M]}$$

we find:

$$\sin\varphi\operatorname{tang}A=\frac{\sin t\,.\sin[\tfrac{1}{2}(t'+t)-M]}{-\sin[\tfrac{1}{2}(t'-t)-M]+\cos t\sin[\tfrac{1}{2}(t'+t)-M]}$$

If we write here

$$\tfrac{1}{2}(t'+t)-M-t \text{ instead of } \tfrac{1}{2}(t'-t)-M,$$

we easily obtain:

$$\operatorname{tang}A=\frac{\operatorname{tang}[\tfrac{1}{2}(t'+t)-M]}{\sin\varphi}. \qquad (B)$$

If the time of both observations is the same or:

$$t'-t=\alpha-\alpha',$$

the formula (A) gives the time, at which two stars are on the same vertical circle.

The places of α Lyrae and α Aquilae are for the beginning of the year 1849:

α Lyrae $\alpha=18^h\,31^m\,47^s.75$ $\delta=+38^\circ\,38'\,52''.2$

α Aquilae $\alpha'=19\;\;43\;\;23\;.43$ $\delta'=+\;8\;\;28\;\;30\;.5.$

Therefore we have:

$$t' - t = -1^h\,11^m\,35^s.68 = -17^0\,53'\,55''.2.$$

If we take then $\varphi = 52^0\,30'\,16''$, we find:

$$M = 192^0\,55'\,53''.0$$

$$\tfrac{1}{2}(t' - t) - M = 158\quad 7\quad 9\;.4$$

and from this we get:

$$\tfrac{1}{2}(t' + t) - M = 142^0\,35'\,38''.6,$$

hence:

$$\tfrac{1}{2}(t' + t) = -24^0\,28'\,28''.4$$

$$= -1^h\,37^m\,53^s.9$$

and

$$t = -1^h\,2^m\,6^s.1,\quad t' = -2^h\,13^m\,41^s.7.$$

Therefore the sidereal time at which the two stars are on the same vertical circle is:

$$\Theta = 17^h\,29^m\,42^s.$$

Hence if we observe the clock-time when two stars are on the same vertical circle, if for instance we observe the clock-time when two stars are bisected by a plumb-line, we can find the error of the clock at least approximately, when we know the latitude of the place and compute the time by means of the formulae given above. It is best to take as one of the stars always the pole-star, since it changes its place very slowly, a circumstance which makes the observation more easy.

V. DETERMINATION OF THE ANGLE BETWEEN THE MERIDIANS OF TWO PLACES ON THE SURFACE OF THE EARTH, OR OF THEIR DIFFERENCE OF LONGITUDE.

26. If the local times, which two different places on the surface of the earth have at the same absolute instant, are known, the hour angle of the vernal equinox for each place is known. But the difference of these hour angles, hence the difference of the local times at the same moment, is equal to the arc of the equator between the meridians passing through the two places and hence equal to their difference of longitude; and since the diurnal motion of the heavenly sphere is going on in the direction from east to west, it follows, that a place, whose local time at a certain moment is earlier than that of another place, is west of this place, and that it is east of it, if its local time is later than that of the other place. For the first meridian, from which the longitudes of all other places are reckoned, usually that of a certain observatory, for instance, that of Paris or Greenwich, is taken. But in geographical works the longitudes are more frequently reckoned from the meridian of Ferro, whose longitude from Paris is $20^{0}\ 0'$ or $1^{h}\ 20^{m}$ West.

In order to obtain the local times which exist simultaneously on two meridians, either artificial signals are observed or such heavenly phenomena as are seen at the same moment from all places. Such phenomena are first the eclipses of the moon. For since the moon at the time of an eclipse enters the cone of the shadow of the earth, the beginning and the end of an eclipse as well as the obscurations of different spots are seen from all places on the earth simultaneously, because the time in which the light traverses the semi-diameter of the earth is insignificant. The same is true for the eclipses of the satellites of Jupiter.

These phenomena therefore would be very convenient for finding differences of longitude, since they are simply equal to the differences of the local times of observations, if they could be observed with greater accuracy. But since the shadow of the earth on the moon's disc is never well defined, and thus the errors of observation may amount to one minute and even more, and since likewise the beginning and end of an eclipse of Jupiter's satellites cannot be accurately observed, these phenomena are at present hardly ever used for finding the longitude. If however the eclipses of Jupiter's satellites should be employed for this purpose, it is absolutely necessary, that the observers at the two stations have telescopes of equal power and that each observes the same number of immersions and emersions and those only of the first satellite, whose motion round Jupiter is the most rapid. The arithmetical mean of all these observations will give a result measurably free of any error, though any very great accuracy cannot be expected.

Benzenberg has proposed to observe the time of disappearance of shooting stars for this purpose. These can be observed with great accuracy, but since it is not known beforehand, when and in what region of the heavens a shooting star will appear, it will always be the case, that even if a great mass of shooting stars have been observed at the two stations, yet very few, which are identical, will be found among them; besides the difference of longitude must be already approximately known, in order to find out these.

Very accurate results can be obtained by observing artificial signals, which are given for instance by lighting a quantity of gunpowder at a place visible from the two stations. Although this method can be used only for places near each other, yet the difference of longitude of distant places may be determined in the following way: Let A and B be the two places, whose difference of longitude l shall be found, and let A_1, A_2, A_3 etc. be other places, lying between those places, whose unknown differences of longitude shall be l_1, l_2, l_3 etc. so that l_1 is the difference of longitude between A_1 and A, l_2 that between A_2 and A_1 etc. If then signals are given at the stations A_1, A_3, A_5 etc. at the local times t_1, t_3, t_5 etc., the signal from A_1 is seen at the place A at the time $t_1 - l_1 = \Theta$, and at the station A_2 at the time $t_1 + l_2 = \Theta_1$. Further the signal given from A_3 is seen at the station A_2 at the time $t_3 - l_3 = \Theta_2$, and at the station A_4 at the time $t_3 + l_4 = \Theta_3$. But since the difference of longitude of the places A and B is equal to $l + l_1 + \ldots + l_n$, if the last signal station is A_{n-1}, or since:

$$l = (\Theta_1 - \Theta) + (\Theta_3 - \Theta_2) + (\Theta_5 - \Theta_4) \text{ etc.},$$

we find:

$$l = \Theta_{n-1} - (\Theta_{n-2} - \Theta_{n-3}) - \ldots - (\Theta_2 - \Theta_1) - \Theta.$$

Therefore at the stations, where the signals are observed, it is not requisite to know the error of the clocks but only their rate, and it is only necessary to know the correct time at the two places, whose difference of longitude is to be found.

Instead of giving the signals by lighting gunpowder, it is better to use a heliotrope, an instrument invented by Gauss, by which the light of the sun can be reflected in any direction to great distances. If the heliotrope is directed to the other station, a signal can be given by covering it suddenly.

The difference of longitude of two places can also be determined by transporting a good portable chronometer from one place to the other and finding at each station the error of the chronometer on local time as well as its rate. For if the error found at the first place be Δu and the daily rate be denoted by $\frac{d\,.\,\Delta u}{dt}$, then the error after a days will be $\Delta u + a\frac{d\,.\,\Delta u}{dt}$. Now if after a days the error of the chronometer at the other place should be found equal to $\Delta u'$, we have, denoting the longitude of the second place east of the first by l:

$$u' - l + \Delta u + \frac{d\,.\,\Delta u}{dt} a = u' + \Delta u',$$

hence

$$l = \Delta u + \frac{d\,.\,\Delta u}{dt} a - \Delta u'.$$

It is assumed here that the chronometer has kept a uniform rate during the interval between the two observations. But since this is never strictly the case, it is necessary, to transport not only one chronometer from one place to the other, but as many as possible, and to take the mean of all the results given by the several chronometers. In this way the difference of longitude of several observatories, for instance that of Greenwich and that of Pulkova has been determined. Likewise the longitude at sea is found by this method, the error of the chronometer as well as its rate being determined at the place from which the ship sails and the time at sea being found by altitudes of the sun.

27. The most accurate method of finding the difference of longitude is that by means of the electric telegraph. Since telegraphic signals can be observed like any other signals, the method is of the same nature as some of those mentioned before, and has no other advantage than perhaps its greater convenience; but when chronographs are used for recording the observations at the two stations, it surpasses all other methods by the accuracy of the results. The chronograph is usually constructed in this way, that a cylinder, about which a sheet of paper is wrapped, is moved around its axis with uniform velocity by a clockwork, which at the same time carries a writing apparatus, resting on the paper, slowly in a direction parallel to the axis of the cylinder. Therefore, if the motion of the cylinder and of the pen is uniform, the latter markes on the paper a spiral, which when the sheet is taken from the cylinder, appears as a system of parallel lines on the paper. Now the writing apparatus is connected with an electro-magnet so that, every time the current is broken for an instant and the armature is pulled away from the magnet by means of a spring attached to it, the pen makes a plain mark on the paper. If then the pendulum of a clock breaks the current by some contrivance at every beat, every second of the clock is thus marked on the sheet of paper, and since the chronograph is always so arranged that the cylinder revolves on its axis once in a minute, there will be on every parallel line sixty marks, corresponding to the seconds of the clock, and the marks corresponding to the same second in different minutes will also lie in a straight line perpendicular to those parallel lines. We will suppose now, that at first the current is broken and that the pen is marking an unbroken line; then if the current be closed just before the second-hand of the clock reaches the zero-second of a certain minute, the first second-mark on the paper will correspond to this certain second, and hence the second corresponding to any other mark is easily found. If then the current can also be broken at any time by a break-key in the hand of the observer, who gives a signal at the instant when a star is seen on the wire of the instrument, the time of this observation is also marked on the sheet, and hence it can be found with great accuracy by measuring the distance of this mark from the nearest second-mark.

If the current goes to another observatory, whose longitude is to be determined, and passes there also through a key in the hand of the observer, the signals given by this observer will be recorded too by the chronograph at the first station; hence if this observer gives also a signal at the time when the same star is seen on the wire of his instrument, the difference of the two times of observation, recorded on the paper and corrected for the deviations of the two instruments from their respective meridians and for the rate of the clock in the interval between the two observations, will be equal to the difference of longitude of the two places.

Since the electrical current, when going to a great distance, is only weak, this main current, which passes through the keys of the two observers, does not act immediately upon the electro-magnet of the chronograph, but merely upon a relay which breaks the local current passing through the chronograph.

If a chronograph is used at each station and the clocks are on the local circuits, the signals from each observer and the seconds of the local clock are recorded by each chronograph, and hence we get a difference of longitude by every star from the records of each chronograph after being corrected for the errors of the instruments and the rate of the clock. But the difference of longitude thus recorded independently at each station is not exactly the same. For since the velocity of electricity is not indefinitely great, there will elapse a very short, but measurable time, at least if the distance of the two stations is great, till the signal given at the station A, being the farthest east, arrives at the station B. Hence the time of the signal recorded at the station B corresponds to a time, when the star was already on the median of a place lying west of A, and the difference of longitude recorded at B is too small by the time, in which the electricity traverses the distance from A to B. But the same time will elapse when the signal from B is given, and the time recorded at the station A will correspond to the time when the star was on the meridian of a place a little west of B, hence the difference of longitude recorded at the station A will be too great by the same quantity. Therefore the mean of the differences of longitude recorded at both stations is the true difference of longitude and half the difference (subtracting the result obtained at the station B from that obtained at the station A) is equal to the time in which the electricity traverses the distance from A to B *).

---

*) The armature-time is also a cause of this difference.

A single star, observed in this way, gives already a more accurate result than a single determination of the longitude made by any other method, and since the number of stars can be increased at pleasure, the accuracy can be driven to a very high degree, provided that also the greatest care is taken in determining the errors of the two instruments. Since the same stars are observed at both stations, the difference of longitude is free from any errors of the places of the stars.

In case that the distance between the two stations is great, sometimes a large number of signals are lost and it is therefore preferable, to let the main current for a short time at the beginning and end of the observations pass through both clocks, so that their beats are recorded by the chronographs at both stations. If then the current is closed at each station at a round minute, after having been broken for a short time, so that the clock-times corresponding to the records on the chronographs are known, the difference of the two clocks can be obtained from every recorded second or better from the arithmetical mean of all. These differences, as obtained at both stations, differ again by twice the time, in which the current passes from one station to the other, and which in this way can be determined even with greater accuracy. A few such comparisons are already sufficient to give a very accurate result, since the accuracy of one comparison probably surpasses the accuracy with which the errors of the clocks can be obtained from observations. Certainly the comparisons obtained during a few minutes are more than sufficient for the purpose so that the telegraphic part of the operation is limited to a few minutes at the beginning and the end of the observations. After the first set of comparisons has been made, the clocks as well as the keys of both observers are put on the local circuit of each observatory and the errors of the clocks determined by each observer. If these errors of the clocks are applied with the proper signs to the difference of the time of the two clocks, the difference of longitude of the two stations is found. Also in this case it is advisable, that the observers use as much as possible the same stars for finding the errors of their respective clocks, in order to eliminate the influence of any errors of the right ascensions of the stars.

Besides errors arising from an inaccurate determination of the errors of the two instruments, there can remain another error in the value of the difference of longitude, produced by the *personal equation* of the two observers, that is, by the relative quickness, with which the two observers perceive any impression upon their senses. But this source of error is not peculiar to this method, but is common to all and even of less consequence, when the observations are recorded by the electro-magnetic method. In this case the error depends upon the time, which elapses between the moment, when the eye of the observer receives an impression and the moment, at which he becomes conscious of this impression and gives the signal by touching the key. If this time is the same for both observers, the determination of the difference of the longitude is not at all affected by it; but if this time is not equal and there exists a personal equation, the difference of longitude is found wrong by a quantity equal to it. But the error arising from this source can be entirely eliminated (at least if the personal equation does not change), if the same observers determine the difference of longitude a second time after having exchanged their stations; the difference of the two results is then equal to twice the personal equation, whilst their arithmetical mean is free from it. The observers can also determine their personal equation, when they meet at one place and observe the transits of stars by an instrument furnished with many wires, so that one observer takes always the transits over some of the wires and the other those over the remainder of the wires. If then these times of observation are reduced to the middle wire, (Section VII No. 20) the results for every star obtained by the two observers will differ by a quantity equal to the personal equation. The observations are then changed so, that now the second observer takes the transits over the first set of wires, and the first one those over the other wires. Then nearly the same difference between the observers will be obtained and the arithmetical mean of the two values thus found will be free from any errors of the wire-distances used for reducing the observations to the middle wire. After the personal equation has thus been found, the value obtained for the difference of longitude must be corrected on account of it. If the observer whose station is farthest to the east observes later than the other, or if the personal equation is $E - W = + a$, the value found for the difference of longitude is too small by the same quantity, and hence $+ a$ must be added to it.

Example. On the 29th of June 1861 the difference of longitude was determined between Ann Arbor in the State of Michigan and Clinton in the State of New York and from 126 comparisons of the clocks recorded by the chronographs of the two stations it was found that:

(recorded at A. A.) $13^h 59^m 3^s.0$ Clinton clock-time $= 19^h 58^m 29^s.56$ A. A. clock-t.
(recorded at Cl.) $13\ 59\ 3\ .0$ „ „ $= 19\ 58\ 29\ .40$ „ „

The clock at the observatory at Clinton was a mean time clock and its error on Clinton sidereal time was at the time $13^h 59^m 3^s.0$ equal to $+ 6^h 33^m 46^s.07$, while the error of the clock at Ann Arbor on local sidereal time was $+ 1^m 1^s.87$. From the records by the chronograph at Ann Arbor we find therefore:

$20^h 32^m 49^s.07$ Cl. sidereal time $= 19^h 59^m 31^s.43$ A. A. sidereal time

and by the chronograph at Clinton:

$20^h 32^m 49^s.07$ Cl. sidereal time $= 19^h 59^m 31^s.27$ A. A. sidereal time.

Hence we find the difference of longitude by the records at Ann Arbor equal to

$$33^m 17^s.64,$$

and by those at Clinton:

$$33^m 17^s.80,$$

or the mean $33^m 17^s.72$.

The personal equation is in this case $E - W = + 0^s.04$ *), hence the corrected difference of longitude is $33^m 17^s.76$.

Note. The electro-magnetic method for finding the difference of longitude is usually called the American method, since it was proposed by Americans. The idea originated with to Sears C. Walker and W. Bond Esq., to whom the honour of inventing it must be accorded, although Mitchel of Cincinnati completed the first instrument for recording the observations.

---

*) Dr. Peters observed at Clinton, the author at Ann Arbor.

28. Besides the observations of natural or artificial signals, which are seen at the same instant at the two stations, whose difference of longitude is to be found, we may use for this purpose also such celestial phenomena, which, though they are not simultaneous for different places, yet can be reduced to the same time; and they afford even this advantage, that they can be observed with great accuracy, and that they are visible over a large portion of the surface of the earth so that it is possible to find the difference of longitude of places very distant from each other. Such phenomena are the occultations of fixed stars and planets by the moon, eclipses of the sun, and transits of the inferior planets Mercury and Venus. Since all these heavenly bodies with the exception of the fixed stars have a parallax, which in the case of the moon is very considerable, they are seen at the same instant from different places on the surface of the earth at different places on the celestial sphere, and hence the occultations as well as the other phenomena mentioned before are not simultaneous for different places. Hence in this case the observations need a correction for parallax, since we must know the time, when those phenomena would have occurred, if there had been no parallax or rather, if they had been observed from the centre of the earth.

Therefore we must find first the parallaxes in longitude and latitude and the apparent semi-diameters of the heavenly bodies at the time of the beginning and the end of the eclipse or occultation (or the parallax in right ascension and declination, if it should be preferable to use these co-ordinates). Then in the triangle between the pole of the ecliptic and the centres of the two bodies the three sides, namely the complements of the apparent latitudes and the sum or the difference of the apparent semi-diameters, are known; hence we can compute the angle at the pole, that is, the difference of the apparent longitudes of the two bodies at the time of observation and, applying the parallaxes in longitude, we find the difference of the true longitudes, as seen from the centre of the earth. From this, the relative velocity of the two bodies being known, we obtain the time of true conjunction, that is, the time, at which the two bodies have the same geocentric longitude, and expressed in local time of the place of observation. If the beginning or end of the same eclipse or occultation has also been observed at another place, we find in the same way the time of true conjunction expressed in local time of that place. Hence the difference of both times is equal to the difference of longitude of the two places.

If the times of observation, as well as the data used for the reduction to the centre of the earth were correct, the difference of longitude thus obtained would also be correct. But since they are subject to errors, we must examine, what influence they have upon the result, and try to eliminate it by the combination of several observations.

This is the method, which formerly was used for finding the difference of longitude by eclipses. At present a different method is employed. Starting from the equation, which expresses the condition of the limbs of the two bodies being in contact with each other and which contains only geocentric quantities, another equation is obtained, in which the unknown quantity is the time of conjunction or rather the difference of longitude.

29. The limbs of two heavenly bodies are seen in contact, when the eye is anywhere in the curved surface enveloping the two bodies. Since the heavenly bodies are so nearly spherical, that we can entirely disregard the small deviation from a spherical form, the enveloping surface will be the surface of a straight cone, and there will always be two different cones, the vertex being in one case between the two bodies, while in the other case it lies beyond the smaller body. If the eye is in the surface of the first cone, we see an exterior contact, whilst when it is in that of the second, we see an interior contact.

The equation of a straight cone is the most simple, if it is referred to a rectangular system of axes, one of which coincides with the axis of the cone. If the cone is generated by a right angled triangle revolving about one of its sides, the equation of its surface is:

$$x^2 + y^2 = (c - z)^2 \operatorname{tang} f^2,$$

where c is the distance of the vertex from the fundamental plane of the co-ordinates, and f is the vertical angle of the generating triangle.

We must now find the equation of the cone enveloping the two bodies and referred to a system of axes one of which passes through the centres of the two bodies. If then we substitute in place of the indeterminate co-ordinates x, y, z the co-ordinates of a place on the surface of the earth, referred to the same system of axes, we obtain the fundamental equation for eclipses. For this purpose we must first determine the position of the line joining the centres of the two bodies. But if a and d be the right ascension and declination of that point, in which the centre of the more distant body is seen from the centre of the nearer body or in which the line passing through both centres intersects the sphere of the heavens, and if G denote the distance of the two centres, further α, δ and Δ be the geocentric right ascension, declination and distance of the nearer body and α', δ', Δ' the same quantities for the more distant body, we have the equations:

$$G\cos d\cos a = \Delta'\cos\delta'\cos\alpha' - \Delta\cos\delta\cos\alpha$$
$$G\cos d\sin a = \Delta'\cos\delta'\sin\alpha' - \Delta\cos\delta\sin\alpha$$
$$G\sin d = \Delta'\sin\delta' - \Delta\sin\delta,$$

or:

$$G\cos d\cos(a-\alpha') = \Delta'\cos\delta' - \Delta\cos\delta\cos(\alpha-\alpha')$$
$$G\cos d\sin(a-\alpha') = -\Delta\cos\delta\sin(\alpha-\alpha')$$
$$G\sin d = \Delta'\sin\delta' - \Delta\sin\delta.$$

If we take as unit the equatoreal semi-diameter of the earth, we must take $\frac{\Delta'}{\sin\pi'}$ and $\frac{1}{\sin\pi}$ instead of Δ' and Δ, since Δ and Δ' are expressed in parts of the semi-major axis of the earth's orbit, where π is the mean horizontal equatoreal parallax of the nearer body, π' the same for the more distant body; thus we obtain:

$$\sin\pi\, G\cos d\cos(a-\alpha') = \Delta'\frac{\sin\pi}{\sin\pi'}\cos\delta' - \cos\delta\cos(\alpha-\alpha')$$
$$\sin\pi\, G\cos d\sin(a-\alpha') = \qquad - \cos\delta\sin(\alpha-\alpha')$$
$$\sin\pi\, G\sin d = \Delta'\frac{\sin\pi}{\sin\pi'}\sin\delta' - \sin\delta.$$

Now since we also have:

$$\sin\pi\, G\cos d = \Delta'\frac{\sin\pi}{\sin\pi'}\cos\delta'\cos(a-\alpha') - \cos\delta\cos(a-\alpha),$$

we find:

$$\operatorname{tang}(a-\alpha')=-\frac{\frac{\sin\pi'}{\Delta'\sin\pi}\,\frac{\cos\delta}{\cos\delta'}\sin(\alpha-\alpha')}{1-\frac{\sin\pi'}{\Delta'\sin\pi}\,\frac{\cos\delta}{\cos\delta'}\cos(\alpha-\alpha')}$$

and:

$$\operatorname{tang}(d-\delta')=-\frac{\frac{\sin\pi'}{\Delta'\sin\pi}\sin(\delta-\delta')}{1-\frac{\sin\pi'}{\Delta'\sin\pi}\cos(\delta-\delta')}\,.$$

Since in the case of an eclipse of the sun $\frac{\sin\pi'}{\sin\pi}$ is a small quantity, we obtain from this by means of the formula (12) in No. 11 of the introduction:

$$\begin{aligned} a&=\alpha'-\frac{\sin\pi'}{\Delta'\sin\pi}\cdot\frac{\cos\delta}{\cos\delta'}(\alpha-\alpha') \\ d&=\delta'-\frac{\sin\pi'}{\Delta'\sin\pi}(\delta-\delta') \end{aligned} \qquad (A)$$

and putting:

$$g=\frac{G\sin\pi'}{\Delta'},$$

we also find:

$$g=1-\frac{\sin\pi'}{\Delta'\sin\pi}\,. \qquad (B)$$

We will imagine now a rectangular system of axes of co-ordinates, whose origin is at the centre of the earth. Let the axis of y be directed towards the north pole of the equator, whilst the axes of z and x are situated in the plane of the equator and directed to points, whose right ascensions are a and $90+a$. Then the co-ordinates of the nearer body with respect to these axes are:

$$z'=\Delta\cos\delta\cos(\alpha-a),\quad y'=\Delta\sin\delta,\quad x'=\Delta\cos\delta\sin(\alpha-a).$$

If now we imagine the axes of y and z to be turned in the plane of yz through the angle $-d$ *), so that the axis of z is directed towards the point whose right ascension and declination are a and d, we find the co-ordinates of the nearer body with respect to the new system of axes:

$$z=\frac{\sin\delta\sin d+\cos\delta\cos d\cos(\alpha-a)}{\sin\pi}$$

$$y=\frac{\sin\delta\cos d-\cos\delta\sin d\cos(\alpha-a)}{\sin\pi}$$

$$x=\frac{\cos\delta\sin(\alpha-a)}{\sin\pi}$$

*) The angle d must be taken negative, since the positive side of the axis of z is turned towards the positive side of the axis of y.

or:

$$z = \frac{\cos(\delta - d)\cos\frac{1}{2}(\alpha - a)^2 - \cos(\delta + d)\sin\frac{1}{2}(\alpha - a)^2}{\sin\pi}$$

$$y = \frac{\sin(\delta - d)\cos\frac{1}{2}(\alpha - a)^2 + \sin(\delta + d)\sin\frac{1}{2}(\alpha - a)^2}{\sin\pi} \qquad (C)$$

$$x = \frac{\cos\delta\sin(\alpha - a)}{\sin\pi}.$$

The axis of z is now parallel to the line joining the centres of the two bodies. If we let the axis of z coincide with this line, the co-ordinates x and y will be the co-ordinates of the centre of the earth with respect to the new origin but taken negative.

Let φ' be the geocentric latitude of a place on the surface of the earth, Θ its sidereal time and ϱ its distance from the centre, then the co-ordinates of this place, taking the origin at the centre of the earth and the axis of ζ parallel to the line joining the centres of the two bodies, are:

$$\zeta = \varrho\,[\sin d \sin\varphi' + \cos d \cos\varphi' \cos(\Theta - a)]$$
$$\eta = \varrho\,[\cos d \sin\varphi' - \sin d \cos\varphi' \cos(\Theta - a)] \qquad (D)$$
$$\xi = \varrho\cos\varphi'\sin(\Theta - a).$$

The co-ordinates of this place with respect to a system of axes, whose axis of z is the line joining the two centres itself, are:

$$\xi - x,\ \eta - y \text{ and } \zeta$$

and the equation, which expresses, that the place on the surface of the earth, given by ϱ, φ' and Θ, lies in the surface of the cone enveloping the two bodies, is:

$$(x - \xi)^2 + (y - \eta)^2 = (c - \zeta)^2 \operatorname{tang} f^2,$$

where c and f are yet to be expressed by quantities referred to the centre of the earth. But the angle f is found, as is easily seen, by the equation:

$$\sin f = \frac{r' \pm r}{G},$$

where r and r' are the semi-diameters of the two bodies and where the upper sign must be used for exterior contacts, the lower one for interior contacts. Now since the unit we use for G is the semi-diameter of the equator of the earth, we must refer r and r' to the same unit. Therefore if k denotes the semi-diameter of the moon expressed in parts of the semi-diameter of the equator of the earth and h the apparent semi-diameter of the sun seen at a distance equal to the semi-major axis of the earth's orbit, we have, since:

$$r' = \frac{\sin h}{\sin \pi'},$$

also:

$$\sin f = \frac{1}{G \sin \pi'} [\sin h \pm k \sin \pi']$$

or:

$$\sin f = \frac{1}{\Delta' g} [\sin h \pm k \sin \pi']. \qquad (E)$$

But we have:

$$\log \sin \pi' = 5.6186145,$$

further we have according to Burkhardt's Lunar Tables $k = 0.2725$ and according to Bessel $h = 15' 59''.788$, hence we have:

$$\log [\sin h + k \sin \pi'] = 7.6688041 \text{ for exterior contacts,}$$
$$\log [\sin h - k \sin \pi'] = 7.6666903 \text{ for interior contacts.}$$

We must still express the quantity c, that is, the distance of the vertex of the cone from the plane of xy. But we easily see, that:

$$c = z \pm \frac{k}{\sin f}, \qquad (F)$$

where again the upper sign is used for an exterior, the lower one for an interior contact. If we then denote by l the quantity $c \operatorname{tang} f$, that is, the radius of the circle in which the plane of xy intersects the cone, and $\operatorname{tang} f$ by λ, the general equation for eclipses, which expresses, that the place on the surface of the earth given by φ', Θ and ϱ, lies in the surface of the cone enveloping both bodies, is as follows:

$$(x - \xi)^2 + (y - \eta^2) = (l - \lambda \zeta)^2.$$

Since l is always positive, we must take $\operatorname{tang} f$ or λ negative, if we find a negative value of c from the equation (F).

The values of the quantities used for computing x, y, z and ξ, η, ζ by means of the equations (C) and (D) are taken from the tables of the sun and the moon. Since these are always a little erroneous, the computed values of x, y etc. will also differ a little from the true values. Therefore if Δx, Δy and Δl are the corrections, which must be applied to the computed values x, y and l in order to obtain the true values, the above equation is transformed into *):

$$(x+\Delta x-\xi)^2+(y+\Delta y-\eta)^2=(l+\Delta l-\lambda\zeta)^2.$$

We will assume now, that the values of α, δ, π, α', δ' and π' have been taken from the tables or almanacs for the time T of the first meridian. Then if the unknown time of the first meridian, at which a phase of the eclipse has been observed, be $T+T'$, we have, denoting by x_0 and y_0 the values of x and y corresponding to the time T and by x' and y' the differential coefficients of x and y:

$$x=x_0+x'\,T' \text{ and } y=y_0+y'\,T'.$$

In the same way the quantities ξ, η and ζ will consist of two parts. But since these quantities change only slowly and an approximate value of the difference of longitude, and hence of the time of the first meridian corresponding to the time of observation is always known, we can assume, that these quantities are known for the time of observation.

Hence the equation is now:

$$[x_0-\xi+x'\,T'+\Delta x]^2+[y_0-\eta+y'\,T'+\Delta y]^2=(l+\Delta l-\lambda\zeta)^2.$$

If the changes of x and y were proportional to the time, x' and y' would be constant, and therefore it would not be necessary to know the time $T+T'$ for their computation. Now this is not the case, but since the variations of x' and y' are very small compared with those of x and y, we can solve the equation by successive approximations.

If we put:

$$x'\,i-y'\,i'=\Delta x$$
$$y'\,i+x'\,i'=\Delta y$$

and:

$$\left.\begin{array}{ll} m\sin M=x_0-\xi & n\sin N=x' \\ m\cos M=y_0-\eta & n\cos N=y' \\ \multicolumn{2}{c}{l-\lambda\zeta=L,} \end{array}\right\}\quad(G)$$

the above equation is transformed into:

$$(L+\Delta l)^2=[m\cos(M-N)+n\,(T'+i)]^2+[m\sin(M-N)-n\,i']^2,$$

and we obtain, neglecting the squares of i' and Δl, the following equation of the second degree for $T'+i$:

$$(T'+i)^2+\frac{2m}{n}\cos(M-N)(T'+i)=\frac{L^2-m^2\sin(M-N)^2}{n^2}-\frac{m^2\cos(M-N)^2}{n^2}$$
$$+\frac{2m}{n}\sin(M-N)\,i'+\frac{2L}{n^2}\Delta l.$$

*) Errors in a, d and λ are here neglected, since they cannot be determined by the observations of eclipses.

Now since:

$$\sqrt{(x+\Delta x)} = \sqrt{x} + \frac{\Delta x}{2\sqrt{x}},$$

putting:

$$L \sin \psi = m \sin (M - N), \qquad (H)$$

we find from this equation:

$$T' = -\frac{m}{n} \cos (M - N) \mp \frac{L \cos \psi}{n} - i \mp \operatorname{tang} \psi \, i' \mp \frac{\Delta l}{n} \sec \psi,$$

or except in case that ψ is very small:

$$T' = -\frac{m}{n} \cdot \frac{\sin (M - N \pm \psi)}{\sin \psi} - i \mp \operatorname{tang} \psi \, i' \mp \frac{\Delta l}{n} \sec \psi.$$

Now since T' for the beginning of the eclipse or any phase of it must have a less positive or greater negative value than for the end, the upper sign must be used for the beginning, the lower sign for the end of the eclipse or any phase, if we take the angle ψ always in the first or fourth quadrant *). But if we take ψ for the beginning of the eclipse or any phase in the first or fourth quadrant and for the end in the second or third quadrant, we have in both cases:

$$T' = -\frac{m \sin (M - N + \psi)}{n \sin \psi} - i - i' \operatorname{tang} \psi - \frac{\Delta l}{n} \sec \psi$$

or:

$$T' = -\frac{m}{n} \cos (M - N) - \frac{L \cos \psi}{n} - i - i' \operatorname{tang} \psi - \frac{\Delta l}{n} \sec \psi. \qquad (J)$$

The equation (J) is solved by successive approximations. For this purpose compute the values of x, y, z, a, d, g, l and λ by means of the formulae (A), (B), (C), (E) and (F) for several successive hours, so that the values x_0 and y_0 and their differential coefficients can be interpolated for any time. Then assume a value of T, as accurately as the approximately known value of the difference of longitude will permit, interpolate for this time the quantities x_0, y_0, x' and y' and find an approximate value of T' by means of the formulae (D), (G), (H) and (J). With the value $T + T'$ repeat, if necessary, the whole computation. If we denote again by T the value assumed in the last approximation and by T' the correction found last, we have $T + T' = t - d$, where t is the time of observation and d is the longitude of the place

*) We find this easily from the first expression for T'.

reckoned from the first meridian, that is, that meridian, for which the quantities x, y, z etc. have been computed, and taken positive when the place is east of the first meridian.

Hence we have:

$$d = t - T + \frac{m}{n}\cos(M - N) + \frac{L}{n}\cos\psi + i + i'\operatorname{tang}\psi + \frac{\Delta l}{n}\sec\psi$$
$$= t - T + \frac{m\sin(M - N + \psi)}{n\sin\psi} + i + i'\operatorname{tang}\psi + \frac{\Delta l}{n}\sec\psi. \qquad (K)$$

Since the values of x' and y' have one mean hour as the unit of time, it is assumed, that d in the above formula is referred to the same unit. Therefore if we wish to find the difference of longitude expressed in seconds of time, we must multiply the formula by the number s of seconds contained in one hour of that species of time, in which the observations are expressed. By this operation $t - T$ is also expressed in seconds of the same species of time, in which t is given or T is expressed in the same species of time as t.

Now the equation (K) does not give the longitude of the place of observation from the first meridian, but only a relation between this longitude and the errors of the several elements used for the reduction. But if the same eclipse has been observed at different places, we obtain for each place as many equations as phases of the ecliptic have been observed. By the combination of these equations we can eliminate, as will be shown hereafter, the errors of several of these elements and thus render the result as independent as possible of the errors of the tables.

It yet remains to develop the quantities i and i', determined by the equations:

$$x'i - y'i' = \Delta x$$
$$y'i + x'i' = \Delta y$$

or:

$$ni = \sin N\Delta x + \cos N\Delta y$$
$$ni' = \sin N\Delta y - \cos N\Delta x.$$

The quantities x and y depend upon $\alpha - a$, $\delta - d$ and π. Therefore if we suppose these quantities to be erroneous, we have:

$$\Delta x = A\Delta(\alpha - a) + B\Delta(\delta - d) + C\Delta\pi$$
$$\Delta y = A'\Delta(\alpha - a) + B'\Delta(\delta - d) + C'\Delta\pi,$$

where A, B, C are the differential coefficients of x with respect to $\alpha - a$, $\delta - d$ and π, and A', B', C' those of y with respect to the same quantities. Now since $\Delta(\alpha - a)$, $\Delta(\delta - d)$ and $\Delta\pi$ are always small quantities, we can neglect in the expressions for the differential coefficients the terms containing $\sin(\alpha - a)$ and $\sin(\delta - d)$ as factors, and can write 1 in place of $\cos(\alpha - a)$ and $\cos(\delta - d)$. Then we obtain:

$$A = \frac{\cos\delta}{\sin\pi}\cos(\alpha - a) = \frac{\cos\delta}{\sin\pi}$$

$$B = -\frac{\sin\delta\,\sin(\alpha - a)}{\sin\pi} = 0$$

$$C = -\frac{\cos\delta\sin(\alpha - a)\cos\pi}{\sin\pi^2} = \frac{x}{\operatorname{tang}\pi}$$

$$A' = +\frac{\cos\delta\sin d\sin(\alpha - a)}{\sin\pi} = 0$$

$$B' = \frac{\cos(\delta - d)}{\sin\pi} = \frac{1}{\sin\pi}$$

$$C' = -\frac{y}{\operatorname{tang}\pi}.$$

Now since i and i', and hence also $\Delta(\alpha - a)$, $\Delta(\delta - d)$ and $\Delta\pi$ are expressed in part of the radius, we must divide the differential coefficients by 206265, if we wish to find the errors of the elements in seconds. Therefore if we put:

$$\frac{s}{206265\,.\,n\sin\pi} = h,$$

we have:

$$i = h\sin N\cos\delta\,\Delta(\alpha - a) + h\cos N\Delta(\delta - d) - h\cos\pi\,\Delta\pi\,[x\sin N + y\cos N]$$

$$i' = -h\cos N\cos\delta\,\Delta(\alpha - a) + h\sin N\Delta(\delta - d) + h\cos\pi\,\Delta\pi\,[x\cos N - y\sin N],$$

or multiplying the upper equation by $\cos\psi$, the lower one by $\sin\psi$ and adding them:

$$[i + i'\operatorname{tang}\psi]\frac{\cos\psi}{h} = \sin(N - \psi)\cos\delta\,\Delta(\alpha - a) + \cos(N - \psi)\,\Delta(\delta - d)$$
$$- \cos\pi\,\Delta\pi\,[x\sin(N - \psi) + y\cos(N - \psi)].$$

From this we obtain:

$$d = t - T + \frac{m}{n}s\frac{\sin(M - N + \psi)}{\sin\psi} + h\frac{\sin(N - \psi)}{\cos\psi}\cos\delta\,\Delta(\alpha - a)$$
$$+ h\frac{\cos(N - \psi)}{\cos\psi}\Delta(\delta - d)$$
$$+ h\frac{1}{\cos\psi}\,206265\sin\pi\,\Delta l$$
$$- h\cos\pi\,\Delta\pi\left(\frac{x\sin(N - \psi) + y\cos(N - \psi)}{\cos\psi}\right)$$

or putting:

$$\begin{aligned}
\varepsilon &= \sin N \cos \delta \Delta (\alpha - a) + \cos N \Delta (\delta - d) \\
\zeta &= -\cos N \cos \delta \Delta (\alpha - a) + \sin N \Delta (\delta - d) \\
\eta &= 206265 \sin \pi \Delta l \qquad\qquad (L) \\
\Theta &= \cos \pi \Delta \pi \\
E &= \frac{x \sin (N - \psi) + y \cos (N - \psi)}{\cos \psi},
\end{aligned}$$

we finally have:

$$d = t - T + \frac{m}{n} \cdot s \frac{\sin (M - N + \psi)}{\sin \psi} + h\varepsilon + h\zeta \operatorname{tang}\psi + h\eta \sec\psi - hE\Theta. \quad (M)$$

Now the observation of every phase of an eclipse gives such an equation and since this contains five unknown quantities, five such equations will be sufficient to find them. However the quantities η and Θ cannot be determined in this way, unless the observations are made at places which are at a great distance from each other. Nevertheless the computation of the coefficients will show us the effect, which errors of π and l can have upon the result. Generally it will only be practicable to free the difference of longitude from the errors of ζ and ε, but the latter quantity can only be determined, if the longitude of one place from the first meridian is already known. When ε and ζ are known, the errors of the tables are obtained by means of the equations:

$$\begin{aligned}
\cos \delta \Delta (\alpha - a) &= \varepsilon \sin N - \zeta \cos N \\
\Delta (\delta - d) &= \varepsilon \cos N + \zeta \sin N.
\end{aligned}$$

If we collect all the formulae necessary for computing the difference of longitude from an eclipse of the sun, they are as follows:

$$\left.\begin{aligned}
a &= \alpha' - \frac{\sin \pi'}{\Delta' \sin \pi} \cdot \frac{\cos \delta}{\cos \delta'} (\alpha - \alpha') \\
d &= \delta' - \frac{\sin \pi'}{\Delta' \sin \pi} (\delta - \delta') \\
g &= 1 - \frac{\sin \pi'}{\Delta' \sin \pi},
\end{aligned}\right\} \quad (1)$$

where α, δ and π are the right ascension, declination and horizontal equatoreal parallax of the moon, α', δ', Δ' and π' the right ascension, declination, distance and mean horizontal equatoreal parallax of the sun.

$$\left.\begin{aligned} x &= \frac{\cos\delta\sin(\alpha - a)}{\sin\pi} \\ y &= \frac{\sin(\delta - d)\cos\tfrac{1}{2}(\alpha - a)^2 + \sin(\delta + d)\sin\tfrac{1}{2}(\alpha - a)^2}{\sin\pi} \\ z &= \frac{\cos(\delta - d)\cos\tfrac{1}{2}(\alpha - a)^2 - \cos(\delta + d)\sin\tfrac{1}{2}(\alpha - a)^2}{\sin\pi} \end{aligned}\right\} \quad (2)$$

$$\sin f = \frac{1}{\Delta'.g}[\sin h \mp k\sin\pi'], \quad (3)$$

where:

$$\log[\sin h + k\sin\pi'] = 7.6588041$$

for exterior contacts and

$$\log[\sin h - k\sin\pi'] = 7.6666903$$

for interior contacts.

$$c = z \pm \frac{k}{\sin f}, \quad (4)$$

where the upper sign is used for exterior contacts, the lower for interior contacts.

$$\begin{aligned} \operatorname{tang} f &= \lambda \\ l &= c\lambda, \end{aligned} \quad (5)$$

where λ has always the same sign as c.

$$\begin{aligned} \xi &= \varrho\cos\varphi'\sin(\Theta - a) \\ \eta &= \varrho[\cos d\sin\varphi' - \sin d\cos\varphi'\cos(\Theta - a)] \\ \zeta &= \varrho[\sin d\sin\varphi' + \cos d\cos\varphi'\cos(\Theta - a)], \end{aligned} \quad (6)$$

where φ' and ϱ are the geocentric latitude and the distance of the place from the centre and Θ is the observed sidereal time of a phase.

If then we have for the time T:

$$x = x_0 \qquad \frac{dx}{dt} = x'$$

$$y = y_0 \qquad \frac{dy}{dt} = y',$$

we compute:

$$\begin{aligned} m\sin M &= x_0 - \xi \qquad & n\sin N &= x' \\ m\cos M &= y_0 - \eta \qquad & n\cos N &= y' \end{aligned} \qquad l - \lambda\zeta = L \quad (7)$$

$$L\sin\psi = m\sin(M - N), \quad (8)$$

where for the beginning ψ must be taken in the first or fourth quadrant and for the end in the second or third quadrant, and:

$$T' = -s\frac{m}{n}\frac{\sin(M - N + \psi)}{\sin\psi} = -\frac{m}{n}\cos(M - N) - \frac{L\cos\psi}{n}. \quad (9)$$

Finally we have:

$$d = t - T - T' + h\varepsilon + h\zeta\operatorname{tang}\psi, \quad (10)$$

where:

$$h = \frac{s}{206265 . n \sin \pi},$$
$$\varepsilon = \sin N \cos \delta \Delta (\alpha - a) + \cos N \Delta (\delta - d),$$
$$\zeta = - \cos N \cos \delta \Delta (\alpha - a) + \sin N \Delta (\delta - d),$$

hence:

$$\cos \delta \Delta (\alpha - a) = \varepsilon \sin N - \zeta \cos N$$
$$\Delta (\delta - d) = \varepsilon \cos N + \zeta \sin N.$$

Example. In 1842 July 7 an eclipse of the sun occurred, which was observed at Vienna and Pulkova as follows:

Vienna:

Beginning of the total eclipse	$18^h 49^m 25^s.0$	Vienna mean time
End of the total eclipse	18 51 22 .0	" " "

Pulkova:

Beginning of the eclipse	$19^h 7^m 3^s.5$	Pulkova mean time
End of the eclipse	21 12 52 .0	" " "

According to the Berlin Jahrbuch we have the following places of the sun and the moon:

Berlin m. t.	α	δ	α'	δ'
17^h	105° 8′49″.93	+ 23° 22′10″.35	106° 50′38″.49	+ 22° 33′24″.46
18^h	47 43 .31	15 0 .34	53 12 .37	33 7 .93
19^h	106 26 34 .14	7 40 .45	55 46 .24	32 51 .36
20^h	107 5 22 .32	0 10 .75	58 20 .09	32 34 .75
21^h	44 7 .75	22 52 31 .29	107 0 53 .94	32 18 .09
22^h	108 22 50 .34	44 42 .13	3 27 .78	32 1 .40

	π	$\log \Delta'$
17^h	59′ 55″.06	0.0072061
18^h	56 .37	56
19^h	57 .65	51
20^h	58 .91	46
21^h	60 0 .14	41
22^h	1 .35	36.

If we compute first the quantities a, d and g by means of the formulae (1) we find:

	a	d	$\log g$
18^h	106° 53′ 21″.53	+ 22° 33′ 2″.04	9.9989808
19^h	55 50 .33	32 46 .47	11
20^h	58 19 .10	32 30 .87	15
21^h	107 0 47 .88	32 15 .25	19.

Then we find by means of the formulae (2), (3), (4) and (5):

	x	y	$\log z$
17^h	-1.5632144	$+0.8246864$	1.7585349
18^h	-1.0061154	$+0.7039354$	1.7584833
19^h	-0.4489341	$+0.5827957$	1.7583923
20^h	$+0.1082514$	$+0.4612784$	1.7582614
21^h	$+0.6653785$	$+0.3393985$	1.7580909
22^h	$+1.2224009$	$+0.2171603$	$1.7578799.$

	l		$\log \lambda$	
	Exterior contact.	Interior contact.	Exterior contact.	Interior contact.
17^h	0.5362314	0.0100548	7.6626222	7.6605084_n
18^h	0.5362001	0.0100860	23	85
19^h	0.5361450	0.0101409	25	87
20^h	0.5360655	0.0102198	26	88
21^h	0.5359622	0.0103227	27	89
22^h	0.5358345	0.0104499	29	91.

Now the time of the beginning of the total eclipse was observed at Vienna at:

$$18^h\, 49^m\, 25^s.0,$$

or at the sidereal time:

$$\Theta = 1^h\, 52^m\, 29^s.8 = 28^\circ\, 7'\, 27''.0;$$

Further we have:

$$\varphi = 48^\circ\, 12'\, 35''.5,$$

hence the geocentric latitude:

$$\varphi' = 48^\circ\, 1'\, 8''.9$$

and:

$$\log \varrho = 9.9991952.$$

If we take $T = 18^h\, 30^m$, we find for this time:

$$x_0 = -0.727530 \qquad y_0 = +0.643413,$$

and by means of the formulae (6):

$$\xi = -0.654897 \qquad \eta = +0.635482 \qquad \log \zeta = 9.606857;$$

moreover by means of the formulae in No. 15 of the introduction:

$$x' = +0.557185 \qquad y' = -0.121140,$$

hence by means of the formulae (7), (8) and (9):

$$M = 276^\circ\, 13'\, 54'' \qquad \log m = 8.863708$$
$$N = 102\;\; 15\;\; 58 \qquad \log n = 9.756030 \qquad \log L = 8.077778$$
$$\psi = 39^\circ\, 57'\, 10''$$
$$T' = -6^m\, 40^s.85.$$

Since in this case it is not necessary to repeat the computation, we obtain by means of the formula (10):

$$d = +0^h\, 12^m\, 44^s.15 + 1.7553\, \varepsilon + 1.4703\, \zeta.$$

In the same way we find from the observation of the end of the total eclipse, if we retain the same value of T:

$$\xi = -0.653763 \qquad \eta = +0.633338 \qquad \log \zeta = 9.612367$$
$$M = 277^\circ\, 46'\, 40'' \qquad \log m = 8.871874 \qquad \log L = 8.078638$$
$$\psi = 150^\circ\, 54'\, 51''.5$$
$$T' = -8^m\, 54^s.74,$$

hence:

$$d = +0^h\, 12^m\, 27^s.26 + 1.7553\, \varepsilon - 0.9764\, \zeta.$$

Likewise from the observations at Pulkova, since:

$$\varphi = 59^\circ\, 46'\, 18''.6,$$

and hence:

$$\varphi' = 59^\circ\, 36'\, 16''.8$$

and:

$$\log \varrho = 9.9989172$$

we find the following equations:

$$d' = 1^h\, 8^m\, 26^s.57 + 1.7559\, \varepsilon + 0.5064\, \zeta,$$
$$d' = 1 \;\; 8 \;\; 22\;.67 + 1.7541\, \varepsilon - 0.3034\, \zeta.$$

We have therefore:

$$d' - d = +55^m\, 42^s.42 - 0.9639\, \zeta,$$
$$d' - d = +55 \;\; 55\;.41 + 0.6730\, \zeta,$$

hence:

$$d' - d = +55^m\, 50^s.07$$

and:

$$\zeta = -7''.94.$$

In order to find the error ε, we must assume the longitude of one place reckoned from the meridian of Berlin as known. But the difference of longitude of Vienna and Berlin is:

$$+0^h\, 11^m\, 56^s.40$$

and with this we obtain from the first equation for d:

$$\varepsilon = -20''.55.$$

Since we have:

$$\cos \delta\, \Delta(\alpha - a) = \varepsilon \sin N - \zeta \cos N$$
$$\Delta(\delta - d) = \varepsilon \cos N + \zeta \sin N,$$

we find:

$$\cos d\, \Delta(\alpha - a) = -21''.78$$

and:

$$\Delta(\delta - d) = -3''.38.$$

30. In the case of occultations of stars by the moon the formulae become more simple. Since then $\pi' = 0$, we have $a = \alpha'$, $d = \delta'$. Hence we need not compute the formulae (1), and the co-ordinates of the place of observation are independent of the place of the moon, since we have simply:

$$\xi = \varrho \cos \varphi' \sin (\Theta - \alpha')$$
$$\eta = \varrho [\sin \varphi' \cos \delta' - \cos \varphi' \sin \delta' \cos (\Theta - \alpha')].$$

The third co-ordinate ζ is also not used, since we have in this case $f = 0$ and hence $\lambda = 0$, so that we have instead of the enveloping cone a cylinder. The radius l of the circle, in which the plane of the co-ordinates intersects this cylinder, is equal to the semi-diameter of the moon or equal to k. Hence we need not compute the co-ordinate z and we have simply:

$$x = \frac{\cos \delta \sin (\alpha - \alpha')}{\sin \pi}$$
$$y = \frac{\sin \delta \cos \delta' - \cos \delta \sin \delta' \cos (\alpha - \alpha')}{\sin \pi}.$$

Thus the fundamental equation for eclipses is transformed into the following:

$$(k + \Delta k)^2 = (x + \Delta x - \xi)^2 + (y + \Delta y - \eta)^2,$$

which is solved in the same way as before. Taking again $t - d = T + T'$ and denoting by x_0 and y_0 the values of x and y for the time T, by x' and y' their differential coefficients, we must compute the auxiliary quantities:

$$m \sin M = x_0 - \xi \qquad n \sin N = x'$$
$$m \cos M = y_0 - \eta \qquad n \cos N = y'$$
$$k \sin \psi = m \sin (M - N)$$

and we find:

$$d = t - T + \frac{m}{n} s \frac{\sin (M - N + \psi)}{\sin \psi} + h \varepsilon + h \zeta \operatorname{tang} \psi,$$

where h, ε and ζ have the same signification as before.

Example. In 1849 Nov. 29 the immersion and emersion of α Tauri was observed at Bilk as follows:

Immersion $8^h\,15^m\,12^s.1$ Bilk mean time
Emersion $9\;\;18\;\;19.8.$

The immersion of the same star was observed at Hamburg at

$8^h\,33^m\,47^s.2$ Hamburg mean time.

The place of the star on that day was according to the Nautical Almanac:

$$\alpha' = 4^h\,11^m\,16^s.24 = 62^\circ\,49'\,3''.6$$
$$\delta' = +15^\circ\,15'\,32''.2.$$

Further we have for Bilk:

$$\varphi' = 51^\circ\ 1'\ 10''.0$$
$$\log \varrho = 9.9991201$$

and for Hamburg:

$$\varphi' = 53^\circ\ 22'\ 4''.2$$
$$\log \varrho = 9.9990624.$$

Finally we have the following places of the moon according to the Nautical Almanac:

	α	δ	π
7^h	$4^h\ 6^m\ 2^s.35$	$+15^\circ\ 47'\ 24''.6$	$60'\ 50''.8$
8^h	$4\ \ 8\ 35\ .69$	$15\ 54\ 48\ .8$	$60\ 51\ .8$
9^h	$4\ 11\ \ 9\ .31$	$16\ \ 2\ \ 6\ .5$	$60\ 52\ .9.$

Hence we find for those three times:

	x	I. Diff.	y	I. Diff.
7^h	-1.240980		$+0.527577$	
		$+0.606752$		$+0.118741$
8^h	-0.634228		$+0.646318$	
		$+0.606864$		$+0.118656.$
9^h	-0.027364		$+0.764974$	

Now we have for the time of the immersion at Bilk:

$$\Theta = 0^h\ 49^m\ 29^s.93$$
$$\Theta - \alpha' = -50^\circ\ 26'\ 34''.6$$

hence:

$$\xi = -0.484015 \text{ and } \eta = +0.643216.$$

Taking then $T = 7^h\ 50^m$, we obtain for this time:

$$x_0 - \xi = -0.251346 \qquad y_0 - \eta = -0.016682$$
$$x' = +0.606789 \qquad y' = +0.118713,$$

hence:

$$M = 266^\circ\ 12'\ 10'' \qquad N = +78^\circ\ 55'\ 50''$$
$$\log m = 9.401226 \qquad \log n = 9.791194$$
$$\psi = -6^\circ\ 43'\ 11''$$
$$T' = +2^m\ 0^s.85.$$

We find therefore from the immersion observed at Bilk the following equation between the difference of longitude from Greenwich and the errors ε and ζ:

$$d = +27^m\ 12^s.95 + 1.5945\,\varepsilon - 0.1879\,\zeta,$$

and in the same way we find from the emersion observed at Bilk: $d = +27^m\ 27^s.10 + 1.5937\,\varepsilon + 0.5336\,\zeta,$

and from the emersion observed at Hamburg:

$$d' = +40^m\ 3^s.76 + 1.5945\,\varepsilon - 0.1362\,\zeta.$$

We have therefore the two equations:

$$d' - d = +12^m\ 50^s.81 + 0.0517\,\zeta,$$
$$d' - d = +12\ \ 36\ .66 - 0.6698\,\zeta,$$

whence we find:

$$d' - d = +12^m\ 49^s.80 \text{ and } \zeta = -19''.61.$$

31. The fundamental equations for eclipses and occultations given in No. 29 and 30 serve also for calculating the time of their occurrence for any place. If we take for T a certain time of the first meridian near the middle of the eclipse, and compute for this time the quantities x_0, y_0, x', y' and L, the fundamental equation for eclipses is:

$$[x_0 + x' T' - \xi]^2 + [y_0 + y' T' - \eta]^2 = L^2 \text{ *)},$$

where ξ and η are the co-ordinates of the place on the earth at the time $T + T'$. Therefore if we denote by Θ_0 the sidereal time corresponding to the time T, $\Theta_0 + d_0$ will be the local sidereal time of the place, for which we calculate the eclipse, and if we denote by ξ_0 and η_0 the values of ξ and η corresponding to the time $\Theta_0 + d_0$, we have:

$$\xi = \xi_0 + \varrho \cos \varphi' \cos(\Theta_0 - a + d_0) \frac{d(\Theta - a)}{dT} . T'$$

$$\eta = \eta_0 + \varrho \cos \varphi' \sin(\Theta_0 - a + d_0) \frac{d(\Theta - a)}{dT} . T' . \sin d.$$

Therefore taking now:

$$m \sin M = x_0 - \xi_0, \quad n \sin N = x' - \varrho \cos \varphi' \cos(\Theta_0 - a + d_0) \frac{d(\Theta - a)}{dT}$$

$$m \cos M = y_0 - \eta_0, \quad n \cos N = y' - \varrho \cos \varphi' \sin(\Theta_0 - a + d_0) \frac{d(\Theta - a)}{dT} \sin d$$

$$\sin \psi = \frac{m}{L_0} \sin(M - N),$$

where L_0 denotes the value of L corresponding to the time T, we find:

$$T' = -\frac{m}{n} \cos(M - N) \mp \frac{L_0}{n} \cos \psi = t - T - d,$$

where ψ must be taken in the first or fourth quadrant, and the upper sign is used for the beginning, the lower for the end of the eclipse, or if we take:

$$-\frac{m}{n} \cos(M - N) - \frac{L_0}{n} \cos \psi = \tau$$

$$-\frac{m}{n} \cos(M - N) + \frac{L_0}{n} \cos \psi = \tau'$$

the time of the beginning expressed in local mean time is:

$$t = T + d + \tau,$$

and the time of the end:

$$t' = T + d + \tau'.$$

*) For an occultation we have $L = k = 0.2725$.

By the first approximation we find the time of the eclipse within a couple of minutes, therefore already sufficiently accurate for the convenience of observers. But if we wish to find it more accurately, we must repeat the calculation, using now $T+\tau$ and $T+\tau'$ instead of T.

It is also convenient to know the particular points on the limb of the sun (or the moon in case of an occultation), where the contacts take place. But if we substitute in

$$x_0 - \xi + x T' \text{ and } y_0 - \eta + y' T'$$

for T' the value:

$$-\frac{m}{n} \cos (M - N) \mp \frac{L}{n} \cos \psi,$$

we find:

$$x - \xi = [m \sin M \cos N \cos N \sin \psi - m \cos M \cos N \sin N \sin \psi$$
$$\mp m \sin M \cos N \sin N \cos \psi \pm m \cos M \sin N \sin N \cos \psi] \frac{1}{\sin \psi},$$

or:

$$x - \xi = \mp \frac{m \sin (M - N)}{\sin \psi} \sin (N \mp \psi)$$
$$= \mp L \sin (N \mp \psi)$$

and likewise:

$$y - \eta = \mp L \cos (N \mp \psi).$$

Hence we have for the beginning of the eclipse:

$$x - \xi = - L \sin (N - \psi) = L \sin (N + 180^\circ - \psi)$$
$$y - \eta = - L \cos (N - \psi) = L \cos (N + 180^\circ - \psi),$$

and for the end:

$$x - \xi = L \sin (N + \psi)$$
$$y - \eta = L \cos (N + \psi).$$

Now we have seen in No. 29 that $\xi - x$ and $\eta - y$ are the co-ordinates of a place on the earth situated in the enveloping surface of the cone and referred to a system of axes, in which the axis of z is the line joining the centres of the two heavenly bodies, whilst the axis of x is parallel to the equator; hence $x - \xi$ and $y - \eta$ are the co-ordinates of that point, which lies in the straight line drawn from the place on the earth to the point of contact of the two bodies, and whose distance from the vertex of the cone is equal to that of the latter point from the place on the surface of the earth. Hence $\frac{x - \xi}{L}$ and $\frac{y - \eta}{L}$ are the sine and cosine of the angle, which the axis of y or the declination circle passing through the point Z *) makes with the line drawn from Z to the point of contact. But since this point is always very near the centre of the sun, we can assume without any appreciable error, that $\frac{x-\xi}{L}$ and $\frac{y-\eta}{L}$ are the sine and the cosine of the angle, which the declination circle passing through the centre of the sun makes with the line from the centre of the sun to the point of contact. Thus this angle is for the beginning of the eclipse or any phase of the eclipse:

$$\left.\begin{array}{l} N+180^0-\psi \\ N+\psi. \end{array}\right\} \quad (A)$$

and for the end:

Therefore the formulae serving for calculating an eclipse are as follows. We first compute for the time T of the first meridian to which the tables or ephemerides of the sun and the moon are referred (for which we take best a round hour near the middle of the eclipse) the formulae (1), (2), (3), (4) and (5) in No. 29 and the differential coefficients x' and y', and then denoting by Θ_0 the sidereal time corresponding to the mean time T and by d_0 the longitude of the place reckoned from the first meridian and taken positive when east, we compute the formulae:

$$\xi_0 = \varrho \cos\varphi' \sin(\Theta_0 + d_0 - a)$$
$$\eta_0 = \varrho [\cos d \sin\varphi' - \sin d \cos\varphi' \cos(\Theta_0 + d_0 - a)]$$
$$\zeta_0 = \varrho [\sin d \sin\varphi' + \cos d \cos\varphi' \cos(\Theta_0 + d_0 - a)].$$

Computing then the formulae:

$$m \sin M = x_0 - \xi_0, \quad n \sin N = x' - \varrho\cos\varphi' \cos(\Theta_0 + d_0 - a)\frac{d(\Theta_0 - a)}{dt}$$

$$m \cos M = y_0 - \eta_0, \quad n \cos N = y' - \varrho\cos\varphi' \sin(\Theta_0 + d_0 - a)\frac{d(\Theta_0 - a)}{dt} \sin d$$

$$L_0 = l_0 - \lambda\zeta_0$$

$$\sin\psi = \frac{m}{L_0}\sin(M-N) \; (\psi \text{ always } < \pm 90^0)$$

$$\tau = -\frac{m}{n}\cos(M-N) - \frac{L_0}{n}\cos\psi$$

$$\tau' = -\frac{m}{n}\cos(M-N) + \frac{L_0}{n}\cos\psi,$$

---

*) The point Z is that point, in which the axis of z or the line joining the centres of the two bodies intersects the sphere of the heavens.

we find the time of the beginning expressed in local mean time:

$$t = T + d_0 + \tau,$$

and the time of the end:

$$t = T + d_0 + \tau'.$$

The expressions (A) give then the particular points on the limb of the sun, where the contact takes place.

For calculating an occultation the formulae are as follows. We compute again for the time T of the first meridian, which is near the middle of the occultation:

$$x_0 = \frac{\cos\delta \sin(\alpha - \alpha')}{\sin\pi}$$

$$y_0 = \frac{\sin\delta \cos\delta' - \cos\delta \sin\delta' \cos(\alpha - \alpha')}{\sin\pi}$$

and the differential coefficients x' and y'. Further we compute, denoting by Θ_0 the sidereal time corresponding to the mean time T:

$$\xi_0 = \varrho \cos\varphi' \sin(\Theta - \alpha' + d_0)$$
$$\eta_0 = \varrho [\sin\varphi' \cos\delta' - \cos\varphi' \sin\delta' \cos(\Theta - \alpha' + d_0)].$$

Then we compute:

$$m \sin M = x_0 - \xi_0, \quad n \sin N = x' - \varrho \cos\varphi' \cos(\Theta_0 + d_0 - \alpha') \frac{d\Theta}{dt}$$

$$m \cos M = y_0 - \eta_0, \quad n \cos N = y' - \varrho \cos\varphi' \sin(\Theta_0 + d_0 - \alpha') \frac{d\Theta}{dt} \sin\delta',$$

where:

$$\log \frac{d\Theta}{dt} = 9.41916\text{ *)}$$

$$\sin\psi = \frac{m}{k} \sin(M - N), \quad \psi < \pm 90^\circ,$$

and:

$$\log k = 9.43537$$

$$-\frac{m}{n} \cos(M - N) - \frac{k}{n} \cos\psi = \tau$$

$$-\frac{m}{n} \cos(M - N) + \frac{k}{n} \cos\psi = \tau'.$$

---

*) As one hour is taken as the unit of the differential coefficients, $\frac{d\Theta}{dt}$ is the change of the hour angle in one mean hour or in $3609^s.86$ of sidereal time. If we multiply by 15 and divide by 206265 in order to express the differential coefficient in parts of the radius, we find:

$$\log \frac{d\Theta}{dt} = 9.41916.$$

Then the immersion takes place at the local mean time:

$$t = T + \tau + d_0$$

and the emersion at the time:

$$t' = T + \tau' + d_0.$$

The angle of position of the particular point on the limb, where the immersion takes place, is found from:

$$Q = N + 180^\circ - \psi$$

whilst for the emersion we have:

$$Q' = N + \psi.$$

Example. If we wish to calculate the time of the beginning and end of the eclipse of the sun in 1842 July 7 for Pulkova, we take $T = 19^h$ Berlin mean time. For this time we have according to No. 29:

$$x_0 = -0.44893,\ y_0 = +0.58280,\ x' = +0.55718,\ y' = -0.12133$$
$$a = 106^\circ\ 55'.8,\ \ d = +22^\circ\ 32'.8,\ l = 0.53614,\ \ \log\lambda = 7.66262.$$

Then we have:

$$\Theta_0 = 2^h\ 3^m\ 8^s,$$

and since the difference of longitude between Pulkova and Berlin is equal to $+1^h\ 7^m\ 43^s$, we get:

$$\Theta_0 + d - a = 300^\circ\ 46'.9,$$

and with this:

$$\xi_0 = -0.43361,\ \eta_0 = +0.69560,\ \log\zeta_0 = 9.75470,\ \log L_0 = 9.72716.$$

Further we find:

$$\frac{d\xi_0}{dt} = \varrho\cos\varphi'\cos(\Theta_0 + d_0 - a)\frac{d(\Theta_0 - a)}{dt} = +0.06762\ ^{*})$$
$$\frac{d\eta_0}{dt} = \varrho\cos\varphi'\sin(\Theta_0 + d_0 - a)\frac{d(\Theta_0 - a)}{dt}\sin d = -0.04352,$$

hence:

$$x' - \frac{d\xi_0}{dt} = +0.48956 \text{ and } y' - \frac{d\eta_0}{dt} = -0.07781.$$

---

*) We have:

$$\frac{d\Theta_0}{dt} = 3609^s.86$$

or:

$$= +57147''.90;$$

Further we have:

$$\frac{da}{dt} = +148''.78$$

hence:

$$\frac{d(\Theta_0 - a)}{dt} = 56999''.12,$$

the logarithm of which number expressed in parts of the radius is 9.41796.

Then we get:

$$M = 187^\circ\,44'.1 \qquad N = 99^\circ\,1'.9$$
$$\log m = 9.05628 \qquad \log n = 9.69522$$
$$\psi = 12^\circ\,19'.0$$

hence:

$$\tau = -1.057 \qquad \tau' = 1.046$$
$$= -1^h\,3^m.4 \qquad = +1^h\,2^m.8,$$

therefore the beginning and the end of the eclipse occur at the times:

$$t = 19^h\,4^m.3$$
$$t' = 21^h\,10^m.5.$$

These times differ only 3^m from the true times. If we repeat the calculation, using $T = 18^h$ and $T = 20^h$, we should find the time still more accurately.

The angle of position of the point on the limb of the sun, where the eclipse begins, is 267° and that of the point, where it ends, is 111° *).

32. Another method for finding the longitude is that by lunar distances, and since this can be used at any time, whenever the moon is above the horizon, it is one of the chief methods of finding the longitude at sea.

For this purpose the geocentric distances of the moon from the sun and the brightest planets and fixed stars are given in the Nautical Almanacs for every third hour of a first meridian. If now at any place the distance of the moon from one of these stars or planets has been measured, it is freed from refraction and parallax, in order to get the true distance, which would have been observed at the centre of the earth. If then the time of the first meridian, to which the same computed distance belongs, is taken from the Almanac, this time compared with the local time of observation gives the difference of longitude. But since it is assumed here, that the tables of the moon give its true place, this method does not afford the same accuracy as that obtained by corresponding observations of eclipses. Besides the

*) Compare on the calculation of eclipses: Bessel, Ueber die Berechnung der Länge aus Sternbedeckungen. Astr. Nachr. No. 151 and 152, translated in the Philosophical Magazine Vol. VIII and Bessel's Astronomische Untersuchungen Bd. II pag. 95 etc. W. S. B. Woolhouse, On Eclipses.

time of the beginning and end of an eclipse of the sun can be observed with greater accuracy than a lunar distance.

In order to compute the refraction and the parallax of the two heavenly bodies, their altitudes must be known. Therefore at sea, a little before and after the lunar distance has been taken, the altitudes of both the moon and the star are taken, and since their change during a short time can be supposed to be proportional to the time, the apparent altitudes for the time of observation are easily found and from these the true altitudes are deduced.

A greater accuracy is obtained by computing the true and the apparent altitudes of the two bodies. For this purpose the longitude of the place, reckoned from the first meridian, must be approximately known, and then for the approximate time of the first meridian, corresponding to the time of observation, the places of the moon and the other body are taken from the ephemerides. Then the true altitudes are computed by means of the formulae in No. 7 of the first section, and, if the spheroidal shape of the earth be taken into account, also the azimuths. The parallax in altitude is then computed by means of the formulae in No. 3 of the third section, the formulae used for the moon being the rigorous formulae:

$$\frac{\Delta'}{\Delta}\sin p' = \varrho \sin p \sin[z - (\varphi - \varphi')\cos A]$$

$$\frac{\Delta'}{\Delta}\cos p' = 1 - \varrho \sin p \cos[z - (\varphi - \varphi')\cos A],$$

and finally for the altitudes affected with parallax the refraction is found with regard to the indications of the meteorological instruments. But since the apparent altitude, affected with parallax and refraction, ought to be used for computing the refraction, this computation must be repeated.

The distance of the centres of the two bodies is never observed, but only the distance of their limbs. Hence we add to or subtract from the observed distance the sum of the apparent semi-diameters of the two bodies, accordingly as the contact of the limbs nearest each other or that of the other limbs has been observed. If r be the horizontal semi-diameter of the moon, the semi-diameter affected with parallax will be:

$$r' = r\,[1 + p \sin h],$$

where p is the horizontal parallax expressed in parts of the radius.

Now since refraction diminishes the vertical semi-diameter of the disc, while it leaves the horizontal semi-diameter unchanged, that in the direction of the measured distance will be the radius vector of an ellipse, whose major and minor axis are the horizontal and the vertical diameter. The effect of refraction on the vertical diameter can be computed by means of the formulae given in VIII of the seventh section, or it can be taken from tables which are given in all Nautical works. If we denote by π the angle, which the vertical circle passing through the centre of the moon makes with the direction towards the other body, by h' the altitude of the latter and by Δ the distance between the two bodies, we have:

$$\sin \pi = \frac{\sin (A' - A) \cos h'}{\sin \Delta}$$

and:

$$\cos \pi = \frac{\sin h' - \cos \Delta \sin h}{\sin \Delta \cos h},$$

hence:

$$\operatorname{tang} \tfrac{1}{2} \pi^2 = \frac{\cos \frac{1}{2} (\Delta + h + h') \sin \frac{1}{2} (\Delta + h - h')}{\sin \frac{1}{2} (\Delta + h' - h) \cos \frac{1}{2} (h + h' - \Delta)}.$$

Then if we denote the vertical and the horizontal semi-diameter by b and a, we find by means of the equation of the ellipse:

$$r = \frac{b}{\sqrt{\cos \pi^2 + \frac{b^2}{a^2} \sin \pi^2}}.$$

After the apparent distance of the centres of the bodies has thus been found, the true geocentric distance is obtained by means of the apparent and true altitudes of the two bodies. For if we denote by H', h' and Δ' the apparent altitudes and the apparent distance of the two bodies and by E the difference of their azimuths, we have in the triangle between the zenith and the apparent places of the two bodies:

$$\begin{aligned}\cos \Delta' &= \sin H' \sin h' + \cos H' \cos h' \cos E \\ &= \cos (H' - h') - 2 \cos H' \cos h' \sin \tfrac{1}{2} E^2.\end{aligned}$$

Likewise we have, denoting by H, h and Δ their true altitudes and the true distance:

$$\cos\Delta = \sin H \sin h + \cos H \cos h \cos E$$
$$= \cos(H - h) - 2\cos H \cos h \sin\tfrac{1}{2}E^2,$$

and if we eliminate $2\sin\frac{1}{2}E^2$ we find:

$$\cos\Delta = \cos(H-h) + \frac{\cos H \cos h}{\cos H' \cos h'}[\cos\Delta' - \cos(H'-h')] \qquad (a)$$

If we take now:

$$\frac{\cos H \cos h}{\cos H' \cos h'} = \frac{1}{C}, \qquad (A)$$

we shall have always $C > 1$, except when the altitude of the moon is great and the other body is very near the horizon. If we then take:

$$H' - h' = d' \text{ and } H - h = d \qquad (B)$$

and take d' and d positive, we can always put:

$$\frac{\cos d'}{C} = \cos d'' \text{ and } \frac{\cos\Delta'}{C} = \cos\Delta'' \qquad (C)$$

because in case that $C < 1$, both $\cos d'$ and $\cos\Delta'$ are small. Thus the equation (a) is transformed into:

$$\cos\Delta - \cos\Delta'' = \cos d - \cos d''$$

or if we introduce the sines of half the sum and half the difference of the angles and write instead of $\sin(\Delta - \Delta'')$ the arc itself:

$$\Delta - \Delta'' = (d - d'')\frac{\sin\frac{1}{2}(d + d'')}{\sin\frac{1}{2}(\Delta + \Delta'')}.$$

If we take here at first $\sin\frac{1}{2}(\Delta' + \Delta'')$ instead of $\sin\frac{1}{2}(\Delta + \Delta'')$ and put:

$$x = (d - d'')\frac{\sin\frac{1}{2}(d + d'')}{\sin\frac{1}{2}(\Delta' + \Delta'')} \qquad (D)$$

we obtain:

$$\Delta = \Delta'' + x, \qquad (E)$$

a value which is only approximately true, but in most cases sufficiently accurate. If Δ should differ considerably from Δ', we must repeat the computation and find a new value of x by means of the formula:

$$x = (d - d'')\frac{\sin\frac{1}{2}(d + d'')}{\sin\frac{1}{2}(\Delta + \Delta'')} \text{ *)}.$$

We have assumed here that the angle E as seen from the centre of the earth is the same as seen from a place on the surface. But we have found in No. 3 of the third section,

---

*) Bremicker, über die Reduction der Monddistanzen. Astronomische Nachrichten No. 716.

that parallax changes also the azimuth of the moon and that, if we denote by A and H the true azimuth and altitude, we have to add to the geocentric azimuth the angle:

$$\Delta A = + \frac{\varrho \sin p\, (\varphi - \varphi') \sin A}{\cos H}$$

in order to find the azimuth as seen from a place on the surface of the earth. Therefore in the formula for $\cos \Delta$ we ought to use $\cos (E - \Delta A)$ instead of $\cos E = \cos (A - a)$, or we ought to add to Δ the correction:

$$d\Delta = - \frac{\cos H \cos h \sin (A - a)}{\sin \Delta} dA$$

or:

$$d\Delta = - \frac{\varrho \sin p\, (\varphi - \varphi') \cos h \sin A \sin (A - a)}{\sin \Delta}.$$

Example. In 1831 June 2 at $23^h\, 8^m\, 45^s$ apparent time the distance of the nearest limbs of the sun and the moon was observed $\Delta' = 96^\circ\, 47'\, 10''$ at a place, whose north latitude was $19^\circ\, 31'$, while the longitude from Greenwich was estimated at $8^h\, 50^m$. The height of the barometer was 29.6 English inches, the height of the interior thermometer 88° Fahrenheit, that of the exterior 90° Fahrenheit.

According to the Nautical Almanac the places of the sun and the moon were as follows:

Greenwich	m. t.	right asc. ☾	decl. ☾	parallax
June 2	12^h	$336^\circ\ 6'\ 24''.0$	$-10^\circ\ 50'\ 58''.0$	$56'\ 44''.0$
	13^h	38 4.7	41 48.4	45.9
	14^h	337 9 45.7	32 35.0	47.9
	15^h	41 27.0	23 17.9	49.9

		right asc. ☉	decl. ☉
June 2	12^h	$70^\circ\ 5'\ 23''.2$	$+22^\circ\ 11'\ 48''.9$
	13^h	7 56.9	12 8.4
	14^h	10 30.5	12 27.9
	15^h	13 4.1	12 47.3

The time of observation corresponds to $14^h\, 18^m\, 45^s$ Greenwich time and for this time we have:

right asc. ☾ =	$337^\circ\ 19'\ 39''.6$	right asc. ☉ =	$70^\circ\ 11'\ 18''.5$
decl. ☾ =	$-10\ \ 29\ \ 41.3$	decl. ☉ =	$+22\ \ 12\ \ 33.9$
$P =$	$56\ \ 48.5$	$\pi =$	$8''.5.$

From this we find the true altitude and azimuth of the moon and the sun for the hour angles:

$$+ 80^\circ\ 2'\ 53''.8$$

and: $-12^{\circ}\,48'\,45''.0$:

$$H = 5^{\circ}\,41'\,58''.4 \qquad h = 77^{\circ}\,43'\,56''.7$$
$$A = +76^{\circ}\,43'.6 \qquad a = -75^{\circ}\,4'.4.$$

The parallax of the moon computed by means of the rigorous formula:

$$\text{tang}\, p' = \frac{\varrho \sin p \sin [z - (\varphi - \varphi') \cos A]}{1 - \varrho \sin p \cos [z - (\varphi - \varphi') \cos A]}$$

is $p' = 56'35''.4$, hence the apparent altitude H' of the moon is $4^{\circ}\,45'\,23''.0$. In order to find the refraction, we first find an approximate value for it, and applying it to H', we repeat the computation of the refraction with regard to the indications of the meteorological instruments. We then find $\varrho = 9'\,3''.2$ and hence the apparent altitude affected with refraction:

$$H' = 4^{\circ}\,54'\,26''.2.$$

For the sun we find in the same way:

$$h' = 77^{\circ}\,44'\,6''.5.$$

Further we find the semi-diameter of the moon by multiplying the horizontal parallax by 0.2725 and obtain:

$$r = 15'\,28''.8$$

and from this the apparent semi-diameter, as increased by parallax:

$$r' = 15'\,30''.1.$$

The vertical semi-diameter is diminished 26''.0 by the refraction, and the angle π being $5^{\circ}\,48'$, the radius of the moon in the direction towards the sun is:

$$r' = 15'\,4''.6,$$

and since the semi-diameter of the sun was $15'\,47''.0$, the apparent distance of the centres of the sun and the moon is:

$$\Delta' = 97^{\circ}\,18'\,1''.6.$$

Further we find by means of the formulae (*A*), (*B*) and (*C*):

$$\log C = 0.000463$$
$$d = 72^{\circ}\ \ 1'\,58''$$
$$d' = 72\ \ 49\ \ 40$$
$$d'' = 72\ \ 50\ \ 48$$
$$\Delta'' = 97\ \ 17\ \ 33$$

and at last, computing x twice by means of the formulae (*D*) and (*E*), we find the true distance of the centres of the sun and the moon:

$$\Delta = 96^{\circ}\,30'\,39''.$$

Now we find according to the Almanac the true distance of the centres of the bodies for Greenwich apparent time from the following table:

12^h	$97^0\,43'\,0''.4$
13^h	$13\;\;4\;.5$
14^h	$96\;\;43\;\;6\;.5$
15^h	$13\;\;6\;.2,$

whence we see, that the distance $96^0\,30'\,39''$ corresponds to the Greenwich apparent time $14^h\,24^m\,55^s.2$, and since the time of observation was $23^h\,8^m\,45^s.0$, the longitude of the place is:

$8^h\,43^m\,49^s.8$ east of Greenwich.

The longitude which we find here is so nearly equal to that, which was assumed, that the error which we made in computing the place of the sun and moon can only be small. If the difference had been considerable, it would have been necessary to repeat the calculation with the places of the sun and moon, interpolated for $14^h\,24^m\,55^s$ Greenwich time.

Bessel has given in the Astronomische Nachrichten No. 220 another method *), by which the longitude can be found with great accuracy by lunar distances. But the method given above or a similar one is always used at sea, and on land better methods can be employed for finding the longitude.

33. An excellent way of finding the longitude is that by lunar culminations. On account of the rapid motion of the moon the sidereal time at the time of its culmination is very different for different places. Hence if it is known, how much the right ascension of the moon changes in a certain time, the longitude can be determined by observing the difference of the sidereal times at the time of culmination of the moon. Since these observations are made on the meridian, neither the parallax nor the refraction will have any influence on the result. In order to render it also independent of the errors of the instruments, the time of culmination of the moon itself is not observed at the two stations, but rather the interval of time between the time of culmination of the moon and that of some fixed stars near her parallel.

---

*) The example given above is taken from this paper.

A list of such stars is always published in the astronomical almanacs, in order that the observers may select the same stars.

The method was proposed already in the last century by Pigott, but was formerly not much used, because the art of observing had not reached that high degree of accuracy which is required for obtaining a good result.

Let α be the right ascension of the moon for the time T of a certain first meridian, and the differential coefficients for the same time be $\frac{d\alpha}{dt}$, $\frac{d^2\alpha}{dt^2}$, etc. We will then suppose, that at a place whose longitude east of the first meridian is d, the time of culmination of the moon was observed at the local time $T+t+d$, corresponding to the time $T+t$ of the first meridian. Then the right ascension of the moon at this time is:

$$\alpha + t \cdot \frac{d\alpha}{dt} + \tfrac{1}{2} t^2 \frac{d^2\alpha}{dt^2} + \tfrac{1}{6} t^3 \frac{d^3\alpha}{dt^3} + \ldots$$

If likewise at another place, whose longitude east from the first meridian is d', the time of culmination of the moon was observed at the time $T+t'+d'$, corresponding to the time $T+t'$ of the first meridian, the right ascension of the moon for this time is:

$$\alpha + t' \cdot \frac{d\alpha}{dt} + \tfrac{1}{2} t'^2 \frac{d^2\alpha}{dt^2} + \tfrac{1}{6} t'^3 \frac{d^3\alpha}{dt^3} + \ldots$$

Now since these observations are made on the meridian, the sidereal times of observation are equal to the true right ascensions of the moon. If we assume, that the tables, from which the values of α and the differential coefficients have been taken, give the right ascension of the moon too small by $\Delta\alpha$, and if we put:

$$T + t + d = \Theta$$

and

$$T + t' + d' = \Theta',$$

we have the following equations:

$$\Theta = \alpha + \Delta\alpha + t \cdot \frac{d\alpha}{dt} + \tfrac{1}{2} t^2 \frac{d^2\alpha}{dt^2} + \tfrac{1}{6} t^3 \frac{d^3\alpha}{dt^3} + \ldots$$

$$\Theta' = \alpha + \Delta\alpha + t' \cdot \frac{d\alpha}{dt} + \tfrac{1}{2} t'^2 \frac{d^2\alpha}{dt^2} + \tfrac{1}{6} t'^3 \frac{d^3\alpha}{dt^3} + \ldots$$

hence:

$$\Theta' - \Theta = (t' - t) \frac{d\alpha}{dt} + \tfrac{1}{2} (t'^2 - t^2) \frac{d^2\alpha}{dt^2} + \ldots \qquad (a)$$

and since we have also:

$$d' - d = (\Theta' - \Theta) - (t' - t), \qquad (b)$$

it is only necessary to find $t' - t$ by means of the equation (a). In order to do this, we will introduce instead of T the arithmetical mean of the times $T + t$ and $T + t'$, that is, the time $T + \frac{1}{2}(t + t')$ which we will denote by T'. Then we must write $T' - \frac{1}{2}(t' - t)$ and $T' + \frac{1}{2}(t' - t)$ in place of $T + t$ and $T + t'$, and if we assume, that the values of α and of $\frac{d\alpha}{dt}$ etc. belong now also to the time T', we have the equations:

$$\Theta = \alpha + \Delta\alpha - \tfrac{1}{2}(t' - t)\frac{d\alpha}{dt} + \tfrac{1}{8}(t' - t)^2\frac{d^2\alpha}{dt^2} - \tfrac{1}{48}(t' - t)^3\frac{d^3\alpha}{dt^3}$$

$$\Theta' = \alpha + \Delta\alpha + \tfrac{1}{2}(t' - t)\frac{d\alpha}{dt} + \tfrac{1}{8}(t' - t)^2\frac{d^2\alpha}{dt^2} + \tfrac{1}{48}(t' - t)^3\frac{d^3\alpha}{dt^3},$$

and hence:

$$\Theta' - \Theta = (t' - t)\frac{d\alpha}{dt} + \tfrac{1}{24}(t' - t)^3\frac{d^3\alpha}{dt^3}.$$

From the last equation we can find $t' - t$, if at first we neglect the second term of the second member and afterwards substitute this approximate value of $t' - t$ in that term. Thus we find:

$$t' - t = \frac{\Theta' - \Theta}{\frac{d\alpha}{dt}} - \tfrac{1}{24}\left[\frac{\Theta' - \Theta}{\frac{d\alpha}{dt}}\right]^3 \frac{d^3\alpha}{dt^3}. \qquad (c)$$

If the difference of longitude does not exceed two hours, the last term is always so small, that is may safely be neglected. The solution of the problem is again an indirect one, since it is necessary to know already the longitude approximately in order to determine the time T'.

For the practical application it is necessary to add a few remarks.

If Θ and Θ' are given in sidereal time, $\Theta' - \Theta$ is expressed in sidereal seconds. Thus in order to find also $t' - t$ expressed in seconds, the same unit must be adopted for $\frac{d\alpha}{dt}$, or $\frac{d\alpha}{dt}$ must be equal to the change of right ascension in one second of time. Therefore if we denote by h the change of the right ascension expressed in arc in one hour sidereal time, we have:

$$\frac{d\alpha}{dt} = \tfrac{1}{15}\cdot\frac{h}{3600}.$$

Now in the ephemerides the places of the moon are not given for sidereal time but for mean time, and we take from them the change of the right ascension of the moon in one hour of mean time. But since 366.24220 sidereal days are equal to 365.24220 mean days or since we have:

one sidereal day $= 0.9972693$ of a mean day

we find, if h' denotes the change of right ascension expressed in time in one hour of mean time:

$$\frac{d\alpha}{dt} = \frac{0.9972693}{3600} h', \qquad (d)$$

hence:

$$t' - t = \frac{15 \times 3600}{0.9972693} \cdot \frac{\Theta' - \Theta}{h'},$$

or from the equation (b):

$$d' - d = (\Theta' - \Theta)\left(1 - \frac{15 \times 3600}{0.9972693\, h'}\right).$$

Now the second term within the parenthesis is always greater than 1, and hence it is better to write the equation in this way:

$$d - d' = (\Theta' - \Theta)\left(\frac{15 \times 3600}{0.9972693\, h'} - 1\right), \qquad (e)$$

and the second place, at which the moon was observed at the time Θ', is west from the other place, if $\Theta' - \Theta$ is positive, and east, if $\Theta' - \Theta$ is negative.

Now the time of culmination of the moon's centre cannot be observed, but only that of one limb; hence the latter must be reduced to the time, at which the culmination of the centre would have been observed. In the seventh section the rigorous methods for reducing meridian observations of the moon will be given, but for the present purpose the following will be sufficient. We call the first limb the one whose right ascension is less than that of the centre, the second limb the one, whose right ascension is greater. Hence if the first is observed, we must add a correction in order to find the time of culmination of the centre, and subtract a correction, if the second limb is observed, and this correction is equal to the time of the moon's semi-diameter passing over the meridian, which according to No. 28 of the first section is equal to $\frac{1}{15}\frac{R}{\cos\delta}\frac{1}{1-\lambda}$, where λ is equal to the value of $\frac{d\alpha}{dt}$ as given by the formula (d). Therefore if ϑ and ϑ'

denote the times at which the moon's limb was observed on the meridian of the two places, we have:

$$\Theta' - \Theta = \vartheta' - \vartheta \pm \tfrac{1}{15}\left(\frac{R'}{\cos\delta'} - \frac{R}{\cos\delta}\right)\frac{1}{1-\lambda},$$

$$\text{where } \lambda = \frac{0.9972693\, h'}{3600},$$

and hence we find from formula (e):

$$d - d' = \left[\vartheta' - \vartheta \pm \tfrac{1}{15}\left(\frac{R'}{\cos\delta'} - \frac{R}{\cos\delta}\right)\frac{1}{1-\lambda}\right]\left(\frac{1}{\lambda} - 1\right), \qquad (A)$$

where h' denotes the change of the right ascension of the moon expressed in time during one hour of mean time and where the upper sign must be used, if the first limb is observed, whilst the lower one corresponds to the second limb.

If the instrument, by which the transit is observed at one place, is not exactly in the plane of the meridian of the place, then the hour angle of the moon at the time of observation is not equal to zero, and if we denote it by s, the difference of longitude which we find, must be erroneous by the quantity:

$$s\left(\frac{15\times 3600}{0.9972693\, h'} - 1\right).$$

Therefore if the instrument is not perfectly adjusted, the longitude found by this method, can be considerably wrong. But any error arising from this cause is at least not increased, if the differences of right ascension of the moon and stars on the same parallel be observed at both places, since these are free from any error of the instruments. Nevertheless since the right ascension of the moon was observed at one place when its hour angle was s, or when it was culminating at a place, whose difference of longitude from that place is equal to s, we find of course the difference of longitude between the two places wrong by the same quantity. Therefore we must add to it the hour angle s, if the meridian of the instrument lies between the meridians of the two places, and subtract s from the difference of longitude, if the meridian of the instrument corresponds to that of a place which is farther from the other place *). How the hour angle s is found

*) We can add also to the observed difference of right ascension of the moon and the star the quantity $\pm \frac{s\lambda}{1-\lambda}$.

from the errors of the instrument, will be shown in No. 18 of the seventh section.

In order that the observers may always use the same comparison stars, a list of stars under the heading moon-culminating stars is annually published in the Nautical Almanac and copied in all other Almanacs, for every day, on which it is possible to observe the moon on the meridian.

Example. In 1848 July 13 the following clock-times of the transit of the moon and the moon-culminating stars were observed at Bilk *):

η Ophiuchi	$17^h\ 1^m\ 52^s.64$
ϱ Ophiuchi	12 6 .59
moon's centre	27 34 .60
μ^1 Sagittarii	18 4 52 .99
λ Sagittarii	18 48 .12.

On the same day the following transits were observed at Hamburg:

η Ophiuchi =	$17^h\ 1^m\ 42^s.61$
ϱ Ophiuchi =	11 56 .91
☾ I. Limb =	25 50 .43
μ^1 Sagittarii =	18 4 43 .53
λ Sagittarii =	18 38 .56.

The semi-diameter of the moon for the time of culmination at Hamburg was $15'\,2''.10$, the declination $-18^0\,10'.1$, and the variation of the right ascension in one hour of mean time equal to $129^s.8$, hence $\lambda = 0.03596$. We find therefore:

$$\tfrac{1}{15}\cdot\frac{R}{(1-\lambda)\cos\delta} = 65^s.66,$$

hence the time of culmination of the moon's centre:

$$17^h\,26^m\,56^s.09.$$

Then we find the differences of right ascension of the stars and the moon's centre:

	for Bilk:	for Hamburg:
η Ophiuchi	$+25^m\ 41^s.96$	$+25^m\ 13^s.48$
ϱ Ophiuchi	+15 28 .01	+14 59 .18
μ^1 Sagittarii	−37 18 .39	−37 47 .44
λ Sagittarii	−51 13 .52	−51 42 .47,

hence the differences of the times of culmination at Bilk and at Hamburg are:

*) Compare No. 21 of the seventh section.

$$\Theta' - \Theta = \begin{array}{r} +28^s.48 \\ 28\ .83 \\ 29\ .05 \\ 28\ .95 \\ \hline \end{array}$$

$$\text{mean} \quad +28^s.83.$$

Now we have found in No. 15 of the introduction the following values of the motion of the moon in one hour for Berlin time:

10^h	$+2^m\ 9^s.77$
11^h	$2\ \ 9\ .91$
12^h	$2\ 10\ .05,$

and since the time of observation at Bilk corresponds to about $10^h\ 30^m$ Berlin time, that at Hamburg to about $10^h\ 16^m$, we have:

$$T' = 10^h\ 23^m$$

hence:

$$h' = 2^m\ 9^s.82$$

and we obtain by means of the formula (e):

$$d - d' = +12^m\ 52^s.83\ ^{*}).$$

---

*) Since h is about $30'$, the value of the coefficient of $\vartheta' - \vartheta$ in the equation (A) is about 29, hence the errors of observation have a great influence on the difference of longitude, since an error of $0^s.1$ in $\vartheta' - \vartheta$ produces an error of 3^s in the longitude.

SIXTH SECTION.

ON THE DETERMINATION OF THE DIMENSIONS OF THE EARTH AND THE HORIZONTAL PARALLAXES OF THE HEAVENLY BODIES.

In the former section we have frequently made use of the dimensions of the earth and the angles subtended at the heavenly bodies by the semi-diameter of the earth or their horizontal parallaxes, and we must show now, by what methods the values of these constants are determined. Only the horizontal parallax of the sun and the moon is directly found by observations, since the distances of planets and comets from the earth, the semi-major axis of the earth's orbit being the unit of distance, are derived from the theory of their orbits, which they describe round the sun according to Kepler's laws. Therefore in order to obtain the horizontal parallaxes of those bodies, it is only necessary to know the horizontal parallax of the sun or of one of these planets.

I. DETERMINATION OF THE FIGURE AND THE DIMENSIONS OF THE EARTH.

1. The figure of the earth is according to theory as well as actual measurements and observations that of an oblate spheroid, that is, of a spheroid generated by the revolution of an ellipse round the conjugate axis. It is true, this would be strictly true only in case that the earth were a fluid mass, but the surface of an oblate spheroid is that curved surface which comes nearest to the true figure of the surface of the earth.

The dimensions of this spheroid are found by measuring the length of a degree, that is, by measuring the linear dimension of an arc of a meridian between two stations by geodetical operations and obtaining the number of degrees corresponding to it by observing the latitudes of the two stations. Eratosthenes (about 300 b. Ch.) made use already of this method, in order to determine the length of the circumference of the earth which he supposed to be of a spherical form. He found that the cities of Alexandria and Syene in Egypt were on the same meridian. Further he knew that on the day of the summer solstice the sun passed through the zenith of Syene, since no shadows were observed at noon on that day, whence he knew the latitude of that place. He observed then at Alexandria the meridian zenith distance of the sun on the day of the solstice and found it equal to $7^0 12'$. Hence the arc of the meridian between Syene and Alexandria must be $7^0 12'$ or equal to the fiftieth part of the circumference. Thus, since the distance between the two places was known to him, he could find the length of the entire circumference. But the result, obtained by him, was very wrong from several causes. First the two places are not on the same meridian, their difference of longitude being about 3 degrees; further the latitude of Syene according to recent determinations is $24^0 8'$, whilst the obliquity of the ecliptic at the time of Eratosthenes was equal to $23^0 44'$, and lastly the latitude of Alexandria and the distance between the two places was likewise wrong. But Eratosthenes has the merit of having first attempted this determination and by a method, which even now is used for this purpose.

Since Newton had proved by theoretical demonstrations, that the earth is not a sphere but a spheroid, it is not sufficient to measure the length of a degree at one place on the surface in order to find the dimensions of the earth, but it is necessary for this purpose to combine two such determinations made at two distant places so as to determine the transverse as well as the conjugate axis of the spheroid.

In No. 2 of the third section we found the following expressions for the co-ordinates of a point on the surface, referred to a system of axes in the plane of the meridian, the origin of the co-ordinates being at the centre of the earth and the axis of x being parallel to the equator:

$$x = \frac{a \cos \varphi}{\sqrt{1 - \varepsilon^2 \sin \varphi^2}},$$

$$y = \frac{a \sin \varphi (1 - \varepsilon^2)}{\sqrt{1 - \varepsilon^2 \sin \varphi^2}},$$

where a and ε denote the semi-transverse axis and the excentricity of the ellipse of the meridian, and φ is the latitude of the place on the surface.

Furthermore the radius of curvature for a point of the ellipse, whose abscissa is x, is:

$$r = \frac{(a^2 - \varepsilon^2 x^2)^{\frac{3}{2}}}{a b},$$

where b denotes the semi-conjugate axis, or if we substitute for x the expression given before:

$$r = \frac{a(1 - \varepsilon^2)}{(1 - \varepsilon^2 \sin \varphi^2)^{\frac{3}{2}}}.$$

Therefore if G is the length of one degree of a meridian expressed in some linear measure and φ is the latitude of the middle of the degree, we have:

$$G = \frac{\pi a (1 - \varepsilon^2)}{180 (1 - \varepsilon^2 \sin \varphi^2)^{\frac{3}{2}}},$$

where π is the number 3.1415927. If now the length of another degree, corresponding to the latitude φ' has been measured, so that:

$$G' = \frac{\pi a (1 - \varepsilon^2)}{180 (1 - \varepsilon^2 \sin \varphi'^2)^{\frac{3}{2}}},$$

we obtain the excentricity of the ellipse by means of the equation:

$$\varepsilon^2 = \frac{1 - \left(\frac{G}{G'}\right)^{\frac{2}{3}}}{\sin \varphi'^2 - \left(\frac{G}{G'}\right)^{\frac{2}{3}} \sin \varphi^2},$$

and when this is known, the semi-transverse axis can be found by either of the equations for G or G'.

Example. The distance of the parallel of Tarqui from that of Cotchesqui in Peru was measured by Bouguer and

Condamine and was found to be equal to 176875.5 toises. The latitudes of the two places were observed as follows:

$$-3^\circ\, 4'\, 32''.068$$

and

$$+0^\circ\, 2'\, 31''.387.$$

Furthermore Swanberg determined the distance of the parallels of Malörn and Pahtawara in Lappland and found it to be equal to 92777.981 toises, the latitudes of the two places being:

$$65^\circ\, 31'\, 30''.265$$

and

$$67^\circ\, 8'\, 49''.830.$$

From the observations in Peru we obtain the length of a degree:

$$G = 56734.01 \text{ toises,}$$

corresponding to the latitude

$$\varphi = -1^\circ\, 31'\, 0''.34,$$

and from the observations in Lappland we get:

$$\varphi' = 66^\circ\, 20'\, 10''.05:$$
$$G' = 57196.15 \text{ toises.}$$

By means of the formulae given above we find from this:

$$\varepsilon^2 = 0.0064351$$
$$a = 3271651 \text{ toises,}$$

and since the ellipticity of the earth α is equal to $1 - \sqrt{1-\varepsilon^2}$, we obtain:

$$\alpha = \frac{1}{310.29}.$$

In this way the length of a degree has been measured with the greatest accuracy at different places. But since the combination of any two of them gives different values for the dimensions of the earth on account of the errors of observation and especially on account of the deviations of the actual shape of the earth from that of a true spheroid, an osculating spheroid must be found, which corresponds as nearly as possible to the values of the length of a degree as measured at all the different places.

2. The length s of an arc of a curve is found by means of the formula:

$$s = \int \sqrt{1 + \frac{dy^2}{dx^2}} \cdot dx.$$

If we differentiate the expressions of x and y, given in the preceding No. with respect to φ and substitute the values of dx and dy in the formula for s, we find the expression for the length of an arc of a meridian, extending from the equator to the place whose latitude is φ:

$$s = a(1-\varepsilon^2)\int \frac{d\varphi}{(1-\varepsilon^2 \sin\varphi^2)^{\frac{3}{2}}}.$$

But we have:

$$[1-\varepsilon^2 \sin\varphi^2]^{-\frac{3}{2}} = 1 + \tfrac{3}{2}\varepsilon^2 \sin\varphi^2 + \frac{\frac{3}{2}\cdot\frac{5}{2}}{1.2}\varepsilon^4 \sin\varphi^4 + \frac{\frac{3}{2}\cdot\frac{5}{2}\cdot\frac{7}{2}}{1.2.3}\varepsilon^6 \sin\varphi^6 + \ldots$$

and if we introduce instead of the powers of $\sin\varphi$ the cosines of the multiples of φ and integrate the terms by means of the formula:

$$\int \cos\lambda x\, dx = \frac{1}{\lambda}\sin\lambda x$$

we obtain:

$$s = a(1-\varepsilon^2)E[\varphi - \alpha \sin 2\varphi + \beta \sin 4\varphi \text{ etc.}],$$

where:

$$E = 1 + \frac{3}{4}\varepsilon^2 + \frac{45}{64}\varepsilon^4 + \frac{175}{256}\varepsilon^6 + \ldots$$

$$E\alpha = \frac{3}{8}\varepsilon^2 + \frac{15}{32}\varepsilon^4 + \frac{525}{1024}\varepsilon^6 + \ldots$$

$$E\beta = \frac{15}{256}\varepsilon^4 + \frac{105}{1024}\varepsilon^6 + \ldots$$

If we take here $\varphi = 180^0$, we obtain, denoting by g the average length of a degree:

$$180\, g = a(1-\varepsilon^2)E.\pi,$$

and hence:

$$s = \frac{180 g}{\pi}[\varphi - \alpha \sin 2\varphi + \beta \sin 4\varphi - \ldots]$$

Therefore the distance of two parallels whose latitudes are φ and φ', is:

$$s' - s = \frac{180 g}{\pi}[\varphi' - \varphi - 2\alpha \sin(\varphi'-\varphi)\cos(\varphi'+\varphi)$$
$$+ 2\beta \sin 2(\varphi'-\varphi)\cos 2(\varphi'+\varphi)],$$

or denoting $\varphi' - \varphi$ by l and the arithmetical mean of the latitudes by L, also expressing l in seconds and denoting 206264.8 by w, we find:

$$\frac{3600}{g}(s'-s) = l - 2w\alpha \sin l \cos 2L + 2w\beta \sin 2l \cos 4L.$$

If we substitute here for l the difference of the observed latitudes and for $s' - s$ the measured length of the arc of the meridian, this equation would be satisfied only in case that we substitute for g and ε and hence for g, α and β some certain values. But if we substitute the values, deduced from the observations at all different places, we can satisfy these equations only by applying small corrections to the observed latitudes. If we write thus $\varphi + x$ and $\varphi' + x'$ instead of φ and φ', where x and x' are small quantities whose squares and products can be neglected, we obtain, neglecting also the influence of these corrections upon L:

$$\frac{3600}{g}(s'-s) = l - 2w\alpha \sin l \cos 2L + 2w\beta \sin 2l \cos 4L + (x'-x)\varrho,$$

where:

$$\varrho = 1 - 2\alpha \cos l \cos 2L + 4\beta \cos 2l \cos 4L.$$

Hence we have:

$$x' - x = \frac{1}{\varrho}\left(\frac{3600}{g}(s'-s) - (l - 2w\alpha \sin l \cos 2L + 2w\beta \sin 2l \cos 4L)\right).$$

and a similar equation is obtained from every determination of the latitudes of two places and of the length of the arc of the meridian between their parallels. Therefore if the number of these equations is greater than that of the unknown quantities, we must determine the values of g and ε so that the sum of the squares of the residual errors $x' - x$ etc. is a minimum. If we take g_0 and α_0 as approximate values of g and α and take:

$$g = \frac{g_0}{1+i} \text{ and } \alpha = \alpha_0 (1+k)$$

we find, if we neglect the squares and the products of i and k:

$$x' - x = \frac{1}{\varrho}\left(\frac{3600}{g_0}(s'-s) - l\right) + \frac{2w}{\varrho}[\alpha_0 \sin l \cos 2L - \beta_0 \sin 2l \cos 4L]$$
$$+ \frac{1}{\varrho}\cdot\frac{3600}{g_0}(s'-s)\, i + \frac{2w}{\varrho}\left[\alpha_0 \sin l \cos 2L - \alpha_0 \frac{d\beta_0}{d\alpha_0} \sin 2l \cos 4L\right] k.$$

Here β_0 denotes the value of β corresponding to α_0, but in order to get this as well as the differential coefficient $\frac{d\beta_0}{d\alpha_0}$, we must first express β as a function of α. Now we find:

$$\alpha = \frac{\frac{3}{8}\varepsilon^2 + \frac{15}{32}\varepsilon^4 + \frac{525}{1024}\varepsilon^6 + \dots}{1 + \frac{3}{4}\varepsilon^2 + \frac{45}{64}\varepsilon^4 + \frac{175}{256}\varepsilon^6 + \dots}$$
$$= \frac{3}{8}\varepsilon^2 + \frac{3}{16}\varepsilon^4 + \frac{111}{1024}\varepsilon^6 + \dots$$

and likewise:

$$\beta = \frac{15}{256}\varepsilon^4 + \frac{15}{256}\varepsilon^6 + \dots$$

If we reverse the series for α we find:

$$\varepsilon^2 = \frac{8}{3}\alpha - \frac{32}{9}\alpha^2 + 4\,\alpha^3 - \dots$$

and if we introduce this in the expression for β:

$$\beta = \frac{5}{12}\alpha^2 + \frac{35}{108}\alpha^4 + \dots$$

hence:

$$\alpha\frac{d\beta}{d\alpha} = \frac{5}{6}\alpha^2 + \frac{35}{27}\alpha^4 + \dots$$

Therefore if we put:

$$n = \frac{1}{\varrho}\left(\frac{3600}{g_0}(s' - s) - l\right)$$
$$+ \frac{2w}{\varrho}\left[\alpha_0 \sin l \cos 2L - \left(\frac{5}{12}\alpha_0{}^2 + \frac{35}{108}\alpha_0{}^4\right)\sin 2l \cos 4L\right] \qquad (A)$$
$$a = \frac{1}{\varrho}\,\frac{3600}{g_0}(s' - s)$$

and:

$$b = \frac{2w}{\varrho}\left[\alpha_0 \sin l \cos 2L - \left(\frac{5}{6}\alpha_0{}^2 + \frac{35}{27}\alpha_0{}^4\right)\sin 2l \cos 4L\right],$$

we obtain the equation:

$$x' - x = n + a\,i + b\,k, \qquad (B)$$

and a similar equation is found from a set of observations for measuring a degree by combining the station which is farthest south with one farther north.

If we treat these equations according to the method of least squares, the equations for the minimum with respect to x, i and k are for this set of observations, if μ is the number of all observed latitudes:

$$\mu x + [a]\,i + [b]\,k + [n] = 0$$
$$[a]\,x + [aa]\,i + [ab]\,k + [an] = 0$$
$$[b]\,x + [ab]\,i + [bb]\,k + [bn] = 0,$$

and if we eliminate x, each set of observations gives the most probable values of i and k by means of the equations:

$$0 = [an_1] + [aa_1]\,i + [ab_1]\,k$$
$$0 = [bn_1] + [ab_1]\,i + [bb_1]\,k.$$

Therefore if we add the different quantities $[an_1]$ which we obtain from different sets of observations made in different localities and designate the sum by (an_1), likewise the sum of all quantities $[a a_1]$ by $(a a_1)$ etc., we find the equations:

$$0 = (an_1) + (aa_1)\,i + (ab_1)\,k$$
$$0 = (bn_1) + (ab_1)\,i + (bb_1)\,k.$$

from which we derive the most probable values of i and k according to all observations made in different localities.

As an example we choose the following observations:

1) Peruvian arc.

	Latitude	l	
Tarqui	— 3° 4′ 32″.068		Distance of the parallels
Cotchesqui	+ 0 2 31 387	3° 7′ 3″. 45	176875.5 toises

2) East Indian arc.

Trivandeporum	+ 11° 44′ 52″. 59		
Paudru	13 19 49 . 02	1° 34′ 56.43	89813.010.

3) Prussian arc.

Truns	54° 13′ 11″. 47		
Königsberg	54 42 50 . 50	0° 29′ 39″. 03	28211.629
Memel	55 43 40 . 45	1 30 28 . 98	86176.975.

4) Swedish arc.

Malörn	65° 31′ 30″. 265		
Pahtawara	67 8 49 . 830	1° 37′ 19″. 56	92777.981.

Taking now:

$$g = \frac{57008}{1+i} \text{ and } \alpha = \frac{1+k}{400},$$

we find:

$$\log \alpha_0 = 7.39794$$
$$\log \left[\frac{15}{2}\alpha_0{}^2 + \frac{35}{108}\alpha_0{}^4\right] = 4.41567$$
$$\log \left[\frac{5}{6}\alpha_0{}^2 + \frac{35}{27}\alpha_0{}^4\right] = 4.71670.$$

If further we put:

$$10000\ i = y$$
$$10\ \ k = z,$$

we obtain the following equations for the four arcs:

1) $x'_1 - x_1 = +1''.97 + 1.1225\,y + 5.6059\,z$
2) $x'_2 - x_2 = +0\ .94 + 0.5697\,y + 2.5835\,z$
3) $x'_3 - x_3 = -0\ .37 + 0.1779\,y - 0.2852\,z$
$x''_3 - x_3 = +3\ .79 + 0.5433\,y - 0.9157\,z$
4) $x'_4 - x_4 = -0\ .51 + 0.5839\,y - 1.9711\,z$

and from these we find:

	$[n]$	$[a]$	$[b]$	$[an]$	$[aa]$	$[ab]$
1)	$+1''.97$	$+1.1225$	$+5.6059$	$+2.2113$	$+1.2600$	$+6.2924$
2)	$+0\ .94$	$+0.5697$	$+2.5835$	$+0.5355$	$+0.3246$	$+1.4718$
3)	$+3\ .42$	$+0.7212$	-1.2009	$+1.9933$	$+0.3268$	-0.5482
4)	$-0\ .51$	$+0.5839$	-1.9711	-0.2978	$+0.3409$	-1.1509

	$[bn]$	$[bb]$
1)	$+11.0436$	$+31.4254$
2)	$+\ 2.4284$	6.6742
3)	$-\ 3.3650$	0.9198
4)	$+\ 1.0026$	3.8853

and:

	$[an_1]$	$[aa_1]$	$[ab_1]$
1)	$+1.1056$	$+0.6300$	$+3.1462$
2)	$+0.2678$	$+0.1623$	$+0.7359$
3)	$+1.1711$	$+0.1534$	-0.2595
4)	-0.1489	$+0.1705$	-0.5755
	$(an_1)=+2.3956,$	$(aa_1)=+1.1162,$	$(ab_1)=+3.0471,$

$[bn_1]$	$[bb_1]$
$+5.5218$	$+15.7127$
$+1.2142$	$+\ 3.3371$
-1.9960	$+\ 0.4391$
$+0.5013$	$+\ 1.9426$
$(bn_1)=+5.2413,$	$(bb_1)=+21.4315.$

Hence the two equations by which y and z are found, are:

$$0=+2.3956+1.1162\,y+\ 3.0471\,z$$
$$0=+5.2413+3.0471\,y+21.4315\,z,$$

and we find:

$$z=+0.099012$$
$$y=-2.4165,$$

hence:

$$i=-0.00024165 \text{ and } k=+0.0099012;$$

therefore:

$$g=\frac{57008}{1-0.00024165}=57021.79$$

and:

$$\alpha=\frac{1+0.0099012}{400}=0.002524753.$$

Now since we had before:

$$\varepsilon^2=\frac{8}{3}\alpha-\frac{32}{9}\alpha^2+4\alpha^3$$

we find:

$$\varepsilon^2=0.006710073,$$

and the ellipticity of the earth $\frac{1}{297.53}$.

Moreover we have:

$$\log \frac{b}{a} = \log \sqrt{1 - \varepsilon^2} = 9.9985380,$$

and since we had:

$$a = \frac{180\, g}{(1 - \varepsilon^2) E\pi}$$

we find:

$$\log a = 6.5147884,$$

and:

$$\log b = 6.5133264.$$

In this way Bessel*) determined the dimensions of the earth from 10 arcs, and found the values, which were given before in No. 1 of the third section:

the ellipticity $\alpha = \frac{1}{299.1528}$

the semi-transverse axis $a = 3272077.14$ toises

the semi-conjugate axis $b = 3261139.33$ „

$\log a = 6.5148235$

$\log b = 6.5133693.$

II. DETERMINATION OF THE HORIZONTAL PARALLAXES OF THE HEAVENLY BODIES.

3. If we observe the place of a heavenly body, whose distance from the earth is not infinitely great, at two places on the surface of the earth, we can determine its parallax or its distance expressed in terms of the equatoreal radius of the earth as unit. Since the length of the latter is known, we can find then the distance of the body expressed in terms of any linear measure.

We will suppose, that the two stations are on the same meridian and on opposite sides of the equator, and that the zenith distance of the body at the culmination is observed at both stations. Then the parallax in altitude will be for one place according to No. 3 of the third section:

$$\sin p' = \varrho \sin p \sin [z - (\varphi - \varphi')],$$

where p is the horizontal parallax, z the observed zenith distance cleared from refraction, φ the latitude, φ' the geocen-

*) In Schumacher's Astronomische Nachrichten No. 333 and 438.

tric latitude and ϱ the distance of the place from the centre of the earth. Hence we have:

$$\frac{1}{\sin p} = \frac{\varrho \sin [z - (\varphi - \varphi')]}{\sin p'}$$

We have also, if φ' is the latitude of the other place, φ'_1 and ϱ_1 the geocentric latitude and the distance from the centre:

$$\frac{1}{\sin p} = \frac{\varrho_1 \sin [z_1 - (\varphi_1 - \varphi'_1)]}{\sin p'_1}.$$

If we now consider the two triangles which are formed by the place of the heavenly body, the centre of the earth and the two stations, the angle at the body in one of the triangles is p', that at the place of observation $180^0 - z + \varphi - \varphi'$, and the angle at the centre $\varphi' \mp \delta$, where δ is the geocentric declination of the body and where the upper or the lower sign must be used, if the heavenly body and the place of observation are on the same side of the equator or on different sides. The angles in the other triangle are p'_1, $180^0 - z_1 + \varphi_1 - \varphi'_1$ and $\varphi'_1 \pm \delta$. We have therefore:

$$p' = z - \varphi' \pm \delta$$
$$p'_1 = z_1 - \varphi'_1 \mp \delta$$

and:

$$p' + p'_1 = z + z_1 - \varphi' - \varphi'_1.$$

Therefore if we denote the known quantity $p' + p'_1$ by π, we have the equation:

$$\frac{\varrho \sin [z - (\varphi - \varphi')]}{\sin p'} = \frac{\varrho_1 \sin [z_1 - (\varphi_1 - \varphi'_1)]}{\sin (\pi - p')},$$

whence follows:

$$\operatorname{tang} p' = \frac{\varrho \sin \pi \sin [z - (\varphi - \varphi')]}{\varrho_1 \sin [z_1 - (\varphi_1 - \varphi'_1)] + \varrho \cos \pi \sin [z - (\varphi - \varphi')]},$$

or:

$$\operatorname{tang} p'_1 = \frac{\varrho_1 \sin \pi \sin [z_1 - (\varphi_1 - \varphi'_1)]}{\varrho \sin [z - (\varphi - \varphi')] + \varrho_1 \cos \pi \sin [z_1 - (\varphi_1 - \varphi'_1)]}.$$

When either p' or p'_1 has been found by means of these equations, we find p either from:

$$\sin p = \frac{\sin p'}{\varrho \sin [z - (\varphi - \varphi')]}$$

or from:

$$\sin p = \frac{\sin p'_1}{\varrho_1 \sin [z_1 - (\varphi_1 - \varphi'_1)}.$$

It was assumed, that the two places are on opposite sides of the equator, a case, which is the most desirable for determining the parallax. But if the two places are on the same side of the equator, the angles at the centre of the earth in the triangles used before are different, namely $\varphi' \mp \delta$ in one triangle and $\varphi'_1 \mp \delta$ in the other. If we put in this case:

$$\pi = p'_1 - p' = z_1 - z - (\varphi_1 - \varphi),$$

we find p' or p'_1 from the same equations as before.

If the two places are not situated on the same meridian, the two observations will not be simultaneous, and hence the change of the declination in the interval of time must be taken into account.

In this way the parallaxes of the moon and of Mars were determined in the year 1751 and 1752. For this purpose Lacaille observed at the Cape of Good Hope the zenith distance of these bodies at their culmination, while corresponding observations were made by Cassini at Paris, Lalande at Berlin, Zanotti at Bologna and Bradley at Greenwich. These places are very favorably situated. The greatest difference in latitude is that between Berlin and the Cape of Good Hope, being $86\frac{1}{2}^{\circ}$, whilst the greatest difference in longitude is that of the Cape and Greenwich, being equal to $1\frac{1}{4}$ hour, a time, for which the change of the declination of the moon can be accurately taken into account.

By these observations the horizontal parallax of the moon at its mean distance from the earth was found equal to 57′ 5″. A new discussion of these observations was made by Olufsen, who, taking the ellipticity of the earth equal to $\frac{1}{302.02}$ found 57′ 2″.64, while the ellipticity given in the preceding No., would give the value 57′ 2″.80 *). Latterly in 1832 and 1833 Henderson observed at the Cape of Good Hope also the meridian zenith distances of the moon, from which in connection with simultaneous observations made at Greenwich he found for the mean parallax the value 57′ 1″.8 **). The value adopted in Burkhardt's Tables of the Moon is 57′ 0″.52, while that in Hansen's is 56′ 59″.59.

The problem of finding the parallax was represented above in its simplest form, but in the case of the moon it

*) Astron. Nachrichten No. 326.

**) Astron. Nachrichten No. 338.

is not quite as simple, since only one limb of the moon can be observed, and hence it is necessary to know the apparent semi-diameter, which itself depends upon the parallax.

If r and r' denote the geocentric and the apparent semi-diameter, Δ and Δ' the distances from the centre of the earth and from the place of observation, we have:

$$\frac{\sin r'}{\sin r} = \frac{\Delta}{\Delta'}.$$

Further in the triangle between the centre of the earth, that of the moon and the place of observation, we have:

$$\frac{\Delta}{\Delta'} = \frac{\sin(180^0 - z')}{\sin(z' - p')},$$

where z' is the angle, which the line drawn from the place of observation to the centre of the moon makes with the radius of the earth produced through the place, and since:

$$z' = z - (\varphi - \varphi') \pm r'$$

where z is the observed zenith distance of the moon's limb and where the upper sign corresponds to the upper limb, we have:

$$\frac{\Delta}{\Delta'} = \frac{\sin[z - (\varphi - \varphi') \pm r']}{\sin[z - (\varphi - \varphi') - p' \pm r']}.$$

If we introduce this expression in the equation for $\frac{\sin r'}{\sin r}$ and eliminate p' by means of the equation:

$$\sin p' = \varrho \sin p \sin[z - (\varphi - \varphi') \pm r'],$$

we obtain, writing for the sake of brevity z instead of $z - (\varphi - \varphi')$ and taking $\varrho = 1$:

$$\sin r' = \sin r + \sin r' \sin p \cos(z \pm r') + \tfrac{1}{2} \sin r' \sin p^2 \sin(z \pm r')^2,$$

or neglecting terms of the third order:

$$r' = r + \sin r \sin p \cos(z \pm r) + \tfrac{1}{2} \sin r \sin p^2 \sin(z \pm r)^2.$$

Now the geocentric zenith distance Z of the moon, expressed by the zenith distance z of the limb, is:

$$Z = z \pm r' - \sin p \sin(z \pm r') - \frac{\sin p^3 \sin(z \pm r')^3}{6},$$

or if we substitute for r' its expression found before:

$$Z = z \pm r \pm \sin r \sin p \cos(z \pm r) \pm \tfrac{1}{2} \sin r \sin p^2 \sin(z \pm r)^2$$
$$- \sin p \sin(z \pm r) - \frac{\sin p^3 \sin(z \pm r)^3}{6}.$$

If we develop this equation and again neglect the terms of a higher order than the third, we find:

$$Z = z \pm r - \sin r^2 \sin p \sin z \pm \tfrac{1}{2} \sin r \sin p^2 \sin z^2$$
$$- \sin p \cos r \sin z + \tfrac{1}{2} \sin p \sin r^2 \sin z - \frac{\sin p^3 \sin z^3}{6},$$

or introducing $1 - \frac{1}{2} \sin r^2$ instead of $\cos r$ and replacing $\sin p$ by $\varrho \sin p$:

$$Z = z \pm r - \varrho \sin p \sin z - \tfrac{1}{2} \varrho \sin p \sin z \sin r^2 \pm \tfrac{1}{2} \varrho^2 \sin p^2 \sin r \sin z^2$$
$$- \frac{\varrho^3 \sin p^3 \sin z^3}{6},$$

and finally, if we take:

$$\sin r = k \sin p,$$

and hence:

$$r = k \sin p + \tfrac{1}{6} k^3 \sin p^3$$

and introduce again $z - \lambda$ in place of z, where $\lambda = \varphi - \varphi'$, we have:

$$Z = z - \lambda - \sin p\,[\varrho \sin (z - \lambda) \mp k] - \frac{\sin p^3}{6} [\varrho \sin (z - \lambda) \mp k]^3.$$

If D is the geocentric declination of the moon's centre, δ the observed declination of the limb, we have also, since $D = \varphi' - z$ and $\delta = \varphi' - (z - \lambda)$:

$$D = \delta + \sin p\,[\varrho \sin (z - \lambda) \mp k] + \frac{\sin p^3}{6} [\varrho \sin (z - \lambda) \mp k]^3.$$

The quantities ϱ and λ depend on the ellipticity of the earth, and since it is desirable, to find the parallax of the moon in such a way, that it can be easily corrected for any other value of the ellipticity, we must transform the expression given above accordingly. But according to No. 2 of the third section we have:

$$\varphi - \varphi' = \frac{a^2 - b^2}{a^2 + b^2} \sin 2\varphi + \ldots$$
$$= \frac{1 - \frac{b^2}{a^2}}{1 + \frac{b^2}{a^2}} \sin 2\varphi + \ldots$$

If we introduce here the ellipticity, making use of the equation:

$$1 - \frac{b^2}{a^2} = 2\alpha - \alpha^2$$

and neglect all terms of the order of α^2, we find:

$$\varphi - \varphi' = \lambda = \alpha \sin 2\varphi.$$

Moreover we had:

$$\varrho^2 = x^2 + y^2 = \frac{\cos \varphi^2}{1 - \varepsilon^2 \sin \varphi^2} + \frac{(1 - \varepsilon^2)^2 \sin \varphi^2}{1 - \varepsilon^2 \sin \varphi^2}$$
$$= \frac{1 - 2\varepsilon^2 \sin \varphi^2 + \varepsilon^4 \sin \varphi^2}{1 - \varepsilon^2 \sin \varphi^2}.$$

If we introduce here also α by means of the equation:

$$\varepsilon^2 = 2\alpha - \alpha^2$$

and neglect all terms of the order of α^2, we find:

$$\varrho = 1 - \alpha \sin\varphi^2.$$

Thus the last expression for D is changed into:

$$D = \delta + [\sin z \mp k] \sin p - [\sin\varphi^2 \sin z + \sin 2\varphi \cos z]\, \alpha \sin p + [\sin z \mp k]^3 \frac{\sin p^3}{6}.$$

Every observation of the limb of the moon, made at a place in the northern hemisphere of the earth, leads to such an equation, in which the upper sign must be taken in case that the upper limb of the moon has been observed, whilst the lower sign corresponds to the lower limb of the moon.

Likewise we find for a place in the southern hemisphere:

$$D_1 = \delta_1 - [\sin z_1 \mp k] \sin p_1 - [\sin z_1 \mp k]^3 \frac{\sin p_1{}^3}{6} + [\sin\varphi_1{}^2 \sin z_1 + \sin 2\varphi_1 \cos z_1] \sin p_1.$$

Now let t and t_1 be the mean times of a certain first meridian, corresponding to the two times of observation, let D_0 be the geocentric declination of the moon for a certain time T and $\frac{dD}{dt}$ its variation in one hour of mean time and taken positive, if the moon approaches the north pole, then we find from the two equations for D and D_1:

$$\begin{aligned}(t_1 - t)\frac{dD}{dt} = \delta_1 - \delta &- [\sin z_1 \mp k - \alpha(\sin\varphi_1{}^2 \sin z_1 + \sin 2\varphi_1 \cos z_1)] \sin p_1 \\ &- [\sin z \mp k - \alpha(\sin\varphi^2 \sin z + \sin 2\varphi \cos z)] \sin p \\ &- [\sin z_1 \mp k]^3 \frac{\sin p_1{}^3}{6} - [\sin z \mp k] \frac{\sin p^3}{6}.\end{aligned}$$

Moreover if p_0 is the parallax for the time T and $\frac{dp}{dt}$ its change in one hour, we have:

$$\sin p = \sin p_0 + \cos p_0 \frac{dp}{dt}(t - T)$$

$$\sin p_1 = \sin p_0 + \cos p_0 \frac{dp}{dt}(t_1 - T),$$

therefore we find the following equation for determining the parallax for the time T:

$$0 = \delta_1 - \delta + (t - t_1)\frac{dD}{dt} - [(\sin z_1 \mp k)^3 + \sin(z \mp k)^3]\frac{\sin p_0{}^3}{6}$$
$$- \frac{dp}{dt}\cos p_0\,[(\sin z \mp k)(t - T) + (\sin z_1 \mp k)(t_1 - T)]$$
$$- [\sin z_1 + \sin z \mp k \mp k]\sin p_0 + \alpha \sin p_0 \left\{ \begin{array}{c} \sin\varphi^2 \sin z + \sin 2\varphi \cos z \\ + \sin\varphi_1{}^2 \sin z_1 \sin 2\varphi_1 \cos z_1 \end{array} \right\} \text{*)}.$$

If at the two places opposite limbs of the moon are observed, the coefficient of $\sin p_0$ is rendered independent of k, and since this quantity thus only occurs in the small terms multiplied by $\sin p_0{}^3$ and $\frac{dp}{dt}$, the value of p_0, which is found from the equation, is independent of any error of k. Since we know the parallaxes from former determinations sufficiently accurately so as to compute the third and the fourth term of the formula without any appreciable error, we can consider the first four terms of the formula as known, since all quantities contained in them have either been observed or can be taken from the tables of the moon. Therefore if we denote the sum of these terms by n, the coefficient of $\sin p_0$ by a and that of $\alpha \sin p_0$ by b, we obtain the equation:

$$0 = n - \sin p_0\,(a - b\alpha),$$

from which p_0 can be found as a function of α. But instead of the parallax p_0 for the time T it is desirable to find immediately the mean parallax, that is, the horizontal parallax for the mean distance of the moon from the earth **). Therefore if K is the value of the mean parallax adopted in the lunar tables, and π the value taken from those tables for the time T, we have, if we denote the sought mean horizontal parallax by Π:

$$\sin p_0 = \frac{\pi}{K}\sin \Pi = \mu \sin \Pi,$$

hence the equation found before is transformed into:

$$0 = \frac{n}{\mu} - \sin \Pi\,(a - b\alpha).$$

*) If the second differential coefficients are taken into account, we must add the term:

$$+ \tfrac{1}{2}[(t - T)^2 - (t_1 - T)^2]\frac{d^2 D}{dt^2}$$

but if we take:

$$T = \tfrac{1}{2}(t_1 + t),$$

this term vanishes.

**) Namely the distance equal to the semi-major axis of the moon's orbit.

Example. In 1752 February 23 Lalande observed at Berlin the declination of the lower limb of the moon:

$$\delta = +20^\circ\,26'\,25''.2,$$

and Lacaille at the Cape of Good Hope the declination of the upper limb:

$$\delta_1 = +21^\circ\,46'\,44''.8.$$

For the arithmetical mean of the times of observation, corresponding to the Paris time:

$$T = 6^h\,40^m,$$

we take from Burkhardt's tables:

$$\frac{dD}{dt} = -34''.15$$

$$\pi = 59'\,24''.54$$

$$\frac{dp}{dt} = +0''.28;$$

finally we have:

$$\varphi = 52^\circ\,30'\,16''$$

and

$$\varphi_1 = 33\quad 56\quad 3 \text{ south.}$$

Since the longitude of the Cape of Good Hope is $20^m\,19^s.5$ East of Berlin and the increase of the right ascension of the moon in one hour was $38'\,10''$, the culmination of the moon took place $21^m\,11^s$ later at Berlin than at the Cape, hence we have:

$$t - t_1 = +21^m\,11^s, \text{ hence } (t - t_1)\frac{dD}{dt} = -12''.06$$

further we have:

$$\delta_1 - \delta = +1^\circ\,20'\,19''.6.$$

The third term, depending on $\sin p^3$, we find equal to $-0''.12$, if we take $k = 0.2725$; therefore if we omit the insignificant term multiplied by $\frac{dp}{dt}$, we find:

$$n = +1^\circ\,20'\,7''.42$$

or expressed in parts of the radius:

$$n = +0.023307$$

and since the value of the mean parallax adopted in Burkhardt's tables is:

$$K = 57'\,0''.52$$

we have:

$$\log \mu = 0.01792,$$

hence:

$$\frac{n}{\mu} = +0.022365.$$

If we compute the coefficients a and b, we find, since:

$$z = 32^0\ 3'\ 51'' \text{ and } z_1 = 55^0\ 42'\ 48''$$

the following values:

$$a = +\ 1.3571 \text{ and } b = +\ 1.9321$$

and hence the equation for determining sin Π is:

$$0 = +\ 0.022365 - \sin \Pi\,(1.3571 - 1.9321\,\alpha).$$

Every combination of two observations gives such an equation of the form:

$$0 = \frac{n}{\mu} - x\,(a - b\,\alpha)$$

If there is only one equation, we can find from it the value of x corresponding to a certain value of α. For instance taking $\alpha = \frac{1}{299\,.\,15}$ we find:

$$\log \sin \Pi = 8.21901$$
$$\Pi = 56'\ 55''.4.$$

But if there are several equations, we find for the equation of the minimum according to the method of least squares:

$$[a\,a]\,x - [a\,b]\,\alpha\,x - \left[a\,\frac{n}{\mu}\right] = 0,$$

hence:

$$x = \frac{\left[a\,\frac{n}{\mu}\right]}{[a\,a]} + \frac{[a\,b]}{[a\,a]}\,\alpha\,x$$

$$= \frac{\left[a\,\frac{n}{\mu}\right]}{[a\,a]} + \frac{\left[a\,\frac{n}{\mu}\right]}{[a\,a]} \cdot \frac{[a\,b]}{[a\,a]}\,\alpha$$

Thus Olufsen found for the mean horizontal parallax of the moon the value $57'\ 2''.80$ *). Since the parallax of the moon is so large, it may even be determined with some degree of accuracy from observations made at the same place by combining observations made near the zenith, for which the parallax in altitude is small, with observations in the neighbourhood of the horizon, where the parallax is nearly at its maximum. In this way the parallax of the moon was discovered by Hipparchus, since he found an irregularity in the motion of the moon, depending on its altitude above the horizon and having the period of a day.

---

*) Astron. Nachrichten No. 326.

4. This method does not afford sufficient accuracy for determining the horizontal parallax of the sun, but the first approximate determinations were obtained in this way. In 1671 meridian altitudes of Mars were observed by Richer in Cayenne and by Picard and Condamine at Paris, and from these the horizontal parallax of Mars was found equal to 25″.5. But as soon as the parallax of one planet is known, the parallaxes of all other planets as well as that of the sun can be found by means of the third law of Kepler, according to which the cubes of the mean distances of the planets from the sun are as the squares of the times of revolution. Thus from this determination the parallax of the sun was found equal to 9″.5. Still less accurate was the value found from the observations of Lacaille and Lalande, namely 10″.25; neither have the observations made latterly in Chili by Gilliss contributed anything towards a more accurate knowledge of this important constant. But allthough all results hitherto obtained by this method have been insufficient, it is still desirable, that they should be repeated again with the greatest care, since the great accuracy of modern observations may lead to more accurate results even by this method *).

The best method for ascertaining the parallax of the sun is that by the transits of Venus over the disc of the sun at her inferior conjunction, which was first proposed by Halley. The computation of such transits can be made in a similar way as that given for eclipses in No. 29 and 31 of the preceding section. The following method, originally owing to Lagrange, was published by Encke in the Berliner Jahrbuch for 1842.

If α, δ, A and D are the geocentric right ascension and declination of Venus and the sun for the time T of a certain first meridian, which is not far from the time of conjunction, then we have in the spherical triangle between the pole of the equator and the centres of Venus and the sun, denoting the distance of the two centres by m and the angles at the sun and Venus by M and $180^0 - M'$:

*) Such observations have been made since during the oppositions of Mars in 1862 and seem to give a greater value of the parallax than the one considered hitherto as the best.

$$\sin \tfrac{1}{2} m \,.\, \sin \tfrac{1}{2} (M' + M) = \sin \tfrac{1}{2} (\alpha - A) \cos \tfrac{1}{2} (\delta + D)$$
$$\sin \tfrac{1}{2} m \,.\, \cos \tfrac{1}{2} (M' + M) = \cos \tfrac{1}{2} (\alpha - A) \sin \tfrac{1}{2} (\delta - D)$$
$$\cos \tfrac{1}{2} m \,.\, \sin \tfrac{1}{2} (M' - M) = \sin \tfrac{1}{2} (\alpha - A) \sin \tfrac{1}{2} (\delta + D)$$
$$\cos \tfrac{1}{2} m \,.\, \cos \tfrac{1}{2} (M' - M) = \cos \tfrac{1}{2} (\alpha - A) \cos \tfrac{1}{2} (\delta - D),$$

or since $\alpha - A$ and $\delta - D$ and hence also m and $M' - M$ are for the times of contact small quantities:

$$\begin{aligned} m \sin M &= (\alpha - A) \cos \tfrac{1}{2} (\delta + D) \\ m \cos M &= \delta - D. \end{aligned} \qquad (A)$$

Taking then:

$$\begin{aligned} n \sin N &= \frac{d(\alpha - A)}{dt} \cos \tfrac{1}{2} (\delta + D) \\ n \cos N &= \frac{d(\delta - D)}{dt}, \end{aligned} \qquad (B)$$

where $\frac{d(\alpha - A)}{dt}$ and $\frac{d(\delta - D)}{dt}$ are the relative changes of the right ascensions and declinationa in the unit of time, and denoting the time of contact of the limbs by $T + \tau$, we have:

$$[m \sin M + \tau n \sin N]^2 + [m \cos M + \tau n \cos N]^2 = [R \pm r]^2,$$

where R and r denote the semi-diameter of the sun and of Venus, and where the upper sign must be used for an exterior contact, the lower sign for an interior contact.

From this equation we obtain:

$$\tau = -\frac{m}{n} \cos (M - N) \mp \frac{R \pm r}{n} \sqrt{1 - \frac{m^2 \sin (M - N)^2}{(R \pm r)^2}}.$$

Therefore if we put:

$$\frac{m \sin (M - N)}{R \pm r} = \sin \psi, \text{ where } \psi < \pm 90^\circ, \qquad (C)$$

we obtain:

$$\tau = -\frac{m}{n} \cos (M - N) \mp \frac{R \pm r}{n} \cos \psi, \qquad (D)$$

where again the upper sign must be used for the ingress and the lower for the egress. Therefore at the centre of the earth the ingress is seen at the time of the first meridian:

$$T - \frac{m}{n} \cos (M - N) - \frac{R \pm r}{n} \cos \psi$$

and the egress at the time:

$$T - \frac{m}{n} \cos (M - N) + \frac{R \pm r}{n} \cos \psi.$$

Finally if $\odot$ is the angle, which the great circle drawn from the centre of the sun towards the point of contact makes with the declination circle passing through the centre of the sun, we have:

$$(R \pm r) \cos \odot = m \cos M + n \cos N \,.\, \tau$$
$$(R \pm r) \sin \odot = m \sin M + n \sin N \,.\, \tau$$

or:

$$\cos \odot = - \sin N \sin \psi \mp \cos N \cos \psi$$
$$\sin \odot = \sin \psi \cos N \mp \cos \psi \sin N,$$

hence for the ingress we have:

$$\odot = 180^0 + N - \psi \qquad (E)$$

and for the egress:

$$\odot = N + \psi. \qquad (F)$$

These formulae serve for computing the times of the ingress and egress for the centre of the earth. In order to find from these the times for any place on the surface of the earth, we must express the distance of the two bodies, seen at any time at the place, by the distance seen from the centre of the earth.

We have:

$$\cos m = \sin \delta \sin D + \cos \delta \cos D \cos (\alpha - A).$$

If α', δ', A' and D' be the apparent right ascensions and declinations of Venus and the sun, seen from the place on the surface of the earth, and m' the apparent distance of the centres of the two bodies, we have also:

$$\cos m' = \sin \delta' \sin D' + \cos \delta' \cos D' \cos (\alpha' - A')$$

and hence:

$$\begin{aligned}\cos m' = \cos m &+ (\delta' - \delta) [\cos \delta \sin D - \sin \delta \cos D \cos (\alpha - A)] \\ &+ (D' - D) [\sin \delta \cos D - \cos \delta \sin D \cos (\alpha - A)] \\ &- (\alpha' - \alpha) \cos \delta \cos D \sin (\alpha - A) \\ &+ (A' - A) \cos \delta \cos D \sin (\alpha - A).\end{aligned}$$

But according to the formulae in No. 4 of the third section we have *):

---

*) We have according to the formulae given there:

$$\delta' - \delta = \pi \sin \varphi \frac{\sin (\delta - \gamma)}{\sin \gamma} = \pi \sin \varphi [\sin \delta \operatorname{cotang} \gamma - \cos \delta].$$

but since:

$$\operatorname{cotang} \gamma = \cos (\alpha - \Theta) \,.\, \operatorname{cotang} \varphi,$$

we have:

$$\delta' - \delta = \pi [\cos \varphi \sin \delta \cos (\alpha - \Theta) - \sin \varphi \cos \delta].$$

$$\delta' - \delta = \pi\,[\cos\varphi \sin\delta \cos(\alpha - \Theta) - \sin\varphi \cos\delta]$$
$$D' - D = p\,[\cos\varphi \sin D \cos(\alpha - \Theta) - \sin\varphi \cos D]$$
$$\alpha' - \alpha = \pi \sec\delta \sin(\alpha - \Theta) \cos\varphi$$
$$A' - A = p \sec D \sin(A - \Theta) \cos\varphi,$$

where π and p are the horizontal parallaxes of Venus and the sun; and if we substitute these expressions in the equation for $\cos m'$, we obtain:

$$\cos m' = \cos m$$
$$+ [\cos\delta \sin D - \sin\delta \cos D \cos(\alpha - A)]\,[\pi \cos\varphi \sin\delta \cos(\alpha - \Theta) - \pi \sin\varphi \cos\delta]$$
$$+ [\sin\delta \cos D - \cos\delta \sin D \cos(\alpha - A)]\,[p \cos\varphi \sin D \cos(\alpha - \Theta) - p \sin\varphi \cos D]$$
$$- \cos D \sin(\alpha - A)\,.\,\pi \sin(\alpha - \Theta) \cos\varphi \qquad (a)$$
$$+ \cos\delta \sin(\alpha - A)\,.\,p \sin(A - \Theta) \cos\varphi.$$

If we develop this equation, we find first for the coefficient of $\cos\varphi$:

$$\pi\,[\sin\delta \cos\delta \sin D \cos(\alpha - \Theta) - \sin\delta^2 \cos D \cos(\alpha - \Theta) \cos(\alpha - A)$$
$$- \cos D \sin(\alpha - \Theta) \sin(\alpha - A)]$$
$$+ p\,[\sin\delta \cos D \sin D \cos(\alpha - \Theta) - \cos\delta \sin D^2 \cos(\alpha - \Theta) \cos(\alpha - A)$$
$$+ \cos\delta \sin(\alpha - \Theta) \sin(\alpha - A)]$$

or since:

$$\sin\delta^2 = 1 - \cos\delta^2 \text{ and } \sin D^2 = 1 - \cos D^2:$$
$$\pi\,[(\sin\delta \sin D + \cos\delta \cos D \cos(\alpha - A)) \cos\delta \cos(\alpha - \Theta) - \cos D \cos(A - \Theta)]$$
$$+ p\,[(\sin\delta \sin D + \cos\delta \cos D \cos(\alpha - A)) \cos D \cos(A - \Theta) - \cos\delta \cos(\alpha - \Theta)],$$

hence:

$$\pi \cos m \cos\delta \cos(\alpha - \Theta) - \pi \cos D \cos(A - \Theta)$$
$$+ p \cos m \cos D \cos(A - \Theta) - p \cos\delta \cos(\alpha - \Theta).$$

This we can transform in the following way:

$$[\pi \cos m \cos\delta \cos\alpha - \pi \cos D \cos A] \cos\Theta$$
$$+ [p \cos m \cos D \cos A - p \cos\delta \cos\alpha] \cos\Theta$$
$$+ [\pi \cos m \cos\delta \sin\alpha - \pi \cos D \sin A] \sin\Theta$$
$$+ [p \cos m \cos D \sin A - p \cos\delta \sin\alpha] \sin\Theta,$$

and hence the term multiplied by $\cos\varphi$ becomes:

$$[(\pi \cos m - p) \cos\delta \cos\alpha - (\pi - p \cos m) \cos D \cos A] \cos\varphi \cos\Theta$$
$$+ [(\pi \cos m - p) \cos\delta \sin\alpha - (\pi - p \cos m) \cos D \sin A] \cos\varphi \sin\Theta. \qquad (b)$$

Further the coefficient of $\sin\varphi$ in the equation (a) is:

$$\pi\,[- \cos\delta^2 \sin D + \sin\delta \cos\delta \cos D \cos(\alpha - A)]$$
$$+ p\,[- \sin\delta \cos D^2 + \sin D \cos D \cos\delta \cos(\alpha - A)],$$

or since $\cos\delta^2 = 1 - \sin\delta^2$ and $\cos D^2 = 1 - \sin D^2$:

$$\pi\,[- \sin D + \sin\delta (\sin\delta \sin D + \cos\delta \cos D \cos(\alpha - A))]$$
$$+ p\,[- \sin\delta + \sin D (\sin\delta \sin D + \cos\delta \cos D \cos(\alpha - A))].$$

Therefore the term of the equation (a), which is multiplied by $\sin\varphi$, is:

$$(\pi \cos m - p) \sin\delta \sin\varphi - (\pi - p \cos m) \sin D \sin\varphi,$$

and thus the equation (a) is transformed into the following:

$$\begin{aligned}\cos m' &= \cos m \\ &+ [(\pi \cos m - p)\cos\delta\cos\alpha - (\pi - p\cos m)\cos D\cos A]\cos\varphi\cos\Theta \\ &+ [(\pi \cos m - p)\cos\delta\sin\alpha - (\pi - p\cos m)\cos D\sin A]\cos\varphi\sin\Theta \quad (c) \\ &+ [(\pi \cos m - p)\sin\delta - (\pi - p\cos m)\sin D]\sin\varphi.\end{aligned}$$

If we take now:

$$\begin{aligned}\pi\cos m - p &= f\sin s \\ -\pi\sin m &= f\cos s,\end{aligned} \quad (d)$$

we have:

$$\pi - p\cos m = f\sin(s-m),$$

and hence:

$$\begin{aligned}\cos m' &= \cos m \\ &+ f[\sin s\cos\delta\cos\alpha - \sin(s-m)\cos D\cos A]\cos\varphi\cos\Theta \\ &+ f[\sin s\cos\delta\sin\alpha - \sin(s-m)\cos D\sin A]\cos\varphi\sin\Theta \quad (e) \\ &+ f[\sin s\sin\delta - \sin(s-m)\sin D]\sin\varphi.\end{aligned}$$

Further if we take:

$$\begin{aligned}\sin s\cos\delta\cos\alpha - \sin(s-m)\cos D\cos A &= P\cos\lambda\cos\beta \\ \sin s\cos\delta\sin\alpha - \sin(s-m)\cos D\sin A &= P\sin\lambda\cos\beta \quad (f) \\ \sin s\sin\delta - \sin(s-m)\sin D &= P\sin\beta,\end{aligned}$$

we find by squaring these equations the following equation for P:

$$\begin{aligned}P^2 &= \sin s^2 + \sin(s-m)^2 - 2\sin s\sin(s-m)\cos m \\ &= \sin s^2 - \sin s^2\cos m^2 + \cos s^2\sin m^2 = \sin m^2.\end{aligned}$$

Hence we may put:

$$\begin{aligned}\sin s\cos\delta\cos\alpha - \sin(s-m)\cos D\cos A &= \sin m\cos\lambda\cos\beta \\ \sin s\cos\delta\sin\alpha - \sin(s-m)\cos D\sin A &= \sin m\sin\lambda\cos\beta \\ \sin s\sin\delta - \sin(s-m)\sin D &= \sin m\sin\beta,\end{aligned}$$

or:

$$\begin{aligned}\sin m\sin(\lambda - A)\cos\beta &= \sin s\cos\delta\sin(\alpha - A) \\ \sin m\cos(\lambda - A)\cos\beta &= \sin s\cos\delta\cos(\alpha - A) - \sin(s-m)\cos D \quad (g) \\ \sin m\sin\beta &= \sin s\sin\delta - \sin(s-m)\sin D.\end{aligned}$$

But we have:

$$\begin{aligned}\sin s\cos\delta\cos(\alpha - A) - \sin(s-m)\cos D &= \sin s[\cos\delta\cos(\alpha - A) - \cos m\cos D] \\ &+ \cos s\,.\,\sin m\cos D\end{aligned}$$

and:

$$\begin{aligned}\sin s\sin\delta - \sin(s-m)\sin D &= \sin s[\sin\delta - \cos m\sin D] \\ &+ \cos s\,.\,\sin m\sin D.\end{aligned}$$

Further we have in the spherical triangle between the pole of the equator and the geocentric places of Venus and the sun, denoting the angle at the sun by M:

$$\begin{aligned}\sin m\sin M &= \cos\delta\sin(\alpha - A) \\ \sin m\cos M &= \sin\delta\cos D - \cos\delta\sin D\cos(\alpha - A) \quad (h) \\ \cos m &= \sin\delta\sin D + \cos\delta\cos D\cos(\alpha - A),\end{aligned}$$

hence we have:

$$\cos\delta\cos(\alpha - A) = \cos D\cos m - \sin D\sin m\cos M$$
$$\sin\delta = \sin D\cos m + \cos D\sin m\cos M,$$

and the equations (g) are thus transformed into the following:

$$\begin{aligned}\sin(\lambda - A)\cos\beta &= \sin s\sin M\\ \cos(\lambda - A)\cos\beta &= \cos s\cos D - \sin s\sin D\cos M \qquad (i)\\ \sin\beta &= \cos s\sin D + \sin s\cos D\cos M,\end{aligned}$$

where s and M must be found by means of the equations (d) and (h). After having obtained λ and β by the equations (i), m' is found according to (e) and (f) by means of the following equation:

$$\begin{aligned}\cos m' &= \cos m + f\sin m\,[\cos\lambda\cos\beta\cos\varphi\cos\Theta + \sin\lambda\cos\beta\cos\varphi\sin\Theta\\ &\qquad + \sin\beta\sin\varphi]\\ &= \cos m + f\sin m\,[\sin\varphi\sin\beta + \cos\varphi\cos\beta\cos(\lambda - \Theta)].\end{aligned}$$

Now let T, as before, be that mean time of a certain first meridian, for which the quantities α, δ, A and D have been computed, and L the sidereal time corresponding to it, further let l be the longitude of the place, to which Θ and φ refer, taken positive when East, we have:

$$\Theta = l + L,$$

therefore:

$$\lambda - \Theta = \lambda - L - l.$$

Hence if we put:

$$\Lambda = \lambda - L,$$

we have:

$$\left.\begin{aligned}\cos\zeta &= \sin\varphi\sin\beta + \cos\varphi\cos\beta\cos(\Lambda - l),\\ \cos m' &= \cos m + f\sin m\cos\zeta\end{aligned}\right\}(k)$$

All places, for which $\cos\zeta$ has the same value, see the same apparent distance m' simultaneously at the sidereal time L of the first meridian, or each place at the local mean time $T + l$. In order to find the time when these places see the distance m, we have: $dm = -f\cos\zeta$,

hence:

$$dt = -\frac{f\cos\zeta}{\frac{dm}{dt}}.$$

But if m is a small quantity, for instance at the time of contact of the limbs, we have according to the formulae (A):

$$m = (\alpha - A)\cos\tfrac{1}{2}(\delta + D)\sin M + (\delta - D)\cos M$$
$$\frac{dm}{dt} = \frac{d(\alpha - A)}{dt}\cos\tfrac{1}{2}(\delta + D)\sin M + \frac{d(\delta - D)}{dt}\cos M,$$

or according to the formulae (B):

$$\frac{dm}{dt} = n\cos(M - N),$$

hence: $$dt = -\frac{f\cos\zeta}{n\cos(M-N)}.$$

Therefore if an observer at the centre of the earth sees at the time T the angular distance m of the bodies, an observer on the surface of the earth sees the same distance at the time of the first meridian:

$$T + \frac{f\cos\zeta}{n\cos(M-N)}$$

or at the local time:

$$T + l + \frac{f\cos\zeta}{n\cos(M-N)}.$$

Therefore in order to find the times of the ingress and egress for a place on the surface of the earth from the times of the ingress and egress for the centre of earth, we need only use $R \pm r$ and $\odot$ instead of m and M, and since we have according to the formulae (E) and (F) for the ingress $\odot = 180^0 + N - \psi$ and for the egress $\odot = N + \psi$, we must add to the times of the ingress and egress for the centre of the earth:

$$-\frac{f\cos\zeta}{n\cos\psi}$$

and:

$$+\frac{f\cos\zeta}{n\cos\psi}.$$

Hence if we collect the formulae for computing a transit of Venus, they are as follows:

For the centre of the earth.

For a time of a certain first meridian, which is near the time of conjunction, compute the right ascensions α, A and the declinations δ, D of Venus and the sun, likewise their semi-diameters r and R. Then compute the formulae:

$$m\sin M = (\alpha - A)\cos\tfrac{1}{2}(\delta + D)$$
$$m\cos M = \delta - D$$
$$n\sin N = \frac{d(\alpha - A)}{dt}\cos\tfrac{1}{2}(\delta + D)$$
$$n\cos N = \frac{d(\delta - D)}{dt}$$
$$\frac{m\sin(M-N)}{R \pm r} = \sin\psi,\ \psi < \pm 90^0$$
$$\tau = -\frac{m}{n}\cos(M-N) - \frac{R \pm r}{n}\cos\psi$$
$$\tau' = -\frac{m}{n}\cos(M-N) + \frac{R \pm r}{n}\cos\psi.$$

Then the time of ingress is:

$$t = T + \tau,$$

and we have for this time:

$$\odot = 180^0 + N - \psi,$$

and the time of egress is:

$$t' = T + \tau',$$

and for this time

$$\odot = N + \psi.$$

For a place whose latitude is φ and whose east longitude is l.

Compute for the ingress as well as for the egress, using the corresponding values of the angle $\odot$, the formulae:

$$\pi \cos (R \pm r) - p = f \sin s$$
$$- \pi \sin (R \pm r) = f \cos s$$
$$\frac{f}{n \cos \psi} = g$$
$$\sin (\lambda - A) \cos \beta = \sin s \sin \odot$$
$$\cos (\lambda - A) \cos \beta = \cos s \cos D - \sin s \sin D \cos \odot$$
$$\sin \beta = \cos s \sin D + \sin s \cos D \cos \odot$$
$$\varDelta = \lambda - L$$
$$\cos \zeta = \sin \beta \sin \varphi + \cos \beta \cos \varphi \cos (\varDelta - l) \text{ *)},$$

where L is the sidereal time corresponding to t or t'. Then the local mean time of the ingress is:

$$t + l - g \cos \zeta,$$

and that of the egress:

$$t' + l + g \cos \zeta.$$

At those places, for which the quantity

$$\sin \beta \sin \varphi + \cos \beta \cos \varphi \cos (\varDelta - l)$$

is equal ± 1, the times of contact are the earliest and the latest. The duration of the transit for a place on the surface may differ by $2g$ from the duration for the centre, and since for central transits we have nearly:

$$g = \frac{\pi - p}{n},$$

the difference of the duration can amount to twice the time, in which Venus on account of her motion relatively to that of the sun, describes an arc equal to twice the difference of her parallax and that of the sun. Now since the difference of the parallaxes is 23″ and the hourly motion of Venus at

*) ζ is the angular distance of the point, whose latitude and longitude are φ and l, from the point, whose latitude and longitude are β and $\varDelta$.

the time of conjunction is 234″, the difference of the duration can amount to 12 minutes, whence we see that the difference of the parallaxes of Venus and the sun, and thus by Keppler's third law the parallax of the sun itself can be determined with great accuracy.

Example. For the transit of Venus in 1761 June 5 we have the following places of the sun and of Venus:

Paris m. t.	A	D	α	δ
16^h	74° 17′ 1″.8	+22° 41′ 3″.7	74° 25′ 50″.3	+22° 33′ 17″.6
17^h	19 36 .4	41 19 .1	24 13 .2	32 32 .4
18^h	22 10 .9	41 34 .5	22 36 .2	31 47 .1
19^h	24 45 .5	41 49 .9	20 59 .2	31 1 .9
20^h	27 20 .1	42 5 .3	19 22 .2	30 16 .6,

further:

$$\pi = 29''.6068 \qquad R = 946''.8$$
$$p = 8''.4408 \qquad r = 29''.0.$$

In order to find the times of exterior contact for the centre of the earth, we take:

$$T = 17^h$$

and find:

$$\alpha - A = +4'\,36''.8,\ \delta - D = -8'\,46''.7,\ \frac{d\alpha}{dt} - \frac{dA}{dt} = -4'\,11''.6$$

$$\frac{d\delta}{dt} - \frac{dD}{dt} = -60''.65,\ R + r = 975''.8.$$

From this we find:

$$M = 154°\,7'.2 \qquad N = 255°\,21'.9$$
$$\log m = 2.76746 \qquad \log n = 2.38028$$
$$M - N = 258°\,45'.3$$
$$\psi = -36\quad 2.6$$

$$-\frac{m}{n}\cos(M-N) = +0.4756 \qquad \tau = -2^h.8114 = -2^h 48^m 41^s.0$$

$$+\frac{(R+r)\cos\psi}{n} = +3.2870 \qquad \tau' = +3\ .7626 = +3\ 45\ 45\ .4$$

Therefore the ingress took place for the centre of the earth:

at $14^h\,11^m\,19^s.0$ Paris mean time,

and it was:

$$\odot = 111°\,24'.5,$$

and the egress took place at

$20^h\,45^m\,45^s.4$ Paris mean time,

and it was:

$$\odot = 219°\,19'.3.$$

If we wish to find then the time of the egress for places on the surface of the earth, we must first compute the constant quantities λ, β and g and find first:

$$s = 90^0\ 22'.7, \quad \log f = 1.32564, \quad \log g = 9.03764,$$

and since:

$$\odot = 219^0\ 19'.3, \quad D = 22^0\ 42'\ 3, \quad A = 74^0\ 29'.3,$$

we obtain:

$$\lambda = 9^0\ 15'.9$$

and

$$\beta = -45^0\ 44'.4.$$

Further since $20^h\ 45^m\ 45^s.4$ Paris mean time corresponds to $1^h\ 45^m\ 34^s.6$ sidereal time, we have:

$$\Delta = -17^0\ 7'.7.$$

If it is required for instance to find the egress for the Cape of Good Hope, for which:

$$l = +1^h\ 4^m\ 33^s.5$$

and

$$\varphi = -33^0\ 56'\ 3'',$$

we find:

$$\log \cos \zeta = 9.94643, \quad g \cos \zeta = +5'\ 47''.0,$$

and hence the local mean time of the egress:

$$t + \lambda + g \cos \zeta = 21^h\ 56^m\ 5^s.9.$$

If we differentiate the equation:

$$T = t + l + g \cos \zeta,$$

we find, if dT is expressed in seconds:

$$\begin{aligned} dT &= \frac{3600 \cos \zeta}{n \cos \psi} d(\pi - p) \\ &= \frac{3600 \cos \zeta}{n \cos \psi} \cdot \frac{\pi - p}{p_0} dp_0 \\ &= 40.49\, dp_0 \text{ *)}, \end{aligned}$$

so that an error of the assumed value of the parallax of the sun equal to $0''.13$ changes the time of the contact of the limbs by 5^s. Conversely any errors of observation will have only a small effect upon the value of the parallax deduced from them, and thus this important element can be found with great accuracy by this method.

5. In order to find the complete equation, to which any observation of the contact of the limbs leads, we start from the following equation:

$$[\alpha' - A']^2 \cos \delta_0{}^2 + [\delta' - D']^2\, [R \pm r]^2, \qquad (a)$$

---

*) Where p_0 is the mean horizontal equatoreal parallax.

where α', A', δ' and D' are the apparent right ascensions and declinations of the sun and Venus, affected with parallax, and δ_0 denotes the arithmetical mean $\frac{\delta' + D'}{2}$. But since the parallaxes of the two bodies are small and likewise the differences of the right ascensions and declinations for the times of contact of the limbs are small quantities, we can take:

$$\alpha' - A' = \alpha - A + (\pi - p) \sec \delta_0 \cos \varphi' \sin (\alpha_0 - \Theta)$$
$$\delta' - D' = \delta - D + (\pi - p) [\cos \varphi' \sin \delta_0 \cos (\alpha_0 - \Theta) - \sin \varphi' \cos \delta_0],$$

where:

$$\alpha_0 = \frac{\alpha + A}{2}$$

If now we introduce the following auxiliary quantities:

$$\left.\begin{aligned} \cos \varphi' \sin (\alpha_0 - \Theta) &= h \sin H \\ \cos \varphi' \sin \delta_0 \cos (\alpha_0 - \Theta) - \sin \varphi' \cos \delta_0 &= h \cos H, \end{aligned}\right\} \quad (A)$$

the equation (a) is transformed into:

$$[\alpha - A + (\pi - p) h \sin H \sec \delta_0]^2 \cos \delta_0{}^2 + [\delta - D + (\pi - p) h \cos H]^2 = [R \pm r]^2.$$

If then α, A, δ, D, π, p, R and r, denote the values which are taken from the tables, whilst $\alpha + d\alpha$, $\delta + d\delta$, $A + dA$, $D + dD$, $\pi + d\pi$, $p + dp$, $R + dR$ and $r + dr$ are the true values, and dl is the error in the assumed longitude of the place of observation, the equation must be written in this way:

$$\left[\begin{aligned} \alpha - A + (\pi - p) h \sin H \sec \delta_0 + d(\alpha - A) \\ + d(\pi - p) h \sin H \sec \delta_0 - \frac{d(\alpha - A)}{dt} dl \end{aligned}\right]^2 \cos \delta_0{}^2$$
$$+ [\delta - D + (\pi - p) h \cos H + d(\delta - D) + d(\pi - p) h \cos H - \frac{d(\delta - D)}{dt} dl]^2$$
$$= [R + dR \pm r + dr]^2.$$

If we develop this equation and neglect the squares and the products of $\pi - p$ and the small increments, and put:

$$\alpha - A + (\pi - p) h \sin H \sec \delta_0 = A'$$
$$\delta - D + (\pi - p) h \cos H \qquad = D',$$

we find:

$$A'^2 \cos \delta_0{}^2 + D'^2 - (R \pm r)^2$$
$$= -2 A' \cos \delta_0{}^2 d(\alpha - A) - 2 [A' h \sin H \cos \delta_0 + D' h \cos H] d(\pi - p)$$
$$- 2 D' d(\delta - D) + 2 \left(A' \frac{d(\alpha - A)}{dt} \cos \delta_0{}^2 + D' \frac{d(\delta - D)}{dt}\right) dl$$
$$+ 2 (R \pm r) d(R \pm r).$$

But if we denote:

$$A'^2 \cos \delta_0{}^2 + D'^2$$

by m^2, and since we have approximately:

$$m^2 - (R \pm r)^2 = 2m [m - (R \pm r)],$$

we find:

$$m[m-(R\pm r)] = -A'\cos\delta_0{}^2\, d(\alpha-A) - D'\,d(\delta-D)$$
$$-[A'h\sin H\cos\delta_0 + D'h\cos H]\,d(\pi-p)$$
$$+\left(A'\frac{d(\alpha-A)}{dt}\cos\delta_0{}^2 + D'\frac{d(\delta-D)}{dt}\right)dl + (R\pm r)\,d(R\pm r).$$

Therefore if we put again:

$$\left.\begin{array}{l} A'\cos\delta_0 = m\sin M \\ D' \qquad = m\cos M \end{array}\right\} \qquad (B)$$

$$\left.\begin{array}{r} \frac{1}{3600}\cos\delta_0\,\frac{d(\alpha-A)}{dt} = n\sin N \\ \frac{1}{3600}\,\frac{d(\delta-D)}{dt} = n\cos N \end{array}\right\} \qquad (C)$$

the equation becomes:

$$dl + \frac{(R\pm r-m)}{n\cos(M-N)} = \frac{\sin M\cos\delta\, d(\alpha-A)}{n\cos(M-N)} + \frac{\cos M\, d(\delta-D)}{n\cos(M-N)}$$
$$+\frac{h\cos(M-H)}{n\cos(M-N)}\,\frac{\pi-p}{p_0}\,dp_0 - \frac{d(R\pm r)}{n\cos(M-N)}. \qquad (D)$$

The difference of longitude dl must be determined by other observations and thus dl can be taken equal to 0. In this case all the divisors might be omitted, but if we retain them, $R\pm r - m$ is expressed in seconds of time, because we have:

$$n\cos(M-N) = \frac{dm}{dt}.$$

Example. The interior contact at the egress was observed at the Cape of Good Hope at

$21^h\,38^m\,3^s.3$ mean time.

This time corresponds to

$20^h\,33^m\,29^s.8$ Paris mean time $= 1^h\,33^m\,16^s.2$ Paris sidereal time.

We have therefore:

$$\Theta = 2^h\,37^m\,49^s.7 = 39^\circ\,27'\,25''.$$

Moreover we have for that time:

$$\begin{array}{ll} \alpha = 74^\circ\,18'\,28''.05 & \delta = 22^\circ\,29'\,51''.32 \\ A = 74\;\;28\;\;46\;.41 & D = 22\;\;42\;\;13\;.90 \\ \hline \alpha - A = -\;\;10'\,18''.36 & \delta - D = -\;\;12'\,22''.58 \end{array}$$

$$\alpha_0 = 74^\circ\,23'37'' \qquad \alpha_0 - \Theta = 34^\circ\,56'\,12'' \qquad \delta_0 = 22^\circ\,36'2''$$
$$(\pi-p)\,h\sin H = +\,10''.07 \qquad H = 31^\circ\,34'.0 \qquad (\pi-p)\,h\sin H\sec\delta_0$$
$$(\pi-p)\,h\cos H = +\,16\;.39 \qquad \log h = 9.95835 \qquad = +\,10''.90$$

$$A' = -\,10'\,7''.46$$
$$D' = -\,12\;\;6\;.19$$

$$M = 217^\circ\,40'.7 \qquad N = 255^\circ\,19'.3$$
$$\log m = 2.96262 \qquad \log n = 8.82412.$$

Now since:

$$R - r = 917''.80$$

and:

$$p_0 = 8''.57116,$$

we find:

$$-5.3 = 10.684\, d(\alpha - A) + 14.986\, d(\delta - D) + 42.240\, dp_0 + 18.934\, d(R - r).$$

Such an equation of the form:

$$0 = n + a\, d(\alpha - A) + b\, d(\delta - D) + c dp_0 + e\, d(R - r)$$

is obtained from each observation of an interior contact and a similar one containing $d(R + r)$ from an exterior contact, and from a great member of such equations, derived from observations at different places on the surface of the earth, the most probable values of dp_0, $d(\alpha - A)$, $d(\delta - D)$ and $d(R \pm r)$ can be found by the method of least squares.

In this way Encke *) found by a careful discussion of all observations made of the transits of Venus in the years 1761 and 1769 the parallax of the sun equal to 8''.5776. More recently after the discovery of the original manuscript of Hell's observations of the transit of 1769 made at Wardoe in Lapland, he has altered this value a little and gives as the best value

$$8''.57116$$

When the parallax of the sun is known, that of any other body, whose distance from the earth, expressed in terms of the semi-major axis of the earth's orbit as unit, is Δ, is found by means of the equation:

$$\sin p = \frac{8''.57116}{\Delta}.$$

Note 1. Although a great degree of confidence has always been placed in the value of the parallax of the sun, as determined by Encke, still not only the theory of the moon and of Venus, but also the recent observations for determining the parallax of Mars and a new discussion of the transit of 1769 by Powalky, who used for the longitudes of several places of observa-

*) Encke, Entfernung der Sonne von der Erde aus dem Venusdurchgang von 1761. Gotha 1822.

Encke, Venusdurchgang von 1769. Gotha 1824.

tion more correct values than were at Encke's disposal, all seem to indicate, that this value must be considerably increased.

Note 2. The transits of Mercury are by far less favourable for determining the parallax of the sun. For since the hourly motion of Mercury at the time of the inferior conjunction is 550″, while the difference of the parallaxes of Mercury and the sun is 9″, the coefficient of dp_0 in the equation (D) in the case of Mercury is to the same coefficient in the case of Venus as:

$$\frac{23}{9}\cdot\frac{550}{234}:1,$$

hence 6 times smaller. Thus an error of observation equal to 5^s produces already an error of $0''.8$ in the parallax of the sun. However on account of the great excentricity of the orbit of Mercury this ratio can become a little more favourable, if Mercury at the time of the inferior conjunction is in its aphelion or at its greatest distance from the sun.

SEVENTH SECTION.

THEORY OF THE ASTRONOMICAL INSTRUMENTS.

Every instrument, with which the position of a heavenly body with respect to one of the fundamental planes can be fully determined, represents a system of rectangular co-ordinates referred to this fundamental plane. For, such an instrument consists in its essential parts of two circles, one of which represents the plane of xy of the system of co-ordinates, whilst the other circle perpendicular to it and bearing the telescope turns around an axis of the instrument perpendicular to the first plane and can thus represent all great circles which are vertical to the plane of xy. If such an instrument were perfectly correct, the spherical co-ordinates of any point, towards which the telescope is directed, could be read off directly on the circles. With every instrument, however, errors must be presupposed, arising partly from the manner, in which it is mounted, and partly from the imperfect execution of the same, and which cause, that the circles of the instrument do not coincide exactly with the planes of the co-ordinates, but make a small angle with them. The problem then is, to determine the deviations of the circles of the instrument from the true planes of co-ordinates, in order to derive from the co-ordinates observed on the circles the true values of these co-ordinates.

Besides other errors occur with instruments, arising partly from the effect of gravity and temperature on the several parts of the instrument, partly from the imperfect execution of particular parts, such as the pivots, the graduation of the circles etc., and means must be had to determine these errors as far as possible, so as to find from the indications of the instrument the true co-ordinates of the heavenly bodies with the greatest possible approximation.

Besides these instruments, with which two co-ordinates of a body perpendicular to each other can be observed, there are still others, with which only a single co-ordinate or merely the relative position of two bodies can be observed. With regard to these instruments likewise the methods must be learned, by which the true values of the observed angles can be obtained from the readings.

I. SOME OBJECTS PERTAINING IN GENERAL TO ALL INSTRUMENTS.

A. *Use of the spirit-level.*

1. The spirit-level serves to find the inclination of a line to the horizon. It consists of a closed glass tube so nearly filled with a fluid that only a small space filled with air remains. Since the upper part of this tube is ground out into a curve, the air-bubble in every position of the level so places itself as to occupy the highest point in this curve. The highest point for the horizontal position of the level is denoted by zero, and on both sides of this point is arranged a graduated scale marked off in equal intervals and counting in both directions from the zero of the scale. If the level could be placed directly on the line, it would only be necessary, in order to render this line horizontal, to change its inclination to the horizon, until the centre of the bubble occupy the highest point, that is, the zero of the scale. Since however this is not practicable, the glass tube for its better protection is first firmly fixed in a brass tube which leaves the graduated scale of the level free, and this tube is itself placed in a wide brass tube of the whole length of the axis of the instrument. The upper middle part of this tube is cut out and covered with a plane glass. In this tube the other is fastened by means of horizontal and vertical screws which also serve as adjusting screws, so that the graduated scale of the level is directly under the plane glass through which it can be read off*). The tube is then provided with two rectangular supports for placing it upon the pivots or for the larger instruments with corresponding hooks for suspending it on the axis of the instrument. Generally however these supports or hooks are not of equal length. Let AB

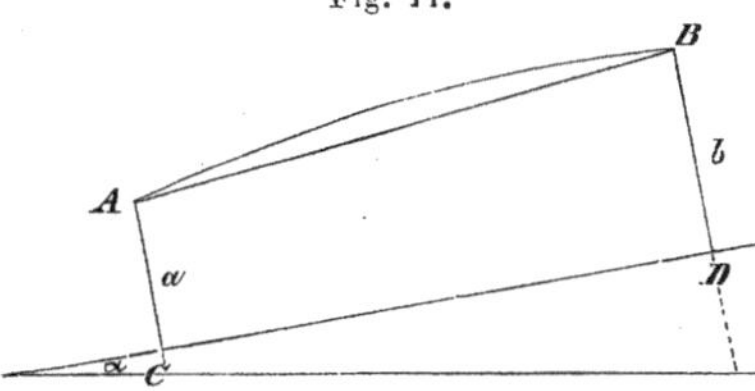

Fig. 11.

Fig. 11 be the level, AC and BD be the two supports, whose length is represented by a and b and suppose the level to be placed on a line, which makes with the horizon an angle α, in such a manner, that BD shall stand upon the higher side. Then will A stand in the height $a + c$ and B in the height:

$$b + c + L \operatorname{tang} \alpha$$

if L is the length of the level. This is, to be sure, not entirely correct, because the supports AC and BD do not stand perpendicularly to the horizontal line; since however only small inclinations of a few minutes, generally of a few seconds, are always here assumed, this approximation suffices perfectly. If now we call the angle which the line AB makes with the horizon x, then we have:

$$\operatorname{tang} x = \frac{b - a + L \operatorname{tang} \alpha}{L},$$

or

$$x = \alpha + \frac{b - a}{L}.$$

If we reverse the level so that B shall stand on the lower side and call x' the angle, which AB now makes with the horizon, then we have:

$$x' = \alpha - \frac{b - a}{L}.$$

If furthermore we now assume, that the zero has been marked erroneously on the level and that it stands nearer to B than to A by λ, then if the level be placed directly on a horizontal line, we read $l + \lambda$ on the side A, if $2l$ be

*) This arrangement is adopted in order that the level may be in a completely closed place and not liable to be disturbed in reading off by the warmth of the observer or of the lamp.

the length of the bubble, and $l - \lambda$ on the side B. Suppose on the other hand the level to be placed on the line AB, whose inclination to the horizon is x, then we read on the side A:

$$A = l + \lambda - rx,$$

where r is the radius of the curve AB, in which the level has been ground out, on the contrary on the higher side B:

$$B = l - \lambda + rx,$$

If the level with its supports be reversed in such a manner that B shall stand upon the lower end, we shall read:

$$A' = l + \lambda + rx'$$
$$B' = l - \lambda - rx'.$$

If we now substitute for x and x' the values already found, we shall find for the four different readings, denoting the inequality of the supports expressed in units of the scale of the level by u:

$$A = l - r\alpha + \lambda - ru$$
$$B = l + r\alpha - \lambda + ru$$
$$A' = l + r\alpha + \lambda - ru$$
$$B' = l - r\alpha - \lambda + ru.$$

It is obvious from the above, that the two quantities λ and ru cannot be separated from each other, and that for the reading off it is one and the same, whether the zero-point be not in the centre or whether the supports be of unequal length. On the other hand by the combination of these equations we can find $\lambda - ru$ and α.

If the end B of the bubble is on a particular side of the axis of an instrument, for instance, on the same side as the circle, which we will call the circle-end, then after the reversion of the level we shall read on this side A'. Now we have:

$$\frac{B - A}{2} = -\lambda + ru + r\alpha$$

$$\frac{A' - B'}{2} = \lambda - ru + r\alpha,$$

therefore:

$$\alpha = \frac{\frac{1}{2}\left(\frac{B - A}{2} + \frac{A' - B'}{2}\right)}{r} 206265,$$

if we wish to have the inclination directly in seconds of arc. The quantity $\frac{206265}{r}$ is then the value of one unit on the scale expressed in seconds of arc.

Therefore, if we wish to determine the inclination of an axis of an instrument by means of the level, we place it in two different positions on the axis and read off both ends of the bubble in each position. We then subtract the reading on the side of the circle from the reading made on the other side and divide the arithmetical mean of the values found in both positions by 2. The result is the elevation of the circle-end of the axis expressed in units of the scale. Finally if this number be multiplied by the value of the unit of the scale in seconds of arc, the result will be the elevation of the circle-end in seconds of arc.

If we can assume, that the length of the bubble during the observation does not change, we have also:

$$a = \tfrac{1}{2}\frac{(A' - A)}{r},$$

or:

$$= \tfrac{1}{2}\frac{(B - B')}{r}$$

i. e. the inclination would be equal to half the movement of the bubble on a determined end. If finally the level were perfectly accurate, then we should have $\lambda - ru = 0$ and it would not be necessary, to reverse the level, but the inclination could be derived merely from one position by taking half the difference of the readings on both ends.

Example. On the prime vertical instrument of the Berlin observatory the following levelings were made:

	Circle-end			Circle-end	
Object glass East	17.0	9.2	Object glass West	6.9	19.5
	8.2	18.0		16.1	10.3

$$\frac{B-A}{2} = +3^p.90 \qquad\qquad -6^p.30$$

$$\lambda - ru = -8^p.80 \qquad\qquad \lambda - ru = -9^p.20$$

$$\frac{A'-B'}{2} = -4\,.90 \qquad\qquad +2\,.90$$

$$-0^p.50 \qquad\qquad -1^p.70$$

Therefore by the mean of both levelings we have $b = -1^p.10$, or since the value of the unit of the scale was equal to $2''(1 - \frac{1}{16})$, $b = -2''.06$.

The above supposes, that a tangent which we imagine drawn to the zero of the level is in the same plane with the axis of the instrument. In order to obtain this result, the level must first be so rectified, that this tangent lies in a plane parallel to the axis, which is the case, when $\lambda - ru$ equals zero. If this value by the leveling is found to be equal to zero, then the level is in this sense rectified; if however, as in the above example, a value different from zero be found, then the inclination of the level must be so changed by means of the vertical adjusting screws as to fulfill the above condition, which will be the case, when A equals A' and B equals B', or when on the side of the circle-end as well as on the opposite side, the bubble has the same position before and after the reversion. In the above example, where $\lambda - ru$ is $9''.00$, it would be necessary to change the inclination of the level, until the bubble in the last position for Object glass West indicates 11.6 and 14.8. Then we should have read on the level so rectified:

Object glass East	12.5	13.7	Object glass West	11.4	15.0
	12.7	13.5		11.6	14.8,

whereby we should have found again the inclinations $-0''.50$ and $-1''.70$, and $\lambda - ru$ equal to zero.

If the level has been thus rectified, the tangent to the zero of the level is in a plane parallel to the axis. If now the level be turned a little on the axis of the instrument in such a manner that the hooks always remain closely in contact with the pivots, then will the tangent to the zero, if it is parallel to the axis, also remain parallel when the level is turned, and the bubble will not change its position by reason of this movement. If however the tangent in the plane parallel to the axis makes an angle with a line parallel to the axis, then will the inclination to the axis be changed when the level is turned, and since the bubble always moves towards the higher end, the end towards which the bubble moves if the level is turned towards the observer, is too near the observer. This end then must be moved by means of the horizontal adjusting screws, until the bubble preserves its position unaffected, when the level is turned, in which case the tangent to the zero is parallel to the axis. By the motion of the horizontal screws, however, the level is generally somewhat changed in a vertical sense so that ordinarily it will be necessary to repeat several times both corrections in a horizontal and vertical sense, before the perfect parallelism of the level with the axis of the instrument can be attained.

2. In order to find the value of the unit of the scale in seconds, the level must be fixed on a vertical circle of an instrument provided with an arrangement for that purpose, and then by means of the simultaneous reading of the level and of the graduated circle, and by repeating the readings in a somewhat different position of the circle, the number of units is found, which corresponds to the number of seconds which the circle has been turned. If the bubble passes through α divisions, whilst the circle revolves through β seconds, then is $\frac{\beta}{\alpha}$ the value of the unit of the scale in seconds.

In making this investigation however it is best, not to remove the level from the tube, in which it is enclosed, since it is to be presumed, that the screws which hold it may produce a somewhat different curve from that which the level itself would have without them, and since a large level cannot be well fastened on a circle of an instrument, it is best to use for this purpose a special instrument which consists in its essential parts of a strong T-shaped supporter, which rests on three screws and on which the level can be placed in two rectangular Y-pieces, in such a manner, that the direction of the level passes through one of the screws and is perpendicular to the line joining the two other screws. The first screw is intended for measuring and is therefore carefully finished and provided with a graduated head and an index, by which the parts of a revolution of the screw can be read off. By means of an auxiliary level the apparatus can be so rectified as to render this screw exactly vertical. If now the level is read off in one position of the screw and then again after the screw has been turned a little, the length of the unit of the scale will be found in parts of the revolution of the screw. If now we know by exact measurement the distance f of the screw from the line joining the two other screws and the distance h between the threads of the screw, then will $\frac{h}{f}$ be the tangent of the angle, which corresponds to one revolution of the screw or $\frac{h}{f}$ 206265 be this angle itself. The perfection of the screw can be easily tested by observing, whether the bubble always advances an equal number of units, when the screw is turned the same number of units of the graduated head. But it is not necessary that the parts of the scale be really of equal length for the whole extent of the scale; it is only essential that this equality exists for those parts, which are liable to be used in leveling and which at least in levels, as they are made now, do not extend far on both sides of the zero. To be sure the bubble of the level changes its length in heat and cold on account of the expansion and contraction of the fluid; but levels are now made so, that there is a small reservoir at one end of the tube, also partly filled with a fluid, which is in communication with that in the level through a small aperture. Then, if the bubble has become too long, the level can be filled from the reservoir by inclining it so that the reservoir stands on the elevated side. If on the contrary the bubble is too short, a portion of the fluid can be drawn off by inclining the level in the opposite direction. In this manner the bubble can be always kept very nearly of the same length, and if care be taken, to have the level always well rectified and the inclination of the axis small, then only a very few parts will be necessary for all levelings and their length can be carefully determined. Besides it would be well to repeat this determination at very different temperatures in order to ascertain, whether the value of the unit of the scale changes with the temperature. If such a dependence is manifest, then the value of the unit of the level must be expressed by a formula of the form:

$$l = a + b\,(t - t_0)$$

where a is the value at a certain temperature t_0, and in which the values of a and b must be determined according to the method of least squares from the values observed by different temperatures.

Instead of a special instrument for determining the unit of the scale an altitude azimuth and a collimator can also be used, if the latter be so arranged, that two rectangular

Ys can be fastened to it, in which the level can be placed so that it is parallel to the axis of the collimator. If then this collimator be mounted before an altitude instrument with a finely graduated circle, and the level be placed in the Ys and read off and likewise the circle, after the wire-cross of the instrument is brought in coincidence with the wire-cross of the collimator, and if this process be repeated after the inclination of the collimator has been somewhat changed by means of one of the foot-screws, then will the length of the unit of the scale be determined by comparing the difference of the two readings of the level with those of the circle.

Theodolites or altitude and azimuth instruments are frequently already so arranged, that the length of the unit of the scale of the level can be determined by means of one of the foot-screws, which is finely cut for this purpose and is provided with a graduated head. These instruments rest namely on three foot-screws which form a equilateral triangle. If now the level be set upon the horizontal axis of such an instrument and the axis be so placed, that the direction of the level shall pass through the screw a provided with the graduated head and therefore be perpendicular to the line joining the two other screws, then can the value of the unit of the scale be determined from the readings of the screw a and the corresponding motion of the bubble of the level, when the distance between the threads of the screw as well as the distance of the screw a from the line joining the two other screws are known. The value of the unit of the scale for the level attached to the supports of the microscopes or the verniers of the vertical circle is determined by directing the telescope to the wire-cross of a collimator or to a distant terrestrial object and then reading off both the circle and the level. If then the inclination of the telescope to the object be changed by means of the foot-screws of the instrument, the amount of the inclination in units of the scale can be read off on the level, whilst the same can be obtained in seconds by turning the telescope towards the object and reading off the circle in the new position.

3. The case hitherto considered, to determine by means of the level the inclination of a line upon which the level can be placed, never actually occurs with the instruments, but the inclination of an axis is always sought which is only given by a pair of cylindrical pivots on which the level must be placed. Even if the axis of the cylinders coincides with the mathematical axis of the instrument, nevertheless the cylinders may be of different diameters, and in that case a level placed upon them will not give the inclination of the axis of the instrument. These pivots always rest on Ys, which are formed by planes making with each other an angle which we will denote by $2i$. Let the angle of the hooks of the level, by which it is held on the axis, be $2i'$ and let the radius of the pivot on one end (for which here again the circle-end is taken) be r_0, then will bC (Fig. 12) or the elevation of the centre of the pivot above the Y be equal to r_0 cosec i, likewise we have:

Fig. 12.

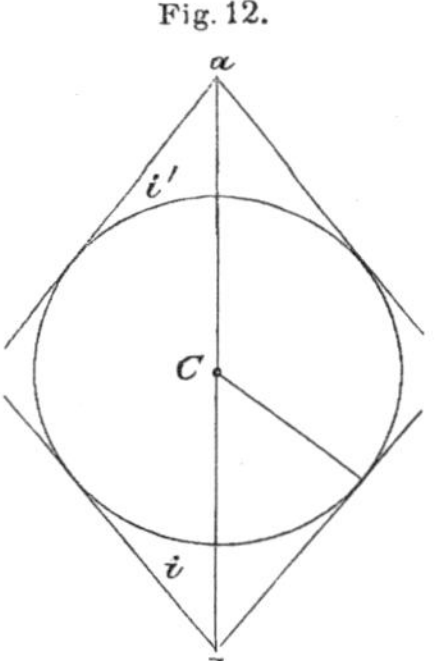

$$aC = r_0 \text{ cosec } i',$$

hence:

$$ab = r_0 \, [\text{cosec } i' + \text{cosec } i],$$

and on the other end of the axis we have:

$$a'b' = r_1 \, [\text{cosec } i' + \text{cosec } i],$$

where r_1 is the radius of the pivot on this side. If now the line through the two Ys makes with the horizon the angle x, then, if the diameters of the pivots be equal, the same inclination x will be found by means of the level. If however the pivots are unequal, then, if x denotes the elevation of the Y of the circle-end, we will have for the elevation b of the circle-end:

$$b = x + \frac{r_0 - r_1}{L} \, [\text{cosec } i' + \text{cosec } i],$$

where L is the length of the axis. If however the instrument be reversed so that the circle shall now rest on the lower Y, then will the elevation of the circle-end be:

$$b' = -x + \frac{r_0 - r_1}{L} \, [\text{cosec } i' + \text{cosec } i].$$

From both equations we derive:

$$\frac{b' + b}{2} = \frac{r_0 - r_1}{L} [\text{cosec } i' + \text{cosec } i],$$

a quantity which remains constant so long as the thickness of the pivots does not change.

Now since we wish to find by means of the level the inclination of the mathematical axis of both cylinders, we must subtract from each b the quantity:

$$\frac{r_0 - r_1}{L} \text{cosec } i',$$

or if $\frac{r_0 - r_1}{L}$ be eliminated, the quantity:

$$\frac{\frac{1}{2}(b + b') \text{cosec } i'}{\text{cosec } i + \text{cosec } i'},$$

or:

$$\frac{\frac{1}{2}(b + b') \sin i}{\sin i + \sin i'}.$$

If the correction, as is generally the case, be small, then we can make $i = i'$ *) and we have therefore to apply to every result of leveling the quantity $-\frac{1}{4}(b + b')$, in which b and b' denote the level-errors found in the two different positions of the instrument.

Example. On the prime vertical instrument of the Berlin Observatory the inclination, that is, the elevation of the circle-end was found according to No. I. to be $b = -2''.06$, when the circle was south. After the reversion of the instrument the leveling was repeated and the inclination found to be $b' = +5''.02$, which value, as before, is the mean of two levelings by which in one case the object glass of the telescope was directed towards the east and in the other case towards the west. In this case therefore is:

$$\tfrac{1}{4}(b' + b) = +0''.74,$$

hence the inclination of the mathematical axis of the pivots was:

$$= -2''.80 \text{ Circle South}$$
$$\text{and } = +4''.28 \text{ Circle North.}$$

Hitherto it has been assumed, that the sections perpendicular to the axis of the pivots are exactly circular. If this is the case, then will the level in every inclination of the telescope give the same inclination of the axis, and the telescope when it is turned round the axis will describe a great

*) Usually i and i' are equal to about 90°.

circle. But if this condition be not fulfilled, then will the inclination be different for different elevations of the telescope and the telescope, when it is turned round the axis, will describe a kind of zigzag line instead of a great circle. By means of the level however we can determine the correction which is to be applied to the inclination in a particular position in order to obtain the inclination for another position. When, namely, the instrument is so arranged, that the level by different elevations of the telescope can be attached to the axis, then can the inclination of the axis in different positions of the telescope be found, for instance for every 15th or 30th degree of elevation, and only when the telescope is directed towards the zenith or the nadir will this be impossible. If these observations are also made in the other position of the instrument, then can the inequality of the pivots or the quantity $\frac{1}{4}(b+b')$ be determined for the different zenith distances, and if this be subtracted from the level-error in the corresponding positions of the telescope, the inclination of the axis for the different zenith distances will be obtained. By a comparison of the same with the inclination found for the horizontal position we can then obtain the corrections, which are to be applied to the inclination in the horizontal position, in order to obtain the inclination for the other zenith distances. These corrections can be found by observations for every tenth or thirtieth degree, and from these values either a periodical series for the correction may be found, or more simply by a graphic construction a curve, the abscissae of the several points being the zenith distances, and the ordinates the observed corrections of the inclination. Then for those zenith distances, for which the correction has not been found from observations, it is taken equal to the ordinate of this curve *).

---

*) The pivots can be examined still better by means of a level, constructed for that purpose, which is placed on the Y in such a manner that one end rests upon the pivot. If the level is first placed on the pivot at the circle-end, and read off by different zenith distances of the telescope and then the mean of the readings in the horizontal position of the telescope is subtracted, it is found, how much higher or lower the highest point of the pivot is than in the horizontal position. These observed differences shall be u_z. Now

B. The vernier and the reading microscope.

4. The vernier has for its object to read and subdivide the space between any two divisions on a circle of an instrument, and consists in an arc of a circle, which can be moved round the centre of the graduated circle, and which is divided into equal parts, the number of which is greater or less than the number of parts which it covers on the limb. The ratio of these numbers determines how far the reading by means of the vernier can be carried.

If we have a scale divided into equal parts, each of which is a, then the distance of any division from the zero can be given by a multiple of a. If then the zero of the vernier or the pointer, which we will denote by y, coincides exactly with one division of the limb, its distance from the zero of the limb is known. But if the zero of the vernier falls between two divisions of the limb, then some one division of the vernier must coincide with a division of the limb, at least so nearly that the distance from it is less than the quantity, which can be read off by means of the vernier. If the distance of this line of the limb from the zero point of the vernier be equal to p parts of the vernier, each of which is a', then its distance from the zero of the limb will be:

$$y + p a'.$$

But it is also $qa + pa$, where qa is that division of the limb, which precedes the zero of the vernier, hence we have:

$$y + p a' = q a + p a,$$

and therefore the distance of the zero of the vernier from the zero of the limb is:

$$y = q a + p (a - a').$$

If we have: $m a = (m + 1) a'$,

that is, if the number of parts on the vernier is greater by

---

if the same observations are made, when the level is placed on the other pivot and the values u'_z are obtained, then the line through the highest points of the pivots will have the same inclination in all the different positions of the instrument, if $u'_z = u_z$. But if this is not the case, then the quantity $\frac{u_z - u'_z}{L} 206265$, where L is the length of the axis, gives the difference of the inclination in this position of the telescope from that in the horizontal position.

one than the number which it covers on the limb, then we have:

$$a' = \frac{m}{m+1} a,$$

therefore:

$$y = q a + \frac{p a}{m+1}.$$

The quantity $\frac{a}{m+1}$ is called the least count of the vernier. Therefore in order to find the distance of the zero of the vernier from the zero of the limb or to read the instrument by means of a vernier: Read the limb in the direction of the graduation up to the division-line next preceding the zero point; this is the reading on the limb: look along the vernier until a line is found, that coincides with one on the limb; multiply the number of the line by the least count; this is the reading on the vernier, and the sum of these two readings is the reading of the instrument.

We see that if we take the number m large enough, we can make the least count of the vernier as small as we like. For instance if one degree on the limb of the instrument is divided into 6 equal parts, each being therefore 10 minutes, and we wish to carry the reading by means of the vernier to 10″, we must divide an arc of the vernier whose length is equal to 590′ in 60 parts, because then we have $\frac{a}{m+1} = 10''$. In order to facilitate the reading of the vernier, the first line following the zero of the vernier ought to be marked 10″, the second 20″ etc., but instead of this only the minutes are marked so that the sixth line is marked 1, the twelfth 2 etc.

In general we find m from the equation:

$$a - a' = \frac{a}{m+1} \quad \text{or} \quad m = \frac{a}{a - a'} - 1,$$

taking for $a - a'$ the least count of the vernier and for a the interval between two divisions of the limb, both expressed in terms of the same unit.

Hitherto we have assumed, that:

$$m a = (m+1) a',$$

therefore that the number of parts of the vernier is greater than the number of parts of the limb, which is covered by the vernier. But we can arrange the vernier also so, that the number of its parts is less, taking:

$$(m+1) a = m a'.$$

In this case we have: $a' - a = \frac{a}{m}$

and $$y = q\,a - p\,\frac{a}{m}.$$

In this case the vernier must be read in the opposite direction.

If the length of the vernier is too great or too small by the quantity Δl, then we have in the first case:

$$m\,a = (m + 1)\,a' - \Delta l,$$

therefore using the same notation as before:

$$y = q\,a + \frac{p\,a}{m+1} - p\,\frac{\Delta l}{m+1}.$$

Therefore if the length of the vernier is too great by Δl, we must add to the reading of the vernier the correction:

$$-\frac{p}{m+1}\,\Delta l,$$

where p is the number of the division of the vernier which coincides with a division of the limb and $m+1$ is the number of parts, into which the vernier is divided. For instance if we have an instrument, whose circle is divided to 10′, and which we can read to 10″ by means of a vernier, so that 59 parts of the circle are equal to 60 parts of the vernier, and if we find that the length of the vernier is 5″ too great, or $\Delta l = +5''$, we must add the correction $-\frac{p}{60}\,5''$. The length of the vernier can always be examined by means of the division of the limb. For this purpose make the zero of the vernier coincident successively with different divisions on the limb, and read the minutes and seconds corresponding to the last division-line on the vernier. Then the arithmetical mean of these readings will be equal to the length of the vernier.

5. If great accuracy is required for reading the circles, the instruments, for instance the meridian circles, are furnished with reading microscopes, which are firmly fastened either to the piers, or to the plates to which the Ys are attached, in such a manner, that they stand perpendicular over the graduation of the circles. The reading is accomplished by a moveable wire at the focus of the microscope, which is moved by means of a micrometer screw whose head is divided into equal parts, depending upon the extent to which the subdivisions are to be carried. The zero of the screw head is so placed that if the wire coincides with a division-line on the circle, the reading of the screw head is zero; in this case the circle is read up to this division-line; but if the wire falls between two division-lines of the circle, it is moved by turning the screw head until it coincides with the next preceding line on the circle, in which position the head of the screw is read, and the reading is then the sum of the reading on the circle and that on the screw head*). Thus the zero of the screw head corresponds to the zero of the vernier, since always the distance of the wire in the position when the reading of the screw is zero from the next preceding division-line of the circle is measured by means of the screw head. The value of one revolution of the screw expressed in seconds of arc is determined beforehand, and since the number of the entire revolutions of the screw can be read by a stationary comb-scale within the barrel of the microscope, whilst the parts of a revolution are read by means of the screw head, this distance can always be found. Now it can always be arranged so that an entire number of revolutions is equal to the interval between two division-lines of the circle, for the object glass of the microscope can be moved farther from or nearer to the eye-piece, and thus the image of the space between two lines can be altered and can be made equal to the space through which the wire is moved by an entire number of revolutions of the screw. If the screw performs more than an entire number of revolutions, when the wire is moved from one division-line to the next, then the object glass of the microscopes must be brought nearer to the eye-piece; but since by this operation the image is thrown off the plane of the wire, the whole body of the microscope must be brought nearer to the circle, until the image is again well defined.

The microscope must be placed so that the wire or the parallel wires are parallel to the division-lines of the circle, and that a plane passing through the axis of the microscope and any radius of the circle is perpendicular to the latter. If

---

*) It is better to use instead of a single wire two parallel wires and to bring the division lines of the circle exactly between these wires.

it is not rectified in this way, the image of a line moves a little sideways, when the circle is gently pressed with the hand, and thus errors would arise in reading off the circle, if it should not be an exact plane or should not be exactly perpendicular to the axis. If such a motion of the image arising from the gentle pressure of the hand be observed, the tube in which the object glass is fastened must be turned until a position is found in which such a pressure has no more effect upon the image.

Since the distance of the microscope from the circle is subject to small changes, the error of run, that is the difference between an entire number of revolutions and the measured distance of two division-lines, must be frequently determined and the reading of the microscope be corrected accordingly *). But it is not indifferent, which two lines of the circle are chosen for measuring their distance, since this can slightly vary on account of the errors of division; therefore the exact distance of two certain lines must first be found and then the run of the microscope always be determined by these two lines.

The micrometer screw itself can be defective so that by equal parts of a revolution of the screw the wires are not moved through equal spaces. In order to determine these errors of the screw, a short auxiliary line (marked so that it cannot be mistaken for a division-line) is requisite at a distance from a division-line, nearly equal to an aliquot part of the space between two lines, for instance at a distance of 10″ or 15″, in general at the distance α'' so that $120 = n\alpha$. If now we turn the micrometer screw to its zero and then by moving the circle bring the line nearest to the auxiliary line between the wires, we can bring the latter line between the

*) The circle of a meridian instrument is usually divided to 2 minutes, and two revolutions of the screw are equal to the interval between two division lines. Hence one revolution of the screw is equal to one minute and the head being divided into 60 parts, each part is one second, whose decimals can be estimated. In that position of the wires to which the zero of the screw head corresponds they bisect a little pointer connected with the comb scale, and if this pointer should be nearer to the following than to the preceding line, then one minute must be added to the reading on the screw head.

wires by the motion of the screw and thus measure the distance of the lines by means of the screw. If we leave now the screw untouched and move the circle, until the first line is again between the parallel wires, we can again by moving the screw bring the second line between the wires, and we can continue this operation, until the screw has made the two entire revolutions which are always used in reading the circle *). If then the different values of the distance of the two lines as measured by the screw are:

$$\begin{array}{ll} \text{from } 0 \text{ to } \alpha & a' \\ \text{from } \alpha \text{ to } 2\alpha & a'' \\ \vdots & \vdots \\ \text{from } (n-1)\,\alpha \text{ to } n\alpha & a^n, \end{array}$$

the last reading on the screw will again be nearly zero, and hence we can assume, that the mean value of all different a', a'' etc. is free from the errors of the screw. These observations must be repeated several times and also be changed so that the intervals are measured in the opposite direction, starting from 120 instead of 0, and then the means of all the several values a', a'' must be taken. If we put then:

$$\frac{a' + a'' + a''' + \ldots + a^n}{n} = a_0,$$

the correction, which must be added to the reading of the screw, if also the interval from $-\alpha$ to 0 and that from $n\alpha$ to $(n+1)\,\alpha$ is measured and the corresponding distances are denoted by a^{-1} and a^{n+1}, will be:

$$\begin{array}{rl} \text{for } -\alpha & -a_0 + a^{-1} \\ 0 & 0 \\ \alpha & a_0 - a' \\ 2\alpha & 2a_0 - a' - a'' \\ \vdots & \vdots \\ (n-1)\,\alpha = & (n-1)\,a_0 - a' - \ldots - a^{n-1} \\ n\alpha = & 0 \\ (n+1)\,\alpha = & a_0 - a^{n+1}. \end{array}$$

*) If there is no auxiliary line on the circle, the two parallel wires can be used for this purpose, if their distance is an aliquot part of 2 minutes. Then, when the screw is turned to its zero point, the circle is moved until a line coincides with one wire, and then the other wire is placed on the same line by moving the screw.

By means of these values the correction for every tenth second can be easily tabulated and then the values for any intermediate seconds be found by interpolation. The reading thus corrected is free from the errors of the screw and gives the true distance of the wires in the zero-position from the next preceding line, expressed in parts of the screw head, each of which is the sixtieth part of a revolution of the screw, and hence if two entire revolutions of the screw should differ from 2 minutes, this distance is not yet the distance expressed in seconds of arc.

Now in order to examine this, two lines on the circle are chosen, whose distance is known and shall be equal to $120 + y$. Then after moving the screw to its zero-point we move the circle until the following one of the two lines is between the wires and then bring by the motion of the screw the preceding line between the wires *). If in this position the corrected reading of the screw is $120 + p$, then the reading of the screw, if we had moved it from zero through exactly 120 seconds, would have been $120 + p - y$; therefore all readings must be corrected by multiplying them by:

$$\frac{120}{120 + p - y}.$$

It must still be shown, how the length of an interval between two certain lines, for instance that between $0^0\ 0'$ and $0^0\ 2'$, can be found. For this purpose first the length of the interval in parts of the screw head is found by moving the circle, after the screw has been turned to its zero, until the line $0^0\ 2'$ is between the wires, and then moving the latter by means of the screw, until the line $0^0\ 0'$ is between them. The length of the interval expressed in parts of the screw head shall be from the mean of many observations $120 + x$. If then in the same way a large number of intervals at different places of the circle are measured, we can assume that there are among them as many too great as there are too small, so that the arithmetical mean will be the true value of an interval equal to $120''$, expressed in parts of the screw

---

*) The reading of the screw increases, when it is turned in the opposite direction in which the division runs.

head. Now if the mean be $120 + u$, the first interval is too large by $x - u = y$ or is equal to $120 + y$.

The correction, which must be applied to the reading for this reason, can also be tabulated so that the argument is the reading on the screw. As long as the error of the run remains the same, this table can be united with the one for the corrections of the screw.

C. Errors arising from an excentricity of the circle and errors of division.

6. A cause of error which cannot be avoided with all astronomical instruments is that the centre round which the circle or the alhidade carrying the vernier revolves is different from that of the division. We will assume that C Fig. 13 be the centre of the division, C' that of the alhidade and that the direction $C'A'$ or the angle OCA' have been measured equal to $A' - O$, supposing that the angles are reckoned from O. Then, if the excentricity were nothing, we should have read the angle $ACO = A'C'O$. Denoting the radius of the circle CO by r and the angle $ACO = A'C'O$ by $A - O$, we have:

Fig. 13.

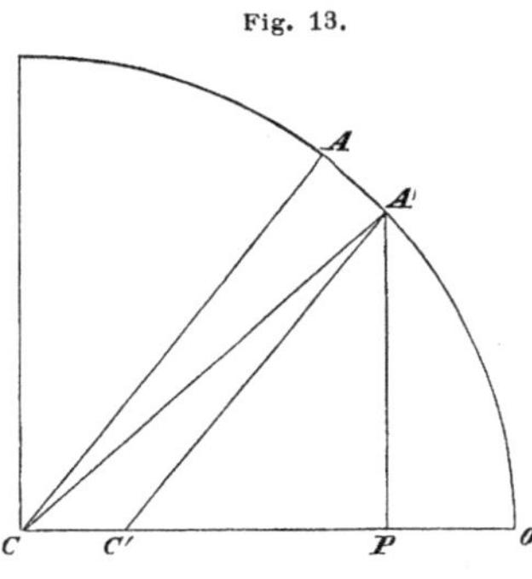

$$A'P = r \sin(A' - O) \quad = A'C' \sin(A - O)$$
$$\text{and } C'P = r \cos(A' - O) - e = A'C' \cos(A - O),$$

where e denotes the excentricity of the circle.

If we multiply the first equation by $\cos(A' - O)$, the second by $\sin(A' - O)$ and subtract the second from the first, we obtain:

$$A'C' \sin(A - A') = e \sin(A' - O).$$

But if we multiply the first by $\sin(A' - O)$, the second by $\cos(A' - O)$ and add them, we find:

$$A'C' \cos(A - A') = r - e \cos(A' - O),$$

therefore we have:

$$\operatorname{tang}(A - A') = \frac{\frac{e}{r} \sin(A' - O)}{1 - \frac{e}{r} \cos(A' - O)}$$

or by means of the formula (12) in No. 11 of the introduction:

$$A - A' = \frac{e}{r} \sin (A' - O) + \tfrac{1}{2} \frac{e^2}{r^2} \sin 2 (A' - O)$$
$$+ \tfrac{1}{3} \frac{e^3}{r^3} \sin 3 (A' - O) + \ldots$$

Now since $\frac{e}{r}$ is always a very small quantity, the first term of this series is always sufficient, and hence we find $A - A'$ expressed in seconds of arc:

$$A - A' = \frac{e}{r} \sin (A' - O)\, 206265,$$

whence we see, that the error $A - A'$ expressed in seconds can be considerable on account of the large factor 206265, although $\frac{e}{r}$ is very small.

In order to eliminate this error of the reading caused by the excentricity, there are always two verniers or microscopes opposite each other used for reading the circle. For if the alhidade consists of two stiff arms, each provided with a vernier, which may make any angle with each other, the correction for the reading B' by the second vernier would be similar so that we have:

$$A = A' + \frac{e}{r} \sin (A' - O)$$

and

$$B = B' + \frac{e}{r} \sin (B' - O),$$

and hence:

$$\tfrac{1}{2} (A + B) = \tfrac{1}{2} (A' + B') + \frac{e}{r} \sin [\tfrac{1}{2} (A' + B') - O] \cos \tfrac{1}{2} [A' - B'].$$

We see therefore, that in case that the angle between the arms of the alhidade $A' - B'$ is 180^0, then the arithmetical mean of the readings by both verniers is equal to the arithmetical mean which we should have found if the excentricity had been nothing. For this reason all instruments are furnished with two verniers exactly opposite each other, and by taking the arithmetical mean of the readings, made by these two verniers, the errors arising from an excentricity of the circle are entirely avoided.

In order to find the excentricity itself, we will subtract the two expressions for A and B. Then we get:

$$B - A = B' - A' + 2\frac{e}{r}\cos\left[\tfrac{1}{2}(A' + B') - O\right]\sin\tfrac{1}{2}(B' - A')$$

or supposing that the angle between the verniers differs from 180^0 by the small angle α:

$$B - A = 180 + \alpha,$$

$$B' - A' = 180^0 + \alpha + 2\frac{e}{r}\sin(A' - O)$$

$$= 180^0 + \alpha + 2\frac{e}{r}\cos O\sin A' - 2\frac{e}{r}\sin O\cos A'.$$

If we take now:

$$B' - A' - 180^0 = [X_{A'}],\ 2\frac{e}{r}\cos O = z \text{ and } 2\frac{e}{r}\sin O = y,$$

we obtain:

$$[X_{A'}] = \alpha + z\sin A' - y\cos A',$$

and hence we can find the unknown quantities α, z and y by readings at different places of the circle.

Example. With the meridian circle at the Berlin Observatory the following values of $B' - A' - 180^0$ were observed for two microscopes opposite each other:

$X_0 = +0''.3$	$X_{180} = +1''.5$
$X_{30} = +3.3$	$X_{210} = -0.6$
$X_{60} = +3.8$	$X_{240} = +0.7$
$X_{90} = +3.1$	$X_{270} = +0.7$
$X_{120} = +4.8$	$X_{300} = -2.5$
$X_{150} = +6.4$	$X_{330} = -4.8.$

From this we find the sum of all these quantities:

$$+16.7 = 12\alpha$$

hence:

$$\alpha = +1''.39.$$

Moreover we find according to No. 27 of the introduction:

A	X_A $+$	X_A $+-$	X_A $-$	X_A $-+$
0^0	$+0.3$	-1.2		
30^0	-1.5	-7.3	$+8.1$	$+15.1$
60	$+1.3$	-4.2	$+6.3$	$+10.4$
90	$+3.8$		$+2.4$	$+2.4$
120	$+5.5$		$+4.1$	
150	$+5.8$		$+7.0$	
180	$+1.5$			

and hence:

$$\tfrac{1}{2}ny = +9''.62$$
$$\tfrac{1}{2}nz = +18.96,$$

therefore:

$$O = 26^0\ 54'.2 \text{ and } \frac{e}{r} = 1''.772.$$

7. If a circle is furnished with several pairs of verniers or microscopes, as it is generally the case, the arithmetical mean of the readings by two verniers ought always to differ from the arithmetical mean of the readings by two other verniers by the same constant quantity, if there were no other errors besides the excentricity. However since the graduation itself is not perfectly accurate, this will never be the case. But, whatever may be the nature of these errors of division, they can always be represented by a periodical series of the form:

$$a + a_1 \cos A + a_2 \cos 2A + \ldots\ldots$$
$$+ b_1 \sin A + b_2 \sin 2A + \ldots\ldots$$

where A is the reading by a single vernier or microscope.

If now we use i verniers equally distributed over the circle, then their readings are:

$$A, A + \frac{2\pi}{i}, A + 2 \cdot \frac{2\pi}{i}, \ldots$$

and

$$A + (i - 1)\frac{2\pi}{i},$$

and if we now take the mean of all readings, a large number of terms of the periodical series for the errors of division will be eliminated, as is easily seen, if we develop the trigonometrical functions of the several angles and make use of the formulae (1) to (5) in No. 26 of the introduction.

In case that the number of verniers is i, only those terms remain, which contain i times the angle. Hence we see that by using several verniers a large portion of the errors of division is eliminated, and that therefore it is of great advantage to use several pairs of verniers or microscopes.

The errors of division are determined by comparing intervals between lines, which are aliquot parts of the circumference, with each other. For instance if the errors of division were to be found for every fifth degree, we should place two microscopes at a distance of about 5 degrees over the graduation. Then we should bring by the motion of the circle the line marked 0^0 under one microscope, which we leave untouched during the entire operation, and measure the distance of the line marked 5^0 by the micrometer screw of the second microscope simply by turning this screw until that line is between the wires and then reading the head of the screw. If now we turn the circle until the line 5^0 is between the wires of the first microscope, the line 10^0 will be under the second microscope and its distance from the line 5^0 can be measured in the same way, and this operation can be continued through the entire circumference, so that we return to the line 0^0 and measure its distance from the line 355^0. The same operation can be repeated, the circle being turned in the opposite direction. If then we take the arithmetical mean of all readings of the screw and denote it by α_0 and the readings for the lines 5^0, 10^0 etc. by α', α'' etc., the error of the line 5^0, taking that of the line 0^0 as nothing, will be $\alpha_0 - \alpha'$, that of the line 10^0, $2\alpha_0 - \alpha' - \alpha''$ etc. But since the circle undergoes during so long a series changes by the change of temperature, it is better, to determine the errors of the several lines in this way, that first the errors of a few lines, for instance those of the lines 0^0 and 180^0, be determined with the utmost accuracy, and then relying upon these, the errors of the lines 90^0 and 270^0 be determined by dividing the arcs of 180^0 into two equal parts; and then by dividing the arcs of 90^0 again into two or three equal parts and going on in the same way, the errors of the intermediate lines are found. Small arcs of 1 degree or 2 degrees may even be divided into five or six equal parts, but for larger arcs it is always preferable to divide them only into two equal parts. These operations can be quickly performed and for the sake of greater accuracy be repeated several times.

In order to make this examination of the graduation, two microscopes are requisite which can be placed at any distance from each other over the graduation. For small intervals, for instance of one degree, one microscope with a divided object glass can be conveniently used. Before the operation is begun, the microscopes must of course be rectified according to No. 5, and it is best, to use always the same microscope for measuring and to arrange the observations even so, that always the same portion of the micrometer screw is used for these measurements. This end can always be attained, if at the beginning of each series the screw of that microscope which is merely used as a Zero is suitably changed.

Example. For the examination of the graduation of the Ann Arbor meridian circle two microscopes were first placed at a distance of 180°. When the line 0° was placed under the first microscope, the reading of the second microscope after being set at the line 180°, was —17″.9; but when the line 180° was brought under the first microscope, then the reading of the other for the division-line 0° was —2″.7. Hence the mean is —10″.3 and the error of the line 180° is 7″.60. The mean of 10 observations gave +7″.61, which value was adopted as the error of that line. In order to find the errors of the lines 90° and 270°, the arcs 0° to 180° and 180° to 0° were divided into two equal parts by placing the two microscopes at a distance of 90°. If then the line 0° was brought under the first microscope, the reading of the second microscope for the line 90° was —6″.5, whilst when the line 90° was brought under the first microscope, the reading of the second microscope for the line 180° was —3″.5 and, if this be corrected for the error of that line, + 4″.11. The arithmetical mean of —6″.5 and +4″.11 gives —1″.19, hence the error of the line 90° is +5″.31. In a like manner the errors of the lines 45°, 135°, 225° and 315° were determined by dividing the arcs of 90° into two equal parts. Then the errors for the arcs of 15° might have been determined by dividing the arcs of 45 degrees into three equal parts. But since the microscopes of the instrument cannot be placed so near each other, arcs of 315 and 225 were divided into three equal parts. For this purpose the microscopes were first placed at a distance of 105 degrees. When the lines 0°, 105° and 210° were in succession brought under the fixed microscope, the readings of the second microscope were respectively —11″.9, —5″.6 and +2″.0 or if we add to the last reading the error of the line 315°, which was found —0″.48, we get —11″.9, —5″.6 and +1″.2. The arithmetical mean of all is —5″.33, hence the error of the line 105° is +6″.57, that of the line 210° is equal to

$2\alpha_0 - \alpha' - \alpha'' = +6''.84$. If the first line which we use is not the line 0^0 but another line, whose error has been found before, the first reading must be corrected also by applying this error with the opposite sign. For instance when the first microscope was set in succession at the lines 90^0, 195^0 and 300^0, the readings of the second microscope for the lines 195^0, 300^0 and 45^0 were successively $-6''.6$, $+2''.1$ and $-7''.9$. Now since the errors of the lines 90^0 and 45^0 have been found to be $+5''.46$ and $+3''.36$, the corrected readings are $-12''.06$, $+2''.10$ and $-4''.54$. The mean is $-4''.83$, and hence the error of the line 195^0 is $+7''.23$, and that of 300^0 is $+0''.30$.

The errors thus found are the sum of the errors of division and of those caused by the excentricity of the circle and by the irregularities of the pivots; finally they contain also the flexure, that is, those changes of the distance between the division-lines produced by the action of the force of gravity on the circle. The errors produced by the latter cause will change according to the position of a line with respect to the vertical line, so that the correction which must be applied to the reading for this reason will be expressed by a series of the form:

$$a' \cos z + b' \sin z + a'' \cos 2z + b'' \sin 2z + a''' \cos 3z + b''' \sin 3z + \ldots$$

where the coefficients of the sines and cosines are different for each line and change according to the distance of the line from a fixed line of the circle. We see therefore, that if a line is in succession at the distance z and $180^0 + z$ from the zenith, all odd terms of the series are in those two cases equal but have opposite signs. Therefore if we measure the distance between two lines first in a position of the circle, in which the zenith distance of that line is z and afterwards in the opposite position, in which its zenith distance is $180^0 + z$, then the mean of the measured distances is nearly free from flexure and only those terms dependent on $2z$, $4z$ etc. remain in the result. If we repeat the observations in 4 positions of the circle, 90^0 different from each other, then only the terms dependent on $4z$, $8z$ remain in the arithmetical mean. Generally already the second terms will be very small, and hence the mean of two values for the distance between two lines determined in two opposite positions of the circle can be considered as free from flexure *).

The errors arising from the excentricity are destroyed, if the arithmetical means of the errors of two opposite lines are taken, and the same is the case with the errors caused by an imperfect form of the pivots. For such deficiencies have only this effect, that the error of excentricity is a little different in different positions of the instrument, since when the instrument is turned round the axis, the centre of the division occupies different positions with respect to the Ys **). If the circle is furnished with 4 microscopes, as is usually the case, the arithmetical means of the errors of every four lines which are at distances of 90^0 from each other are taken and used as the corrections which are to be applied to the arithmetical mean of the readings by the 4 microscopes in order to free it from the errors of division.

By the method given above, the errors of every degree of the graduation and even of the arcs of 30′ may be determined. If a regularity is perceptible in these corrections, at least a portion of them can be represented by a series of the form $a \cos 4z + b \sin 4z + a_1 \cos 8z + b_1 \sin 8z$ etc. and thus the *periodical errors of division* are obtained which can be tabulated. But the accidental errors of the lines must be found by subdividing the arcs of half a degree into smaller ones according to the above method, and since this would be an immense labor if excecuted for all lines, Hansen has proposed a peculiar construction of the circle and the micros-

*) Bessel in No. 577, 578, 579 of the Astron. Nachr. has investigated the effect of the force of gravity on a circle in a theoretical way and has found for the change of the distance between two lines the expression $a' \cos z + b' \sin z$. However the case of a perfectly homogoneous circle, which he considered, wlll hardly ever occur. Usually the higher powers of the expression for flexure will be very small, but it is always advisable, to examine this by a special investigation.

**) The errors arising from the excentricity of the circle and from the irregularities of the pivots are of the form:

$$[e + e' \cos z + e'' \sin z + e'_2 \cos 2z + e''_2 \sin 2z] \sin (A - O_z),$$

where A is the reading of the circle, z the zenith distance of the zero of the circle, and O_z the direction of the line through the centre of the division and that of the axis, which is likewise a function of z.

copes, for which the number of lines, whose errors must be determined, is greatly diminished. (Astron. Nachr. No. 388 and 389.) The determination of these errors will always be of great importance for those lines, which are used for the determination of the latitude, the declination of the standard stars and the observations of the sun; and after the errors for arcs of half a degree have been obtained, the errors of the intermediate lines of any such arc can be found by measuring all intervals of 2 minutes by means of the screw of the microscope. For this purpose we turn the screw of the microscope to its zero, then bring by the motion of the circle the line of a degree between the wires and measure the distance of the next line by means of the screw. After this the screw is turned back to its zero and when the same line has been brought between the wires by turning the circle, the distance of the following line is measured and so on to the next line of half a degree. These measurements are also made in the opposite direction, and the means taken of the values found for the same intervals by the two series of observation. Then if x and x' are the errors of division of the first and the last line, and α', α'' etc. are the observed intervals between the first and the second, the second and the third line etc., we have:

$$\frac{\alpha' + \alpha'' + \alpha''' + \ldots + x' - x}{15} = \alpha_0$$

equal to an interval of 2 minutes as measured by the screw, and hence the error of the line following the degree line is:

$$x + \alpha_0 - \alpha'$$

that of the second $x + 2\alpha_0 - \alpha' - \alpha''$

that of the third $x + 3\alpha_0 - \alpha' - \alpha'' - \alpha'''$

and so forth.

Compare on the determination of the errors of division: Bessel, Königsberger Beobachtungen Bd. I und VII, also Astronomische Nachrichten No. 841. Struve, Astronomische Nachrichten No. 344 and 345, and Observ. Astron. Dorpat. Vol. VI sive novae seriae Vol. III; Peters, Bestimmung der Theilungsfehler des Ertelschen Verticalkreises der Pulkowaer Sternwarte.

D. On flexure or the action of the force of gravity upon the telescope and the circle.

8. The force of gravity alters the figure of a circle in a vertical position. If we imagine the point, from which the division is reckoned, to be directed to the zenith, every line of the graduation will be a little displaced with respect to the zero, and for a certain line A the produced displacement shall be denoted by α_0. If now we turn the circle so that its zero has the zenith distance z, that is so that the line z of the graduation is directed towards the zenith, the displacement of the line A will be different from α_0. If we denote by α_ζ the displacement of the line A, when the zero has the zenith distance ζ, which shall be reckoned in the same direction from 0^0 to 360^0, then α_ζ can be expressed by a periodical series of the following form:

$$a' \cos \zeta + a'' \cos 2\zeta + a''' \cos 3\zeta + \ldots$$
$$+ b' \sin \zeta + b'' \sin 2\zeta + b''' \sin 3\zeta + \ldots$$

But if we take now another line, the displacement of it will be expressed by a similar series, in which only the coefficients a', b' etc. will have different values. These coefficients themselves can thus be expressed by periodical series, depending on the reading of the circle, so that the displacement of any line u of the graduation, when the zero has the zenith distance ζ, can be expressed by a periodical series of the form:

$$a'_u \cos \zeta + a''_u \cos 2\zeta + a'''_u \cos 3\zeta + \ldots$$
$$+ b'_u \sin \zeta + b''_u \sin 2\zeta + b'''_u \sin 3\zeta + \ldots,$$

where a'_u, b'_u etc. are periodical functions of u. The sign of this expression shall be taken so, that the correction given by the expression is to be applied to the reading of the circle in order to free it from flexure.

Now a complete reading of the instrument is the arithmetical mean of the readings of the different microscopes, the number of which is usually 4. These microscopes we will suppose to be so placed, that one of them indicates 0^0, when the telescope is directed to the zenith. The zenith distance of this microscope which always gives the zenith distance of the telescope shall be denoted by m. If now the telescope is turned so that it is directed to the zenith distance z, the line z will be under this microscope, and since in this case the zenith distance of the zero is $z + m$, we have in this case $u = z$, $\zeta = z + m$; hence the correction which is to be applied to the reading of the microscope, is:

$$a'_z \cos(z+m) + a''_z \cos 2(z+m) + a'''_z \cos 3(z+m) + \dots$$
$$+ b'_z \sin(z+m) + b''_z \sin 2(z+m) + b'''_z \sin 3(z+m) + \dots$$

For the other microscope, whose reading is $90 + z$, we have $u = 90 + z$, $\zeta = z + m$; hence the coefficients in the expression for flexure become a'_{90+z}, b'_{90+z} etc. and thus we see, that when we use four microscopes at a distance of 90° from each other, and take the mean of all 4 readings, then we have to apply to this mean the correction:

$$\alpha'_z \cos(z+m) + \alpha''_z \cos 2(z+m) + \alpha'''_z \cos 3(z+m) + \dots$$
$$+ \beta'_z \sin(z+m) + \beta''_z \sin 2(z+m) + \beta'''_z \sin 3(z+m) + \dots,$$

where the several α and β are periodical functions of z, but contain only terms in which $4z$, $8z$ etc. occur, since all the other terms are eliminated by taking the mean of four readings. If these terms should be equal to zero, then the force of gravity has no effect at all on the arithmetical mean of the readings of four microscopes; otherwise there exists flexure, and since m is constant, the expression for the correction which is to be applied to the mean of the readings of 4 microscopes will have the form:

$$\begin{array}{l} a' \cos z + a'' \cos 2z + a''' \cos 3z + \dots \\ + b' \sin z + b'' \sin 2z + b''' \sin 3z + \dots \end{array} \qquad (A)$$

But the force of gravity acts also on the tube of the telescope, bending down both ends of it, except when it is in a vertical position. If the flexure at both ends is the same so that the centre of the object glass is lowered exactly as much as the centre of the wire-cross, it is evident, that it has no influence at all upon the observations, since in that case the line joining those two centres (the line of collimation) remains parallel to a certain fixed line of the circle. But if the flexure at both ends is different, the line of collimation changes its position with respect to a fixed line of the circle, and hence the angles, through which the line of collimation moves, do not correspond to the angles as given by the readings of the circle. The correction which is to be applied on this account to the readings can again be expressed by a periodical function, and hence we may assume, that the expression (A) represents these two kinds of flexure, that of the circle and that of the telescope.

There are two methods of arranging the observations in such a manner, that the result is free from flexure, at least from the greatest portion of it. For if we observe a star at the zenith distance z, its image reflected from an artificial horizon will be seen at the zenith distance $180 - z$, hence the division-lines corresponding to these zenith distances will be under that microscope, whose reading gives the zenith distance. Now if we reverse the instrument, the division of the circle runs in the opposite direction, and hence the reading for the direct observation is now $360^0 - z$ and that for the reflected observation $180^0 + z$. Therefore if we denote the four complete readings, corrected for the errors of division, for those four observations by z, z', z'' and z''', and by ζ the true zenith distance free from flexure, we have the following four equations, in which N denotes the nadir point:

$$\begin{array}{lll} \text{Direct} & \zeta = z & + a' \cos z + a'' \cos 2z + a''' \cos 3z + \ldots + b' \sin z \\ & & + b'' \sin 2z + b''' \sin 3z + \ldots - (180^0 + N) + a' - a'' + a'''\,{}^{*)} \\ \text{Reflected} & 180^0 - \zeta = z' & - a' \cos z + a'' \cos 2z - a''' \cos 3z + \ldots + b' \sin z \\ & & - b'' \sin 2z + b''' \sin 3z - \ldots - (180^0 + N) + a' - a'' + a''' \\ \text{Direct} & 360^0 - \zeta = z'' & + a' \cos z + a'' \cos 2z + a''' \cos 3z + \ldots - b' \sin z \quad (B \\ & & - b'' \sin 2z - b''' \sin 3z - \ldots - (180^0 + N) + a' - a'' + a''' \\ \text{Reflected} & 180^0 + \zeta = z''' & - a' \cos z + a'' \cos 2z - a''' \cos 3z + \ldots - b' \sin z \\ & & + b'' \sin 2z - b''' \sin 3z + \ldots - (180^0 + N) + a' - a'' + a'''. \end{array}$$

From these equations we obtain:

$$90^0 - \zeta = \frac{z' - z}{2} - a' \cos z - a''' \cos 3z - \ldots - b'' \sin 2z - \ldots$$

$$90^0 - \zeta = \frac{z'' - z'''}{2} + a' \cos z + a''' \cos 3z - \ldots - b'' \sin 2z - \ldots,$$

hence by taking the mean:

$$90^0 - \zeta = \tfrac{1}{2} \left\{ \frac{z' - z}{2} + \frac{z'' - z'''}{2} \right\} - b'' \sin 2z - \ldots,$$

and we see therefore, that if a star is observed direct and reflected in both positions of the instrument, only that portion of flexure, which is expressed by the terms $b'' \sin 2z$

*) The correction which is to be applied to the nadir point is namely $- a' + a'' - a''' + \ldots$

$+ b^{IV} \sin 4z$ etc. remains in the mean of those four observations.

We obtain also from the mean of the first two equations (B):

$$90^0 = \frac{z+z'}{2} + a'' \cos 2z + \ldots + b' \sin z + b''' \sin 3z + \ldots$$
$$- (180^0 + N) + a' - a'' + a''',$$

likewise:

$$270^0 = \frac{z''+z'''}{2} + a'' \cos 2z + \ldots - b' \sin z - b''' \sin 3z - \ldots$$
$$- (180^0 + N') + a' - a'' + a''',$$

from which we find:

$$360^0 = \frac{z+z'}{2} + \frac{z''+z'''}{2} + 2a'' \cos 2z + \ldots - (N+N') + 2(a' - a'' + a''')$$

$$180^0 = \frac{z''+z'''}{2} - \frac{z+z'}{2} - 2b' \sin z - 2b''' \sin 3z + \ldots + N - N'.$$

Therefore if we observe different stars direct and reflected in both positions of the instrument, we can find from those equations the most probable values of the coefficients a'', a^{IV} etc. and b', b''' etc.

Since these observations are made on different days, it is of course necessary to reduce the zenith distances z, z', z'' and z''' to the same epoch, for instance to the beginning of the year by applying to the reading of the circle the reduction to the apparent place with the proper sign. Since, besides, the microscopes change continually their position with respect to the circle, it is also necessary, to determine the zenith or nadir point after each observation (VII, 24) and thus to eliminate the change of the microscopes. Another correction is required for the reflected observations. For if we observe a star reflected, we strictly do not observe the star from the place where the instrument stands, but from that in which the artificial horizon stands, and thus the latitude of the place for those observations is different. Now since the artificial horizon is placed in the prolongation of the axis of the telescope, its distance from the point vertically below the centre of the telescope will be $h \tang z$, where h is the height of the axis of the instrument above the artificial horizon. Since an arc of the meridian equal to a toise corresponds to a change of latitude equal to $0''.063$, we must add to the zenith distance of the reflected image of the star, if h is expressed in Paris feet, the quantity $0''.011\, h \tang z$.

A second method of eliminating the flexure was proposed by Hansen and requires a peculiar construction of the telescope. The tube of the telescope, namely, is made in such a manner, that the heads, in which the object glass and the eye-piece are fastened, can be taken of and their places be exchanged, without changing the distance off the centres of gravity of both ends of the tube from the axis of the instrument. Thus in exchanging the object glass and the eye-piece the equilibrium is not at all disturbed and it can be assumed, that the effect of the force of gravity on the telescope is the same in both cases. Now if in one case the line 180^0 of the circle is directed to the nadir, and the reading of one microscope is the zenith distance, then in the other case the line 0^0 will correspond to the nadir, and the reading of the same microscope will be $180^0 +$ the zenith distance. Therefore if ζ is the zenith distance free from flexure, and if the readings corrected for the errors of division are in the first case z, and in the other z', we have:

$$\begin{aligned}\zeta &= z + a'\cos z + a''\cos 2z + a'''\cos 3z + \ldots + b'\sin z \\ &\quad + b''\sin 2z + b'''\sin 3z \ldots - (180^0 + N) + a' - a'' + a''' - \ldots \\ \zeta &= z' - a'\cos z + a''\cos 2z - a'''\cos 3z + \ldots - b'\sin z \\ &\quad + b''\sin 2z - b'''\sin 3z \ldots - (180^0 + N') - a' - a'' - a''' - \ldots\end{aligned}$$

Therefore we obtain from the mean of those two equations, denoting the zenith points $180^0 + N$ and $180^0 + N'$ by Z and Z':

$$\zeta = \frac{z - Z + z' - Z'}{2} + a''\cos 2z \ldots + b''\sin 2z - \ldots - a'' - \ldots$$

whence we see that the arithmetical mean of the zenith distances in the two cases contains only that portion of flexure, which is expressed by the terms dependent on $2z$, $4z$ etc.

We also obtain by subtracting the above equations:

$$\begin{aligned}0^0 = \frac{z' - Z' - (z - Z)}{2} - a'\cos z - a'''\cos 3z - \ldots - b'\sin z \ldots - b'''\sin 3z - \ldots \\ - a' - a''' - \ldots,\end{aligned}$$

hence we see, that we can determine the coefficients of the terms dependent on z, $3z$, etc. by observing stars at various zenith distances or by means of a collimator placed at various zenith distances.

In general we can find these coefficients by placing the telescope in two positions which differ exactly 180^0. In order to accomplish this, we mount two collimators so, that their axes produced pass through the centre of the axis of the instrument, and direct them towards each other through apertures, made for this purpose in the cube of the axis of the instrument, so that the centres of their wire-crosses coincide. Then the telescope being directed first to the wire-cross of one collimator and then to that of the other, will describe exactly 180^0. Hence if we read the circle in the two positions of the telescope, and denote the true zenith distance of the collimator by ζ, we have in one position:

$$\zeta = z + a' \cos z + a'' \cos 2z + a''' \cos 3z + \ldots + b' \sin z + b'' \sin 2z + b''' \sin 3z + \ldots - Z + a' - a'' + a'''$$

and in the other position:

$$180 + \zeta = z' - a \cos z + a'' \cos 2z - a''' \cos 3z + \ldots - b' \sin z + b'' \sin 2z - b''' \sin 3z + \ldots - Z + a' - a'' + a''',$$

therefore:

$$0 = \frac{z' - z - 180}{2} - a' \cos z - a''' \cos 3z - \ldots - b' \sin z - b''' \sin 3z - \ldots$$

Since we use in reading the circle both times the same division-lines, the observed quantity $z' - z$ is entirely free from the errors of division. If we make these observations by different inclinations of the telescope, that is, at different zenith distances, we obtain a number of such equations, from which we can find the most probable values of the coefficients.

There is no difficulty in making these observations when the telescope is in a horizontal position; but when the inclination is considerable, it would become necessary to place one of the collimators very high, in which case it might be difficult to give it a firm stand. However one can use instead of this collimator a plane mirror which is placed at some distance in front of the object glass or better held by an arm, which is fastened to the pier of the instrument so that by turning this arm it may easily be placed in any position *). If then outside of the eye-piece of the lower collimator a plane glass is fastened at an angle of 45^0 **), by

*) The mirror must admit of a motion by which it can be placed so that a horizontal line in its plane is perpendicular to the axis of the telescope.

**) This plane glass must be fixed so, that one can change its inclination to the eye-piece and that it can be moved around the axis of the means of which, light is reflected into the telescope and which, while it is not used, can be turned off, and if the telescope of the collimator is directed to the mirror, then looking into the telescope through this plane glass we see not only the wire-cross of the collimator but also its image reflected from the mirror. Hence by turning the collimator, until the wire-cross and the reflected image coincide, we place its axis perpendicular to the mirror. If then we place by the same means the telescope of the instrument perpendicular to the mirror, and afterwards direct it to the wire-cross of the collimator, the angle, through which the telescope is turned, will be exactly 180°, and hence we can find, as before, those terms of the expression for the flexure, which depend upon z, $3z$, etc. It is best to make these observations in a dark room and to reflect the light from a lamp into the telescope, since then the reflected images of the wires are better seen. The only difficulty will be, to find a plane mirror which will bear a high magnifying power. But since it need not be larger than the aperture of the collimator, it will not be impossible, to excecute such a mirror, especially as it is used only for rays falling upon it perpendicularly.

The coefficients of the terms dependent upon the cosines can be determined also by observing the zenith distances of objects in both positions of the circle, and for this purpose again either a collimator or the mirror described above can be used. We find namely from the first and the third of the equations (B):

$$180^0 = \frac{z - Z + z'' - Z'}{2} + a' \cos z + a'' \cos 2z + a''' \cos 3z + \ldots + a' - a'' + a''',$$

where $Z = 180 + N$, $Z' = 180 + N'$ and where z and z'' are the readings in both positions, corrected for the errors of division.

We thus see, that all coefficients can be determined by simple observations, except those of the sines of even multiples of z. In order to find these, we must have means to

---

telescope so as to reflect the light well towards the mirror. It is also better, to use for these observations an eye-piece with one lens only, since then the reflected image of the wire-cross is better seen.

turn the telescope exactly through certain angles different from 90^0 or 180^0. There is no contrivance known by which the telescope may be turned any desired angle; but by means of the mirror described before and of two collimators the telescope may be placed at the zenith distance of 45^0, and thus at least the coefficient b'' may be determined. In order to do this, the mirror is placed so, that the telescope, when directed to it, has nearly the zenith distance 135^0, and in this position of the mirror, a small telescope is placed above the mirror and directed towards the nadir, while a collimator is placed horizontal in front of it. Both telescopes are placed so that their axes are directed to the centre of the mirror, and this can be accomplished by putting covers with a small hole at the centre over the object glasses, and likewise covering all but the central part of the mirror, and then moving the two telescopes until the light from the uncovered portion of the mirror is reflected into the telescopes. When this is done, the mirror is turned away, and the line of collimation of the vertical telescope is made exactly vertical by means of an artificial horizon, whilst that of the collimator is made exactly horizontal by means of a level. Then the angle between the lines of collimation of the two telescopes will be a right angle. If now the mirror is turned back to its original place, there is one position of it, in which rays coming from the wire-cross of one collimator are reflected from the mirror into the other telescope so that its image coincides with the wire-cross of that telescope, and when this is the case, the angle which the mirror makes with the vertical line is exactly 45^0. A small correction is to be applied also in this case on account of the different latitude of the places of the collimators. If y is the small angle, which the vertical collimator makes with the vertical line of the instrument, and x the angle, which the horizontal collimator makes with the horizon of the instrument, then the angle which the telescope, when directed to the mirror, makes with the line towards the nadir is:

$$45^0 + \tfrac{1}{2}(x - y),$$

if we assume, that the two collimators are placed on different sides of the instrument; and if we denote by h and h' the distance of the horizontal and the vertical collimator from the vertical line of the instrument, and if we further denote by b the inclination of the horizontal collimator as found by means of the level, taken positive when the side nearer to the instrument is the higher one, then this angle will be:

$$45^0 + 0''.0052\,(h - h') + \tfrac{1}{2}\,b.$$

If we denote this angle by ζ, and the two readings of the circle when the telescope is directed to the nadir point and to the mirror, that is, for the zenith distance 180^0 and 135^0, by z' and z, we have:

$$\zeta = z' - z - a'\,(1 - \tfrac{1}{2}\sqrt{2}) + a'' - a'''\,(1 + \tfrac{1}{2}\sqrt{2}) - b'\tfrac{1}{2}\sqrt{2} + b'' - b'''\tfrac{1}{2}\sqrt{2}.$$

If we make now the same observation, when the zenith distance of the telescope is 225^0, and if we denote again the nadir point by z' and by z'' the reading of the circle, when the telescope is directed to the mirror, then we have in this case:

$$\zeta' = z'' - z' + a'\,(1 - \tfrac{1}{2}\sqrt{2}) - a'' + a'''\,(1 + \tfrac{1}{2}\sqrt{2}) - b'\,\tfrac{1}{2}\sqrt{2} + b'' - b'''\tfrac{1}{2}\sqrt{2},$$

therefore we have:

$$\tfrac{1}{2}\,(\zeta + \zeta') = \frac{z'' - z}{2} - b'\tfrac{1}{2}\sqrt{2} + b'' - b'''\tfrac{1}{2}\sqrt{2}\ldots,$$

provided that the nadir point is the same for both observations.

E. On the examination of the micrometer screws.

9. The measurement of the distance of two points by means of a micrometer screw presupposes that the linear motion of the screw and the micrometrical apparatus moved by it, for instance that of the wire, is proportional to the indications of the head of the screw and of the scale, by which the entire revolutions of the screw are indicated. However this condition is never rigorously fulfilled, since not only the threads of the screw are not exactly equal for different parts, and hence cause that the amount of the linear motion produced by an entire revolution varies, but also equal parts of the same revolution move the wire over different spaces. It has been shown already, how the irregularities of the screws of the reading microscopes can be determined, but since in that case only very few threads of the screw are really used in measuring, the case shall be treated now, when the entire length of the screw is employed.

The corrections which must be applied to the readings of the screw head, in order to find from them the true linear motion of the screw, can again be represented by a periodical series of the form:

$$a_1 \cos u + b_1 \sin u + a_2 \cos 2u + b_2 \sin 2u + \ldots$$

where u is the reading of the screw head. These corrections will be nearly the same for several successive threads, so that the coefficients a_1, b_1 etc. can be considered to be equal for them. Hence these coefficients are determined from the mean of the observations made for several successive threads, and these determinations are repeated for different portions of the screw.

If we measure the linear distance between two points, whose true value is f (for instance, the distance between two wires of a collimator) by bisecting each point by the moveable wire of the micrometer, then, if u and u' are the indications of the screw for those positions of the moveable wire, we have:

$$f = u' - u + a_1 (\cos u' - \cos u) + b_1 (\sin u' - \sin u) + a_2 (\cos 2u' - \cos 2u)$$
$$+ b_2 (\sin 2u' - \sin 2u) + \ldots$$

Now if the distance is an aliquot part of a revolution, and we measure the same distance by different parts of the screw arranging the observations so, that first we read $0^r.00$, when the moveable wire bisects one point, the next time $0^r.10$, then $0^r.20$ and so on through one entire revolution of the screw, then, if these coefficients are small, as is usually the case, we can assume, that f is equal to the arithmetical mean of all observed values of $u - u'$, and we can take $u + f$ instead of u'. Therefore if we denote this arithmetical mean by f, every observed value of $u' - u$ gives an equation of the form:

$$u' - u - f = 2a_1 \sin \tfrac{1}{2} f \sin (u + \tfrac{1}{2} f) - 2b_1 \sin \tfrac{1}{2} f \cos (u + \tfrac{1}{2} f)$$
$$+ 2a_2 \sin f \sin (2u + f) - 2b_2 \sin f \cos (2u + f)$$
$$\ldots\ldots$$

and since we have ten such equations, because we suppose that the screw has made one entire revolution, we find the following equations:

$$10\,a_1 \sin \tfrac{1}{2} f = \Sigma (u' - u - f) \sin (u + \tfrac{1}{2} f)$$
$$10\,b_1 \sin \tfrac{1}{2} f = -\Sigma (u' - u - f) \cos (u + \tfrac{1}{2} f)$$
$$10\,a_2 \sin f = \Sigma (u' - u - f) \sin (2u + f)$$
$$10\,b_2 \sin f = -\Sigma (u' - u - f) \cos (2u + f),$$

from which we can determine the values of the coefficients.

Example. Bessel measured by the micrometer screw of the heliometer the distance between two objects, which was nearly equal to half a revolution of a screw, in the way just described, and found from the mean of the observations made on ten successive threads of the screw: *)

	Measured distance $u' - u$
Starting point 0,0	$0^r.50045$
0,1	0.49690
0,2	0.49440
0,3	0.49240
0,4	0.49260
0,5	0.49555
0,6	0.49905
0,7	0.50140
0,8	0.50340
0,9	0.50350
	$f = 0.497965 = 179^\circ\ 16'.0.$

From this we find:

$u' - u - f$	$(u' - u - f) \sin (u + \frac{1}{2} f)$
+ 0.002485	+ 0.002485
− 0.001065	− 0.000865
− 0.003565	− 0.001123
− 0.005565	+ 0.001686
− 0.005365	+ 0.004320
− 0.002415	+ 0.002415
+ 0.001085	− 0.000882
+ 0.003435	− 0.001083
+ 0.005435	+ 0.001646
+ 0.005535	+ 0.004457
	sum + 0.013056,

and since $\sin \frac{1}{2} f = 1$, we have:

$$10\,a_1 = +0.013056$$
as: $$10\,b_1 = -0.024874$$
$$0.128\,a_2 = +0.000147$$
$$0.128\,b_2 = +0.000337.$$

*) Astronomische Untersuchungen Bd. 1, pag. 79.

Bessel made then a similar series of observations by measuring a distance, which was nearly equal to one fourth of one revolution and found:

$$7.339\,a_1 = +0.015915$$
$$7.339\,b_1 = -0.016126$$
$$9.970\,a_2 = -0.004987$$
$$9.970\,b_2 = -0.000576,$$

and from these two determinations he obtained according to Note 2 to No. 24 of the introduction:

$$a_1 = +0^r.001608$$
$$b_1 = -0.002386$$
$$a_2 = -0.000499$$
$$b_2 = -0.000057.$$

These periodical corrections of the screw must be applied to all readings of the screw head. But the observations can also be arranged in such a manner that these periodical errors are entirely eliminated. For, if we measure the same distance first, when the indication of the screw at the bisection of one object is $-0^r.25$ and then again, when the reading is $+0^r.25$ at the bisection of the same object, so that u for these two observations is equal to -90^0 and $+90^0$, then in the expression for f the terms $a_1 (\cos u'_0 - \cos u) + b_1 (\sin u' - \sin u)$ will be in one case $+ a_1 \cos u' + b' (\sin u' + 1)$ and in the other case $- a_1 \cos u' - b_1 (\sin u' + 1)$, and hence this portion of the correction, dependent on a_1 and b_1, will be eliminated by taking the arithmetical mean of both observations. Likewise the result will be free from that portion of the correction dependent on a, b, a_2 and b_2, if we take the mean of 5 observations, arranging them so that the reading of the screw for the bisection of one object is in succession $-0^r.4$, $-0^r.2$, 0, $+0^r.2$ and $+0^r.4$.

Now in order to examine, whether the threads of the screw are equal, we must measure the same distance, which is nearly equal to one revolution of the screw or to a multiple of it, by different parts of the screw, and it will be best to arrange these observations in the manner just described in order that the periodical errors may be eliminated.

Bessel measured by the same screw a distance between two points nearly equal to ten revolutions of the screw, the indications of the scale at the bisection of one point being in succession 0^r, 10^r, 20^r, etc. Thus he found:

Reading of the scale at the beginning 0^r	10.0142
10	20.0147
20	30.0131
30	40.0122
40	50.0107

etc.,

where each value is the mean of 5 observations, for instance the second value that of five observations made when the indications of the scale were $9^r.6$, $9^r.8$, 10, 10.2 and 10.4. If now the true distance is $10^r + x$, and the corrections of the screw for the readings of the scale 10, 20, etc. are f_{10}, f_{20}, etc. then we have, since we can take $f_0 = 0$:

$$x_1 = +0.0142 + f_{10}$$
$$x_1 = +0.0147 + f_{20} - f_{10}$$
$$x_1 = +0.0131 + f_{30} - f_{20}$$
etc.

Likewise he measured a distance, which was equal to $20^r + x_2$, in the same way and obtained thus another system of equations:

$$x_2 = a + f_{20}$$
$$x_2 = a + f_{40} - f_{20}$$
etc.

Similar systems were obtained by measuring a distance equal to $30^r + x_3$, and from all these equations he found the values of x, x_2, x_3, etc. as well as the corrections of the screw for the readings 10, 20, etc., that is, f_{10}, f_{20}, etc.

II. THE ALTITUDE AND AZIMUTH INSTRUMENT.

10. One circle of the altitude and azimuth instrument represents the plane of the horizon and must therefore be exactly horizontal. Therefore it rests on a tripod by whose screws its position with respect to the true horizon can be adjusted by means of a level, as will be shown afterwards. But since this adjustment is hardly ever perfect, we will suppose that the circle has still a small inclination to the horizon. Let therefore P be the pole of this circle of the instrument, whilst the pole of the true horizon is the zenith Z, and let i be the angle, which the plane of the circle makes with the plane of the horizon, and whose measure is the arc of the great circle between P and Z. In the centre of this circle, which has a graduation, is a short conical axis carrying another circle to which the verniers are attached. On the circle stand two pillars of equal length, which are furnished at their top with Ys, one of which can be raised or lowered by means of a screw. On these Ys rest the pivots of the horizontal axis supporting the telescope and the vertical circle. The concentrical circle carrying the verniers can be firmly connected with the Y, but the telescope and the graduated circle are turning with the horizontal axis. Since also the vernier circle turns about a vertical axis, the telescope can be directed to any object, and the spherical co-ordinates of it can be obtained from the indications of the circles. We will denote by i' the angle, which the line through both Ys makes with the horizontal circle, and by K the point, in which this line produced beyond that end on which the circle is, intersects the celestial sphere. The altitude of this point shall be denoted by b. Now since only differences of azimuth are measured by this instrument (if we set aside at present the observations with the vertical circle) it will be indifferent, from what point we begin to reckon the azimuth, and since the points P and Z remain the same, though K moves through 360 degrees if the vernier circle is turned on its axis, we can choose as zero of the azimuth that reading, which corresponds to the position the instrument has, when K is on the same vertical circle with P and Z. We will denote this reading by a_0. For any other position we will suppose that we read always that point of the circle, in which the arc PK intersects the plane of the circle, and this is allowable, because the difference of this point and the point indicated by the zero of the vernier is always constant. The azimuth reckoned in the horizon, but from the same zero, shall be denoted by A.

If now we imagine three rectangular axes of co-ordinates, one of which is vertical to the plane of the horizon, whilst the two others are in the plane of the horizon so that the axis of y is directed to the zero of the azimuth, adopted above, then the co-ordinates of the point K referred to these axes will be:

$$z = \sin b\,,\ y = \cos b \cos A$$

and

$$x = \cos b \sin A.$$

Moreover the co-ordinates of K referred to three rectangular axes, one of which is perpendicular to the horizontal plane of the instrument, whilst the two others are situated in this plane so that the axis of x coincides with the same axis in the former system, are:

$$z = \sin i'\,,\ y = \cos i' \cos (a - a_0)\,,\ x = \cos i' \sin (a - a_0).$$

Now since the axis of z in the first system makes with the axis of z of the other system the angle i, we have according to the formulae (1) for the transformation of co-ordinates:

$$\sin b = \cos i \sin i' - \sin i \cos i' \cos (a - a_0)$$
$$\cos b \sin A = \cos i' \sin (a - a_0)$$
$$\cos b \cos A = \sin i \sin i' + \cos i \cos i' \cos (a - a_0).$$

We can obtain these equations also from the triangle between the zenith Z, the pole of the horizontal circle P and the point K, whose sides PZ, PK and ZK are respectively i, $90^0 - i'$ and $90^0 - b$, whilst the angles opposite the sides PK and ZK are A and $180^0 - (a - a_0)$.

Now since b, i and i' are small quantities, if the instrument is nearly adjusted, we can write unity instead of the cosine and the arc instead of the sine, and thus we obtain:

$$b = i' - \cos (a - a_0) \qquad (a)$$
$$A = a - a_0.$$

The telescope is perpendicular to the horizontal axis. The line of collimation ought also to be perpendicular to this axis, but we will assume, that this is not the case, but that it makes the angle $90^0 + c$ with the side of the axis towards the circle. The angle c is called the error of collimation. It can be corrected by means of screws which move the wire-cross in a direction perpendicular to the line of collimation.

The telescope shall be directed to the point O, whose zenith distance and azimuth are z and e, and whose co-ordinates with respect to the axes of z and y are therefore $\cos z$ and $\sin z \cos e$. Now we will suppose that the division increases from the left to the right, that is, in the direction of the azimuth. Therefore if the circle-end be on the left side, the telescope is directed to an azimuth greater than that of the point K; and hence if we suppose, that the axis of y is turned so that it lies in the same vertical circle with K, the co-ordinates will then be: $\cos z$ and $\sin z \cos (e - A)$. This is true, when the circle is on the left side, whilst we must take $A - e$ instead of $e - A$, when the circle is on the right side. If further we imagine the point O to be referred to a system of axes, of which the axes x and y are in the plane of the instrument, the axis of y being directed to the point K, then the co-ordinate y of the point O is equal to $-\sin c$, and since the angle between the axes of z of the two systems is b, we have according to the formulae for the transformation of co-ordinates:

$$-\sin c = \cos z \sin b + \sin z \cos b \cos (e - A).$$

We can find this equation also from the triangle between the zenith Z, the point K and the point O, towards which the telescope is directed. The sides ZO, ZK and OK are respectively equal to z, $90^0 - b$ and $90^0 + c$, and the angle KZO is equal to $PZO - PZK = e - A$.

Since b and c are small quantities, we obtain:

$$-c = b \cos z + \sin z \cos (e - A),$$

or finally, substituting for A its value from the equations (a):

$$0 = c + b \cos z + \sin z \cos [e - (a - a_0)].$$

Hence it follows, that

$$\cos [e - (a - a_0)]$$

is a small quantity of the same order as b and c. Therefore if we write instead of it:

$$\sin [90^0 - e + (a - a_0)],$$

we can take the arc instead of the sine and obtain:

$$0 = c + b \cos z + \sin z [90^0 - e + (a - a_0)].$$

This formula is true, as was stated before, when the circle is on the left side. If it is on the right side, we must take $A - e$ instead of $e - A$ and we obtain then:

$$0 = c + b \cos z + \sin z [90^0 - (a - a_0) + e].$$

Therefore we obtain the true azimuth e by means of the formulae:

$$e = a - a_0 + 90^0 + \frac{c}{\sin z} + b \text{ cotang } z \qquad \text{Circle left}$$

and:

$$e = a - a_0 - 90^0 - \frac{c}{\sin z} - b \text{ cotang } z \qquad \text{Circle right,}$$

and if we call A the azimuth as indicated by the vernier, and ΔA the index error of the vernier, so that $A + \Delta A$ is the azimuth reckoned on the circle from the zero of azimuth, then we have:

$$e = A + \Delta A \pm c \text{ cosec } z \pm b \text{ cotang } z,$$

where the upper sign must be used, when the circle is on the left side and the lower one, when the circle is on the right side.

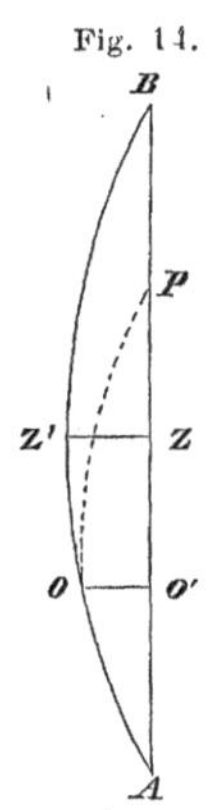

Fig. 14.

11. We can find these formulae also by a geometrical method. Let AB Fig. 14 be the vertical circle of the object and Z the zenith. If we assume now that the telescope turns round an axis, whose inclination to the horizon is b, it will describe a vertical circle which passes through the points A and B and the point Z' whose distance from the zenith is equal to b. Therefore while we read the azimuth of the vertical circle AZ, the telescope will be directed to a point on the great circle $AZ'B$, say O, and hence, when the circle is on the left side, we shall find the azimuth too small. Now we have:

$$\begin{aligned} \sin OO' &= \sin AO \sin b \\ &= \cos z \,.\, \sin b. \end{aligned}$$

But we read the angle at Z subtended by OO', and therefore the angle OZO' is the sought correction ΔA of the azimuth. Now since:

$$\sin OO' = \sin ZO \sin \Delta A,$$

and hence:

$$\sin \Delta A = \text{cotang } z \sin b,$$

we must add to the reading of the circle on account of the error b, when the circle is left:

$$+ b \text{ cotang } z.$$

In a similar way we can find the correction for the error of collimation. Let AB again be the vertical circle, which the line of collimation of the telescope would describe, if

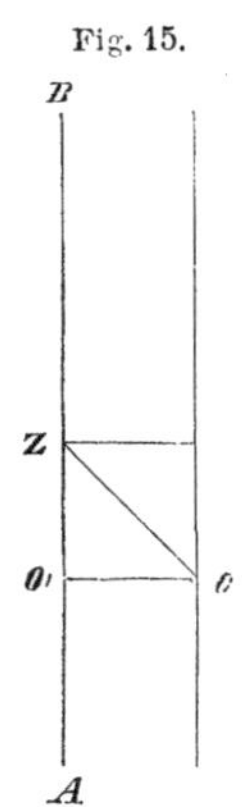

Fig. 15.

there were no error of collimation. But if the angle between this line and the side of the axis towards the circle be $90 + c$, the line of collimation will describe, when the telescope is turned around, the surface of a cone, which intersects the sphere of the heavens in a small circle, whose distance from the great circle AB is equal to c. Fig. 15. In this case the reading of the circle is again too small, when the circle is on the left, and if we denote again the angle AZO by ΔA, we have:

$$\sin \Delta A = \frac{\sin c}{\sin z}$$

or:

$$\Delta A = + c \operatorname{cosec} z.$$

12. It shall now be shown, how the errors of the instrument can be determined.

The level-error is found according to the rules given in No. 1 of this section by placing a spirit-level upon the pivots of the horizontal axis. But we have according to the equation (a) in No. 10:

$$b = i' - i \cos (a - a_0),$$

where i is the inclination of the horizontal circle to the horizon, i' the inclination of the horizontal axis, which carries the telescope, to the horizontal circle. This equation contains three unknown quantities, namely i', i and a_0, and hence three levelings in different positions of the axis will be sufficient for their determination. We will assume that the inclination b is found by means of the level in a certain position of the axis, when the reading of the circle is a, then it is best, to find also the inclinations b_1 and b_2 in two other positions of the instrument corresponding to the readings $a + 120^0$ and $a + 140^0$. For if we substitute these values in the above formula, develop the cosines and remember that:

$$\cos 120^0 = -\tfrac{1}{2}$$

and

$$\sin 120^0 = +\tfrac{1}{2}\sqrt{3},$$

moreover:

$$\cos 240^0 = -\tfrac{1}{2}$$

and

$$\sin 240^0 = -\tfrac{1}{2}\sqrt{3},$$

we obtain the following three equations:

$$b = i' - i \cos(a - a_0)$$
$$b_1 = i' + \tfrac{1}{2} i \cos(a - a_0) + \tfrac{1}{2} i \sin(a - a_0) \sqrt{3}$$
$$b_2 = i' + \tfrac{1}{2} i \cos(a - a_0) - \tfrac{1}{2} i \sin(a - a_0) \sqrt{3}.$$

If we add these three equations, we find:

$$i' = \frac{b + b_1 + b_2}{3}.$$

But if we subtract the third equation from the second, we obtain:

$$i \sin(a - a_0) = \frac{b_1 - b_2}{\sqrt{3}},$$

and if we add the two last equations and subtract the first after being multiplied by 2, we find:

$$i \cos(a - a_0) = \frac{b_1 + b_2 - 2b}{3}.$$

Therefore if we level the axis in three positions of the instrument, which are 120° apart, we find by means of these formulae, i, i' and a_0, and then we obtain the inclination for any other position by means of the formula:

$$b = i' - i \cos(a - a_0).$$

In order to find the collimation-error, the same distant terrestrial object must be observed both, when the axis is on the left, as well, when it is on the right, and the circle be read each time. If the reading in the first case is a, that in the second case a', we shall have the two equations:

$$e = A + \Delta A + b \operatorname{cotang} z + c \operatorname{cosec} z$$
$$e = A' + \Delta A - b' \operatorname{cotang} z - c \operatorname{cosec} z,$$

from which we find:

$$c \operatorname{cosec} z = \frac{A' - A}{2} - \frac{b' + b}{2} \operatorname{cotang} z.$$

Therefore if the inclinations b and b' in both positions are known and we get the zenith distance from the reading of the vertical circle, we can find the collimation-error by observing the same object in both positions of the instrument.

It is assumed here, that the telescope is fastened to the centre of the axis or that, if this is not the case, a very distant object has been observed. Otherwise we must apply a correction to the collimation-error, as found by the above method. For, if we observe the object O Fig. 16 with a telescope, which is fastened to one extremity of the axis, it is seen in the direction OF. The angle OFK shall be $90^\circ + c_0$.

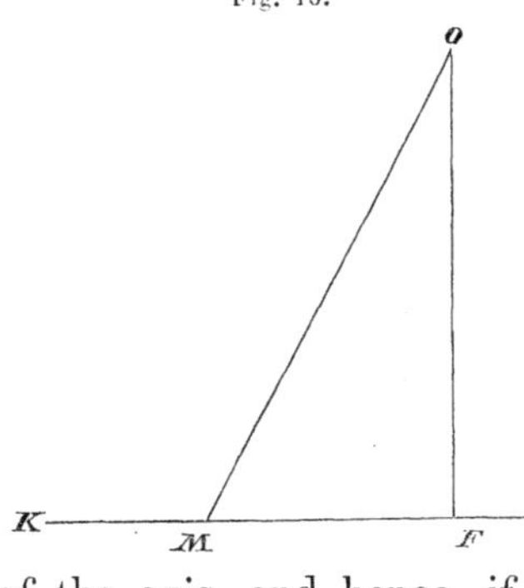

Fig. 16.

Now if we imagine a telescope at the centre M of the axis, and directed to O, then the angle OMK will be $90^0 + c$. We have therefore:

$$c = c_0 + MOF.$$

But we have:

$$\text{tang}\, MOF = \frac{\varrho}{d}$$

where d is the distance of the object OM, and ϱ is half the length of the axis, and hence, if c_0 is very small, we get:

$$c = c_0 + \frac{\varrho}{d}.$$

Therefore if we observe a terrestrial object with an instrument whose telescope is at one extremity of the axis, the reading of the circle will be too small by the quantity $\frac{\varrho}{d}$ cosec z, when the circle is on the left, and too large, when the circle is on the right side. Therefore if these two readings be denoted by A and A', we have the two equations:

$$e = A + \Delta A + b \text{ cotang } z + \left(c + \frac{\varrho}{d}\right) \text{cosec } z$$

$$e = A' + \Delta A - b' \text{cotang } z - \left(c + \frac{\varrho}{d}\right) \text{cosec } z,$$

from which we can find the collimation-error, if d is known.

If the telescope is attached to one extremity of the axis, its weight can produce a flexure of the axis, which renders the collimation-error variable with the zenith distance. When the telescope is horizontal, the flexure has no influence on the collimation-error, since it merely lowers the line of collimation, but leaves it parallel to the position it would have, if there were no flexure. But when the telescope is vertical, the flexure increases the angle, which the line of collimation makes with the axis. Hence the collimation-error in this case can be expressed by the formula $c + a \cos z$. In order to find c and a, the error of collimation must be determined in the vertical as well as in the horizontal position of the telescope (See No. 22 of this section).

If no terrestrial object can be used for finding the collimation-error, it may be determined by observations of the pole-star. For, if we observe the pole-star at the time t, read the circle and then reverse the instrument and observe the pole-star a second time at the time t', we shall have the two equations:

$$e = A + \Delta A + b \text{ cotang } z + c \text{ cosec } z$$

and

$$e' = A' + \Delta A - b' \text{cotang } z - c \text{ cosec } z,$$

and since we have:

$$e' = e + \frac{dA}{dt}(t' - t)$$

where $\frac{dA}{dt}$ denotes the change of the azimuth at the time $\frac{t' + t}{2}$, we obtain:

$$c \text{ cosec } z = \frac{A' - A}{2} - \frac{dA}{dt} \cdot \frac{t' - t}{2} - \frac{b' + b}{2} \text{ cotang } z.$$

Finally, in order to find the index error ΔA, we observe again a star, whose place is known, for instance the pole-star and read the circle. If then the hour angle of the star is t, we compute the true azimuth e by means of the formulae:

$$\sin z \sin e = \cos \delta \sin t$$
$$\sin z \cos e = -\cos \varphi \sin \delta + \sin \varphi \cos \delta \cos t,$$

and we obtain:

$$\Delta A = e - A \mp b \text{ cotang } z \mp c \text{ cosec } z,$$

where A is the reading of the circle and where the upper sign is used, when the circle is on the left side, the lower sign, when it is on the right side.

13. If the instrument serves only for observing the azimuth, it is called a theodolite. But often the vertical circle of such an instrument has also a fine graduation so that it can be used for observing altitudes as well as azimuths. In this case the vernier-circle is clamped to the Y, whilst the graduated circle is attached to the horizontal axis and turns with it. Such an instrument is directed to an object and the vertical circle having been read in this position, it is turned 180^0 in azimuth and again directed to the same object. If then we subtract the reading in the second position from that in the first position or conversely, according to the direction in which the division increases, half the difference of these readings will be the zenith distance of the object or more strictly its distance from the point denoted before by P. But this presupposes, that the angles i and i' as well as the error of collimation are equal to 0. Now we can assume again, that the reading of the circle indicates always the point, where a plane perpendicular to the circle and passing through the line of collimation, intersects the circle. Then the telescope will be directed to P, when the great circles KO and KP coincide. (Compare No. 10 of this section.)

When the line of collimation is turned from here to point O, the telescope will describe the angle PKO, but the side PO will be the measure of this angle only in case that OP and PK are 90^0. On the contrary, if these sides are equal to $90^0 + c$ and $90^0 - i'$, we have, denoting PO by ζ and the reading of the circle, that is, the angle PKO by ζ':

$$\begin{aligned}\cos\zeta &= -\sin c \sin i' + \cos c \cos i' \cos\zeta' \\ &= \cos(i' + c)\cos\tfrac{1}{2}\zeta'^2 - \cos(i' - c)\sin\tfrac{1}{2}\zeta'^2.\end{aligned}$$

If we subtract $\cos\zeta'$ from both members and write $(\zeta' - \zeta)\sin\zeta'$ instead of $\cos\zeta - \cos\zeta'$, which is allowable, because $\zeta - \zeta'$ is small, we obtain:

$$\zeta = \zeta' + \sin\tfrac{1}{2}(c + i')^2 \operatorname{cotg}\tfrac{1}{2}\zeta' - \sin\tfrac{1}{2}(i' - c)^2 \operatorname{tang}\tfrac{1}{2}\zeta'$$

or:

$$\zeta = \zeta' + \frac{c^2 + i'^2}{2}\operatorname{cotg}\zeta' + i'c \operatorname{cosec}\zeta';$$

ζ is then the zenith distance referred to the pole of the instrument P. But if P does not coincide with the zenith, it is not yet the true zenith distance. However in this case all is the same as before, with this difference, that instead of using the inclination i' of the horizontal axis of the instrument to the horizontal circle, we must take its inclination to the horizon, that is:

$$i' - i\cos(a - a_0) = b$$

and besides, we must subtract from the reading of the vertical circle the projection of PZ on the circle or the angle $PKZ = i\sin(a - a_0)$. This angle is always found by means of a spirit-level attached to the vertical circle. If we denote by p the reading of the level on that side, on which the division, starting from the highest point, increases, and that on the opposite side by n, and finally the point of the circle, corresponding to the middle of the bubble, by Z, then the zenith point of the circle will be in one position of the instrument $Z+\frac{1}{2}(p-n)$ and in the other $Z+\frac{1}{2}(p'-n')$. Therefore if we denote the readings in the two positions by ζ' and ζ'_1, then the zenith distance in one position will be:

$$\zeta' - Z - \tfrac{1}{2}(p-n)\,\varepsilon,$$

where ε expresses the value of one part of the scale of the level in seconds, and we shall have in the other position:

$$Z - \zeta'_1 + \tfrac{1}{2}(p'-n')\,\varepsilon,$$

and hence we find from the arithmetical mean the zenith distance:

$$z' = \frac{\zeta' + \zeta'_1}{2} - \frac{\frac{1}{2}(p-n)\,\varepsilon + \frac{1}{2}(p'-n')\,\varepsilon}{2}$$

and in order to obtain from this the true zenith distance, we must add the correction:

$$+\sin\tfrac{1}{2}(b+c)^2 \operatorname{cotg}\tfrac{1}{2}z' - \sin\tfrac{1}{2}(b-c)^2 \operatorname{tang}\tfrac{1}{2}z'$$

or:

$$+\frac{c^2+b^2}{2}\operatorname{cotg} z' + b\,c\operatorname{cosec} z'.$$

If we take $b=0$, since we have it always in our power to make this error small, we have simply to add:

$$+\frac{c^2}{2}\operatorname{cotang} z'.$$

If, for instance, $c=10'$, we find $\frac{c^2}{2} = 0''.87$. Therefore if z' is a small angle, that is, if the object is near the zenith, this correction can become very considerable. In case therefore that the zenith distances are less than 45^0, we must always take care that we observe the object at the middle of the field, that is, as near as possible to the wire-cross.

14. We can deduce the formulae for all other instruments from the formulae for the azimuth and altitude instrument. An equatoreal differs from this instrument only so far as its fundamental plane is that of the equator, whilst for the other instrument it was that of the horizon. Therefore if we simply substitute for the quantities which are referred to the horizon, the corresponding quantities with respect to the equator, we find immediately the formulae for the equatoreal. The quantity a will then be the reading of the hour circle, i' will be the inclination of the axis, which carries the telescope, to the hour circle which should be parallel to the equator. Further i will be the inclination of the hour circle to the equator, and $90^0 + c$ is again the angle, which the line of collimation of the telescope makes with the axis.

We can also easily find the formulae for those instruments, which serve for making only observations in a certain plane. For instance, the transit instrument, is used only in the plane of the meridian, therefore for this instrument the quantity $a - a_0 + 90^0$ must always be very small. Denoting the small quantity by which it differs from zero, by $-k$, the formulae given in No. 10 are changed into:

$$e = -k + b \operatorname{cotang} z + c \operatorname{cosec} z \quad \text{Circle left}$$
$$e = -k - b \operatorname{cotang} z - c \operatorname{cosec} z \quad \text{Circle right.}$$

When e is not equal to zero, the body will not be observed exactly in the plane of the meridian, and if e has a negative value, it will be observed before the culmination. Now let τ be the time which is to be added to the time of observation in order to find the time of culmination, then τ is the hour angle of the body at the time of observation, taken positive on the east side of the meridian. Now since:

$$\sin \tau = -\sin e \cdot \frac{\sin z}{\cos \delta}$$

or:

$$\tau = -e \cdot \frac{\sin z}{\cos \delta},$$

the formulae given above change into:

$$\tau = -b \frac{\cos z}{\cos \delta} + k \frac{\sin z}{\cos \delta} - c \sec \delta \quad \text{Circle left (east)}$$

and:

$$\tau = +b \frac{\cos z}{\cos \delta} + k \frac{\sin z}{\cos \delta} + c \sec \delta \quad \text{Circle right (west).}$$

These are the formulae for the transit instrument. The quantity b denotes now the inclination of the horizontal axis to the horizon, and k is the azimuth of the instrument, taken positive when east of the meridian.

In a similar way the formulae for the prime vertical instrument are deduced. We have, namely, according to No. 7 of the first section:

$$\operatorname{cotang} A \sin t = -\cos \varphi \operatorname{tang} \delta + \sin \varphi \cos t$$

or, if we reckon the azimuth e from the prime vertical, so that $A = 90^0 + e$:

$$\operatorname{tang} e \cdot \sin t = \cos \varphi \operatorname{tang} \delta - \sin \varphi \cos t.$$

Now if Θ is the time at which the star is on the prime vertical, we have:

$$0 = \cos\varphi \operatorname{tang}\delta - \sin\varphi\cos\Theta$$

and if we subtract both equations:

$$\operatorname{tang} e \sin t = 2\sin\varphi \sin\tfrac{1}{2}(t-\Theta)\sin\tfrac{1}{2}(t+\Theta).$$

From this we find, if e is small and therefore t is nearly equal to Θ:

$$e = (t-\Theta)\sin\varphi$$

or:

$$\Theta = t - \frac{e}{\sin\varphi}.$$

If we substitute here for e the expression found before:

$$e = -k \pm b \operatorname{cotang} z \pm c \operatorname{cosec} z,$$

we obtain the following formulae for the prime vertical instrument:

$$\Theta = t + \frac{k}{\sin\varphi} \mp b\frac{\operatorname{cotang} z}{\sin\varphi} \mp c\frac{\operatorname{cosec} z}{\sin\varphi}.$$

The direct deduction of these formulae will be given for each instrument in the sequel.

III. THE EQUATOREAL.

15. As the altitude and azimuth instrument corresponds to the first system of co-ordinates, that of the altitudes and azimuths, so the equatoreal corresponds to the second system, that of the hour angles and declinations. With this instrument therefore that circle, which with the other was horizontal, is parallel to the equator. Now let P be the pole of the heavens, Π that of the hour circle of the instrument. Further let λ be the arc of the great circle between those two points, and h the hour angle of the pole of the instrument. Finally let i' be the angle, which the axis carrying the declination circle (the declination axis) makes with the hour circle, and let K be the point, in which this axis, produced beyond the end on which the circle is, intersects the sphere of the heavens, and finally let D be the declination of this point. As zero of the hour angle we will take again at first that reading of the hour circle, which we obtain, when K, P and Π are on the same declination circle. And we will assume that every other reading gives us that point of the circle, in which it is intersected by the great circle passing through P and Π. This point differs from the reading of the circle only by a constant quantity. Let the hour angle reckoned on the true equator, but from the same zero, be T.

If now we imagine again three rectangular axes of co-ordinates, of which one is perpendicular to the plane of the true equator, whilst the other two are situated in the plane of the equator so, that the axis of y is directed to the adopted zero of the hour angle, then the three co-ordinates of the point K, referred to these axes, are:

$$z = \sin D, \quad y = \cos D \cos T, \quad x = \cos D \sin T.$$

Further, the co-ordinates of K, referred to three rectangular axes, one of which is perpendicular to the hour circle of the instrument, whilst the other two are situated in its plane, the axis of x coinciding with that of the former system, are:

$$z = \sin i', \quad y = \cos i' \cos(t - t_0), \quad x = \cos i' \sin(t - t_0).$$

Now since the axes of z of these two systems make with each other the angle λ, we have the following equations:

$$\begin{aligned} \sin D &= \cos\lambda \sin i' - \sin\lambda \cos i' \cos(t - t_0) \\ \cos D \sin T &= \cos i' \sin(t - t_0) \\ \cos D \cos T &= \sin\lambda \sin i' + \cos\lambda \cos i' \cos(t - t_0). \end{aligned}$$

Since λ, i' and D are small quantities, if the instrument is nearly rectified, we obtain:

$$\begin{aligned} D &= i' - \lambda \cos(t - t_0) \\ T &= t - t_0. \end{aligned}$$

The telescope is attached to the declination axis and we will assume, that the part of its line of collimation towards the object-glass makes with the side of the axis, on which the circle is, the angle $90^0 + c$, c being called the collimation-error. Now if the telescope be directed to a point, whose declination is δ and whose hour angle, reckoned from the adopted zero, is τ_1, then the co-ordinates of this point will be:

$$z = \sin\delta, \quad y = \cos\delta \cos\tau_1 \quad \text{and} \quad x = \cos\delta \sin\tau_1.$$

We will assume, that the division of the circle increases in the direction from south towards west from 0^0 to 360^0 or from 0^h to 24^h. Therefore if the circle-end is west of the telescope, the latter is directed towards a point, whose hour angle is less than that of the point K. Therefore if we imagine the axis of y to be turned so that it lies in the same declination circle with K, if the telescope is directed to the object, then the co-ordinates will be:

$$z = \sin\delta,\ y = \cos\delta\cos(T - \tau_1),\ x = \cos\delta\sin(T - \tau_1).$$

On the contrary, when the circle-end is east of the telescope, these co-ordinates will be:

$$z = \sin\delta,\ y = \cos\delta\cos(\tau_1 - T),\ x = \cos\delta\sin(\tau_1 - T).$$

If now we refer the place of the point O, towards which the telescope is directed, to a system of axes, of which the axis of y is parallel to the declination axis of the instrument and hence directed to K, whilst the axis of x coincides with the corresponding axis of the former system, then the three co-ordinates of the point O will be, δ' denoting the reading of the declination circle:

$$z = \sin\delta'\cos c,\ y = -\sin c$$

and

$$x = \cos\delta'\cos c.$$

Now since the axes of z of the two systems make with each other the angle D, we have:

$$-\sin c = \cos\delta\cos(\tau_1 - T)\cos D + \sin\delta\sin D,$$

or

$$-c = \cos\delta\cos(\tau_1 - T) + D\,.\,\sin\delta,$$

and hence, if we substitute for D and T the values found before:

$$-c = [i - \lambda\cos(t - t_0)]\sin\delta + \cos\delta\cos[\tau_1 - (t - t_0)].$$

From this it follows, that:

$$\cos[\tau_1 - (t - t_0)]$$

is a small quantity. Therefore if we write:

$$\sin[90^0 - \tau_1 + (t - t_0)]$$

instead of

$$\cos[\tau_1 - (t - t_0)],$$

we can take the arc instead of the sine and we find the true hour angle:

$$\tau_1 = 90^0 + (t - t_0) - \lambda\cos(t - t_0)\operatorname{tang}\delta + i'\operatorname{tang}\delta + c\sec\delta,$$

when the circle-end is east of the telescope, and:

$$\tau_1 = (t - t_0) - 90^0 + \lambda\cos(t - t_0)\operatorname{tang}\delta - i'\operatorname{tang}\delta - c\sec\delta,$$

when the circle-end is west of the telescope.

If we add h to both members of these equations, we

reckon the angles from the meridian. Then $\tau_1 + h$ will be the true hour angle reckoned from the meridian and:

$$h + t - t_0 + 90^0$$
$$\text{and } h + t - t_0 - 90^0$$

are the hour angles, as given by the instrument in the two positions. Therefore if we introduce the reading of the circle and call it t', and the index error Δt, we have:

$$\tau = t' + \Delta t - \lambda \sin [t' + \Delta t - h] \operatorname{tang} \delta \pm c \sec \delta \pm i' \operatorname{tang} \delta,$$
$$\text{or: } \tau = t' + \Delta t - \lambda \sin (\tau - h) \operatorname{tang} \delta \pm c \sec \delta \pm i' \operatorname{tang} \delta,$$

where the upper sign is used, when the circle-end is west, the lower one, when it is east.

We can also find these equations and the corresponding ones for the declination from the spherical triangle between the pole of the heavens P, the pole of the instrument Π and the point O, towards which the telescope is directed, in connection with the other triangle formed by Π, O and K, that is, the point in which the declination axis produced intersects the sphere of the heavens.

The sides of the first triangle OP, $O\Pi$ and $P\Pi$ are respectirely the true polar distance $90^0 - \delta$ of the point towards which the telescope is directed, the distance from the pole of the instrument $90^0 - \delta'$, and λ, whilst the angles opposite the two first sides are $180^0 - (\tau' - h)$ and $\tau - h$, where $\tau - h$ is the hour angle, referred to the meridian of the instrument, and $\tau_1 - h$ the hour angle referred to the pole of the instrument and reckoned from the meridian of the instrument. Hence we have the rigorous equations:

$$\cos \delta \cos (\tau - h) = \sin \delta' \sin \lambda + \cos \delta' \cos \lambda \cos (\tau' - h)$$
$$\cos \delta \sin (\tau - h) = \cos \delta' \sin (\tau' - h)$$
$$\sin \delta = \sin \delta' \cos \lambda - \cos \delta' \sin \lambda \cos (\tau' - h),$$

from which we obtain in case that λ is a small quantity:

$$\tau = \tau' - \lambda \operatorname{tang} \delta' \sin (\tau' - h)$$
$$\delta = \delta' - \lambda \cos (\tau' - h).$$

But τ' and δ' are only then equal to the readings of the circle, when i' and c as well as the index error of the vernier are equal to zero. First it is evident, that the angle $90^0 - \delta'' - \Delta\delta$ obtained by the reading of the declination circle (where $\Delta\delta$ is the index error of the declination circle) is equal to the angle at K in the triangle $\Pi K O$. The angle $S \Pi O$, S being a point on the great circle $P\Pi$, is

$\tau' - h$; the reading of the instrument is the angle between the position of ΠK at the time of observation and that, in which ΠP coincides with ΠS. If the above conditions were fulfilled, this angle would be $\tau' - h$, whilst the angle $S \Pi K$ would be $90^0 + \tau - h$, when the axis is west, and $\tau' - h - 90^0$, when the axis is east of the telescope. If for the general case we denote the latter angle by $90^0 + \tau'' - h + \Delta t$ and $\tau'' - h + \Delta t - 90^0$, then the angle $O \Pi K$ will be equal to $90^0 + \tau'' + \Delta t - \tau'$, when the axis is west and $\tau' - (\tau'' + \Delta t - 90^0)$, when the axis is east of the telescope, or equal to $90^0 \mp (\tau' - \tau'' - \Delta t)$. Now since the opposite side in the triangle is $90^0 + c$, and since the side ΠO, opposite the angle $90^0 - \delta'' - \Delta\delta$, is $90^0 - \delta'$, and $\Pi K = 90^0 - i'$, we have:

$$\cos\delta' \cos(\tau' - \tau'' - \Delta t) = \cos c \cos(\delta'' + \Delta\delta),$$
$$\pm \cos\delta' \sin(\tau' - \tau'' - \Delta t) = -\sin c \cos i' - \cos c \sin i' \sin(\delta'' + \Delta\delta),$$
$$\sin\delta' = -\sin c \sin i' + \cos c \cos i' \sin(\delta'' + \Delta\delta),$$

from which we obtain:

$$\tau' = \tau'' + \Delta t \mp c \sec(\delta'' + \Delta\delta) \mp i' \operatorname{tang}(\delta'' + \Delta\delta),$$

and in the same way as in No. 13 of this section:

$$\delta' = \delta'' + \Delta\delta - \sin\tfrac{1}{2}(i' + c)^2 \operatorname{tang}\left[45^0 + \tfrac{1}{2}(\delta'' + \Delta\delta)\right]$$
$$+ \sin\tfrac{1}{2}(i' - c)^2 \operatorname{cotang}\left[45^0 + \tfrac{1}{2}(\delta'' + \Delta\delta)\right],$$

or also $\delta' = \delta'' + \Delta\delta - \frac{1}{2}(i'^2 + c^2)\operatorname{tang}(\delta'' + \Delta\delta) - i' c \sec(\delta'' + \Delta\delta)$,

and substituting these expressions in the equations above, we find:

$$\tau = \tau'' + \Delta t - \lambda \operatorname{tang}\delta \sin(\tau' - h) \mp c \sec\delta \mp i' \operatorname{tang}\delta$$
$$\delta = \delta'' + \Delta\delta - \lambda \cos(\tau' - h) - \tfrac{1}{2}(i'^2 + c^2)\operatorname{tang}\delta - i' c \sec\delta,$$

where the upper sign must be taken, when the axis is west, the lower one, when it is east. The last equation is true, when the divison of the circle increases in the direction of the declination, otherwise we have:

$$\delta = 360^0 - \delta''_1 - \Delta\delta - \lambda \cos(\tau - h) - \tfrac{1}{2}(i'^2 + c^2)\operatorname{tang}\delta - i' c \sec\delta.$$

16. It shall now be shown, how the errors of the instrument can be determined by observations. First we find from the two last equations for δ:

$$\Delta\delta = 180^0 - (\delta''_1 + \delta''),$$

and hence we see, that the index error of the declination circle can be found by directing the telescope in both positions of the instrument to the same object. As such we can choose either a star in the neighbourhood of the meridian, or the pole-star, for then the change of the apparent declination during the interval between the observations will be insignificant.

The errors i' and c can be determined by observing two stars, of which one is near the pole, the other near the equator, each being observed in both positions of the instrument. We have namely for each star the two equations:

$$\tau = \tau' + \Delta\tau - \lambda \sin(\tau - h) \operatorname{tang} \delta + i' \operatorname{tang} \delta + c \sec \delta,$$

when the circle is east, and:

$$\tau_1 = \tau'_1 + \Delta\tau - \lambda \sin(\tau_1 - h) \operatorname{tang} \delta - i' \operatorname{tang} \delta - c \sec \delta,$$

when the circle is west. Therefore if the interval between the two observations is short so that $\tau_1 - \tau$ is a small quantity, we obtain, denoting the sidereal times of the two observations by Θ and Θ_1:

$$i' \operatorname{tang} \delta + c \sec \delta = \frac{[\tau - \tau'] - [\tau_1 - \tau'_1]}{2}$$
$$= \frac{[\Theta - \tau'] - [\Theta_1 - \tau'_1]}{2}$$

and from this equation and the similar one which is deduced from the observations of the second star, the values of the unknown quantities i' and c can be found.

When the errors i' and c have thus been determined as well as the index error $\Delta\delta$, then the errors λ and h as well as the index error Δt are found by the observations of two stars whose places are known. For, if we assume that the readings are corrected for the errors i' and c and for the index error $\Delta\delta$, we have:

$$\tau = \tau' + \Delta t - \lambda \sin(\tau - h) \operatorname{tang} \delta$$
$$\delta = \delta' - \lambda \cos(\tau - h),$$

and likewise for the second star:

$$\tau_1 = \tau'_1 + \Delta t - \lambda \sin(\tau_1 - h) \operatorname{tang} \delta_1$$
$$\delta_1 = \delta'_1 - \lambda \cos(\tau_1 - h).$$

From these equations we easily find:

$$\lambda \sin\left[\frac{\tau_1 + \tau}{2} - h\right] = \frac{\delta - \delta' - (\delta_1 - \delta'_1)}{2 \sin \frac{\tau - \tau_1}{2}}$$

$$\lambda \cos\left[\frac{\tau_1 + \tau}{2} - h\right] = \frac{\delta - \delta' + (\delta_1 - \delta'_1)}{2 \cos \frac{\tau - \tau_1}{2}},$$

and from these the values of h and λ can be obtained.

The index error Δt is then found by means of one of the equations for τ or τ_1.

Since all the quantities obtained by the readings of the circles are affected with refraction, we must understand by τ, τ_1, δ and δ_1 also the apparent hour angles and declinations affected with refraction. But if the observations are not taken very near the horizon, we can use the simple expression:

$$dh = \alpha \text{ cotang } h,$$

for computing the refraction, and then we obtain the corresponding changes of the hour angle and declination by means of the formulae:

$$dt = -\alpha \text{ cotang } h \, . \, \frac{\sin p}{\cos \delta}$$
$$d\delta = +\alpha \text{ cotang } h \, . \, \cos p,$$

where p is the parallactic angle, which is found by means of the formulae:

$$\cos \varphi \cos t = n \sin N$$
$$\sin \varphi = n \cos N$$
$$\text{tang } p = \frac{\cos \varphi \sin t}{n \cos (N + \delta)},$$

or:

$$\cos h \sin p = \cos \varphi \sin t$$
$$\cos h \cos p = n \cos (N + \delta).$$

The altitude h is found by means of the equation:

$$\sin h = n \sin (N + \delta).$$

If we substitute these values in the expressions for dt and $d\delta$, we have also:

$$dt = -\frac{\alpha \cos \varphi \sin t}{\cos \delta \sin (N + \delta)}$$
$$d\delta = +\alpha \text{ cotang } (N + \delta).$$

Now since $\sin p$ has always the same sign as $\sin t$, the hour angle is diminished by refraction in the first and second quadrant, but it is increased, or its absolute value is diminished also, in the third and fourth quadrant.

If $\delta < \varphi$, then $\sin \delta \cos \varphi$ is less than $\cos \delta \sin \varphi$ and hence $\cos p$ is always positive. Therefore the declination is then increased by refraction. But if $\delta > \varphi$, then $\cos p$ is always positive when t lies in the second or third quadrant, therefore then also the declination is always increased by refraction. But in the first and the fourth quadrant it may be diminished, and this is the case for all hour angles which are less than that of the greatest elongation, for which:

$$\cos t > \frac{\tang \varphi}{\tang \delta}.$$

When the errors h and λ have been determined and it is desirable to correct them, this can be accomplished simply by changing the position of the polar axis of the instrument in a vertical as well as a horizontal direction. For if y is the arc of a great circle drawn from the pole perpendicular to the meridian, and if x is the distance of the pole from the point of intersection of this arc with the meridian, then we have:

$$\tang x = \tang \lambda \cos h$$

and:

$$\sin y = \sin \lambda \sin h.$$

Therefore it is only necessary to move the lower end of the polar axis by the adjusting screws through the distance y in the horizontal direction and through the distance x in the vertical direction.

The formulae given above for determining λ and h presuppose, that λ is a small quantity. But this condition can always be fulfilled, since the instrument can very easily be approximately adjusted. For this purpose the instrument is set at the declination of a culminating star (the index error $\Delta\delta$ having been determined before) and then by means of those foot-screws which act in the plane of the meridian (or if the instrument is mounted on a stone pier, by the vertical adjusting screws of the plate on which the polar axis rests) the star is brought to the wire-cross. The same operation is then performed for a star whose hour angle is about 6^h, using now those screws which turn the entire instrument round a horizontal line in the plane of the meridian (or using the horizontal adjusting screws of the polar axis).

No regard has been paid to the effect of the force of gravity upon the several parts of the instrument. This produces a flexure of the telescope as well as of the two axes. Now the flexure of the polar axis need not be taken into consideration, if the centre of gravity of all parts of the instrument, which are moveable on this axis, falls within it, and this must always be the case, at least very nearly, if the instrument is to be in equilibrium in all different positions. Only the pole of the instrument will have a different position on the sphere of the heavens than that which it would have without flexure, but this position remains constant in whatever position the instrument may be. The flexure of the telescope, which may be assumed equal to $\gamma \sin z$, can be determined by the method given in No. 8, and since like the refraction it affects only the zenith distance, the correction for it can be united with that for refraction by using in the formulae given above α tang $z + \gamma \sin z$ instead of α tang z. The flexure of the declination axis has the effect, that the angle i' is variable with the zenith distance. Now if the force of gravity changes the zenith distance of the point K by $\beta \sin z$, then the corresponding change of its declination D is $\beta \sin z \cos p$, and that of its hour angle T is $-\beta \dfrac{\sin z \sin p}{\cos D}$, or since in this case D is very nearly equal to zero, the change of declination is $\beta \sin \varphi$ and that of the hour angle $\beta \cos \varphi \sin T$. But since we have:

$$T = 90^0 + \tau'' \text{ if the circle-end is west}$$
$$\text{and } = \tau'' - 90^0 \text{ if the circle-end is east,}$$

we have to take instead of this hour angle:

$$90^0 + \tau'' - \beta \cos \varphi \cos \tau''$$
$$\text{or } \tau'' - 90^0 + \beta \cos \varphi \cos \tau'',$$

and hence we must use in the formulae given before $\tau'' \mp \beta \cos \varphi \cos \tau''$ instead of τ'' and $i' + \beta \sin \varphi$ instead of i', since now $\Pi K = 90^0 - i' - \beta \sin \varphi$. Thus we obtain:

$$\tau = \tau'' + \Delta t - \lambda \operatorname{tg} \delta \sin(\tau - h) \mp c \sec \delta \mp i' \operatorname{tg} \delta \mp \beta \operatorname{tg} \delta [\sin \varphi + \cos \varphi \operatorname{cotg} \delta \cos \tau].$$

Therefore i' is in this case not constant, but we must take instead of it:

$$i' + \beta [\sin \varphi + \cos \varphi \operatorname{cotang} \delta \cos \tau].$$

Now the observation of a star in both positions of the instrument gives an equation of the form:

$$c \sec \delta + i' \operatorname{tang} \delta + \beta \operatorname{tang} \delta [\sin \varphi + \cos \varphi \operatorname{cotg} \delta \cos \tau] = \frac{\Theta - \tau' - (\Theta_1 - \tau'_1)}{2},$$

and therefore we can determine c, i' and β by observing three different stars in both positions of the instrument.

17. If the equatoreal is well constructed so that the errors can be supposed to remain constant at least for moderate intervals of time, and if the circles have a fine graduation and are furnished with reading microscopes, such an instrument can be advantageously employed to determine differences of right ascension and declination, and hence to determine the places of planets and comets. For this purpose the telescope must have two parallel wires which are a few seconds apart and parallel to the motion of the stars, and another wire perpendicular to those. The object, which is observed, is then brought between the parallel wires by means of the motion of the instrument round the declination axis, and the transit over the perpendicular wire is observed, (if there should be several such wires parallel to each other, then the times of observations are reduced to the middle wire according to No. 20) and then the two circles of the instrument are read. Then in the same way also the star, whose place is known, is observed. If the readings of the circle are corrected for the errors of the instrument and for refraction, the differences of the right ascensions and declinations of the star and the unknown object are obtained, and if these are added to the apparent right ascension and declination of the star, the apparent place of the object is found. This method has this advantage, that one can never be in want of a comparison star and can always choose stars whose places are well known, even standards stars. However it is best not to take the comparison stars at too great a distance from the object, because otherwise mistakes made in determining the errors of the instrument would have too much influence on the results. But when the star is near, those errors will have very little influence, since both observations will be nearly equally affected.

Usually however the equatoreal is not perfect enough for determining the differences of right ascension and declination by it, and these determinations are made by means of a micrometer connected with the telescope, whilst the parallactic mounting of the instrument serves merely for greater convenience. Such micrometers, whose theory will be given in the sequel, are used also to determine the distance of two objects and the angle of position, that is, the angle, which the line joining the two objects makes with the declination circle passing through the middle of this line. This angle is obtained from the reading of the circle of the micrometer, whose centre is in the line of collimation of the telescope. If the equatoreal is perfectly adjusted, then in every position of the instrument the same point of the position circle will correspond to the declination circle of that object, to which the telescope is directed. But otherwise this point varies, and hence the readings of the position circle must be corrected by the angle, which the great circle passing through the object and the pole of the instrument makes with the declination circle. If we denote this angle by π, we have in the triangle between the object, the pole and the pole of the instrument:

$$\cos\delta \sin\pi = \sin\lambda \sin(\tau' - h)$$

$$\text{or} \quad \pi = \lambda \sin(\tau' - h) \sec\delta.$$

Therefore we obtain from the reading of the circle P' the true angle of position P, reckoned as usually from north towards east from 0^0 to 360^0, by means of the equation:

$$P = P' + \Delta P + \lambda \sin(\tau' - h) \sec\delta,$$

where ΔP is the index error of the position circle.

Compare on the equatoreal: Hansen, die Theorie des Aequatoreals, Leipzig 1855 and Bessel, Theorie eines mit einem Heliometer versehenen Aequatoreals. Astronomische Untersuchungen. Bd. I.

IV. THE TRANSIT INSTRUMENT AND THE MERIDIAN CIRCLE.

18. The transit instrument is an azimuth instrument which is fixed in the plane of the meridian. The horizontal axis of the instrument is therefore perpendicular to the meridian so that the telescope can be turned in the plane of the meridian.

With portable transit instruments this axis rests again on two supports which stand on an azimuth circle. But the large instruments have no such circle and the Ys on which the pivots of the axis rest are fastened to two insulated stone piers. One of the Ys is provided with adjusting screws, by which it can be raised or lowered in order to rectify the horizontal axis, whilst the other Y admits of a motion parallel to the meridian, by which the azimuth of the instrument can be corrected.

One end of the axis supports the circle, which, if the instrument is a mere transit, serves only for setting the instrument. If the circle has a fine graduation, so that the meridian altitudes can be observed with the instrument, it is called a meridian circle. The modern instruments of this kind have all two circles, one on each end of the axis. Sometimes both these circles have a fine graduation, but usually only one of them is finely divided, whilst the other serves for setting the instrument. At first we will pay no regard to the circle of such an instrument and treat it as a mere transit instrument.

We will suppose that the axis produced beyond the circle end, which shall be on the west side, intersects the sphere of the heavens in a point, whose altitude and azimuth are b and $90^0 - k$, reckoning the azimuths as usually from the south point through west etc. from 0^0 to 360^0. Then we have the rectangular co-ordinates of this point, referred to a system, whose axis of z is vertical, whilst the axes of x and y are situated in the plane of the horizon so that the positive sides of the axes of x and y are directed respectively to the south and west points:

$$\begin{aligned} z &= \sin b \\ y &= \cos b \cos k \\ x &= \cos b \sin k. \end{aligned}$$

If we denote the declination and the hour angle of this point by n and $90^0 - m$, then we have the co-ordinates of this point, referred to a system whose axis of z is perpendicular to the equator, whilst the axis of y coincides with the corresponding axis of the former system:

$$\begin{aligned} z &= \sin n \\ y &= \cos n \cos m \\ x &= \cos n \sin m. \end{aligned}$$

Now since the axes of z of the two systems make an angle equal to $90^0 - \varphi$ with each other, we have:

$$\begin{aligned} \sin n &= \sin b \sin \varphi - \cos b \sin k \cos \varphi \\ \cos n \sin m &= \sin b \cos \varphi + \cos b \sin k \sin \varphi \\ \cos n \cos m &= \cos b \cos k. \end{aligned}$$

The same formulae can be deduced from the triangle between the pole, the zenith and the point Q, towards which the east end of the axis is directed. For in this triangle we have $ZP = 90^0 - \varphi$, $ZQ = 90^0 + b$, $PQ = 90^0 + n$ and $PZQ = 90^0 - k$, $ZPQ = 90^0 + m$.

If the instrument is nearly adjusted so that b and k as well as m and n are small quantities, whose sines can be taken equal to the arcs and whose cosines are equal to unity, we find the formulae:

$$n = b \sin \varphi - k \cos \varphi$$
$$m = b \cos \varphi + k \sin \varphi,$$

or the converse formulae:

$$b = n \sin \varphi + m \cos \varphi$$
$$k = - n \cos \varphi + m \sin \varphi.$$

Now if we assume, that the line of collimation of the telescope makes with the side of the axis on which the circle is the angle $90^0 + c$, and that it is directed to an object, whose declination is δ and whose east hour angle is τ, which quantity therefore is equal to the interval of time between the time of observation and the time of culmination of the star, then the co-ordinates of the star with respect to the equator, the axis of x being in the plane of the meridian, are:

$$z = \sin \delta, \quad y = - \cos \delta \sin \tau$$

and

$$x = \cos \delta \cos \tau,$$

or if we suppose, that the axis of x is perpendicular to the axis of the instrument:

$$z = \sin \delta, \quad y = - \cos \delta \sin (\tau - m)$$

and

$$x = \cos \delta \cos (\tau - m).$$

Here $\tau - m$ is the interval between the time of observation and the time at which the star passes over the meridian of the instrument.

If now we imagine another system of co-ordinates, so that the axis of x coincides with that of the former system, whilst the axis of y is not in the plane of the equator, but parallel to the axis of the instrument, then we have:

$$y = - \sin c,$$

and since the axes of z of these two systems make with each other the angle n, we have:

$$\sin c = - \sin n \sin \delta + \cos n \cos \delta \sin (\tau - m).$$

In the case of the lower culmination, $\tau - m$ is on the same side of the meridian, but since then the star is observed after it has passed the meridian of the instrument, we must take $\tau - m$ negative. Therefore in this case the co-ordinates of the point to which the telescope is directed will be:

$$z = \sin\delta, \quad y = +\cos\delta \sin(\tau - m),$$

and hence we have:

$$\sin c = -\sin n \sin\delta - \cos n \cos\delta \sin(\tau - m).$$

Therefore in this case we have only to change the sign of the second term in the formula for sin c and we can take:

$$\sin c = -\sin n \sin\delta + \cos n \cos\delta \sin(\tau - m)$$

as the general formula, if for lower culminations we use $180^0 - \delta$ instead of δ. These formulae can also be deduced from the triangle between P, Q and the star O, of which the sides are $PO = 90^0 - \delta$, $PQ = 90^0 + n$, $OP = 90^0 - c$, whilst the angle OPQ is equal to $90^0 + m - \tau$ for upper culminations and equal to $90^0 - m + \tau$ for lower culminations.

From the above formula we find:

$$\cos n \sin(\tau - m) = \sin n \operatorname{tang}\delta + \sin c \sec\delta,$$

and adding to this the identical equation:

$$\cos n \sin m = \cos n \sin m,$$

we obtain:

$$2\cos n \sin\tfrac{1}{2}\tau \cos\left[\tfrac{1}{2}\tau - m\right] = \cos n \sin m + \sin n \operatorname{tang}\delta + \sin c \sec\delta. \quad (a)$$

Now if we suppose the instrument to be so nearly adjusted that m, n and τ are small quantities, we find from this:

$$\tau = m + n \operatorname{tang}\delta + c \sec\delta\ ^{*)}.$$

This is Bessel's formula for reducing observations made with a transit instrument.

If τ is known and T is the clock-time of observation, the clock-time of the culmination of the star is $T + \tau$. If then Δt is the error of the clock on sidereal time, then $T + \tau + \Delta t$ will be the sidereal time of the culmination of the star or be equal to its right ascension α. Hence we have:

$$\alpha = T + \Delta t + m + n \operatorname{tang}\delta + c \sec\delta.$$

Therefore if Δt is known, the right ascension of the star can be determined, and conversely, if the right ascension of the star is known, the error of the clock can be found.

---

*) The same we get immediately from the equation for $\cos n \sin(\tau - m)$.

We can express τ in terms of b and k, if we substitute the expressions:

$$\cos n \sin m = \sin b \cos \varphi + \cos b \sin \varphi \sin k$$
$$\sin n = \sin b \sin \varphi - \cos b \cos \varphi \sin k$$

in the equation (a). We find then:

$$2 \sin \tfrac{1}{2} \tau \cos n \cos [\tfrac{1}{2} \tau - m] = \sin b \frac{\cos (\varphi - \delta)}{\cos \delta}$$
$$+ \cos b \sin k \frac{\sin (\varphi - \delta)}{\cos \delta} + c \sec \delta,$$

and from this:

$$\tau = b \frac{\cos (\varphi - \delta)}{\cos \delta} + k \frac{\sin (\varphi - \delta)}{\cos \delta} + c \sec \delta.$$

This formula is called Mayer's formula, since Tobias Mayer used it for reducing his meridian observations. It is the same formula which was deduced before from the formulae for the azimuth instrument.

Hansen has proposed still another form of the equation for τ, which is the most convenient of all. For if we add the two equations:

$$\sin n \operatorname{tang} \varphi = \sin b \frac{\sin \varphi^2}{\cos \varphi} - \cos b \sin k \sin \varphi$$

and

$$\cos n \sin m = \sin b \cos \varphi + \cos b \sin k \sin \varphi,$$

we find:

$$\cos n \sin m = \sin b \sec \varphi - \sin n \operatorname{tang} \varphi$$

and if we substitute this value of $\cos n \sin m$ in the equation (a), we obtain easily:

$$\tau = b \sec \varphi + n [\operatorname{tang} \delta - \operatorname{tang} \varphi] + c \sec \delta.$$

All these formulae are true, if the circle is on the west side. But if the circle is east, then the altitude of the west end of the axis is $-b$, and the angle, which the line of collimation makes with the west end of the axis, will be $90^0 - c$, whilst k remains the same. Therefore in this case we have only to change the sign of b and c and we have according to Mayer's formula:

For upper culminations

Circle West $\alpha = T + \Delta t + b \dfrac{\cos (\varphi - \delta)}{\cos \delta} + k \dfrac{\sin (\varphi - \delta)}{\cos \delta} + c \sec \delta$

Circle East $\alpha = T + \Delta t - b \dfrac{\cos (\varphi - \delta)}{\cos \delta} + k \dfrac{\sin (\varphi - \delta)}{\cos \delta} - c \sec \delta.$

For lower culminations we take $180^0 - \delta$ instead of δ and obtain:

$$\text{Circle West} \quad \alpha + 12^h = T + \Delta t + b \frac{\cos(\varphi + \delta)}{\cos \delta} + k \frac{\sin(\varphi + \delta)}{\cos \delta} - c \sec \delta$$

$$\text{Circle East} \quad \alpha + 12^h = T + \Delta t - b \frac{\cos(\varphi + \delta)}{\cos \delta} + k \frac{\sin(\varphi + \delta)}{\cos \delta} + c \sec \delta.$$

When a large mass of stars is to be reduced, Mayer's formula is not very convenient, and it is better to employ then Bessel or Hansen's formula. If we choose Bessel's formula, we must apply to each observation the correction:

$$n \operatorname{tang} \delta + c \sec \delta$$

and the error of the clock is then:

$$\alpha - T - m.$$

If we take Hansen's form we apply the correction:

$$n [\operatorname{tang} \delta - \operatorname{tang} \varphi] + c \sec \delta$$

and obtain the error of the clock form:

$$\alpha - T - b \sec \varphi.$$

19. These formulae can be deduced easily in the following way: If the circle is West, and b is the altitude of the point to which the circle-end of the axis is directed, then the telescope will not move in the plane of the meridian, but it will describe the great circle $AZ'B$ Fig. 14 pag. 433. If now the star O is observed, we must add to the time of observation the hour angle:

$$\tau = OPO'$$

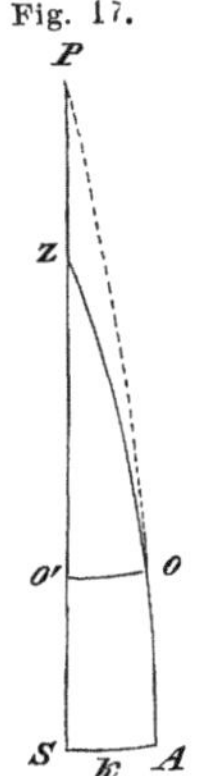

Fig. 17.

But we have:

$$\sin \tau = \frac{\sin OO'}{\cos \delta}$$

and

$$\operatorname{tang} OO' = \operatorname{tang} b \cos O'Z = \operatorname{tang} b \cos(\varphi - \delta),$$

therefore:

$$\tau = b \frac{\cos(\varphi - \delta)}{\cos \delta}.$$

If the azimuth of the instrument is k, the telescope will describe the vertical circle ZA Fig. 17. But we have again, if O is the star:

$$\sin OPO' = \sin \tau = \frac{\sin OO'}{\cos \delta}$$

and

$$\text{tang } O\,O' = \text{tang } k \sin O'Z,$$

therefore:

$$\tau = k\,\frac{\sin(\varphi - \delta)}{\cos\delta}.$$

Finally, if the line of collimation of the telescope makes with the side of the axis on which the circle is, the angle $90 + c$, it will describe a small circle parallel to the meridian and we must add to the time of observation the hour angle (see Fig. 15 pag. 434):

$$\tau = \frac{O\,O'}{\cos\delta} = c \sec\delta.$$

For lower culminations we find the corresponding formulae in the same way.

20. The normal wire of the transit when perfectly adjusted, is a visible representation of the meridian, and the times are observed, when the stars cross this wire. Now in order to give a greater weight to these observations, the transits over several other wires, placed on each side of this wire (which is called the middle wire) and parallel to it, are also observed. Then in order that these transits may be taken always at the same points of the wires, a horizontal wire is stretched across these wires, in the neighbourhood of which the transits are always observed. In order to place this wire perfectly horizontal and thus the other wires perfectly vertical, we let an equatoreal star run along the wire, and turn the diaphragm, to which the wires are fastened, by means of two counteracting screws about the axis of the telescope, until the star does not leave the wire during its passage through the field. If the wires on both sides are equally distant from the middle wire, the arithmetical mean of all observations will give the time of the transit over the middle wire. However usually these distances are not perfectly equal; besides, it has some interest, to find the time of transit over the middle wire from the time of observation on each wire, since we can judge then of the accuracy of the observations by the deviations of the single results from their mean. Therefore we must have a method for reducing the time of observation on any lateral wire to the middle wire, and for this purpose we must know the distances of the wires from the middle wire. This distance f of a wire is the angle at the centre of the object glass between the line towards the middle wire and that towards the other wire. But we had:

$$\sin(\tau - m)\cos n = \sin n \operatorname{tang}\delta + \sin c \sec\delta.$$

Now if an observation was taken on a lateral wire whose distance is f, then the angle which the line from the centre of the object glass to this wire makes with that side of the axis on which the circle is, will be:

$$90^0 + c + f\,^{*}),$$

where f is positive, if the star comes to this wire before it comes to the middle wire. If then τ' is the east hour angle of the star at the time of crossing the wire, we have:

$$\sin(\tau' - m)\cos n = \sin n \operatorname{tang}\delta + \sin(c + f)\sec\delta,$$

and subtracting from this the former equation:

$$2\sin\tfrac{1}{2}(\tau - \tau')\cos\left[\tfrac{1}{2}(\tau' + \tau) - m\right]\cos n = 2\sin\tfrac{1}{2}f\cos\left[c + \tfrac{1}{2}f\right]\sec\delta.$$

Now when the instrument is nearly adjusted, so that c, n and m are small quantities, we find from this the following formula, if we denote by t the time $\tau - \tau'$, which is to be added to the time of observation on a lateral wire in order to find the time of transit over the middle wire:

$$\sin t = \sin f \sec\delta.$$

This rigorous formula is used for stars near the pole, the value of $\sec\delta$ being then very great; but for stars farther from the pole it is sufficient to take:

$$t = f\sec\delta.$$

If it is not required to reduce the lateral wires to the middle wire, we can proceed also in the following way. Let f', f'', f''', etc. be the distances of the lateral wires on the side towards the circle, and φ', φ'', φ''', etc. those on the other side, then compute:

$$\frac{f' + f'' + f''' \ldots - \varphi' - \varphi'' - \varphi''' \ldots}{n} = a,$$

where n is the number of wires. Then we must add to the arithmetical mean of the transits over all the wires the quantity:

$$\pm a \sec\delta$$

*) See Fig. 16 pag. 436, where O is the centre of the object glass, M the middle wire and F the other wire.

where the upper or lower sign is to be used accordingly as the circle is West or East. For lower culminations the opposite sign is taken.

The equation

$$\sin t = \sin f \sec \delta$$

serves also for determining the wire-distances by observing the transits of a star near the pole and computing:

$$f = \sin t \cos \delta,$$

where t is the difference of the transit over the lateral wire and the middle wire, converted into arc. In this way the wire-distances are found very accurately. For the pole-star, for instance, we have:

$$\cos \delta = 0.02609,$$

and hence we see, that an error of one second of time in the difference of the times of transit produces only an error of $0^s.03$ in the value of the wire-distance.

Gauss has proposed another method for determining the wire-distances.

Since rays, which strike the object glass of a telescope parallel, are collected in the focus of the telescope, it follows, that rays coming from the focus of a telescope are parallel after being refracted by the object glass. If the rays come from different points near the focus, their inclinations to each other after their refraction are equal to the angles between the lines drawn from the centre of the object glass to those different points. Now if another telescope, which is adjusted for rays coming from an infinite distance, is placed in front of the first telescope, so that their axes coincide, we can see through it distinctly any point at the focus of the first telescope. Therefore if there is at the focus of the first telescope a system of wires, it is seen plainly through the second telescope, provided that those wires are suitably illuminated. But this is simply done by directing the eye-piece of the first telescope towards the sky or any other bright object. If then the second telescope is that of an azimuth instrument, the apparent distances of the wires can be measured by it like any other angles.

In order to bring the wires exactly in the focus of the object glass, the position of the eye-piece with respect to the wires is first changed until they appear perfectly distinct. Then the wires are at the focus of the eye-piece. After that the telescope is directed to a star, and the entire tube containing the wires and the eye-piece is moved towards or from the object glass, until the star is seen distinctly. When this is the case, the wires are at the focus. In order to examine this more fully, we direct the telescope to an object at an infinite distance and bring it on the wire, and then slighty shifting the eye before the eye-piece we see, whether the object remains on the wire notwithstanding the motion. If this should not be the case, it shows, that the wires are not exactly at the focus, and they are too far from the object glass, if the eye and the image of the object move towards the same side from the wire. But if the eye and the image move to different sides, the wires are too near the object glass *).

In 1850 June 20 Polaris was observed at the lower culmination with the transit-instrument of the observatory at Bilk, and the following transits over the wires were obtained:

Circle West.

I	*II*	*III*	*IV*	*V*
$13^h\,32^m\,7^s$	$19^m\,4^s$	$13^h\,5^m\,7^s$	$52^m\,7^s$	$12^h\,38^m\,9^s$.

Hence the differences of the times are:

I—III	*II—III*	*III—IV*	*III—V*
$27^m\,0^s$	$13^m\,57^s$	$13^m\,0^s$	$26^m\,58^s$.

Since the declination of Polaris on that day was:

$$88^0\,30'\,18''.01$$

we find by means of the formula:

$$f = \sin t \cos \delta$$

the following values of the wire-distances:

$I—III = 42^s.17$, $II—III = 21^s.84$, $III—IV = 20^s.34$, $III—V = 42^s.12$.

On the same day the star η Ursae majoris was observed:

		I	*II*	*III*	*IV*	*V*
η Ursae maj.	Upper culm.	18 . 5	50 . 3	$13^h\,41^m\,24^s.3$	56 . 0	30 . 0.

*) It is best to use for this the pole-star. — Since the wire-distances remain the same only as long as the distance of the wires from the object-glass is not changed, it is necessary to bring the wires exactly in the focus before determining the wire-distances, and then leave them always in the same position.

The declination is $50^0\,4'$. Hence the wire-distances are found by means of the formula:

$$t = f \sec \delta$$

$I - III = 65^s.70$, $II - III = 34^s.02$, $III - IV = 31^s.69$, $III - V = 65^s.62$.

Since the star was first seen on the first wire, we find the transits over the middle wire from these wires as follows:

$$\begin{array}{r} 13^h\,41^m\,24^s.20 \\ 24\;.32 \\ 24\;.30 \\ 24\;.31 \\ 24\;.38 \\ \hline 13^h\,41^m\,24^s.30. \end{array}$$

The arithmetical mean of all wire-distances, taking them positive for the wires *I* and *II* (these being on the side of the circle) and negative for the wires *IV* and *V*, is:

$$a = +\,0^s.31.$$

Now if we take the arithmetical mean of the transits of η Ursae majoris over the several wires, we find:

$$13^h\,41^m\,23^s.82,$$

and adding to it the quantity:

$$a \sec \delta = +\,0^s.48$$

taken with the positive sign, because the circle was West, we find the transit over the middle wire from the mean of all wires, as before:

$$13^h\,41^m\,24^s.30.$$

21. If the body have a proper motion, this must be taken into account in reducing the lateral wires to the middle wire. But since such a body has also a visible disc and a parallax, we will now consider the general case, that one limb of such a body has been observed on a lateral wire, and that we wish to find the time of transit of the centre of the disc over the middle wire.

We have found before the following equation, which is true for circle West:

$$\sin c = -\sin n \sin \delta + \cos n \cos \delta \sin (\tau - m).$$

Now if the body has been observed on a lateral wire, whose distance is f, where f is again positive, when the wire is on the same side from the middle wire as the circle, then we must use in this formula $c + f$ instead of c. But if we have not observed the centre but only one limb of the body, whose apparent semi-diameter is h', we must take instead of c now:

$$c + f \pm h'$$

where the upper or lower sign must be used accordingly as the preceding or the following limb has been observed *). If then Θ is the sidereal time of observation, and α' is the apparent right ascension of the body, then its east hour angle is:

$$\tau = \alpha' - \Theta,$$

and hence we have the following equation, denoting the apparent declination by δ':

$$\sin [c + f \pm h'] = -\sin n \sin \delta' + \cos n \cos \delta' \sin [\alpha' - \Theta - m],$$

where the upper or lower sign is to be taken accordingly as the preceding or the following limb has been observed. If then Δ denotes the distance of the body from the earth, the distance from the centre of the earth being taken as the unit, we have also:

$$\begin{aligned}\Delta \sin [c + f \pm h'] = &- \Delta \sin n \sin \delta' \\ &- \Delta \cos n \cos m \cos \delta' \sin (\Theta - \alpha') \\ &- \Delta \cos n \sin m \cos \delta' \cos (\Theta - \alpha'),\end{aligned}$$

and since:

$$c,\ n,\ m,\ f,\ h',$$

and therefore also $\Theta - \alpha'$ are small quantities, their sines can be taken equal to the arcs and their cosines equal to unity, and we obtain:

$$\Delta \cos \delta' (\alpha' - \Theta) = + \Delta . f \pm \Delta . h' + m \Delta . \cos \delta' + n \Delta . \sin \delta' + c \Delta.$$

The apparent quantities here can be expressed by geocentric quantities. For we have according to the formulae (a) in No. 4 of the third section, introducing the horizontal parallax instead of the distance from the centre of the earth:

$$\begin{aligned}\Delta \cos \delta' \cos \alpha' &= \cos \delta \cos \alpha - \varrho \sin \pi \cos \varphi' \cos \Theta \\ \Delta \cos \delta' \sin \alpha' &= \cos \delta \sin \alpha - \varrho \sin \pi \cos \varphi' \sin \Theta \\ \Delta \sin \delta' &= \sin \delta - \varrho \sin \pi \sin \varphi',\end{aligned}$$

from which we easily obtain:

$$\begin{aligned}\Delta \cos \delta' \cos (\Theta - \alpha') &= \cos \delta \cos (\Theta - \alpha) - \varrho \sin \pi \cos \varphi' \\ \Delta \cos \delta' \sin (\Theta - \alpha') &= \cos \delta \sin (\Theta - \alpha)\end{aligned}$$

or in case that $\Theta - \alpha$ is a small angle:

---

*) For if the preceding limb is observed on the middle wire, then the centre would be seen at the same moment on a lateral wire, whose distance f is equal to $+ h'$.

$$\Delta \cos\delta' (\Theta - \alpha') = \cos\delta (\Theta - \alpha)$$
$$\Delta \cos\delta' = \cos\delta - \varrho \sin\pi \cos\varphi'$$
$$\Delta \sin\delta' = \sin\delta - \varrho \sin\pi \sin\varphi'.$$

From the two last equations we find also with sufficient accuracy:

$$\Delta = 1 - \varrho \sin\pi \cos(\varphi' - \delta).$$

Finally we have, denoting by h the true geocentric semidiameter of the body:

$$\Delta h' = h.$$

If we substitute these expressions for the apparent quantities in the above equation for:

$$\Delta \cos\delta' (\alpha' - \Theta),$$

we find:

$$\cos\delta (\alpha - \Theta) = f[1 - \varrho \sin\pi \cos(\varphi' - \delta)] \pm h$$
$$+ [\cos\delta - \varrho \sin\pi \cos\varphi'][m + n \operatorname{tang}\delta' + c \sec\delta']$$

or:

$$\alpha = \Theta \pm \frac{h}{\cos\delta} + f \frac{1 - \varrho \sin\pi \cos(\varphi' - \delta)}{\cos\delta}$$
$$+ \left[1 - \varrho \sin\pi \frac{\cos\varphi'}{\cos\delta'}\right][m + n \operatorname{tang}\delta' + c \sec\delta'], \qquad (a)$$

where δ' has been retained in the last term instead of δ, because it is more convenient in this form. The apparent declination δ' is found with sufficient accuracy by the reading ot the small circle for setting the instrument. But if this is not the case, we must use in the last term also the true geocentric quantities. Now the last term in the equation for $\Delta \cos\delta' (\alpha' - \Theta)$ is:

$$+ m \Delta \cos\delta' + n \Delta \sin\delta' + c \Delta.$$

If we substitute here for $\Delta \cos\delta'$, $\Delta \sin\delta'$ and Δ the expressions given before, and introduce the following notation:

$$m' = m - c \cos\varphi' \varrho \sin\pi$$
$$n' = n - c \sin\varphi' \varrho \sin\pi$$
$$c' = c - [m \cos\varphi' + n \sin\varphi'] \varrho \sin\pi,$$

those three terms are transformed into:

$$\cos\delta [m' + n' \operatorname{tang}\delta + c' \sec\delta],$$

and hence we obtain:

$$\alpha = \Theta \pm \frac{h}{\cos\delta} + f \frac{1 - \varrho \sin\pi \cos(\varphi' - \delta)}{\cos\delta} + m' + n' \operatorname{tang}\delta + c' \sec\delta. \quad (b)$$

Now if the body has a proper motion, we find the time of culmination from the time of observation Θ on one of the lateral wires by adding to Θ the time, in which the body moves through the hour angle $\alpha - \Theta$. But this time is equal to the hour angle itself divided by $1 - \lambda$, if λ denotes again the increase of the right ascension expressed in time in one second of sidereal time. If we put therefore:

$$\frac{1 - \varrho \sin \pi \cos (\varphi' - \delta)}{(1 - \lambda) \cos \delta} = F,$$

the reduction to the meridian is:

$$= \pm \frac{h}{(1 - \lambda) \cos \delta} + fF + \frac{m' + n' \operatorname{tang} \delta + c' \sec \delta}{1 - \lambda}$$

or:

$$= \pm \frac{h}{(1 - \lambda) \cos \delta} + fF + \frac{1 - \varrho \sin \pi \cos \varphi' \sec \delta'}{1 - \lambda} [m + n \operatorname{tang} \delta' + c \sec \delta'].$$

If we omit the term $\frac{h \sec \delta}{1 - \lambda}$, we find the time of culmination for the observed limb instead for the centre. Moreover, if we omit $1 - \lambda$ in the denominator of the last term, the right ascension of the limb, which is obtained thus, is not referred to the time of culmination, but to the time of the transit over the middle wire. Since:

$$1 - \varrho \sin \pi \cos \varphi' \sec \delta'$$

always differs little from unity, we can use instead of this factor unity, if m, n and c are very small quantities *).

Bessel has given a table in his Tabulae Regiomontanae, which facilitates the computation of the quantity F for the moon. This table gives the logarithm of

$$1 - \varrho \sin \pi \cos (\varphi' - \delta)$$

the argument being:

$$\log \varrho \sin \pi \cos (\varphi' - \delta),$$

and besides it gives the logarithm of $1 - \lambda$, the argument being the change of the right ascension of the moon in 12 hours. Another table gives the logarithm of F and the quantity $\frac{h}{(1 - \lambda) \cos \delta}$ for the sun, the arguments being the days of the year.

If a body, which has a proper motion, has been observed on all the wires, then it is not necessary to know the quantity F, since we may take again the arithmetical mean of all the wires and add the small quantity $a \sec \delta$, as was shown before in No. 20.

---

*) Compare: Bessel, Tabulae Regiomontanae pag LII.

Example. In 1848 July 13 the transit of the first limb of the moon was observed with the transit instrument at Bilk, when the circle was West:

I	$17^h\ 25^m\ 42^s.9$
II	$26\ \ 5\ .0$
III	$28\ .8$
IV	$51\ .0$
V	$27\ \ 14\ .8.$

The wire distances were at that time:

I $42^s.23$ *II* $21^s.96$ *IV* $20^s.32$ *V* $42^s.30.$

Now in order to reduce the several wires to the middle wire, we must first compute the quantity *F*. But on that day was:

$$\delta = -18^0\ 10'.6,$$

further the increase of the right ascension in one hour of mean time was:

$$129^s.8, \text{ and } \pi = 55'\ 11''.0,\ h = 60^s.15;$$

moreover we have for Bilk:

$$\varphi' = 50^0\ 1'.2,\ \log\varrho = 9.99912.$$

Now since one hour of mean time is equal to $3609^s.86$ sidereal, we find:

$$\lambda = 0.03596,$$

and hence:

$$F = 0.03565.$$

If we multiply the wire-distances by this factor, we find:

$45^s.84$ $23^s.84$ $22^s.06$ $45^s.92.$

Hence the times of observation reduced to the middle wire are:

	$17^h\ 26^m\ 28^s.74$
	$28\ .84$
	$28\ .80$
	$28\ .94$
	$28\ .88$
mean value	$17^h\ 26^m\ 28^s.84.$

The term

$$+\frac{h}{(1-\lambda)\cos\delta}$$

is equal to:

$$+65^s.67,$$

and hence the time of transit of the moon's centre over the middle wire is:

$$17^h\ 27^m\ 34^s.51.$$

30

Now on that day b and k and therefore also m and n were equal to zero, but:

$$c = +0^s.09.$$

Therefore taking the factor:

$$\frac{1 - \varrho \sin \pi \cos \varphi' \sec \delta'}{1 - \lambda}$$

equal to unity, we find for the time of culmination of the moon's centre:

$$17^h\ 27^m\ 34^s.60.$$

If the parallax of the body is equal to zero or at least very small, as in case of the sun, the formula for the reduction to the meridian becomes more simple. For then we have:

$$F = \frac{1}{(1-\lambda)\cos\delta}.$$

In observing the sun usually the transits of both limbs over the wires are observed. Then it is only necessary to take the arithmetical mean of the observations of both limbs, and thus the computation of the term $\frac{h}{(1-\lambda)\cos\delta}$ is avoided in this case.

22. It shall be shown now, how the errors of the transit instrument are determined by observations.

First the instrument must be nearly adjusted according to the methods given in No. 5 of the fourth section. The level-error can then be accurately determined by means of the spirit-level according to No. 1 of this section, when the inequality of the pivots is known from a large number of observations in both positions of the instrument. The inclination of the axis can also be found by direct and reflected observations of a star near the pole, for instance, the pole-star. For if we observe such a star on several wires and call T the arithmetical mean of the times of observation reduced to the middle wire, then we have for the upper culmination the equation:

$$\alpha = T + \Delta t + i\frac{\cos z}{\cos\delta} + k\frac{\sin z}{\cos\delta} \pm c \sec\delta,$$

where $i = b$, when the circle is West, and $i = -b'$, when the circle is East, if b and b' denote the elevation of the circle-end in the two positions. But if we observe the image of the star reflected from an artificial horizon, in which case the zenith distance is $180^0 - z$, we have, denoting now the arithmetical mean of the times of observation reduced to the middle wire by T':

$$\alpha = T' + \Delta t - i \frac{\cos z}{\cos \delta} + k \frac{\sin z}{\cos \delta} \pm c \sec \delta,$$

and hence we find:

$$i = \frac{T' - T}{2} \cdot \frac{\cos \delta}{\cos z}.$$

Since the value of $\cos \delta$ is small, we can find i by such observations with great accuracy.

Then in order to determine the error c, we observe the same star in the two positions of the instrument, when the circle is West and when it is East. For these observations we must choose again a star near the pole, α, δ or λ Ursae minoris, because for other stars there is no time for reversing the instrument between the observations on the several wires, and because for these stars the coefficient $\sec \delta$ of c is very great so that errors of observation have only little influence on the determination of c. If we observe the star on several wires when the circle is West, and denote by t the arithmetical mean of the times of observation, reduced to the middle wire and corrected for the level-error, we have:

$$\alpha = t + \Delta t + k \frac{\sin (\varphi - \delta)}{\cos \delta} + c \sec \delta,$$

Then if we reverse the instrument and observe the star again on several wires, when the circle is East, we have, denoting now the arithmetical mean of the times of observation reduced to the middle wire and corrected for the level-error, by t':

$$\alpha = t' + \Delta t + k \frac{\sin (\varphi - \delta)}{\cos \delta} - c \sec \delta.$$

From the two equations we find therefore:

$$c = \frac{t' - t}{2} \cos \delta.$$

If there is a very distant terrestrial object in the horizon in the direction of the meridian (a meridian mark), furnished with a scale, the value of whose parts is known in seconds, we can determine the collimation-error by observing this object in the two positions of the instrument, since, if we read the point of the scale in which it is intersected by the middle wire in the two positions, the collimation-error is equal to half the difference of the readings. Still better is it to use a collimator for this purpose. But then the telescope must have besides the vertical wires, which serve for observing the transits of the stars, also a moveable micrometer-wire, parallel to them, whose position can be easily determined by means of a scale, which gives the entire revolutions of the micrometer-screw, and of the divided screw head whose readings give the parts of one revolution of the screw. If the telescope is furnished with such a wire, it is directed to the wire-cross of the collimator in both positions, and the moveable wire is moved until it coincides with it each time. Now if the readings for the moveable wire in the two positions are a and b, it is easily seen, that $\frac{1}{2}(a+b)$ corresponds to that position of the moveable wire, in which a line drawn from it to the centre of the object glass is perpendicular to the axis of the instrument. Therefore if the moveable wire is moved until it coincides with the middle wire, and if the reading in this position is C, then $C - \frac{1}{2}(a+b)$ or $\frac{1}{2}(a+b) - C$ is the error of collimation, and its sign is positive, if the moveable wire in the position $\frac{1}{2}(a+b)$ and the circle-end of the axis are on opposite sides of the middle wire.

When there are two collimators opposite each other, one north, the other south of the telescope, the error of collimation can be determined without reversing the instrument. For, the two collimators being directed to each other *), one of them is moved until the two wire-crosses coincide so that the axes of the two collimators are parallel. Then the telescope is directed in succession to each of the collimators, and the moveable wire is placed exactly on their wire-crosses. If the readings for the moveable wire in the two positions be a and b, then the error of collimation is again $\frac{1}{2}(a+b) - C$ or $C - \frac{1}{2}(a+b)$, and we can decide about its sign by the same rule as was given before.

---

*) In order that this may be possible if the collimators are on the same level with the instrument, the cube of the axis of the latter has two apertures opposite each other, through which the two collimators can be directed to each other, when the telescope of the instrument is in a vertical position.

Another method of determining the error of collimation is that by means of the collimating eye-piece. For this purpose the telescope is directed to the nadir and an artificial horizon placed underneath *). If then the line of collimation deviates a little from the vertical line, one sees in the telescope besides the middle wire its reflected image, whose distance from the wire will be double the deviation of the line of collimation from the vertical line, which can be easily measured by means of the moveable wire **). For this purpose it is best, to place first the moveable wire so, that the middle wire is exactly half way between the reflected image and the moveable wire and afterwards so, that the reflected image is half way between the middle wire and the moveable wire. Since there is also a reflected image of the moveable wire, in the first position the two wires and by their side the two reflected images are seen at equal distances, whilst in the other position the wires and their images alternately are seen at equal distances. The difference of the two readings for the moveable wire is equal to three times the distance of the middle wire from its reflected image.

In order to see the image reflected from the mercury horizon, it is requisite, that light be so reflected towards the mercury as to show the wires on a light ground. This is accomplished by placing inside the tube of the eye-piece a plane glass inclined by an angle of 45^0 to the axis of the telescope, an aperture being opposite in the tube, through which light can be thrown upon it. In order to have then the

---

*) Usually a mercury horizon, that is, a very flat copper basin filled with mercury, which is poured into the basin after this has been well rubbed with cotton dipped into nitric acid. The mercury then dissolves some of the copper and gives in this impure state a more steady horizontal surface. The oxyde which is formed on the surface can be easily taken off by means of the edge of a paper, and thus a perfectly pure reflecting surface is easily obtained.

**) For all these determinations it is requisite to know the value of one revolution of the micrometer-screw of the moveable wire in seconds. But this can be easily found, if the known interval between two wires is measured also in revolutions of the screw by placing the moveable wire over each of these wires, and reading the scale and the screw head.

whole field uniformely illuminated, it is necessary, as was first shown by Gauss, that there be no lens between the wires and the reflector. But since it is always troublesome, to exchange the common eye-piece so often for this collimating eye-piece, Bessel proposed, to place simply outside upon the common eye-piece a plane glass in the right inclination or a small prism, and to reflect by means of it light into the telescope. It is true, a small part of the field is then only illuminated, but there is no difficulty in observing the reflected image, provided that the glass or the prism is fastened in a frame so that its inclination to the axis can be changed.

The error of collimation is then determined in the following way. Let b denote the inclination of the line passing through the Ys, taken positive, when the side on which the circle is, is the highest; further let u denote the inequality of the pivots expressed in seconds and taken positive, when the pivot on the side of the circle is the thickest one of the two; finally let c be the error of collimation, taken positive, when the angle, which the end of the axis towards the circle makes with the part of the line of collimation towards the object glass, is greater than 90^0; then we have, denoting by d the distance of the middle wire from its reflected image, and taking it positive, when the reflected image is on that side of the middle wire, on which the circle is:

$$\tfrac{1}{2}\, d = b + u - c.$$

Therefore if $b + u$ is known by means of the spirit-level, the error of collimation can be found from this equation, and conversely, if the error of collimation has been determined by other methods, the inclination of the axis of the pivots is found. Now if the instrument is reversed, and d' denotes again the distance of the middle wire from its reflected image, taken again positive, when it is on the side towards the circle, we have:

$$\tfrac{1}{2}\, d' = -b + u - c,$$

and from both equations we obtain:

$$c - u = -\tfrac{1}{4}\,(d + d')$$
$$b = +\tfrac{1}{4}\,(d - d').$$

Therefore by observing the reflected image in both positions of the instrument, we can find c as well as the inclination of the axis, if the inequality of the pivots is known.

With small portable instruments, which usually are not furnished with a moveable wire, we can find the error of collimation according to the same method but by means of the spirit-level. For if one end of the axis is raised or lowered by means of the adjusting screws, until the reflected image is made coincident with the middle wire, we have $d=0$ and hence $c=b+u$. Therefore if $b+u$ is found by the spirit-level according to No. 3 of this section, this value is equal to the error of collimation.

With the meridian circle at Ann Arbor the following observations were made in the two positions of the instrument.

By means of the level the inclination of the axis of the pivots was found, when the circle was West, $b'=+2''.77$ and when the circle was East, $b'_1=-2''.45$. The distance of the middle wire from the reflected image was found in parts of a revolution of the micrometer-screw:

$$d=+0^p.2260 \quad \text{Circle West}$$
$$d'=-0\ .3107 \quad \text{Circle East.}$$

We have therefore:

$$c-u=+0^p.0212=+0''.43$$
$$b=+0\ .1342=+2''.73;$$

since one revolution of the screw is equal to $20''.33$, and since $u=+0''.17$, we have:

$$c=+0''.60,$$

and the inclination of the axis, when the circle was West, $b'=+2''.90$, and when the circle was East, $b'_1=-2''.56$.

Then the instrument was directed to one of the collimators, and when the moveable wire was made coincident with the wire-cross, the reading of the screw was:

$$21^p.132 \quad \text{Circle West}$$
$$21\ .999 \quad \text{Circle East.}$$

We have therefore $\frac{1}{2}(a+b)=21.5655$; the coincidence of the wires was $21^p.5397$, and since we must take $\frac{1}{2}(a+b)-C$, in order to find the error of collimation with the right sign, we obtain:

$$c=+0^p.0258=+0''.52.$$

Finally the two collimators were directed towards each other and the moveable wire was made coincident with the wire-crosses. Then the readings of the screw were:

for the south collimator	$21^{r}.1190$
for the north collimator	$22\ .0127$
Hence we have $\frac{1}{2}(a+b) =$	$21\ .5658$
$C =$	$21\ .5397$
$c = +$	$0^{r}.0261 = +0''.53.$

The inclination and the error of collimation being thus determined, it is still necessary, to find the azimuth of the instrument and the error of the clock.

For this purpose we can combine the observations of two stars, whose right ascensions are known. But in case that the rate of the clock is not equal to zero, we must first reduce the error of the clock to the same time by correcting one time of observation for the rate of the clock in the interval of time between the two observations. Then Δt in both equations will have the same value. If then t_0 and t'_0 are the two times of transit over the middle wire, corrected for the level-error, the collimation-error and the rate of the clock, we have the two equations:

$$\alpha = t_0 + \Delta t + k \frac{\sin(\varphi - \delta)}{\cos\delta}$$

$$\alpha' = t'_0 + \Delta t + k \frac{\sin(\varphi - \delta')}{\cos\delta'},$$

by means of which we can find the values of the two unknown quantities Δt and k; for we have:

$$\alpha' - \alpha = t'_0 - t_0 + k \frac{\sin(\delta - \delta')}{\cos\delta\cos\delta'}\cos\varphi,$$

hence $$k = \frac{\alpha' - \alpha - (t'_0 - t_0)}{\cos\varphi} \cdot \frac{\cos\delta\cos\delta'}{\sin(\delta - \delta')}.$$

After having found k we obtain the error of the clock from one of the equations for α or α'. We see from the equation for k, that it is best, when $\delta - \delta'$ is as nearly as possible 90^0, and that it is of the greatest advantage, to combine a star near the pole with an equatoreal star, because then the divisor $\sin(\delta - \delta')$ is equal to unity and the numerator is very small. If it is impossible to observe a star near the pole, we can combine a star culminating near the zenith with another near the horizon. But in either case it is always advisable to observe more than two stars, and to find the most probable values of Δt and k from all the observations.

For these determinations the standard stars, whose right ascensions are well known and whose apparent places are given in the almanacs for every tenth day, are always used. But these apparent places do not contain the diurnal aberration, since this depends on the latitude of the place. Now according to No. 19 of the third section the diurnal aberration for culminating stars is:

$$\pm 0''.3113 \cos \varphi \sec \delta,$$

where the upper sign corresponds to the upper culmination, the lower one to the lower culmination. We see therefore, that it will be very convenient, to apply this correction with the opposite sign to the observations, since then it can be united with the error of collimation. Therefore the diurnal aberration is taken into account, by writing in all the formulae given before $c - 0''.3113 \cos \varphi$ instead of c or, expressed in time, $c - 0^s.0208 \cos \varphi$ instead of c and $-(c + 0^s.0208 \cos \varphi)$ instead of $-c$.

The methods given above for determining the azimuth are generally used for small instruments, which have no very firm mounting, and they may also be used for larger instruments, especially the first method of the two, when only relative determinations are made. The following may serve as a complete example for determining the errors of an instrument of the smaller class.

Example. In 1849 April 5 the following observations were made with the transit instrument at Bilk.

Circle West.

	I	*II*	*III*	*IV*	*V*	Mean
β Orionis	$54^s.8$	$15^s.3$	$5^h 8^m 37^s.4$	$58^s.0$	$20^s.1$	$5^h 8^m 37^s.44$
Polaris U	$38^m 13^s.0$	$51^m 14^s.0$	0^h			1 5 15 .25

$$b = -0^s.03.$$

Circle East.

	II	*III*	Mean
Polaris U	$19^m 26^s.0$	$1^h 5^m 25^s.0$	1 5 24 .57

$$b = +0^s.05.$$

The apparent-places of the two stars were on that day:

Polaris	$\alpha = 1^h 4^m 17^s.92$	$\delta = 88^0 30' 15''.5$
β Orionis	$\alpha' = 5\ 7\ 16\ .66$	$\delta' = -8\ 22\ .8.$

If we reduce the observations to the middle wire and apply the correction for the level-error, we find:

Circle West	β Orionis	$5^h\ 8^m\ 37^s.42$
	Polaris	$1\ \ 5\ \ 14\ .33$
Circle East	Polaris	$1\ \ 5\ \ 23\ .05.$

From the observations of Polaris in both positions of the instrument, we find the error of collimation

$$=+0^s.114,$$

and since the diurnal aberration for Bilk is equal to $0^s.013$ sec δ, we must take for c now $+0^s.101$, when the circle is West, and $+0^s.127$, when the circle is East. If then we correct the observations in the first position for the error of collimation, we find:

$$\beta \text{ Orionis} = t'_0 = 5^h\ 8^m\ 37^s.52$$
$$\text{Polaris} = t_0 = 1\ \ 5\ \ 18\ .20.$$

Hence we have:

$$t'_0 - t_0 = 4^h\ 3^m\ 19^s.32 \qquad \alpha' - \alpha = 4^h 2^m\ 58^s.74,$$

and since:

$$\varphi = 51^0\ 12'.5$$

we find:

$$k = -0^s.85.$$

Therefore the observation of β Orionis corrected for the errors of the instrument is:

$$5^h\ 8^m\ 36^s.78,$$

and hence:

$$\Delta t = -1^m\ 20^s.12.$$

The methods for determining k, which were given before, have this disadvantage, that they are dependent on the places of the stars. It is therefore desirable to have another method, which gives k independent of any errors of the right ascensions, and which therefore can be employed when absolute determinations are made with an instrument. For this purpose the observations of the upper and lower culminations of the same star are used, as has been stated already in No. 5 of the fourth section. In this case we have $\alpha' - \alpha = 12^h + \Delta\alpha$ and $\delta' = 180^0 - \delta$, where $\Delta\alpha$ is the change of the right ascension in the interval between the two culminations, and therefore the formula for k, which was found before, is transformed into:

$$k = \frac{12^h + \Delta\alpha - (t'_0 - t_0)}{\cos\varphi} \cdot \frac{\cos\delta^2}{\sin 2\delta}$$
$$= \frac{12^h + \Delta\alpha - (t'_0 - t_0)}{2\cos\varphi \operatorname{tang}\delta}.$$

Also for this purpose it is best to observe stars very near the pole at both culminations, because then the divisor tang δ becomes very great. But the method requires, that the instrument remains exactly in the same position during the time between both observations, or at least, if this is not the case, that any change of the azimuth can be determined and taken into account.

In order to dispense with frequent determinations of the azimuth by means of the pole-star, a meridian-mark is usually erected at a great distance from the instrument. This consists of a stone pillar on a very solid foundation, which bears a scale on the same level with the instrument. If then by a great many observations of the pole-star that point of the scale, which corresponds to the meridian, has been determined, the azimuth of the instrument can be immediately found by observing the point, in which the scale is intersected by the middle wire, at least, if the scale remains exactly in the same position, and if either the error of collimation is known or the instrument is reversed and the scale is observed in the two positions of the instrument; for the distance of the middle wire from the point of the scale, which corresponds to the meridian, is in one position equal to $k + c$ and in the other equal to $k - c$. But the distance of the meridian-mark must be great, if great accuracy shall be obtained, since one inch subtends an angle of 1″ at a distance of 17189 feet, and therefore in this case a displacement of the scale equal to $\frac{1}{10}$ of an inch would produce an error of the azimuth equal to 0″.1. However such a great distance is not favorable for making these observations, since the disturbed state of the atmosphere will very seldom admit of an accurate observation of the scale. And since, besides, the observation of such a meridian-mark is limited to the time of daylight, Struve has proposed a different kind of meridian-mark, which is in use at the observatory at Pulkova. In front of the telescope, namely, a lens of great focal length is placed (Struve uses lenses of about 550 feet focal length) in a very firm position and so that the axis coincides with that of the telescope. The meridian-mark at its focus is a small hole in a vertical brass plate, which in the telescope appears like a small and very distinct circle. The lens is mounted on an insulated pier and is well protected by suitable coverings against any change. Likewise the meridian-mark is placed on a insulated pier in a small house and carefully protected against any external disturbing causes. Since thus the same care is taken as in the mounting of the instrument itself, it can be supposed, that the changes of the lens and of the meridian-mark will not be greater that those of the two Ys of the instrument, and since experience shows, that the azimuth of a well mounted instrument does not change more than a second during a day, the probable change of the line of collimation of the meridian-mark (that is, of the line from the centre of the lens to the centre of the small hole) will be less in the same ratio, as the length of the axis of the instrument is less than the focal length of the lens. Therefore if the length of the axis is 3 feet and the focal length of the lens is 550 feet, this change will not exceed $\frac{1}{183}$ of a second. The chief advantage of such a meridian-mark is this, that it can be observed at any time of the day, and thus any change in the position of the instrument can be immediately noticed and taken into account. When there are two such meridian-marks, one south, the other north of the telescope, we can find, by observing both, the change of the error of collimation as well as that of the azimuth, whilst the observation of one alone gives only the change of the line of collimation and thus requires, that the error of collimation has been determined by other methods. If the readings for the north and south mark are a and b, and at another time a' and b', and if we take them positive, when the middle wire appears east of the mark, then we obtain the changes dc and da of the error of collimation and of the azimuth by means of the equations:

$$dc = \frac{a' - a + (b' - b)}{2}$$

$$da = \frac{b' - b - (a' - a)}{2},$$

where dc must be taken with the opposite sign, when the circle is East.

23. If the transit instrument has a divided circle so that not only the transits but also the meridian zenith distances of the stars can be observed, it is called a meridian circle.

When a star is placed between the horizontal wires of such an instrument at some distance from the middle wire, the angle obtained from the reading of the circle is not the meridian zenith distance or the declination of the star, because the horizontal wire intersects the celestial sphere in a great circle, whilst the star describes a small circle. Therefore a correction must be applied on this account to the reading of the circle.

The co-ordinates of a point of the celestial sphere, referred to a system, whose fundamental plane is the plane of the equator, whilst the axis of x is perpendicular to the axis of the instrument, are:

$$x = \cos\delta\cos(\tau - m),\quad y = -\cos\delta\sin(\tau - m)\ \text{and}\ z = \sin\delta.$$

If we imagine now a second system of co-ordinates, whose axis of x coincides with that of the former system, whilst the axis of y is parallel to the horizontal axis of the instrument, and if we denote by δ' the angle through which the telescope moves and which is given by the reading of the circle, and if further we remember, that the telescope describes an arc of a small circle, whose radius is cos c, then the three co-ordinates of the point, to which the telescope is directed, are:

$$x = \cos\delta'\cos c,\quad y = -\sin c,\ \text{and}\ z = \sin\delta'\cos c.$$

Now since the axes of the two systems make with each other an angle equal to n, we obtain:

$$\begin{aligned}\sin\delta &= -\sin c\sin n + \cos c\cos n\sin\delta' \\ \cos\delta\cos(\tau - m) &= \cos\delta'\cos c \\ \cos\delta\sin(\tau - m) &= \sin\delta'\cos c\sin n + \sin c\cos n\end{aligned}$$

and hence:

$$\operatorname{cotang}\delta\cos(\tau - m) = \frac{\cos\delta'\cos c}{-\sin n\sin c + \cos n\cos c\sin\delta'}.$$

This formula can be developed in a series, but since n is always very small and c, even if the star is observed on the most distant lateral wire, is never more than 15 or 20 minutes, we can write simply:

$$\tang \delta = \tang \delta' \cos (\tau - m),$$

and from this we obtain according to formula (17) of the introduction:

$$\delta = \delta' - \tang \tfrac{1}{2} (\tau - m)^2 \sin 2 \delta + \tfrac{1}{2} \tang (\tau - m)^4 \sin 4 \delta.$$

This formula is still transformed so that the coefficients contain the quantities

$$2 \sin \tfrac{1}{2} (\tau - m)^2 \text{ and } 2 \sin \tfrac{1}{2} (\tau - m)^4$$

because these quantities can always be taken from tables. (V. No. 7).

For this purpose we write instead of

$$\tang \tfrac{1}{2} (\tau - m)^2$$

now:

$$\frac{\sin \tfrac{1}{2} (\tau - m)^2}{1 - \cos \tfrac{1}{2} (\tau - m)^2}$$

and develop this into the series:

$$\sin \tfrac{1}{2} (\tau - m)^2 + \sin \tfrac{1}{2} (\tau - m)^4 + \ldots$$

and since:

$$\tfrac{1}{2} \tang \tfrac{1}{2} (\tau - m)^4 = \tfrac{1}{2} \sin \tfrac{1}{2} (\tau - m)^4 + \ldots,$$

we obtain:

$$\delta = \delta' - 2 \sin \tfrac{1}{2} (\tau - m)^2 \,.\, \tfrac{1}{2} \sin 2 \delta - 2 \sin \tfrac{1}{2} (\tau - m)^4 \cos \delta^2 \sin 2 \delta,$$

the first term of which formula is usually sufficient.

The sign of this formula corresponds to the case, when the division of the circle increases in the direction of the declination and when the star is observed at its upper culmination.

When the division increases in the opposite direction, the corrected reading is:

$$\delta' + 2 \sin \tfrac{1}{2} (\tau - m)^2 \,.\, \tfrac{1}{2} \sin 2 \delta + 2 \sin \tfrac{1}{2} (\tau - m)^4 \cos \delta^2 \sin 2 \delta.$$

Since the circle is numbered in the same direction from 0^0 to 360^0, it follows, that if for upper culminations the division increases in the direction of the declination, the reverse takes place for lower culminations, and hence also for lower culminations the sign of the formula must be changed.

We can find the formula also in the following way. Let PO' Fig. 18 represent the meridian and O a star, whose

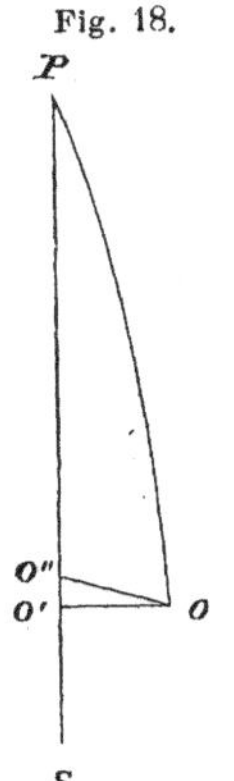

hour angle shall be t. If we direct the telescope to this star and bring it on the horizontal or axial wire, we observe the polar distance PO', where the point O' is found by laying through O an arc of a great circle perpendicular to PS. Then we have $PO' = 90^0 - \delta'$, $PO = 90^0 - \delta$ and hence:

$$\text{tang}\,\delta = \cos t\,.\,\text{tang}\,\delta'.$$

Now we will further suppose, that the axial wire is not parallel to the equator, but that it makes an angle equal to $90^0 + J$ with the meridian, where J is called the inclination of the wire; then we observe the polar distance PO'', where O'' is found by laying through O a great circle making with the meridian an angle equal to $90^0 + J$. If we denote again the observed declination by δ', and take $OO'' = c$, we have:

$$\begin{aligned} \sin c \sin J &= -\sin\delta\cos\delta' + \cos\delta\sin\delta'\cos t \\ \sin c \cos J &= \cos\delta\sin t, \end{aligned}$$

and therefore:

$$\begin{aligned} \text{tang}\,\delta &= \text{tang}\,\delta'\left[\cos t - \sin t\frac{J}{\sin\delta'}\right] \\ &= \text{tang}\,\delta'\cos(t+y), \end{aligned}$$

where:

$$y = \frac{J}{\sin\delta'}.$$

When $J = 0$, the formula gives simply the reduction to the meridian. But this reduction *plus* the correction for the inclination of the wires is, if we take only the first term of the series:

$$\delta - \delta' = -\tfrac{1}{2}\sin 2\delta\,.\,2\sin\tfrac{1}{2}(t+y)^2.$$

In order to determine the inclination of the wires, a star near the pole is observed at a great distance from the middle wire on each side of it. For, every such observation gives an equation of the form:

$$\delta = \delta' - \tfrac{1}{2}\sin 2\delta\,.\,2\sin\tfrac{1}{2}t^2 - \cos\delta\sin t\,.\,J,$$

where also the second term, dependent on $\sin\frac{1}{2}t^4$, can be added, if it is necessary. Therefore from two such equations we can find δ and J, or when more than two observations have been made, we can find the most probable values of J and $\Delta\delta$, if we assume for δ the approximate value δ_0 so that $\delta = \delta_0 + \Delta\delta$. The above equation becomes then:

$$0 = \delta_0 - \delta' + \tfrac{1}{2} \sin 2\delta \,.\, 2 \sin \tfrac{1}{2} t^2 + \Delta\delta + \cos\delta \sin t \,.\, J.$$

It is also easy to find the correction which must be applied to the observed declination in case, that a body has been observed, which has a parallax and a proper motion, for instance, the moon. If such a body has been observed on a lateral wire, we have the equations:

$$\cos c \cos \delta' = \cos \delta \cos (\tau - m)$$
$$\cos c \sin \delta' = \cos \delta \sin (\tau - m) \sin n + \sin \delta \cos n.$$

Here δ is the apparent declination of the observed point of the limb, and τ is the east hour angle of that point at the time of observation, whilst δ' is the declination given by the reading of the circle. But if we denote by δ the apparent declination of the centre of the moon, and by τ its apparent hour angle, we have:

$$\cos c \cos (\delta' \mp x) = \cos \delta \cos (\tau - m)$$
$$\cos c \sin (\delta' \mp x) = \cos \delta \sin (\tau - m) \sin n + \sin \delta \cos n,$$

where

$$\sin x \cos c = \sin h'$$

if h' is the apparent semi-diameter *), and where the upper or lower sign must be taken accordingly as the upper or lower limb has been observed. If we substitute in these equations $\sin h'$ instead of $\sin x \cos c$, eliminate $\cos c \cos x$ and multiply the resulting equation by Δ, which denotes the ratio of the distance of the body from the place of observation to the distance from the centre of the earth, we find:

$$\begin{aligned} \pm \Delta \sin h' = \; & \Delta \cos \delta \sin \delta' \cos (\tau - m) \\ & - \Delta \cos \delta \cos \delta' \sin (\tau - m) \sin n \\ & - \Delta \sin \delta \cos \delta' \cos n, \end{aligned}$$

or since the quantity $\sin (\tau - m) \sin n$ can be neglected and $\cos n$ be taken equal to unity:

$$\begin{aligned} \pm \Delta \sin h' = \; & \Delta \cos \delta \,.\, \sin \delta' \cos (\tau - m) \\ & - \Delta \sin \delta \,.\, \cos \delta'. \end{aligned}$$

If we express now the apparent quantities in terms of the geocentric quantities, taking:

---

*) We find this immediately from the right angled triangle between the pole of the circle of the instrument, the centre of the moon and the observed point of the limb, the angle at the pole being x and the opposite side h'.

$$\Delta \sin h' = \sin h$$
$$\Delta \cos \delta = \cos \delta_0 - \varrho \sin \pi \cos \varphi'$$
$$\Delta \sin \delta = \sin \delta_0 - \varrho \sin \pi \sin \varphi',$$

we easily find:

$$\pm \sin h - \varrho \sin \pi \sin (\varphi' - \delta')$$
$$= \sin (\delta' - \delta_0) - \cos \delta_0 \sin \delta' \tfrac{1}{2} (\tau - m)^2 \frac{1}{206265^2}.$$

Now if the time of observation is Θ, and the time of culmination of the moon is Θ_0, we have:

$$\tau = \Theta - \Theta_0.$$

But when the body has a proper motion and λ denotes the increase of the right ascension in one second, we have:

$$\tau = (\Theta - \Theta_0)(1 - \lambda) . 15,$$

if $\Theta - \Theta_0$ is expressed in seconds of time.

Now if we neglect the small quantity m in $(\tau - m)^2$ and take:

$$\sin p = \varrho \sin \pi \sin (\varphi' - \delta'),$$

we have:

$$\sin (\delta_0 - \delta') = \sin p \mp \sin h - \tfrac{1}{4} \sin 2\delta' (\Theta - \Theta_0)^2 (1 - \lambda)^2 \frac{15^2}{206265^2}.$$

And since:

$$\sin (p \pm h) = \sin p \pm \sin h - 2 \sin p \tfrac{1}{2} h^2 \mp 2 \sin h \sin \tfrac{1}{2} p^2,$$

and hence:

$$\sin p \pm \sin h = \sin (p \pm h) \pm \frac{p \pm h}{2} \sin p \sin h \frac{1}{206265},$$

we finally obtain:

$$\delta_0 = \delta' + p \mp h \mp \frac{(p \mp h)}{2} \sin p \sin h$$
$$- \frac{15^2}{4} \cdot \frac{1}{206265} \sin 2\delta' (1 - \lambda)^2 (\Theta - \Theta_0)^2.$$

This is the formula given by Bessel in the introduction to the Tabulae Regiomontanae pag. LV. The last term of this formula corresponds to the first term of the formula for the reduction to the meridian, which was found before, multiplied by $(1 - \lambda)^2$.

This true declination of the moon's centre corresponds to the time Θ. If we wish to have it for the time Θ', we must add the term:

$$+ \frac{d\delta}{dt} (\Theta' - \Theta)$$

where $\frac{d\delta}{dt}$ is the change of the declination in the unit of time.

24. In order that the observations with the meridian circle may give the true declinations or zenith distances, the readings of the circle must be corrected for the errors of division and for flexure, which must be determined according to No. 7 and 8 of this section. Finally the zenith point or the polar point of the circle must be known. In order to find the latter, the pole-star must be observed at the upper and lower culmination. When the readings are freed from refraction, and from the errors of division and from flexure, the arithmetical mean of the two readings gives the polar point, provided, that the microscopes have not changed their position during the interval between the observations. But since it is necessary for examining the stability of the microscopes and for determining any change of their position, to observe the nadir point at the time of the two observations, it is at once the most simple and the most accurate method, to refer all observations to the zenith point, that is, to determine the zenith distances of the stars, and to deduce from them the declinations with the known value of the latitude.

As has been shown before, the nadir point is determined, by turning the telescope towards the nadir and observing the image of the wires reflected from an artificial horizon, which must be made coincident with the wires themselves. Usually such an instrument has two axial wires parallel to each other at a distance of about 10 seconds, and in making an observation the instrument is turned, until the star is exactly half way between these wires. For determining the nadir point the reflected images of the two wires are placed in succession half way between the wires, and then the arithmetical mean of the readings of the circle in these two positions of the telescope gives the nadir point. The observations are then freed from flexure according to the equations (B) in No. 8 of this section and from the errors of division. In order to obtain the utmost accuracy, it would be necessary to determine the nadir point after every observation of a star; but since the displacements of the microscopes are only small and are going on slowly, it is sufficient, to determine it at intervals, and then to interpolate the value of the nadir point for every observation. In this way the errors produced by any changes of the microscopes are entirely eliminated, and since the observation of the nadir point is so simple and so accurate, this method for determining zenith distances is the most recommendable.

Horizontal collimators, of which one is north, the other south of the telescope, can also be used for determining the zenith point. For this purpose the collimators are constructed so, that the line of collimation of the telescope is also the axis of the instrument, the cylindrical tube of the telescope being provided with two exactly circular rings of bell metal, with which it lies in the Ys. These Ys have the usual adjusting screws for altitude and azimuth, and the wire-cross is likewise furnished with such screws, by which it can be moved in the plane perpendicular to the axis of the telescope. When the collimators have been placed so that their line of collimation coincides nearly with that of the telescope, the line of collimation of the telescope of each collimator is rectified so that it coincides with the axis of revolution. This is accomplished by directing one collimator to the other and turning it 180^0 about its axis. If the point of intersection of the wires after this motion of the telescope remains in the same position with respect to that of the other collimator, then the line of collimation is rectified; if this is not the case, the wire-cross is moved by means of the adjusting screws, until the point of intersection remains exactly in the same position when the telescope is turned 180^0. The inclination of the axis and hence also of the line of collimation is then found by means of the level, and since the collimator can be reversed so that the object glass is on that side on which the eye-piece was before, the inequality of the pivots can be determined and taken into account in the usual way. In order then to find the horizontal point of the circle, the collimator is levelled, and the telescope of the meridian circle turned until its wire-cross is coincident with that of the collimator. In this position the circle is read. The same operation is repeated after the collimator has been turned 180^0 about its axis, to eliminate any error of the line of collimation. Then the same observations are repeated with the other collimator, and when a and b denote the arithmetical means of the readings of the circle for each collimator, $\frac{a+b}{2}$ is the zenith point of the circle, if the collimators are at equal distances from the axis of the instrument *). If x is the elevation of the object-end of the collimator, corrected already for the inequality of the pivots, then the zenith distance of the telescope when it is directed to the wire-cross of the collimator, is $90^0 + x$, taking no account of the angle between the vertical lines of the two instruments, and hence we must subtract x from the reading or add it, accordingly as the division increases or decreases in the direction of the zenith distance.

This method being more complicated and therefore probably less accurate than the one mentioned before, the latter is always preferable.

The latitude is determined best by direct and reflected observations of the circumpolar stars. For we obtain from the observations made at one culmination according to the equations (B) in No. 8 of this section:

$$90^0 - \zeta = \tfrac{1}{2}\left(\frac{z' - z}{2} + \frac{z'' - z'''}{2}\right) - b'' \sin 2z - \ldots$$

and a similar equation is found for the lower culmination. The arithmetical mean of these two equations gives the latitude independent of the declination of the star, but affected with those terms of flexure which depend on the sine of $2z$, $4z$ etc., the first of which can be determined by the method given in that No. The angle between the vertical lines of the instrument and the artificial horizon must likewise be taken into account, as was shown in the same No.

V. THE PRIME VERTICAL INSTRUMENT.

25. If we observe the transit of a star and its zenith distance with a transit circle mounted in the plane of the prime vertical, we can determine two quantities, namely a

*) The readings must be corrected for flexure, if there are any terms, which have an influence upon the mean of the two readings.

and δ or φ. But since the observation of zenith distances in this case is more difficult, usually only the transits of stars are observed with such an instrument, in order to find the latitude or the declinations of the stars. For this purpose a method is required, by which the true time of passage over the prime vertical can be deduced from the observed time and the known errors of the instrument.

We will suppose, that the axis of the instrument produced towards north meets the celestial sphere in a point Q, whose apparent altitude is b and whose azimuth, reckoned from the north point and positive on the east side of the meridian, is k. If we imagine now three axes of co-ordinates, of which the axis of z is perpendicular to the horizon, whilst the axes of x and y are situated in the plane of the horizon so that the positive axis of x is directed to the north point and the positive axis of y to the east point, then the three co-ordinates of the point Q are:

$$z = \sin b\,,\; y = \cos b \sin k \text{ and } x = \cos b \cos k.$$

Further if we imagine another system of co-ordinates, whose axis of z is parallel to the axis of the heavens, and whose axis of y coincides with the corresponding axis of the first system so that the positive axis of x is directed to the point in which the equator intersects the meridian below the horizon, then the three co-ordinates of the point Q, denoting its hour angle (reckoned in the same way as the azimuth) by m, and 180^0 *minus* its declination by n, are:

$$z = \sin n\,,\; y = \cos n \sin m\,,\; x = \cos n \cos m,$$

and since the axes of z in both systems make with each other an angle equal to $90^0 - \varphi$, we have the equations:

$$\begin{aligned}\sin b &= \sin n \sin \varphi - \cos n \cos m \cos \varphi\\ \cos b \sin k &= \cos n \sin m\\ \cos b \cos k &= \cos n \cos m \sin \varphi + \sin n \cos \varphi\end{aligned}$$

and

$$\begin{aligned}\sin n &= \cos b \cos k \cos \varphi + \sin b \sin \varphi\\ \cos n \sin m &= \cos b \sin k\\ \cos n \cos m &= \cos b \cos k \sin \varphi - \sin b \cos \varphi.\end{aligned}$$

If we then assume, that the line of collimation of the telescope makes with the end of the axis towards the circle an angle equal to $90^0 + c$, and that it is directed to an object, whose declination is δ and whose hour angle is t, then the three co-ordinates of this point with respect to the equator and supposing the axis of x to be directed towards north, are:

$$z = \sin\delta,\ y = \cos\delta \sin t \text{ and } x = -\cos\delta\cos t,$$

and if we take the axis of x in the plane of the equator, but in the direction of the axis of the instrument:

$$z = \sin\delta$$
$$x = -\cos\delta\cos(t - m).$$

Now if we imagine another system, of which the axis of y coincides with that of the former system, whilst the axis of x coincides with the axis of the instrument, we have:

$$x = -\sin c,$$

and since the angle between the axes of x in the two systems is n, we have:

$$\sin c = -\sin\delta\sin n + \cos\delta\cos(t - m)\cos n.$$

We can deduce these formulae also from the triangle between the pole, the zenith and the point Q, towards which the side of the axis opposite to that on which the circle is, is directed. In this triangle we have, when the circle is north, $PQ = 180^0 - \varphi - n$, $ZQ = 90^0 + b$ and $PZ = 90^0 - \varphi$, whilst the angle $QPZ = m$ and $QZS = k$. The formula for $\sin c$ is deduced from the triangle PSQ, where S is that point of the sphere of the heavens, to which the telescope is directed, and in which we have $S = 90^0 - c$, when S is west of the meridian and $SP = 90^0 - \delta$, $PQ = 180^0 - \varphi - n$, whilst the angle $SPQ = t - m$.

From the last equation we obtain by substituting for $\sin n$, $\cos n \cos m$ and $\cos n \sin m$ the values found before, and taking instead of the sines of b, k and c the arcs themselves and instead of the cosines unity:

$$\begin{aligned} c = & -\sin\delta\cos\varphi + \cos\delta\sin\varphi\cos t \\ & -[\sin\delta\sin\varphi + \cos\delta\cos\varphi\cos t]\, b \\ & +\cos\delta\sin t\,.\,k, \end{aligned}$$

and since:

$$\sin\delta\sin\varphi + \cos\delta\cos\varphi\cos t = \cos z$$

and

$$\cos\delta\sin t = \sin z\sin A,$$

or, since A is nearly 90^0:

$$\cos\delta\sin t = \sin z,$$

we obtain, when the star is west of the meridian:

$$c + b\cos z - k\sin z = -\sin\delta\cos\varphi + \cos\delta\sin\varphi\cos t.$$

If then Θ is the true sidereal time, at which the star is on the prime vertical, and if therefore $\Theta - \alpha$ is the hour angle of the star at that moment, we have:

$$\cos(\Theta - \alpha) = \frac{\operatorname{tang}\delta}{\operatorname{tang}\varphi},$$

or:

$$0 = -\sin\delta\cos\varphi + \cos\delta\sin\varphi\cos(\Theta - \alpha).$$

Subtracting this equation from the other, we obtain:

$$c + b\cos z - k\sin z = \cos\delta\sin\varphi \,.\, 2\sin\tfrac{1}{2}[\Theta - \alpha - t]\sin\tfrac{1}{2}[\Theta - \alpha + t].$$

Now since c, b and k are small quantities and hence $\Theta - \alpha$ and t are nearly equal, we can put:

$$\sin t \quad \text{instead of} \quad \sin\tfrac{1}{2}[\Theta - \alpha + t]$$

and

$$\tfrac{1}{2}[\Theta - \alpha - t] \quad \text{instead of} \quad \sin\tfrac{1}{2}[\Theta - \alpha - t]$$

and then, remembering that

$$\cos\delta\sin t = \sin z$$

we obtain:

$$\Theta - \alpha = t + \frac{c}{\sin z\sin\varphi} + \frac{b}{\operatorname{tang} z\sin\varphi} - \frac{k}{\sin\varphi}.$$

If then a star has been observed on the middle wire of the instrument at the clock-time T, the true sidereal time will be $T + \Delta t$, and the hour angle:

$$T + \Delta t - \alpha = t.$$

Therefore we have:

$$\Theta = T + \Delta t + \frac{c}{\sin z\sin\varphi} + \frac{b}{\operatorname{tang} z\sin\varphi} - \frac{k}{\sin\varphi}.$$

This formula is true, when the circle is North and the star West. When the star is East, we have:

$$\cos\delta\sin t = -\sin z.$$

Therefore, since the signs of the quantities c, b and k remain the same, we must change in the above formula the signs of the divisors $\sin z$ and $\operatorname{tang} z$ and thus we have:

$$\Theta = T + \Delta t - \frac{c}{\sin z\sin\varphi} - \frac{b}{\operatorname{tang} z\sin\varphi} - \frac{k}{\sin\varphi} \quad \left\{\begin{matrix}\text{Circle North}\\ \text{Star East}\end{matrix}\right\}.$$

When the circle is South, the quantities b and c have the opposite sign, and therefore we have:

$$\Theta = T + \Delta t - \frac{c}{\sin z\sin\varphi} - \frac{b}{\operatorname{tang} z\sin\varphi} - \frac{k}{\sin\varphi} \quad \left\{\begin{matrix}\text{Circle South}\\ \text{Star West}\end{matrix}\right\}$$

and

$$\Theta = T + \Delta t + \frac{c}{\sin z\sin\varphi} + \frac{b}{\operatorname{tang} z\sin\varphi} - \frac{k}{\sin\varphi} \quad \left\{\begin{matrix}\text{Circle South}\\ \text{Star East}\end{matrix}\right\}.$$

If we know Θ and α, we obtain by means of the formula:

$$\operatorname{tang}\varphi\cos(\Theta-\alpha)=\operatorname{tang}\delta$$

either φ, when the declination of the star is known, or the declination, when the latitude is known. If Θ and Θ' be the times, at which the star was on the prime vertical east and west of the meridian, then $\frac{1}{2}(\Theta'-\Theta)$ will be the hour angle of the star at those times, and therefore we have:

$$\operatorname{tang}\varphi\cos\tfrac{1}{2}(\Theta'-\Theta)=\operatorname{tang}\delta,$$

so that it is not necessary to know the right ascension of the star, in order to find φ or δ. When the instrument is reversed between the two observations, so that one transit is observed when the circle is North, the other when the circle is South, then we have:

$$\tfrac{1}{2}(\Theta'-\Theta)=\tfrac{1}{2}(T'-T),$$

and hence in that case it is not necessary to know the error of the clock nor the errors of the instrument except the level-error. An example is given in No. 24 of the fifth section.

26. The formulae given before are used, when the instrument is nearly adjusted so that b, c and k are small quantities, whose squares and products can be neglected. But this method of determining the latitude by observing stars on the prime vertical is often resorted to by travellers, who sometimes cannot adjust their instrument sufficiently and thus make the observation at a greater distance from the prime vertical. In that case the formulae given above cannot be employed. But we found before the rigorous equation:

$$\sin c=-\sin\delta\sin n+\cos\delta\cos n\cos(t-m),$$

or if we substitute the values of $\sin n$, $\cos n\cos m$ and $\cos n\sin m$

$$\sin c=-\sin b\sin\delta\sin\varphi-\sin b\cos\delta\cos\varphi\cos t-\cos b\cos k\sin\delta\cos\varphi$$
$$+\cos b\cos k\sin\varphi\cos\delta\cos t+\cos b\sin k\cos\delta\sin t.$$

Now if the observation were made on the prime vertical, we should have:

$$\sin\delta=\cos z\sin\varphi,\qquad\cos\delta\cos t=\cos z\cos\varphi$$

and

$$\cos\delta\sin t=\sin z.$$

But since we assume, that the instrument makes a considerable angle with the prime vertical, we will introduce the following auxiliary quantities:

$$\sin\delta = \cos z' \sin\varphi'$$
$$\cos\delta\cos t = \cos z'\cos\varphi'$$
$$\cos\delta\sin t = \sin z',$$

by means of which the formula for $\sin c$ is transformed into:

$$\sin c = -\sin b\cos z'\cos(\varphi-\varphi') + \cos b\cos k\cos z'\sin(\varphi-\varphi') + \cos b\sin k\sin z',$$

so that we obtain:

$$\text{tang}(\varphi-\varphi') = \frac{\sin c\sec z'}{\cos b\cos k\cos(\varphi-\varphi')} + \frac{\text{tang}\, b}{\cos k} - \frac{\text{tang}\, k\,\text{tang}\, z'}{\cos(\varphi-\varphi')}.$$

We see from this formula, that it is best to observe stars which pass as nearly as possible by the zenith, because in that case, even if k is not very accurately known, we can obtain a good result for the latitude. And observing the star on the east and west side in the two different positions of the instrument, we can combine the observations so, that the errors of the instrument are entirely eliminated. For the above formula is true when the circle is North and the star West. For the other cases we find the formulae in the same way as before, taking z negative when the star is East, and we have:

$$\text{tang}(\varphi-\varphi') = \frac{\sin c\sec z'}{\cos b\cos k\cos(\varphi-\varphi')} + \frac{\text{tang}\, b}{\cos k} + \frac{\text{tang}\, k\,\text{tang}\, z'}{\cos(\varphi-\varphi')} \quad \begin{Bmatrix}\text{Circle North}\\ \text{Star East}\end{Bmatrix}$$

$$\text{tang}(\varphi-\varphi') = -\frac{\sin c\sec z'}{\cos b\cos k\cos(\varphi-\varphi')} - \frac{\text{tang}\, b}{\cos k} - \frac{\text{tang}\, k\,\text{tang}\, z'}{\cos(\varphi-\varphi')} \quad \begin{Bmatrix}\text{Circle South}\\ \text{Star West}\end{Bmatrix}$$

$$\text{tang}(\varphi-\varphi') = -\frac{\sin c\sec z'}{\cos b\cos k\cos(\varphi-\varphi')} - \frac{\text{tang}\, b}{\cos k} + \frac{\text{tang}\, k\,\text{tang}\, z'}{\cos(\varphi-\varphi')} \quad \begin{Bmatrix}\text{Circle South}\\ \text{Star East}\end{Bmatrix}$$

Therefore when we reverse the instrument between the observations, and compute $\varphi-\varphi'$ from each observation, the arithmetical mean is free from all errors of the instrument except the level-error. If we cannot observe the same star east and west of the meridian, we may observe one star east and another star west of the meridian after the instrument has been reversed. If we choose two stars, whose zenith distances on the prime vertical are nearly equal, at least a large portion of the errors of the instrument will be eliminated, and the accuracy of the result for the latitude depends then merely on the accuracy with which φ' has been found. But we have:

$$\text{tang}\,\varphi' = \frac{\text{tang}\,\delta}{\cos t},$$

therefore if we write the formula logarithmically and differentiate it, we have:

$$d\varphi' = \frac{\sin 2\varphi'}{\sin 2\delta} d\delta + \tfrac{1}{2} \sin 2\varphi' \operatorname{tang} t \, dt.$$

From this formula we see again, that it is best to observe stars which pass over the prime vertical near the zenith. For since we have:

$$\operatorname{tang} t = \frac{\operatorname{tang} z'}{\cos \varphi},$$

we see that the coefficient of dt is equal to $\sin \varphi' \operatorname{tang} z'$, and that it is very small for stars near the zenith, and since for such stars δ is nearly equal to φ, an error of the declination is at least non increased.

If the observations have been made on several wires, it is not even necessary, to reduce them to the middle wire, an operation which for this instrument is a little troublesome, but we can find a value of the latitude by combining two observations made east and west of the meridian, but on the same wire *).

If we write the formula for $\operatorname{tang}(\varphi - \varphi')$ in this way:

$$\sin(\varphi - \varphi') = \frac{\sin c}{\cos b \cos k} \sec z' + \frac{\operatorname{tang} b}{\cos k} \cos(\varphi - \varphi') - \operatorname{tang} k \operatorname{tang} z',$$

then develop $\sin(\varphi - \varphi')$, and substitute for $\sin \varphi'$ and $\cos \varphi'$ the values:

$$\sin \delta \sec z' \text{ and } \cos \delta \cos t \sec z'$$

and take $\cos(\varphi - \varphi')$ equal to unity, we obtain:

$$\sin(\varphi - \delta) = \cos \delta \sin \varphi \,.\, 2 \sin \tfrac{1}{2} t^2 + \frac{\sin c}{\cos b \cos k}$$
$$+ \frac{\operatorname{tang} b}{\cos k} \cos z' - \operatorname{tang} k \sin z'.$$

When b, c and k are small quantities, we thus find the following convenient formulae for determining the latitude by stars near the zenith, writing $c + f$ instead of c:

$$\begin{aligned} \varphi - \delta = \sin \varphi \cos \delta \,.\, 2 \sin \tfrac{1}{2} t^2 \pm f & + b + c - k \sin z \text{ [Circle North, Star West]} \\ & + b + c + k \sin z \text{ [Circle North, Star East]} \\ & - b - c - k \sin z \text{ [Circle South, Star West]} \\ & - b - c + k \sin z \text{ [Circle South, Star East]}. \end{aligned}$$

*) For when we observe on a lateral wire, whose distance is f, it is the same as if we observe with an instrument whose error of collimation is $c + f$.

With the prime vertical instrument at the observatory of Berlin the star β Draconis was observed in 1846 Sept. 10:

Circle North, Star East.

I	*II*	*III*	*IV*	*V*	*VI*	*VII*
		$19^m 9^s.0$,	$17^h 10^m 48^s.0$,	$5^m 24^s.0$,	$1^m 16^s.5$,	$16^h 55^m 6^s.3$

Circle South, Star West.

$1^m 5^s.0$, $54^m 59^s.7$, $50^m 47^s.8$, $17^h 45^m 28^s.0$, $37^m 38^s.0$.

The inclination of the instrument was:

$$\text{Circle North} = +4''.64$$
$$\text{Circle South} = -3\;.49.$$

Further was:

$$\alpha = 17^h\, 26^m\, 58^s.59$$
$$\delta = 52^0\; 25'\; 27''.77$$
$$\Delta t = \quad -54^s.52,$$

and the wire-distances expressed in arc were:

I	12′ 31″. 16
II	6 43 . 78
III	3 25 . 17
V	3 23 . 14
VI	6 34 . 21
VII	12 22 . 32.

Now in order to compute $\varphi - \delta$, we must know already an approximate value of φ. Assuming:

$$\varphi = 52^0\; 30'\; 16'',$$

we have:

$$\log \sin\varphi \cos\delta = 9.684686,$$

and we obtain:

Circle North.

	III	*IV*	*V*	*VI*	*VII*
t	$8^m 44^s.11$	$17^m 5^s.11$	$22^m 29^s.11$	$26^m 36^s.61$	$32^m 46^s.81$
$\log 2 \sin\frac{1}{2} t^2$	2 . 17552	2 . 75807	2 . 99648	3 . 14264	3 . 32351
$\sin\varphi \cos\delta\, 2 \sin\frac{1}{2} t^2$	1 12 . 48	4 37 . 18	7 59 . 92	11 11 . 94	16 59 . 07
$\varphi - \delta$	4 37 . 65	4 37 . 18	4 36 . 78	4 37 . 73	4 36 . 75,

and hence from the mean:

$$\varphi - \delta = 4'\, 37''.22 + 4''.64 + c + k \sin z.$$

Likewise we find from the observations made when the circle was South:

$$\varphi - \delta = 4'\, 53''.53 + 3''.49 - c - k \sin z,$$

therefore combining these two results, we find:

$$\varphi - \delta = 4'\, 49''.44$$
$$\varphi = 52^0\; 30'\; 17''.21$$
$$c + k \sin z = +7''.58.$$

This method is the very best for determining the zenith distance of a star near the zenith with great accuracy, and it can therefore be used with great advantage to determine the change of the zenith distance of a star on account of aberration, nutation and parallax, and hence to find the constants of these corrections. For this purpose is has been used by Struve with the greatest success. Since the level-error of the instrument has a great influence upon the result, because it remains in the result at its full amount, the instrument used for such observations must be built so, that it can be levelled with the greatest accuracy. The instrument built for the Pulkova observatory according to Struve's directions is therefore arranged so that the spirit-level remains always on the axis, even when the instrument is being reversed, so that any disturbance of the level, which can be produced by its being placed on the axis, is avoided. When the level is reversed on the axis and observed in each position, b and b' are obtained; but it is only necessary to leave it in the same position when the instrument is reversed, because the two readings of the level give then immediately $b - b'$, which quantity alone is used for obtaining the value of $\varphi - \delta$.

A difficulty in making these observations arises from the oblique motion of the stars with respect to the wires. A chronograph is therefore very useful in making these observations, since it is easier to observe the moment when a star is bisected by the wire, than to estimate the decimal of a second, at which a star passes over the wire.

If the constant of aberration, that of nutation, or the parallax of a star is to be determined by this method, such stars must be selected, which are near the pole of the ecliptic, because for such the influence of these corrections upon the declination is the greatest.

27. The formulae by means of which the observations on a lateral wire can be reduced to the middle wire, are found in the same way as for the transit instrument. For when we have observed on a lateral wire, whose distance is f, it is the same as if we have observed with an instrument, whose error of collimation is $c + f$. Therefore we have the equation:

$$\sin(c+f) = -\sin\delta \sin n + \cos\delta \cos n \cos(t'-m),$$

where t' is the hour angle of the star at the time of the observation on the lateral wire. If we subtract from this the equation:

$$\sin c = -\sin\delta \sin n + \cos\delta \cos n \cos(t-m),$$

we obtain:

$$2\sin\tfrac{1}{2}f \cos\left[\tfrac{1}{2}f + c\right] = 2\cos\delta \cos n \sin\tfrac{1}{2}(t-t') \sin\left[\tfrac{1}{2}(t+t') - m\right].$$

Now since f is only a few minutes, we can put f instead of the first member of the equation and thus we find:

$$2\sin\tfrac{1}{2}(t-t') = \frac{f}{\cos\delta \sin\tfrac{1}{2}(t+t') \cos n \cos m - \cos\delta \cos\tfrac{1}{2}(t+t') \cos n \sin m},$$

or if we substitute for $\cos n \cos m$ and $\cos n \sin m$ the expressions given in the preceding No., we find:

$$2\sin\tfrac{1}{2}(t-t') = \frac{f}{\cos\delta \sin\varphi \sin\tfrac{1}{2}(t+t')\left[1 - b\,\text{cotang}\,\varphi - k\,\text{cotang}\,\tfrac{1}{2}(t+t')\,\text{cosec}\,\varphi\right]}.$$

Therefore for reducing the observations on a lateral wire to the middle wire we must use instead of the wire distance f the quantity:

$$\frac{f}{1 - b\,\text{cotang}\,\varphi - k\,\text{cotang}\,\tfrac{1}{2}(t+t')\,\text{cosec}\,\varphi} = f',$$

and then we have:

$$2\sin\tfrac{1}{2}(t-t') = \frac{f'}{\cos\delta \sin\varphi \sin\tfrac{1}{2}(t+t')}.$$

In order to solve this equation we ought to know already t'. But we have:

$$\sin\tfrac{1}{2}(t+t') = \sin\left[t - \tfrac{1}{2}(t-t')\right].$$

If we take then for $\frac{1}{2}(t-t')$ half the interval of time between the passages over the lateral wire and over the middle wire, the second member of the equation is known, and we can compute $t-t'$. When the value found differs much from the assumed value, the computation must be repeated with the new value. But this supposes that the value of f' has been computed before. Now in the formula for this the term b cotang φ can always be neglected, because b will always be very small, and likewise if k is small, and the star is not too near the zenith, the term dependent on k can also be neglected, so that then simply f is used instead of f'. But when the star is near the zenith, the correction dependent on k can become considerably large, if k is not very small. For we have:

$$\text{tang}\, t \cos\varphi = \text{tang}\, z,$$

and since f is small, we also have approximately:

$$\operatorname{tang} t' \cos \varphi = \operatorname{tang} z'$$

and hence:

$$\operatorname{tang} \tfrac{1}{2}(t + t') \cos \varphi = \operatorname{tang} \tfrac{1}{2}(z + z').$$

Therefore we can write instead of the factor of k:

$$\operatorname{cotang} \varphi \operatorname{cotang} \tfrac{1}{2}(z + z'),$$

and thus we see, that the correction can be large, when the star is near the zenith.

Instead of solving the equation

$$2 \sin \tfrac{1}{2}(t - t') = \frac{f'}{\cos \delta \sin \varphi \sin \frac{1}{2}(t + t')}$$

by an indirect method, we can develop it in a series. For we can write it in this way:

$$\cos t' - \cos t = \frac{f'}{\cos \delta \sin \varphi},$$

and from this we obtain according to formula (19) in No. 11 of the introduction:

$$t' = t - \frac{f'}{\cos \delta \sin \varphi \sin t} - \tfrac{1}{2} \operatorname{cotang} t \left[\frac{f'}{\cos \delta \sin \varphi \sin t}\right]^2 - \tfrac{1}{6}\left[\frac{f'}{\cos \delta \sin \varphi \sin t}\right]^3 (1 + 3 \operatorname{cotang} t^2).$$

Now when the instrument is nearly adjusted, we have:

$$\cos \delta \sin t = \sin z,$$

and hence:

$$t' = t - \frac{f'}{\sin z \sin \varphi} - \tfrac{1}{2} \operatorname{cotang} t \left[\frac{f'}{\sin z \sin \varphi}\right]^2 - \tfrac{1}{6}[1 + 3 \operatorname{cotang} t^2]\left[\frac{f'}{\sin z \sin \varphi}\right]^3 - \ldots.$$

Since this formula contains also the even powers of f, we see, that wires, which are equally distant from the middle wire on both sides of it, give different values of $t' - t$. For when f is negative, we have:

$$t' = t + \frac{f'}{\sin z \sin \varphi} - \tfrac{1}{2} \operatorname{cotang} t \left[\frac{f'}{\sin z \sin \varphi}\right]^2 + \tfrac{1}{6}[1 + 3 \operatorname{cotang} t^2]\left[\frac{f'}{\sin z \sin \varphi}\right]^3 - \ldots.$$

In order to compute this series more conveniently, we can construct a table, from which we take the quantities $\sin \varphi \sin z$, $\frac{1}{2} \operatorname{cotang} t$, and $\frac{1}{6}(1 + 3 \operatorname{cotang} t^2)$ with the argument δ.

But this series can be used only, when the star is far from the zenith, because if the star is near the zenith these terms of the series would not be sufficient and some higher terms would come into consideration.

In this case, when the zenith distance is small, the following method for computing t' can be used with advantage. We had:

$$\cos t' = \cos t + \frac{f'}{\cos\delta \sin\varphi}.$$

If we subtract both members of the equation from unity and also add them to it, we obtain, dividing the two resulting equations:

$$\operatorname{tang} \tfrac{1}{2} t'^2 = \frac{2 \sin \frac{1}{2} t^2 \cos\delta \sin\varphi - f'}{2 \cos \frac{1}{2} t^2 \cos\delta \sin\varphi + f'}.$$

Now since:

$$\cos t = \frac{\operatorname{tang}\delta}{\operatorname{tang}\varphi}$$

we have:

$$1 - \cos t = 2 \sin \tfrac{1}{2} t^2 = \frac{\sin(\varphi - \delta)}{\cos\delta \sin\varphi}$$

and

$$1 + \cos t = 2 \cos \tfrac{1}{2} t^2 = \frac{\sin(\varphi + \delta)}{\cos\delta \sin\varphi};$$

therefore we get:

$$\operatorname{tang} \tfrac{1}{2} t'^2 = \frac{\sin(\varphi - \delta) - f'}{\sin(\varphi + \delta) + f'},$$

and if f is negative:

$$\operatorname{tang} \tfrac{1}{2} t'^2 = \frac{\sin(\varphi - \delta) + f'}{\sin(\varphi + \delta) - f'}.$$

The values of the wire-distances are determined by observing a star near the zenith on all the wires. If we compute for each observation the quantity:

$$\sin\varphi \cos\delta \,.\, 2 \sin \tfrac{1}{2} t^2,$$

the differences of these quantities give us the wire-distances, because we have for stars near the zenith:

$$\varphi - \delta = \sin\varphi \cos\delta \,.\, 2 \sin \tfrac{1}{2} t^2 \pm f + c + b + k \sin z.$$

Thus in the example of the preceding No. the following wire-distances would be obtained from the observations made when the circle was North:

$III = 3' \, 24''.70$
$V = 3 \; 22 \; .74$
$VI = 6 \; 34 \; .76$
$VII = 12 \; 21 \; .89.$

In 1838 Oct. 2 α Bootis was observed with the prime vertical instrument at the Berlin observatory:

Circle South, Star West.

	I	II	III	IV	V	VI	VII
α Bootis	$44^s.7$	$8^s.3$	$50^s.2$	$19^h\,2^m\,32^s.2$	$13^s.8$	$55^s.4$	$1^m\,19^s.2$.

The wire-distances expressed in time were then:

$$I = 51^s.639$$
$$II = 25\ .814$$
$$III = 12\ .610$$
$$V = 13\ .305$$
$$VI = 26\ .523$$
$$VII = 52\ .397;$$

moreover we have:

$$\Delta t = +47^s.5,\quad \alpha = 14^h\,8^m\,16^s.5,\quad \delta = +20^\circ\,1'\,39'',\quad \varphi = 52^\circ\,30'\,16''.$$

The quantities b and k were so small, that it was not necessary to compute the reduced wire-distances f'. Then we have:

$$t = 4^h\,55^m\,3^s.2 = 73^\circ\,45'\,48''.0,\quad \log\cos\delta\sin t\sin\varphi = 9.85244$$

and
$$\log\operatorname{cotang}\tfrac{1}{2}t = 9.14552.$$

Now in order to compute the second term of the series, we must express $\dfrac{f'}{\sin\varphi\cos\delta\sin t}$ in terms of the radius, that is, we must multiply it by 15, and divide it by 206265. Then we must square it, and in order to express the term in seconds of time, we must multiply it by 206265 and divide by 15. Thus the factor of:

$$\left[\frac{f'}{\sin\varphi\cos\delta\sin t}\right]^2$$

will be:

$$\frac{15}{206265}\cdot\tfrac{1}{2}\operatorname{cotang} z,$$

the logarithm of the numerical factor being 5.00718. Likewise the coefficient of the second term, expressed in seconds of time, will be:

$$\frac{1}{6}\left[\frac{15}{206265}\right]^2[1+3\operatorname{cotang} t^2].$$

But in this case this term is already insignificant. Now if we compute for instance the reduction for wire I, we have, since f is negative:

$$-\frac{f}{\sin\varphi\cos\delta\sin t} = -72^s.533$$
$$+\frac{15}{206265}\cdot\tfrac{1}{2}\operatorname{cotang} t\left[\frac{f}{\cos\delta\sin t\sin\varphi}\right]^2 = +0.053,$$

hence the reduction to the middle wire is:

$$I = -1^m\,12^s.48.$$

In the same way we find:

$$II = -36^s.25$$
$$III = -17.71$$
$$V = +18.69$$
$$VI = +37.24$$
$$VII = +73.54,$$

and hence the observations on the several wires reduced to the middle wire are:

$19^h\ 2^m\ 32^s.22$
32.05
32.49
32.20
32.49
32.64
32.74

mean value $19^h\ 2^m\ 32^s.40.$

In order to give an example for the other method of reduction, we will take the following observation of α Persei:

Circle South, Star West.

	I	*II*	*III*	*IV*	*V*
α Persei	$4^m\ 26^s.0$	$2^m\ 38^s.0$	$1^m\ 43^s.0$	$5^h\ 0^m\ 49^s.2$	$59^m\ 52^s.0$

VI	*VII*
$58^m\ 55^s.2$	$57^m\ 2^s.0.$

If we compute first:

$$\operatorname{tang} \tfrac{1}{2} t^2 = \frac{\sin(\varphi - \delta)}{\sin(\varphi + \delta)},$$

taking:

$$\delta = 49^\circ\ 16'\ 26''.7$$

and

$$\varphi = 52^\circ\ 30'\ 16''.0$$

we find:

$$t = 26^\circ\ 58'\ 58''.88.$$

If we compute the reduction for the first wire, we have f negative, and hence we must compute the formula:

$$\operatorname{tang} \tfrac{1}{2} t'^2 = \frac{\sin(\varphi - \delta) + f}{\sin(\varphi + \delta) + f}.$$

Now since

$$f = 51^s.639 = 12'\ 54''.585,$$

or expressed in terms of the radius $f = 0.0037553$, we find:

$$t' = 27^\circ\ 53'\ 6''.72,$$

hence:

$$t' - t = 0^\circ\ 54'\ 7''.84$$
$$= 0^h\ 3^m\ 36^s.52.$$

Likewise we find for the other wires:

$$\begin{array}{lrl} II = & 1^m & 49^s.05 \\ III & & 53.48 \\ V & & 56.85 \\ VI & 1 & 53.85 \\ VII & 3 & 46.77. \end{array}$$

However for this star the series is used with greater convenience, since the influence of the third term for wires *III* and *V* amounts to nothing and for wires *I* and *VII* it is only $0^s.12$.

28. It must still be shown, how the errors of the instrument are determined by observations.

The inclination of the axis is always found by means of a spirit-level. The collimation-error can be determined by observing stars near the zenith east and west of the meridian in the two different positions of the instrument. Or we can obtain it by combining the observations of the same star east and west of the meridian, made in the same position of the instrument. For we have, when the circle is North:

$$\Theta = T + \Delta t - \frac{c}{\sin z \sin \varphi} - \frac{k}{\sin \varphi} \text{ [Star East]}$$

$$\Theta' = T' + \Delta t + \frac{c}{\sin z \sin \varphi} - \frac{k}{\sin \varphi} \text{ [Star West]},$$

if we assume, that the times of passage over the middle wire have been corrected for the error of level. Hence we have:

$$c = \sin \varphi \sin z \left[\tfrac{1}{2}(\Theta' - \Theta) - \tfrac{1}{2}(T' - T)\right].$$

where the value of $\frac{1}{2}(\Theta' - \Theta)$ is obtained by means of the equation:

$$\cos \tfrac{1}{2}(\Theta' - \Theta) = \frac{\operatorname{tang} \delta}{\operatorname{tang} \varphi},$$

or more accurately, taking $\frac{1}{2}(\Theta' - \Theta) = t$, from the equation:

$$\operatorname{tang} \tfrac{1}{2} t^2 = \frac{\sin(\varphi - \delta)}{\sin(\varphi + \delta)}.$$

In order that the errors of observation in T and T' may have as little influence as possible on the determination of c, we must select such stars which pass over the prime vertical as near as possible to the zenith.

Adding the two equations for Θ and Θ', we find:

$$k = \sin \varphi \left[\tfrac{1}{2}(T' + T) + \Delta t - \tfrac{1}{2}(\Theta + \Theta')\right],$$

or since $\frac{1}{2}(\Theta + \Theta') = \alpha$:

$$k = \sin\varphi\,[\tfrac{1}{2}(T + T') + \Delta t - \alpha].$$

For the determination of the azimuth k it is best to take stars, which pass over the prime vertical at a considerable distance from the zenith, because their transits can be observed with greater precision. With the prime vertical instrument at the Berlin observatory the following observations were made in 1838:

Circle South:

June 25	α Bootis West	19^h	3^m	$1^s.44$	
26	α Bootis East	9	12	54 .49,	

these times being the mean of the observations on seven wires. On June 25 the level-error was $b = +6''.42$ and on June 26 $b = +7''.98$. If we correct the times by adding the correction $+\frac{b}{15\,\text{tang}\,z\,\sin\varphi}$, we must add to the first observation $-0^s.26$, and add to the second $+0^s.32$ so that we obtain:

$$T = 19^h\ 3^m\ 1^s.18$$
$$T' = 9\ \ 12\ \ 54\ .81.$$

Hence we have:

$$\tfrac{1}{2}(T + T') = 14^h\ 7^m\ 58^s.00,$$

and since:

$$\Delta t = +20^s.27 \text{ and } \alpha = 14^h\ 8^m\ 16^s.48$$

we find:

$$k = +1^s.42.$$

Note. Compare on the prime vertical instrument: Encke, Bemerkungen über das Durchgangsinstrument von Ost nach West. Berliner astronomisches Jahrbuch für 1843 pag. 300 etc.

VI. ALTITUDE INSTRUMENTS.

29. The altitude instruments are either entire circles, quadrants or sextants. The entire circle is fastened to a horizontal axis attached to a vertical pillar. By means of a spirit-level placed upon the horizontal axis, the vertical position of the pillar can be examined and corrected by means of the three foot-screws. The adjustment is perfect, when the bubble of the level remains in the same position while the pillar is turned about its axis. By reversing the level upon the horizontal axis, the inclination of the latter is found, which can also be corrected by adjusted screws so that the circle is vertical.

The horizontal axis carries the divided circle, which turns at the same time with the telescope, whilst the concentric vernier circle is firmly attached to the pillar. When the circle is read by means of microscopes, the arm to which the microscopes are fastened is firmly attached to the pillar and furnished with a spirit-level. By observing a star in two positions of the horizontal axis which differ 180°, double the zenith distance is determined in the same way as with the altitude and azimuth instrument, and everything that was said about the observation of zenith distances with that instrument can be immediately applied to this one.

Since the telescope is fastened at one extremity of the axis, this has the effect, that the error of collimation is variable with the zenith distance, so that it can be assumed to be of the form $c + a \cos z$. With larger instruments of this kind the error of collimation in the horizontal position of the telescope can be determined by two collimators, and the error in the vertical position by means of the collimating eye-piece, as was shown in No. 22. The difference of the two values obtained gives the quantity a, which however will always amount only to a few seconds, and hence have no influence upon the determination of the zenith distances.

Note. The quadrant is similar to the above instrument, but instead of an entire circle it has only an arc of a circle equal to a quadrant, round the centre of which the telescope fastened to an alhidade is turning. When such a quadrant is firmly attached to a vertical wall in the plane of the meridian, it is called a mural quadrant. These instruments are now antiquated, since the mural quadrants or mural circles have been replaced by the meridian circle, and the portable quadrants by the altitude and azimuth instruments and by entire circles.

30. The most important altitude instrument is the sextant, or as it is called after the inventor, Hadley's sextant [*]). But this instrument is used not only for measuring altitudes, but for measuring the angle between two objects in any inclination to the horizon; and since it requires no firm mounting, but on the contrary the observations are made, while the instrument is held in the hand, it is especially useful for making observations at sea, as well for determining the time and the latitude by altitudes of the sun or of stars, as for determining the longitude by lunar distances.

The sextant consists of a sector of a circle equal to about one sixth of the entire circle, which is divided and about the centre of which an alhidade is moving, carrying a plane-glass reflector whose plane is perpendicular to the plane of the sector and passing through its centre. Another smaller reflector is placed in front of the telescope; its plane is likewise perpendicular to the plane of the sextant and parallel to the line joining the centre of the divided arc with the zero of the division. The two reflectors are parallel when the index of the alhidade is moved to the zero of the division. Of the small reflector only the lower half is covered with tinfoil so that through the upper part rays of light from an object can reach the object glass of the telescope. Now when the alhidade is turned, until rays of light from another object are reflected from the large reflector to the small one and from that to the object glass of the telescope, then the images of the two objects are seen in the telescope; and when the alhidade is turned until these images are coincident, the angle between the two reflectors, and hence the angle through which the alhidade has been turned from that position in which the two reflectors were parallel, is half the angle subtended at the eye by the line between those two objects.

First it is evident, that when the two reflectors are parallel, the direct ray of light and the ray which is reflected twice are also parallel. For if we follow the way of these rays in the opposite direction, that is, if we consider them as emanating from the eye of the observer, they will at first

---

*) In fact Newton is the inventor of this instrument, since after Hadley's death a copy of the description in Newton's own hand-writing was found among his papers. But Hadley first made the invention known.

coincide. Then one ray passes through the upper uncovered part of the small reflector to the object A. If α is the angle, which the direction of the two rays makes with the small reflector, then the other ray after being reflected makes the same angle with it, and since the large reflector is parallel to the small reflector, the angle of incidence and that of reflection for the large reflector are also equal to α. Hence this ray will also reach the object A, if this is at an infinitely great distance so that the distance of the two reflectors is as nothing compared to the distance of the object.

But when the angle between the large and the small reflector is equal to γ, the ray whose angle of reflection from the small reflector is α, will make a different angle, which we will denote by β, with the large reflector. But in the triangle formed by the direction of the two reflectors and by the direction of the reflected ray we have:

$$180^0 - \alpha + \gamma + \beta = 180^0$$

or:

$$\gamma = \alpha - \beta.$$

The angle of reflection from the large reflector is then β, and the direction of this twice reflected ray will make with the original direction of the ray emanating from the eye an angle δ, which is equal to the angle subtended by the line between the two objects, which are seen in the telescope. But in the triangle formed by the direct ray, the direction of the ray reflected from the small reflector and that of the twice reflected ray, we have:

$$180^0 - 2\alpha + \delta + 2\beta = 180^0,$$

and hence we have:

$$\delta = 2\alpha - 2\beta$$

or:

$$\delta = 2\gamma.$$

The angle between the two objects which are seen coincident in the telescope is therefore equal to double the angle, which the two reflectors make with each other and which is obtained by the reading of the circle. Hence for greater convenience the arc of measurement is divided into half-degree spaces, which are numbered as whole degrees, and thus the reading gives immediately the angle between the two objects.

When altitudes are observed with the sextant, an artificial horizon, usually a mercury horizon, is used, and the angle between the object and its image reflected from the mercury is observed, which is double the altitude of the object. But at sea the altitudes of a heavenly body are observed by measuring its distance from the horizon of the sea.

In this case the altitude is measured too great, since the sensible horizon on account of the elevation of the eye above the surface of the water is depressed below the rational horizon and is therefore a small circle. It is formed by the intersection of the surface of a cone, tangent to the surface of the earth and having its vertex at the eye of the observer, with the sphere of the heavens, whilst the rational horizon is the great circle in which a horizontal plane passing through the eye intersects the apparent sphere. If we denote the zenith distance of the sensible horizon by $90^0 + c$, we easily see, that c is the angle at the centre of the earth between the two radii, one passing through the plane of observation, the other drawn through a point of the small circle in which the surface of the cone is tangent to the earth. Hence if a denotes the radius of the earth, h the elevation of the eye above the surface of the water, we have:

$$\cos c = \frac{a}{a+h},$$

and hence: $$2 \sin \tfrac{1}{2} c^2 = \frac{h}{a+h},$$

or: $$c = \sqrt{\frac{2h}{a+h}}.$$

By means of this formula the angle c, which is called the *dip of the horizon*, can be computed for any elevation of the eye, and must then be subtracted from the observed altitude.

31. We will now examine, what influence any errors of the sextant have upon the observations made with it. If we imagine the eye to be at the centre of a sphere, the plane of the sextant will intersect this sphere in a great circle, which shall be represented by BAC Fig. 19,

Fig. 19.

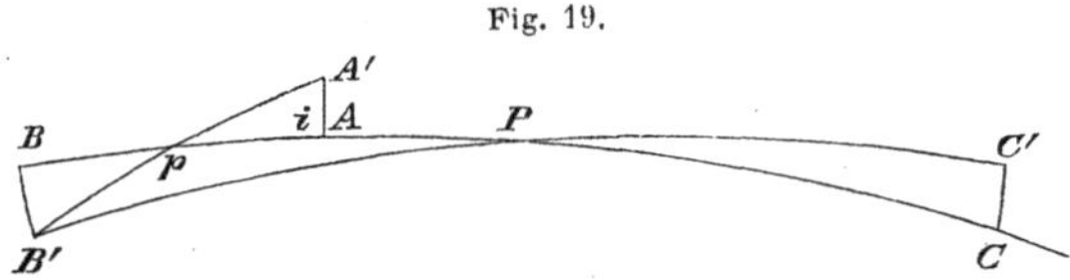

and which at the same time represents the plane in which the two objects are situated. Let OA be the line of vision towards the object A. When this ray falls upon the small reflector (which is also called the horizon-glass) it is reflected to the large reflector, and if p is the pole of the small reflector, that is, the point in which a line perpendicular to its centre intersects the great circle, the ray after being reflected will intersect the great circle in the point B so that

$$Bp = pA.$$

Further if P is the pole of the large reflector (which is also called the index-glass) the ray after being reflected twice will intersect the great circle in the point C so that

$$PC = PB$$

and in this direction the second observed object will lie. The angle between the two objects is then measured by AC, the angle between the two reflectors by pP, and it is again easily seen that AC is equal to $2pP$.

This is the case, if the line of collimation of the telescope is parallel to the plane of the sextant, and both reflectors are perpendicular to this plane. We will now suppose, that the inclination of the line of collimation to the plane of the sextant is i. If then BAC represents again the great circle in which the plane of the sextant intersects the sphere, the line of collimation will not intersect the sphere in the point A but in A', the arc AA' being perpendicular to BAC and equal to i. After the reflexion from the small and the large reflector the ray will intersect the sphere in the points B' and C', the arcs BB' and CC' being likewise equal to i and perpendicular to BAC. If the pole of the great circle BAC is Q, then the angle QAC is the angle given by the reading of the sextant, whilst the arc $A'C'$ is equal to the angle between the two observed objects, and denoting the first by α, the other by α', we have in the spherical triangle $A'QC'$:

$$\begin{aligned}\cos\alpha' &= \sin i^2 + \cos i^2 \cos\alpha\\ &= \cos\alpha + 2\,i^2 \sin\tfrac{1}{2}\alpha^2,\end{aligned}$$

and hence according to the formula (19) of the introduction:

$$\alpha' = \alpha - i^2 \operatorname{tang}\tfrac{1}{2}\alpha.$$

Therefore when the telescope is inclined to the plane of the sextant, all measured angles will be too great. The amount of the error can be easily found. For in the telescope of the sextant there are two parallel wires, which are also parallel to the plane of the sextant, and the line from the centre of the object glass to a point half way between these wires is taken as the line of collimation. Now if the images of two objects are made coincident near one of these wires and the sextant is turned so that the images are seen near the other wire, then the images must still be coincident, if the line of collimation is parallel to the plane of the sextant, because each time the line of vision was in the same inclination to the plane of the sextant. But if the two images are not coincident in the second position of the sextant, it indicates, that the line of collimation is inclined to the plane of the sextant. Now let the two readings, when the images are made coincident near each wire, be s and s', the inclination of the telescope i, the distance of the two wires δ, and the true distance of the objects b, then we have in one case:

$$s = b + \left(\frac{\delta}{2} - i\right)^2 \operatorname{tang}\tfrac{1}{2}s,$$

and in the other case:

$$s' = b + \left(\frac{\delta}{2} + i\right)^2 \operatorname{tang}\tfrac{1}{2}s';$$

therefore putting:

$$\operatorname{tang}\tfrac{1}{2}s' = \operatorname{tang}\tfrac{1}{2}s$$

we have:

$$i = \frac{s' - s}{2\,\delta} \operatorname{cotang}\tfrac{1}{2}s.$$

It is easily seen that the smaller angle corresponds to that wire which is nearest to the plane of the sextant, and that a line parallel to the plane of the sextant would pass through a point whose distance from this wire is equal to $\frac{\delta}{2} - i$. A third wire must then be placed at this distance, and all observations must be made near it, or, if they are made midways between the two original wires, the correction $-i^2 \tang \frac{1}{2} s$ must be applied to all measured angles.

It is necessary, that the plane of the horizon-glass be parallel to that of the index-glass, when the index of the vernier is at the zero of the scale, and that these two reflectors be perpendicular to the plane of the sextant. It is easy to examine whether the first condition is fulfilled, and if there is any error, it can be easily corrected. For the horizon-glass has two adjusting screws. One is on the back-side of the reflector, which by means of it is turned round an axis perpendicular to the plane of the sextant, the other screw serves to render the plane of the reflector perpendicular to the plane of the sextant. Now when the index of the vernier is nearly at the zero of the scale, the telescope is directed to an object at an infinitely great distance, and the direct and reflected images are made coincident. If this is possible, the two reflectors are parallel and the reading of the circle is then the index error. But if it is impossible to make the two images coincident, and they pass by each other when the alhidade is turned, it shows, that the planes of the two reflectors are not parallel. If the images are then placed so that their distance is as little as possible, then the lines of intersection of the two reflectors with the plane of the sextant are parallel, and then by means of the second of the screws mentioned before the horizon-glass can be turned until the two images coincide and the two glasses are parallel. The reading in this position is the index error, which must be subtracted from all readings, in order to find the true angles between the observed objects. In order to correct this error, the alhidade is turned until the index is exactly at the zero of the scale and then the images of an object at an infinitely great distance are made coincident by turning the horizon-glass by means of the screw on its back. Usually however this error is not corrected, but its amount is determined and subtracted from all readings. For this observation the sun is mostly used, the reflected image being brought in contact first with one limb of the direct image and then with the other. If the reading the first time is a, the second time b, then $\frac{a+b}{2}$ is the index-error, and $\frac{b-a}{2}$ or $\frac{a-b}{2}$ is the diameter of the sun, accordingly as a is less or greater than b. One of these readings will be on the arc of excess, and therefore be an angle in the fourth quadrant; but the readings on the arc of excess may also be reckoned from the zero and must then be taken negative.

For observing the sun colored glasses are used to qualify its light. When these are not plane glasses, the value of the index-error found by the sun is wrong. When afterwards altitudes of the sun are taken, this error has no influence, as long as the same colored glasses are employed which were used for finding the index error. But when other observations are made, for instance when lunar distances are taken, the index-error must be found by a star or by a terrestrial object.

But when a terrestrial object is observed, whose distance is not infinitely great compared to the distance between the two reflectors, the index-error c as found by these observations must be corrected, in order to obtain the true index-error c_0, which would have been found by an object at an infinitely great distance. For if Δ denotes the distance of the object from the horizon-glass, f the distance between the two reflectors, β the angle which the line of collimation of the telescope makes with a line perpendicular to the horizon-glass, then we find the angle c, which the direct and the twice reflected ray make at the object, when the two images are coincident, from the equation:

$$\text{tang}\, c = \frac{f \sin 2\beta}{\Delta + f \cos 2\beta},$$

and hence we have:

$$c = \frac{f}{\Delta} \sin 2\beta - \tfrac{1}{2} \frac{f^2}{\Delta^2} \sin 4\beta,$$

where the second member of the equation must be multiplied by 206265, in order to find c in seconds. Now if the two reflectors had been parallel, the ray reflected from the index-glass would have met an object whose distance from the observed object is c, and the true index-error would have been obtained, if these two objects had been made coincident. Therefore if the reading was c_1, when the object and its reflected image were coincident, we have:

$$c_0 = c_1 + \frac{f}{\Delta} \sin 2\beta - \tfrac{1}{2} \frac{f^2}{\Delta^2} \sin 4\beta.$$

The angle β, which was used already before, can be easily determined, if the sextant is fastened to a stand, and the index-error c_1 is found by means of a terrestrial object. If we then direct a telescope furnished with a wire-cross to the index-glass, make the wire-cross coincident with the reflected image of the object, and then measure with the sextant the angle between the object and the wire-cross of the telescope, we have:

$$s - c_0 = 2\beta - \frac{f}{\Delta} \sin 2\beta,$$

and since:

$$c_0 = c_1 + \frac{f}{\Delta} \sin 2\beta,$$

we obtain:

$$2\beta = s - c_1.$$

If the inclination of the horizon-glass to the plane of the sextant is i, its pole will be at p' (Fig. 20), the arc pp' being equal to i and perpendicular to BAC.

Fig. 20.

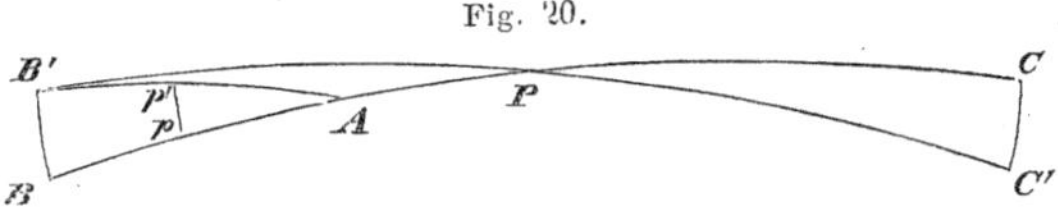

The ray after being reflected from the horizon-glass intersects the sphere in B' and after its reflexion from the index-glass in C'. In this case again AC is the angle α obtained by the reading, while AC' is really the angle α', which is measured. We have then, as is easily seen:

$$BB' = CC' = 2 \cos \beta \,.\, i,$$

where β is, as before, the angle between the line of collimation of the telescope and a line perpendicular to the horizon-glass, which is equal to Ap. Moreover we have:

$$\begin{aligned} \cos \alpha' &= \cos \alpha \cos CC' \\ &= \cos \alpha - 2 \cos \beta^2 \, i^2 \cos \alpha, \end{aligned}$$

and according to the formula (19) of the introduction:

$$\alpha' = \alpha + \frac{2 \cos \beta^2 \, i^2}{\operatorname{tang} \alpha}.$$

If the inclination of the index-glass to the plane of the sextant were i, and the horizon-glass were parallel to it and the telescope perpendicular to both, then p', P', A' and likewise B' and C' would lie on a small circle, whose distance from the great circle BAC would be equal to i. Then $p'P'$ or the angle $\frac{1}{2}\alpha'$ between the two reflectors would be, as in the former case, when the inclination of the telescope was equal to i:

$$\tfrac{1}{2}\alpha' = \tfrac{1}{2}\alpha - i^2 \operatorname{tang} \tfrac{1}{4}\alpha,$$

or:

$$\alpha' = \alpha - 2\,i^2 \operatorname{tang} \tfrac{1}{4}\alpha.$$

For correcting this error two metal pieces are used, which when placed on the sextant, are perpendicular to its plane. One of these pieces has a small round hole, and the other piece is cut out and a fine silver-wire is stretched across the opening so that it is at the same height as the centre of the hole, when the two pieces are placed on the sextant. For correcting the error the sextant is laid horizontal and the piece with the hole is placed in front of the index-glass which is turned, until the image of the piece is seen through the pole. Then the other piece is likewise placed before the index-glass so, that the wire is also seen through the hole. If then the wire passes exactly through the centre of the reflected image of the hole, the index-glass is perpendicular to the plane of the sextant, because then the hole, its reflected image and the wire lie in a straight line, which on account of the equal height of the wire and the hole is parallel to the plane of the sextant. If this is not the case, the position of the index-glass must be changed by means of the correcting screws, until the above condition is fulfilled.

The same can be accomplished in this way, though perhaps not as accurately: If we hold the instrument horizontally with the index-glass towards the eye, and then look into this glass so that we see the circular arc of the sextant as well direct as reflected by it, then, if the index-glass is perpendicular, the arc will appear continuous, and if it appears broken, the position of the glass must be altered until this is the case.

It may also be the case, that the two surfaces of the plane-glas reflectors, which ought to be parallel, make a small angle with each other so that the reflectors have the form of prisms. Let then AB (Fig. 21) be the ray striking the

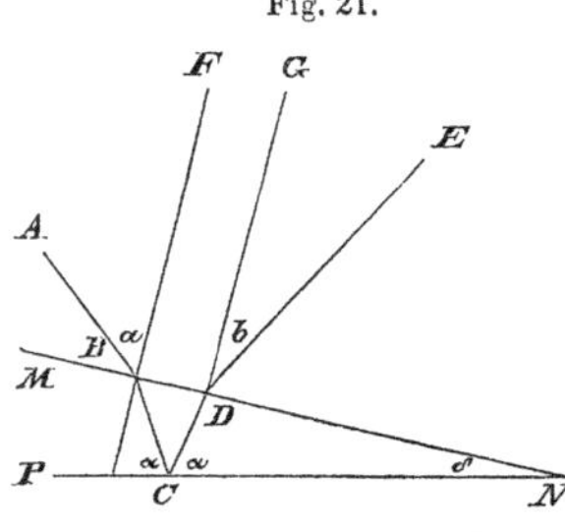

Fig. 21.

front surface of the index-glass, which will be refracted towards C. After its reflection from the back surface it will be refracted at the front surface and leave this surface in the direction DE. When the two surfaces are parallel, the angle ABF will be equal to GDE, but this will not be the case, when the surfaces are inclined to each other. Now if we take $MNP = \delta$, and denote the angles of incidence ABF and GDE by a and b, and the angles of refraction by a_1 and b_1, we have:

$$a_1 + a = 90^0 + \delta$$
$$b_1 + a = 90^0 - \delta,$$

and hence:

$$b_1 = a_1 - 2\delta.$$

Now if $\frac{n}{m}$ is the refractive index for the passage from atmospheric air into glass, we have also:

$$\sin a_1 = \frac{n}{m} \sin a, \ \sin b_1 = \frac{n}{m} \sin b;$$

and hence:

$$\sin a - \sin b = \frac{m}{n} [\sin a_1 - \sin a_1 \cos 2\delta + \cos a_1 \sin 2\delta]$$

or:

$$a - b = \frac{m}{n} 2\delta . \frac{\cos a_1}{\cos a} = 2\delta \sqrt{\frac{m^2}{n^2} \sec a^2 - \operatorname{tang} a^2}$$
$$= 2\delta \sqrt{\frac{m^2 - n^2}{n^2} \sec a^2 + 1}.$$

Now a is the angle, which the line from the eye to the second object makes with the line perpendicular to the index-glass. If we denote by β the angle, which the line of collimation of the telescope makes with the line perpendicular to the horizon-glass, and by γ the angle between the two objects, then we have:

$$a = \tfrac{1}{2}(\gamma + \beta)$$

and hence:

$$a - b = 2\delta \sqrt{\frac{m^2 - n^2}{n^2} \sec \left(\frac{\beta + \gamma}{2}\right)^2 + 1}.$$

Now the correction which must be applied to the angle γ is the difference of the above value and that for $\gamma = 0$, because the index-error is also found wrong, when the two surfaces of the glasses are not parallel. Therefore if we denote this correction by x, we have:

$$x = 2\delta \sqrt{\frac{m^2 - n^2}{n^2} \sec\left(\frac{\beta+\gamma}{2}\right)^2 + 1} - 2\delta \sqrt{\frac{m^2 - n^2}{n^2} \sec\tfrac{1}{2}\beta^2 + 1},$$

and we must add this correction, if the side of the glass towards the direct ray is the thicker one, because then the reflected ray is less inclined to the line perpendicular to the glass than the direct ray, and hence the angle read off is too small. If the side towards the direct ray is the thinner one, the correction must be subtracted.

The formula for x can be written more simply thus:

$$x = 2\delta \frac{m}{n} \left\{ \sec\frac{\beta+\gamma}{2} \sqrt{1 - \frac{n^2}{m^2} \sin\left(\frac{\beta+\gamma}{2}\right)^2} - \sec\frac{\beta}{2} \sqrt{1 - \frac{n^2}{m^2} \sin\tfrac{1}{2}\beta^2} \right\},$$

or since $\frac{n}{m}$ is nearly equal to $\frac{2}{3}$:

$$x = 3\delta \left\{ \sec\frac{\beta+\gamma}{2} \sqrt{1 - \tfrac{4}{9}\sin\left(\frac{\beta+\gamma}{2}\right)^2} - \sec\frac{\beta}{2} \sqrt{1 - \tfrac{4}{9}\sin\tfrac{1}{2}\beta^2} \right\}.$$

Now in order to find x, we measure after having determined the index-error the distance of two well defined objects, for instance, of two fixed stars, which must however be over 100°. Then we take the index-glass out of its setting, put it back in the reversed position and determine the index-error and the same distance a second time. If then Δ be the true distance of the stars, we find the second time

$$\Delta - x = s',$$

if the first observation gave:

$$\Delta + x = s''$$

and hence we have:

$$\delta = \frac{s' - s''}{6 \sec\frac{\beta+\gamma}{2} \sqrt{1 - \tfrac{4}{9}\sin\left(\frac{\beta+\gamma}{2}\right)^2}}.$$

Since rays coming from the index-glass strike the horizon-glass always at the same angle, it follows, that the error arising from a prismatic form of this glass is the same for all positions of the index-glass and hence it has no effect upon the measured distances.

Finally the sextant may have an excentricity, the centre on which the alhidade turns being different from that of the graduation. This error must be determined by measuring known angles between two objects. If the angle is α and the reading of the circle gives s, we have according to No. 6 of this section:

$$\alpha - s = \frac{e}{r} \sin \tfrac{1}{2}(s - O)\, 206265,$$

or:

$$\alpha - s = \left[\frac{e}{r} \cos \tfrac{1}{2} O \,.\, \sin \tfrac{1}{2} s - \frac{e}{r} \sin \tfrac{1}{2} O \,.\, \cos \tfrac{1}{2} s\right] 206265.$$

Therefore if we measure two such angles, we can find $\frac{e}{r} \cos \frac{1}{2} O$ and $\frac{e}{r} \sin \frac{1}{2} O$, and hence $\frac{e}{r}$ and O, and then every reading must be corrected by the quantity:

$$+ \frac{e}{r} \sin \tfrac{1}{2}(s - O)\, 206265,$$

Since the error of excentricity is entirely eliminated with an entire circle, when the readings are made by means of two verniers which are diametrically opposite, reflecting circles are for this reason preferable to sextants. Especially convenient are those invented by Pistor & Martins in Berlin, which instead of the horizon-glass have a glass-prism. They have the advantage, that any angles from 0^0 to 180^0 can be measured with them. All that has been said about the sextant can be immediately applied to these instruments.

Note. Compare: Encke, Ueber den Spiegelsextanten. Berliner astron. Jahrbuch für 1830.

VII. INSTRUMENTS, WHICH SERVE FOR MEASURING THE RELATIVE PLACE OF TWO HEAVENLY BODIES NEAR EACH OTHER. (MICROMETER AND HELIOMETER).

32. *Filar micrometer.* For the purpose of measuring the differences of right ascension and declination of stars, which are near each other, equatoreals are furnished with a filar micrometer, which consists of a system of several parallel wires and one or more normal wires. This system of wires can be turned about the axis of the telescope so that the parallel wires can be placed parallel to the diurnal motion of the stars, and this is accomplished, when these wires are turned so that an equatoreal star does not leave the wire while it is moving through the field of the telescope. In this position the normal wire represents a declination circle. Therefore when a known and an unknown star pass through the field, and the times of transit over this wire are observed, the difference of these two times is equal to the difference of the right ascensions of the two stars. In order to measure also the difference of the declinations, the micrometer is furnished with a moveable wire, which is also parallel to the diurnal motion of the stars, and which can be moved by means of a screw so that it is always perpendicular to the normal wire. The number of entire revolutions of the screw can be read on a scale, and the parts of one revolution on the graduated screw-head. Therefore if the equivalent in arc of one revolution is known, and the screw is regularly cut or its irregularities are determined by the methods given in No. 9 of this section, we can always find, through what arc of a great circle the wire has been moved by means of the screw. Hence if we let a star run through the field along one of the parallel wires and move the moveable wire, until it bisects the other star, and then make it coincident with the wire on which the first star was moving, then the difference of the readings in these two positions of the moveable wire will be equal to the difference of the declinations of the two stars. In case that one of the bodies has a proper motion, the difference of the right ascensions belongs to the time, at which the moveable body crossed the normal wire, and the difference of the declinations to that time, at which the moveable body was placed on one of the parallel wires or bisected by the moveable wire.

The coincidence of the wires is observed so, that the moveable wire is placed very near the other wire first on one side and then on the other; it is then equal to the arithmetical mean of the readings in the two positions of the wire. If this observation is made not only in the middle of the field, but also on each side near the edge, and the values obtained are the same, it shows, that the moveable wire is parallel to the others.

The equivalent of one revolution of the screw in seconds of arc is found in the same way that the wire-distances of a transit instrument are determined. The micrometer is turned so that the normal wire is parallel to the diurnal motion of the stars, and then the times of transit of the pole-star over the parallel wires are observed, since these now represent declination circles. Thus the distances between the wires are found in seconds of arc, and since they are also found expressed in revolutions of the screw, if the coincidence of the moveable wire with each of the parallel wires is observed, the equivalent of one revolution of the screw in seconds of arc is easily deduced. This method is especially accurate, when a chronograph is used for these observations.

Another method is that by measuring the distance between the threads of the screw, and the focal length of the telescope, because if the first is denoted by m, the other by f, we find one revolution of the screw expressed in seconds:

$$r = \frac{m}{f}\, 206265.$$

We can also find by Gauss's method the distances between the parallel wires and then the same expressed in revolutions of the screw. Finally we may measure any known angle, for instance the distance between two known fixed stars, by means of the screw; but in either case the accuracy is limited, in the first by the accuracy with which angles can be measured with the theodolite, and in the other by the accuracy of the places of the stars.

Since the focal length of the telescope and likewise the distance between the threads of the screw vary with the temperature, the equivalent of one revolution of the screw is not the same for all temperatures. Hence every determination of it is true only for that temperature, at which it was made, and when such determinations have been made at different temperatures, we may assume r to be of the form:

$$r = a - b\,(t - t_0),$$

and then determine the values of a and b by means of the method of least squares.

Usually such a micrometer is arranged so, that it serves also for measuring the distances and the angles of position of two objects, that is, the angle, which the great circle joining the two objects makes with the declination circle. In this case there is a graduated circle (called the position circle) connected with it, by means of which the angles through which the micrometer is turned about the axis of the telescope, can be determined. The distance is then observed in this way, that the micrometer is turned until the normal wire bisects both objects, and then one of the objects is placed on the middle wire while the other is bisected by the moveable wire. When afterwards the coincidence of the wires is observed, the difference of the two readings of the screw-head is equal to the distance between the two objects. If another observation is made by placing now the second object on the middle wire and bisecting the first object by the moveable wire, then it is not necessary to determine the coincidence of the wires, since one half of the difference of the two readings is equal to the distance between the two objects. If also the position-circle is read, first when the normal wire bisects the two objects, and then, when this wire is parallel to the diurnal motion of the stars, the difference of these two readings is the angle of position, but reckoned from the parallel; however these angles are always reckoned from the north part of the declination circle towards east from 0^0 to 360^0, and therefore 90^0 must be added to the value found.

In order to make the centre of the micrometer coincident with the centre of the position angle, we must direct the telescope to a distant object and turn the position circle 180^0. If the object remains in the same position with respect to the parallel wires, this condition is fulfilled; if not, the diaphragm holding the parallel wires must be moved by means of a screw opposite the micrometer screw, until the error is corrected. When this second screw is turned, of course the coincidence of the wires is changed, and hence we must always be careful, that this screw is not touched during a series of observations, for which the coincidence of the wires is assumed to be constant.

In order to find from such observations of the distance and the angle of position the difference of the right ascensions and the declinations of the two bodies, we must find the relations between these quantities. But in the triangle between the two stars and the pole of the equator the sides are equal to Δ, $90^0 - \delta$ and $90^0 - \delta'$, whilst the opposite angles are $\alpha' - \alpha$, $180^0 - p'$ and p, where p and p' are the two angles of position and Δ is the distance, and hence we have according to the Gaussian formulae:

$$\sin \tfrac{1}{2} \Delta \sin \tfrac{1}{2} (p' + p) = \sin \tfrac{1}{2} (\alpha' - \alpha) \cos \tfrac{1}{2} (\delta' + \delta)$$
$$\sin \tfrac{1}{2} \Delta \cos \tfrac{1}{2} (p' + p) = \cos \tfrac{1}{2} (\alpha' - \alpha) \sin \tfrac{1}{2} (\delta' - \delta)$$
$$\cos \tfrac{1}{2} \Delta \sin \tfrac{1}{2} (p' - p) = \sin \tfrac{1}{2} (\alpha' - \alpha) \sin \tfrac{1}{2} (\delta' + \delta)$$
$$\cos \tfrac{1}{2} \Delta \cos \tfrac{1}{2} (p' - p) = \cos \tfrac{1}{2} (\alpha' - \alpha) \cos \tfrac{1}{2} (\delta' - \delta).$$

In case that $\alpha' - \alpha$ and $\delta' - \delta$ are small quantities so that we can take the arc instead of the sines and 1 instead of the cosines, Δ is also a small quantity, and since we can take then $p = p'$, we obtain:

$$\cos \tfrac{1}{2} (\delta' + \delta) [\alpha' - \alpha] = \Delta \sin p$$
$$\delta' - \delta = \Delta \cos p.$$

For observing distances and angles of position it is requisite that the telescope be furnished with a clockwork, by which it is turned so about the polar axis of the instrument, that the heavenly body is always kept in the field. But if the instrument has no clockwork or at least not a perfect one, the micrometer in connection with a chronograph can still be advantageously used for such observations, for instance, the measurement of double stars, without the aid of the screw. For this purpose the moveable wire is placed at a small, but arbitrary distance from the middle wire, and the position circle is clamped likewise in an arbitrary position. The transit of the star A is then observed over the first wire and that of the star B over the second; let the interval of time be t. Then the star B is observed on the first wire and the star A on the second wire, and if the interval of time is t', and if Δ denotes the distance between the two stars, p the angle of position, i the inclination of the wires to the parallel circle reckoned from the west part of the parallel through north, which is given by the position circle, we have:

$$a = \cos \delta \,.\, \tfrac{1}{2} (t - t') = \Delta \frac{\cos (p - i)}{\sin i}.$$

For, a is the arc of the parallel circle of A between A and a great circle passing through B and making the angle i

with the parallel circle. If we consider the arcs as straight lines, we have a triangle, in which two sides are Δ and a, whilst the opposite angles are i and $90^0 + p - i$. When these observations are made in two different positions of the position circle, we can find from the two values of a the two unknown quantities Δ and p, and when the observations have been made in more than two positions, each observation leads to an equation of the form:

$$0 = \frac{\Delta \cos (p-i)}{\sin i} - a + d\Delta \frac{\cos (p-i)}{\sin i} - dp \,.\, \Delta \frac{\sin (p-i)}{\sin i} \frac{3600}{206265},$$

and from all these equations the values of $d\Delta$ and dp can be found by the method of least squares.

At the observatory at Ann Arbor the following observations of ε Hydrae were made, where every a is the mean of ten transits:

$$\begin{array}{lll} i = 99^0\,24' & 50^0\,24' & 141^0\,40' \\ a = -1''.062 & -4''.239 & +2''.382. \end{array}$$

If we take $p = 207^0$, $\Delta = 3''.5$, we obtain the equations:

$$\begin{array}{lll} 0 = -0''.011 & -0.306\, d\Delta & -0.590\, dp' \\ 0 = +0''.070 & -1.191\, d\Delta & -0.315\, dp' \\ 0 = -0''.044 & +0.668\, d\Delta & -0.089\, dp', \end{array}$$

where $p' = \frac{1}{10} p$. From these we find $d\Delta = +0''.056$, $dp = +0^0.208$, and the residual errors are $-0''.040$, $-0''.004$ and $+0''.024$.

33. Besides this kind of filar micrometer others were used formerly, which now however are antiquated and shall be only briefly mentioned.

Fig. 22.

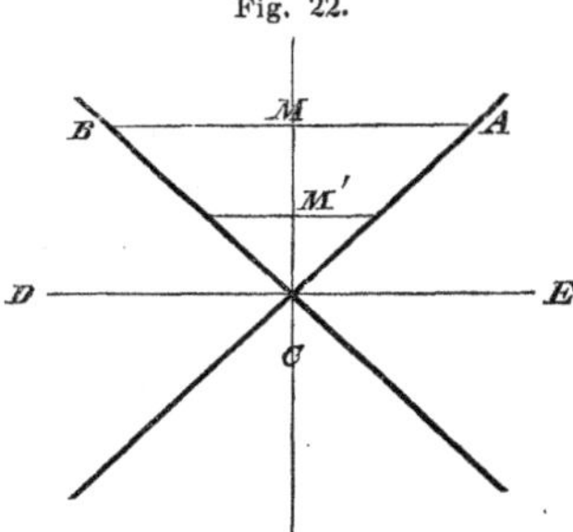

One is a micrometer, whose wires make angles of 45^0 with each other, Fig. 22. If one wire is placed parallel to the diurnal motion, we can find from the time in which a star moves from A to B, its distance from the centre, for we have:

$$MC = \frac{t' - t}{2} 15 \cos \delta.$$

and since we have for another star:

$$M'C = \frac{\tau' - \tau}{2} 15 \cos \delta',$$

the difference of the declinations of the two stars can be found. The arithmetical mean of the times t and t' is the time at which the star was on the declination circle CM; if $\frac{\tau' + \tau}{2}$ is the same for the second star, the difference is equal to the difference of the right ascensions.

Fig. 23.

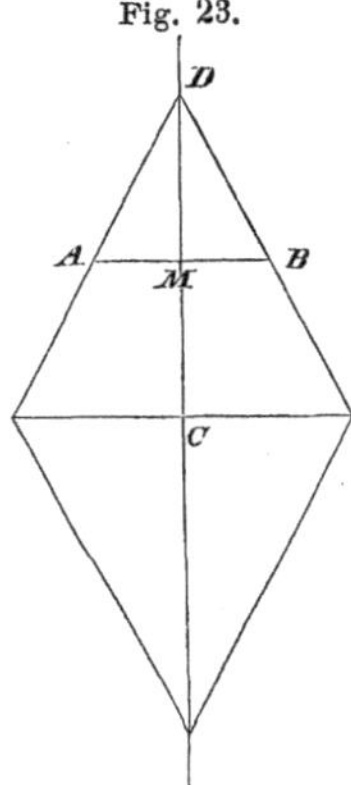

A second micrometer is that invented by Bradley, whose wires form a rhombus, the length of one diagonal being one half of that of the other, Fig. 23. The shorter diagonal is placed parallel to the diurnal motion. If then a star is observed on the wires at A and B, MD will be equal to the interval between the observations expressed in arc and multiplied by cos δ, so that:

$$MD = 15\,(t' - t)\cos\delta.$$

And if we have for another star:

$$M'D = 15\,(\tau' - \tau)\cos\delta'.$$

we easily find the difference of the declinations, whilst the difference of the right ascensions is found in the same way as with the other micrometer.

Before these micrometers can be used, it must be examined, whether the wires make the true angles with each other. They have this inconvenience that the wires must be illuminated, so that they cannot be employed for observing any very faint objects. For this reason ring-micrometers are preferable, since they do not require any illumination, and besides can be executed with the greatest accuracy.

34. The ring-micrometer consists in a metallic ring, turned with the greatest accuracy, which is fastened on a plane glass at the focus of the telescope, and hence is distinctly seen in the field of the telescope. If the emersions as well as the immersions of stars are observed, the arithmetical mean of the two times is the time at which the star was on the declination circle passing through the centre of the field. Therefore the difference of the right ascensions is found in the same way as with the other micrometers. And since the length of the chords can be obtained from the interval of the times of emersion and immersion, the difference of the declinations can be found, if the radius of the ring is known.

Let t and t' be the times of emersion and of immersion of a star, whose declination is δ, and let τ and τ' be the same for another star, whose declination is δ', then we have:

$$\alpha' - \alpha = \tfrac{1}{2}(\tau' + \tau) - \tfrac{1}{2}(t' + t).$$

If then μ and μ' denote half the chords which the stars describe, we have:

$$\mu = \frac{15}{2}(t' - t)\cos\delta$$

and

$$\mu' = \frac{15}{2}(\tau' - \tau)\cos\delta'.$$

Putting:

$$\sin\varphi = \frac{\mu}{r}$$

$$\sin\varphi' = \frac{\mu'}{r},$$

where r denotes the radius of the ring, we obtain, if we denote by D the declination of the centre of the ring:

$$\delta - D = r\cos\varphi$$
$$\delta' - D = r\cos\varphi',$$

and hence:

$$\delta' - \delta = r\,[\cos\varphi' \pm \cos\varphi],$$

accordingly as the stars move through the field on different sides or on the same side of the centre.

In 1848 April 11 Flora was observed at the observatory at Bilk with a ring-micrometer, whose radius was 18′ 46″.25. The declination of Flora was

$$\delta' = 24^\circ\ 5'.4$$

and the place of the comparison star was:

$$\alpha = 91^\circ\ 12'\ 59''.01$$
$$\delta = 24\quad 1\quad 9\ .01.$$

The observations were:

$\tau =$	$11^h\,16^m\,35^s.0$ Sider. time	$t =$	$11^h\,17^m\,53^s.0$
$\tau' =$	17 25 .5	$t' =$	19 46 .5
$\tau' - \tau =$	$50^s.5$	$t' - t =$	$1^m\,53^s.5.$

We have therefore:

$\log \tau' - \tau$	1.70329	$\log t' - t$	2.05500
$\log \mu'$	2.53878	$\log \mu$	2.89070
$\cos\varphi'$	9.97850	$\cos\varphi$	9.85941
$\delta' - D$	17′ 51″.9	$\delta - D$	13′ 34″.8,

and since the two bodies passed through the field on the same side of the centre, namely both north of it, we have:

$$\delta' - \delta = + 4' 17''.1.$$

The time at which the bodies were on the declination circle of the centre were:

$$\tfrac{1}{2}(\tau' + \tau) = 11^h 17^m 0^s.25 \qquad \tfrac{1}{2}(t' + t) = 11^h 18^m 49^s.75.$$

Therefore at

$$11^h 17^m 0^s.25$$

the difference of the right ascensions and declinations were:

$$\alpha' - \alpha = - \ 1^m 49^s.50 \qquad \delta' - \delta = + 4' 17''.1$$
$$= - 27' 22''.50.$$

If the exterior edge of such a ring is turned as accurately circular as the other, we can observe the immersions and emersions on both edges. However it is not necessary in this case to reduce the observations made on each edge with the radius pertaining to it, but the following shorter method can be used.

Let μ and r be the chord and the radius of the interior ring, and μ' and r' the same for the exterior ring, then we have:

$$\frac{15}{2} \cos \delta \, (t' - t) = \mu = r \sin \varphi$$

$$\frac{15}{2} \cos \delta' (t'_1 - t_1) = \mu' = r' \sin \varphi',$$

hence:

$$\mu + \mu' = (a + b) \sin \varphi + (a - b) \sin \varphi'$$

and:

$$\mu - \mu' = (a + b) \sin \varphi - (a - b) \sin \varphi',$$

putting:

$$\frac{r + r'}{2} = a \text{ and } \frac{r - r'}{2} = b.$$

From this we find:

$$\frac{\mu + \mu'}{2} = a \sin \frac{\varphi + \varphi'}{2} \cos \frac{\varphi - \varphi'}{2} + b \cos \frac{\varphi - \varphi'}{2} \sin \frac{\varphi - \varphi'}{2}$$

$$\frac{\mu - \mu'}{2} = a \cos \frac{\varphi + \varphi'}{2} \sin \frac{\varphi - \varphi'}{2} + b \sin \frac{\varphi + \varphi'}{2} \cos \frac{\varphi - \varphi'}{2}.$$

Adding and subtracting the two equations:

$$\delta - D = r \cos \varphi$$
$$\delta' - D = r' \cos \varphi'$$

we further obtain:

$$(a - b) \cos \varphi' - (a + b) \cos \varphi = 0,$$

or:

$$b = a \,.\, \frac{\sin\dfrac{\varphi+\varphi'}{2}\sin\dfrac{\varphi-\varphi'}{2}}{\cos\dfrac{\varphi+\varphi'}{2}\cos\dfrac{\varphi-\varphi'}{2}}$$

and

$$\delta - D = a\cos\frac{\varphi+\varphi'}{2}\cos\frac{\varphi-\varphi'}{2} - b\sin\frac{\varphi+\varphi'}{2}\sin\frac{\varphi-\varphi'}{2},$$

therefore if we substitute the value of b in the expressions for:

$$\frac{\mu+\mu'}{2},\ \frac{\mu-\mu'}{2} \text{ and } \delta - D$$

we find:

$$\frac{\mu+\mu'}{2} = a \,.\, \frac{\sin\dfrac{\varphi+\varphi'}{2}}{\cos\dfrac{\varphi-\varphi'}{2}}$$

$$\frac{\mu-\mu'}{2} = a \,.\, \frac{\sin\dfrac{\varphi-\varphi'}{2}}{\cos\dfrac{\varphi+\varphi'}{2}}$$

and

$$\delta - D = a \,.\, \frac{\cos\left(\dfrac{\varphi+\varphi'}{2}\right)^2 . \cos\left(\dfrac{\varphi-\varphi'}{2}\right)^2 - \sin\left(\dfrac{\varphi+\varphi'}{2}\right)^2 \sin\left(\dfrac{\varphi-\varphi'}{2}\right)^2}{\cos\dfrac{\varphi+\varphi'}{2}\cos\dfrac{\varphi-\varphi'}{2}}$$

$$= a\,\frac{\cos\varphi\cos\varphi'}{\cos\dfrac{\varphi+\varphi'}{2}\cos\dfrac{\varphi-\varphi'}{2}}.$$

Therefore if we put:

$$\frac{\mu+\mu'}{2a} = \sin A \text{ and } \frac{\mu-\mu'}{2a} = \sin B, \qquad (A)$$

we obtain:

$$\cos A = \frac{\sqrt{\cos\varphi\cos\varphi'}}{\cos\dfrac{\varphi-\varphi'}{2}}$$

and

$$\cos B = \frac{\sqrt{\cos\varphi\cos\varphi'}}{\cos\dfrac{\varphi+\varphi'}{2}},$$

hence:

$$\delta - D = a\cos A\cos B. \qquad (B)$$

Hence for the computation of the distance of the chord from the centre of the ring only the simple formulae (**A**) and (**B**) are required.

In 1850 June 24 a comet discovered by Petersen was observed with a ring-micrometer at the observatory at Bilk and compared with a star, whose apparent place was:

$$\alpha = 223^{0}\ 22'\ 41''.30 \qquad \delta = 59^{0}\ 7'\ 12''.19,$$

whilst the declination of the comet was assumed to be $59^{0}\,20'.0$. The radius of the exterior ring was $11'\,21''.09$, that of the interior ring $9'\,26''.29$, hence we have:

$$a = 10'\ 23''.69.$$

The observations were as follows:

C. north of the centre		Star south	
Immersion*)	Emersion	Immersion	Emersion
$18^{h}\,15^{m}\,54^{s}\,20^{s}$	$17^{m}\,21^{s}\,48^{s}$	$18^{m}\,55^{s}.3 \quad 13^{s}.0$	$21^{m}\,20^{s}.5 \quad 37^{s}.5.$

With this we obtain:

$\tau' - \tau$ Exterior ring	$1^{m}\,54^{s}$	$t' - t$ $E.R.$	$2^{m}\,42^{s}.2$
Interior ring	1 1		2 7.5
log of the sum	2.24304		2.46195
log of the diff.	1.72428		1.54033
$\cos A$	9.92623		9.65138
$\cos B$	9.99418		9.99749
	9.92041		9.64887
	$\delta' - D = +8'\,39''.26$		$\delta - D = -4'\,37''.88,$

hence:

$$\delta' - \delta = +13'\ 17''.14,$$

and the difference of right ascension is found:

$$\alpha' - \alpha = -3^{m}\ 25^{s}.82 = -51'\ 27''.30.$$

35. In order to see, how the observations are to be arranged in the most advantageous manner, we differentiate the formulae:

$$r \sin\varphi = \mu, \quad r \sin\varphi' = \mu', \quad r\cos\varphi' \mp r\cos\varphi = \delta' - \delta.$$

Then we obtain:

$$\begin{aligned} \sin\varphi\, dr + r\cos\varphi\, d\varphi &= d\mu \\ \sin\varphi' dr + r\cos\varphi' d\varphi' &= d\mu' \\ [\cos\varphi' \mp \cos\varphi]\, dr - r\sin\varphi' d\varphi' \pm r\sin\varphi\, d\varphi &= d(\delta' - \delta) \end{aligned}$$

or eliminating in the last equation $d\varphi$ and $d\varphi'$ by means of the two first equations:

$$\begin{aligned} [\cos\varphi \mp \cos\varphi']\, dr - \sin\varphi' \cos\varphi\, d\mu' \pm \sin\varphi \cos\varphi' d\mu \\ = \cos\varphi \cos\varphi' d(\delta' - \delta); \end{aligned}$$

---

*) For the immersion the first second belongs to the exterior, the second to the interior ring. The reverse in the case for the emersion.

$d\mu$ and $d\mu'$ are the errors of half the observed intervals of time. Now the observations made at different points of the micrometer are not equally accurate, since near the centre the immersion and emersion of the stars is more sudden than near the edge. But the observations can always be arranged so that they are made at similar places with respect to the centre, and hence we may put $d\mu = d\mu'$ so that we obtain the equation:

$$[\cos\varphi \mp \cos\varphi']\, dr - \sin[\varphi' \mp \varphi]\, d\mu = \cos\varphi \cos\varphi'\, d(\delta' - \delta).$$

Therefore in order to find the difference of the declinations of two stars, we must arrange the observations so that $\cos\varphi \cos\varphi'$ is as nearly as possible equal to 1; hence we must let the stars pass through the field as far as possible from the centre. If the stars are on the same parallel, in which case the upper sign must be taken and we have $\varphi = \varphi'$, then an error of r has no influence whatever upon the determination of the declination. For finding the difference of right ascension as accurately as possible, it is evident, that the stars must pass as nearly as possible through the centre, since there the immersions and emersions can be observed best.

36. Frequently the body, whose place is to be determined by means of the ring-micrometer, changes its declination so rapidly that we cannot assume any more, that it moves through 15″ in one sidereal second, and that an arc perpendicular to the direction of its motion is an arc of a declination circle. In this case we must apply a correction to the place found simply by the method given before. If we denote by d the distance of the chord from the centre, we have:

$$d^2 = r^2 - (15\, t \cos\delta)^2,$$

where $t = \frac{1}{2}(t' - t'')$ is equal to half the interval of time between the immersion and emersion. Now if we denote by $\Delta\alpha$ the increase of the right ascension in one second of time, then the correction Δt which we must apply to t on account of it so that $t + \Delta t$ is half the interval of time which would have been observed, if $\Delta\alpha$ had been equal to zero, is:

$$\Delta t = -\frac{1}{15}\, t \,.\, \Delta\alpha.$$

But we have:

$$\Delta d = -\frac{15^2\, t \cos\delta^2}{d}\,\Delta t,$$

hence:
$$\Delta d = 15\,.\,\frac{t^2 \cos\delta^2\,\Delta\alpha}{d},$$

or since we have $15\, t \cos\delta = \mu$:

$$\Delta d = \Delta(\delta - D) = \frac{\mu^2}{d}\cdot\frac{\Delta\alpha}{15}. \qquad (A)$$

Further the tangent of the angle n, which the chord described by the body makes with the parallel, is:

$$\operatorname{tang} n = \frac{\Delta\delta}{(15 - \Delta\alpha)\cos\delta},$$

where $\Delta\delta$ is the increase of the declination in one second of time.

Therefore if we denote by x that portion of the chord between the declination circle of the centre of the ring and the arc drawn from the centre perpendicularly to the chord, we have:

$$x = d \operatorname{tang} n = \frac{d\Delta\delta}{(15 - \Delta\alpha)\cos\delta},$$

and since we must add to the time $\frac{\tau' + \tau}{2}$ the correction $\frac{x}{\cos\delta}$ or:

$$+\frac{d\Delta\delta}{15\cos\delta^2 - \Delta\alpha\cos\delta^2}$$

we have, neglecting the product of $\Delta\delta$ and $\Delta\alpha$:

$$\Delta\left(\frac{\tau' + \tau}{2}\right) = +\frac{d\,.\,\Delta\delta}{15\cos\delta^2}. \qquad (B)$$

In the example given above the change of the right ascension in 24^h was $-1^0\, 15'$, and that of the declination was $-1^0\, 17'$, hence we have:

$$\log\Delta\alpha = 8.71551\, n$$

and

$$\log\Delta\delta = 8.72694\, n;$$

further we have:

$$\log d = 2.71538, \qquad \log\mu = 2.52468,$$

and with this we find:

$$\Delta(\delta - D) = -0''.75 \text{ and } \Delta\left(\frac{\tau' + \tau}{2}\right) = -7''.10.$$

The change of the right ascension is also taken into account, if we multiply the chord by $\frac{3600 - \Delta'\alpha}{3600}$, where $\Delta'\alpha$

is the hourly change of the right ascension in time, and then compute with this corrected chord the distance from the centre. But we have:

$$\log \frac{3600 - \Delta' \alpha}{3600} = -\frac{M . \Delta' \alpha}{3600},$$

where M is the modulus of the common logarithms, that is, 0.4343. Now since this number is nearly equal 48 times 15 multiplied by 60 and divided by 100000, we have approximately:

$$\frac{M \Delta' \alpha}{3600} = \frac{\Delta' \alpha . 48 . 15}{60 . 100000},$$

therefore we must subtract from the constant logarithm of $\frac{15}{2} \frac{\cos \delta'}{r}$ as many units of the fifth decimal as the number of minutes of arc, by which the right ascension changes in 48 hours.

In the above example the change of the right ascension in 48 hours is equal to $-2^0\, 30' = -150'$, and since the constant logarithm of $\frac{15}{2} \frac{\cos \delta'}{2a}$ was 7.48667, we must now take instead of it 7.48817, and we obtain:

$$\begin{array}{rl} & 2.24304 \\ & 1.72428 \\ \hline \cos A & 9.92563 \\ \cos B & 9.99415 \\ \hline \delta' - D = & 8'38''.50. \end{array}$$

37. Thus far we have supposed, that the path which the body describes while it is passing through the field of the ring, can be considered to be a straight line. But when the stars are near the pole, this supposition is not allowable, and hence we must apply a correction to the difference of declination computed according to the formulae given before. But the right ascension needs no correction, since also in this case the arithmetical mean of the times of immersion and emersion gives the time at which the body was on the declination circle of the centre.

In the spherical triangle between the pole of the equator, the centre of the ring and the point where the body enters or quits the ring, we have, denoting half the interval of time between the immersion and emersion by τ:

$$\cos r = \sin D \sin \delta + \cos D \cos \delta \cos 15\,\tau,$$

or:

$$\sin \tfrac{1}{2} r^2 = \sin \tfrac{1}{2} (\delta - D)^2 + \cos D \cos \delta \sin \left(\frac{15}{2}\tau\right)^2,$$

hence:

$$\begin{aligned}(\delta - D)^2 &= r^2 - \cos \delta^2 (15\tau)^2 - [\cos D - \cos \delta] \cos \delta (15\tau)^2 \\ &= r^2 - \cos \delta^2 (15\tau)^2 - (\delta - D) \sin \delta \cos \delta (15\tau)^2.\end{aligned}$$

If we take the square root of both members and neglect the higher powers of $\delta - D$, we have:

$$\delta - D = [r^2 - \cos \delta^2 (15\,\tau)^2]^{\frac{1}{2}} - \frac{(\delta - D) \sin \delta \cos \delta (15\tau)^2}{2\,[r^2 - \cos \delta^2 (15\tau)^2]^{\frac{1}{2}}}.$$

The first term is the difference of declination, which is found, when the body is supposed to move in a straight line, the second term is the correction sought. We have therefore:

$$\delta - D = d - \tfrac{1}{2} \sin \delta \cos \delta (15\tau)^2,$$

where the second term must be divided by 206265, if we wish to find the correction expressed in seconds. For the second star we have likewise:

$$\delta' - D = d' - \tfrac{1}{2} \sin \delta' \cos \delta' (15\,\tau')^2,$$

and hence:

$$\delta' - \delta = d' - d + \tfrac{1}{2} [\operatorname{tang} \delta \cos \delta^2 (15\tau)^2 - \operatorname{tang} \delta' \cos \delta'^2 (15\tau')^2],$$

instead of which we can write without any appreciable error:

$$\delta' - \delta = d' - d + \tfrac{1}{2} \operatorname{tang} \tfrac{1}{2} (\delta + \delta') [\cos \delta^2 (15\tau)^2 - \cos \delta'^2 (15\tau')^2],$$

or since:

$$\cos \delta^2\, 15^2\, \tau^2 = r^2 - d^2$$

and

$$\cos \delta'^2\, 15^2\, \tau'^2 = r^2 - d'^2,$$

also

$$\delta' - \delta = d' - d + \tfrac{1}{2} \operatorname{tang} \tfrac{1}{2} (\delta' + \delta) (d' + d) (d' - d).$$

Hence the correction which is to be applied to the difference of declination computed according to the formulae of No. 34, is:

$$+ \tfrac{1}{2} \operatorname{tang} \tfrac{1}{2} (\delta' + \delta) \frac{(d' + d)(d' - d)}{206265}.$$

In 1850 May 30 Petersen's comet, whose declination was $74^0\ 9'$ was compared with a star, whose declination was $73^0\ 52'.5$. The computation of the formulae of No. 34 gave:

$$d = -8'\,56''.7, \qquad d' = +7'\,36''.9.$$

With this we find:

$$
\begin{aligned}
\log (d' + d) &= 1\,.\,90200_n \\
\log (d' - d) &= 2\,.\,99721 \\
\text{Compl}\log 206265 &= 4\,.\,68557 \\
\text{Compl}\log 2 &= 9\,.\,69897 \\
\text{tang}\,\tfrac{1}{2}(\delta' + \delta) &= 0\,.\,54286 \\
\hline
&\ 9\,.\,82661_n \\
\text{Correct.} &= -0''.\,67.
\end{aligned}
$$

Hence the corrected difference of declination was:

$$+16'\,32''.93.$$

38. For determining the value of the radius of the ring, various methods can be used.

If we observe two stars, whose declination is known, we have:

$$\mu + \mu' = r\,[\sin\varphi + \sin\varphi'] = 2\,r\sin\tfrac{1}{2}(\varphi + \varphi')\cos\tfrac{1}{2}(\varphi - \varphi')$$

$$\mu - \mu' = r\,[\sin\varphi - \sin\varphi'] = 2\,r\cos\tfrac{1}{2}(\varphi + \varphi')\sin\tfrac{1}{2}(\varphi - \varphi').$$

Further we have:

$$r = \frac{\delta' - \delta}{\cos\varphi + \cos\varphi'} = \frac{\delta' - \delta}{2\cos\frac{1}{2}(\varphi + \varphi')\cos\frac{1}{2}(\varphi - \varphi')},$$

and hence:

$$\frac{\mu + \mu'}{\delta' - \delta} = \text{tang}\,\tfrac{1}{2}(\varphi + \varphi') \qquad \frac{\mu - \mu'}{\delta' - \delta} = \text{tang}\,\tfrac{1}{2}(\varphi - \varphi').$$

Therefore if we put:

$$\frac{\mu + \mu'}{\delta' - \delta} = \text{tang}\,A \quad \text{and} \quad \frac{\mu - \mu'}{\delta' - \delta} = \text{tang}\,B,$$

we obtain:

$$
\begin{aligned}
r &= \frac{\delta' - \delta}{2\cos A\cos B} \\
&= \frac{\mu + \mu'}{2\sin A\cos B} \\
&= \frac{\mu - \mu'}{2\cos A\sin B} \\
&= \frac{\mu}{\sin(A + B)} \\
&= \frac{\mu'}{\sin(A - B)}.
\end{aligned}
$$

The differential equation given in No. 35 shows, that the two stars must pass through the field on opposite sides of the centre and as near as possible to the edge, because then the coefficient of dr is a maximum, being nearly equal to 2, and the coefficient of $d\mu$ is very small. We must select therefore such stars, whose difference of declination is little less than the diameter of the ring.

The radius of the interior ring of the micrometer at the Bilk observatory was determined by means of the stars Asterope and Merope of the Pleiades, whose declinations are:

$$\delta = 24^{0}\ 4'\ 24''.26$$

and

$$\delta' = 23^{0}\ 28'\ 6''.85$$

and half the observed intervals of time were *):

$$18^{s}.5 \text{ and } 56^{s}.2.$$

With this we find:

$$\begin{aligned}
\log(\mu + \mu') &= 2.71038 \\
\log(\mu - \mu') &= 2.41490 \\
\cos A &= 9.98825 \\
\cos B &= 9.99693 \\
& 9.98518 \\
r &= 18'\ 46''.5.
\end{aligned}$$

The radius of the ring can also be determined by observing two stars near the pole, but in this case we cannot use the above formulae, since the chords of the stars are not straight lines. But in the triangle between the pole, the centre of the ring and the point, where the immersion or emersion takes place, we have, if we denote half the interval of time between the two moments converted into arc, for one star by τ and for the other by τ':

$$\begin{aligned}
\cos r &= \sin\delta \sin D + \cos\delta \cos D \cos\tau \\
\cos r &= \sin\delta' \sin D + \cos\delta' \cos D \cos\tau'.
\end{aligned}$$

If we write:

$$\frac{\delta+\delta'}{2} + \frac{\delta-\delta'}{2} \text{ instead of } \delta \text{ and } \frac{\delta+\delta'}{2} - \frac{\delta-\delta'}{2} \text{ instead of } \delta'$$

and then subtract the two equations, we obtain:

$$\begin{aligned}
\operatorname{tang} D = &\operatorname{cotang}\frac{\delta-\delta'}{2}\sin\frac{\tau-\tau'}{2}\sin\frac{\tau+\tau'}{2} \\
&+ \operatorname{tang}\frac{\delta+\delta'}{2}\cos\frac{\tau-\tau'}{2}\cos\frac{\tau+\tau'}{2}.
\end{aligned}$$

Therefore if we put:

---

*) The stars of the Pleiades are especially convenient for these observations since it is always easy to find among them suitable stars for any ring. Their places have been determined by Bessel with great accuracy and have been published in the Astronomische Nachrichten No. 430 and in Bessel's Astronomische Untersuchungen, Bd. I.

$$\text{cotang}\,\frac{\delta-\delta'}{2}\,\sin\frac{\tau-\tau'}{2}=a\cos A$$
$$\text{tang}\,\frac{\delta+\delta'}{2}\,\cos\frac{\tau-\tau'}{2}=a\sin A, \qquad (A)$$

we find D from the equation:

$$\text{tang}\,D=a\sin\left[\frac{\tau+\tau'}{2}+A\right]. \qquad (B)$$

When thus D has been found, we can compute r by means of one of the following equations:

$$\sin\tfrac{1}{2}r^2=\sin\tfrac{1}{2}(\delta-D)^2+\cos\delta\cos D\sin\tfrac{1}{2}\tau^2,$$

or

$$\sin\tfrac{1}{2}r^2=\sin\tfrac{1}{2}(\delta'-D)^2+\cos\delta'\cos D\sin\tfrac{1}{2}\tau'^2.$$

If we put here:

$$\text{tang}\,y=\frac{\sin\frac{1}{2}\tau}{\sin\frac{1}{2}(\delta-D)}\sqrt{\cos\delta\cos D},$$

or:

$$\text{tang}\,y'=\frac{\sin\frac{1}{2}\tau'}{\sin\frac{1}{2}(\delta'-D)}\sqrt{\cos\delta'\cos D}, \qquad (C)$$

we obtain:

$$\sin\tfrac{1}{2}r^2=\sin\tfrac{1}{2}(\delta-D)^2\sec y$$
$$=\sin\tfrac{1}{2}(\delta'-D)^2\sec y',$$

and

$$r=\frac{\delta-D}{\cos y}=\frac{\delta'-D}{\cos y'}. \qquad (D)$$

The solution of the problem is therefore contained in the formulae (*A*), (*B*), (*C*) and (*D*).

When the radius of the ring is determined by one of these methods, the declinations of the stars must be the apparent declinations affected with refraction. But according to No. 16 of this section the apparent declinations are, if the stars are not very near the horizon:

$$\delta+57''\,\text{cotang}\,(N+\delta)$$

and

$$\delta'+57''\,\text{cotang}\,(N+\delta'),$$

where

$$\text{tang}\,N=\text{cotg}\,\varphi\cos t,$$

and where t is the arithmetical mean of the hour angles of the two stars.

Hence the difference of the apparent declinations of the two stars is:

$$\delta'-\delta-\frac{57''\sin(\delta'-\delta)}{\sin(N+\delta)\sin(N+\delta')},$$

instead of which we may write:

$$\delta' - \delta - \frac{57'' \sin(\delta' - \delta)}{\sin[N + \frac{1}{2}(\delta + \delta')]^2}.$$

The difference of declination thus corrected must be employed for computing the value of the radius of the ring.

These methods of determining the radius of the ring are entirely dependent on the declinations of the stars. Therefore stars of the brighter class, whose places are very accurately known, ought to be chosen for these observations; but it is desirable, to use also faint stars for determining the radius of the ring, because the objects observed with a ring micrometer are mostly faint, and it may be possible that there is a constant difference between the observations of bright and faint objects; therefore Peters of Clinton has proposed another method, by which the radius is found by observing a star passing nearly through the centre of the field, and another, which describes only a very small chord and whose difference of declination need not be very accurately known.

We find namely from the equation $\mu = r \sin \varphi$:

$$r = \mu + 2r \sin(45^0 - \tfrac{1}{2}\varphi)^2.$$

Now if the star passes very nearly through the centre of the ring, the second term, that is, the correction which must be applied to μ is very small. For finding its amount the observation of the other star is used. We have namely according to the equations which where found in No. 38:

$$\frac{\mu + \mu'}{\delta' - \delta} = \operatorname{tang} A, \qquad \frac{\mu - \mu'}{\delta' - \delta} = \operatorname{tang} B:$$

$$\varphi = A + B.$$

Hence we have:

$$r = \mu + 2r \sin[45^0 - \tfrac{1}{2}(A + B)]^2,$$

or because the last term is very small:

$$r = \mu [1 + 2 \sin(45^0 - \tfrac{1}{2}(A + B))]^2$$
$$= \mu [2 - \sin(A + B)].$$

Since suitable stars for this method can be found anywhere, it is best, to select stars near the meridian and high above the horizon so that the refraction has no influence upon the result. In case that a chronograph is used for the observations, this method is especially recommendable.

We can use also the method proposed by Gauss for determining the radius of the ring by directing the telescope of a theodolite to the telescope furnished with the ring micrometer and finding the diameter of the ring by immediate measurement.

When solar spots have been observed with the ring micrometer, it is best to determine the radius of the ring also by observations of the sun, because the immersions and emersions of the limb of the sun are usually observed a little differently from those of stars. For this purpose the exterior and interior contacts of the limb of the sun with the ring are employed. Now when the first limb of the sun is in contact with the ring, the distance of the sun's centre from that of the ring is $R + r$, if R denotes the semi-diameter of the sun and r that of the ring. If we assume the centre of the sun to describe a straight line while passing through the field, we have a right angled triangle, whose hypothenuse is $R + r$, whilst one side is equal to the difference of the declination of the sun's centre and that of the ring, and the other equal to half the interval of time between the exterior contacts, expressed in arc and multiplied by the cosine of the declination. Therefore, denoting half this interval of time by t, we have the equation:

$$(R + r)^2 = (\delta - D)^2 + (15\, t \cos \delta)^2.$$

For interior contacts we find a similar equation in which t', i. e. half the interval of time between the interior contacts occurs instead of t, and $R - r$ instead of $R + r$:

$$(R - r)^2 = (\delta - D)^2 + (15\, t' \cos \delta)^2.$$

In these two equations the times t and t' must be expressed in apparent solar time in order to account for the proper motion of the sun. If we eliminate now $(\delta - D)^2$, we obtain:

$$(R + r)^2 - (R - r)^2 = (15 \cos \delta)^2\, [t^2 - t'^2],$$

and

$$r = \frac{(15 \cos \delta)^2\, [t + t']\, [t - t']}{4\, R}.$$

The sun was observed with one of the ring micrometers at the Bilk observatory, when its declination was $+ 23^0\, 14'\, 50''$ and its semi-diameter $15'\, 45''.07$, as follows:

Exterior contact:		Interior contact:
Immersion	$10^h\,31^m\,8^s.2$ Sidereal time	$10^h\,32^m\,30^s.8$
Emersion	$34^m\,47^s.5$	33 25 .3.

From this we find half the intervals of time expressed in sidereal time equal to $1^m\,49^s.65$ and $0^m\,27^s.25$, and these must be multiplied by 0.99712, in order to be expressed in apparent time, since the motion of the sun in 24 hours was equal to $4^m\,8^s.7$. We have therefore:

$$t = 109^s.33 \text{ and } t' = 27^s.17,$$

and we find:

$$r = 9'\,23''.52.$$

Note. It is evident, that the radius of the ring has the same value only as long as its distance from the object glass is not changed. Therefore, when the radius has been determined by one of the above methods, we must mark the position in which the tube containing the eye-piece was at the time of the observation so that we can always place the ring micrometer at the same distance from the object glass.

On the ring micrometer compare the papers by Bessel in Zach's Monatliche Correspondenz Bd. 24 and 26.

39. *The Heliometer* is a micrometer essentially different from those which have been treated so far. It consists of a telescope whose object glass is cut in two halves, each of which can be moved by means of a micrometer screw parallel to the dividing plane or plane of section and perpendicularly to the optical axis. The entire number of revolutions which the screws make in moving the two semi-lenses can be read on the scales attached to the slides which hold the lenses, and the parts of one revolution are obtained by the readings of the graduated heads of the screws. Therefore if the equivalent of one revolution of the screw in seconds of arc is known, we can find the distance through which the centres of the semi-lenses are moved with respect to each other. When the semi-lenses are placed so that they form one entire lens, that is, when their centres coincide, we shall see in the telescope the image of any object, to which it is directed, in the direction from the focus of the lens to its centre. If then we move one of the semi-lenses through a certain number of revolutions of the screw, the image, made by that semi-lens which is not moved, will remain in the same position, but near it we shall see another image made by the other semi-lens in the direction from its focus to its centre. Therefore if there is another object in the direction from the centre of this semi-lens to the focus of the fixed lens, then the image of the first object made by this lens and that of the second object made by the semi-lens which was moved, will coincide, and the angular distance between these two objects can be obtained from the number of revolutions of the screw, through which one of the semi-lenses was moved.

In order that the plane of section may always pass through the two observed objects, the frame-work supporting the two slides with the semi-lenses is arranged so, that it can be turned around the optical axis of the telescope. Therefore if the heliometer has a position circle whose readings indicate the position of the plane of section, then we can measure with such an instrument angles of position. But for this purpose it is requisite, that the telescope have a parallactic mounting.

The eye-piece is also fastened on a slide, whose position is indicated by a scale, and this can likewise be turned about the axis, and its position be obtained by the readings of a small position circle whose division increases in the same direction as that of the position circle of the object glass. This arrangement serves to bring the focus of the eye-piece always over the images of the object made by the semi-lenses. For if one of them is moved so that its centre does not coincide with that of the other, its focus moves also from the axis of the telescope, and hence the focus of the eye-piece does not coincide with the image of an object made by this semi-lens. Therefore in order to see it distinctly, we must move the eye-piece just as far from the axis of the telescope and in the right direction, so that its focus and the image of the object coincide.

Now the plane of section will not pass exactly through the centre of the position circle. We will call the reading of the moveable slide *), when the distance of the optical

---

*) We will assume here, that only one of the slides is moved and that the other always remains in a fixed position.

centre of the lens from the centre of the circle is a minimum, the zero-point. It can easily be determined, if we find that position, in which the image of an object seen in the telescope does not change its place in the direction of the plane of section, when the object glass is turned 180°. When this position has been found, the index of the scale of the slide can be moved so that it is exactly at the middle of the scale. In the same way we can find the zero-point of the eye-piece, and we will assume, that for this position the readings of the three scales, namely those on the slides of the two semi-lenses and that on the slide of the eye-piece, are the same and equal to h. Then the wire-cross of the telescope must likewise be placed so that its distance from the axis of revolution is a minimum, and this is accomplished by directing the telescope to a very distant object and turning both position circles 180°. If the image remains in the same position with respect to the point of intersection of the wires, then this condition is fulfilled, but if it changes its place, the wire-cross must be corrected by means of its adjusting screws.

We will assume, that when the image of an object made by one of the semi-lenses is on the wire-cross, the reading of the scale is s and that of the position circle, corrected for the index-error, p; at the same time let the reading of the scale of the eye-piece be σ, and that of its position circle π. Let a be the distance of the zero-point from the centre of the position circle, and t and δ the corrected readings of the hour-circle and the declination-circle of the instrument; these belong to that point of the heavens, towards which the axis of the telescope is directed. We will imagine then a rectangular system of axes, the axis of ξ and η being in the plane of the wire-cross so that the positive axis of ξ is directed to 0^0, and the positive axis of η directed to 90^0 of the position circle, that is, to the east when the telescope is turned to the zenith. Finally let the positive axis of ζ be perpendicular to the plane of the wire-cross and directed towards the object glass. If we put then:

$$s - h = e \text{ and } \sigma - h = \varepsilon,$$

and denote by l the focal length of the object glass expressed in units of the scale, and take a positive, if the zero-point is on the side where η is positive, and if the angle of position is either in the first or the fourth quadrant, then the co-ordinates of the point s are:

$$e \cos p - a \sin p, \quad e \sin p - a \cos p, \quad l$$

and those of the point σ:

$$\varepsilon \cos \pi - a \sin \pi, \quad \varepsilon \sin \pi - a \cos \pi, \quad 0.$$

Hence the relative co-ordinates of s with respect to σ will be:

$$\begin{aligned} \xi &= e \cos p - \varepsilon \cos \pi - a [\sin p - \sin \pi] \\ \eta &= e \sin p - \varepsilon \sin \pi + a [\cos p - \cos \pi] \qquad (a) \\ \zeta &= l, \end{aligned}$$

and if celestial objects are observed, whose distance from the focus of the telescope is infinitely great compared to ε, we can assume, that these expressions are also those of the co-ordinates of the point s with respect to the focus.

The co-ordinates must now be changed into such which are referred to the plane of the equator and the meridian, the positive axis of x being in the plane of the meridian and directed to the zero of the hour-angles, whilst the positive axis of y is directed to 90^0, and the positive axis of z is parallel to the axis of the heavens and directed to the north pole.

For this purpose we first imagine the axis of ξ to be turned in the plane of $\xi\zeta$ towards the axis of ζ through the angle $90^0 - \delta$; then the new co-ordinates will be in the plane of the equator, and we shall have:

$$\begin{aligned} \xi' &= \xi \sin \delta + \zeta \cos \delta \\ \eta' &= \eta \\ \zeta' &= \zeta \sin \delta - \xi \cos \delta. \end{aligned}$$

Then we turn the new axis of ξ' in the plane of $\xi'\eta'$ forwards through the angle $270^0 + t$, in order that it may become the positive axis of y, and we obtain:

$$\begin{aligned} x &= \xi' \cos t + \eta' \sin t \\ y &= \xi' \sin t - \eta' \cos t \\ z &= \zeta'. \end{aligned}$$

If we eliminate now ξ', η', ζ' we find:

$$\begin{aligned} x &= \zeta \cos \delta \cos t + \xi \sin \delta \cos t + \eta \sin t \\ y &= \zeta \cos \delta \sin t + \xi \sin \delta \sin t - \eta \cos t \\ z &= \zeta \sin \delta \qquad - \xi \cos \delta, \end{aligned}$$

or substituting the values of ξ, η, ζ taken from the equations (a):

$$\begin{aligned}
x &= l\cos\delta\cos t + [e\cos p - \varepsilon\cos\pi]\sin\delta\cos t + [e\sin p - \varepsilon\sin\pi]\sin t \\
&\quad - a[\sin p - \sin\pi]\sin\delta\cos t + a[\cos p - \cos\pi]\sin t \\
y &= l\cos\delta\sin t + [e\cos p - \varepsilon\cos\pi]\sin\delta\sin t - [e\sin p - \varepsilon\sin\pi]\cos t \\
&\quad - a[\sin p - \sin\pi]\sin\delta\sin t - a[\cos p - \cos\pi]\cos t \\
z &= l\sin\delta - [e\cos p - \varepsilon\cos\pi]\cos\delta + a[\sin p - \sin\pi]\cos\delta.
\end{aligned}$$

From this we find the square of the distance r of the point s from the origin of the co-ordinates:

$$r^2 = l^2 + [e\cos p - \varepsilon\cos\pi]^2 + [e\sin p - \varepsilon\sin\pi]^2 + 4a^2\sin\tfrac{1}{2}(p-\pi)^2.$$

The line drawn from the origin of the co-ordinates to the point s makes then the following angles with the three axes of co-ordinates:

$$\cos\alpha = \frac{x}{r},\quad \cos\beta = \frac{y}{r} \text{ and } \cos\gamma = \frac{z}{r}.$$

But if we denote by δ' and t' the declination and the hour angle of the observed star, that is, of the point, in which the line joining the wire-cross of the telescope and the point s intersects the celestial sphere, we have also:

$$\cos\alpha = \cos\delta'\cos t',\quad \cos\beta = \cos\delta'\sin t',\quad \cos\gamma = \sin\delta',$$

therefore if we put:

$$\frac{e}{l} = D,\ \frac{\varepsilon}{l} = \Delta \text{ and } \frac{a}{l} = d,$$

and also for the sake of brevity:

$$1 + [D\cos p - \Delta\cos\pi]^2 + [D\sin p - \Delta\sin\pi]^2 + 4d^2\sin\tfrac{1}{2}(p-\pi)^2 = A$$

we obtain:

$$\begin{aligned}
\cos\delta'\cos t' &= \frac{\cos\delta\cos t + [D\cos p - \Delta\cos\pi]\sin\delta\cos t}{\sqrt{A}} \\
&\quad + \frac{[D\sin p - \Delta\sin\pi]\sin t}{\sqrt{A}} \\
&\quad - \frac{d[\sin p - \sin\pi]\sin\delta\cos t - d[\cos p - \cos\pi]\sin t}{\sqrt{A}} \\
\cos\delta'\sin t' &= \frac{\cos\delta\sin t + [D\cos p - \Delta\cos\pi]\sin\delta\sin t}{\sqrt{A}} \\
&\quad - \frac{[D\sin p - \Delta\sin\pi]\cos t}{\sqrt{A}} \qquad (b) \\
&\quad - \frac{d[\sin p - \sin\pi]\sin\delta\sin t + d[\cos p - \cos\pi]\cos t}{\sqrt{A}} \\
\sin\delta' &= \frac{\sin\delta - [D\cos p - \Delta\cos\pi]\cos\delta}{\sqrt{A}} \\
&\quad + \frac{d[\sin p - \sin\pi]\cos\delta}{\sqrt{A}}.
\end{aligned}$$

Now we observe always two objects with the heliometer, and since thus there will be also the image of another star made by the second semi-lens on the wire-cross, we shall have three similar equations, in which

$$\delta,\ t,\ \Delta,\ \pi,\ d \text{ and } p$$

remain the same, while instead of D, δ' and t' other quantities referring to this star occur, which shall be denoted by D', δ'' and t''. We have thus six equations, which however really correspond only to four, if we find the angles by tangents; and all quantities occurring in the second members of these equations will be obtained by the readings of the instrument, namely δ and t by the readings of the declination-circle and the hour-circle, D and Δ by the readings of the slides of the object glass and the eye-piece, and p and π by the readings of the two position circles. Hence we can find by means of these equations δ', t', δ'' and t''. It is true, the instrument does not give the quantities δ, t, Δ and π with the same accuracy as the other quantities; but since the observed stars are near each other so that the errors of those quantities have the same influence upon the places of the two stars, we shall find the differences $\delta'' - \delta'$ and $t'' - t'$ perfectly accurate.

In case that the observed stars are near the pole, we must find δ'', δ', t'' and t' by means of the rigorous formulae (b), but in most cases we can use formulae, which give immediately $\delta'' - \delta'$ and $\alpha'' - \alpha'$, although they are only approximately true. First we may take d equal to zero. If then we develop the divisor in the equation for $\sin\delta'$ in a series, and retain only the first terms, we find:

$$\sin\delta - \sin\delta' = [D\cos p - \Delta\cos\pi]\cos\delta + \tfrac{1}{2}[D\cos p - \Delta\cos\pi]^2\sin\delta + \tfrac{1}{2}[D\sin p - \Delta\sin\pi]^2\sin\delta,$$

or according to the formula (20) of the introduction, retaining only the squares of the quantities put in parenthesis:

$$\delta' - \delta = -[D\cos p - \Delta\cos\pi] - \tfrac{1}{2}[D\sin p - \Delta\sin\pi]^2\operatorname{tang}\delta.$$

For the other star we find in the same way:

$$\delta'' - \delta = -[D'\cos p - \Delta\cos\pi] - \tfrac{1}{2}[D'\sin p - \Delta\sin\pi]^2\operatorname{tang}\delta,$$

and hence we obtain:

$$\delta'' - \delta' = [D - D']\cos p + \tfrac{1}{2}\operatorname{tang}\delta[(D + D')\sin p - 2\Delta\sin\pi][D - D']\sin p, \quad (c)$$

an equation, by means of which the difference of the declinations of the two stars is found from the readings of the instrument.

In order to find also the difference of the right ascensions we multiply the first of the equations (b) by $\sin t$, the second by $-\cos t$ and add them. Then we get:

$$\cos\delta'\sin(t-t')=\frac{D\sin p-\Delta\sin\pi}{\sqrt{1+[D\cos p-\Delta\cos\pi]^2+[D\sin p-\Delta\sin\pi]^2}},$$

and in a similar way:

$$\cos\delta''\sin(t-t'')=\frac{D'\sin p-\Delta\sin\pi}{\sqrt{1+[D'\cos p-\Delta\cos\pi]^2+[D'\sin p-\Delta\sin\pi]^2}}.$$

If we neglect the squares of D, D' and Δ, and introduce the right ascensions instead of the hour angles, these equations are changed into:

$$\cos\delta'(\alpha'-\alpha)=D\sin p-\Delta\sin\pi$$
$$\cos\delta''(\alpha''-\alpha)=D'\sin p-\Delta\sin\pi,$$

and if we write here instead of δ' and δ'':

$$\delta'=\tfrac{1}{2}(\delta'+\delta'')+\tfrac{1}{2}(\delta'-\delta'')$$
$$\delta''=\tfrac{1}{2}(\delta'+\delta'')-\tfrac{1}{2}(\delta'-\delta'')$$

and write $\delta'-\delta''$ instead of $\sin(\delta'-\delta'')$, and 1 instead of $\cos(\delta'-\delta'')$, we obtain:

$$(\alpha'-\alpha)\cos\tfrac{1}{2}(\delta'+\delta'')=[D\sin p-\Delta\sin\pi]\,[1+\tfrac{1}{2}\operatorname{tang}\delta(\delta''-\delta')]$$
$$(\alpha''-\alpha)\cos\tfrac{1}{2}(\delta'+\delta'')=[D'\sin p-\Delta\sin\pi]\,[1+\tfrac{1}{2}\operatorname{tang}\delta(\delta''-\delta')],$$

and hence:

$$(\alpha''-\alpha')\cos\tfrac{1}{2}(\delta'+\delta'')=(D'-D)\sin p+\tfrac{1}{2}\operatorname{tang}\delta\,[\delta''-\delta']\,[D'+D]\sin p$$
$$-\operatorname{tang}\delta\,\Delta\sin\pi\,[\delta''-\delta'],$$

and if we substitute instead of $\delta''-\delta'$ the value found before

$$(D-D')\cos p$$

we find:

$$(\alpha''-\alpha')\cos\tfrac{1}{2}(\delta'+\delta'')=(D'-D)\sin p$$
$$-\tfrac{1}{2}\operatorname{tang}\delta\,[(D'+D)\sin p-2\Delta\sin\pi]\,[D'-D]\cos p. \quad (d)$$

If now we put:

$$u=-\tfrac{1}{2}\operatorname{tang}\delta\,[(D'+D)\sin p-2\Delta\sin\pi], \qquad (A)$$

we can write in the equations (c) and (d) $\sin u$ instead of the small quantity u, and add in the first terms of the equations the factor $\cos u$. Then we obtain:

$$\left.\begin{aligned}\delta''-\delta'&=-(D'-D)\cos(p+u)\\ \alpha''-\alpha'&=+(D'-D)\sin(p+u)\sec\tfrac{1}{2}(\delta'+\delta'').\end{aligned}\right\}\quad (B)$$

We have assumed thus far, that simply the distance between the two stars has been measured, and that s is the reading of the slide in that position, in which the images made by the two semi-lenses coincide. But when we have two objects a' and b' near each other, and we move one of the semi-lenses, we see in the telescope two new images a' and b', and we can make the images a and b' coincident. Then if we turn the screw back beyond the point, at which the centres of the semi-lenses coincide, we can make also the images b and a' coincident, and the difference of the readings of the slide in those two positions will be double the distance.

When the observations have been made in this way, we must put $\frac{1}{2}(D' - D)$ instead of $D' - D$ in the above formulae. Instead of the angle $p + u$, we obtain from the two observations now $p' + u'$ and $p' + u''$, and hence we shall have:

$$p = \frac{p' + p''}{2}, \quad D' + D = s + s' - 2h, \quad \Delta = \sigma - h$$

and

$$u = -\tfrac{1}{2} \operatorname{tang} \delta \left[(s + s' - 2h) \sin p - 2(\sigma - h) \sin \pi\right]$$
$$\delta'' - \delta' = -\tfrac{1}{2}(D' - D) \cos(p + u)$$
$$\alpha'' - \alpha' = +\tfrac{1}{2}(D' - D) \sin(p + u) \sec \tfrac{1}{2}(\delta' + \delta'').$$

If we wish to find $\delta'' - \delta'$ and $\alpha'' - \alpha'$ expressed in seconds and u expressed in minutes, we must multiply $\frac{D' - D}{2}$ by the equivalent of one unit of the scale in seconds of arc and the expression for u by $\frac{206265}{60 \, . \, l}$. Now we can always arrange the observations so, that we can neglect the term dependent on $p - \pi$, because we have

$$u = 0, \text{ when } \sigma = \frac{s' + s}{2} \text{ and } \pi = p.$$

Therefore we must place the eye-piece always, at least approximately in the position, in which these conditions are fulfilled, and this is the more necessary, since the images in this position are seen the most distinctly.

We have assumed thus far, that the coincidence of the images is observed exactly on the wire-cross. But unless the stars are very near the pole, it is sufficient, to observe the coincidence near the middle of the field.

40. If one of the bodies has a proper motion in right ascension and declination, this must be taken into account in reducing the observations. If we compute from each observed distance and the angle of position the differences of the right ascensions and declinations of the two bodies, then their arithmetical means will belong to the mean of the times of observation, since it will be allowable to consider the motion in right ascension and declination to be proportional to the time. However it is more convenient to calculate the difference of the right ascensions and declinations only once from the arithmetical mean of all the observed distances and angles of position. But since these do not change proportionally to the time, their arithmetical mean will not correspond to the arithmetical mean of the times of observation, and hence a correction must be applied similar to that used in No. 5 of the fifth section for reducing a number of observed zenith distances to the mean of the times of observation.

Let t, t', t'' etc. be the times of observation, and T their arithmetical mean, and put:

$$t - T = \tau, \quad t' - T = \tau', \quad t'' - T = \tau'', \text{ etc.}$$

Further let p, p', p'' etc. be the angles of position corresponding to those times, P that corresponding to the time T, and $\Delta\alpha$ and $\Delta\delta$ the change of the right ascension and declination in one second of time, assuming that τ, τ' etc. are likewise expressed in seconds of time. Then we have:

$$p = P + \frac{dP}{d\alpha} . \Delta\alpha . \tau + \tfrac{1}{2}\frac{d^2P}{d\alpha^2}\Delta\alpha^2 . \tau^2$$
$$+ \frac{dP}{d\delta}\Delta\delta . \tau + \tfrac{1}{2}\frac{d^2P}{d\delta^2}\Delta\delta^2 . \tau^2 + \frac{d^2P}{d\alpha\, d\delta} . \Delta\alpha . \Delta\delta . \tau^2.$$

We shall have as many equations as angles of position have been observed, and if n is the number of observations, we obtain:

$$P = \frac{p + p' + p'' + \ldots .}{n}$$
$$- \left\{ \tfrac{1}{2}\frac{d^2P}{d\alpha^2}\Delta\alpha^2 + \frac{d^2P}{d\alpha\, d\delta}\Delta\alpha\,\Delta\delta + \tfrac{1}{2}\frac{d^2P}{d\delta^2}\Delta\delta^2 \right\} \frac{\Sigma\tau^2}{n},$$

where we can take:

$$\frac{2\,\Sigma\, 2\sin\tfrac{1}{2}\tau^2}{n} \text{ instead of } \frac{\Sigma\tau^2}{n}$$

if we have tables for these quantities.

Likewise we obtain from the observed distances the distance D corresponding to the arithmetical mean of the times:

$$D=\frac{d+d'+d''+\ldots.}{n}$$
$$-\left\{\tfrac{1}{2}\frac{d^2 D}{d\alpha^2}\Delta\alpha^2+\frac{d^2 D}{d\alpha\, d\delta}\Delta\alpha\,\Delta\delta+\tfrac{1}{2}\frac{d^2 D}{d\delta^2}\Delta\delta^2\right\}\frac{\Sigma\tau^2}{n}.$$

We must now find the expressions for the differential coefficients. But we have:

$$D\sin P=(\alpha-\alpha')\cos\delta$$
$$D\cos P=\delta-\delta',$$

or:

$$\operatorname{tang} P=\frac{\alpha-\alpha'}{\delta-\delta'}\cos\delta$$
$$D^2=(\alpha-\alpha')^2\cos\delta^2+(\delta-\delta')^2,$$

and we easily find:

$$\frac{dP}{d\alpha}=\frac{\cos\delta\cos P}{D},\ \frac{dP}{d\delta}=-\frac{\sin P}{D},\ \frac{dD}{d\alpha}=\cos\delta\sin P,\ \frac{dD}{d\delta}=\cos P$$
$$\frac{d^2 P}{d\alpha^2}=-\frac{2\cos\delta^2\sin P\cos P}{D^2},\ \frac{d^2 P}{d\delta^2}=\frac{2\sin P\cos P}{D^2}$$
$$\frac{d^2 P}{d\alpha\, d\delta}=\frac{2\cos\delta\sin P^2}{D^2}-\frac{\cos\delta}{D^2}$$
$$\frac{d^2 D}{d\alpha^2}=\frac{\cos\delta^2\cos P^2}{D},\ \frac{d^2 D}{d\delta^2}=\frac{\sin P^2}{D},\ \frac{d^2 D}{d\alpha.d\delta}=-\frac{\cos\delta\sin P\cos P}{D}.$$

If we put:

$$\Delta\alpha\cos\delta=c\sin\gamma$$
$$\Delta\delta=c\cos\gamma,$$

we obtain:

$$P=\frac{p+p'+p''+\ldots}{n}-\frac{\sin(P-\gamma)\cos(P-\gamma)}{D^2}c^2\frac{\Sigma\tau^2}{n}$$
$$D=\frac{d+d'+d''+\ldots}{n}-\tfrac{1}{2}\frac{\sin(P-\gamma)^2}{D}c^2\frac{\Sigma\tau^2}{n},$$

or denoting by M the modulus of the common logarithms:

$$\log D=\log\frac{d+d'+d''+\ldots}{n}-\tfrac{1}{2}\frac{M\sin(P-\gamma)^2}{D^2}c^2\frac{\Sigma\tau^2}{n}.$$

It is desirable to find the second term of P expressed in minutes of arc, and the second term of $\log D$ in units of the fifth decimal. Therefore, if R is the equivalent of the unit of the scale in seconds of arc, and if D is expressed in units of the scale, and $\Delta\alpha$ and $\Delta\delta$ denote the changes of the right ascension and declination in 24 hours, both expressed in minutes of arc, we must multiply the second term in the equation for P by

$$\frac{60}{86400^2}\frac{206265}{R^2},$$

and the term in the equation for D by:

$$\frac{100000.60^2}{86400^2.R^2}.$$

But if we make use of the tables for $2 \sin \frac{1}{2} \tau^2$, so that we take:

$$P = \frac{p + p' + p'' + \ldots}{n} - 2 \frac{\sin(P-\gamma)\cos(P-\gamma)}{D^2} c^2 \frac{\Sigma 2 \sin \frac{1}{2} \tau^2}{n}$$

and

$$\log D = \log \frac{d + d' + d'' + \ldots}{n} - \frac{M \sin(P-\gamma)^2}{D^2} c^2 \frac{\Sigma 2 \sin \frac{1}{2} \tau^2}{n},$$

we must multiply these terms respectively by

$$\frac{60 \,.\, 206265^2}{86400^2 \,.\, 15^2 \,.\, R^2}$$

and

$$\frac{100000 \,.\, 60^2 \,.\, 206265}{86400^2 \,.\, R^2 \,.\, 15^2}.$$

41. It is still to be shown, how the zero of the position circle and the value in arc corresponding to one unit of the scale can be determined.

The index of the position circle should be at the zero of the limb, when the plane of section is perpendicular to the declination axis. Therefore, when the two semi-lenses have been separated considerably, turn the frame of the object glass so that the index of the position circle is at the zero, and then make one image of an object coincident with the point of intersection of the wires *). If then also the other image can be brought to this point merely by turning the telescope round the declination-axis, the plane of section will be parallel to the plane in which the telescope is moving, and hence the collimation-error of the position circle will be zero. But if this should not be the case, then the object glass must be turned a little, until both images of an object pass over the point of intersection of the wires when the telescope is moved about the declination-axis. Then the reading of the position circle in this position is its error of collimation.

But this presupposes, that the slides move on a straight line. If this is not the case, the error of collimation will be variable with the distance between the two images.

If the wire-cross is placed so, that an equatoreal star during its passage through the field moves always on one of the

---

*) For this purpose it is convenient to have double parallel wires, so that the middle of the field is indicated by a small square.

wires, this must be parallel to the equator. If then the semi-lenses are separated, and the object-glass is turned about the axis of the telescope until the two images of an object move along this wire, then the reading of the position circle ought to be 90^0 or 270^0. But if it is in this position $90^0 - c$ or $270^0 - c$, then c is the error of collimation, which must be added to all readings.

The equivalent in arc of one unit of the scale can be found by measuring the known diameter of an object, for instance, that of the sun, or the distance between two stars, whose places are accurately known. For this purpose stars of the Pleiades may be chosen, as their places have been observed by Bessel with the greatest accuracy.

The method proposed by Gauss can be used also for this purpose. For since the axes of the semi-lenses, even when they are separated, are parallel, it follows, that if we direct a telescope, whose eye-piece is adjusted for objects at an infinite distance, to the object-glass of a heliometer, we see distinctly the double image of the wire at its focus. Therefore if one of the semi-lenses is in that position, in which the index is exactly at the middle of the scale, while the other semi-lens is moved so that the index of its scale is at a considerable distance from the middle, we measure the distance between the two images of the wire by means of a theodolite. Comparing then with this angular distance the difference of the readings of the two scales, we can easily find the equivalent in arc of one unit of the scale. In case that one of the semi-lenses has no micrometer, the observations must be made in two different positions of that semi-lens which is furnished with a graduated screw-head.

Let then S be the reading of the scale of the latter semi-lens and S_0 the reading of the scale of the other semi-lens which remains always in the same position, finally s that of the scale of the eye-piece, then we have, if b and c are the angles, which straight lines drawn from the points S_0 and S to the focus make with the axis of the telescope:

$$(s - S_0)\, R = 206265'' \operatorname{tang} b$$
$$(S - s)\, R = 206265'' \operatorname{tang} c,$$

where R is the value in arc of one unit of the scale. Further let a be the measured angular distance between the two images of the wire, then we have

$$a = b + c.$$

If we eliminate b and c by means of the last equation, we find the following equation of the second degree:

$$(s - S_0)(S - s) \operatorname{tang} a \frac{R^2}{206265^2} + (S - S_0) \frac{R}{206265} = \operatorname{tang} a,$$

from which we obtain:

$$\frac{R}{206265} = -\frac{(S - S_0) - \sqrt{(S - S_0)^2 + 4(s - S_0)(S - s) \operatorname{tang} a^2}}{2(s - S_0)(S - s) \operatorname{tang} a}.$$

Let then S' be the reading of the scale in the second position of the semi-lens, s' that of the scale of the eye-piece and a' the observed angular distance between the two images, then we shall obtain a similar equation for R, in which S', s' and a' take the place of S, s and a. Now we can always arrange the observations in such a way that:

$$S' - S_0 = S_0 - S \text{ and } s - S_0 = S_0 - s'$$

and then we find from the difference of the two equations:

$$\frac{R}{206265} = -\frac{(S' - S) - \sqrt{(S' - S)^2 + 16(s - S_0)(S - s) \operatorname{tang} \frac{1}{2}(a + a')^2}}{4(s - S_0)(S - s) \operatorname{tang} \frac{1}{2}(a + a')}.$$

When $s - S_0$ and $S - s$ have the same sign, and if we put:

$$\operatorname{tang} \alpha = 4 \frac{\operatorname{tang} \frac{1}{2}(a + a')}{S' - S} \sqrt{(s - S_0)(S - s)},$$

we find for R:

$$R = 206265 \frac{[\sec \alpha - 1]}{\operatorname{tang} \alpha \sqrt{(s - S_0)(S - s)}}$$

$$= 206265 \frac{\operatorname{tang} \frac{1}{2} \alpha}{\sqrt{(s - S_0)(S - s)}}.$$

But when $s - S_0$ and $S - s$ have opposite signs, and if we put:

$$\sin \beta = 4 \frac{\operatorname{tang} \frac{1}{2}(a + a')}{S' - S} \sqrt{(s - S_0)(S - s)},$$

we find for R:

$$R = 206265 \frac{1 - \cos \beta}{\sin \beta \sqrt{(s - S_0)(S - s)}}$$

$$= 206265 \frac{\operatorname{tang} \frac{1}{2} \beta}{\sqrt{(s - S_0)(S - s)}}.$$

When $s = S$ and $s' = S'$, we obtain for R instead of the equations of the second degree the following:

$$(S - S_0) \frac{R}{206265} = \text{tang}\, a$$

$$(S_0 - S') \frac{R}{206265} = \text{tang}\, a',$$

hence:

$$R = 206265 \frac{2 \,\text{tang}\, \frac{1}{2}(a + a')}{S - S'},$$

for which we can also write:

$$R = \frac{a' + a}{S - S'}.$$

These formulae can be used also in case, that the diameter of the sun or the distance between two fixed stars is observed. Then a and a' will be equal to the diameter of the sun or to the distance between the two stars.

When the heliometer is furnished with a wire-cross, we can also place one of the wires parallel to the equator and then, after the two semi-lenses have been separated and turned so that the two images of a star move along this wire, observe the transits of the two images over the normal wires.

The value in arc of one revolution of the screw is variable with the temperature and hence it must be assumed to be of the form:

$$R = a - b\,(t - t_0).$$

Hence the value of R must be determined at different temperatures and the values of a and b be deduced from all these different determinations.

Note. Compare:

Hansen, Methode mit dem Fraunhoferschen Heliometer Beobachtungen anzustellen.

and

Bessel, Theorie eines mit einem Heliometer versehenen Aequatoreals. Astronomische Untersuchungen, Bd. I. Königsberger Beobachtungen Bd. 15.

VIII. METHODS OF CORRECTING OBSERVATIONS MADE BY MEANS OF A MICROMETER FOR REFRACTION.

42. The observations made by means of a micrometer give the differences of the apparent right ascensions and declinations of stars either immediately or so that they can be computed from the results of observation. If the refraction were the same for the two stars, the observed difference of the apparent places would also be equal to the difference of the true places. But since the refraction varies with the altitude of the objects, the observations made with a micrometer will need a correction on this account. Only in case that the two stars are on the same parallel, there will be no correction, because then the observations are made at the same point of the micrometer and hence at the same altitude *).

The common tables of refraction, for instance, those published in the Tabulae Regiomontanae give the refraction for the normal state of the atmosphere (that is, for a certain height of the barometer and thermometer) in the form:

$$\alpha \tang z,$$

where z denotes the apparent zenith distance and α is a factor variable with the zenith distance, which for

$$z = 45^0 \text{ is equal to } 57''.682$$

and decreases when the zenith distance is increasing so that

$$\text{for } z = 85^0 \text{ it is equal to } 51''.310.$$

By means of these tables others can be calculated, whose argument is the true zenith distance ζ and by means of which the refraction is found by the formula:

$$\varrho = \beta \tang \zeta,$$

where β is again a function of ζ. We have therefore:

$$\zeta = z + \beta \tang \zeta$$
$$\zeta' = z' + \beta' \tang \zeta',$$

hence:

$$\zeta' - \zeta = z' - z + \beta' \tang \zeta' - \beta \tang \zeta,$$

or denoting:

$$\zeta' - \zeta - (z' - z) \text{ by } \Delta (z' - z)$$

also:

$$\Delta (z' - z) = \beta' \tang \zeta' - \beta \tang \zeta. \qquad (a)$$

This is the expression for the correction, which must be applied to the observed difference of the apparent zenith distances in order to find the difference of the true zenith distances.

---

*) This remark is not true for micrometers with which distances and angles of position are measured.

If we denote by β_0 that value of β, which corresponds to:

$$\frac{\zeta' + \zeta}{2} = \zeta_0$$

and which is derived from the equation:

$$\varrho_0 = \beta_0 \text{ tang } \zeta_0 ,$$

we have:

$$\beta' \text{ tang } \zeta' = \beta_0 \text{ tang } \zeta' + \tfrac{1}{2} \frac{d\beta_0}{d\zeta_0} \text{ tang } \zeta' (\zeta' - \zeta) + \ldots$$

$$\beta \text{ tang } \zeta = \beta_0 \text{ tang } \zeta - \tfrac{1}{2} \frac{d\beta_0}{d\zeta_0} \text{ tang } \zeta (\zeta' - \zeta) + \ldots$$

If we write in all terms of the second member, except the first, tang ζ_0 instead of tang ζ and tang ζ', the terms containing the second differential coefficients will be the same, and we have with a considerable degree of accuracy:

$$\beta' \text{ tang } \zeta' - \beta \text{ tang } \zeta = \beta_0 [\text{tang } \zeta' - \text{tang } \zeta]$$
$$+ \frac{d\beta_0}{d\zeta_0} \text{ tang } \zeta_0 \; \frac{\text{tang } \zeta' - \text{tang } \zeta}{\sec \zeta_0{}^2} \, 206265.$$

Therefore if we put:

$$k = \beta_0 + \frac{d\beta_0}{d\zeta_0} \, \frac{\text{tang } \zeta_0}{\sec \zeta_0{}^2} \, 206265,$$

we obtain by means of (a):

$$\Delta (z' - z) = k [\text{tang } \zeta' - \text{tang } \zeta]$$

where k must be computed with the value:

$$\zeta_0 = \frac{\zeta' + \zeta}{2}$$

and since we can take, neglecting the second power of $\zeta' - \zeta$:

$$\text{tang } \zeta' - \text{tang } \zeta = \frac{\zeta' - \zeta}{\cos \zeta_0{}^2}$$

we have:

$$\Delta (z' - z) = k \; \frac{\zeta' - \zeta}{\cos \zeta_0{}^2} . \qquad (b)$$

But this formula assumes that the difference of the true zenith distances is given. If we introduce instead of it the difference of the apparent zenith distances, we must multiply the formula by $\frac{d\zeta_0}{dz_0}$ and we find:

$$\Delta (z' - z) = k \, \frac{d\zeta_0}{dz_0} \cdot \frac{z' - z}{\cos \zeta_0{}^2} ,$$

or if we put now:

$$k = \frac{d\zeta_0}{dz_0}\left\{\beta_0 + \frac{d\beta_0}{d\zeta_0}\frac{\operatorname{tang}\zeta_0}{\sec\zeta_0{}^2}\,206265\right\}$$

$$= \frac{d\zeta_0}{dz_0}\left\{\beta_0 + \tfrac{1}{2}\frac{d\beta_0}{d\zeta_0}\sin 2\,\zeta_0\,206265\right\}, \qquad (A)$$

we finally obtain:

$$\Delta\,(z' - z) = k\,.\,\frac{z' - z}{\cos\zeta_0{}^2}\,. \qquad (B)$$

The following example will serve to show how accurately the difference of the true zenith distances can be found from the difference of the apparent zenith distances by means of this formula:

True zenith distance ζ	Apparent zenith distance z	Refraction
87° 20′	87° 5′ 27″.4	14′ 32″.6
30	14 54 .8	15 5 .2
40	24 20 .7	39 .3
50	33 44 .5	16 15 .5
88 0	43 6 .4	53 .6.

From this we obtain the following values of β:

87° 20′	40″.6427
30	39 .5209
40	38 .2727
50	36 .9073,

and from these we find by means of the formulae in No. 15 of the introduction the values of $\frac{d\beta_0}{d\zeta_0}$, that is, the variations of β_0 corresponding to a change of ζ_0 equal to one second:

87° 30′	— 0″.0019750
40	0 .0021767
50	0 .0023967.

If we compute now the values of k, we find, since the logarithms of $\frac{d\zeta}{dz}$ are:

87° 30′	0.0271
40	0.0287
50	0.0307,

the following values for the logarithms of k:

	k	
87° 30′	6.0505	
		350
40	6.0155	
		384
50	5.9771	

where k is expressed in parts of the radius.

If we take now:

$$z = 87^\circ\, 10' \text{ and } z' = 87^\circ\, 50',$$

and hence:

$$z' - z = 40',$$

we have by means of the common tables of refraction:

$$\zeta = 87^\circ\, 24'\, 47''.8$$
$$\zeta' = 88 \quad 7 \;\; 23 \;.0,$$

hence:

$$\zeta' - \zeta = +\, 42'\, 35''.2$$
$$\zeta_0 = 87^\circ\, 46'\, 5''.4.$$

If we suppose now that $z' - z$ and ζ_0 are given, and compute $\Delta\,(z' - z)$ by means of the formulae (A) and (B), we find, since the value of log k corresponding to ζ_0 is 5.9925:

$$\Delta\,(z' - z) = +\;\; 2'\, 35''.4,$$

hence:

$$\zeta' - \zeta = +\, 42'\, 35''.4,$$

which is nearly the same value, which was obtained from the tables of refraction.

The values of k may be taken from tables whose argument is the zenith distance. Such tables have been published in the third volume of the Astronomische Nachrichten in Bessel's paper „Ueber die Correction wegen der Strahlenbrechung bei Micrometerbeobachtungen“ and in his work Astronomische Untersuchungen Bd. I. In the last mentioned work there are also tables, which give the variations of k for any change of the height of the thermometer and barometer.

For computing the difference of the true zenith distances ζ_0 itself must be known. But since the right ascensions and declinations of the two stars are known, we can find this quantity with sufficient accuracy, if we compute it from the arithmetical mean of the right ascensions and declinations. For this purpose the following formulae are the most convenient, since it is also necessary, to know the parallactic angle:

$$\sin\zeta\,\sin\eta = \cos\varphi\,\sin t_0$$
$$\sin\zeta\,\cos\eta = \cos\delta_0\,\sin\varphi - \sin\delta_0\,\cos\varphi\,\cos t_0$$
$$\cos\zeta = \sin\delta_0\,\sin\varphi + \cos\delta_0\,\cos\varphi\,\cos t_0.$$

Putting:

$$\cos n = \cos \varphi \sin t_0$$
$$\sin n \sin N = \cos \varphi \cos t_0$$
$$\sin n \cos N = \sin \varphi,$$

we have:

$$\sin \zeta \sin \eta = \cos n$$
$$\sin \zeta \cos \eta = \sin n \cos (N + \delta_0)$$
$$\cos \zeta = \sin n \sin (N + \delta_0),$$

or:

$$\text{tang}\, \zeta \sin \eta = \text{cotang}\, n \,.\, \text{cosec}\, (N + \delta_0)$$
$$\text{tang}\, \zeta \cos \eta = \text{cotang}\, (N + \delta_0).$$

The quantities cotang n and N can again be tabulated for any place, the argument being t. In case that the tables, mentioned in No. 7 of the first section, have been computed, they can also be used for finding the zenith distance and the parallactic angle. The connection between the above formulae and those used for constructing the tables is easily discovered.

43. The difference of the true zenith distances having been found from that of the apparent zenith distances, the difference of the true right ascensions and declinations of two stars is also easily derived from the observed apparent differences of these co-ordinates. For if β tang ζ is the refraction for the zenith distance ζ,

$\beta \,.\, \dfrac{\text{tang}\, \zeta \sin \eta}{\cos \delta}$ is the refraction in right ascension

and

β tang ζ cos η the refraction in declination.

But we have:

$$\beta' \,\text{tang}\, \zeta' \frac{\sin \eta'}{\cos \delta'} - \beta \,\text{tang}\, \zeta \frac{\sin \eta}{\cos \delta} = k \,\text{tang}\, \zeta' \frac{\sin \eta'}{\cos \delta'} - k \,\text{tang}\, \zeta \frac{\sin \eta}{\cos \delta}$$
$$= k \,.\, \frac{d \,.\, \dfrac{\text{tang}\, \zeta_0 \sin \eta_0}{\cos \delta_0}}{d \delta_0} (\delta' - \delta) + k \,.\, \frac{d \,.\, \dfrac{\text{tang}\, \zeta_0 \sin \eta_0}{\cos \delta_0}}{d \alpha_0} (\alpha' - \alpha),$$

and likewise we find:

$$\beta' \,\text{tang}\, \zeta' \cos \eta' - \beta \,\text{tang}\, \zeta \cos \eta = k \,.\, \frac{d \,.\, \text{tang}\, \zeta_0 \cos \eta_0}{d \delta_0} (\delta' - \delta)$$
$$+ k \,.\, \frac{d \,.\, \text{tang}\, \zeta_0 \cos \eta_0}{d \alpha_0} (\alpha' - \alpha),$$

where $\delta' - \delta$ and $\alpha' - \alpha$ denote the differences of the apparent right ascensions and declinations.

Differentiating the formulae for:

$$\frac{\operatorname{tang}\zeta \sin\eta}{\cos\delta} \text{ and } \operatorname{tang}\zeta \cos\eta$$

we obtain:

$$\frac{d.\dfrac{\operatorname{tang}\zeta \sin\eta}{\cos\delta}}{d\delta} = -\frac{\operatorname{tang}\zeta^2 \sin\eta \cos\eta - \operatorname{tang}\zeta \sin\eta \operatorname{tang}\delta}{\cos\delta}$$

$$\frac{d.\dfrac{\operatorname{tang}\zeta \sin\eta}{\cos\delta}}{dt} = 1 - \operatorname{tang}\zeta \cos\eta \operatorname{tang}\delta + \operatorname{tang}\zeta^2 \sin\eta^2$$

$$\frac{d.\operatorname{tang}\zeta\cos\eta}{d\delta} = -[\operatorname{tang}\zeta^2\cos\eta^2 + 1]$$

$$\frac{d.\operatorname{tang}\zeta\cos\eta}{dt} = \operatorname{tang}\zeta^2 \cos\eta \sin\eta \cos\delta + \operatorname{tang}\zeta \sin\eta \sin\delta,$$

and these expressions being found we can now treat of the several micrometers, whose theory was given in No. VII of this section. But since those mentioned in No. 33 are at present entirely out of use, we will omit the corrections for them.

44. *The micrometer, by which the difference of right ascension is found from the transits over wires perpendicular to the parallel of the stars, whilst the difference of declination is found by direct measurement.* With these micrometers refraction has an influence only at the moment when the two stars pass over the same declination circle, and hence we need only to consider the difference of refraction, dependent on the difference of declination.

Therefore the correction of the apparent right ascension and declination is for the first star:

$$\Delta\alpha = -\beta\frac{\operatorname{tang}\zeta \sin\eta}{\cos\delta} \qquad \Delta\delta = -\beta \operatorname{tang}\zeta\cos\eta,$$

for the second:

$$\Delta\alpha' = -\beta'\frac{\operatorname{tang}\zeta' \sin\eta'}{\cos\delta'} \qquad \Delta\delta' = -\beta' \operatorname{tang}\zeta'\cos\eta';$$

and hence we obtain by means of the formulae in No. 43:

$$\Delta(\alpha' - \alpha) = -k.\frac{d.\dfrac{\operatorname{tang}\zeta_0 \sin\eta_0}{\cos\delta_0}}{d\delta_0}(\delta' - \delta)$$

$$\Delta(\delta' - \delta) = -k.\frac{d.\operatorname{tang}\zeta_0\cos\eta_0}{d\delta_0}(\delta' - \delta),$$

or substituting the values of the differential coefficients:

$$\Delta(\alpha' - \alpha) = k(\delta' - \delta)\frac{\operatorname{tang}\zeta_0{}^2 \sin\eta_0 \cos\eta_0 - \operatorname{tang}\zeta_0 \sin\eta_0 \operatorname{tang}\delta_0}{\cos\delta_0}$$

$$\Delta(\delta' - \delta) = k(\delta' - \delta)[\operatorname{tang}\zeta_0{}^2 \cos\eta_0{}^2 + 1].$$

These formulae receive a more convenient form if we introduce the auxiliary quantities cotang n and N. For, substituting the values given in No. 42 for:

$$\operatorname{tang}\zeta \sin\eta \text{ and } \operatorname{tang}\zeta\cos\eta$$

we obtain:

$$\Delta(\alpha' - \alpha) = k(\delta' - \delta)\frac{\operatorname{cotang} n \cos(N + 2\delta_0)}{\sin(N + \delta_0)^2 \cos\delta_0{}^2}$$

and

$$\Delta(\delta' - \delta) = \frac{k(\delta' - \delta)}{\sin(N + \delta_0)^2}.$$

45. *The ring micrometer.* If the refraction were the same during the passage of the stars through the field of the ring micrometer, they would describe chords parallel to the equator and it would only be necessary, to correct the observed differences of right ascension and declination for the difference of refraction at the moment when the stars pass over the declination circle of the centre of the ring. Therefore we would have the same corrections as for the filar micrometer:

$$\Delta(\alpha' - \alpha) = k(\delta' - \delta)\frac{\operatorname{tang}\zeta_0{}^2 \sin\eta_0 \cos\eta_0 - \operatorname{tang}\zeta_0 \sin\eta_0 \operatorname{tang}\delta_0}{\cos\delta_0}$$

and $\qquad\qquad\qquad\qquad\qquad\qquad\qquad\qquad\qquad\qquad\qquad\qquad (a)$

$$\Delta(\delta' - \delta) = k(\delta' - \delta)[\operatorname{tang}\zeta_0{}^2 \cos\eta_0{}^2 + 1].$$

But since the refraction really changes while the stars are passing through the field of the ring, it is the same, as if the stars have a proper motion in right ascension and declination. Now if h and h' denote the variations of the right ascension and declination of a star in one second of time, we must add according to No. 36 of this section the following correction to the differences of right ascension and declination computed from the observations:

$$\Delta\alpha = +\frac{\delta - D}{\cos\delta^2}h'$$

$$\Delta\delta = +\frac{\mu^2}{\delta - D}h,$$

where D is the declination of the centre of the ring and μ is half the chord. Since:

$$h = k \, . \, \frac{d \, . \, \dfrac{\operatorname{tang} \zeta \, \sin \eta}{\cos \delta}}{dt}$$

and

$$h' = k \, . \, \frac{d \, . \operatorname{tang} \zeta \cos \eta}{dt} ,$$

we have:

$$\Delta \alpha = k \, (\delta - D) \frac{\operatorname{tang} \zeta^2 \cos \eta \sin \eta + \operatorname{tang} \zeta \sin \eta \operatorname{tang} \delta}{\cos \delta} ,$$

and likewise for the other star:

$$\Delta \alpha' = k \, (\delta' - D) \frac{\operatorname{tang} \zeta'^2 \cos \eta' \sin \eta' + \operatorname{tang} \zeta' \sin \eta' \operatorname{tang} \delta'}{\cos \delta'} ,$$

or if we write in both equations ζ_0, η_0 and δ_0 instead of ζ, η, δ and ζ', η', δ', that is, if we neglect terms of the order of $k(\delta - D)^2$, we obtain:

$$\Delta \, (\alpha' - \alpha) = k \, (\delta' - \delta) \frac{\operatorname{tang} \zeta_0{}^2 \cos \eta_0 \sin \eta_0 + \operatorname{tang} \zeta_0 \sin \eta_0 \operatorname{tang} \delta_0}{\cos \delta_0} .$$

If we unite this with the first part of the correction, which is given by the first of the equations (a), we find:

$$\Delta \, (\alpha' - \alpha) = k \, (\delta' - \delta) \frac{\operatorname{tang} \zeta_0{}^2 \sin 2 \eta_0}{\cos \delta_0} . \qquad (A)$$

Further we have:

$$\Delta \delta = \frac{\mu^2}{\delta - D} \, h$$

$$= \frac{r^2 - (\delta - D)^2}{\delta - D} \, h = \frac{r^2 - d^2}{d} \, h.$$

If we put $\delta' - D = d'$ and denote by h_0 the value of h for the centre of the field, we have:

$$\Delta \, (\delta' - \delta) = \left\{ \frac{r^2 - d'^2}{d'} - \frac{r^2 - d^2}{d} \right\} h_0$$

$$= \frac{r^2 \, (d - d')}{d d'} \, h_0 + \frac{d d' \, (d - d')}{d d'} \, h_0 ,$$

hence:

$$\Delta \, (\delta' - \delta) = - \frac{k \, (\delta' - \delta) \, r^2}{(\delta - D) \, (\delta' - D)} \, [1 - \operatorname{tang} \zeta_0 \cos \eta_0 \operatorname{tang} \delta_0 + \operatorname{tang} \zeta_0{}^2 \sin \eta_0{}^2]$$

$$- \, k \, (\delta' - \delta) \, [1 - \operatorname{tang} \zeta_0 \cos \eta_0 \operatorname{tang} \delta_0 + \operatorname{tang} \zeta_0{}^2 \sin \eta_0{}^2],$$

and if we unite this with the first part of the correction, given by the second of the equations (a), we find:

$$\Delta(\delta'-\delta) = k(\delta'-\delta)\,[\text{tang}\,\zeta_0{}^2 \cos 2\eta_0 + \text{tang}\,\zeta_0 \cos\eta_0 \,\text{tang}\,\delta_0]$$
$$- k(\delta'-\delta)\frac{r^2}{(\delta-D)(\delta'-D)}$$
$$\times [1 + \text{tang}\,\zeta_0{}^2 \sin\eta_0{}^2 - \text{tang}\,\zeta_0 \cos\eta_0\,\text{tang}\,\delta_0]$$

for the expression of the complete correction of the difference of declination. Here we can in most cases neglect the terms multiplied by tang ζ_0 and thus we obtain simply:

$$\Delta(\alpha'-\alpha) = k(\delta'-\delta)\frac{\text{tang}\,\zeta_0{}^2 \sin 2\eta_0}{\cos\delta_0}$$
$$\Delta(\delta'-\delta) = k(\delta'-\delta)\,\text{tang}\,\zeta_0{}^2 \cos 2\eta_0 \qquad (B)$$
$$- k(\delta'-\delta)\frac{r^2}{(\delta-D)(\delta'-D)}[\text{tang}\,\zeta_0{}^2 \sin\eta_0{}^2 + 1].$$

Example. In 1849 Sept. 9 the planet Metis was observed at Bilk and compared with a star, whose apparent place was:

$$\alpha = 22^h\,1^m\,59^s.63, \quad \delta = -21^\circ\,43'\,27''.08.$$

The observations corresponding to $23^h\,23^m\,19^s.3$ sidereal time, were:

$$\alpha'-\alpha = +1^m\,9^s.65 = +17'\,24''.75$$
$$\delta'-D = -5'\,17''.5, \qquad \delta-D = +6'\,34''.2$$
$$\delta'-\delta = -11'\,51''.7 \text{ and we have } r = 9'\,26''.29.$$

Now if we compute ζ and η with

$$t_0 = 1^h\,20^m\,45^s = 20^\circ\,11', \quad \delta_0 = -21^\circ\,49'.4 \text{ and } \varphi = 51^\circ\,12'.5$$

we obtain:

$$\text{cotang}\,n = 9.34516 \qquad N = 37^\circ\,1'.9$$

and

$$\eta = 12^\circ\,55'.3 \qquad \zeta = 75^\circ\,9'.6.$$

From the tables for k we find for this zenith distance:

$$\log k = 6.4214,$$

and then the computation of the corrections by means of the formulae (B) is as follows:

$\log k =$	6.4214	$\sin 2\eta_0$	9.6394		0.0667_n
$\log(\delta'-\delta) =$	2.8523_n		0.4273	$\cos\delta_0$	9.9677
$\text{tang}\,\zeta^2 =$	1.1536	$\cos 2\eta_0$	9.9542	$\Delta(\alpha'-\alpha) =$	$-1''.25$
	0.4273_n	I term of $\Delta(\delta'-\delta) =$	$-2''.41$		
$\sin\eta^2$	8.6990				

$\log(\text{tang}\,\zeta^2 \sin\eta^2 + 1) =$	0.2335
$\log r^2$	5.5061
$k(\delta'-\delta)$	9.2737_n
	5.0133_n
$\log(\delta-D)(\delta'-D)$	5.0975_n
II term of $\Delta(\delta'-\delta)$	$+0''.82$

$$\Delta(\alpha'-\alpha) = -1''.25$$
$$\Delta(\delta'-\delta) = -3''.23.$$

Hence the corrected differences of right ascension and declination are:

$$\alpha' - \alpha = +17' 23''.50$$
$$\delta' - \delta = -11' 54''.93.$$

46. *The micrometer with which angles of position and distances are measured.* If $\alpha' - \alpha$ and $\delta' - \delta$ denote the differences of right ascension and declination affected with refraction, and $a' - a$ and $d' - d$ the same differences freed from it, we have:

$$a' - a = \alpha' - \alpha - k(\delta' - \delta)\frac{d.\frac{\tang \zeta \sin \eta}{\cos \delta}}{d\delta}$$
$$- k(\alpha' - \alpha)\frac{d.\frac{\tang \zeta \sin \eta}{\cos \delta}}{d\alpha},$$

where the values of the differential coefficients ought to be computed with the arithmetical means $\frac{\zeta + \zeta'}{2}$, $\frac{\eta + \eta'}{2}$ and $\frac{\delta + \delta'}{2}$. We have therefore:

$$d(a' - \alpha) = -k(\delta' - \delta)\frac{d.\frac{\tang \zeta \sin \eta}{\cos \delta}}{d\delta}$$
$$+ k(\alpha' - \alpha)\frac{d.\frac{\tang \zeta \sin \eta}{\cos \delta}}{dt},$$

and likewise:

$$d(\delta' - \delta) = -k(\delta' - \delta)\frac{d.\tang \zeta \cos \eta}{d\delta} + k(\alpha' - \alpha)\frac{d.\tang \zeta \cos \eta}{dt}.$$

Substituting the values of the differential coefficients found in No. 43, we get:

$$d(\alpha' - \alpha) = k(\delta' - \delta)\frac{\tang \zeta^2 \sin \eta \cos \eta - \tang \zeta \sin \eta \tang \delta}{\cos \delta}$$
$$+ k(\alpha' - \alpha)[\tang \zeta^2 \sin \eta^2 - \tang \zeta \cos \eta \tang \delta + 1]$$
$$d(\delta' - \delta) = k(\delta' - \delta)[\tang \zeta^2 \cos \eta^2 + 1]$$
$$+ k(\alpha' - \alpha)[\tang \zeta^2 \cos \eta \sin \eta \cos \delta + \tang \zeta \sin \eta \sin \delta].$$

But, if Δ and π denote the apparent distance and the apparent angle of position, we have:

$$\cos \delta (\alpha' - \alpha) = \Delta \sin \pi$$

and

$$\delta' - \delta = \Delta \cos \pi,$$

hence:

$$\tang \pi = \frac{\cos \delta (\alpha' - \alpha)}{\delta' - \delta}$$

and

$$\Delta = \cos \delta (\alpha' - \alpha) \sin \pi + (\delta' - \delta) \cos \pi.$$

If then Δ' and π' denote the true distance and the true angle of position, we have:

$$\pi' = \pi + \frac{\cos\pi\cos\delta\, d(\alpha'-\alpha) - \sin\pi\, d(\delta'-\delta)}{\Delta}$$

$$\Delta' = \Delta + \sin\pi\cos\delta\, d(\alpha'-\alpha) + \cos\pi\, d(\delta'-\delta).$$

If now we substitute here the values of $d(\alpha'-\alpha)$ and $d(\delta'-\delta)$ which were found before, and introduce in them Δ and π instead of $\alpha'-\alpha$ and $\delta'-\delta$, we obtain:

$$\begin{aligned}\pi' = \pi + k \operatorname{tang}\zeta^2\, [&\sin\pi\cos\eta\cos\pi\cos\pi + \sin\eta\sin\eta\sin\pi\cos\pi \\ &- \cos\eta\cos\eta\cos\pi\sin\pi - \sin\eta\cos\eta\sin\pi\sin\pi] \\ - k \operatorname{tang}\zeta\, [&\cos\pi\cos\pi\sin\eta\operatorname{tang}\delta + \sin\pi\cos\pi\cos\eta\operatorname{tang}\delta \\ &+ \sin\pi\sin\pi\sin\eta\operatorname{tang}\delta] \\ + k\sin\pi\cos\pi &- k\sin\pi\cos\pi,\end{aligned}$$

or if we neglect the terms multiplied by $\operatorname{tang}\zeta$:

$$\pi' = \pi - k\operatorname{tang}\zeta^2\sin(\pi-\eta)\cos(\pi-\eta).$$

Further we get:

$$\begin{aligned}\Delta' = \Delta + k\Delta\operatorname{tang}\zeta^2\, [&\sin\pi\cos\pi\sin\eta\cos\eta + \sin\pi^2\sin\eta^2 + \cos\pi^2\cos\eta^2 \\ &+ \sin\pi\cos\pi\sin\eta\cos\eta] \\ - k\Delta\operatorname{tang}\zeta\, [&\cos\pi\sin\pi\sin\eta\operatorname{tang}\delta + \sin\pi\sin\pi\cos\eta\operatorname{tang}\delta \\ &- \sin\pi\cos\pi\sin\eta\operatorname{tang}\delta] \\ + k\Delta\, [&\sin\pi^2 + \cos\pi^2],\end{aligned}$$

or if we neglect the terms multiplied by $\operatorname{tang}\zeta$:

$$\Delta' = \Delta + k\,\Delta\,[\operatorname{tang}\zeta^2\cos(\pi-\eta)^2 + 1].$$

IX. ON THE EFFECT OF PRECESSION, NUTATION AND ABERRATION UPON THE DISTANCE BETWEEN TWO STARS AND THE ANGLE OF POSITION.

47. The lunisolar precession and the nutation changes the position of the declination circle and hence the angles of position of the stars. From the triangle between the pole of the ecliptic, that of the equator and the star we easily find by means of the formulae in No. 11 of the first section and the third of the differential equations (11) in No. 9 of the introduction the variation of the angle η, which the declination circle makes with the circle of latitude:

$$\cos\delta\, d\eta = -\sin\varepsilon\,.\,\sin\alpha\, d\lambda + \cos\alpha\, d\varepsilon,$$

as $\sin a\; dB$ is equal to zero, because the lunisolar precession and the nutation do not change the latitude of the stars.

The sum of this angle η and of the angle of position p of another star relatively to this star is equal to the angle, which the circle of latitude makes with the great circle passing through the two stars, and since this is not changed by precession and nutation, it follows that the change of p is equal to that of η taken with the opposite sign, and that therefore:

$$\cos\delta\, dp = \sin\varepsilon \sin\alpha\, d\lambda - \cos\alpha\, d\varepsilon. \qquad (a)$$

Since the lunisolar precession does not change the obliquity of the ecliptic, we find the annual change of the angle of position by precession from the equation

$$\cos\delta \frac{dp}{dt} = \sin\alpha \sin\varepsilon \frac{d\lambda}{dt},$$

or:

$$\frac{dp}{dt} = n \sin\alpha \sec\delta$$

$$\text{where } n = 20''.06442 - 0''.0000970204\, t.$$

When this formula is employed for computing the change during a long interval of time, it is necessary to compute the values of n, α and δ for the arithmetical mean of the times, and to multiply the value of $\frac{dp}{dt}$ found from them by the interval of time.

In order to find the changes produced by nutation, we must substitute in (a) instead of $d\lambda$ and $d\varepsilon$ the expressions given in No. 5 of the second section. If we neglect the small terms, we obtain thus the complete change of p by precession and nutation from the formula:

$$\begin{aligned} dp = +\,20''.0644 \sin\alpha\sec\delta + [&-6''.8650 \sin\Omega + 0''.0825 \sin 2\Omega \\ &- 0''.5054 \sin 2\odot] \sin\alpha \sec\delta \\ - [&9''.2231 \cos\Omega - 0''.0897 \cos 2\Omega \\ &+ 0''.5509 \cos 2\odot] \cos\alpha\sec\delta, \end{aligned}$$

or if we make use of the notation adopted in No. 1 of the fourth section:

$$dp = A\,.\,n \sin\alpha \sec\delta + B\cos\alpha\sec\delta,$$

which formula gives the difference of the angle of position affected with precession and nutation from that referred to the mean equinox and the mean equator for the beginning of the year.

In order to find the effect of aberration upon the distance and the angle of position we must remember that according to the expressions in No. 1 of the fourth section we have:

for the aberration in right ascension: $Cc + Dd$
and for the aberration in declination: $Cc' + Dd'$,

$$\text{where } C = -20''.445 \cos\varepsilon \cos\odot, \quad D = -20''.445 \sin\odot$$
$$c = \sec\delta \cos\alpha, \quad c' = \operatorname{tang}\varepsilon \cos\delta - \sin\delta \sin\alpha$$
$$d = \sec\delta \sin\alpha, \quad d' = \sin\delta \cos\alpha.$$

Now if λ and ν denote the differences of the right ascensions and the declinations of the two stars, we find the changes of these differences by aberration, which are equal to the difference of the aberration for the two stars, by means of the equations:

$$\Delta\lambda = C.\Delta c + D.\Delta d$$
$$\Delta\nu = C.\Delta c' + D.\Delta d',$$

where:
$$\Delta c = -\sec\delta \sin\alpha.\lambda + \sec\delta \operatorname{tang}\delta \cos\alpha.\nu$$
$$\Delta d = \sec\delta \cos\alpha.\lambda + \sec\delta \operatorname{tang}\delta \sin\alpha.\nu$$
$$\Delta c' = -\sin\delta \cos\alpha.\lambda - [\operatorname{tang}\varepsilon \sin\delta + \cos\delta \sin\alpha]\nu$$
$$\Delta d' = -\sin\delta \sin\alpha.\lambda + \cos\delta \cos\alpha.\nu.$$

Hence, substituting these expressions we have:

$$\cos\delta\,\Delta\lambda = C[-\sin\alpha.\lambda + \operatorname{tang}\delta \cos\alpha.\nu] + D[\cos\alpha.\lambda + \operatorname{tang}\delta \sin\alpha.\nu]$$
$$\Delta\nu = -C[\sin\delta\cos\alpha.\lambda + (\operatorname{tang}\varepsilon \sin\delta + \cos\delta \sin\alpha)\nu]$$
$$- D[\sin\delta \sin\alpha.\lambda - \cos\delta \cos\alpha.\nu].$$

But, if we denote the distance and the angle of position by s and P, we have:

$$s.\sin P = \lambda \cos\delta$$
$$s.\cos P = \nu,$$

hence:

$$s^2 = \lambda^2 \cos\delta^2 + \nu^2, \quad \operatorname{tang} P = \frac{\lambda\cos\delta}{\nu},$$

and therefore:

$$s.\Delta s = \cos\delta^2\,\lambda.\Delta\lambda + \nu\,\Delta\nu - \cos\delta \sin\delta\,\lambda^2\,(Cc' + Dd').$$

If we substitute herein the values of $\Delta\lambda$ and $\Delta\nu$ found before as well as the values of c' and d', we find after an easy reduction:

$$s.\Delta s = [\lambda^2 \cos\delta^2 + \nu^2][-C(\operatorname{tang}\varepsilon \sin\delta + \cos\delta \sin\alpha) + D\cos\delta\cos\alpha]$$

or:
$$\Delta s = -C.s[\operatorname{tang}\varepsilon \sin\delta + \cos\delta\sin\alpha] + D.s\cos\delta\cos\alpha.$$

Further we have:

$$s^2\,dP = \nu\cos\delta.\Delta\lambda - \lambda\cos\delta\,\Delta\nu - \lambda\sin\delta\,\nu\,[Cc' + Dd'],$$

and if we substitute the values of $\Delta\lambda$, $\Delta\nu$, c' and d', we find again after a simple reduction:

$$dP = C \operatorname{tang}\delta \cos\alpha + D \operatorname{tang}\delta \sin\alpha.$$

Therefore if we introduce the following notation:

$$a' = \frac{n}{60} \sec \delta \sin \alpha$$

$$b' = \frac{\sec \delta \cos \alpha}{60}$$

$$c' = \frac{\operatorname{tang} \delta \cos \alpha}{60} \qquad c = -\frac{s}{w} [\operatorname{tang} \varepsilon \sin \delta + \cos \delta \sin \alpha]$$

$$d' = \frac{\operatorname{tang} \delta \sin \alpha}{60} \qquad d = \frac{s}{w} \cos \delta \cos \alpha,$$

where the factors $\frac{1}{60}$ and $\frac{1}{w} = \frac{1}{206265}$ have been added in order to find the corrections of the distance and of the angle of position expressed respectively in seconds of arc and minutes of arc, then we have:

Observed distance = True distance $+ cC + dD$

Observed angle of position = True angle of position for the beginning of the year $+ a'A + b'B + c'C + d'D$.

Since c, d, c' and d' are independent of the angle of position, it follows, that aberration changes the distances, whatever be their direction, in the same ratio, and all angles of positions by the same quantity. Therefore if the circumference of a small circle described round a star is occupied by stars, such a circle will appear enlarged or diminished by aberration and at the same time turned a little about its centre; but it always will remain a circle, and the angles between the radii of the stars will remain the same.

Berlin, printed by A. W. SCHADE, Stallschreiberstr. 47.

www.ingramcontent.com/pod-product-compliance
Lightning Source LLC
LaVergne TN
LVHW021228110826
845150LV00002B/270
* 9 7 8 1 4 2 5 5 6 3 4 6 2 *